駿台

2024
大学入学共通テスト
実戦問題集

英語 リーディング

駿台文庫編

は じ め に

　2021 年度より始まった大学入学共通テストは，2020 年度までのセンター試験とは出題内容や形式が大きく変わりました。英語の 4 技能と呼ばれる「読む」，「聞く」，「書く」，「話す」のうち，リーディング問題においては，「読む」ことに関する能力が試されるわけですが，共通テストにおいて重視される能力は，極端に難しい英文を読む能力ではなく，実際のコミュニケーションにおける，様々な目的や場面，状況に対応できる読解力です。このような出題方針から，従来のセンター試験で出題されていたような，発音・文法・語法・語句整序などを単独で問うような問題は廃止され，すべてが「読解問題」の形式になりました（ただし発音や文法などの知識は，リスニングやリーディングの問題の中で重要なポイントとなることもあるので，軽視せずに学習を続けていくことが大事です）。そして設問内容は，与えられた文章の要点を把握したり，必要な情報を読み取ったりする力を見るものが中心となります。より具体的には，以下のような特徴があります。

　英文の難易度は，従来のセンター試験と大きな変化はなく，極端に難しいものはありません。共通テストの大問数は 6 題ですが，その中の 4 題は A と B の 2 つのセクションに分かれているため，問題の分量はかなり多めです。そのため，時間配分を誤ると，すべての問題に取り組むことができなくなるおそれがあります。一言で言えば，「難しくはないが，分量が多い」というのが，共通テストの特徴と言えます。したがって，時間配分に十分留意しつつ，各問題を手際よく片付けていく必要があります。そのため，本問題集を活用して，各問題の形式・特徴を掴み，効率よく解答する方法を探ることは，間違いなく本番で大きな助けになることでしょう。

　出題される英文のジャンルは，高校生から大学生ぐらいの日本人が日常生活や学業の中で触れる機会が多い SNS，メール，ブログ，行事などの案内文，討論や発表のための記事や資料などが中心となります（会話文を素材とする問題はリーディングからはなくなりました。会話の内容を理解する力はリスニング問題で問われることになります）。加えて，一部の問題文ではイギリス英語が使用されるなど，現代のグローバルな状況に対する意識が反映されていることにも注意しておきましょう。

　形式的な特徴としては，本文や問いの中に，図表・イラスト・グラフが数多く用いられていることが挙げられます。また，すべての問題で “You are planning …” などの場面が設定されており，受験者に当事者意識を持たせ，あたかも実際のコミュニケーションにおける目的・場面・状況などに応じて英語の理解力を考査しているような作りになっているのも，共通テスト独自の特徴と言えるでしょう。さらに問いの中には，「事実と意見を区別するもの」，「図表中の空所を埋めるもの」，「本文の内容と一致する図（表）を選ぶもの」など，他の試験にはほとんど見られない独特の形式が含まれるため，本番で戸惑うことがないよう，本問題集を活用して慣れておくことが大事です。

　このように，出題される英文のジャンルや問いの形式は独特なものが多いので，共通テストに向けての対策としては，確実な英文読解力を養成していくことは言うまでもありませんが，それに加えて，各設問に合わせた情報検索スキルを高めていくことも非常に重要なものとなります。そのことを忘れずに日々の学習を積み重ねていってください。そうすれば必ずや良い結果が得られることでしょう。本問題集がその一助となれば幸いです。

（編集責任者）　鈴木貴之

本書の特長と利用法

特　長

1　オリジナル予想問題＆過去問を掲載

　　共通テスト「英語（リーディング）」対策のために，オリジナル予想問題5回分と，3年分の共通テスト過去問題を掲載しています。予想問題は，形式・分量はもちろん，題材・レベルに至るまで，実際の試験と遜色のないよう工夫を凝らしてあります。

2　傾向と対策をわかりやすく解説

　　「共通テスト英語　攻略のポイント」では，本試験の問題例を具体的に示しながら，リーディングの学習方法や解き方のポイントを簡潔に解説しています。

3　重要事項の総復習ができる

　　解答冊子の巻頭には，共通テストの英語（リーディング）における重要事項をまとめた「直前チェック総整理」を掲載しています。コンパクトにまとめてありますので，限られた時間で効率よく重要事項をチェックすることができます。

4　学力の客観的評価が可能

　　2023年度・2022年度共通テスト（本試験）および2021年度共通テスト（第1日程）の［解答・解説］の扉には「得点別偏差値表」を掲載していますので，「自分の得点でどの程度のレベルになるのか」が一目でわかります。

5　試験関連情報が満載

　　① 2024年度大学入学共通テスト出題教科・科目，② 2018 〜 2023年度共通テスト・センター試験の受験者数・平均点の推移，③ 2023年度共通テストのデータネット自己採点集計による得点別人数グラフを掲載しました。

利用法

1　問題は，本番の試験に臨むつもりで，マークシート解答用紙を用いて，必ず制限時間を設けて取り組んでください。マークシート解答用紙は本冊の巻末にありますので，切り取って使用してください。

2　解答したあとは，自己採点をし（結果は解答ページの自己採点欄に記入しておく），ウイークポイントの発見に役立ててください。ウイークポイントがあったら再度解き，わからないところを教科書や辞書で調べるなどして克服しましょう！

2024年度　大学入学共通テスト　出題教科・科目

以下は，大学入試センターが公表している大学入学共通テストの出題教科・科目等の一覧表です。
最新のものについて調べる場合は，下記のところへ原則として志願者本人がお問い合わせください。
●問い合わせ先　大学入試センター
　　　　TEL　03-3465-8600　（土日祝日を除く　9時30分〜17時）　　http://www.dnc.ac.jp

教　科	グループ	出題科目	出題方法等	科目選択の方法等	試験時間(配点)
国　語		『国　語』	「国語総合」の内容を出題範囲とし，近代以降の文章，古典（古文，漢文）を出題する。		80分 (200点)
地理歴史		「世界史A」 「世界史B」 「日本史A」 「日本史B」 「地理A」 「地理B」	『倫理，政治・経済』は，「倫理」と「政治・経済」を総合した出題範囲とする。	左記出題科目の10科目のうちから最大2科目を選択し，解答する。 　ただし，同一名称を含む科目の組合せで2科目を選択することはできない。 　なお，受験する科目数は出願時に申し出ること。	1科目選択 60分（100点） 2科目選択 130分（うち解答時間120分） (200点)
公　民		「現代社会」 「倫　理」 「政治・経済」 『倫理，政治・経済』			
数　学	①	「数学I」 『数学I・数学A』	『数学I・数学A』は，「数学I」と「数学A」を総合した出題範囲とする。 　ただし，次に記す「数学A」の3項目の内容のうち，2項目以上を学習した者に対応した出題とし，問題を選択解答させる。 〔場合の数と確率,整数の性質,図形の性質〕	左記出題科目の2科目のうちから1科目を選択し，解答する。	70分 (100点)
	②	「数学II」 『数学II・数学B』 『簿記・会計』 『情報関係基礎』	『数学II・数学B』は，「数学II」と「数学B」を総合した出題範囲とする。 　ただし，次に記す「数学B」の3項目の内容のうち，2項目以上を学習した者に対応した出題とし，問題を選択解答させる。 〔数列，ベクトル，確率分布と統計的な推測〕	左記出題科目の4科目のうちから1科目を選択し，解答する。	60分 (100点)
理　科	①	「物理基礎」 「化学基礎」 「生物基礎」 「地学基礎」		左記出題科目の8科目のうちから下記のいずれかの選択方法により科目を選択し，解答する。 A　理科①から2科目 B　理科②から1科目 C　理科①から2科目及び理科②から1科目 D　理科②から2科目 　なお，受験する科目の選択方法は出願時に申し出ること。	2科目選択 60分（100点）
	②	「物　理」 「化　学」 「生　物」 「地　学」			1科目選択 60分（100点） 2科目選択 130分（うち解答時間120分）（200点）
外国語		『英　語』 『ドイツ語』 『フランス語』 『中国語』 『韓国語』	『英語』は，「コミュニケーション英語I」に加えて「コミュニケーション英語II」及び「英語表現I」を出題範囲とし，【リーディング】と【リスニング】を出題する。 　なお，【リスニング】には，聞き取る英語の音声を2回流す問題と，1回流す問題がある。	左記出題科目の5科目のうちから1科目を選択し，解答する。	『英　語』 【リーディング】 80分（100点） 【リスニング】 60分（うち解答時間30分）（100点） 『ドイツ語』，『フランス語』，『中国語』，『韓国語』 【筆記】 80分（200点）

備考

1．「　」で記載されている科目は，高等学校学習指導要領上設定されている科目を表し，『　』はそれ以外の科目を表す。
2．地理歴史及び公民の「科目選択の方法等」欄中の「同一名称を含む科目の組合せ」とは，「世界史A」と「世界史B」，「日本史A」と「日本史B」，「地理A」と「地理B」，「倫理」と『倫理，政治・経済』及び「政治・経済」と『倫理，政治・経済』の組合せをいう。
3．地理歴史及び公民並びに理科②の試験時間において2科目を選択する場合は，解答順に第1解答科目及び第2解答科目に区分し各60分間で解答を行うが，第1解答科目及び第2解答科目の間に答案回収等を行うために必要な時間を加えた時間を試験時間とする。
4．理科①については，1科目のみの受験は認めない。
5．外国語において『英語』を選択する受験者は，原則として，リーディングとリスニングの双方を解答する。
6．リスニングは，音声問題を用い30分間で解答を行うが，解答開始前に受験者に配付したICプレーヤーの作動確認・音量調節を受験者本人が行うために必要な時間を加えた時間を試験時間とする。

2018～2023年度　共通テスト・センター試験　受験者数・平均点の推移（大学入試センター公表）

センター試験←→共通テスト

科目名	2018年度 受験者数	2018年度 平均点	2019年度 受験者数	2019年度 平均点	2020年度 受験者数	2020年度 平均点	2021年度第1日程 受験者数	2021年度第1日程 平均点	2022年度 受験者数	2022年度 平均点	2023年度 受験者数	2023年度 平均点
英語 リーディング（筆記）	546,712	123.75	537,663	123.30	518,401	116.31	476,173	58.80	480,762	61.80	463,985	53.81
英語 リスニング	540,388	22.67	531,245	31.42	512,007	28.78	474,483	56.16	479,039	59.45	461,993	62.35
数学Ⅰ・数学A	396,479	61.91	392,486	59.68	382,151	51.88	356,492	57.68	357,357	37.96	346,628	55.65
数学Ⅱ・数学B	353,423	51.07	349,405	53.21	339,925	49.03	319,696	59.93	321,691	43.06	316,728	61.48
国　語	524,724	104.68	516,858	121.55	498,200	119.33	457,304	117.51	460,966	110.26	445,358	105.74
物理基礎	20,941	31.32	20,179	30.58	20,437	33.29	19,094	37.55	19,395	30.40	17,978	28.19
化学基礎	114,863	30.42	113,801	31.22	110,955	28.20	103,073	24.65	100,461	27.73	95,515	29.42
生物基礎	140,620	35.62	141,242	30.99	137,469	32.10	127,924	29.17	125,498	23.90	119,730	24.66
地学基礎	48,336	34.13	49,745	29.62	48,758	27.03	44,319	33.52	43,943	35.47	43,070	35.03
物　理	157,196	62.42	156,568	56.94	153,140	60.68	146,041	62.36	148,585	60.72	144,914	63.39
化　学	204,543	60.57	201,332	54.67	193,476	54.79	182,359	57.59	184,028	47.63	182,224	54.01
生　物	71,567	61.36	67,614	62.89	64,623	57.56	57,878	72.64	58,676	48.81	57,895	48.46
地　学	2,011	48.58	1,936	46.34	1,684	39.51	1,356	46.65	1,350	52.72	1,659	49.85
世界史B	92,753	67.97	93,230	65.36	91,609	62.97	85,689	63.49	82,985	65.83	78,185	58.43
日本史B	170,673	62.19	169,613	63.54	160,425	65.45	143,363	64.26	147,300	52.81	137,017	59.75
地理B	147,026	67.99	146,229	62.03	143,036	66.35	138,615	60.06	141,375	58.99	139,012	60.46
現代社会	80,407	58.22	75,824	56.76	73,276	57.30	68,983	58.40	63,604	60.84	64,676	59.46
倫　理	20,429	67.78	21,585	62.25	21,202	65.37	19,954	71.96	21,843	63.29	19,878	59.02
政治・経済	57,253	56.39	52,977	56.24	50,398	53.75	45,324	57.03	45,722	56.77	44,707	50.96
倫理, 政治・経済	49,709	73.08	50,886	64.22	48,341	66.51	42,948	69.26	43,831	69.73	45,578	60.59

(注1) 2020年度までのセンター試験『英語』は，筆記200点満点，リスニング50点満点である。
(注2) 2021年度以降の共通テスト『英語』は，リーディング及びリスニングともに100点満点である。
(注3) 2021年度第1日程及び2023年度の平均点は，得点調整後のものである。

2023年度　共通テスト本試「英語（リーディング）」「英語（リスニング）」データネット（自己採点集計）による得点別人数

英語

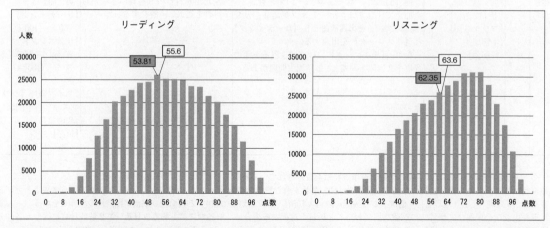

上のグラフは，2023年度センター試験データネット（自己採点集計）に参加したリーディング：392,260名，リスニング：391,270名の得点別人数をグラフ化したものです。
2023年度データネット集計による平均点はリーディング 55.6 ／リスニング 63.6 ，2023年度大学入試センター公表の本試験平均点はリーディング 53.81 ，リスニング 62.35 です。

共通テスト英語　攻略のポイント

2023年度　本試験：**英語（リーディング）**

1. 英語（リーディング）の概要

2023年度本試験の概要と，各問題の内容は，以下のとおりです：

・試験時間：80分　　・配点：100点　　・平均点：53.81点（前年度の平均点は61.80点）
・問題数　大問：6題　小問：39題（マーク箇所は49ヵ所）
・問題構成：

大問 （配点）	状況設定	素材	内容	*総語数	小問数	難易度	解答時間 （目安）
第1問 （10点）	案内文を読み，希望する活動を申し込む	A：配布プリント	観劇の申込書	231語	2題	易	6分程度
		B：ウェブサイト	英語サマーキャンプの案内文	369語	3題	標準	
第2問 （20点）	自分の必要や目的に合う情報を読む	A：広告文 （レビュー付き）	新しいシューズの広告	450語	5題	標準	14分程度
		B：レポート （感想コメント付き）	「通学チャレンジ」についてのレポート	468語	5題	標準	
第3問 （15点）	自分が関心を持つ活動の体験談とアドバイスを読む	A：クラブの会報	キャンプ参加者へのアドバイス	328語	2題	標準	10分程度
		B：ブログ	「アドベンチャールーム」の作り方	460語	3題	標準	
第4問 （16点）	同じ問題に関する2つの意見を読んで比較する	2つの投稿記事	効果的な学習法について	766語	5題	標準	10分程度
第5問 （15点）	気持ちを高めるストーリーを読んで発表する	ストーリー	卓球から学んだこと	1,002語	5題	標準	10分程度
第6問 （24点）	文章を読んで討論や発表のためにまとめる	A：記事	コレクション活動	887語	4題	標準	30分程度
		B：抜粋文	緩歩動物の生態	1,155語	5題	やや難	

* 「総語数」とは，指示文・問題文・設問に含まれるすべての語の合計です。

—7—

上の表からわかるように，リーディングの問題はその名の通り，すべて読解問題で，設問も英文の内容に関する理解を問うものばかりです（文法・語法・熟語の知識のみを問う問題は原則として出題されません）。各問題に用いられる英文の素材は，高校生や大学生が日常生活や学校生活の中で触れる英文という想定のもとに選ばれます。そのため，各問題の冒頭には，上の表の「状況設定」にあるように，受験者（リード文中では you で示されます）が置かれている状況を説明する英文が付され，そこでは以下の本文が，自分の生活や学業とどのような関わり合いを持っているかが説明されます。自分がその状況に置かれていると想定して本文に取り組むことが大事です。また，本文や設問を理解するのに有用な情報が含まれていることもあるので，必ず目を通して，状況を把握してください。

　設問は，すべて英語で出題されます。原則として本文中には，空所や下線など，設問との対応箇所を示す記号は設けられません。設問内容は上で述べたように，すべて英文の理解度を問うものですが，さまざまな形式が用いられます。以下に各問題の主な特徴を挙げていきます。

2. 各問題の特徴

第1問：

　第1問は，AとBの2部構成です。どちらも実用的な文書を素材とする問題で，本年度はイベントの申込書が素材となりました。設問は，質問に対する適切な解答文を選択するいわゆる英問英答形式と，本文の内容と一致する英文を完成させる空所補充形式からなります。

　Aは，本文は短く平易ですが，情報量は多く，解答の決め手となる情報が本文中の複数の箇所に分散している場合があるので，必要な情報を素早く的確に選び取る力が求められます。また，実用的な内容の素材文であることから，問1の「このプリントを読んだ後であなたは何をせよと言われているか」のように，受験生が現実の生活の中で本文の内容を実践することを想定した質問文が用いられることがあります（例1）。設問数は2題と少ないことから，短時間で解答することが大事ですが，細かい情報を正しく読み取らないと間違える恐れがあるので注意が必要です。

例1

```
問1  What are you told to do after reading the
     handout?  1
```

　Bは，Aよりも長めの文書を素材とする問題です。情報量も増え，設問数も1題多いことから，速く読み，必要な情報を的確に見つけることがより重要となります。

第2問：

　第2問もAとBの2部構成です。ここでは自分の必要や目的に合う文書を読むという状況を想定して問題が出されます。また，どちらの問題にも，本文には複数の人物によるレビューや感想が添えられているという特徴があります。

　Aはスマートシューズの商品広告が素材で，素材文は「商品の説明」と「ユーザーによるレビュー」の2つの部分からなっています。設問形式は，第1問と同様に，「英問英答問題」と「空所補充による英文完成問題」ですが，問3では「（客観的な事実ではなく）意見」を問う問題が出題されているのが特徴的です（例2）。第1問と同様に，解答の手がかりとなる情報が分散していることが多く，異なる箇所で示される情報を組み合わせることで正解が決まる問題もあるので，本文中の必要な情報を素早く見つけ出す力が鍵となります。

例2

```
問3  One opinion stated by a customer is that
     8 .
```

　Bは，交換学生が書いた通学チャレンジについてのレポートが素材で，記事は「交換学生が書いたレポート」と「チャレンジに参加した生徒の感想」からなっています。設問形式は，Aの問3とは対照的に，「（主観的な意見ではなく客観的な）事実」を問う問題が出題されています（問2）。また，問3では同一の選択肢群から2つの正解を選ぶ問題が出されています。そして問5は，前半のレポートの中で筆者が提起した問題について，後半の感想の中でその答えに相当する発言をした参加者の氏名（イニシャル）を答えさせるという形式で，かなり特徴的な出題形式と言えます（例3）。

例3

```
問5  The author's question is answered by  15 .

     ① HS  ② JH  ③ KF  ④ MN  ⑤ SS
```

第3問：

　第3問もＡとＢの2部構成です。どちらの問題文も，自分が関心を持っている活動についての体験談とアドバイスを読むという状況設定で，アドバイスの内容を正しく把握できているかどうかが1つの鍵となります。Aは，キャンプクラブの会報を素材とする問題で，キャンプに参加した会報記事の筆者が，自分の経験に基づくアドバイスをするという内容です。設問はイラストを用いた選択問題と，英文の空所補充問題です。

　Bは，ブログ記事が素材で，「アドベンチャールーム」を実際に作った筆者が，自分の経験を語りアドバイスをするという内容です。設問には，出来事の起こった順序を問うもの（問1／**例4**）が含まれるのが特徴的です。これは「出来事が述べられる順序」とは同じではないことがあるので，注意が必要です。

例4

問1　Put the following events (①〜④) into the
　　 order in which they happened.
　　 18 → 19 → 20 → 21

第4問：

　第4問では，共通のテーマを持つ2つの文章が出題されます。本年度は，「効果的な学習法」をテーマとする2つの投稿記事が出題されました。設問内容は，2人の筆者の主張の共通点や相違点を問うものが中心となります。両者の論点を的確に把握する力が求められています。設問形式としては，問3のように，英文中の2つの空所を，共通する選択肢群から適切な語を選んで埋める問題が出題されます。また問5のような，本文の主張の裏付けとなる追加情報を選ばせる問題，つまり本文に直接書かれていないことを，本文の内容から予想させる問題も出題されることを覚えておきましょう（**例5**）。

例5

問5　Which additional information would be
　　 the best to further support Lee's argument for
　　 spaced learning?　29

第5問：

　長めの英文を読み，その要点をまとめることを主な狙いとする問題です。問題は「本文」とその要点をまとめた「メモ」の2つからなり，本文中には空所は設けられませんが，メモの中に空所が設けられ，それを適切な表現で埋めるという出題形式です。本文の素材はストーリーで，メモは「主な登場人物の紹介」，「主な出来事」，「ストーリーから得られる教訓」などからなります。設問の中には，起こった出来事を時系列に沿った順序に並べることを問う問題が含まれます（**例6**）。これは第3問Bの問1と似ていますが，一部の出来事の位置があらかじめ指定されていて，空所よりも選択肢の数が多い（つまりいずれの空所にも入らない選択肢が1つ含まれる）ので，より注意する必要があります。本文がかなり長いので，設問との対応箇所をいかに速くかつ的確に見つけられるかどうかが鍵となります。

例6

Influential events in Ben's journey to becoming
a better communicator
Began playing table tennis
→ 32 → 33 → 34 → 35

- -

問3　Choose **four** out of the five options (①〜⑤)
　　 and rearrange them in the order they happened.
　　 32 → 33 → 34 → 35
① Became a table tennis champion
② Discussed with his teacher how to play well
③ Refused a party in his honour
④ Started to study his opponents
⑤ Talked to his brother about table tennis

—9—

第6問：
　第6問はAとBの2部構成です。第5問と同様に，長い文章を読んで，その要点をまとめたメモやスライドの中の空所を埋めるという形式の問題です。

　Aの素材文は，「コレクション活動」をテーマにした解説調の記事です。設問は，原則として本文の記述の順序通りに配列されているので，本文を1段落読み進めるごとに，設問を問1から順にチェックして，解答可能な問題を見つけ次第解答するのが要領のいい取り組み方です。そして正解に確信が持てない場合は，本文の該当箇所に戻り，内容を再確認する姿勢が大事です。

　Bの素材文は，「緩歩動物の生態」をテーマにした解説調の文章です。本文を読んだ後で，発表用のスライドを作成するという設定で，スライド内の空所を埋めることが求められます。素材文は情報量のかなり多い英文で，細かい情報を読み取って整理する力が求められます。本年度は，動物の体の部位を表す語を，具体的な位置を表すスライドと組み合わせる問題が出されました（例7）。かなり分量の多い問題ですが，本文を1段落読むごとに，スライドの内容を確認しながら取り組んでいけば，効率よく解答できるでしょう。また，問5のように，本文の内容から「推測できること」を問う問題が出されているのも特徴的です。

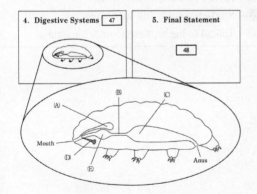

例7

問3　Complete the missing labels on the illustration of a tardigrade for the **Digestive Systems** slide. 47

① (A) Esophagus　　(B) Pharynx
　 (C) Middle gut　　(D) Stylets
　 (E) Salivary gland
② (A) Pharynx　　　(B) Stylets
　 (C) Salivary gland (D) Esophagus
　 (E) Middle gut
③ (A) Salivary gland (B) Esophagus
　 (C) Middle gut　　(D) Stylets
　 (E) Pharynx
④ (A) Salivary gland (B) Middle gut
　 (C) Stylets　　　 (D) Esophagus
　 (E) Pharynx
⑤ (A) Stylets　　　 (B) Salivary gland
　 (C) Pharynx　　　(D) Middle gut
　 (E) Esophagus

3．学習対策

教科書レベルの英文を速く正確に読める力をつけよう。

　共通テストのリーディング問題の最大の特徴を一言で言えば，「難解ではないが分量が多い」ということです。どの問題の英文も，極端に難しいものはなく，設問についても，本文が正しく読めれば正誤の判断に迷うものは少ないので，標準的な学力がある受験生が落ち着いて時間をかけて取り組めば，かなりの高得点が取れると思います。しかしながら，80分という制限時間の中で，すべての問題に取り組んで正解を出すのはかなり難しいことです。したがって，「平易な英文を速く正確に読めるようにする」ことが，リーディング問題への最大の対策であることは間違いありません。そのためには，高校の教科書レベルの英文をしっかり理解した上で，止まったり戻ったりすることなく読めるようになるまで読み込むことが大事です。このような訓練を日々繰り返して，習熟した英文の量を増やしていくことが，共通テストで高得点が取れる学力を養うための最大の鍵となります。そしてそのプロセスで語彙力を自然に身につけていくのが，望ましい単語の覚え方です。なお，文法や語法や熟語の知識のみを問う問題は出題されませんが，これらの知識を間接的な形で問う問題もあり，英文を正しく読む上でも文法や語法や熟語の知識は大切ですから，標準的なレベルの学習は怠らないようにしましょう。こういった学習を日々積み重ねた上で，本書を利用して，過去に出題された問題の形式，特徴，効率のよい取り組み方などを頭に入れておけば，制限時間内に全ての問題に正解するのは不可能ではありません。本書がその一助となれば幸いです。

第 1 回

（80分）

実 戦 問 題

━━● 標 準 所 要 時 間 ●━━

第 1 問　7 分程度	第 4 問 12 分程度
第 2 問 13 分程度	第 5 問 14 分程度
第 3 問 12 分程度	第 6 問 22 分程度

英 語(リーディング)

各大問の英文や図表を読み，解答番号 $\boxed{1}$ ～ $\boxed{47}$ にあてはまるものとして最も適当な選択肢を選びなさい。

第1問 （配点 10）

A You are studying in Canada, and you need to decide which sounds more interesting out of two suggestions for a morning activity. Your teacher gives you this voting instruction sheet.

Saturday Activity Suggestions

<u>Vancouver Harbor</u>	<u>Stanley Park</u>
Wet and Wild	***Culture on Wheels***
Sail with whales	Explore Vancouver by bicycle
▶ Departs every hour between 9:00 and 13:00 (50-minute tours) ▶ Detailed staff announcements about local marine life and geography ▶ View from decks or through large windows (vending machines available for drinks) ▶ The first customer to see a whale gets a free cap!	▶ A two-hour tour beginning at 10:30, stopping for 20 minutes for included refreshments (choose drinks and vegetarian options when booking) ▶ Hear facts about famous landmarks from trained guides ▶ Spend over $30 on souvenirs at the bicycle drop-off for 10% off

Voting: Write your name on blue paper (*Wet and Wild*) or red paper (*Culture on Wheels*) and put it in the box.

— 2 —

第1回　英語（リーディング）

問1　What are you told to do after reading the sheet?　1

① Choose a colored box for your paper.

② Contact a tour company directly.

③ Place your name in a box.

④ Prepare to vote in the next lesson.

問2　Which is true about both activities?　2

① Drinks are available for no extra cost.

② Employees know a lot about the tour areas.

③ They go ahead several times every morning.

④ You can get discounts on some special goods.

B You are thinking of joining a fitness club which just opened near your house. You visit its website.

Lexus Fitness

Lexus Fitness offers flexible plans, affordable rates, and brand new equipment. Our simple goal is to provide a modern, welcoming environment specifically designed to help you achieve all of your health and fitness goals. You can't help but be motivated to elevate your workout to new levels.

All new members will receive a special towel with the **Lexus Fitness** logo on it. In addition, if you enroll by the end of April, you will have a chance to win our original gym bag in a lottery. Plus, as a special promotion, if you become a platinum member by the end of April, you will be given our original T-shirt! Please don't miss this wonderful opportunity to join our club and achieve your goals.

Please choose from the membership options below.

When you can use the facility and what is included (✔)	Membership Options		
	Daytime ($60/month)	Gold ($80/month)	Platinum ($100/month)
Monday to Friday, 9:00 AM ~ 5:00 PM	✔		✔
Monday to Friday, 5:00 PM ~		✔	✔
Saturday and Sunday (All day)	✔	✔	✔
Free Parking	✔	✔	✔
Group exercise class		✔	✔
Pool & Spa		✔	✔
Free Rental of Bathing Suit			✔
Free Rental of Gym Shoes			✔
Personal Training Program			✔

第1回 英語（リーディング）

☆ We charge $50 as an enrollment fee.
☆ Join before April 20, and you won't need to pay the membership fees for April!
☆ Membership fees are to be paid at the beginning of each month.

Whether you are a Daytime, Gold, or Platinum member, you will love being a member of the Lexus Fitness club. For more information, or to join, click *here*.

問1　Every new member will receive 　3　.

① a fitness bag and a towel
② a set of essential gym items
③ a towel and a T-shirt
④ at least one practical gift

問2　You will be able to 　4　 if you become a Gold member.

① join group exercise classes on Tuesday mornings
② rent gym footwear for free
③ swim in the pool on Saturday mornings
④ take one-on-one lessons on Sundays

問3　If you become a Daytime member on April 15, you will have paid 　5　 in total by the end of December.

① $480
② $530
③ $540
④ $590

第２問 （配点 20）

A Your mattress is uncomfortable, and you often feel irritable after getting up suddenly when your noisy alarm clock rings. You are reading an article about sleep on a UK website and find this advertisement.

Forty Winks presents the new *Sweet Sleep Sheet*

You can use the refreshing *Sweet Sleep Sheet* with your existing mattress. It is intelligent and improves sleep.

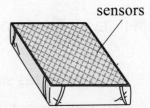

Unique Aspects

Download the *Sweet Sleep Sheet* app to link it to the sensors which check your quality of sleep and control temperature. This product not only tells you how much you move around during the night, but how to rest more deeply. Subscribe to the app for regular sleeping tips!

Benefits

Climate Setting: Select the perfect temperature for when you climb into bed and let it change throughout the night in relation to your body heat in all seasons.

Gentle Rising: Begin your day calmly as your mattress starts to vibrate gradually more quickly, avoiding the shock of loud alarms.

Improved Health: Track how well you sleep to understand when you are stressed or sick.

Individual Feedback: Receive advice to suit you particularly by answering a few questions in the app about your preferred sleeping habits.

第1回　英語（リーディング）

Customers' Comments

● Though it is a bit noisy, it's quieter than a fan, heater or other smart mattresses.

● You can try it for free! If you don't like it after two weeks, send it back!

● Make sure you have strong wi-fi in your bedroom to avoid losing connection.

● The personalised breathing exercises really improved my sleep!

● This mattress cover is neither too soft nor too hard.

● It takes a long time to set up, but other than that no complaints from me!

● The water-controlled temperature system needs only a couple of spoons of water added every month.

問1　According to the company's words, which best describes the mattress cover?　 6

① Adaptable for all year

② Refreshing and seasonal

③ Smart with clear alarms

④ Washable and convenient

問2　Which benefit offered by the cover is most likely to suit you?　 7

① Comparing various sleeping techniques

② Reducing feelings of anxiety

③ Understanding sleep patterns scientifically

④ Waking up more leisurely

— 7 —

問3　One **opinion** stated by a user is that 　8　 .

① The cover is likely to break quickly

② The cover's firmness is just right

③ The temperature system is too loud

④ The temperature system needs water regularly

問4　One user's comment mentions personalised breathing exercises. Which benefit is the comment related to? 　9　

① Climate Setting

② Gentle Rising

③ Improved Health

④ Individual Feedback

問5　According to one customer's opinion, 　10　 is advised.

① answering the questions in the app honestly

② comparing the cover with various mattresses

③ installing wi-fi with a good signal in your bedroom

④ testing the cover for thirty days before buying it

— 8 —

第 1 回　英語（リーディング）

（下 書 き 用 紙）

英語（リーディング）の試験問題は次に続く。

B You need to decide on a hotel before going to Miyakojima, Okinawa for your holidays, so you are reading the information on one hotel and a guest's comment about it.

The Imgya

Location:
　Located on Miyakojima, the Imgya is a twenty-minute drive from Miyako airport and is located on a beautiful private beach. Hirara Bridge and Karimata Shrine are notable nearby landmarks, and some of the area's popular attractions include Shimoji American Village and Shigira Botanical Garden. With scuba diving, snorkeling and waterskiing nearby, you'll be able to have plenty of adventures in the water.

Hotel description:
　Spend the day enjoying the wonderful beach and then return to dine at one of the Imgya's 5 restaurants. All 180 soundproofed rooms feature free Wi-Fi and room service. For a bit of entertainment, LCD TVs come with satellite channels, and guests can also enjoy conveniences like fridges and coffee makers.

Hotel amenities:
- Free airport shuttle
- Gift shop / General store
- Laundry facilities
- Parking (JPY 1,000 per night)
- Seasonal outdoor pool
- 24-hour front desk
- 18-hole golf course
- Internet
- Elevator
- Spa services
- Tennis courts

Room amenities:
- Hairdryer
- Towels
- Phone-chargers
- Separate bathtub and shower
- Free bottled water

Prices (breakfast included):
- Standard Double/Twin, Garden View　　JPY 15,000 for 1 night
- Standard Double/Twin, Ocean View　　 JPY 21,000 for 1 night
- Superior Double/Twin, Ocean View　　 JPY 33,000 for 1 night
- Deluxe Double/Twin, Ocean View　　　JPY 42,000 for 1 night

第1回 英語 (リーディング)

Guest reviews (129 reviewers)　　　　　　★★★★★ (Average 4.8)

Cynthia from the UK

　If you are coming to Miyakojima this is the best place to stay. The beach is gorgeous white sand and the ocean is an amazing blue. The hotel rooms are very clean and comfortable. The pool and beach have lifeguards and are good for children. A breakfast buffet was included, and it was good, with a lot of options. The only drawback was the humidity on the island.

問1　The hotel is located ⬚ 11 ⬚ .

① far away from a golf course

② in front of a famous entertainment park

③ near a famous bridge

④ within walking distance of the airport

問2　One **fact** about the hotel is that ⬚ 12 ⬚ .

① it is the best place in Miyakojima

② the guests can park their cars for free

③ the guests cannot use the pool all year round

④ the only problem is the humidity

問3　To stay in a room with a sea view for three nights, you will pay ⬚ 13 ⬚ .

① at least 63,000 yen

② at most 99,000 yen

③ less than 42,000 yen

④ only 30,000 yen

問4 One **opinion** expressed about the hotel is that ☐14☐ .

① food and souvenirs are readily available to the guests

② it is safe for children to play on the beach

③ most of the guests are satisfied with the stay

④ the guests can go scuba diving in the nearby sea

問5 What is one of the attractions of the hotel? ☐15☐

① Free Wi-Fi in all areas

② Several restaurants to choose from

③ The indoor tennis courts

④ The public beach in front

— 12 —

第1回　英語（リーディング）

（下書き用紙）

英語（リーディング）の試験問題は次に続く。

— 13 —

第3問 （配点 15）

A You are planning to travel in Europe and go from London to Dublin by plane. You found useful information in the Q&A section of a travel advice website.

I'm considering taking an aeroplane to Dublin from London in April 2022. Can anyone tell me what the best way to get there is? I want to save as much money as possible. I live in Bloomsbury. Thanks in advance.

(Grace)

- -

Answer

I happen to live in the same area of London, and I often go to Dublin on business. I prefer to use the train to get to Hamlet Airport (it takes only about one hour and costs three pounds) and then to take Darwin Airlines. From Bloomsbury to Hamlet Airport by express bus you can save ten minutes, but it costs much more (about eight pounds).

Let me suggest some alternatives.

If you choose Tempest Airport instead of Hamlet Airport, you can take Lion Airlines, the cheapest airline in Europe. However, to get to Tempest Airport you need to take an express train, which costs about twenty pounds.

Here's another suggestion. If you take Ants Airways from Hamlet Airport, you can almost always save money compared to taking Darwin Airlines from there, although I do not recommend that airline. The service is poor and the staff is not well trained.

Prices of flights depend on your departure date, so check online.

Enjoy your trip!

(Robin)

— 14 —

How to get to Dublin

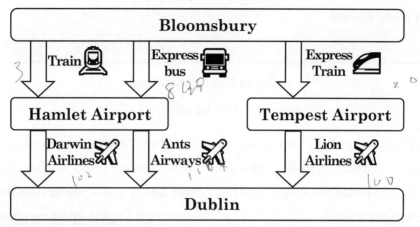

Flight Price Comparison (22 May 2022)

Airline	Price	Departure	Free Baggage Allowance	Excess Baggage Charge
Darwin Airlines	102 pounds	Hamlet	2	20 pounds / 1 piece
Ants Airways	84 pounds	Hamlet	1	30 pounds / 1 piece
Lion Airlines	60 pounds	Tempest	1	40 pounds / 1 piece

問1　From Robin's answer, you learn that Robin ☐16☐ .

① does not recommend Darwin Airlines
② lives in Bloomsbury and often visits Dublin
③ strongly suggests buying tickets online
④ usually takes an express bus to Hamlet Airport

問2　You are departing from Bloomsbury on 22 May 2022. You are going to carry two pieces of baggage. What is the most economical way to get to Dublin? ☐17☐

① By express bus and Ants Airways
② By express train and Lion Airlines
③ By train and Ants Airways
④ By train and Darwin Airlines

B You found the following article in a magazine for those who are hoping to study abroad.

Gap in Communication

Tim Leach

Let me tell you my experience of miscommunication resulting from the gap in conversational styles between Japanese and English.

As a high school student, I went to Japan as part of a cultural exchange program. I had been learning Japanese for two years then, so I thought it was time for me to have a real conversation with Japanese people. When I was introduced to the class, I was warmly welcomed. At first I had a little trouble understanding what they said, but soon I got used to it.

One day, when I was in a group-discussion, I found a strange thing. While I was expressing my opinion, one of the group members nodded and said "Hai," which is supposed to mean "Yes" in Japanese. So I thought he agreed with my opinion. However, when I finished speaking, he started to disagree with what I had just said. I was slightly confused. Just a while ago he said "Hai" and nodded, and now he disagreed with my opinion.

After the class, I talked about it to the teacher, who teaches English and has a good understanding of cultures in English-speaking countries. She told me that Japanese people sometimes use "Hai" as a sign that they understand what you are saying. This is called "aizuchi" in Japanese, and it is often accompanied by nodding. This means that even when Japanese people say "Hai" and nod, it doesn't always mean that they agree with what you say. I understood, but at the same time I thought this could lead to a serious misunderstanding.

So, here is a suggestion. Why don't we collect accounts of this kind of experience, in which you felt that the gap in communication styles might have caused a negative result? Please write an e-mail to the editor about your experiences. Our contact address is given on the last page of this magazine. We are going to make a list of your experiences in this section of next month's issue.

第 1 回 英語 (リーディング)

問1 Put the following events (① ~ ④) into the order in which they happened. 18 → 19 → 20 → 21

① Tim considered one classmate's reactions to his opinion inconsistent.

② Tim felt he could generally follow what his classmates were saying.

③ Tim had a discussion with his teacher about what had happened.

④ Tim stated an opinion of his during the class.

問2 From this article, you learn that when listening to foreigners, Japanese people might 22 .

① give a wrong impression of what they actually think

② nod when they do not understand

③ not state their opinion clearly

④ say "Hai" instead of saying "Yes"

問3 You have decided to send an account of your experiences to the editor. What should you do first? 23

① Find out the website address.

② Give a suggestion to the editor.

③ Look at the last page of the magazine.

④ Make a list of your experiences.

— 17 —

第4問 (配点 16)

You are preparing a presentation on students in foreign countries. You emailed data about it to your classmates, Jack and Mary. Based on their responses, you draft a presentation outline.

The data:

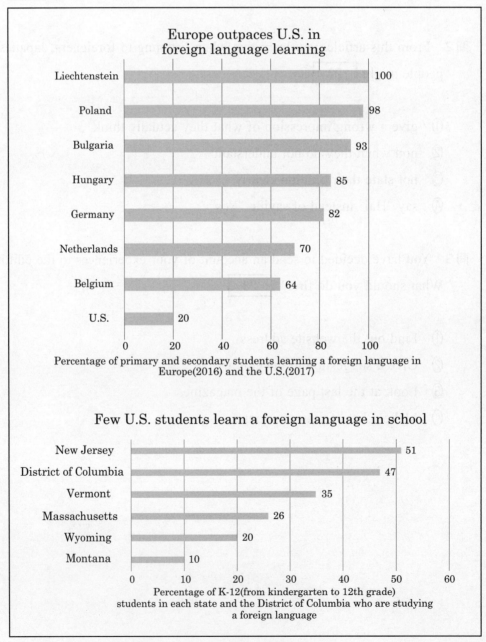

第1回　英語（リーディング）

The responses to your email:

Hi,

Thanks for your email. That's interesting data. Most primary and secondary school students across Europe study at least one foreign language as part of their education. I've also heard that studying a second foreign language for at least one year is compulsory in more than 20 European countries. Learning a foreign language is a common experience for students throughout Europe. I'd like to make a presentation on this.

However, I'd like to know more about this issue. For example, I need to find out the reason for this high percentage. I suppose many Europeans have a strong motive for studying a foreign language in order to be successful in business, or even to get a job, but I need to do further research on this in the near future.

Best,
Jack
P.S. This message is going to Mary, too.

Hi,

Thank you for sending your data. It was really informative!

I was surprised that very few students in the U.S. learn a foreign language, and I also wonder what they are learning when they do not learn a foreign language. I'll talk about this. In addition, I will look for information about

---

— 19 —

what American students think is indispensable in searching for a job. I agree with Jack in thinking that finding a job is an important factor for European students when they learn a foreign language. So what about American students? I want to know what they put emphasis on when they are preparing themselves to get a job.

I would like you to talk about the differences among the fifty states in the U.S., which will make the presentation more worth listening to. As is shown in the graph you sent, there is no national standard about foreign language learning in the U.S. and many differences exist in the one country. I'm sure many people want to know why. However, this needs further study.

All the best,
Mary
P.S. This message is going to Jack, too.

The presentation draft:

Presentation Title: 24

Presenter   **Topic**

Jack : 25

Mary : 26

me : *Gaps among U.S. states regarding foreign language learning*

Although a kind of uniformity exists in Europe, with the percentage of foreign language learning in Belgium being about 27 *of that in Liechtenstein, in the U.S. the percentage in Montana is only about* 28 *of that in New Jersey.*

Themes for Future Research: 29

第1回　英語（リーディング）

問1　Which is the best for ☐ 24 ☐ ?

① Fierce competition in the U.S. for a limited number of rewarding career opportunities
② Foreign language education in European and American schools
③ Rising expenditure on foreign language learning in the world
④ The uniformity of European schools in foreign language education

問2　Which is the best for ☐ 25 ☐ ?

① Comparing European schools with American ones
② How foreign language learning is becoming more diverse in Europe
③ The popularity of Japanese as a second foreign language
④ The widespread practice of foreign language learning in Europe

問3　Which is the best for ☐ 26 ☐ ?

① American students' struggle for well-paid jobs
② Different school policies of the states in the U.S.
③ The reason for many European students studying French
④ The subjects American students study instead of foreign languages

— 21 —

問4　You agree with Mary's suggestion and look at the graph.　Choose the best for 　27　 and 　28　 .

① a fifth

② two-thirds

③ three quarters

④ four-fifths

問5　Which is the best combination for 　29　 ?

A : The future tendency toward English as the global language

B : The impact of learning a foreign language on one's mother tongue

C : The reason for the difference in foreign language learning in the U.S.

D : Why many students are learning a foreign language in Europe

① A and B

② A and C

③ A and D

④ B and C

⑤ B and D

⑥ C and D

— 22 —

第1回　英語（リーディング）

（下書き用紙）

英語（リーディング）の試験問題は次に続く。

— 23 —

第5問 （配点　15）

Using an international news report, you are going to take part in an English oral presentation contest. Read the following news story from the United States to make notes for your talk.

Anais Bordier and Samantha Futerman have the same laugh and the same freckled cheeks. They wear their hair the same way. The pair tease and poke each other like they've grown up together, but they didn't. Neither Samantha nor Anais knew she had an identical twin sister. The twins met for the first time in London in May 2013. When the twins came face to face in the living room of the Airbnb apartment, all they could do was stare. At first, they felt a little awkward, as they were on a first date, but their discomfort quickly disappeared; they even took a nap together that first day.

Anais, a French student who grew up in Paris, was studying fashion design in London. On a Saturday in December 2012, while she was on a bus, a friend of hers sent her a screen shot of a YouTube video featuring Samantha. Anais automatically thought, "Oh, who posted a video of me on YouTube?" But later she found out that it was not her but an American actress. Samantha, a Los Angeles-based actress who had appeared in the 2005 movie *Memoirs of a Geisha*, was born in South Korea, like Anais — and was born on the same day, November 19, 1987. They were both adopted soon after birth — Anais by a couple in Paris and Samantha by a New Jersey family with three boys. She decided to contact Samantha via Facebook, sending her a friend request and a message.

On February 21, 2013, Samantha went to a friend's apartment to have her nails done for the opening day of her new film. While her friend was painting her nails, she fiddled with her cellphone and saw a request on Facebook from a young woman named Anais. She studied the woman's photo and thought it was an old picture of hers. She tapped the image and saw its profile; they shared a birthdate and similar activities. Samantha at first didn't know what to make

— 24 —

第 1 回　英語 （リーディング）

of Anais's friend request and message. It took her a few days to respond, but eventually she accepted the friend request.

Several days after they connected on Facebook, Samantha and Anais talked for the first time, using Skype. For them, it was like going on a blind date, and they didn't know what to ask first. They talked about how it all happened, and what their friends were saying. They compared their noses, their teeth, their ears, and their hands. They talked about their current boyfriend status. They talked until they were just staring at each other. They were supposed to chat for 90 minutes but ended up talking for three hours.

Later they took a DNA test, which proved what they already knew — that they were, in fact, twins. They discovered similarities, beyond their long hair and the spray of freckles across their noses. Both hate bell peppers and cooked carrots, prefer Coke to Pepsi, and enjoy Korean barbecue and Halloween. They share a love of the same color nail polish and the need to nap when stressed and sleep 10 hours a day. However, their differences are notable, too: Samantha is more outgoing, which is a result, she believes, of growing up with two older brothers. On the other hand, Anais, an only child, is much moodier, struggling with her adoption and with feelings of abandonment.

They have tried to contact their Korean birth mother but she has not been interested in connecting with them. "If one day she wants to contact us, then we're here, and we're willing, and we're ready," Samantha says. Though they still live halfway around the world from each other, Anais, who is now a handbag designer in Paris, and Samantha in Los Angeles send text messages multiple times every day. Anais says Samantha always wakes her up in the morning via text. She gets messages like, "Wake up, you're late." They may have been torn apart as babies, but they say they are now forever bonded.

Your notes:

[30] Central High School
English Oral Presentation Contest

Who's Who?
- Anais: ☐
- Samantha: ☐ } [31]

Storyline of the Twin's Encounter
They were born as twins.
→ They were adopted by different families.
→ [32] → [33] → [34] → [35]

The Twins' Shared Characteristics
They have the same:
- freckles.
- hair style.
- way of laughing.
- tastes in color.
- [36] .
- [37] .

The Twins Now
The twins today:
- [38] .
- feel connected to each other.
- send multiple messages to each other.

— 26 —

第1回 英語 (リーディング)

問1　Which is the best title for your presentation?　30

    ① Twins Always Staying Together

    ② Twins Looking for their Mother

    ③ Twins Pursuing their Dreams

    ④ Twins Reunited in a Modern Way

問2　Which is the best combination for　31　?

	Anais	Samantha
①	a French designer of Korean descent	an American actress of Korean descent
②	a Korean actress of American descent	a Korean designer of French descent
③	a Korean designer of French descent	a Korean actress of American descent
④	an American actress of Korean descent	a French designer of Korean descent

問3　Choose **four** out of the five options (① ～ ⑤) and rearrange them in the order they happened.　32　→　33　→　34　→　35

    ① Anais saw Samantha on YouTube.

    ② Samantha sent a friend request to Anais.

    ③ They became "friends" on Facebook.

    ④ They met in person for the first time.

    ⑤ They talked on Skype.

問4 Choose the best two options for ☐36☐ and ☐37☐ . (The order does not matter.)

① food preferences
② home environment
③ personality
④ professions
⑤ sleep pattern

問5 Choose the best option for ☐38☐ .

① are in touch with their biological mother
② call each other every morning
③ frequently visit each other
④ live far away from each other

— 28 —

第1回　英語（リーディング）

（ 下 書 き 用 紙 ）

英語（リーディング）の試験問題は次に続く。

第6問 （配点 24）

A You are working on a class project about dress codes in modern society and found the following article. You are reading it and making notes to speak about your findings to your classmates.

Is Wearing a Tie Really Necessary?

Is wearing a tie really necessary? Why do intelligent men loop rags around their necks and tighten them? U.S. journalist Linda Ellerbee asked, "If men can run the world, why can't they stop wearing neckties?" A lot of people may answer that men, like women, do many silly things in the name of fashion.

Many businesspeople in the world now argue that today's necktie is useless: a tie does not protect the body from heat or cold, as a hat, shirt, pants, and shoes do. A tie is a thin strip of cloth, so it is not large enough to cover the body in bad weather. Also, it does not hold up other clothing items, as a belt does. A tie hangs from the top of a shirt, so it holds nothing up. A tie does not provide any comfort to the wearer, unlike socks, which allow a person to wear shoes comfortably. In fact, most men say that neckties are uncomfortable. Clearly, the tie has no practical purpose.

The tie hasn't always been useless, however. In second-century Rome, speakers and soldiers wore neck scarves called fascalias to protect their throats from heat, cold, and dust. Later, Croatians adopted the Roman neck cloths to guard against the weather. In 18th-century England, neck cloths were so thick that they reportedly prevented injuries in battle. From Asia to North and South America, bandanas have served as practical means of protecting working men's necks.

As time passed, though, the tie lost its usefulness. In the 1600s, men wore ties only because they symbolized the fashion of the upper class. King

— 30 —

第1回　英語（リーディング）

Louis XIV of France wore lace and fine silk neck coverings. Consequently, many men followed the king's style. European paintings of the 17th to 19th centuries show men belonging to the military, government, and upper class in neck cloths so high and stiff that they could barely turn their heads. In the end, neck cloths became essential clothing for well-dressed men.

Many men today also wear neckties as a result of their desire for upward status in certain professions. Hopeful executives, clerks, and technicians wear neckties because their bosses do. These men wear ties to show they belong in business, politics, and other professions and to look successful or please their bosses. Due to these factors, the tyranny of the tie has spread across the globe. A necktie is a necessary part of formal male clothing in Asia, Africa, and South America. In fact, people in China and Japan now think a man without a tie is not serious about work and believe that he is disrespecting tradition, though their parents and grandparents had never even heard of the tie.

Some people have seen this as a bad convention and tried to get rid of ties. More and more companies are allowing their workers to dress more casually on Fridays, so that is a day when male professionals may go to work without ties. Also, men sometimes dress in shirts without ties in the summer when it is hot. And in more and more workplaces today, men are no longer expected to wear ties at all. Nevertheless, many men are still expected to wear ties to work.

In a few centuries, or perhaps just decades from today, people may look back and shake their heads in disbelief. They will not be able to understand why men actually put these things around their necks and thought them necessary to wear. So why are men in today's world considered inappropriately dressed if they appear at a business meeting or a wedding without a tie? In the future, perhaps comfort will be more important than the unofficial fashion rules of society to most people in such situations.

Your notes:

Is wearing a tie really necessary?

Some arguments against today's tie

A tie does not have such practical functions as

◆ protecting the body from the weather

◆ [39]

◆ providing physical comfort

Historical context of the tie

◆ **Practical purposes of the tie in history**

◇ Ancient Rome: Protecting men's throats from the weather

→ Croatians [40]

◇ 18th-century England: Protecting against injuries in battle

◇ Asia and Americas: Protecting working men's necks

▽

◆ **Change in the meaning of the tie**

◇ Europe from the 17th century on: Functioning as a symbol of the upper class

◇ Modern society: Showing [41] and [42]

Recent trends

Many people regard wearing a tie as a bad convention

◆ A lot of companies allow no-tie dress codes on certain occasions

◆ Some companies do not require ties at all

→Despite these attempts, the pressure to wear a tie hasn't completely disappeared

Author's expectation

The majority of people in the future will [43] .

— 32 —

第1回　英語（リーディング）

問1　Choose the best option for ☐ 39 ☐.

① helping the wearer achieve success

② making the wearer look better

③ protecting against an enemy's attacks

④ securing other pieces of clothing

問2　Choose the best option for ☐ 40 ☐.

① criticized the Romans' dress code

② guarded against their invasion

③ imitated the Romans' custom

④ invented a way of weather forecasting

問3　Choose the best two options for ☐ 41 ☐ and ☐ 42 ☐. (The order does not matter.)

① people's ambition to succeed at work

② people's expectations of succeeding without effort

③ people's friendly attitudes toward others

④ people's rebellious attitudes toward their bosses

⑤ people's sense of belonging to their organizations

問4　Choose the best option for ☐ 43 ☐.

① abandon the custom of wearing a tie to avoid the physical discomfort

② consider people without a tie on official occasions inappropriately dressed

③ not believe they need to follow any rules

④ not underestimate the practical value of the tie

— 33 —

B You are studying the effects of light on the environment. You are going to read the following passage from an Internet site to learn more about it.

Most of us are familiar with air, water, and land pollution, but did you know that light can also be a pollutant? Inappropriate or excessive use of artificial light — known as light pollution — can have serious environmental consequences on humans, wildlife, and our climate.

One kind of light pollution is sky glow, which is the brightening of the night sky, mostly over urban areas, due to the electric lights of cars, streetlamps, offices, factories, and outdoor advertising, turning night into day for people who work and play long after sunset. According to a 2016 survey, 80 percent of the world's population lives under sky glow. In the United States and Europe 99 percent of the public can't experience a natural night sky! There are three other kinds of light pollution: clutter, light trespass, and glare. Clutter is bright, confusing, and excessive groupings of light sources. Light trespass is when light extends into an area where it is not wanted or needed. Glare is excessive brightness that can cause visual discomfort.

Light pollution is a side effect of industrial civilization. The fact is that much of the outdoor lighting used at night is inefficient, overly bright, poorly targeted, improperly shielded, and, in many cases, completely unnecessary. This light, and the electricity used to create it, is being wasted by being spilled into the sky rather than focused on the actual objects and areas that people want illuminated.

With much of the Earth's population living under light-polluted skies, over-lighting is an international concern. If you live in an urban or suburban area, all you have to do to see this type of pollution is go outside at night and look up at the sky. For three billion years, life on Earth existed in a rhythm of light and dark that was created solely by the illumination of the sun, moon and stars. Now, artificial lights have power over the darkness,

— 34 —

第1回　英語（リーディング）

and our cities glow at night, disrupting the natural day-night pattern and shifting the delicate balance of our environment. The negative effects of the loss of this natural resource might seem invisible. But a growing body of evidence links the brightening night sky directly to negative impacts including increased energy consumption, disruption of the ecosystem and wildlife, the harming of human health, and adverse effects regarding crime and safety. Light pollution affects every citizen. Fortunately, concern about light pollution is rising dramatically. A growing number of scientists, environmental groups and civic leaders are taking action to restore the natural night. Each of us can adopt practical solutions to combat light pollution locally, nationally and internationally.

The good news is that light pollution, unlike many other forms of pollution, is reversible, and each one of us can make a difference! Just being aware that light pollution is a problem is not enough: the need is for action. You can start by minimizing the light from your own home at night. So spread the word to your family and friends and tell them to pass it on. Many people either don't know or don't understand a lot about light pollution and the negative impacts of artificial light at night. By being an ambassador and explaining the issues to others, you will help bring awareness of this growing problem and inspire more people to take the necessary steps to protect our natural night sky.

問1 You learn that light pollution has been caused by 44 .

① destruction of natural light sources by humans

② economic depression in industrialized countries

③ increasing awareness of the dangers of darkness

④ the use of unnecessary light in the wrong places

問2 You are summarizing the information you have just studied. How should the table be finished? 45

The kind of light pollution	Brief description
(A)	Brightness above inhabited areas
(B)	Brightness making it hard to see
(C)	Light gathered from various light sources
(D)	Light falling where it is not intended

① (A) clutter   (B) glare

    (C) light trespass   (D) sky glow

② (A) clutter   (B) light trespass

    (C) sky glow   (D) glare

③ (A) light trespass   (B) glare

    (C) clutter   (D) sky glow

④ (A) sky glow   (B) clutter

    (C) light trespass   (D) glare

⑤ (A) sky glow   (B) glare

    (C) clutter   (D) light trespass

第1回 英語 (リーディング)

問3 Which of the following should you **not** include for the negative effects of light pollution? 46

① hazard to human life and limb
② ineffective use of electricity
③ interference in the natural environment
④ the development of civilization
⑤ the weakening of security in society

問4 According to the article you read, which of the following are true? (Choose two options. The order does not matter.) 47 · 48

① It is possible to get rid of light pollution.
② Life on Earth followed the rhythm of light and dark for a very long time.
③ People should know more about other kinds of pollution apart from light pollution.
④ The bad influences of light pollution are easy to understand.
⑤ We have no control over the amount of light on Earth.

問5 To describe the author's position, which of the following is most appropriate? 49

① The author argues that reducing light pollution requires public awareness and action.
② The author believes that humans should be reminded of the beauty of natural light.
③ The author states that the effort of governments rather than individuals is needed to stop light pollution.
④ The author talks about the need to create products emitting less light.

— 37 —

第 2 回

（80分）

実 戦 問 題

● 標 準 所 要 時 間 ●

第1問　7分程度	第4問 12分程度
第2問 13分程度	第5問 14分程度
第3問 12分程度	第6問 22分程度

第２回　実戦問題

英　語(リーディング)

各大問の英文や図表を読み，解答番号 $\boxed{1}$ ～ $\boxed{48}$ にあてはまるものとして最も適当な選択肢を選びなさい。

第1問　(配点　10)

A　You are preparing for a trip to Copenhagen, Denmark. You found a website introducing some of the main districts of the city and what tourists can enjoy in them.

Main Districts of Copenhagen	
Islands Brygge ▶ Young artists have their studios here, including those who design for well-known brands. ▶ You can also enjoy boat trips on a solar-powered motor boat.	**Christianshavn** ▶ *Christianshavn* is largely residential. ▶ You can enjoy strolling or cycling along the beautiful tree-lined canals. ▶ You can find many cafes and shops selling fashionable clothes that the locals love.
Vesterbro ▶ This district used to be the city's meatpacking area and is now filled with restaurants and art galleries. ▶ You can join workshops held by artists here.	**Nørrebro** ▶ *Nørrebro* is one of the best places in the city to find good coffee. ▶ You can shop for nice secondhand clothes and furniture and for vintage records.

— 2 —

第2回　英語（リーディング）

問1　Both in *Islands Brygge* and *Christianshavn*, you can enjoy ☐ 1 ☐ .

① an outdoor activity

② exotic food

③ meeting famous people

④ window-shopping

問2　If you want to look at some artworks and also eat out, you should
visit ☐ 2 ☐ .

① *Christianshavn*

② *Islands Brygge*

③ *Nørrebro*

④ *Vesterbro*

— 3 —

B You are looking at the website for Monthly Book Club, a book-reading circle. You are thinking about taking part in the next meeting, to be held on June 17th.

Monthly Book Club with Tyler Bloom
Read books and cultivate your mind!

Hello, booklovers! We are having another Monthly Book Club meeting!

This month, it's not just another meeting, because we are having as a guest Tyler Bloom, a young, talented writer who very recently won the Mayor's Book Prize for 2022.

Meeting Schedule

Discussion	June 17th, Saturday, 15:30-17:00
Talk by Tyler Bloom	June 17th, Saturday, 17:00-18:00

How to Join the Next Monthly Book Club Meeting

◆ Fill in the web application form.　　　　　→ Click **HERE**!
  ・You should apply to join the meeting by June 15th.
◆ Read the selected book and join the Monthly Book Club meeting!
  ・Check the list for which book we are going to discuss this month.
　　　　　　　　　　　　　　　　　→ The List is **HERE**!
  ・Location → Click **HERE** for the map.
  ・You can also join the meeting (both the discussion and the talk) online. → **See below**.
  ・As for the discussion, you can come and leave at any time you like, as long as you have submitted the web application form and you have read the book.

How to join the meeting online:
Please email us (monthlybookclub@example.com) after you have completed the application process. We'll send you the link for the online meeting.

About the fee:
◆ The discussion is free of charge.
◆ To listen to the talk, please go to **this LINK** and get a ticket ($15). You can either pay by credit card or by bank transfer.

第2回　英語（リーディング）

問1　You should apply for the next meeting at least ⬛3⬛ before the meeting.

① a day

② two days

③ a week

④ two weeks

問2　If you want to attend the discussion, you must ⬛4⬛ .

① attend it online

② buy a ticket for 15 dollars

③ read the book on the list

④ stay until it ends at 17:00

問3　You are asked to send an email to the organizer if ⬛5⬛ .

① you are planning to join the event online

② you can't complete the application form

③ you don't have a credit card

④ you want to apply after June 15th

—5—

第2問 (配点 20)

A You are going to participate in a summer programme held by a university in the UK, during which you can stay in the college dormitory. You are reading the information about the dormitory.

Commonwealth Hall
Life in Dormitory Guidebook 2022

Study Room: Room 21 on the first floor

Open from 10 am to 6 pm every day except Sundays. On Sundays it's open from 1 pm to 6 pm. Free Wi-Fi is available. You are allowed to drink bottled water only. You can read any book in this room, but you are not allowed to take them out of the room.

Dining Hall: Room 5 on the ground floor

Open from 7 am to 9 am (for breakfast) and from 6 pm to 8 pm (for dinner). On Saturdays and Sundays brunch is served from 9 am to 11 am instead of breakfast. You need to present your student ID card to get your meal.

Laundry Room: located on each floor

In order to use the laundry room, you must first purchase a laundry card, which is £3.00. Then you need to charge the card to do the laundry. Washing and drying cost £1.00 each. Please do not forget to pick up your clothes and clean the area after you use it.

Comments from Past Students

- Usually many people are studying enthusiastically in the study room, but there are lots of seats there, so it never happens that all seats are occupied.

- We can eat a good meal at our dining hall. The amount of food is fairly large, so I am always full after the meal.

- The laundry room is always kept clean, which suggests that residents in this dormitory are willing to follow the rules.

- I think the machines in the laundry room are easy to use, so you don't have to worry about it. Just note that there are no chairs to sit on in the rooms. You should wait in your own room while your clothes are being washed.

- There is a common room for students on the third floor where you can sit, relax, and talk with friends. I love the atmosphere!

— 6 —

第2回　英語（リーディング）

問1　6　are two things you can do at the dormitory.

　　A : connect to a Wi-Fi network in the study room

　　B : eat breakfast at 8 am every day

　　C : purchase a meal card at the dining hall

　　D : sit and wait in the laundry room

　　E : use the study room until dinner is ready

　　① A and B

　　② A and E

　　③ B and C

　　④ C and D

　　⑤ D and E

問2　You are in the common room for students and want to go to the study room. You need to　7　.

　　① go down one floor

　　② go down two floors

　　③ go up one floor

　　④ stay on the same floor

問3　The dormitory has several rooms for　8　.

　　① eating breakfast

　　② studying

　　③ talking with friends

　　④ washing clothes

—7—

問4　If you don't have a laundry card and you want to do both washing and drying at the laundry room, you'll need to pay ☐ 9 ☐ in total.

① £3.00

② £4.00

③ £5.00

④ £6.00

問5　One **fact** stated by a previous student is that ☐ 10 ☐ .

① the dining hall is located on the ground floor

② the washing machines are easy to use for new students

③ usually there are few people in the study room

④ you can talk with friends in the common room

― 8 ―

B You are the editor of a school English paper at a high school in Tokyo. Hugh, an exchange student from the UK, has written an article for the paper.

Where in Japan should I visit? This is the question I asked you guys the other day, and I finished collecting answers, with the help of Tomomi and Takuya. I expected Kyoto would rank first, but in reality Osaka was chosen as the most recommended place. Actually, Hokkaido was more popular than Kyoto. Next to Kyoto ranked Kagoshima.

Why is Osaka so popular? Here are some comments on the questionnaire.

- Osaka is famous as "The Nation's kitchen." Food is really lovely there!
- People are friendly. I'm sure they are happy to help foreigners.
- The coexistence of history and modernity in Osaka will surely satisfy you!
- The location is ideal. From Osaka you can easily visit Nara, Kyoto, Kobe, and Nagoya.

What interests me most is the last comment. I want to visit as many cities in Japan as possible, so it's a good idea to go to Osaka first, and then take short trips to several cities accessible from there! Also, I heard Osaka has easy access to the Shinkansen. So if I stay in Osaka, I might be able to go by the Shinkansen as far as Hiroshima, where a friend of mine lives. Or do you think it is better to use an overnight bus to get there? Tell me about it! Anyway, I will definitely visit Osaka. Thanks for your answer!

問1 Which shows the recommended prefectures' ranking from **highest to lowest**? ___11___

① Osaka — Hokkaido — Kagoshima — Kyoto
② Osaka — Hokkaido — Kyoto — Kagoshima
③ Osaka — Kagoshima — Hokkaido — Kyoto
④ Osaka — Kagoshima — Kyoto — Hokkaido
⑤ Osaka — Kyoto — Hokkaido — Kagoshima
⑥ Osaka — Kyoto — Kagoshima — Hokkaido

問2 According to the comments on the questionnaire, one advantage of visiting Osaka is that ___12___ .

① it has a lot of popular tourist attractions
② many people there work as tourist guides
③ you can enjoy both the old and the new
④ you can usually get food at a low price

問3 Which best summarises Hugh's idea about his trip to Osaka? ___13___

① He'll base himself in Osaka and make trips from there.
② He'll eat as many kinds of food as possible.
③ He'll offer as much help as he can to foreigners.
④ He'll use the Shinkansen to go to Osaka from Tokyo.

— 10 —

第2回　英語（リーディング）

問4　Why does Hugh want to visit Hiroshima?　14

① Because he has a friend there.

② Because he has never visited there.

③ Because he really likes the food there.

④ Because he wants to ride the Shinkansen.

問5　What information are Hugh's classmates most likely to give him after reading this article?　15

① How to get an overnight bus ticket to Osaka.

② Places he should visit in Hiroshima.

③ Recommended restaurants in the Kansai region.

④ The best way to get to Hiroshima from Osaka.

— 11 —

第3問 (配点 15)

A You've become acquainted with an exchange student from the UK. You are reading her blog post in order to become friendlier with her.

Helen Potter
Monday, 28 February, 10.00 pm

The other day, I came back to my flat to find a letter in my postbox. It was from Kenta, a classmate at my Japanese college. He asked me to go to an event called 'A World Fountain Pen Fair' held at a department store in Tokyo.

Usually I use a pencil or a ballpoint pen to study and assumed that rich adults use fountain pens because they were expensive. However, I became interested when I saw a brochure of the fair with pictures of beautiful pens Kenta attached, so I texted him to accept his offer.

Today, I met Kenta at an underground station near the department store. At the fair, there were a lot of fountain pens from around the world. As a student majoring in Japanese literature, I was interested in those made in Japan. A clerk let me try a Japanese one, so I wrote my own name, but it felt a bit strange using it. The clerk said Japanese fountain pens are suitable for writing Japanese characters including *kanji*, so if I use one for writing English, I should use one made in a European country.

At first Kenta said he would buy a model made in Germany, but as he overheard our conversation, he decided to buy a Japanese one advertised on a flier because he mainly writes in Japanese. Actually, I usually write in English, but I bought a Japanese one shown on the flier, too, though one that was cheaper than his, because I eventually want to master writing in Japanese.

第2回 英語（リーディング）

Square Department Store
Held from 25 February to 10 March (10.00 am – 5.00 pm)

International Sale: Splendid pens from around the world are available.

Example	Model A	Model B	Model C	Model D
Price	¥3,000	¥12,000	¥30,000	¥75,000
Country	Japan	Japan	Germany	Italy

Pen Clinic : Professional craftspeople will fix your pen for nothing.
　Note : One pen per person

問 1　From Helen's blog, you learn that she 16 .

① can write her name in Japanese
② has a good command of Japanese
③ has always longed to have her own fountain pen
④ wants to learn to write *kanji*

問 2　Kenta most likely bought a fountain pen 17 .

① Model A
② Model B
③ Model C
④ Model D

— 13 —

B You enjoy outdoor sports and have found an interesting story in a cycling magazine.

Over 1,400 Kilometres in Under Five Days

Several years ago, I participated in a long-distance bicycle ride across the United Kingdom called "London Edinburgh London", which takes place every four years, and in which participants ride from London, the capital of England, to Edinburgh, the capital of Scotland, and then back to London in under five days. To make up for my lack of experience I teamed up with Anne and Ted, both much more experienced riders than me, from my local cycling club.

On 30 July, we started northwards from London at 6 am. There was a checkpoint about every 80 kilometres. Thanks to the rather flat route, I enjoyed cycling with my teammates. After it got dark we reached Pocklington Checkpoint, and we spent the night there. But as there were more participants than beds, everyone was allowed to sleep in bed for only three hours! This made us decide to book hotel rooms after that. The next day, despite our lack of sleep, we pressed on. At the end of the day, we managed to find hotel rooms in Moffat.

On the 3rd day, we got up at 4 am and set off before 5 am, arriving in Edinburgh at 9 am. Now it was time to set out on our southbound leg. But soon after that, it started to rain very hard, and then my right leg began aching. I took painkillers, and we somehow managed to arrive at Barnard Castle after dark. The next morning, although Ted had started complaining about his neck, we set off anyway. But the hills got steeper, and then came the head winds. My right leg started aching again. When we got to Louth at the end of the day, Ted and I were in great pain and exhausted. Anne offered to give us massages, even when she, too, was obviously tired!

第2回 英語（リーディング）

On the last morning, thanks to Anne's massage, my pain had eased a lot. But Ted was still in pain, and at Great Easton he completely stopped cycling. Anne and I spent an hour trying to persuade him to keep going, but to no effect. At last we decided to leave him behind. Now we had to go really fast to finish the challenge before the time ran out. Finally we reached the goal with 25 minutes to spare, and I was happy about that. But I wished Ted were with us at the finish line.

問1 Put the following events (① ～ ④) into the order in which they happened.

| 18 | → | 19 | → | 20 | → | 21 |

① Heavy rain began to come down as they rode.

② One team member chose not to finish the ride.

③ The team reached the capital of Scotland.

④ The team slept at one of the checkpoints.

問2 What was the reason that the writer's team started to sleep in hotels?

| 22 |

① Hotels turned out to be less expensive than checkpoints.

② The checkpoint they stayed at was too noisy.

③ They couldn't find any place to sleep at one of the checkpoints.

④ They couldn't get enough sleep the first night.

問3 From this story, you learnt that the writer | 23 | .

① only suffered from pain in the leg for one day

② reached the final destination within the time limit

③ was completely satisfied with the result

④ was the most experienced rider in the team

— 15 —

第4問 （配点 16）

You have just moved to South City. You are reading two posts about bicycle use. One was posted by a bicycle shop, and the other by Amy.

Come and enjoy cycling in South City!
Posted by bicycle shop BEN at 5:00 p.m. on April 2, 2022

Cycling is an environmentally sustainable means of transportation and good for your health. Why don't you enjoy cycling around South City? You can reach the backstreets that are not accessible by bus or car. We are renting bicycles near Central Park. You can choose a bicycle you like depending on the place you want to ride to. Different types of bicycle are available for rent and the prices are as follows:

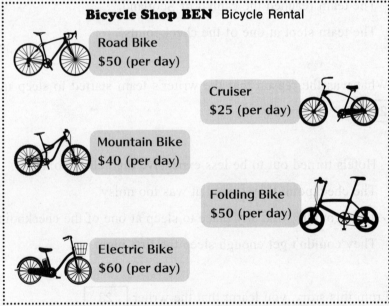

Information on other types → https://rentalcycleben.example.web

Fees are for one day. Bicycles can be checked out from 10:00 a.m. to 1:00 p.m. The bicycle you use must be returned to our shop by 8:00 p.m. on the same day. You can ride anywhere as long as you return your bicycle on time.

Would you like to experience riding a shared bicycle?
Posted by Amy at 11:18 a.m. on May 5, 2020

Have you heard of a bicycle sharing service? This service has recently been started in South City. Once you have downloaded the app and registered, you can start using this service. Bicycles are locked to docks at bicycle stations. Enter your membership number to unlock them, and you can use a bicycle any time you like. Bicycles can be returned anytime and anywhere as long as there is a dock available. I have created a list comparing what is available at different companies, and their fees. One of the companies has as many as 20 stations in South City. There are companies that offer the same services in neighboring cities. I often use bike sharing services and find them very convenient. South City has many hills, and electric bicycles are very convenient but expensive to buy. Rental bicycles must be returned to the place where they were rented, which can be a bit troublesome when you are far from where you picked your bicycle up and the weather turns bad. Why don't you take this opportunity to experience an environmentally friendly bicycle sharing service?

Companies	Pedal More	BJ Cycles	Amazing Wheels
Price per hour	$12	$15 (Electric bike) $10 (Cruiser)	$12 (Electric bike) $10 (Cruiser)
The number of stations in South City	12	20	15
Type of bicycle	Electric Bike	Electric Bike Cruiser	Electric Bike Cruiser
The number of docks per station	8	5	6
Services in neighboring cities	Available	Available	Unavailable

Note that bicycles can be returned when a bicycle dock is available. You can check the location of the bike station and availability of docks on the app, but you should bear in mind that there might not be any docks available near where you want to finish using your bike.

問1　The bicycle shop BEN recommends that in South City you should
　　　24　.

　　　① choose and rent the cheapest bicycle
　　　② not go out on a bicycle on rainy days
　　　③ not ride a bicycle at night
　　　④ visit places you can't reach by car

問2　Regarding shared bicycle services, Amy writes that　25　.

　　　① some companies have more than double the number of docks of
　　　　 other companies
　　　② the same services are always available outside South City
　　　③ there are few restrictions on when and where to pick up a bicycle
　　　④ they offer many different types of bicycle to suit your taste

問3　Both the bicycle shop BEN and Amy suggest that　26　.

　　　① bicycle sharing is less troublesome than renting
　　　② bicycles don't harm the environment
　　　③ riding a bicycle is healthy
　　　④ using bicycles can save money

— 18 —

第2回　英語（リーディング）

問4　If you want to begin using any type of bike at the lowest rate after 6:00 p.m., you should ☐ 27 ☐ .

① access the shop's URL address
② check the list Amy made
③ contact the bicycle shop
④ use services in other cities

問5　You are considering riding an electric bike belonging to ☐ 28 ☐ from 10:00 a.m. to 5:00 p.m. because it is the cheapest electric bike. However, you are also thinking about riding a cruiser belonging to ☐ 29 ☐ because you might want to return your bicycle in a neighboring city.　(Choose the best one for each box from options ① ～ ④.)

① Amazing Wheels
② Bicycle shop BEN
③ BJ Cycles
④ Pedal More

— 19 —

第5問 (配点 15)

You are a high school student and are learning English as a foreign language. Next week you have to make a presentation on a researcher. You found the following article and have prepared notes for your presentation.

English grammar is studied in the field called linguistics, and countless facts about it have been revealed and discovered over many decades. One scholar who everyone says contributed most to the study of English grammar is Otto Jespersen, a Danish linguist.

Otto Jespersen

He was born in the town of Randers in 1860. When he was young, he loved languages and learned several foreign languages, including Italian and Spanish, by himself. He entered Copenhagen University in 1877. At first he studied law, as his father and grandfather had, but when he had free time, he enjoyed literature in foreign languages. At that time, in order to earn a living, he worked part-time as a schoolteacher and as a shorthand reporter in the Danish parliament.

In 1881 came a major turning-point in his academic career: he gave up law altogether and decided to devote himself entirely to the study of languages, which was something he had really wanted to pursue. Among his teachers there was Vilhelm Thomsen, who was later to have a great influence on him. Jespersen's main research topic was French, but he also studied English and German. In 1887, he earned his master's degree in French.

After graduating from the university in 1887, Jespersen spent nearly one year in England, Germany, and France, where he attended some linguistic classes. When he visited England, he met Henry Sweet, then a very famous and influential linguist. During his stay overseas, Thomsen advised him to specialize in the English language, since an academic post in that field would soon be vacant. Jespersen followed this advice and returned to Copenhagen in August 1888 and began work on his doctoral thesis on English. In 1891 he finally received a doctoral degree. Jespersen was a professor of English at the University of Copenhagen from 1893 to 1925. From 1920 to 1921, he also served as the president of the university.

He published a lot of articles and books on English, most of which have been highly regarded. One of his most important works is *A Modern English Grammar on Historical Principles*. This consists of seven volumes published from 1909 to 1949. Those volumes are considered the best literature on the English language written by a non-native speaker of English. Explanations found in them are so detailed that some even suggest that Jespersen knew much more about English than native speakers do.

What is special about Jespersen's research and works? First, example sentences for explaining each grammatical feature are adopted from authentic materials, such as works by Shakespeare. Often, researchers who analyze English grammar make example sentences by themselves just for explanatory purposes. Those kinds of linguists tend to unknowingly present English as they want it to be seen rather than as it is. On the other hand, Jespersen always tried to depict the truth about English by referring to actual instances of language use.

Second, he coined a lot of new technical terms to explain English grammar. It is true that many researchers invented new concepts and tools by which to describe English grammar, but most of them have gone out of use or have been ignored by other researchers. By contrast, even about 80 years after his death, most of what Jespersen invented and revealed is still used and considered as valid, especially for English pedagogical grammar. Pedagogical grammar refers to a description of how to use grammar in communication for foreign language learners.

Also, most linguists today still cite and mention Jespersen's research in their articles. Furthermore, many linguists often find that what they feel they have discovered was already described in works by Jespersen. Noam Chomsky, one of the most renowned linguists alive today, wrote that even though Jespersen's works involve a lot of problems from a theoretical point of view, his observations of English were largely correct.

Your presentation notes:

Otto Jespersen (1860-1943)

— 30 —

Early Days

  — born in 1860

  — 31

  — 32

Sequence of Some Events in His Life

      Jespersen changed his major to languages.

      33

      34

      Jespersen became a professor of English.

      35

      36

One Important Characteristic of His Research and Books

  — Jespersen explained the grammatical phenomena of English by 37 .

Influence and Recognition

  — Jespersen is sometimes regarded as knowing about English far better than native speakers.

  — 38

第2回 英語 (リーディング)

問1 Which is the best subtitle for your presentation? 30

① A Famous Linguist and Lawyer

② A Strong Love of His Native Language

③ English Grammar for Beginners

④ His Contribution to the Description of English

問2 Choose the best two options for 31 and 32 to complete Early Days. (The order does not matter.)

① became a reporter with an English newspaper

② broke some laws without noticing it

③ followed his father's path for several years

④ learned European languages without help from others

⑤ started studying linguistics by himself before entering university

問3 Choose **four** out of the five events (① ~ ⑤) in the order they happened to complete Sequence of Some Events in His Life.

33 → 34 → 35 → 36

① Jespersen became the university president.

② Jespersen began working as a schoolteacher.

③ Jespersen started his project to gain a doctoral degree.

④ The first volume of *A Modern English Grammar on Historical Principles* was published.

⑤ Vilhelm Thomsen encouraged Jespersen to major in English.

— 23 —

問4　Choose the best option for 　37　 to complete One Important Characteristic of His Research and Books.

① employing traditional theoretical frameworks
② making suitable example sentences by himself
③ quoting English sentences that were actually used
④ writing English textbooks for beginners

問5　Choose the best option for 　38　 to complete Influence and Recognition.

① As a linguist, Jespersen is viewed as great as Henry Sweet.
② Jespersen's research has great significance both for language learning and linguistic investigations.
③ Noam Chomsky totally agreed with Jespersen's theories on English.
④ Teaching methods developed by Jespersen vastly improved language education around the world.

― 24 ―

第2回　英語（リーディング）

（下 書 き 用 紙）

英語（リーディング）の試験問題は次に続く。

— 25 —

第6問 （配点 24）

A Your study group is learning about "whether music can help plants grow." You have found an article you want to share. Complete the summary notes for your next meeting.

Fact or Myth: Does Music Affect Plant Growth?

Have you ever wondered if there's any truth to the theory that playing music for plants helps them grow? How do they "hear?" Do they prefer Vivaldi or Harry Styles? While there have been studies conducted that suggest that plants do indeed respond well to music, the truth of the matter is still up in the air. That being said, the evidence that supports the idea is very convincing!

It may not surprise you to learn that this idea took root at the height of New Age thinking. *The Secret Life of Plants*, published in 1973 and written by Christopher Bird and Peter Tompkins, is an account of the "physical, emotional and spiritual relations between plants and man" that helped popularize the idea. Bird and Tompkins cited scientific studies that suggested that not only does music help plants grow, but that they have a level of consciousness and can intelligently respond to people.

One of the earliest studies of the effect of music on plants was conducted in 1962 by Dr. T. C. Singh, Head of Botany at Annamalai University. He exposed balsam plants to classical music and found that their growth rate increased by 20% compared to a control group. He then exposed crops to raga (a kind of melody found in Indian music) over loudspeakers and found they yielded 25% – 60% more than the national average.

The same year that *The Secret Life of Plants* was published, researcher Dorothy Retallack of Colorado's Women's College experimented with different types of music, including classical, jazz, and rock. Plants exposed to the more soothing classical and jazz music grew towards the speaker and even wrapped themselves around it. Plants exposed to rock music, on the other hand, grew away from the speakers and showed signs similar to overwatering.

— 26 —

Many of the researchers who conducted these experiments, Singh and Retallack among them, concluded that plants respond as if they were calmed by the music they were hearing. It is worth noting that they also believed plants had some magical abilities — Retallack also thought that plants had supernatural powers and stayed away from rock music because they were afraid of the words used in it.

The best scientific theory as to how music helps plants grow is through how the vibration of the sound waves affects the plant. Plants transport nutrients such as proteins in their fluids (cytoplasm) through a process called cytoplasmic streaming. The vibration of certain types of music and sound may help stimulate this process — in nature, the plants may grow advantageously around bird song or areas with strong breezes.

A post from The University of California, Santa Barbara points out that there are so many things in these experiments that may not have been properly managed or accounted for, such as light and water, air pressure, and soil conditions. They also suggest that it may simply be that it's not the plants that benefit from the music, but their caretakers! This may also be why it is said that talking to plants helps their growth, as those caretakers are simply more attentive.

But the idea is still plausible, at least according to a popular TV show. They tackled this topic in 2004, setting up six greenhouses with different conditions: one had no music, one played classical music, one played death metal, two played recordings of negative speech and one played positive speech. In this experiment, it was the death metal plant that grew better than the rest! Classical music was second, followed by the greenhouses playing speech, both negative and positive, exhibiting similar growth. The plant exposed to no sound was dead last.

Music is food for the soul, but is it food for plants? We're still waiting for a definitive answer. But regardless of whether or not playing music actually aids in plant growth, at the very least it couldn't hurt as long as you don't put the plant right next to a speaker and turn the volume up too high!

Your summary notes:

Fact or Myth: Does Music Affect Plant Growth?

Past Research (1960s - 1970s)

• The hypothesis that music influenced plant growth was born.

• Some scientists believed that plants possessed spiritual powers, and that plants ⬜39⬜ humans.

Current Views

• There is no conclusive evidence that music has a positive effect on plant growth.

• Scientifically, ⬜40⬜ .

Interesting Details

• One experiment in the 1970s and another in the 2000s ⬜41⬜ .

• Some studies show that not only music but also ⬜42⬜ may have something to do with plant growth.

• The author of this article concludes that music probably has no negative effect on plants, except for ⬜43⬜ .

問1　Choose the best option for ⬜39⬜ .

① had some awareness of

② kept away from

③ were able to communicate like

④ were capable of imitating

— 28 —

第2回　英語（リーディング）

問2　Choose the best option for ☐40☐.

① a noisy environment usually hinders plants from growing steadily

② plants have an ability to distinguish music from noise

③ the sound of certain types of music may damage tissues in plants' bodies

④ the vibrations of sound waves could improve the circulation of nutrients in plants

問3　Choose the best option for ☐41☐.

① explain that the relationship between humans and plants is gradually changing

② indicate that all types of music make plants grow at the exact same rate

③ show different results in terms of the genre of music that plants seem to prefer

④ support the idea that plants like classical music more than any other kind of music

問4　Choose the best options for ☐42☐ and ☐43☐.

① complex rhythm

② death metal

③ some kinds of natural sound

④ total silence

⑤ traffic noise

⑥ unusually loud sound

— 29 —

B You are in a student group preparing a poster for a scientific presentation contest with the theme "What can we do in order to protect the environment?" You are reading the following passage to make the poster.

You can help fight climate change:
Even nonscientists can take part in research

Climate change can seem like a problem too big for any one person to bother tackling. Scientists, of course, do research to help inform the public about what's happening to the world around us. Many of those scientists could use some help. And sometimes they don't need scientific experts. Average citizens can supply what they need. Experts refer to these helpers as citizen scientists.

There are some really great volunteer programs, which are roughly divided into two types: Many involve observing wild plants and animals and the natural environment, while others are related to reporting human activities that cause climate change and environmental destruction.

SciStarter and Zooniverse are two websites that list citizen-science projects in which you can take part. An internet search for "citizen science" and your city, state or country can also bring up local projects that may be seeking volunteers. Here are some examples of such projects and what they might involve:

Bird Count: In this project, volunteers around the world count birds in their neighborhoods. The counts provide scientists data on where different birds are found and how many there are, and allow them to find out how these patterns may be changing with time. That includes how climate change may be affecting these populations. The project also asks volunteers to share as many pictures from their birdwatching as possible.

Household Waste Audit: According to the Environmental Protection Agency, the average American generates 4.51 pounds of waste per day, and the burning of this waste generates greenhouse gases such as carbon dioxide. In this project, students will be asked to actually measure the amount of waste generated in their homes in a week and devise creative ways in which they can reduce, reuse and/or recycle to take an active role in protecting the environment around them.

Lunch Food Waste Audit: In the United States, food reaches landfills more than any other material. When food goes to the landfill, it rots and produces methane — a greenhouse gas more potent than carbon dioxide. We could reduce roughly 6% - 8% of all human-caused greenhouse gas emissions if we just stopped wasting food. Lunch Food Waste Audit is an at-home project that asks you to track your lunch waste and change some habits. Measure as best you can and take photos.

MeadoWatch: This project, out of the University of Washington, is looking at how climate change is affecting wildflowers on Mount Rainier. Volunteers collect data along hiking trails about when wildflowers bud, flower, provide fruit, and produce seed. The project is also collecting photos of wildflowers from across Mount Rainier National Park.

Redmap: Gretta Pecl is a marine ecologist in Australia at the University of Tasmania in Hobart. She studies where marine animals are moving to in response to climate change. She set up a program called Redmap. It asks people to report "uncommon" marine species that they've seen in Australian waters. "We wanted to have an early indication of what species were changing where they live," she explains.

Water Monitoring: Residents of Minnesota can sign up to be a volunteer water monitor for the Minnesota Pollution Control Agency. Volunteers are assigned a lake or stream. Twice a month during the summer, they take measurements of water clarity. This data lets the government see whether water clarity has been changing over time as well as assess the health of those waterways.

Weather Rescue: People have collected weather data for a very long time. But for scientists to use it, data from handwritten, paper records needs to be digitized — entered into a computer. With Weather Rescue, British researchers are asking online volunteers to transcribe past weather measurements taken in Europe back in the 1860s, using their own computers at home. That was before temperatures began to rise because of global warming. This data will provide a useful baseline for future research.

第２回　英語（リーディング）

Your presentation poster draft:

What can ordinary citizens do to prevent climate change?

About citizen scientists and projects focusing on climate change

- Citizen scientists are ordinary people who help experts conduct scientific research.
- There are two types of projects concerning climate change: observing nature and reporting human activities.
- 44

Examples of citizen science projects

Name of Projects	An Example of the Activities	Types
Bird Count	This project is studying 45 .	observing nature
Household Waste Audit	This project asks you to know the amount of waste in your house and 46 .	reporting human activities
Lunch Food Waste Audit	This project encourages you to change your habits to reduce food waste.	reporting human activities
MeadoWatch		

Some of the projects share common characteristics:

47

48

— 33 —

問1 Your group wants to introduce the citizen-science projects explained in the passage. Which of the following is the most appropriate? 44

① Average citizens often do better research about climate change than scientists.

② You can find such projects around your place of residence by searching the internet.

③ Your community will choose projects suitable for you if you apply online.

④ Zooniverse is one of the citizen-science projects ordinary people can take part in.

問2 You have been asked to write descriptions of Bird Count and Household Waste Audit. Choose the best options for 45 and 46 .

Bird Count 45

① birds' ability to fly long distances

② how birds adapt to new environments

③ seasonal changes in bird behavior

④ the effects of changes in climate on birds

Household Waste Audit 46

① consider how you can reduce it for the sake of the environment

② follow the garbage separation rules in your community

③ learn about the effects of greenhouse gases

④ think about appropriate ways of burning it

— 34 —

第2回　英語（リーディング）

問3　You found that some of these projects share common characteristics. According to the article, which two of the following are appropriate? (The order does not matter.) 　47　・　48

① Household Waste Audit, Lunch Food Waste Audit, Water Monitoring and Weather Rescue don't involve doing research on plants and animals.

② It is necessary to do research on water in Bird Count, Redmap and Water Monitoring.

③ Redmap and Water Monitoring require volunteers to report on marine animals.

④ Studies in Bird Count, MeadoWatch, and Redmap involve looking at ecosystems of wild animals.

⑤ Volunteers in Bird Count, Lunch Food Waste Audit and MeadoWatch are asked to take photos.

⑥ You have to do research outdoors except in Household Waste Audit and Lunch Food Waste Audit.

— 35 —

第 3 回

（80分）

実 戦 問 題

●標 準 所 要 時 間●

第1問　7分程度	第4問 12分程度
第2問 13分程度	第5問 14分程度
第3問 12分程度	第6問 22分程度

第3回　実戦問題

英　　語（リーディング）

各大問の英文や図表を読み，解答番号 $\boxed{1}$ 〜 $\boxed{48}$ にあてはまるものとして最も適当な選択肢を選びなさい。

第 1 問（配点　10）

A In your home economics classes, you are studying about seeds you can eat or use as seasoning. You find four kinds of seeds you want to try.

---

4 Seeds I Should Be Eating

Chia Seeds

▶ Contain a lot of fiber
▶ The perfect crunchy topping for yogurt or salads
▶ Soak them in juice or almond milk to make them soft and become like pudding

Pomegranate Seeds

▶ Sweet, jewel-like beads from inside the pomegranate fruit
▶ High in vitamin C, and low in calories
▶ They can add a juicy pop of flavor and color to a salad or whole-grain dish.

Flax Seeds

▶ Have been eaten since 9,000 B.C.
▶ They contain healthy fats and a good dose of fiber.
▶ Add them to oatmeal, pancakes, or fresh vegetables

Hemp Seeds

▶ Contain plenty of protein: even more than flax or chia seeds
▶ You can use the seeds whole, sprinkled on salads or whole-grain dishes, or use them to make hemp milk to cut out some of the dairy you consume.

第3回　英語（リーディング）

問1 　　1　　 can be recommended for people who feel they are eating too much dairy.

① Chia Seeds

② Flax Seeds

③ Hemp Seeds

④ Pomegranate Seeds

問2　All of the seeds go well with 　　2　　 .

① milk

② salad

③ whole-grain dishes

④ yogurt

B You are the chief leader of the English club at your school, and the club is going to attend a contest explained in a flyer as follows:

The 1st Youth English Drama Contest

The Youth English Drama Society will have its first contest. We aim to encourage young Japanese people to learn English through drama, which is one of the best forms of entertainment.

There are three stages to this competition. Winners will be selected at each stage, and if you pass all three stages, you can participate in the Grand Final.

The Grand Final	Place: Century Hall Date: February 5, 2023

GRAND PRIZE

The winning team can join The International English Camp in Canberra, Australia in March 2023.

Contest information:

Stages	Things to Upload & Events	Details	2022 Deadlines & Dates
Stage 1	Answers to a questionnaire, and an English essay	Number of words for the essay: 150 - 200	Upload by 12 p.m. on August 13
Stage 2	A video of your team giving its performance	Time: 25-30 minutes	Upload by 12 p.m. on October 25
Stage 3	Regional Contests	On this site we'll show you the winners, who will go on to the Grand Final.	Held on December 23

Grand Final Grading Information

Pronunciation & Intonation, etc.	Gestures & Performance	Voice & Eye Contact	Teamwork	Answering Questions from Judges
40%	10%	10%	30%	10%

第3回　英語（リーディング）

◆ You must download the questionnaire as well as the title of your English essay and the script for your play online.

click here.

◆ You must upload your materials online. All dates and times are Japan Standard Time (JST).

◆ You can get to know the results of Stage 1 and 2 on the website seven days after the deadline for each stage.

For more details, **click here**.

問1　To take part in the first stage, you should ⬚3⬚ .

① answer the questions and make a video of your performance

② answer the questions and write an essay in English

③ write an English essay and make a video of your performance

④ write an English essay and write a play

問2　When can you start to check the result of the first stage? ⬚4⬚

① August 6

② August 13

③ August 20

④ August 27

問3　You should put the greatest effort into speaking natural English and ⬚5⬚ to earn a high score in the Grand Final.

① controlling your voice and expressions

② explaining your story carefully to the judges

③ using dramatic gestures

④ working better as a group

—5—

第2問 （配点 20）

A You are planning to participate in a summer programme in England, so you are reading information about the course you will join and a comment of a student who joined the same course last year.

INTERMEDIATE LEVEL OF PRACTICAL ENGLISH CLASS

Dr Mary White
white.mary@example-u.ac.uk
Call: 020-8765-xxxx
Office Hours:
Monday & Thursday   1.00 pm – 2.00 pm

4-30 August 2022
Monday & Thursday
2.00 pm – 3.30 pm
8 classes – 1 credit

Course description:
You will be learning how to interact better with people from different countries in English. English must not be the first language of participants. You are also expected to have already mastered basic English grammar.

In this course, students are going to make an English speech or presentation to introduce one of their country's unique cultures.

Goals:
After this course you should be able to:
— communicate with people in English about general topics in daily life and speak about them in front of people.
— write text messages in English without any particular difficulties.
— exchange ideas on some social issues with people in English.

Textbook:
Samuel, B. (2020). *Go Forward! [INTERMEDIATE]*. London: SDBK Inc.

Participants' evaluations (76 reviewers)
★★★★★ （Average: 4.78）

● Mary is an experienced teacher. She is strict but very kind and thoughtful.

● At first you may find this course difficult, but soon you'll get used to it. You can surely make your English skills better.

● I enjoyed the email classes. They really help me communicate with people now.

● I wanted to learn about how to make the most of the computer translation technology, which will be more and more useful and helpful in communication in the future.

● I realized there are many kinds of English in the world; this course made me confident in *my* English. English is surely a common worldwide language.

— 6 —

第3回　英語（リーディング）

Evaluation:
70% overall score required to pass
— achievement tests: 60%
— an English speech or presentation: 30%
— participation: 10%

問1　What is the aim of this course? 　6

① Learning English through doing sports activities

② Learning to improve English communication skills

③ Studying famous English speeches

④ Studying the history of many English-speaking countries

問2 　7　 are two things you will be able to do after this course.

A：master advanced English grammar

B：read English newspapers

C：speak English in public

D：understand English culture

E：write emails in English

① A and B

② A and D

③ B and C

④ C and E

⑤ D and E

— 7 —

問3   One **fact** about Dr White is that ☐8☐ .

   ① she is always in her office an hour before her class

   ② she is good at team-teaching in English

   ③ she is severe and gives lots of homework

   ④ she teaches students how to use a handy translation machine

問4   Which best summarises one participant's opinion about the class?
☐9☐

   ① Achievement tests are most highly valued.

   ② Email classes are not recommended.

   ③ It will turn out to be not so difficult.

   ④ Students take classes for three hours a week.

問5   What is required most to get a credit of this course?   ☐10☐

   ① Getting good scores in the tests

   ② Joining discussions actively

   ③ Making a good speech and presentation

   ④ Not being absent from the classes

B You and John, an exchange student from the UK, are the editors of a school English paper. He has written an article for the paper.

Do you like using a tablet in class? The UK has been promoting ICT (Information and Communication Technology) education, but I don't think it's going smoothly. How about in Japan? Results of some surveys about Japanese high schools give us some answers.

> The number of schools which didn't provide a tablet for each student was about five times as large as that of schools which did in 2018.

In 2020, the situation was as follows:
> The number of schools which didn't think of introducing tablets was more than three times as large as that of schools which did.
> 43.8% of private high schools got tablets for each of their students, while only 5.4% of public ones provided each student with one.
> There were many more private than public high schools which planned to give all students tablets.

As you know, in our school we are luckily provided with individual tablets. However, I wonder if they are properly and fully used by each student. Are the teachers skillful enough to use one? Are they trying to have each student make the most of his or her tablet in their everyday classes? I've got some information from the head teacher; four in ten of  our math teachers are eager to promote ICT education. This is higher than the number of English teachers. Three in eleven of them are having their students use their tablets. And the lowest percentage goes to the Japanese teachers.

In fact, I wonder whether we will need to depend on such electronic tools more or not in the future. I think we've got to give questionnaires or something to the students and teachers at our school, and we may get hints about the usage of tablets which will lead to the improvement of the present situation.

問1 In terms of the ratios of your school's teachers who are trying ICT education eagerly, which shows the subject teachers' ranking from **highest to lowest**? ☐ 11 ☐

① English teachers — Japanese teachers — math teachers
② English teachers — math teachers — Japanese teachers
③ Japanese teachers — English teachers — math teachers
④ Japanese teachers — math teachers — English teachers
⑤ math teachers — English teachers — Japanese teachers
⑥ math teachers — Japanese teachers — English teachers

問2 John's comments on the current ICT education at his school show that ☐ 12 ☐.

① he feels ICT education in his own country is inferior
② he is satisfied with the effective way of using tablets at the school
③ he is skeptical about whether tablets are being used effectively at the school
④ he wants to see more kinds of online learning

問3 The statement that best reflects one finding from the survey is ☐ 13 ☐

① 'I wish I were a public school student because I could get my own tablet.'
② 'My school is public and isn't planning to promote ICT education now.'
③ 'One out of three schools provided tablets for each student in 2018.'
④ 'The majority of schools intend to improve their ICT education classes.'

— 10 —

第3回　英語（リーディング）

問4　Which best summarises John's opinions about ICT education at his school?　| 14 |

① Some surveys are necessary to make the situation better.

② Tablets are not as useful as we expected.

③ We have to hold classes for teachers to teach them how to use tablets.

④ We need to make it easier for students to use tablets.

問5　Which is the most suitable title for the article?　| 15 |

① Cost and Performance of Tablets

② Introducing Tablets and Their Future

③ Strategy for Distributing Tablets to Public Schools

④ Usefulness of and Problems with Tablets

— 11 —

第3問 （配点 15）

A Your Canadian friend, Sue, visited a new Zoo & Aquarium Park and posted a blog about her experience.

Posted by Sue
at 8:47 p.m. on October 3, 2021

Sunrise Zoo & Aquarium Park: A Wonderful Place to Visit

I had a great time with my friends at Sunrise Zoo & Aquarium Park, which opened three weeks ago. It's a huge park with two main areas of a zoo and an aquarium.

We were really looking forward to seeing pandas and enjoying a dolphin show. We first headed for the zoo area to meet the pandas, but we found it full with too many people, so we went to the dolphin show instead. We stood in a line for a while to enter the aquarium area. However, it was worth it because the show was so great and exciting! We were going to have lunch at the open cafe and visit the zoo area to see the pandas. But both the cafe and the panda sections were so crowded that we decided to go to the park shops to buy some sandwiches and drinks, and we had them at a nearby rest stop. In the afternoon, we were finally able to meet the pandas. They were incredibly cute! We dropped in at the park shops again lastly, where we bought souvenirs for our friends and family.

Sunrise Zoo & Aquarium Park is super! This unforgettable experience will certainly never be forgotten!

第3回　英語（リーディング）

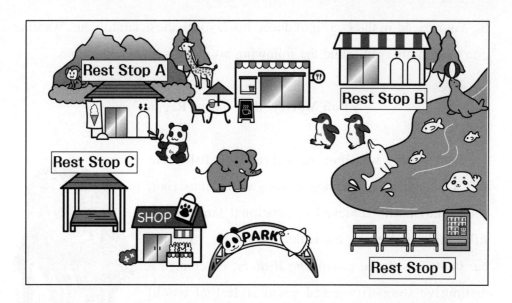

問1　From Sue's post, you understand that ☐16☐ .

① it took too much time to see the pandas and Sue got tired
② Sue and her friends didn't regret changing their plan
③ Sue stood to see the dolphin show because it was crowded
④ the restaurant was more crowded than the open cafe

問2　At which rest stop did Sue and her friends have lunch? ☐17☐

① Rest Stop A
② Rest Stop B
③ Rest Stop C
④ Rest Stop D

B Your friend in the U.S. introduced his favorite musician to you. Wanting to learn more, you found the following article in a music magazine.

Bob Marley, the Soul of Reggae

Bob Marley was born on February 6, 1945. He was a Jamaican reggae singer, songwriter, musician, and guitarist who achieved international fame and is still highly praised by his enthusiastic fans. Starting out in 1963 with the group *The Wailers*, he created a distinctive songwriting and vocal style that would soon be received with admiration by audiences worldwide. After *The Wailers* broke up in 1974, Marley pursued a solo career that reached its peak with the release of the album *Exodus* in June, 1977. It is certain that the album established his worldwide reputation and led to his status as one of the world's best-selling artists of all time, with sales of more than 75 million records.

Bob Marley was a committed Rastafarian, an Abrahamic religion which developed in Jamaica in the 1930s. This religion inspired him and filled his music with a sense of spirituality. The *Rastafari movement* was a key element in the development of reggae. As a passionate supporter of Rastafari, Bob Marley took reggae music out of the socially deprived areas of Jamaica and onto the international music scene.

In July, 1977, Marley was found to be suffering from a type of a fatal disease under the nail of one of his toes. His doctors strongly advised him to have an operation on it. However, Marley turned down their advice, citing his religious beliefs. In spite of his illness, he continued touring until his health grew worse as the cancer spread throughout his body. He died on 11 May 1981 at Cedars of Lebanon Hospital in Miami (now University of Miami Hospital) at the age of 36. The spread of the cancer to his lungs and brain caused his death. His final words to his son Ziggy were: "Money can't buy life."

問1　Put the following events (①〜④) into the order in which they happened.

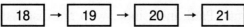

① Marley began to sing solo.
② Marley didn't stop his tours after he discovered his disease.
③ Marley joined the group *The Wailers*.
④ The album *Exodus* was released.

問2　Marley refused to be taken care of by his doctors because 22 .

① he thought it was too late to have an operation
② he was busy doing concert tours
③ he was following his faith
④ his cancer was at an early stage

問3　From this story, you learned that 23 .

① a religion had an influence on Marley's music
② a religion made Marley move to Jamaica
③ Marley didn't get along with his band members
④ Marley's music deprived his country of money

第4問 （配点 16）

You are now studying at Robert University in the US. In a social studies class, you are asked to report on how smartphones affect people. You found the blogs of two students, Paul and Linda, who are discussing the usage of smartphones.

Smartphone Addiction?
Posted by Paul at 4:52 p.m. on September 5, 2022

Since the world saw the first iPhone in 2007, smartphone usage has steadily become an accepted part of our daily lives — and the smartphone addiction statistics prove it. Now, in 2022, we are glued to our phones. Because we rely on our phones for communication and connection, it can be hard to determine when excessive smartphone use becomes an addiction. However, it's necessary to know the following statistics:

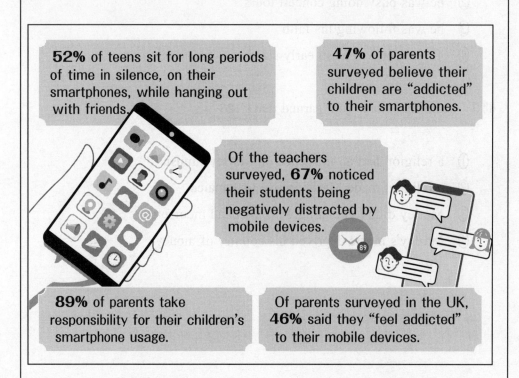

52% of teens sit for long periods of time in silence, on their smartphones, while hanging out with friends.

47% of parents surveyed believe their children are "addicted" to their smartphones.

Of the teachers surveyed, **67%** noticed their students being negatively distracted by mobile devices.

89% of parents take responsibility for their children's smartphone usage.

Of parents surveyed in the UK, **46%** said they "feel addicted" to their mobile devices.

第3回　英語（リーディング）

In fact, I once suffered from sleep deprivation, increased stress levels, depression, and anxiety because of, I believe, my smartphone. And I've stopped using it. While being addicted to your digital devices doesn't negatively impact your health as seriously as other types of addiction, it does indeed impact not only your mental health but your physical wellbeing. Why don't you stop and think about how you use YOUR smartphone?

Smartphone (over)usage in school
Posted by Linda at 11:22 a.m. on September 6, 2022

If there's anything that most deserves the claim to being a man's best friend in the modern age, it has got to be the smartphone. Mobile devices have penetrated every type of human activity. Nearly everyone uses one at home, school, work, and during times of leisure. So much so that not having access to a mobile phone has paved the way for "nomophobia", the fear of being out of mobile phone contact. As such, understanding the current smartphone addiction statistics is important to get a grasp of how serious it really is.

Here, I'd like to shine a light on smartphone usage and habits in school. Given that smartphones are mini-computers, they can take on a wide variety of functions which can be useful in class. This allows users to enjoy their devices in a lot of different ways. Unfortunately, too much enjoyment can be counterproductive. As the smartphone addiction statistics suggest, mobile phones prove to be huge distractions in schools. This causes dips in productivity.

Percentage	What does the percentage show?
20%	The time spent by students in class texting and checking social media
45%	Students who are constantly online. This includes the time that they are in class.
46%	Parents who want educators to find ways to integrate the use of smartphones into lessons more
49%	Students who are distracted by smartphones and other digital gadgets in class
80%	Schools which have a policy that restricts the use of mobile phones in class

If you're uncomfortable with your attachment to your smartphone, there are ways to cultivate a healthier relationship with the technology in your life. Try limiting the time spent on your smartphone by using an app that tracks your daily usage and sends reminders to log off. You can also access your average screen time in the settings of your phone. Another trick that helps limit smartphone use is to turn your color settings to black and white. Late night scrolling isn't as stimulating when you're seeing black and white visuals, which encourages putting down your device.

問 1　Paul recommends stopping using smartphones because ⬜24⬜ .

① they are harmful to our health

② they can damage human relationships

③ they cost a lot of money

④ they prevent face-to-face communication

問 2　Linda suggests that ⬜25⬜ .

① you should be careful about your physical health being affected by your smartphone

② you should change the color of the screen of your smartphone

③ you should install an app which turns off your smartphone automatically

④ you should limit the time you use your smartphone using other digital gadgets

— 18 —

第3回　英語（リーディング）

問3　Both Paul and Linda recommend that you ☐ 26 ☐ .

① appreciate the advance of communication technologies
② look into how effectively smartphones are utilized by people
③ realize how dangerous using social networking services is
④ understand how affected people are by smartphones through statistics

問4　The percentage of students who are distracted by digital gadgets in class is higher than the percentage of students who ☐ 27 ☐ .

① are always connected to the Internet
② are using their smartphones properly
③ use apps that limit their phone use
④ use their smartphones late at night

問5　In ☐ 28 ☐ blog, you can find that less than half of parents ☐ 29 ☐ . (Choose the best one for each box from options ① ～ ④.)

① are satisfied with the way smartphones are used at school
② think their children are using their smartphones too much
③ Linda's
④ Paul's

— 19 —

第5問 (配点 15)

In your English class, you will give a presentation about a great writer in the world. You found the following article and prepared notes for your presentation.

Edgar Allan Poe was born on January 19, 1809 in Boston, Massachusetts. He was an American author, poet, editor, and literary critic. He is widely regarded as a central figure of Romanticism in the United States, and of American literature. Poe is best known for his tales of mystery. He was one of the earliest American practitioners of the short story, and is generally considered the inventor of the detective fiction genre.

Edgar Allan Poe

Both Poe's father and mother were professional actors. They died before the poet was three years old. John and Frances Allan never formally adopted him but raised him as a foster child in Richmond, Virginia. Poe attended the University of Virginia for one semester but left due to lack of money. Poe quarreled with John over the funds for his education and his gambling debts. In 1827, he enlisted in the United States Army under a false name. It was at this time his writing career began with his first publication, although humbly, with an anonymous collection of poems, *Tamerlane and Other Poems* (1827), credited only to "a Bostonian". With the death of Frances Allan in 1829, Poe and John Allan reached a temporary reestablishing of good relations. Poe later failed as a military officer's trainee at West Point. He firmly stated his strong wish to be a poet and writer and parted ways with John Allan.

Although Poe began earnestly in his attempts to start his career as a poet, he chose a difficult time to do so. The American publishing industry was particularly hurt by the Panic of 1837, a financial crisis in the United States: profits, prices, and wages went down. Unemployment

第3回 英語 (リーディング)

went up, and pessimism prevailed. Publishers often refused to pay their writers or paid them much later than they had promised. Poe had to have had a hard time. After his early attempts at poetry, Poe turned his attention to prose. He spent the next several years working for literary journals and periodicals. He became well-known, acting as a critic of literature in his own unique way. His work forced him to move between several cities, including Baltimore, Philadelphia, and New York City. In Baltimore in 1835, he married his cousin Virginia Clemm, which may have inspired some of his writing.

In January 1845 Poe published the poem, "*The Raven*", which became a popular sensation. It made Poe a household name almost instantly, though he was paid only $9 for its publication. His wife died of tuberculosis two years after its publication. For years, he had been planning to produce his own journal, *The Penn* (later renamed *The Stylus*), though he died before it could be published. On October 7, 1849, at age 40, Poe died in Baltimore; the cause of his death is unknown and has been variously attributed to alcohol, brain disease, cholera, drugs, heart disease, suicide, tuberculosis, and other causes.

Edgar Allan Poe and his works influenced literature in the United States and around the world, as well as being responsible for the start of specialized areas of writing. He is considered as one of the originators of both horror and detective fiction. He is also credited as the "architect" of the modern short story. As a critic he was one of the first writers to put emphasis on the effect of style and structure. He was thus a forerunner in the "art for art's sake" movement. Poe is particularly respected in France, in part due to early translations by Charles Baudelaire. Baudelaire's translations became definitive artistic performances of Poe's work throughout Europe.

Poe and his work appear throughout popular culture in literature, music, films, and television. A number of his homes are dedicated as museums today. The Mystery Writers of America present an annual award known as the Edgar Award for distinguished work in the mystery genre.

— 21 —

Your presentation notes:

Edgar Allan Poe

He was born on January 19, 1809 and is considered the inventor of the detective fiction genre.

Early Life
— He was taken care of by John and Frances Allan.
— He argued with John but, later, made up with him.
— 30

A New Life and Marriage
— He switched his focus to 31 .
— He became famous for his own style of 32 .
— He married his cousin, Virginia Clemm.

Success and Death

33

He joined the Army under a false name.

34

35

36

He died in Baltimore from an unknown cause.

Influence
— He and his work appear throughout popular culture in literature, music, films, and television.
— 37

Achievements and Recognition
— He invented the field of horror and detective fiction.
— He first focused on how style and structure affect a story.
— 38

第3回　英語 (リーディング)

問1　Choose the best statement for 　30　 .

① He cut off contact with John, declaring that he would be a poet and writer.

② His father abandoned the family and left home.

③ His first collection of poems made his name well-known to people.

④ Poe became on bad terms with John again just after he joined the army.

問2　Choose the best two items for 　31　 and 　32　 to complete A New Life and Marriage.

① detective stories

② editing magazines

③ literary criticism

④ plotting mysteries

⑤ prose writing

問3　Choose **four** out of the five events (① ～ ⑤) in the order they happened to complete Success and Death.

　33　 → 　34　 → 　35　 → 　36　

① An anonymous collection of poems was published.

② He entered the University of Virginia.

③ His wife passed away because of a disease.

④ *The Penn* was published.

⑤ *"The Raven"* was published and was a big hit.

— 23 —

問4 Choose the best option for [37] to complete Influence.

① He improved the style and structure of fiction which was popular at that time.

② He inspired Baudelaire, whose works were translated by him.

③ His literary criticism on short stories made an impact on mysteries.

④ His work was translated into French and became highly valued in Europe.

問5 Choose the best option for [38] to complete Achievements and Recognition.

① A prominent mystery writer is honored in the name of Poe every year.

② As an architect, he changed his homes into museums.

③ He established the Mystery Writers of America organization.

④ He was against the trend of criticizing mysteries artistically.

— 24 —

第3回　英語（リーディング）

（下書き用紙）

英語（リーディング）の試験問題は次に続く。

— 25 —

第6問 （配点 24）

A You are a member of the student council at your school. You happened to find an English article on a website which could give your school a suggestion on how to contribute to achieving one of the SDGs (Sustainable Development Goals). Complete the summary notes for your next meeting.

What Can Schools Do about the Climate Change Issue?

Climate change, including global warming, poses a major threat to humanity. Researchers and communities have shown us that climate change affects where people can live, grow food, maintain infrastructure, and stay healthy. Climate change is connected to many other global issues. For example, climate change is linked to inequality and ethics because developing countries are the least responsible for climate change, yet they are the most at risk from its effects.

What can we do to solve the problem? As one person or a group of people, for example, at school, there must be something we can do. Yes. Everyone in your school can play a role in working towards your school's climate goals. In fact, by having everyone participate, you are giving everyone a chance to develop the empathy needed for creating a more sustainable society.

Students, teachers, support staff, families, and local community members all have a role to play. Girls and boys, women and men should be equally engaged and active. For example, cafeteria staff can prepare healthy snacks and meals made with local ingredients, students can study about their energy consumption, and families can reinforce what students are learning at school by adopting climate-friendly practices at home. It is

---

— 26 —

recommended that you involve everyone in your school in deciding which roles they will take on. Each group should elect representatives that will speak and act on their behalf to the climate action team which is in charge of coordinating the development, implementation and review of the school's action plan on climate change.

Colégio Israelita Brasileiro A. Liessen, a school in Rio de Janeiro, Brazil, is working to create a culture of environmental responsibility. The school believes that everyone in the school — 800 students and 200 employees — should know why environmental projects are taking place. Also, everyone should feel like they are part of the process. To this end, the school's environment team has invited teachers, students, engineers and others to participate in experiential, non-formal learning activities. They have created a green roof, built solar ovens and bamboo bicycle racks, planted spices, flowers, created meditation gardens, and converted used cooking oil into fuel. These activities have created bonds between different members of the school community, awakened a sense of belonging and pride in the school, and built an environment where ideas and information are shared freely. The environment team has also offered training for school community members in order to succeed in their projects. For example, training on waste sorting and cooking oil collection was offered to employees. Also, a gardening workshop was organized for student volunteers, so they could assist maintenance staff in caring for the expanding school gardens.

Your summary notes:

What Can Schools Do about the Climate Change Issue?

The Aim of the Action

Taking part in climate action can [39].

The Main Points

- Climate change, including global warming, is a big problem for human beings.
- Schools should [40].
- Some groups should be organized at school so that they can discuss and carry out better plans systematically.

Interesting Details

- A school in Brazil is introduced to prove that it [41].
- The Brazilian school tries to have its people engage in [42], so it has created [43].

問1　Choose the best option for [39].

① let students appeal to their teachers for information about climate change

② make students aware of the necessity of maintaining a sustainable society

③ make students realize how much damage their schools cause to the environment

④ reduce students' sense of guilt about producing CO_2

第3回　英語（リーディング）

問2　Choose the best option for ［ 40 ］.

① cooperate with each other to create a nationwide network of student volunteers

② have every student and staff member participate in activities that help achieve their climate goals

③ introduce a subject which focuses on climate change in their curriculum

④ try harder to avoid cancellations of school events due to changes in weather patterns

問3　Choose the best option for ［ 41 ］.

① can teach us how to prevent miscommunication within a community

② has been carrying out climate action for a very long time

③ is a good example showing that anyone can take some action

④ is working in cooperation with families of students

問4　Choose the best options for ［ 42 ］ and ［ 43 ］.

① a sense of identification with the school

② advanced academic discussions

③ earth-friendly activities

④ food waste problems

⑤ money saving activities

⑥ some ideas about recycling

— 29 —

B You are in a group preparing for a poster presentation whose title is "How we can Send Messages." Your group is interested in pictograms, a way of sending messages through pictorial symbols, and is planning to use the following passage to create the poster.

Hazard Pictograms
— Symbols Quick to Send a Message —

Pictograms introduced here are graphic images that immediately show the user of a hazardous product what type of hazard is present. With a quick glance you can see, for example, if the product is flammable (capable of burning quickly), or if it might be a health hazard in another way.

Some pictograms have a diamond shape. Inside this diamond is a symbol that represents the potential hazard (e.g., fire, harmful if eaten, strong acid, etc.). Together, the symbol and the design of the diamond are referred to as a pictogram. Pictograms are assigned specific hazard classes or categories.

Hazard pictograms form part of the international Globally Harmonized System of Classification and Labelling of Chemicals (GHS). Two sets of pictograms are included within the GHS: one for the labeling of containers and for workplace hazard warnings, and a second for use during the transport of dangerous goods. Either one or the other is chosen, depending on the target audience, but the two are not used together. The two sets of pictograms use the same symbols for the same hazards, although certain symbols are not required for transport pictograms. Transport pictograms come in a wider variety of colors and may contain additional information such as a subcategory number.

Hazard pictograms are one of the key elements for the labeling of containers under GHS, along with other information such as:

— 30 —

- a description of the product
- a signal word – either 'Danger' or 'Warning' — where necessary
- hazard statements, indicating the nature and degree of the risks posed by the product
- precautionary statements, indicating how the product should be handled to minimize risks to the user (as well as to other people and the general environment)
- the identity of the supplier (who might be a manufacturer or importer)

The GHS chemical hazard pictograms are intended to provide the basis for or to replace national systems of hazard pictograms. In fact, GHS transport pictograms are the same as those recommended in the UN Recommendations on the Transport of Dangerous Goods, widely implemented in national regulations in many countries.

The figure below shows some examples of hazard pictograms.

Figure 1. Hazard Pictograms

Can you guess what each pictogram means? They are divided into two groups. One group (numbers 1 and 2) shows the first set of pictograms mentioned above, physical hazards pictograms. On the other hand, the other group (numbers 3, 4, 5, 6 and 7) contains the second set, transport pictograms. Now, we will look at each of them, beginning with the first group.

The pictograms of the first group have their own names; No. 1 is called "Flame," and No. 2 is named "Flame over Circle." The former means flammable materials or substances liable to catch fire by themselves when exposed to water or air, or which emit flammable gas and cause other materials to burn, while the latter identifies oxidizers, which are chemicals that help something burn or make fires burn hotter and last longer.

Next, let us move on to the second group. No. 3 shows flammable solids or self-reactive substances. Under conditions encountered in transport, they could possibly catch fire, may cause or contribute to fire through friction, or may explode if not treated carefully. No. 4 means flammable liquids — liquids which have a flash point of less than 60℃ and which are capable of sustaining burning. No. 5 means substances liable to burn spontaneously — substances which are liable to spontaneously heat up under normal conditions encountered in transport, or to heat up due to contact with air, and are then liable to catch fire. No. 6 shows influential substances — substances which, while in themselves not necessarily burnable, may, generally by releasing oxygen, cause, or contribute to, the burning of other material. Finally, No. 7 means organic poisons — organic substances which contain harmful matter or hazardous materials with certain chemical structures.

Each pictogram covers a specific type of hazard and is designed to be immediately recognizable to anyone handling hazardous material, though those pictograms are not so easy for general people to understand.

第3回　英語（リーディング）

Your presentation poster draft:

> **Do you know hazard pictograms?**

> **What are hazard pictograms?**

· They are graphic images that show what type of hazard is present in a product.

· ☐ 44

> **Some kinds of hazard pictograms**

No.	Pictogram	Hazards	General Meaning
1		· flammable materials or substances	They are materials or substances which can burn or ☐ 45 .
2		· oxidizers	They are chemicals which ☐ 46 .
3		· flammable solids · self-reactive substances	They are materials or substances which can catch fire easily due to friction.

> **Pictograms with common messages**

☐ 47

☐ 48

— 33 —

問1　Under the first poster heading, your group wants to introduce hazard pictograms as explained in the passage.　Which of the following is the most appropriate?　44

① The same hazards may be represented by different symbols.

② There are two sets, and you can use both sets at the same time.

③ They are accompanied by other information about a product.

④ They were invented by the UN and are widely accepted around the world.

問2　You have been asked to write general meanings of No. 1 and No. 2 pictograms.　Choose the best options for 45 and 46 .

No. 1　45

① contain a deadly poison

② explode near a fire

③ melt even in low temperatures

④ release gases that burn

No. 2　46

① can be active and catch fire without proper controls

② can shorten the time in which materials explode

③ contain substances which can absorb oxygen

④ increase the temperature and length of fire

— 34 —

第3回　英語（リーディング）

問3　You are making statements about some pictograms which share common messages. According to the article, which two of the following are appropriate?　(The order does not matter.)　 47 ・ 48

① No.1 and 5 can be dangerous when air is brought into contact with them.

② No.1 and 6 release gases that can cause a fire.

③ No. 1, 6, and 7 mean that they can emit poisonous gas.

④ No. 1, and No. 7 mean that they burn easily and produce harmful gas.

⑤ No. 2 and No. 6 indicate that they are flammable and can cause big fires.

⑥ No. 3, 4 and 6 show that they start to burn at low temperatures.

第 4 回
（80分）

実 戦 問 題

●標 準 所 要 時 間●

第1問　7分程度	第4問 12分程度
第2問 13分程度	第5問 14分程度
第3問 12分程度	第6問 22分程度

第4回　実戦問題

英　　語(リーディング)

各大問の英文や図表を読み，解答番号 | 1 | ～ | 47 | にあてはまるものとして最も適当な選択肢を選びなさい。

第1問 (配点　10)

A　You are preparing for a cooking competition organized by some Indian students at your senior high school. Your goal is to make a new dish using unfamiliar flavors. You find an article about spices that are not so well-known in Japan.

Delicious Spices	
Urfa Biber	**Porcini Powder**
· Sweet chocolatey taste but the smoky smell can ruin soups · Great with meat but not in cakes · Make vegetables exciting with it	· Unique mushroom smell · Despite its nutty taste, it's better for soups and vegetables than cakes · Perfect with pasta
Blade Mace	**Cardamom**
· Use this mild seed whole for great flavor · Just as delicious in fruit cakes as in meatballs · Warm yourself up with it in soup	· Two types, green and black · Make your soup and pasta dishes extra spicy with it and avoid it in cakes · Has a strong smell, like pork

— 2 —

第4回 英語 (リーディング)

問1 Both Urfa Biber and Blade Mace can be used for ☐ 1 ☐ .

① cakes
② meatballs
③ mushrooms
④ soups

問2 If you want to improve your pasta with a hot, meaty spice you should choose ☐ 2 ☐ .

① Blade Mace
② Cardamom
③ Porcini Powder
④ Urfa Biber

— 3 —

B A student in the hallway gave you an interesting piece of paper.

Join Animal Awareness Week

Calling international students! For Animal Awareness Week, we'd like to hear about animals on your continent that are dying out. Participants will join various activities until, at the end of the week, students make thirty-minute presentations on "Endangered Animals Worldwide," using visuals and explanations about what could be done to save their chosen animals.

We are hoping to attract ten representatives each from the continents of Asia, Europe, Oceania, North America, and South America.

Schedule

August 16	Morning — Welcome speech from the Head of Biology.
	Afternoon — Self-introductions and forming groups.
August 17	Safari park
	Morning — Tour of the park and documentary on endangered animals.
	Afternoon — Lecture on current conservation projects.
August 18	Morning — Natural History Museum workshop — extinct animal DNA harvesting workshop.
	Afternoon — Presentation preparation.
August 19	Morning — Debate — Recreating historical animals through science — acceptable or unacceptable?
	Afternoon — Presentation preparation.
August 20	Morning — Presentations.
	Afternoon — 'Most Educational Presentation' award ceremony.

- All activities / presentations will be conducted in English.
- Tablets / Materials needed will be provided by the university where possible.

— 4 —

第4回　英語（リーディング）

The first ten students from each continent who apply to the program will be accepted.

＊ Stop by the Science Department desk to ask for more details or to apply.

問1　The purpose of this event is for international students to ☐ 3 ☐ .

① consider threatened animals' futures

② create stronger animals scientifically

③ help weaker animals using historical knowledge

④ introduce unique animals

問2　Which of the following are the students going to do during the program?　☐ 4 ☐

① Attend a class on collecting DNA

② Decide which animals are most at risk

③ Discuss recent advances in biology

④ Interact with unusual zoo animals

問3　The event will benefit science students by causing them to ☐ 5 ☐ .

① consider opinions for and against cloning extinct animals

② explain ideas better in more scientific ways

③ listen to theories of world-renowned scientists

④ utilize modern life-saving techniques

第2問 （配点 20）

A You are thinking of running for the school council next year. On a UK website you found some great suggestions by high school election winners on how to win support and succeed.

Popularity isn't enough! How to win a student election!

Considerations

1. No formula for being elected has been found! Talk to as many students as possible — not just to your mates!
   - ◇ Find out what people want.
   - ◇ Join classes actively.

2. Set up social networking accounts.
   - ◇ Post your thoughts. Encourage comments.

3. Design a character and a catchphrase!
   - ◇ Make recognisable goals.

4. Let people help you.
   - ◇ Ask mates to wear support stickers!

5. Find weaknesses in your ideas.
   - ◇ Ask mates to challenge your ideas.
   - ◇ Prepare clever election-debate answers!

6. Plan a strong speech.
   - ◇ Make the benefits for classmates clear.
   - ◇ Mix humour into your speech. You'll sound good-natured.

7. Film your speech for YouTube!
   - ◇ Wear the school uniform correctly (be serious).

8. Tackle stress!
   - ◇ Breathe, and stretch to relax when under pressure.

— 6 —

第4回　英語（リーディング）

Judgement on advice by high school election winners:

Useful Considerations (Score) → High School ↓	Most (+2)	Second Best (+1)	Least (-1)
Granger High School	2 & 5	1 & 6	3 & 8
Longbottom Academy	6	5 & 7	1 & 2
Potter Academy	3 & 6	1, 2 & 4	7 & 8
Weasley Secondary School	4 & 7	5	3

問1　Based on the feedback from the four high schools, which advice is the least useful? ☐6☐

① Chat to everyone.

② Control your stress.

③ Create a character and a catchphrase.

④ Get help from students.

問2　If you take the advice when running for student council, you will use ☐7☐ .

① gorgeous clothes

② lesson time

③ video equipment

④ well-known characters

問3　According to the website, one **fact** about running for student council is that ☐8☐ .

① assistance is necessary to succeed

② no one knows what makes winning certain

③ some people will reject your ideas

④ technology is important today

— 7 —

問4　According to the website, one **opinion** about running for student council is that ☐9☐ .

① borrowing well-known phrases gets votes

② responding to comments improves communication

③ taking deep breaths relieves panic completely

④ telling jokes attracts listeners

問5　Which of the following are the most effective pieces of advice based on the winners' judgement? ☐10☐

	1 st	2 nd	3 rd
①	Find weaknesses in your ideas.	Let people help you.	Plan a strong speech.
②	Find weaknesses in your ideas.	Plan a strong speech.	Let people help you.
③	Let people help you.	Find weaknesses in your ideas.	Plan a strong speech.
④	Let people help you.	Plan a strong speech.	Find weaknesses in your ideas.
⑤	Plan a strong speech.	Find weaknesses in your ideas.	Let people help you.
⑥	Plan a strong speech.	Let people help you.	Find weaknesses in your ideas.

— 8 —

第4回　英語（リーディング）

（下 書 き 用 紙）

英語（リーディング）の試験問題は次に続く。

—9—

B You've come across an online forum about learning styles, at a high school in the UK where you are studying this summer. You are reading some discussions from the forum.

Learning Styles < Posted on 21 July 2021 >
To: S. Perkins
From: J. Harley

Dear Ms Perkins,

Problem-based learning (pbl), solving real world problems in groups, in student-centred lessons, will leave teachers who are unaccustomed to pbl feeling overwhelmed.

Cooperation among teachers is vital because pbl often makes it necessary to have subjects overlap. Statistics prove that this causes students to feel uncertain in national tests divided by subject. It's also expensive. More teachers are required to monitor discussions and hold regular meetings with students. And it consumes time as students evaluate various sources of information, often unproductively. Isn't traditional lecture-learning better?

Regards,
Joe Harley
School Prefect

第4回　英語（リーディング）

Re: Learning Styles < Posted on 22 July 2021 >
To: J. Harley
From: S. Perkins

Dear Joe,

Thanks for a valuable opinion! Though worthwhile, memorising is less powerful than you think. A study conducted at Harvard University indicated that, though students feel they learn more in lectures, it isn't actually true.

It has been proved that previous knowledge is essential for problem-tackling, so pbl demands students learn continuously. They consider different possibilities and select what seems to them the best, and therefore analyse pros and cons seriously, rather than accepting a 'correct' answer.

Regards,
Shauna Perkins
Head of Curriculum

問1　Problem-based learning 　11　 .

① doesn't necessarily focus on a specific textbook
② helps Earth become a better place
③ is controversial all over the world
④ makes teachers' roles irrelevant

－ 11 －

問2　One **fact** stated in Joe Harley's forum post about pbl is that ☐ 12 ☐ .

① it is expensive, and schools already struggle with budgets

② standard tests distinguished by subject often confuse students

③ teachers have to familiarise themselves with numerous subjects

④ time needed to succeed is not necessarily used wisely

問3　One **opinion** that Shauna Perkins believes supports pbl is that ☐ 13 ☐ .

① facing several potential answers seems to make us consider problems earnestly

② it is just as affordable as other learning styles

③ learning through lectures is not old-fashioned even today

④ we cannot solve problems without grasping background knowledge first

問4　Who showed students learn less than they think in conventional classes?
☐ 14 ☐

① Joe Harley

② Shauna Perkins

③ Those who did a study at Harvard University

④ Young teachers

問5　What might you try to find to help Joe Harley oppose pbl? ☐ 15 ☐

① Exam result scores from the last twenty years

② Proof that university studies are often inaccurate

③ Scientific data about the merits of memorisation

④ Stories of teachers who are unfamiliar with pbl

— 12 —

第4回　英語（リーディング）

（下書き用紙）

英語（リーディング）の試験問題は次に続く。

— 13 —

第3問 (配点 15)

A　You want to see the view from the top of a mountain in the UK.　You found helpful information on a backpacker website.

I want to go up Mt. George but have limited time.　Does anyone know the best way there from Perth Station?　　　　　　　　　　　　　　　(Tim)

Answer

A cable car goes to the top.　Take a free coach from the train station to the cable car station.　As it's popular, you'll probably have to wait at the station — I'd say about 10 minutes.　Once you're on it, it will take you up in only 3 minutes!

You can also take a taxi, but you may have to wait for ten or twenty minutes. Just be warned, neither free coaches nor taxis will take you if it has rained a lot and the road is slightly flooded.

You can also hike to the ski lift, which is available from November to March but which is five times as slow as the cable car.　Pass the newspaper stand outside the station, and you'll find the entrance to the mountain trail.　You might spot salmon in the river beside it if you're really lucky!

　　　　　　　　　　　　　　　　　　　　　　　　　　　　　　　(Regina)

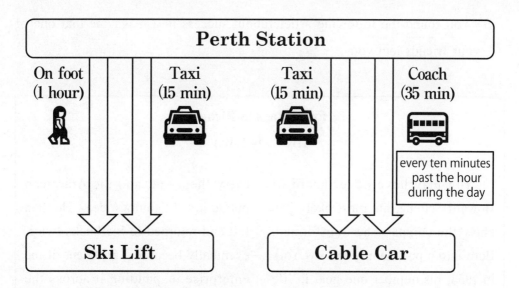

問1　From Regina's answer you learn that ┌16┐ .

① the river is full of salmon
② there's a store by the train station
③ storms are common in the area
④ you can book a taxi online in advance

問2　You arrive at Perth Station at 9.00 am on the 7th March. The weather has been sunny for three days. What is the fastest way to get to the mountain top? ┌17┐

① By coach and cable car
② By taxi and cable car
③ By taxi and ski lift
④ On foot and by ski lift

B You found the following article about success in a magazine that one of your friends lent you.

From Rags to Riches

(By Sally Ellis)

You may have never heard of Howard Schultz, but most likely you know the company he transformed. Born into a poor family in New York in 1953, his number one goal in life was to succeed and build a brighter future, and he fought hard at school to achieve good grades.

Schultz later proved to be a natural at sports, and was offered a free place at university because of his ability. After graduation Schultz did sales for a small coffee-maker company, as well as for other companies, and was promoted quickly there. Eventually he became an advertising manager for a coffee bean company with a few stores in Seattle. The name of this small chain? Starbucks.

On an Italian trip, Schultz was impressed by the café culture there, and suggested Starbucks open coffee shops where people could socialize and chat comfortably. Even when the top managers doubted that ideas would suit their organization, they sometimes allowed their staff to carry them out; and the American public loved Schultz's idea. He then left and returned to Starbucks twice, eventually becoming president of the enterprise, expanding it across the USA and further, incorporating it into 39 countries by 2012. Ironically, some neighboring Starbucks stores have closed because they were competing with each other. Soon after, Schultz was listed in Forbes Magazine as one of America's richest.

Schultz has used any power he had in positive ways since he climbed to the top of his company, and once famously criticized an investor for being against gay marriage, even suggesting he spend his money boosting another company. He received an award for never lying at work, and was invited to teach a course on fair business practices at an American university. He supports the concept of an environmentally friendly business world, and wants oil and gas to be taxed more harshly.

第4回 英語 (リーディング)

問1 Put the following events (①～④) into the order in which they happened. | 18 | → | 19 | → | 20 | → | 21 |

① Schultz became the head of Starbucks.

② Schultz proposed introducing a new business style to Starbucks.

③ Schultz quit working at Starbucks.

④ Schultz started using his influence constructively.

問2 One **fact** we know about Schultz's life is that he | 22 | .

① caused constant trouble at school

② preferred traditional American customs

③ used expensive energy sources

④ was among the wealthiest persons in the USA

問3 From this story, you learned that Starbucks | 23 | .

① began as a cheap store accessible to people living in poverty

② faced considerable challenges early on and almost went out of business

③ itself collected ideas from restaurants worldwide to build an international chain

④ listened to proposals of employees and was willing to try new things

— 17 —

第4問 （配点 16）

You have a friend from the U.S. who is an exchange student at your university. She is looking for a room and has found two articles from two different real estate companies introducing rooms for foreign students. You are reading them with her.

Looking for an apartment?
AP real estate company

Here are two apartments for rent for foreign students looking for a place to live alone near X University.

Apartment A is 40 years old and made of reinforced concrete. The room size is 18m^2. The rent is 50,000 yen, the management fee is 5,000 yen, and the insurance to guarantee the monthly payment is 1,000, which makes the total amount of 56,000 yen per month.

B is a 45-year-old, wooden apartment. The room size is 15m^2. The rent is 40,000 yen, the management fee is 2,000 yen, and the insurance is 1,000 yen every month.

Both rooms are in good condition and have a kitchen, a toilet, and a bath. Both apartment owners require the initial cost of 20,000 yen to exchange the front door key for a new one. No deposit nor key money, which is a fee paid to the owner for agreeing to sign a contract with you, is required.

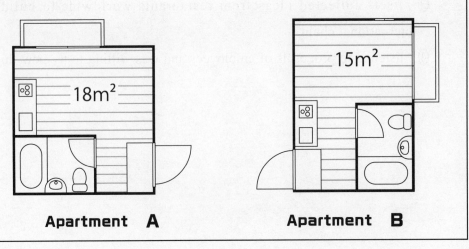

Why not a share house?
SH real estate company

We recommend share houses to exchange students who are looking for a place to live.

Share house C is 10 years old and located very close to X University. It is three stories high and is made of reinforced concrete. Each floor has a living room and three private bedrooms of 8m^2. The living room and kitchen are shared spaces, and the bath and toilet are also shared. You can lock the door of your bedroom, so privacy is protected. The rent is 25,000 yen and the management fee is 15,000 yen every month. The insurance is 9,600 yen for a year, so 800 yen per month. There are no other costs. As there are many international students at X University living in this share house, the shared space is a great place for international exchanges.

Share house D is a 9-year-old building and the building's structure is similar to C's. It is located a little far from the university but within a 5-minute walk of the station. The monthly rent is 30,000 yen as private floor space is slightly larger in this property with each room being 10m^2. The other fees are the same as those for share house C.

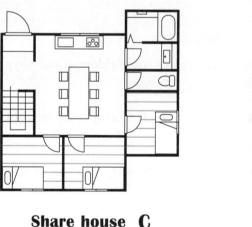
Share house C

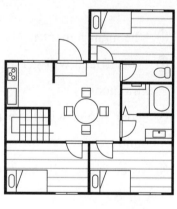
Share house D

問1　The rooms of apartment A and B have the same ┃ 24 ┃.

① building structure

② floor space size

③ monthly insurance money

④ monthly management fee

問2　If your friend wants to live in apartment B, she needs to pay ┃ 25 ┃

as the initial cost including the rent.

① 42,000 yen

② 43,000 yen

③ 54,000 yen

④ 63,000 yen

問3　A good point of living in share house C is that ┃ 26 ┃.

① the management fee is less than apartment A's or B's

② your friend will get a new key for her room's door if she pays some

extra money

③ your friend will have a good chance of making friends from other

countries

④ your friend will have a larger kitchen than if she lives in apartment

A or B

— 20 —

第4回　英語（リーディング）

問4　If your friend's monthly budget is less than 45,000 yen after the 2nd month, she can afford ☐ 27 ☐.

① apartment A and apartment B

② apartment B and share house C

③ apartment B, share house C and share house D

④ only apartment B

問5　If your friend wants to live in a place with a kitchen, a toilet, and a bath of her own in a concrete building, her choice will be ☐ 28 ☐. If she is planning to use trains quite often, ☐ 29 ☐ is a good choice. (Choose the best one for each box from options ① ~ ④.)

① apartment A

② apartment B

③ share house C

④ share house D

— 21 —

第5問 （配点 15）

You are going to give a presentation about a person you admire for achieving great things in spite of great difficulties. Read the following passage about the person you have chosen and finish your presentation slides.

Kenya has produced some amazing runners. Tegla Loroupe, born in rural Kenya in 1973, was put to work looking after cows, as well as her 24 brothers and sisters, almost as soon as she started walking. Aged seven, she started running the ten kilometer journey to school without shoes every day; and it was at school, often winning races against older kids, that she realized her running potential, and this created her ambition to become an accomplished athlete — a dream her mother alone supported her in. At the age of 21, she won the New York marathon — the first African woman to do so — and became a role model across her continent.

Nicknamed 'Chametia,' a reference to her relaxed personality, Tegla faced and overcame countless obstacles. Not only did her father insist running was unladylike and demand she quit, but when first spotted by the Kenyan Athletics Federation, she was judged too weak to become anything special. She refused to listen to negative criticism or to give up; and in 1988 she won a well-known long-distance race, and Kenyan sports officials finally began to take notice. A year later, she received her first pair of running shoes, though she preferred to compete without them where possible.

Tegla became more and more successful, not only beating her rivals in several distances, but breaking several world records. In the 2000 Sydney Olympics marathon in Australia, Tegla was the firm favorite to earn the gold medal, but she ate something that made her very ill the night before. However, even after that, she refused to drop out and came 13th in the event regardless of her terrible condition. Her motivation? A sense of duty to all of her supporters in Africa. Between 1998 and 2001, she had the women's world record for the

— 22 —

第4回　英語（リーディング）

full marathon, breaking her own record in 1999 in Germany, even though she was in poor health for much of this three-year period.

Tegla is now retired from professional sports, and a spokesperson for the worldwide charity Oxfam describes her humanitarian work as 'brilliant.' In 2011 she invested in and helped found *Tegla Loroupe Peace and Leadership Centre*, a school set up for students from many warring communities across four countries. Her objective is to erase deeply rooted negative feelings and to provide a decent education to impoverished kids, especially girls — she herself defied her father and joined her brothers at school — who often miss out; many from her background believing formal learning is a male luxury.

In fact, when the Kenyan Athletics Federation made clear their opinion that she could never stand out, Tegla genuinely considered dedicating her life to God. She was sick of the attitudes of the men around her, and working for the church, living simply with other women, seemed appealing. Luckily, her drive to prove those people with discouraging attitudes toward her wrong was strong. Though society is slowly recognizing that men and women are all humans who should be treated equally, she notes that it can still be tougher for women than men to be taken seriously, and doesn't understand why it should still be a struggle.

Women's rights are not the only cause that Tegla advocates. Coming from a tribe in an area inhabited by several enemy races, Tegla has always dreamed of using her fame to end disputes. She established the annual 10km Peace Race in 2006, and in the first one, 2,000 fighters from six rival communities came together to compete in a friendly manner. Furthermore, the United Nations nominated her as Ambassador of Sports the same year. Instead of telling tribes at war to just 'stop,' she offers them faith in a future without battles. The Tegla Loroupe Peace Foundation she began in 2003 continues to change lives. Ever the peacemaker, Germany-based Tegla describes her father, who, in his own words, "was close to destroying her career," as her friend — but jokes that she is grateful she never listened to him!

Presentation Slides

30

Johnson High School
Presentation
Event

Tegla Loroupe — the Person

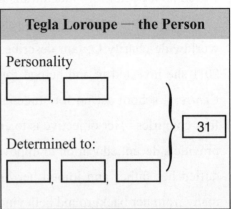

Personality

☐ , ☐

Determined to:

☐ , ☐ , ☐   } 31

Tegla's Life

Runs to and from school in Kenya
↓
| 32 |
↓
| 33 |
↓
| 34 |
↓
| 35 |
↓
Lives in Germany

Effects of Tegla's Actions

- Athletes saw that struggling on in imperfect conditions earns respect.
- Ordinary people realized that it is possible for enemies to cooperate and get along.
- | 36 |
- | 37 |

Why Didn't Tegla Ever Give Up?

- Her mother always encouraged her.
- | 38 |
- She wanted to repay her supporters.

— 24 —

第4回　英語（リーディング）

問1　Which is the best title for your presentation?　30

① A Male-Oriented World? No, an Equal World.

② Believe In Yourself: Make Change Real!

③ End Conflict with Action! Words Are NOT Enough.

④ Female? Poor? Sick? Stop Making Excuses!

問2　Which is the best combination for the **Tegla Loroupe — the Person** slide?　31

	Personality	Determined to:
①	Angry, hardworking	become famous, help poor kids, stop tribal fighting
②	Calm, hardworking	be an outstanding athlete, help poor kids, stop tribal fighting
③	Careless, friendly	become famous, stop tribal fighting, lead a religious life
④	Shy, friendly	be an outstanding athlete, help poor kids, lead a religious life

問3　Choose the events in the order in which they happened to complete the timeline of **Tegla's Life**.　32　～　35

① Badly injured herself at the Olympics

② Built a school for children in need

③ Considered giving up sports and focusing on religion

④ Set up an organization to promote friendship

⑤ Used sports to stop enemy tribes fighting

— 25 —

問4 Choose the best two items for the **Effects of Tegla's Actions** slide.
(The order does not matter.) 36 · 37

① More girls began to receive an education.

② Physically weak teenagers tried harder.

③ The UN recognized Tegla's efforts.

④ Ways of thinking rapidly became more modern.

⑤ Young kids began challenging adults' ideas.

問5 Complete the **Why Didn't Tegla Ever Give Up?** slide with the most
appropriate item. 38

① She dreamed of breaking a world record.

② She feared for her safety at home.

③ She knew she was talented.

④ She wanted to escape farm life.

第4回　英語（リーディング）

（下書き用紙）

英語（リーディング）の試験問題は次に続く。

— 27 —

第6問 （配点 24）

A You are working on a geography project about natural disasters and their effect on certain regions and found the following article. You are reading it and making a poster to present your findings to your classmates.

Natural Disasters on the Increase ― the Bigger Picture

The number of natural disasters ― earthquakes, volcanoes erupting, typhoons, floods and droughts ― is rising. Noticeable changes in weather began in the 1960s; and compared to 1990, there are 35% more such disasters today. The Red Cross says more than eight out of ten disasters can be linked to climate. Its "World Disasters Report" published in 2020 states that extreme heat and storms in particular have killed thousands.

Since the beginning of this century parts of Australia have suffered from continuing drought. Intense heat and lack of rain have destroyed crops of vegetables and fruits, as well as killed animals. The 2019-2020 forest fire season was one of the worst on record, forcing many people to desert their homes before they burnt down. Scientists are not surprised, stating that models based on predictions regarding the destruction of the ozone layer fit.

Location is also significant. More people than ever reside near the coast. Agriculture benefits from nutritious land on volcano slopes and close to river systems. Similarly, communities near the ocean attract jobseekers because of the abundance of established companies. Seaside cities have taken advantage of convenient overseas access and profit generously from foreign trade and business.

A relatively new term is 'climate migrant'. People used mainly to flee their nations to escape war, discrimination for their beliefs, or other hardships. Between 1845 and 1849, half a million people left Ireland for the United States after a disease almost completely wiped out the potato crop. Though the

---

― 28 ―

第4回 英語 (リーディング)

original reasons for people fleeing their homes still exist, today people are far more likely to be simply trying to escape their homelands, which have, sadly, become inhospitable to them, just as in Ireland two centuries ago.

The first country to disappear could be Kiribati, a Pacific nation consisting of numerous islands. The ocean is swallowing it, and land is disappearing under water quickly. In 1999 two uninhabited islands sank completely. In preparation for the inevitable — the whole country going underwater by 2100 — Kiribati's president has gone so far as to buy an island from Fiji for the purpose of relocating the population. Despite taking measures such as strictly enforcing laws to reduce erosion of the coast, the government has already begun to encourage its citizens to migrate.

Elsewhere, international migrants often face dangerous, illegal journeys, and even professionals can get only menial jobs on arrival at their destinations. Of course, reversing the effects of global warming will take decades, and experts believe it is essential that refugees from natural disasters caused by weather get protection by law. A New York politician has proposed The Embrace Act — a law that would give health and financial benefits to everyone, regardless of nationality or reason for living in the USA. The number of natural disasters is unlikely to decrease soon, and governments must understand the need to help victims.

Natural Disasters & Climate

The Facts:
· Weather changes first noticed in the 1960s.
· There are 35% more natural disasters today than in 1990.
· 80% of natural disasters can be linked to climate.

Australian Climate Disaster in This Century

What?	Effects
· ⬚39⬚ · Too little rainfall	· ⬚40⬚ · Animals being killed · Major forest fires · People leaving their homes

Why are more people today living near the coast?

· Land is good for farming
· ⬚41⬚
· It's convenient for international trade

Reasons for migration

Traditional	New
· War · Beliefs · Other hardships	· CLIMATE

The Island Nation of Kiribati	Problems Often Faced by Migrants in Other Areas
 Citizens are being urged to migrate by the government	· ⬚42⬚ · They can't get jobs that match their skills

第4回　英語（リーディング）

問1　Choose the best option for ▢39 on your poster.

① Earthquakes
② Poor air quality
③ Storms and typhoons
④ Too hot temperatures

問2　Choose the best option for ▢40 on your poster.

① Agriculture being ruined
② An increasing number of deserts
③ Faster damage to Earth's atmosphere
④ Not enough drinking water

問3　Choose the best option for ▢41 on your poster.

① Access to surrounding islands is good
② Many organizations have offices there
③ People migrating tend to travel by boat
④ Power produced by water is common

問4　Choose the best option for ▢42 on your poster.

① Journeys are often against the law
② They are not accustomed to the climate of their destinations
③ They arrive in new countries in ill health
④ They don't have enough money to settle down

― 31 ―

B You are one of a group of students preparing a poster for a presentation about the history of exercise. You have been reading the following passage to help you create a poster to demonstrate how fitness has changed.

The Search for Good Health

We live in a health-obsessed society, and gyms are everywhere. With access to the worldwide web, at the click of a button we can surf through the latest exercise and diet trends in an instant. What is more, we are becoming amateur doctors. We check any symptoms of illness we might have and try to identify and solve the problem ourselves. This may be one of the reasons for the increase in mental health problems. Today we recognize the importance of how we feel mentally as well as physically, with millions of people around the world chasing the secret to happiness and, of course, the 'perfect' body shape, though this in itself varies vastly according to location and culture.

Naturally, physical exercise isn't a new concept, but our oldest ancestors stayed fit following instinct. Humans living in the wilds of nature ran, crawled, jumped, carried heavy objects of all different sizes, threw things, and were getting into fights constantly to survive. Then, around ten thousand years ago, the age of agriculture arrived. We stopped hunting and gathering and instead began to farm land, repeating the same actions and movements over and over again through our unvaried daily tasks. Life was simpler. For example, going up a ladder requires far less effort and movement than rushing to the top of a tree, so existence became less physically demanding.

After this peaceful period, as nations were formed and leaders appointed, hunger for land and power resulted in an era of war, and training males for battle became a major operation. Through drills and specific training activities, these disciplined soldiers moved in similar ways to ancient man, but their routines followed more structure. Fitness was the key to success,

— 32 —

第4回　英語（リーディング）

and drove them to be incredible athletes. Later still, the great civilizations connected strong bodies with sharp minds, and people believed that by being muscular and tight they could also be more intelligent. Though physical activity was not as intense, people took care of themselves, and sporting events to celebrate athletic ability, such as the Olympics, became common.

Between 500 and 1500, attitudes to sport encountered a major reversal. Religion started to dominate the way societies functioned and taught us that bodies were unimportant. In fact, our bones, skin and organs were deemed essentially just elaborate containers for carrying our souls until we entered the afterlife. Moreover, this was a period of time that brought tragedies in the form of a variety of sicknesses and natural calamities that left people weak. But this state of affairs did not last for long. Science brought about a change in mindset along with advances in medicine, and universities provided opportunities to expand biological knowledge. Vittorino da Feltre, considered a pioneer of modern education, included P.E. classes in the timetables at the institution where he worked. Another Italian, Mercurialis, published a guide promoting exercise and regular washing routines to ensure cleanliness, and championed the necessity of eating balanced meals. He had a profound influence on current approaches to health.

The twentieth century saw an increase in organized sports and various fashionable diets, and health and fitness featured significantly in the media. The desire to look attractive resulted in billion-dollar businesses. Yet despite all the tools we have to build perfect bodies today, life expectancy began to fall worldwide in the 1990s. To tell the truth, nowadays being slightly overweight is not regarded as terribly embarrassing; and, though spoiled by the wide range of health and fitness apps on our electronic devices, we are equally indulged by functions allowing us to order fast food at the touch of a button and have it delivered. Perhaps, ultimately, the trick for getting good health is natural food, movement, and fresh air, not machines or apps. Nature can be your gym.

Your presentation poster:

The History of Exercise

1. Modern Attitudes to Health

A. A tendency to try and diagnose our own problems
B. Access to information on the latest fitness fashions
C. Awareness of mental as well as physical health issues
D. Different health goals depending on our backgrounds
E. Many facilities for staying in shape

2. 44

- Cultivation of land instead of collecting sources of food from nature
- Appreciation of what the human body can achieve, generating a love of sporting competitions
- Development of religion and science

3. In Which Era Was the Body More Important?

45

Problems in Society Today

46
47

第4回　英語（リーディング）

問1　Under the first poster heading, your group wants to describe modern attitudes to health as explained in the passage. Everyone agrees that one item does not fit well. Which of the following should you **not** include?　43

① A
② B
③ C
④ D
⑤ E

問2　You have been asked to write the second heading for the poster. Which of the following is the most appropriate?　44

① Health in Rural and Urban Environments
② Man's Competitive Nature and Health
③ Social Shifts Impacting Health
④ The Evolution of Our Bodies and Health

問3 Out of the following four sets of formulas, which one is the most appropriate for your poster? ⬚45⬚

```
[Meaning]

More important  >  Less important
Less important  <  More important
```

① Ancient Man   > Farming Man
   Farming Man   > Fighting Man
   Religious Man > Scientific Man

② Ancient Man   > Farming Man
   Farming Man   < Fighting Man
   Religious Man < Scientific Man

③ Ancient Man   < Farming Man
   Farming Man   > Fighting Man
   Religious Man < Scientific Man

④ Ancient Man   < Farming Man
   Farming Man   < Fighting Man
   Religious Man < Scientific Man

問4 Under the last poster heading, you want to point out some problems in today's society based on the passage. Which two of the following statements could you use? ⬚46⬚ · ⬚47⬚

① It is very expensive to stay in shape.
② People aren't living as long as they once did.
③ The media cause people to feel unattractive.
④ There's little shame in being larger than average.
⑤ We get food delivered more than we cook.

第 5 回

（80分）

実 戦 問 題

●標準所要時間●

第1問 7分程度	第4問 12分程度
第2問 13分程度	第5問 14分程度
第3問 12分程度	第6問 22分程度

第5回　実戦問題

英　　語（リーディング）

各大問の英文や図表を読み，解答番号 ┃ 1 ┃ 〜 ┃ 47 ┃ にあてはまるものとして最も適当な選択肢を選びなさい。

第1問　（配点　10）

A　You are studying abroad in France. You get a text message from your British friend who is studying at another school in the same city.

Simon

Hi! The city hall is organising a 'Sing!' day at the community centre, with the opportunity to sing and listen to songs in various languages, as a way of introducing people from around the world! The music will be karaoke style, with no musical instruments or stage. Come! And bring your classmates! ☺

Hey, Simon. I heard! I'll be there ♡! Song categories haven't been decided yet, right? People tend to like different kinds of music. What should I sing?

Simon

Well, most people will be young so I should think that lively songs would be better, so that people can dance to their favourite ones. I'll go early, but see you at the centre!

第5回 英語 (リーディング)

問1 Your friend wants you to ☐1☐ .

① find some people to form a rock band

② invite other people to attend the event

③ perform a traditional dance on the stage

④ teach students songs from your country

問2 How will you reply to Simon's second message? ☐2☐

① Got it. I'll start translating song words!

② OK! I'd better research old songs!

③ Sorry, I can't go there so early.

④ Sure! I'll choose some cool J-pop!

― 3 ―

B Your teacher has given you a notice of interesting lectures.

Special Lectures on English Language

Professor Swain, one of the leading scholars in the field of language, is giving a series of free lectures on English at our high school next month. This special course consists of three sections:

	DATE	PLACE	Content
Lesson A	March 6	South Hall	· syntax of English
Lesson B	March 8	Center Hall	· vocabulary of English · phonology of English
Lesson C	March 10	Auditorium	· history of English

☆ Each student can register for up to two lessons.
☆ No prior knowledge is required.
☆ You will have to write a short report after each lesson.

About the lecturer
He is a professor at Bolic University. He has published many articles mainly on English syntax, a field that deals with the grammar of English, but he is also famous for his research on English phonology, the study of the sounds of English.

Message from the lecturer
Hi everyone! I like Japanese culture and food very much. So I am really looking forward to talking about them with you after each lesson! I hope this will be a good opportunity for you to practice speaking English.

* You must hand in your application to Ms. Takahashi by the end of this month.
* You can invite your family members to these lectures.

第5回 英語 (リーディング)

問1 In order to take part in the special lectures, you have to ☐ 3 ☐ .

① attend at least two lessons
② have some background knowledge
③ submit your application in February
④ take your family members with you

問2 After the lectures, Professor Swain is likely to ☐ 4 ☐ .

① eat Japanese food with the other teachers
② have conversations about Japan
③ publish a book on Japanese customs
④ write a brief report about Japan

問3 If you want to learn about the grammar of English, you are most likely to ☐ 5 ☐ .

① attend the lecture held at South Hall
② go to the Auditorium on March 10
③ participate in the lecture given on March 8
④ take lessons at Bolic University

—5—

第2問 （配点 20）

A You are looking for a restaurant in London, the UK, for Valentine's Day, and are reading about a restaurant battle in the area. You hope to book one for your date.

Restaurant critics' star ★ ranking				
Condition ＼ Restaurants	Food ★★★★★	Service ★★★★★	Décor ★★★★★	Total
Funk Shack	1.3	2.0	1.7	5
Meadow Inn	3.9	3.8	5.0	12.7
O'Sullivan's	4.1	4.7	3.9	12.7
The Rose Pub	4.3	3.9	4.5	12.7

Comments of the critics	
Mr Frome	I felt that the servers' timing was excellent at The Rose Pub, especially compared to the slow, humourless delivery at Meadow Inn! O'Sullivan's fusion of Chinese and British food was clever, but didn't always work.
Ms King	O'Sullivan's served up some unexpected dishes! Not for everyone perhaps, but winners for me! The wait staff knew the menu well. At The Rose Pub, they seemed unsure. I loved Meadow Inn's cheerful atmosphere!
Ms Tucker	Thanks O'Sullivan's for my favourite dish! But take a hint from Meadow Inn. Paint the walls a brighter, more cheerful colour!

Critic's shared decision (summarised by Ms King)

With one exception, all the restaurants tied in scores! When it comes to food, none of those three were bad at all, so we critics all agreed that service should be the factor that tops the ranking.

When deciding second and third place, Ms Tucker pointed out that most people don't care much about the décor if the food is good. Mr Frome and I think so too.

— 6 —

第5回　英語（リーディング）

問1　Based on the critics' final decisions, which restaurant was decorated the best? ⬜6

① Funk Shack

② Meadow Inn

③ O'Sullivan's

④ The Rose Pub

問2　Which judges gave both positive and critical comments? ⬜7

① All of them

② Mr Frome

③ Ms King

④ Ms Tucker

問3　One **fact** from the critics' original comments is that ⬜8 .

① at The Rose Pub you never wait long for food

② O'Sullivan's mixes the food culture of two countries

③ the judges couldn't agree about Funk Shack

④ the wall colors at Meadow hill are pleasant

問4　One **opinion** from the critics' shared evaluation is that ⬜9 .

① all three best restaurants serve decent food

② décor takes less skill to improve than food quality

③ Ms Tucker indicated something and the others agreed

④ the critics picked a winner through discussion

—7—

問5 Which of the following is the final ranking based on the critics' shared evaluation? ☐10☐

	1 st	2 nd	3 rd
①	Meadow Inn	O'Sullivan's	The Rose Pub
②	Meadow Inn	The Rose Pub	O'Sullivan's
③	O'Sullivan's	Meadow Inn	The Rose Pub
④	O'Sullivan's	The Rose Pub	Meadow Inn
⑤	The Rose Pub	Meadow Inn	O'Sullivan's
⑥	The Rose Pub	O'Sullivan's	Meadow Inn

— 8 —

第5回　英語（リーディング）

（下書き用紙）

英語（リーディング）の試験問題は次に続く。

B Your English teacher gave you an article to help you prepare for a debate in the next class. A part of this article with one of the comments is shown below.

Should students wear school uniforms?

By Roger White, New York
20 October 2019 5:15PM

The United States is slowly adopting the use of school uniforms. According to figures published in 2018 by the National Center for Education Statistics, the proportion of public schools requiring students to wear school uniforms increased from 12 percent in 1999 to 21 percent in 2015. Another survey showed that 41 percent of students at public schools in big cities wear uniforms. In Philadelphia, especially, all the students at public schools are required to wear uniforms.

So what are the advantages of wearing school uniforms? One teacher said, "First, we can promote equality among students and reduce bullying. Some students have expensive clothes, but others do not. This sometimes leads to bullying. Besides, if outsiders come into our school, we can recognize them more easily. In terms of security, too, this policy is desirable."

Not all parents, however, agree with this policy. Some parents said, "The school uniform policy violates the students' freedom of expression. Students should wear their favorite clothes." And others said, "Now there are a lot of immigrant children who have different values and customs from ours. In this day and age we have to respect diversity, not *uniformity*."

17 Comments

Newest

Kate Thompson 22 October 2019 9:05 PM
I understand this policy. You don't need to think about what to wear every morning. Moreover, a sense of togetherness can be built. But at the same time some students can't afford uniforms, perhaps. I hear the price sometimes reaches over $500.

— 10 —

第5回 英語（リーディング）

問1 According to the article, students at public schools in Philadelphia are ☐11☐ .

① forced to ask their parents to buy school uniforms
② free to wear anything they like
③ not permitted to dress the way they want
④ not willing to change their clothes every day

問2 Your team will support the debate topic, "All students should wear school uniforms." In the article, one **opinion** helpful for your team is that ☐12☐ .

① it will cost less to wear school uniforms than to choose what to wear
② school uniforms will create a safer environment for students
③ the image of public schools will be really improved
④ the number of students committing crimes will decrease

問3 The other team will oppose the debate topic. In the article, one **opinion** helpful for that team is that ☐13☐ .

① it is not fair for teachers at public schools to dress as they like
② requiring uniforms has no effect on the social status of public schools
③ school uniforms will limit students' ability to express themselves
④ some parents cannot buy their favorite clothes for their children

— 11 —

問4 In the 3rd paragraph of the article, "In this day and age" means "In the times when 14 ".

① all people have to wear some kind of uniform
② individual human rights are restricted to some extent
③ information plays a very important role in people's lives
④ people from various cultural backgrounds live together

問5 Judging from her comment, Kate Thompson 15 the policy mentioned in the article.

① has no interest in
② partly agrees with
③ totally agrees with
④ totally disagrees with

— 12 —

第5回　英語（リーディング）

（下 書 き 用 紙）

英語（リーディング）の試験問題は次に続く。

— 13 —

第3問 （配点 15）

A Your British friend, Pippa, just got back from a cool museum, and posted about it on her webpage.

Welcome to Alternative Worlds: Pebbleton Science Museum!

〈Posted by Pippa at 20:21 on 16th March 2021〉

....

I'd heard amazing things about Pebbleton Science Museum, and finally went there today! There is plenty of cool stuff, and it's so interactive!

The 4D theatre was fantastic. I was so looking forward to experiencing flying to the moon in the rocket show. Before that we had time to take a guided tour through the dinosaur area on the ground floor, or so we thought. The modern models were terribly realistic! It was so good we lost track of time, and by the time we found our way through the slightly confusing 'streets' of the model city of the future two floors up to reach the escalator for the rocket show, it was half over. Never mind, we were able to see a different show instead just before going home!

Don't miss the model city of the future. The driverless vehicles and environmentally-friendly technology were impressive, and AI robots actually quite cute! There are lots of buttons to press with exciting results — I won't say anymore! Oh, don't forget to go to the café after a long, exciting day if you are hungry. I recommend the moon cakes. Your visit won't be complete without stepping inside! I had a nice break there before going up one floor to our last stop.

— 14 —

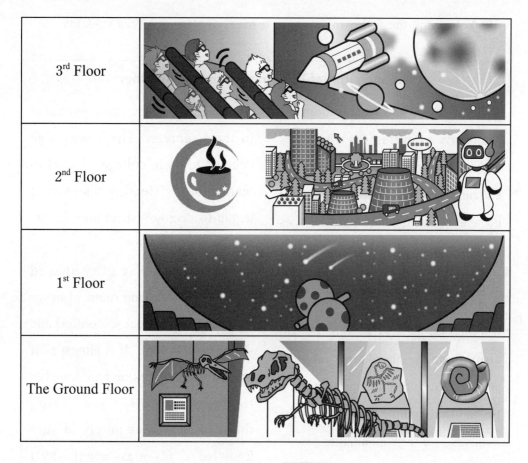

問1 From Pippa's post, you learn that 16 .

① the layout of the model city was a bit complicated
② the stories told by the dinosaur guides were frightening
③ you can experience sitting in a real rocket
④ you can take the café's food into the model city

問2 What floor did Pippa finish her day at the museum on? 17

① The ground floor
② The first floor
③ The second floor
④ The third floor

B You found the following story in a magazine for overseas students.

The meaning of learning for my grandfather

One day, when I came home, I found my grandfather, who lives with us, reading a book about college entrance exams. When I asked why he was reading it, he said he was preparing to go to college again. At first, I didn't believe him, thinking he was just making a joke. However, it turned out he was serious; he had also bought textbooks on subjects such as English and mathematics. He had said nothing to anyone in the family, so we were all amazed.

A few days later, I dared to ask him what he was going to study. I thought it would be a subject related to his career as a teacher, like child psychology. He didn't tell me directly, but said, "When I was young, living in the country, I loved looking up at the night sky and trying to name the stars and planets. I found them completely fascinating. Even when I was working as a history teacher, I read a lot of books

that made me all the more interested in their secrets. That's why I've decided to go to college. I want to learn more." Hearing his story, I began to deeply respect him for his intellectual curiosity.

Since then, we've often studied together in the living room. I never thought I would feel so comfortable sitting next to him. It is almost as if we are friends working hard together toward our goals. And seeing the way he studies purely to gain knowledge, my ideas about why I should study have changed. It's clear to me that I don't need a practical purpose to study something. Now I don't necessarily regard passing the entrance exam as a practical matter. It may actually be a way of entering a huge world of knowledge.

Satoru Akiyama
(high school student)

第5回 英語 (リーディング)

問1 According to the story, Satoru's feelings toward his grandfather changed in the following order: ⬚18 → ⬚19 → ⬚20 → ⬚21 .

① admiration

② closeness

③ doubt

④ surprise

問2 Satoru's grandfather is probably planning to learn about ⬚22 in college.

① child psychology

② country life

③ the universe

④ world history

問3 From this story, you learned that Satoru's grandfather ⬚23 .

① felt very unhappy in college because he didn't understand the meaning of learning

② made Satoru realize that studying can be done simply to learn new things

③ studied very hard when he was young in order to make his wishes come true

④ talked about his family in order to help Satoru discover the meaning of life

— 17 —

第4問 （配点 16）

You are planning to hold a seminar about pets. After e-mailing the data about international pet keeping habits you found to your two British partners, Melanie and Dustin, you come up with a draft for your talk.

The data:

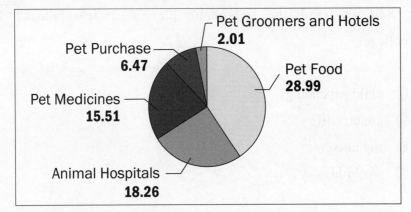

Figure 1. *The Costs of Owning Pets* (billion dollars)

Table 1. *Global Pet Populations*

Country	Pet dogs (millions)	Country	Pet cats (millions)
United States	55.3	United States	80.6
Brazil	35.7	China	58.1
China	27.4	Russia	18.0
Russia	12.5	Brazil	12.5
Japan	12.0	France	11.4
Philippines	11.6	UK	8.5
India	10.2	Germany	8.2
Argentina	9.2	Italy	7.5
UK	8.5	Japan	7.3
France	7.4	Turkey	3.1

(参考：Euromonitor, APPA, FEDIAF and sportrichlist.com, via GfK: "*Finding your opportunities in the Chinese pet food & treats market,*" Petfood Forum China 2015)

第5回　英語（リーディング）

The responses to your email:

Hi,

Thanks for the mail! I had no idea pet products were such big business! The Brazilians really love their dogs. I read you'll find dogs in around half of the homes in Brazil! This makes sense I guess, as I know Brazil has become wealthier over the last decade. I heard that many Brazilians are keeping pets instead of having kids these days, too.

I see pet shops all over our city, and I'm not surprised so much money is spent on pet health. I wish people would realise this before purchasing pets. I'm fed up of hearing about them being abandoned in the streets. I'd like to focus on this point, please.

I wonder what pets will be popular in another few years? The latest trend for urban living is snakes and lizards! But it'd be better for you to talk about cat and dog keeping trends for now?

Chat soon,
Melanie
P.S. I also sent this message to Dustin.

Hi,

Excellent data! How useful!

The chart on pet owner spending might be misleading in terms of money spent on pet hotels. This industry is growing rapidly, along with the number of pet-sitting services available. I want to explain this to everyone.

It's interesting that although the USA tops the charts for the number of cats and dogs, in the near future this may not be true. Did you know pet dogs used to be illegal in Beijing? Not anymore. Apparently especially older people there keep them for company.

Melanie's point about people throwing away animals is good. There are millions of animals without homes, but this is changing, due to an increased improvement in animal rights. In Russia's capital city the homeless dogs are famous, and often travel on metro escalators where kind strangers pet and feed them! I'll find out more. It could be a fun topic to present another time.

Cheers,
Dustin.
P.S. This message is going to Melanie, too.

第５回　英語（リーディング）

Your talk draft:

Talk Theme:	24

Speaker	**Topic**
Melanie:	25
Dustin:	26
me:	Current pet keeping statistics

Example observation:
The citizens of 27 have about two-thirds as many dogs as cats, and keep roughly as many dogs as people in 28 have cats.

Themes to Study More: 29

問1　Which is the best for 24 ?

① Cats Versus Dogs: Which Win the People's Vote?

② Communities Globally Welcoming Our Pets More Warmly

③ Humans' Relationships With and Tastes for Animals

④ The Main Reasons Why People Keep Pets

問2　Which is the best for 25 ?

① Educating people on where to get pets

② Organisations dedicated to keeping pets safe

③ The financial success of pet services

④ Think carefully before buying a pet

— 21 —

問3　Which is the best for 26 ?

① China overtaking America in keeping pets

② How to spot a homeless animal

③ Pet care services getting more popular

④ Pets being allowed on public transport

問4　You agree with Melanie's idea, and look at the data. Choose the best for 27 and 28 .

① France

② Japan

③ Russia

④ UK

問5　Which is the best combination for 29 ?

A : Animals filling the gap left by lack of family and friends

B : Laws about pet keeping becoming more relaxed

C : Stories of people helping animals living on the streets

D : Types of pet that are becoming more fashionable

① A and B

② A and C

③ A and D

④ B and C

⑤ B and D

⑥ C and D

第5回 英語（リーディング）

（下 書 き 用 紙）

英語（リーディング）の試験問題は次に続く。

第5問 （配点 15）

You are doing your homework, which requires you to create presentation notes about a man who greatly influenced America, using information from a magazine article below, to present your findings to your classmates.

Called "the man who shaped America," Raymond Loewy must be one of the most influential designers of all time. He revolutionized the design industry, working as a consultant for more than 200 companies and creating designs for everything from packaging to refrigerators, from cars to the interiors of spacecraft. He achieved fame for the importance of his design efforts across a variety of industries.

Raymond Loewy was born in Paris in 1893. He started exhibiting a great talent for design when he was still a teenager. The model aircraft he designed was so successful that it won a famous award for model airplanes in 1908. After World War I, during which he served in the French army, he moved to New York in 1919. On arriving there, he found a job as a fashion illustrator. He started his career in industrial design in 1929 by re-designing a copying machine for a British manufacturer. Thanks to his design, the sales of the machine increased greatly. This led to people paying greater attention to the importance of the design of the industrial products. Further commissions followed, including the styling of a refrigerator. It was this product that established his reputation as an industrial designer. After 1937, he established relations with various companies, such as the Pennsylvania Railroad, American car maker Studebaker, and so on.

Loewy's designs all had one thing in common. They were shaped by the principle that designs must be very progressive and at the same time moderate. His idea was that people were attracted to novel things but were afraid of unknown things. The external feature of Loewy's designs was streamlining. A streamlined object has a shape that allows it to move quickly or efficiently through air or water. The copying machine in 1929 was the beginning of many designs which used streamlining.

— 24 —

He described streamlining as "beauty through function and simplification." After his invention of streamlining, its use became a growing trend in various fields of industrial design over the decades. It was seen as the symbol for speed, progress, and modernity. He spent the next 50 years streamlining everything from postage stamps and company logos to the interiors of stores.

Loewy is perhaps most famous for his re-design of the packaging of Lucky Strike, an American cigarette brand. In 1940, he changed the background of the packet from green to white. Then he put the red lucky strike target on both sides of the packet. This made it more eye-catching and greatly increased sales. Loewy's logo designs aimed at "visual retention." He wanted to make sure that anyone who saw the logo, even for a short while, would never forget it. He designed many highly visible logos for famous companies.

By the mid-20th century, his industrial design firm was so famous that Loewy could say "the average person leading a normal life is bound to be in daily contact with some of the things, services or structures" designed by his firm. Late in life, Loewy worked for NASA. He improved the psychology, safety, and comfort of people in manned spacecraft. Loewy retired at the age of 87 in 1980 and returned to his native France, where he died in 1986.

Presentation notes:

Title: 30

The Life of Raymond Loewy

☆ Loewy spent his childhood in France.

☆ 31

☆ 32

☆ 33

☆ 34

☆ Loewy returned to his mother country.

About Loewy's Designs

☆ The concept common to all his designs was " 35 ."

☆ There are some distinctive characteristics in his designs: 36 · 37

Loewy, a revolutionist in design

☆ He revolutionized the design industry.

☆ He made great achievements in design in a number of ways: 38

第5回 英語（リーディング）

問1 Which is the best title for your presentation? 　30

   ① An American Master of Advertising

   ② Complex and Cool Designs Show Quality

   ③ Redesigning the Face of Industry

   ④ The Journey from Fashion to Space

問2 You listed the important events in Loewy's life. Put the events into
the boxes 　31　 ～ 　34　 in the order that they happened.

   ① Loewy began working as a fashion illustrator.

   ② Loewy re-designed a copying machine.

   ③ Loewy took on work for a railway company and a car maker.

   ④ Loewy won an award for his model airplane.

問3 Which of the following best describes Loewy's designs? 　35

   ① Advanced and also acceptable

   ② Both beautiful and traditional

   ③ Combining speed and comfort

   ④ Following the latest fashion

— 27 —

問4 Which two of the following descriptions are the most appropriate for use in the poster? (The order does not matter.) 36 · 37

① A combination of specific colors and letters was used in them.
② A motif of circles and straight lines was used in them.
③ People could remember them after only a glance.
④ People couldn't understand them because they were too artistic.
⑤ They were beautiful despite being simple and functional.

問5 Which combination of the following events is the most appropriate for use in the poster? 38

A : Loewy created progressive and modern industrial design.
B : Loewy established the trend of design from the 1930s onward.
C : Loewy found out that sales increased even though designs were complicated.
D : Loewy improved the engine design of spacecraft at the request of NASA.
E : Loewy made people aware of the importance of industrial design.
F : Loewy proved the effectiveness of changing design regularly.

① A and C
② D and E
③ A, B and D
④ A, B and E
⑤ C, D and E
⑥ C, E and F

— 28 —

第5回　英語（リーディング）

（下 書 き 用 紙）

英語（リーディング）の試験問題は次に続く。

第6問 (配点 24)

A You are working on a class project about the effects of reading for your class. You have found the article below. You are reading it and making a poster to present your findings to your classmate.

What makes reading a social justice issue?

A recent study reported in The New York Times determined that people who read books live an average of almost two years longer than nonreaders. Indeed, the lives of readers are likely to be not only longer but deeper. Reading can help develop the ability to understand other people's feelings and build the capacity for more joy and love.

Americans' current engagement in reading is somewhat difficult to evaluate. More than a decade ago, a report called "Reading at Risk" (2004) concluded that the percentage of adult Americans reading literature had dropped dramatically. But a survey in 2005 found the exact opposite. Almost half of all Americans were reading a book at the time of the survey, an increase over the 1990 rate and more than double the 1957 rate. More recently, a report in 2015 found that 80 percent of Americans between the ages of 16 and 29 had read a book in the past year and even showed that people in that age range were more likely than those over 30 to be book readers.

As encouraging as some of that data may be, however, there are also clear causes for concern. Literacy survey data collected in 2012 and 2014, the most recent available, show that 17 percent of Americans between the ages of 16 and 65 read at or below the lowest of the four levels of reading ability evaluated. Furthermore, the share of those lacking reading skills is higher among the population that is unemployed.

Whatever the relationship is between socioeconomic status and reading ability, it is complicated. Unequal distribution of resources and insufficient funding in school systems surely contribute, as does the fact

---

— 30 —

第5回　英語（リーディング）

that better-off families enjoy more time and flexibility for parents to act on their desire to read with children. Regardless of what, exactly, links poverty and literacy, these statistics serve as a reminder that reading must not be treated as a luxury but as a basic and necessary human need that calls for a community response.

Commitment to reading in schools should also be strengthened, not only to develop students' reading skills but also to introduce them to the worlds and insights that books present to readers. Both the traditional Great Books and more recent works from a wider variety of authors are important to help broaden students' horizons and encourage curiosity about the lives of others. A writer who recently spent a year monitoring English classes in three different public high schools found teachers at all three determined to motivate their students to read not only classics like Hemingway but also recent authors such as Alice Walker and Amy Tan.

These students became passionately involved through creative assignments and earnest classroom debates. Books, one of our oldest technologies, helped connect them to different experiences, cultures and ideas with greater depth than even the most modern social media networks can offer.

Reading skills are necessary for any participation in the modern economy. But even more important, reading — especially of fiction — inspires readers, making them more interested in others' feelings and helping them grow in spirituality and political responsibility. Encouraging a love for reading is likely not only to improve the economic quality of life but also to deepen and enrich life shared together in society.

Why Everyone Should Read

Reading at risk? Who reads literature?
- 1957 — Around 1/4 of adults
- 2005 — Around 1/2 of adults
- 2015 — Around 80% of adults
⇒ More people are reading today

Main Problem: 17% of Americans aged 16 ~ 65 lack basic reading skills

Why are some people more likely to lack reading skills?

Who	Possible Reasons
· The unemployed	· Lack of resources at the schools they attended
	· 39
	· Parents had no time to read to them
	· Parents had no desire/ability to read to them

Classroom Solutions
- More commitment to reading
- Using traditional and recent books
- Giving creative assignments
- 40

→

Benefits of Reading
- Living two years longer
- 41
- Building capacity for love
- Broadening students' horizons

Summary

Reading is important for our society.

It makes us more caring people as well as it 42 .

第5回　英語（リーディング）

問1　Choose the best option for ☐ 39 ☐ on your poster.

① Do not see reading as important

② Long absences from school

③ Not enough money given to education

④ The high cost of books

問2　Choose the best option for ☐ 40 ☐ on your poster.

① Explaining links to other cultures

② Incorporating social networking sites

③ Sharing teacher experiences

④ Starting serious class discussions

問3　Choose the best option for ☐ 41 ☐ on your poster.

① Comprehension of emotions

② Desire to describe experiences

③ Improving students manners

④ Motivation to write better

問4　Choose the best option for ☐ 42 ☐ on your poster.

① boosts the economy

② develops technology

③ encourages us to pay taxes

④ lowers the crime rate

— 33 —

B You are interested in the importance of having adequate sleep. You are going to read the following article about the sleep patterns of different groups of people.

Sleep is important. In fact, recent data suggest that keeping a consistent sleep schedule might be just as important as getting the right amount of quality sleep. Compared with other primates, human evolution featured a shift toward sleeping more deeply over shorter time periods, providing more time for learning new skills and knowledge as cultures expanded. Humans also evolved an ability to revise sleep schedules based on daily work schedules and environmental factors.

Interestingly, not everyone in the world keeps to the same types of sleep schedules. In recent studies, scientists looked at the sleep patterns of four groups of people. The Hadza are hunter-gatherers that live in Tanzania, a nation in East Africa. The Malagasy live in villages on the large island nation of Madagascar, off Africa's lower East Coast. Both groups live without electricity. These people were compared to those living in the West (places like the United States and Europe) and also to Western Europeans who lived before the Industrial Revolution, some 200 to 500 years ago.

Contrary to conventional wisdom, people in societies without electricity do not always sleep more than those in industrial societies. This might be, in part, because non-Western hunter-gatherers and villagers, including the Malagasy and Hadza groups in the studies, spend more of their days in natural sunlight. Napping once or twice a day may also have some effect on them. Hunter-gatherers and villagers usually sleep in spaces with various family and group members and often wake up more frequently during the night than has been reported among Westerners.

Except for the naps, the Malagasy villagers' sleep pattern is very similar to that of preindustrial Western Europeans. In both cases, adults went to sleep a little after 6 p.m. Then they slept in two shifts. The first shift ended around midnight. Then, after remaining up for an

— 34 —

第5回　英語（リーディング）

hour or so, they would fall back to sleep again. By comparison, present-day Westerners such as adults working 9 to 5 jobs in the U.S. typically go to sleep just before midnight and get up around 6 a.m. And no mid-day naps for the majority of them.

Different sleep patterns in each of these groups highlight the flexibility of human sleep and also point to potential health dangers in the way Westerners today sleep. Hunter-gatherers and villagers are exposed to less blue light from indoor lighting and computer screens, which can confuse the body's internal clock. Blue-wave light emitted by smartphones and other digital devices can suppress the production of melatonin, a hormone helping people fall asleep, and delay sleep. People in modern societies can learn lessons from this research; that is, they should get more sunlight exposure during the day and less blue-wave light exposure after dark in order to get a good-quality sleep.

問1　Humans evolved to sleep more deeply in a shorter time, which 　43　 .

　① allowed them to revise sleep schedules on their own
　② enabled them to become more intelligent and competent
　③ offered more opportunities to take a nap during the day
　④ provided much more time for hunting and gathering

— 35 —

問2 Out of the four charts, which is consistent with the article? 44

①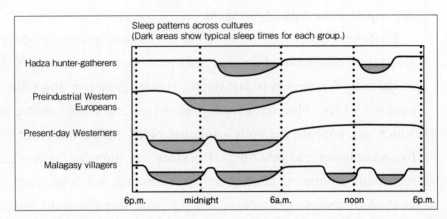

②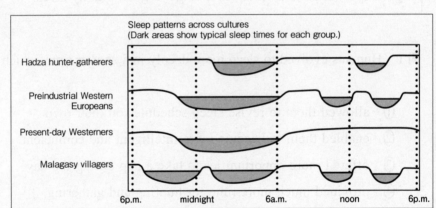

③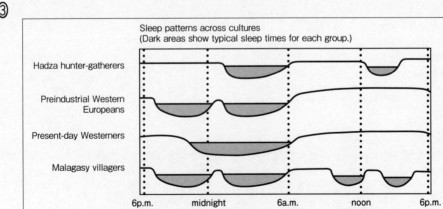

④

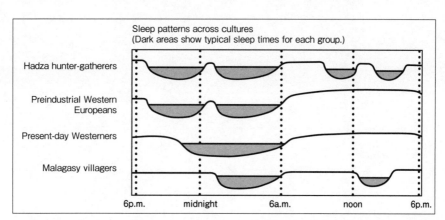

問3 According to the article, which two of the following statements are true? (The order does not matter.) 45 ・ 46

① Blue-wave light can pose some health hazards to humans.
② Hunter-gatherers should get more exposure of natural sunlight.
③ One kind of blue light can stimulate production of the sleep hormone.
④ Western people today should take daytime naps regularly.
⑤ Westerners' body clocks today are very easy to confuse.

問4 The best title for this article is 47 .

① Evolution of Human Sleep Quantity
② Flexible Sleep Patterns in Humans
③ Sleep Disorders in the Modern Age
④ Sleeping Habits Without Electricity

'23
本試験問題

2023年度

大学入学共通テスト

本試験

英語（リーディング）

（100点　80分）

・標 準 所 要 時 間・

第1問　7分程度	第4問 12分程度
第2問 13分程度	第5問 14分程度
第3問 12分程度	第6問 22分程度

英　語（リーディング）

各大問の英文や図表を読み，解答番号　1　～　49　にあてはまるものとして
最も適当な選択肢を選びなさい。

第1問　（配点　10）

A　You are studying in the US, and as an afternoon activity you need to choose
one of two performances to go and see. Your teacher gives you this handout.

Performances for Friday

Palace Theater *Together Wherever*	**Grand Theater** *The Guitar Queen*
A romantic play that will make you laugh and cry	A rock musical featuring colorful costumes
▸ From 2:00 p.m. (no breaks and a running time of one hour and 45 minutes)	▸ Starts at 1:00 p.m. (three hours long including two 15-minute breaks)
▸ Actors available to talk in the lobby after the performance	▸ Opportunity to greet the cast in their costumes before the show starts
▸ No food or drinks available	▸ Light refreshments (snacks & drinks), original T-shirts, and other goods sold in the lobby
▸ Free T-shirts for five lucky people	

Instructions: Which performance would you like to attend? Fill in the form
below and hand it in to your teacher today.

✂ –

Choose (✔) one: *Together Wherever*　☐　　*The Guitar Queen*　☐

Name: _____

— 2 —

2023 本試 英語 (リーディング)

問 1 What are you told to do after reading the handout? ⬚1

① Complete and hand in the bottom part.

② Find out more about the performances.

③ Talk to your teacher about your decision.

④ Write your name and explain your choice.

問 2 Which is true about both performances? ⬚2

① No drinks can be purchased before the show.

② Some T-shirts will be given as gifts.

③ They will finish at the same time.

④ You can meet performers at the theaters.

— 3 —

B You are a senior high school student interested in improving your English during the summer vacation. You find a website for an intensive English summer camp run by an international school.

GIS

Intensive English Summer Camp

Galley International School (GIS) has provided intensive English summer camps for senior high school students in Japan since 1989. Spend two weeks in an all-English environment!

Dates: August 1-14, 2023
Location: Lake Kawaguchi Youth Lodge, Yamanashi Prefecture
Cost: 120,000 yen, including food and accommodation (additional fees for optional activities such as kayaking and canoeing)

Courses Offered

◆**FOREST**: You'll master basic grammar structures, make short speeches on simple topics, and get pronunciation tips. Your instructors have taught English for over 20 years in several countries. On the final day of the camp, you'll take part in a speech contest while all the other campers listen.

◆**MOUNTAIN**: You'll work in a group to write and perform a skit in English. Instructors for this course have worked at theater schools in New York City, London, and Sydney. You'll perform your skit for all the campers to enjoy on August 14.

◆**SKY**: You'll learn debating skills and critical thinking in this course. Your instructors have been to many countries to coach debate teams and some have published best-selling textbooks on the subject. You'll do a short debate in front of all the other campers on the last day. (Note: Only those with an advanced level of English will be accepted.)

▲Application

Step 1: Fill in the online application **HERE** by May 20, 2023.

Step 2: We'll contact you to set up an interview to assess your English ability

and ask about your course preference.

Step 3: You'll be assigned to a course.

問 1　All GIS instructors have 　3　 .

   ① been in Japan since 1989

   ② won international competitions

   ③ worked in other countries

   ④ written some popular books

問 2　On the last day of the camp, campers will 　4　 .

   ① assess each other's performances

   ② compete to receive the best prize

   ③ make presentations about the future

   ④ show what they learned at the camp

問 3　What will happen after submitting your camp application? 　5　

   ① You will call the English instructors.

   ② You will take a written English test.

   ③ Your English level will be checked.

   ④ Your English speech topic will be sent.

第2問　(配点　20)

A　You want to buy a good pair of shoes as you walk a long way to school and often get sore feet. You are searching on a UK website and find this advertisement.

Navi 55 presents the new *Smart Support* shoe line

Smart Support shoes are strong, long-lasting, and reasonably priced. They are available in three colours and styles.

nano-chip

Special Features

Smart Support shoes have a nano-chip which analyses the shape of your feet when connected to the *iSupport* application. Download the app onto your smartphone, PC, tablet, and/or smartwatch. Then, while wearing the shoes, let the chip collect the data about your feet. The inside of the shoe will automatically adjust to give correct, personalised foot support. As with other Navi 55 products, the shoes have our popular Route Memory function.

Advantages

Better Balance: Adjusting how you stand, the personalised support helps keep feet, legs, and back free from pain.

Promotes Exercise: As they are so comfortable, you will be willing to walk regularly.

Route Memory: The chip records your daily route, distance, and pace as you walk.

Route Options: View your live location on your device, have the directions play automatically in your earphones, or use your smartwatch to read directions.

2023 本試 英語 (リーディング)

Customers' Comments

● I like the choices for getting directions, and prefer using audio guidance to visual guidance.

● I lost 2 kg in a month!

● I love my pair now, but it took me several days to get used to them.

● As they don't slip in the rain, I wear mine all year round.

● They are so light and comfortable I even wear them when cycling.

● Easy to get around! I don't need to worry about getting lost.

● They look great. The app's basic features are easy to use, but I wouldn't pay for the optional advanced ones.

問 1 According to the maker's statements, which best describes the new shoes?

 6

① Cheap summer shoes

② High-tech everyday shoes

③ Light comfortable sports shoes

④ Stylish colourful cycling shoes

問 2 Which benefit offered by the shoes is most likely to appeal to you?

 7

① Getting more regular exercise

② Having personalised foot support

③ Knowing how fast you walk

④ Looking cool wearing them

— 7 —

問 3　One **opinion** stated by a customer is that ⬚8⬚ .

① the app encourages fast walking

② the app's free functions are user-friendly

③ the shoes are good value for money

④ the shoes increase your cycling speed

問 4　One customer's comment mentions using audio devices.　Which benefit is this comment based on?　⬚9⬚

① Better Balance

② Promotes Exercise

③ Route Memory

④ Route Options

問 5　According to one customer's opinion, ⬚10⬚ is recommended.

① allowing time to get accustomed to wearing the shoes

② buying a watch to help you lose weight

③ connecting to the app before putting the shoes on

④ paying for the *iSupport* advanced features

— 8 —

B You are a member of the student council. The members have been discussing a student project helping students to use their time efficiently. To get ideas, you are reading a report about a school challenge. It was written by an exchange student who studied in another school in Japan.

Commuting Challenge

Most students come to my school by bus or train. I often see a lot of students playing games on their phones or chatting. However, they could also use this time for reading or doing homework. We started this activity to help students use their commuting time more effectively. Students had to complete a commuting activity chart from January 17th to February 17th. A total of 300 students participated: More than two thirds of them were second-years; about a quarter were third-years; only 15 first-years participated. How come so few first-years participated? Based on the feedback (given below), there seems to be an answer to this question:

Feedback from participants

HS: Thanks to this project, I got the highest score ever in an English vocabulary test. It was easy to set small goals to complete on my way.

KF: My friend was sad because she couldn't participate. She lives nearby and walks to school. There should have been other ways to take part.

SS: My train is always crowded and I have to stand, so there is no space to open a book or a tablet. I only used audio materials, but there were not nearly enough.

JH: I kept a study log, which made me realise how I used my time. For some reason most of my first-year classmates didn't seem to know about this challenge.

MN: I spent most of the time on the bus watching videos, and it helped me to understand classes better. I felt the time went very fast.

問 1　The aim of the Commuting Challenge was to help students to 　11　 .

① commute more quickly

② improve their test scores

③ manage English classes better

④ use their time better

問 2　One **fact** about the Commuting Challenge is that 　12　 .

① fewer than 10% of the participants were first-years

② it was held for two months during the winter

③ students had to use portable devices on buses

④ the majority of participants travelled by train

問 3　From the feedback, 　13　 were activities reported by participants.

A : keeping study records

B : learning language

C : making notes on tablets

D : reading lesson notes on mobile phones

① A and B

② A and C

③ A and D

④ B and C

⑤ B and D

⑥ C and D

— 10 —

2023 本試 英語（リーディング）

問 4 One of the participants' opinions about the Commuting Challenge is that ⬚14⬚ .

① it could have included students who walk to school

② the train was a good place to read books

③ there were plenty of audio materials for studying

④ watching videos for fun helped time pass quickly

問 5 The author's question is answered by ⬚15⬚ .

① HS

② JH

③ KF

④ MN

⑤ SS

— 11 —

第3問 (配点 15)

A You are studying at Camberford University, Sydney. You are going on a class camping trip and are reading the camping club's newsletter to prepare.

Going camping? Read me!!!

Hi, I'm Kaitlyn. I want to share two practical camping lessons from my recent club trip. The first thing is to divide your backpack into three main parts and put the heaviest items in the middle section to balance the backpack. Next, more frequently used daily necessities should be placed in the top section. That means putting your sleeping bag at the bottom; food, cookware and tent in the middle; and your clothes at the top. Most good backpacks come with a "brain" (an additional pouch) for small easy-to-reach items.

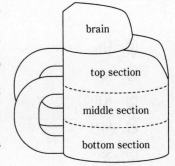

Last year, in the evening, we had fun cooking and eating outdoors. I had been sitting close to our campfire, but by the time I got back to the tent I was freezing. Although I put on extra layers of clothes before going to sleep, I was still cold. Then, my friend told me to take off my outer layers and stuff them into my sleeping bag to fill up some of the empty space. This stuffing method was new to me, and surprisingly kept me warm all night!

I hope my advice helps you stay warm and comfortable. Enjoy your camping trip!

問 1 If you take Kaitlyn's advice, how should you fill your backpack?　16

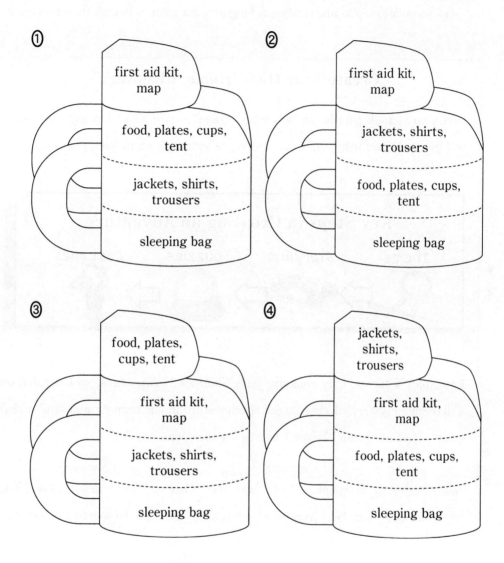

問 2 According to Kaitlyn,　17　is the best method to stay warm all night.

① avoiding going out of your tent
② eating hot meals beside your campfire
③ filling the gaps in your sleeping bag
④ wearing all of your extra clothes

B Your English club will make an "adventure room" for the school festival. To get some ideas, you are reading a blog about a room a British man created.

Create Your Own "Home Adventure"

Last year, I took part in an "adventure room" experience. I really enjoyed it, so I created one for my children. Here are some tips on making your own.

First, pick a theme. My sons are huge Sherlock Holmes fans, so I decided on a detective mystery. I rearranged the furniture in our family room, and added some old paintings and lamps I had to set the scene.

Next, create a storyline. Ours was *The Case of the Missing Chocolates*. My children would be "detectives" searching for clues to locate the missing sweets.

The third step is to design puzzles and challenges. A useful idea is to work backwards from the solution. If the task is to open a box locked with a three-digit padlock, think of ways to hide a three-digit code. Old books are fantastic for hiding messages in. I had tremendous fun underlining words on different pages to form mystery sentences. Remember that the puzzles should get progressively more difficult near the final goal. To get into the spirit, I then

2023 本試 英語 (リーディング)

had the children wear costumes. My eldest son was excited when I handed him a magnifying glass, and immediately began acting like Sherlock Holmes. After that, the children started to search for the first clue.

This "adventure room" was designed specifically for my family, so I made some of the challenges personal. For the final task, I took a couple of small cups and put a plastic sticker in each one, then filled them with yogurt. The "detectives" had to eat their way to the bottom to reveal the clues. Neither of my kids would eat yogurt, so this truly was tough for them. During the adventure, my children were totally focused, and they enjoyed themselves so much that we will have another one next month.

問 1 Put the following events (①~④) into the order in which they happened.

$$\boxed{18} \rightarrow \boxed{19} \rightarrow \boxed{20} \rightarrow \boxed{21}$$

① The children ate food they are not fond of.
② The children started the search for the sweets.
③ The father decorated the living room in the house.
④ The father gave his sons some clothes to wear.

問 2 If you follow the father's advice to create your own "adventure room," you should $\boxed{22}$.

① concentrate on three-letter words
② leave secret messages under the lamps
③ make the challenges gradually harder
④ practise acting like Sherlock Holmes

— 15 —

問 3 From this story, you understand that the father ☐23☐ .

① became focused on searching for the sweets
② created an experience especially for his children
③ had some trouble preparing the adventure game
④ spent a lot of money decorating the room

2023 本試 英語 (リーディング)

（下 書 き 用 紙）

英語（リーディング）の試験問題は次に続く。

— 17 —

第4問 （配点 16）

Your teacher has asked you to read two articles about effective ways to study. You will discuss what you learned in your next class.

How to Study Effectively: Contextual Learning!
Tim Oxford
Science Teacher, Stone City Junior High School

As a science teacher, I am always concerned about how to help students who struggle to learn. Recently, I found that their main way of learning was to study new information repeatedly until they could recall it all. For example, when they studied for a test, they would use a workbook like the example below and repeatedly say the terms that go in the blanks: "Obsidian is igneous, dark, and glassy. Obsidian is igneous, dark, and glassy...." These students would feel as if they had learned the information, but would quickly forget it and get low scores on the test. Also, this sort of repetitive learning is dull and demotivating.

To help them learn, I tried applying "contextual learning." In this kind of learning, new knowledge is constructed through students' own experiences. For my science class, students learned the properties of different kinds of rocks. Rather than having them memorize the terms from a workbook, I brought a big box of various rocks to the class. Students examined the rocks and identified their names based on the characteristics they observed.

Thanks to this experience, I think these students will always be able to describe the properties of the rocks they studied. One issue, however, is that we don't always have the time to do contextual learning, so students will still study by doing drills. I don't think this is the best way. I'm still searching for ways to improve their learning.

Rock name	Obsidian
Rock type	igneous
Coloring	dark
Texture	glassy
Picture	

— 18 —

How to Make Repetitive Learning Effective
Cheng Lee
Professor, Stone City University

Mr. Oxford's thoughts on contextual learning were insightful. I agree that it can be beneficial. Repetition, though, can also work well. However, the repetitive learning strategy he discussed, which is called "massed learning," is not effective. There is another kind of repetitive learning called "spaced learning," in which students memorize new information and then review it over longer intervals.

The interval between studying is the key difference. In Mr. Oxford's example, his students probably used their workbooks to study over a short period of time. In this case, they might have paid less attention to the content as they continued to review it. The reason for this is that the content was no longer new and could easily be ignored. In contrast, when the intervals are longer, the students' memory of the content is weaker. Therefore, they pay more attention because they have to make a greater effort to recall what they had learned before. For example, if students study with their workbooks, wait three days, and then study again, they are likely to learn the material better.

Previous research has provided evidence for the advantages of spaced learning. In one experiment, students in Groups A and B tried to memorize the names of 50 animals. Both groups studied four times, but Group A studied at one-day intervals while Group B studied at one-week intervals. As the figure to the right shows, 28 days after the last learning session, the average ratio of recalled names on a test was higher for the spaced learning group.

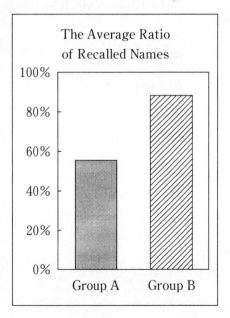

I understand that students often need to learn a lot of information in a short period of time, and long intervals between studying might not be practical. You should understand, though, that massed learning might not be good for long-term recall.

問 1 Oxford believes that ☐24☐ .

① continuous drilling is boring

② reading an explanation of terms is helpful

③ students are not interested in science

④ studying with a workbook leads to success

問 2 In the study discussed by Lee, students took a test ☐25☐ after their final session.

① four weeks

② immediately

③ one day

④ one week

問 3 Lee introduces spaced learning, which involves studying at ☐26☐ intervals, in order to overcome the disadvantages of ☐27☐ learning that Oxford discussed. (Choose the best one for each box from options ①～⑥.)

① contextual

② extended

③ fixed

④ irregular

⑤ massed

⑥ practical

— 20 —

2023 本試 英語（リーディング）

問 4 Both writers agree that 　28　 is helpful for remembering new information.

  ① experiential learning

  ② having proper rest

  ③ long-term attention

  ④ studying with workbooks

問 5 Which additional information would be the best to further support Lee's argument for spaced learning? 　29　

  ① The main factor that makes a science class attractive

  ② The most effective length of intervals for spaced learning

  ③ Whether students' workbooks include visuals or not

  ④ Why Oxford's students could not memorize information well

— 21 —

第5問 (配点 15)

Your English teacher has told everyone in your class to find an inspirational story and present it to a discussion group, using notes. You have found a story written by a high school student in the UK.

Lessons from Table Tennis

Ben Carter

The ball flew at lightning speed to my backhand. It was completely unexpected and I had no time to react. I lost the point and the match. Defeat... Again! This is how it was in the first few months when I started playing table tennis. It was frustrating, but I now know that the sport taught me more than simply how to be a better athlete.

In middle school, I loved football. I was one of the top scorers, but I didn't get along with my teammates. The coach often said that I should be more of a team player. I knew I should work on the problem, but communication was just not my strong point.

I had to leave the football club when my family moved to a new town. I wasn't upset as I had decided to stop playing football anyway. My new school had a table tennis club, coached by the PE teacher, Mr Trent, and I joined that. To be honest, I chose table tennis because I thought it would be easier for me to play individually.

At first, I lost more games than I won. I was frustrated and often went straight home after practice, not speaking to anyone. One day, however, Mr Trent said to me, "You could be a good player, Ben, but you need to think more about your game. What do you think you need to do?" "I don't know," I replied, "focus on the ball more?" "Yes," Mr Trent continued, "but you also need to study your opponent's moves and adjust your play accordingly. Remember, your opponent is a person, not a ball." This made a deep impression on me.

— 22 —

I deliberately modified my style of play, paying closer attention to my opponent's moves. It was not easy, and took a lot of concentration. My efforts paid off, however, and my play improved. My confidence grew and I started staying behind more after practice. I was turning into a star player and my classmates tried to talk to me more than before. I thought that I was becoming popular, but our conversations seemed to end before they really got started. Although my play might have improved, my communication skills obviously hadn't.

My older brother Patrick was one of the few people I could communicate with well. One day, I tried to explain my problems with communication to him, but couldn't make him understand. We switched to talking about table tennis. "What do you actually enjoy about it?" he asked me curiously. I said I loved analysing my opponent's movements and making instant decisions about the next move. Patrick looked thoughtful. "That sounds like the kind of skill we use when we communicate," he said.

At that time, I didn't understand, but soon after our conversation, I won a silver medal in a table tennis tournament. My classmates seemed really pleased. One of them, George, came running over. "Hey, Ben!" he said, "Let's have a party to celebrate!" Without thinking, I replied, "I can't. I've got practice." He looked a bit hurt and walked off without saying anything else.

Why was he upset? I thought about this incident for a long time. Why did he suggest a party? Should I have said something different? A lot of questions came to my mind, but then I realised that he was just being kind. If I'd said, "Great idea. Thank you! Let me talk to Mr Trent and see if I can get some time off practice," then maybe the outcome would have been better. At that moment Patrick's words made sense. Without attempting to grasp someone's intention, I wouldn't know how to respond.

I'm still not the best communicator in the world, but I definitely feel more confident in my communication skills now than before. Next year, my friends and I are going to co-ordinate the table tennis league with other schools.

Your notes:

Lessons from Table Tennis

About the author (Ben Carter)

- Played football at middle school.
- Started playing table tennis at his new school because he [30].

Other important people

- Mr Trent: Ben's table tennis coach, who helped him improve his play.
- Patrick: Ben's brother, who [31].
- George: Ben's classmate, who wanted to celebrate his victory.

Influential events in Ben's journey to becoming a better communicator

Began playing table tennis → [32] → [33] → [34] → [35]

What Ben realised after the conversation with George

He should have [36].

What we can learn from this story

- [37]
- [38]

— 24 —

2023 本試 英語 (リーディング)

問 1　Choose the best option for ☐30☐.

① believed it would help him communicate

② hoped to become popular at school

③ thought he could win games easily

④ wanted to avoid playing a team sport

問 2　Choose the best option for ☐31☐.

① asked him what he enjoyed about communication

② encouraged him to be more confident

③ helped him learn the social skills he needed

④ told him what he should have said to his school friends

問 3　Choose **four** out of the five options (①～⑤) and rearrange them in the order they happened. ☐32☐ → ☐33☐ → ☐34☐ → ☐35☐

① Became a table tennis champion

② Discussed with his teacher how to play well

③ Refused a party in his honour

④ Started to study his opponents

⑤ Talked to his brother about table tennis

— 25 —

問 4　Choose the best option for ☐ 36 ☐.

① asked his friend questions to find out more about his motivation

② invited Mr Trent and other classmates to the party to show appreciation

③ tried to understand his friend's point of view to act appropriately

④ worked hard to be a better team player for successful communication

問 5　Choose the best two options for ☐ 37 ☐ and ☐ 38 ☐. (The order does not matter.)

① Advice from people around us can help us change.

② Confidence is important for being a good communicator.

③ It is important to make our intentions clear to our friends.

④ The support that teammates provide one another is helpful.

⑤ We can apply what we learn from one thing to another.

2023 本試 英語（リーディング）

（下書き用紙）

英語（リーディング）の試験問題は次に続く。

— 27 —

第6問 （配点 24）

A You are in a discussion group in school. You have been asked to summarize the following article. You will speak about it, using only notes.

Collecting

Collecting has existed at all levels of society, across cultures and age groups since early times. Museums are proof that things have been collected, saved, and passed down for future generations. There are various reasons for starting a collection. For example, Ms. A enjoys going to yard sales every Saturday morning with her children. At yard sales, people sell unwanted things in front of their houses. One day, while looking for antique dishes, an unusual painting caught her eye and she bought it for only a few dollars. Over time, she found similar pieces that left an impression on her, and she now has a modest collection of artwork, some of which may be worth more than she paid. One person's trash can be another person's treasure. Regardless of how someone's collection was started, it is human nature to collect things.

In 1988, researchers Brenda Danet and Tamar Katriel analyzed 80 years of studies on children under the age of 10, and found that about 90% collected something. This shows us that people like to gather things from an early age. Even after becoming adults, people continue collecting stuff. Researchers in the field generally agree that approximately one third of adults maintain this behavior. Why is this? The primary explanation is related to emotions. Some save greeting cards from friends and family, dried flowers from special events, seashells from a day at the beach, old photos, and so on. For others, their collection is a connection to their youth. They may have baseball cards, comic books, dolls, or miniature cars that they have kept since they were small.

— 28 —

2023 本試 英語 (リーディング)

Others have an attachment to history; they seek and hold onto historical documents, signed letters and autographs from famous people, and so forth.

For some individuals there is a social reason. People collect things such as pins to share, show, and even trade, making new friends this way. Others, like some holders of Guinness World Records, appreciate the fame they achieve for their unique collection. Cards, stickers, stamps, coins, and toys have topped the "usual" collection list, but some collectors lean toward the more unexpected. In September 2014, Guinness World Records recognized Harry Sperl, of Germany, for having the largest hamburger-related collection in the world, with 3,724 items; from T-shirts to pillows to dog toys, Sperl's room is filled with all things "hamburger." Similarly, Liu Fuchang, of China, is a collector of playing cards. He has 11,087 different sets.

Perhaps the easiest motivation to understand is pleasure. Some people start collections for pure enjoyment. They may purchase and put up paintings just to gaze at frequently, or they may collect audio recordings and old-fashioned vinyl records to enjoy listening to their favorite music. This type of collector is unlikely to be very interested in the monetary value of their treasured music, while others collect objects specifically as an investment. While it is possible to download certain classic games for free, having the same game unopened in its original packaging, in "mint condition," can make the game worth a lot. Owning various valuable "collector's items" could ensure some financial security.

This behavior of collecting things will definitely continue into the distant future. Although the reasons why people keep things will likely remain the same, advances in technology will have an influence on collections. As technology can remove physical constraints, it is now possible for an individual to have vast digital libraries of music and art that would have been unimaginable 30 years ago. It is unclear, though, what other impacts technology will have on collections. Can you even imagine the form and scale that the next generation's collections will take?

2023 本試 英語 (リーディング)

Your notes:

Collecting

Introduction
◆ Collecting has long been part of the human experience.
◆ The yard sale story tells us that [39] .

Facts
◆ [40]
◆ Guinness World Records
  ◇ Sperl: 3,724 hamburger-related items
  ◇ Liu: 11,087 sets of playing cards

Reasons for collecting
◆ Motivation for collecting can be emotional or social.
◆ Various reasons mentioned: [41] , [42] , interest in history, childhood excitement, becoming famous, sharing, etc.

Collections in the future
◆ [43]

— 31 —

問 1　Choose the best option for 　39　.

① a great place for people to sell things to collectors at a high price is a yard sale

② people can evaluate items incorrectly and end up paying too much money for junk

③ something not important to one person may be of value to someone else

④ things once collected and thrown in another person's yard may be valuable to others

問 2　Choose the best option for 　40　.

① About two thirds of children do not collect ordinary things.

② Almost one third of adults start collecting things for pleasure.

③ Approximately 10% of kids have collections similar to their friends.

④ Roughly 30% of people keep collecting into adulthood.

問 3　Choose the best options for 　41　 and 　42　. (The order does not matter.)

① desire to advance technology

② fear of missing unexpected opportunities

③ filling a sense of emptiness

④ reminder of precious events

⑤ reusing objects for the future

⑥ seeking some sort of profit

問 4　Choose the best option for 　43　.

① Collections will likely continue to change in size and shape.

② Collectors of mint-condition games will have more digital copies of them.

③ People who have lost their passion for collecting will start again.

④ Reasons for collecting will change because of advances in technology.

— 32 —

2023 本試 英語（リーディング）

B You are in a student group preparing for an international science presentation contest. You are using the following passage to create your part of the presentation on extraordinary creatures.

Ask someone to name the world's toughest animal, and they might say the Bactrian camel as it can survive in temperatures as high as 50℃, or the Arctic fox which can survive in temperatures lower than −58℃. However, both answers would be wrong as it is widely believed that the tardigrade is the toughest creature on earth.

Tardigrades, also known as water bears, are microscopic creatures, which are between 0.1 mm to 1.5 mm in length. They live almost everywhere, from 6,000-meter-high mountains to 4,600 meters below the ocean's surface. They can even be found under thick ice and in hot springs. Most live in water, but some tardigrades can be found in some of the driest places on earth. One researcher reported finding tardigrades living under rocks in a desert without any recorded rainfall for 25 years. All they need are a few drops or a thin layer of water to live in. When the water dries up, so do they. They lose all but three percent of their body's water and their metabolism slows down to 0.01% of its normal speed. The dried-out tardigrade is now in a state called "tun," a kind of deep sleep. It will continue in this state until it is once again soaked in water. Then, like a sponge, it absorbs the water and springs back to life again as if nothing had happened. Whether the tardigrade is in tun for 1 week or 10 years does not really matter. The moment it is surrounded by water, it comes alive again. When tardigrades are in a state of tun, they are so tough that they can survive in temperatures as low as −272℃ and as high as 151℃. Exactly how they achieve this is still not fully understood.

Perhaps even more amazing than their ability to survive on earth — they have been on earth for some 540 million years — is their ability to survive in space. In 2007, a team of European researchers sent a number of living

— 33 —

tardigrades into space on the outside of a rocket for 10 days. On their return to earth, the researchers were surprised to see that 68% were still alive. This means that for 10 days most were able to survive X-rays and ultraviolet radiation 1,000 times more intense than here on earth. Later, in 2019, an Israeli spacecraft crashed onto the moon and thousands of tardigrades in a state of tun were spilled onto its surface. Whether these are still alive or not is unknown as no one has gone to collect them — which is a pity.

Tardigrades are shaped like a short cucumber. They have four short legs on each side of their bodies. Some species have sticky pads at the end of each leg, while others have claws. There are 16 known claw variations, which help identify those species with claws. All tardigrades have a place for eyes, but not all species have eyes. Their eyes are primitive, only having five cells in total — just one of which is light sensitive.

Basically, tardigrades can be divided into those that eat plant matter, and those that eat other creatures. Those that eat vegetation have a ventral mouth — a mouth located in the lower part of the head, like a shark. The type that eats other creatures has a terminal mouth, which means the mouth is at the very front of the head, like a tuna. The mouths of tardigrades do not have teeth. They do, however, have two sharp needles, called stylets, that they use to pierce plant cells or the bodies of smaller creatures so the contents can be sucked out.

Both types of tardigrade have rather simple digestive systems. The mouth leads to the pharynx (throat), where digestive juices and food are mixed. Located above the pharynx is a salivary gland. This produces the juices that flow into the mouth and help with digestion. After the pharynx, there is a tube which transports food toward the gut. This tube is called the esophagus. The middle gut, a simple stomach/intestine type of organ, digests the food and absorbs the nutrients. The leftovers then eventually move through to the anus.

Your presentation slides:

Tardigrades: Earth's Ultimate Survivors

1. Basic Information
- 0.1 mm to 1.5 mm in length
- shaped like a short cucumber
-
- 44
-
-

2. Habitats
- live almost everywhere
- extreme environments such as...
  - ✓ 6 km above sea level
  - ✓ 4.6 km below sea level
  - ✓ in deserts
  - ✓ −272℃ to 151℃
  - ✓ in space (possibly)

3. Secrets to Survival

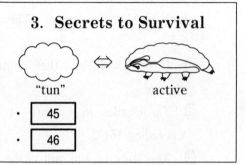

"tun" ⇔ active

- 45
- 46

4. Digestive Systems 47

5. Final Statement

48

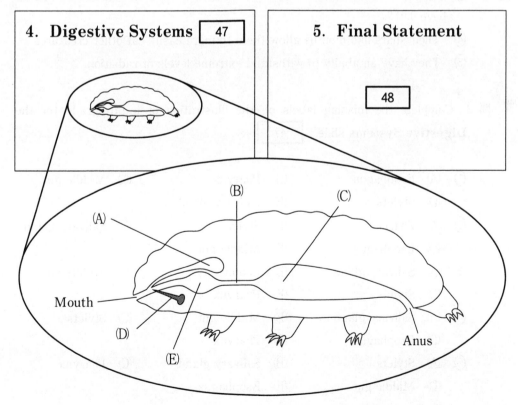

問 1   Which of the following should you **not** include for   44   ?

① eight short legs

② either blind or sighted

③ plant-eating or creature-eating

④ sixteen different types of feet

⑤ two stylets rather than teeth

問 2   For the **Secrets to Survival** slide, select two features of the tardigrade which best help it survive. (The order does not matter.)   45   ·   46

① In dry conditions, their metabolism drops to less than one percent of normal.

② Tardigrades in a state of tun are able to survive in temperatures exceeding 151℃.

③ The state of tun will cease when the water in a tardigrade's body is above 0.01%.

④ Their shark-like mouths allow them to more easily eat other creatures.

⑤ They have an ability to withstand extreme levels of radiation.

問 3   Complete the missing labels on the illustration of a tardigrade for the **Digestive Systems** slide.   47

① (A) Esophagus   (B) Pharynx   (C) Middle gut
  (D) Stylets   (E) Salivary gland

② (A) Pharynx   (B) Stylets   (C) Salivary gland
  (D) Esophagus   (E) Middle gut

③ (A) Salivary gland (B) Esophagus   (C) Middle gut
  (D) Stylets   (E) Pharynx

④ (A) Salivary gland (B) Middle gut   (C) Stylets
  (D) Esophagus   (E) Pharynx

⑤ (A) Stylets   (B) Salivary gland (C) Pharynx
  (D) Middle gut   (E) Esophagus

— 36 —

2023 本試 英語 (リーディング)

問 4 Which is the best statement for the final slide? ☐48☐

  ① For thousands of years, tardigrades have survived some of the harshest conditions on earth and in space. They will live longer than humankind.

  ② Tardigrades are from space and can live in temperatures exceeding the limits of the Arctic fox and Bactrian camel, so they are surely stronger than human beings.

  ③ Tardigrades are, without a doubt, the toughest creatures on earth. They can survive on the top of mountains; at the bottom of the sea; in the waters of hot springs; and they can also thrive on the moon.

  ④ Tardigrades have survived some of the harshest conditions on earth, and at least one trip into space. This remarkable creature might outlive the human species.

問 5 What can be inferred about sending tardigrades into space? ☐49☐

  ① Finding out whether the tardigrades can survive in space was never thought to be important.

  ② Tardigrades, along with other creatures that have been on earth for millions of years, can withstand X-rays and ultraviolet radiation.

  ③ The Israeli researchers did not expect so many tardigrades to survive the harsh environment of space.

  ④ The reason why no one has been to see if tardigrades can survive on the moon's surface attracted the author's attention.

— 37 —

2022年度

大学入学共通テスト

本試験

英語(リーディング)

(100点　80分)

───● 標 準 所 要 時 間 ●───

第1問　7分程度　　第4問 12分程度

第2問 13分程度　　第5問 14分程度

第3問 12分程度　　第6問 22分程度

英　　語（リーディング）

各大問の英文や図表を読み，解答番号 1 ～ 48 にあてはまるものとして最も適当な選択肢を選びなさい。

第1問 （配点 10）

A You are studying about Brazil in the international club at your senior high school. Your teacher asked you to do research on food in Brazil. You find a Brazilian cookbook and read about fruits used to make desserts.

Popular Brazilian Fruits

Cupuaçu
- Smells and tastes like chocolate
- Great for desserts, such as cakes, and with yogurt
- Brazilians love the chocolate-flavored juice of this fruit.

Jabuticaba
- Looks like a grape
- Eat them within three days of picking for a sweet flavor.
- After they get sour, use them for making jams, jellies, and cakes.

Pitanga
- Comes in two varieties, red and green
- Use the sweet red one for making cakes.
- The sour green one is only for jams and jellies.

Buriti
- Orange inside, similar to a peach or a mango
- Tastes very sweet, melts in your mouth
- Best for ice cream, cakes, and jams

（編集注：写真は類似のものに変更しています。）

2022 本試 英語（リーディング）

問 1　Both *cupuaçu* and *buriti* can be used to make ☐ 1 ☐ .

①　a cake

②　chocolate

③　ice cream

④　yogurt

問 2　If you want to make a sour cake, the best fruit to use is ☐ 2 ☐ .

①　*buriti*

②　*cupuaçu*

③　*jabuticaba*

④　*pitanga*

— 3 —

B You are looking at the website for the City Zoo in Toronto, Canada and you find an interesting contest announcement. You are thinking about entering the contest.

Contest!
Name a Baby Giraffe

Let's welcome our newest animal to the City Zoo!

A healthy baby giraffe was born on May 26 at the City Zoo.
He's already walking and running around!
He weighs 66 kg and is 180 cm tall.
Your mission is to help his parents, Billy and Noelle, pick a name for their baby.

How to Enter

◆ Click on the link here to submit your idea for his name and follow the directions. → **Enter Here**

◆ Names are accepted starting at 12:00 a.m. on June 1 until 11:59 p.m. on June 7.

◆ Watch the baby giraffe on the live web camera to help you get ideas.
→ **Live Web Camera**

◆ Each submission is $5. All money will go towards feeding the growing baby giraffe.

Contest Schedule

June 8	The zoo staff will choose five finalists from all the entries. These names will be posted on the zoo's website by 5:00 p.m.
June 9	How will the parents decide on the winning name? Click on the live stream link between 11:00 a.m. and 12:00 p.m. to find out! → **Live Stream** Check our website for the winning name after 12:00 p.m.

Prizes

All five contest finalists will receive free one-day zoo passes valid until the end of July.
The one who submitted the winning name will also get a special photo of the baby giraffe with his family, as well as a private Night Safari Tour!

2022 本試 英語 (リーディング)

問 1 You can enter this contest between ⬚3⬚ .

① May 26 and May 31

② June 1 and June 7

③ June 8 and June 9

④ June 10 and July 31

問 2 When submitting your idea for the baby giraffe's name, you must ⬚4⬚ .

① buy a day pass

② pay the submission fee

③ spend five dollars at the City Zoo

④ watch the giraffe through the website

問 3 If the name you submitted is included among the five finalists, you will ⬚5⬚ .

① get free entry to the zoo for a day

② have free access to the live website

③ meet and feed the baby giraffe

④ take a picture with the giraffe's family

— 5 —

第2問 (配点 20)

A You are on a *Future Leader* summer programme, which is taking place on a university campus in the UK. You are reading the information about the library so that you can do your coursework.

Abermouth University Library
Open from 8 am to 9 pm
2022 Handout

Library Card: Your student ID card is also your library card and photocopy card. It is in your welcome pack.

Borrowing Books

You can borrow a maximum of eight books at one time for seven days. To check books out, go to the Information Desk, which is on the first floor. If books are not returned by the due date, you will not be allowed to borrow library books again for three days from the day the books are returned.

Using Computers

Computers with Internet connections are in the Computer Workstations by the main entrance on the first floor. Students may bring their own laptop computers and tablets into the library, but may use them only in the Study Area on the second floor. Students are asked to work quietly, and also not to reserve seats for friends.

Library Orientations

On Tuesdays at 10 am, 20-minute library orientations are held in the Reading Room on the third floor. Talk to the Information Desk staff for details.

Comments from Past Students

- The library orientation was really good. The materials were great, too!
- The Study Area can get really crowded. Get there as early as possible to get a seat!
- The Wi-Fi inside the library is quite slow, but the one at the coffee shop next door is good. By the way, you cannot bring any drinks into the library.
- The staff at the Information Desk answered all my questions. Go there if you need any help!
- On the ground floor there are some TVs for watching the library's videos. When watching videos, you need to use your own earphones or headphones. Next to the TVs there are photocopiers.

— 6 —

2022 本試 英語 (リーディング)

問 1　6　are two things you can do at the library.

A : bring in coffee from the coffee shop

B : save seats for others in the Study Area

C : use the photocopiers on the second floor

D : use your ID to make photocopies

E : use your laptop in the Study Area

① A and B

② A and C

③ B and E

④ C and D

⑤ D and E

問 2　You are at the main entrance of the library and want to go to the orientation. You need to　7　.

① go down one floor

② go up one floor

③ go up two floors

④ stay on the same floor

問 3　8　near the main entrance to the library.

① The Computer Workstations are

② The Reading Room is

③ The Study Area is

④ The TVs are

— 7 —

問 4 If you borrowed three books on 2 August and returned them on 10 August, you could 9 .

① borrow eight more books on 10 August

② borrow seven more books on 10 August

③ not borrow any more books before 13 August

④ not borrow any more books before 17 August

問 5 One **fact** stated by a previous student is that 10 .

① headphones or earphones are necessary when watching videos

② the library is open until 9 pm

③ the library orientation handouts are wonderful

④ the Study Area is often empty

— 8 —

B You are the editor of a school English paper. David, an exchange student from the UK, has written an article for the paper.

Do you like animals? The UK is known as a nation of animal-lovers; two in five UK homes have pets. This is lower than in the US, where more than half of homes have pets. However, Australia has the highest percentage of homes with pets!

Why is this so? Results of a survey done in Australia give us some answers.

Pet owners mention the following advantages of living with pets:
- The love, happiness, and friendship pets give (90%);
- The feeling of having another family member (over 60% of dog and cat owners);
- The happy times pets bring. Most owners spend 3-4 hours with their 'fur babies' every day and around half of all dog and cat owners let their pets sleep with them!

One disadvantage is that pets have to be cared for when owners go away. It may be difficult to organise care for them; 25% of owners take their pets on holidays or road trips.

These results suggest that keeping pets is a good thing. On the other hand, since coming to Japan, I have seen other problems such as space, time, and cost. Still, I know people here who are content living in small flats with pets. Recently, I heard that little pigs are becoming popular as pets in Japan. Some people take their pig(s) for a walk, which must be fun, but I wonder how easy it is to keep pigs inside homes.

問 1　In terms of the ratios for homes with pets, which shows the countries' ranking from **highest to lowest**?　11

① Australia — the UK — the US
② Australia — the US — the UK
③ The UK — Australia — the US
④ The UK — the US — Australia
⑤ The US — Australia — the UK
⑥ The US — the UK — Australia

問 2　According to David's report, one advantage of having pets is that　12　.

① you can save money
② you can sleep longer
③ you will become popular
④ your life can be more enjoyable

問 3　The statement that best reflects one finding from the survey is　13

① 'I feel uncomfortable when I watch TV with my cat.'
② 'I spend about three hours with my pet every day.'
③ 'Most pets like going on car trips.'
④ 'Pets need a room of their own.'

— 10 —

2022 本試 英語（リーディング）

問 4　Which best summarises David's opinions about having pets in Japan?
　　　| 14 |

① It is not troublesome to keep pets.

② People might stop keeping pets.

③ Pet owners have more family members.

④ Some people are happy to keep pets inside their homes.

問 5　Which is the most suitable title for the article?　| 15 |

① Does Your Pet Sleep on Your Bed?

② What Does Keeping Pets Give Us?

③ What Pet Do You Have?

④ Why Not Keep a Pet Pig?

— 11 —

第3問 (配点 15)

A You are interested in how Japanese culture is represented in other countries. You are reading a young UK blogger's post.

Emily Sampson
Monday, 5 July, 8.00 pm

On the first two Sundays in July every year, there is an intercultural event in Winsfield called A Slice of Japan. I had a chance to go there yesterday. It is definitely worth visiting! There were many authentic food stands called *yatai*, hands-on activities, and some great performances. The *yatai* served green-tea ice cream, *takoyaki*, and *yakitori*. I tried green-tea ice cream and *takoyaki*. The *takoyaki* was especially delicious. You should try some!

I saw three performances. One of them was a *rakugo* comedy given in English. Some people were laughing, but somehow I didn't find it funny. It may be because I don't know much about Japanese culture. For me, the other two, the *taiko* and the *koto*, were the highlights. The *taiko* were powerful, and the *koto* was relaxing.

I attended a workshop and a cultural experience, which were fun. In the workshop, I learnt how to make *onigiri*. Although the shape of the one I made was a little odd, it tasted good. The *nagashi-somen* experience was really interesting! It involved trying to catch cooked noodles with chopsticks as they slid down a bamboo water slide. It was very difficult to catch them.

If you want to experience a slice of Japan, this festival is for you! I took a picture of the flyer. Check it out.

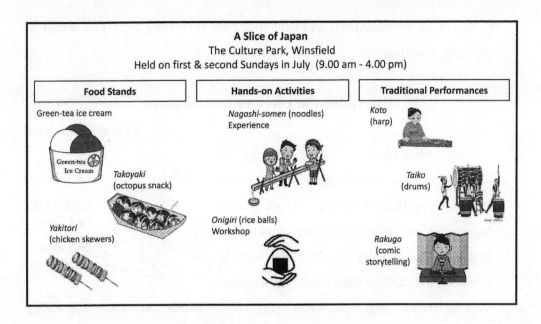

問1 In Emily's blog, you read that she [16].

① enjoyed Japanese traditional music
② learnt how to play Japanese drums
③ made a water slide from bamboo
④ was able to try all the *yatai* foods

問2 Emily was most likely [17] when she was listening to the *rakugo* comedy.

① confused
② convinced
③ excited
④ relaxed

B You enjoy outdoor sports and have found an interesting story in a mountain climbing magazine.

Attempting the Three Peaks Challenge

By John Highland

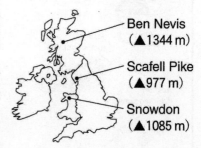

Last September, a team of 12 of us, 10 climbers and two minibus drivers, participated in the Three Peaks Challenge, which is well known for its difficulty among climbers in Britain. The goal is to climb the highest mountain in Scotland (Ben Nevis), in England (Scafell Pike), and in Wales (Snowdon) within 24 hours, including approximately 10 hours of driving between the mountains. To prepare for this, we trained on and off for several months and planned the route carefully. Our challenge would start at the foot of Ben Nevis and finish at the foot of Snowdon.

We began our first climb at six o'clock on a beautiful autumn morning. Thanks to our training, we reached the summit in under three hours. On the way down, however, I realised I had dropped my phone. Fortunately, I found it with the help of the team, but we lost 15 minutes.

We reached our next destination, Scafell Pike, early that evening. After six hours of rest in the minibus, we started our second climb full of energy. As it got darker, though, we had to slow down. It took four-and-a-half hours to complete Scafell Pike. Again, it took longer than planned, and time was running out. However, because the traffic was light, we were right on schedule when we started our final climb. Now we felt more confident we could complete the challenge within the time limit.

Unfortunately, soon after we started the final climb, it began to rain heavily and we had to slow down again. It was slippery and very difficult to see ahead. At 4.30 am, we realised that we could no longer finish in 24 hours.

2022 本試 英語 (リーディング)

Nevertheless, we were still determined to climb the final mountain. The rain got heavier and heavier, and two members of the team decided to return to the minibus. Exhausted and miserable, the rest of us were also ready to go back down, but then the sky cleared, and we saw that we were really close to the top of the mountain. Suddenly, we were no longer tired. Even though we weren't successful with the time challenge, we were successful with the climb challenge. We had done it. What a feeling that was!

問 1 Put the following events (①~④) into the order they happened.

18 → 19 → 20 → 21

① All members reached the top of the highest mountain in Scotland.

② Some members gave up climbing Snowdon.

③ The group travelled by minibus to Wales.

④ The team members helped to find the writer's phone.

問 2 What was the reason for being behind schedule when they completed Scafell Pike? 22

① It took longer than planned to reach the top of Ben Nevis.

② It was difficult to make good progress in the dark.

③ The climbers took a rest in order to save energy.

④ The team had to wait until the conditions improved.

問 3 From this story, you learnt that the writer 23 .

① didn't feel a sense of satisfaction

② reached the top of all three mountains

③ successfully completed the time challenge

④ was the second driver of the minibus

— 15 —

第4問 (配点 16)

You are a new student at Robinson University in the US. You are reading the blogs of two students, Len and Cindy, to find out where you can buy things for your apartment.

New to Robinson University?
Posted by Len at 4:51 p.m. on August 4, 2021

Getting ready for college? Do you need some home appliances or electronics, but don't want to spend too much money? There's a great store close to the university called Second Hand. It sells used goods such as televisions, vacuum cleaners, and microwaves. A lot of students like to buy and sell their things at the store. Here are some items that are on sale now. Most of them are priced very reasonably, but stock is limited, so hurry!

Second Hand Sale for New Students!

Television **$250**
2016 model
50 in.

Vacuum Cleaner **$30**
2017 model
W 9 in. x L 14 in. x H 12 in.

Rice Cooker **$40**
2018 model
W 11 in. x D 14 in. x H 8 in.

Microwave **$85**
2019 model
1.1 cu. ft. 900 watts

Kettle **$5**
2018 model
1ℓ

https://secondhand.web

Purchasing used goods is eco-friendly. Plus, by buying from Second Hand you'll be supporting a local business. The owner is actually a graduate of Robinson University!

Welcome to Robinson University!

Posted by Cindy at 11:21 a.m. on August 5, 2021

Are you starting at Robinson University soon? You may be preparing to buy some household appliances or electronics for your new life.

You're going to be here for four years, so buy your goods new! In my first year, I bought all of my appliances at a shop selling used goods near the university because they were cheaper than brand-new ones. However, some of them stopped working after just one month, and they did not have warranties. I had to replace them quickly and could not shop around, so I just bought everything from one big chain store. I wish I had been able to compare the prices at two or more shops beforehand.

The website called save4unistu.com is very useful for comparing the prices of items from different stores before you go shopping. The following table compares current prices for the most popular new items from three big stores.

Item	Cut Price	Great Buy	Value Saver
Rice Cooker (W 11 in. x D 14 in. x H 8 in.)	$115	$120	$125
Television (50 in.)	$300	$295	$305
Kettle (1ℓ)	$15	$18	$20
Microwave (1.1 cu. ft. 900 watts)	$88	$90	$95
Vacuum Cleaner (W 9 in. x L 14 in. x H 12 in.)	$33	$35	$38

https://save4unistu.com

Note that warranties are available for all items. So, if anything stops working, replacing it will be straightforward. Value Saver provides one-year warranties on all household goods for free. If the item is over $300, the warranty is extended by four years. Great Buy provides one-year warranties on all household goods, and students with proof of enrollment at a school get 10% off the prices listed on the table above. Warranties at Cut Price are not provided for free. You have to pay $10 per item for a five-year warranty.

Things go fast! Don't wait or you'll miss out!

問 1 Len recommends buying used goods because ☐24☐ .

① it will help the university

② most of the items are good for the environment

③ they are affordable for students

④ you can find what you need in a hurry

問 2 Cindy suggests buying ☐25☐ .

① from a single big chain store because it saves time

② from the website because it offers the best prices

③ new items that have warranties for replacement

④ used items because they are much cheaper than new items

問 3 Both Len and Cindy recommend that you ☐26☐ .

① buy from the store near your university

② buy your appliances as soon as you can

③ choose a shop offering a student discount

④ choose the items with warranties

— 18 —

2022 本試 英語 (リーディング)

問 4　If you want to buy new appliances at the best possible prices, you should ⬜27⬜ .

　① access the URL in Cindy's post

　② access the URL in Len's post

　③ contact one big chain store

　④ contact shops close to the campus

問 5　You have decided to buy a microwave from ⬜28⬜ because it is the cheapest.　You have also decided to buy a television from ⬜29⬜ because it is the cheapest with a five-year warranty.　(Choose one for each box from options ①〜④.)

　① Cut Price

　② Great Buy

　③ Second Hand

　④ Value Saver

— 19 —

第5問 (配点 15)

In your English class, you will give a presentation about a great inventor. You found the following article and prepared notes for your presentation.

Farnsworth in 1939

Who invented television? It is not an easy question to answer. In the early years of the 20th century, there was something called a mechanical television system, but it was not a success. Inventors were also competing to develop an electronic television system, which later became the basis of what we have today. In the US, there was a battle over the patent for the electronic television system, which attracted people's attention because it was between a young man and a giant corporation. This patent would give the inventor the official right to be the only person to develop, use, or sell the system.

Philo Taylor Farnsworth was born in a log cabin in Utah in 1906. His family did not have electricity until he was 12 years old, and he was excited to find a generator—a machine that produces electricity—when they moved into a new home. He was very interested in mechanical and electrical technology, reading any information he could find on the subject. He would often repair the old generator and even changed his mother's hand-powered washing machine into an electricity-powered one.

One day, while working in his father's potato field, he looked behind him and saw all the straight parallel rows of soil that he had made. Suddenly, it occurred to him that it might be possible to create an electronic image on a screen using parallel lines, just like the rows in the field. In 1922, during the spring semester of his first year at high school, he presented this idea to his chemistry teacher, Justin Tolman, and asked for advice about his concept of an electronic television system. With sketches and diagrams on blackboards, he

2022 本試 英語 (リーディング)

showed the teacher how it might be accomplished, and Tolman encouraged him to develop his ideas.

On September 7, 1927, Farnsworth succeeded in sending his first electronic image. In the following years, he further improved the system so that it could successfully broadcast live images. The US government gave him a patent for this system in 1930.

However, Farnsworth was not the only one working on such a system. A giant company, RCA (Radio Corporation of America), also saw a bright future for television and did not want to miss the opportunity. They recruited Vladimir Zworykin, who had already worked on an electronic television system and had earned a patent as early as 1923. Yet, in 1931, they offered Farnsworth a large sum of money to sell them his patent as his system was superior to that of Zworykin's. He refused this offer, which started a patent war between Farnsworth and RCA.

The company took legal action against Farnsworth, claiming that Zworykin's 1923 patent had priority even though he had never made a working version of his system. Farnsworth lost the first two rounds of the court case. However, in the final round, the teacher who had copied Farnsworth's blackboard drawings gave evidence that Farnsworth did have the idea of an electronic television system at least a year before Zworykin's patent was issued. In 1934, a judge approved Farnsworth's patent claim on the strength of handwritten notes made by his old high school teacher, Tolman.

Farnsworth died in 1971 at the age of 64. He held about 300 US and foreign patents, mostly in radio and television, and in 1999, *TIME* magazine included Farnsworth in *Time 100: The Most Important People of the Century*. In an interview after his death, Farnsworth's wife Pem recalled Neil Armstrong's moon landing being broadcast. Watching the television with her, Farnsworth had said, "Pem, this has made it all worthwhile." His story will always be tied to his teenage dream of sending moving pictures through the air and those blackboard drawings at his high school.

Your presentation notes:

Philo Taylor Farnsworth (1906 – 1971)

— [30] —

Early Days

- born in a log cabin without electricity
- [31]
- [32]

Sequence of Key Events

[33]

[34]

Farnsworth successfully sent his first image.

[35]

[36]

↓ RCA took Farnsworth to court.

Outcome

- Farnsworth won the patent battle against RCA thanks to [37].

Achievements and Recognition

- Farnsworth had about 300 patents.
- *TIME* magazine listed him as one of the century's most important figures.
- [38]

2022 本試 英語（リーディング）

問 1 Which is the best subtitle for your presentation? | 30 |

① A Young Inventor Against a Giant Company

② From High School Teacher to Successful Inventor

③ Never-Ending Passion for Generating Electricity

④ The Future of Electronic Television

問 2 Choose the best two options for | 31 | and | 32 | to complete Early Days. (The order does not matter.)

① bought a generator to provide his family with electricity

② built a log cabin that had electricity with the help of his father

③ enjoyed reading books on every subject in school

④ fixed and improved household equipment for his family

⑤ got the idea for an electronic television system while working in a field

問 3 Choose **four** out of the five events (①~⑤) in the order they happened to complete Sequence of Key Events.

| 33 | → | 34 | → | 35 | → | 36 |

① Farnsworth rejected RCA's offer.

② Farnsworth shared his idea with his high school teacher.

③ RCA won the first stage of the battle.

④ The US government gave Farnsworth the patent.

⑤ Zworykin was granted a patent for his television system.

— 23 —

問 4　Choose the best option for ☐37☐ to complete Outcome.

① the acceptance of his rival's technological inferiority

② the financial assistance provided by Tolman

③ the sketches his teacher had kept for many years

④ the withdrawal of RCA from the battle

問 5　Choose the best option for ☐38☐ to complete Achievements and Recognition.

① He and his wife were given an award for their work with RCA.

② He appeared on TV when Armstrong's first moon landing was broadcast.

③ His invention has enabled us to watch historic events live.

④ Many teenagers have followed their dreams after watching him on TV.

— 24 —

2022 本試 英語 (リーディング)

（下 書 き 用 紙）

リスニングの試験問題は次に続く。

— 25 —

第6問 (配点 24)

A Your study group is learning about "how time of day affects people." You have found an article you want to share. Complete the summary notes for your next meeting.

When Does the Day Begin for You?

When asked "Are you a morning person?" some reply "No, I'm a night owl." Such people can concentrate and create at night. At the other end of the clock, a well-known proverb claims: "The early bird catches the worm," which means that waking early is the way to get food, win prizes, and reach goals. The lark is a morning singer, so early birds, the opposite of *owls*, are *larks*. Creatures active during the day are "diurnal" and those emerging at night are "nocturnal."

Yet another proverb states: "Early to bed, early to rise makes a man healthy, wealthy, and wise." *Larks* may jump out of bed and welcome the morning with a big breakfast, while *owls* hit the snooze button, getting ready at the last minute, usually without breakfast. They may have fewer meals, but they eat late in the day. Not exercising after meals can cause weight gain. Perhaps *larks* are healthier. *Owls* must work or learn on the *lark* schedule. Most schooling occurs before 4:00 p.m., so young *larks* may perform certain tasks better. Business deals made early in the day may make some *larks* wealthier.

What makes one person a *lark* and another an *owl*? One theory suggests preference for day or night has to do with time of birth. In 2010, Cleveland State University researchers found evidence that not only does a person's internal clock start at the moment of birth, but that those born at night might have lifelong challenges performing during daytime hours. Usually, their world

— 26 —

experience begins with darkness. Since traditional study time and office work happen in daylight, we assume that day begins in the morning. People asleep are not first in line, and might miss chances.

Does everyone follow the system of beginning days in the morning? The Jewish people, an approximately 6,000-year-old religious group, believe a day is measured from sundown until the following sundown—from eve to eve. Christians continue this tradition with Christmas Eve. The Chinese use their system of 12 animals not only to mark years, but to separate each two-hour period of the day. The hour of the rat, the first period, is from 11:00 p.m. to 1:00 a.m. Chinese culture also begins the day at night. In other words, ancient customs support how *owls* view time.

Research indicates *owls* are smarter and more creative. So, perhaps *larks* are not always wiser! That is to say, *larks* win "healthy" and sometimes "wealthy," but they may lose "wise." In an early report, Richard D. Roberts and Patrick C. Kyllonen state that *owls* tend to be more intelligent. A later, comprehensive study by Franzis Preckel, for which Roberts was one of the co-authors, came to the same conclusion. It is not all good news for *owls*, though. Not only can schoolwork be a challenge, but they may miss daytime career opportunities and are more likely to enjoy the bad habits of "nightlife," playing at night while *larks* sleep. Nightlife tends to be expensive. A University of Barcelona study suggests *larks* are precise, seek perfection, and feel little stress. *Owls* seek new adventures and exciting leisure activities, yet they often have trouble relaxing.

Can people change? While the results are not all in, studies of young adults seem to say no, we are hard-wired. So, as young people grow and acquire more freedom, they end up returning to their *lark* or *owl* nature. However, concerns arise that this categorization may not fit everyone. In addition to time of birth possibly being an indication, a report published in *Nature Communications* suggests that DNA may also affect our habits concerning time. Other works focus on changes occurring in some people due to aging or illness. New research in this area appears all the time. A study of university students in Russia suggests that there are six types, so *owls* and *larks* may not be the only birds around!

Your summary notes:

When Does the Day Begin for You?

Vocabulary

Definition of diurnal: ⬚ 39

⇔ opposite: nocturnal

The Main Points

- Not all of us fit easily into the common daytime schedule, but we are forced to follow it, especially when we are children.
- Some studies indicate that the most active time for each of us is part of our nature.
- Basically, ⬚ 40 .
- Perspectives keep changing with new research.

Interesting Details

- The Jewish and Christian religions, as well as Chinese time division, are referred to in the article in order to ⬚ 41 .
- Some studies show that ⬚ 42 may set a person's internal clock and may be the explanation for differences in intelligence and ⬚ 43 .

問 1　Choose the best option for ⬚ 39 .

① achieves goals quickly

② likes keeping pet birds

③ lively in the daytime

④ skillful in finding food

— 28 —

2022 本試 英語（リーディング）

問 2　Choose the best option for ⬚40⬚ .

① a more flexible time and performance schedule will be developed in the future

② enjoying social activities in the morning becomes more important as we age

③ it might be hard for us to change what time of day we perform best

④ living on the *owl* schedule will eventually lead to social and financial benefits

問 3　Choose the best option for ⬚41⬚ .

① explain that certain societies have long believed that a day begins at night

② indicate that nocturnal people were more religious in the past

③ say that people have long thought they miss chances due to morning laziness

④ support the idea that *owls* must go to work or school on the *lark* schedule

問 4　Choose the best options for ⬚42⬚ and ⬚43⬚ .

① amount of sleep

② appearance

③ behavior

④ cultural background

⑤ religious beliefs

⑥ time of birth

— 29 —

B You are in a student group preparing a poster for a scientific presentation contest with the theme "What we should know in order to protect the environment." You have been using the following passage to create the poster.

Recycling Plastic
—What You Need to Know—

The world is full of various types of plastic. Look around, and you will see dozens of plastic items. Look closer and you will notice a recycling symbol on them. In Japan, you might have seen the first symbol in Figure 1 below, but the United States and Europe have a more detailed classification. These recycling symbols look like a triangle of chasing pointers, or sometimes a simple triangle with a number from one to seven inside. This system was started in 1988 by the Society of the Plastics Industry in the US, but since 2008 it has been administered by an international standards organization, ASTM (American Society for Testing and Materials) International. Recycling symbols provide important data about the chemical composition of plastic used and its recyclability. However, a plastic recycling symbol on an object does not always mean that the item can be recycled. It only shows what type of plastic it is made from and that it might be recyclable.

Figure 1. Plastic recycling symbols

So, what do these numbers mean? One group (numbers 2, 4, and 5) is considered to be safe for the human body, while the other group (numbers 1, 3, 6, and 7) could be problematic in certain circumstances. Let us look at the safer group first.

High-density Polyethylene is a recycle-type 2 plastic and is commonly called HDPE. It is non-toxic and can be used in the human body for heart

2022 本試 英語 (リーディング)

valves and artificial joints. It is strong and can be used at temperatures as low as −40℃ and as high as 100℃. HDPE can be reused without any harm and is also suitable for beer-bottle cases, milk jugs, chairs, and toys. Type 2 products can be recycled several times. Type 4 products are made from Low-density Polyethylene (LDPE). They are safe to use and are flexible. LDPE is used for squeezable bottles, and bread wrapping. Currently, very little Type 4 plastic is recycled. Polypropylene (PP), a Type 5 material, is the second-most widely produced plastic in the world. It is light, non-stretching, and has a high resistance to impact, heat, and freezing. It is suitable for furniture, food containers, and polymer banknotes such as the Australian dollar. Only 3% of Type 5 is recycled.

Now let us look at the second group, Types 1, 3, 6, and 7. These are more challenging because of the chemicals they contain or the difficulty in recycling them. Recycle-type 1 plastic is commonly known as PETE (Polyethylene Terephthalate), and is used mainly in food and beverage containers. PETE containers — or PET as it is often written in Japan — should only be used once as they are difficult to clean thoroughly. Also, they should not be heated above 70℃ as this can cause some containers to soften and change shape. Uncontaminated PETE is easy to recycle and can be made into new containers, clothes, or carpets, but if PETE is contaminated with Polyvinyl Chloride (PVC), it can make it unrecyclable. PVC, Type 3, is thought to be one of the least recyclable plastics known. It should only be disposed of by professionals and never set fire to at home or in the garden. Type 3 plastic is found in shower curtains, pipes, and flooring. Type 6, Polystyrene (PS) or Styrofoam as it is often called, is hard to recycle and catches fire easily. However, it is cheap to produce and lightweight. It is used for disposable drinking cups, instant noodle containers, and other food packaging. Type 7 plastics (acrylics, nylons, and polycarbonates) are difficult to recycle. Type 7 plastics are often used in the manufacture of vehicle parts such as seats, dashboards, and bumpers.

Currently, only about 20% of plastic is recycled, and approximately 55% ends up in a landfill. Therefore, knowledge about different types of plastic could help reduce waste and contribute to an increased awareness of the environment.

Your presentation poster draft:

Do you know the plastic recycling symbols?

What are plastic recycling symbols?

44

Types of plastic and recycling information

Type	Symbol	Description	Products
1	PETE (PET)	This type of plastic is common and generally easy to recycle.	drink bottles, food containers, etc.
2	HDPE	This type of plastic is easily recycled 45 .	heart valves, artificial joints, chairs, toys, etc.
3	PVC	This type of plastic is 46 .	shower curtains, pipes, flooring, etc.
4			

Plastics with common properties

47

48

— 32 —

2022 本試 英語 (リーディング)

問 1 Under the first poster heading, your group wants to introduce the plastic recycling symbols as explained in the passage. Which of the following is the most appropriate? 44

① They are symbols that rank the recyclability of plastics and other related problems.

② They provide information on the chemical make-up and recycling options of the plastic.

③ They tell the user which standards organization gave them certificates for general use.

④ They were introduced by ASTM and developed by the Society of the Plastics Industry.

問 2 You have been asked to write descriptions of Type 2 and Type 3 plastics. Choose the best options for 45 and 46 .

Type 2 45
① and commonly known as a single-use plastic
② and used at a wide range of temperatures
③ but harmful to humans
④ but unsuitable for drink containers

Type 3 46
① difficult to recycle and should not be burned in the yard
② flammable; however, it is soft and cheap to produce
③ known to be a non-toxic product
④ well known for being easily recyclable

— 33 —

問 3 You are making statements about some plastics which share common properties. According to the article, which two of the following are appropriate? (The order does not matter.) 47 · 48

① Boiling water (100℃) can be served in Type 1 and Type 6 plastic containers.

② It is easy to recycle products with Type 1, 2, and 3 logos.

③ Products with the symbols 1, 2, 4, 5, and 6 are suitable for food or drink containers.

④ Products with Type 5 and Type 6 markings are light in weight.

⑤ Type 4 and 5 plastics are heat resistant and are widely recycled.

⑥ Type 6 and 7 plastics are easy to recycle and environmentally friendly.

— 34 —

2021年度

大学入学共通テスト

第1日程

英語(リーディング)

(100点　80分)

● 標 準 所 要 時 間 ●

第1問　7分程度　　第4問12分程度
第2問13分程度　　第5問14分程度
第3問12分程度　　第6問22分程度

英　語（リーディング）

各大問の英文や図表を読み，解答番号 | 1 | ～ | 47 | にあてはまるものとして最も適当な選択肢を選びなさい。

第1問　（配点　10）

A　Your dormitory roommate Julie has sent a text message to your mobile phone with a request.

Help!!!
Last night I saved my history homework on a USB memory stick. I was going to print it in the university library this afternoon, but I forgot to bring the USB with me. I need to give a copy to my teacher by 4 p.m. today. Can you bring my USB to the library? I think it's on top of my history book on my desk. I don't need the book, just the USB. ♡

Sorry Julie, I couldn't find it. The history book was there, but there was no USB memory stick. I looked for it everywhere, even under your desk. Are you sure you don't have it with you? I'll bring your laptop computer with me, just in case.

You were right! I did have it. It was at the bottom of my bag.
What a relief!
Thanks anyway. ☺

— 2 —

2021 第 1 日程 英語（リーディング）

問 1　What was Julie's request?　　1

① To bring her USB memory stick

② To hand in her history homework

③ To lend her a USB memory stick

④ To print out her history homework

問 2　How will you reply to Julie's second text message?　　2

① Don't worry. You'll find it.

② I'm really glad to hear that.

③ Look in your bag again.

④ You must be disappointed.

— 3 —

B Your favorite musician will have a concert tour in Japan, and you are thinking of joining the fan club. You visit the official fan club website.

TYLER QUICK FAN CLUB

Being a member of the **TYLER QUICK** (**TQ**) fan club is so much fun! You can keep up with the latest news, and take part in many exciting fan club member events. All new members will receive our New Member's Pack. It contains a membership card, a free signed poster, and a copy of **TQ**'s third album *Speeding Up*. The New Member's Pack will be delivered to your home, and will arrive a week or so after you join the fan club.

TQ is loved all around the world. You can join from any country, and you can use the membership card for one year. The **TQ** fan club has three types of membership: Pacer, Speeder, and Zoomer.

Please choose from the membership options below.

What you get (♫)	Membership Options		
	Pacer ($20)	Speeder ($40)	Zoomer ($60)
Regular emails and online magazine password	♫	♫	♫
Early information on concert tour dates	♫	♫	♫
TQ's weekly video messages	♫	♫	♫
Monthly picture postcards		♫	♫
TQ fan club calendar		♫	♫
Invitations to special signing events			♫
20% off concert tickets			♫

- ◇Join before May 10 and receive a $10 discount on your membership fee!
- ◇There is a $4 delivery fee for every New Member's Pack.
- ◇At the end of your 1st year, you can either renew or upgrade at a 50% discount.

Whether you are a Pacer, a Speeder, or a Zoomer, you will love being a member of the **TQ** fan club. For more information, or to join, click *here*.

問 1　A New Member's Pack ☐ 3 ☐ .

① includes TQ's first album
② is delivered on May 10
③ requires a $10 delivery fee
④ takes about seven days to arrive

問 2　What will you get if you become a new Pacer member? ☐ 4 ☐

① Discount concert tickets and a calendar
② Regular emails and signing event invitations
③ Tour information and postcards every month
④ Video messages and access to online magazines

問 3　After being a fan club member for one year, you can ☐ 5 ☐ .

① become a Zoomer for a $50 fee
② get a New Member's Pack for $4
③ renew your membership at half price
④ upgrade your membership for free

第2問 (配点 20)

A As the student in charge of a UK school festival band competition, you are examining all of the scores and the comments from three judges to understand and explain the rankings.

Judges' final average scores				
Qualities Band names	Performance (5.0)	Singing (5.0)	Song originality (5.0)	Total (15.0)
Green Forest	3.9	4.6	5.0	13.5
Silent Hill	4.9	4.4	4.2	13.5
Mountain Pear	3.9	4.9	4.7	13.5
Thousand Ants	(did not perform)			

Judges' individual comments	
Mr Hobbs	Silent Hill are great performers and they really seemed connected with the audience. Mountain Pear's singing was great. I loved Green Forest's original song. It was amazing!
Ms Leigh	Silent Hill gave a great performance. It was incredible how the audience responded to their music. I really think that Silent Hill will become popular! Mountain Pear have great voices, but they were not exciting on stage. Green Forest performed a fantastic new song, but I think they need to practice more.
Ms Wells	Green Forest have a new song. I loved it! I think it could be a big hit!

— 6 —

Judges' shared evaluation (summarised by Mr Hobbs)
Each band's total score is the same, but each band is very different. Ms Leigh and I agreed that performance is the most important quality for a band. Ms Wells also agreed. Therefore, first place is easily determined. To decide between second and third places, Ms Wells suggested that song originality should be more important than good singing. Ms Leigh and I agreed on this opinion.

問 1 Based on the judges' final average scores, which band sang the best?
  6

① Green Forest
② Mountain Pear
③ Silent Hill
④ Thousand Ants

問 2 Which judge gave both positive and critical comments? 7

① Mr Hobbs
② Ms Leigh
③ Ms Wells
④ None of them

問 3　One **fact** from the judges' individual comments is that ⬚ 8 ⬚.

① all the judges praised Green Forest's song

② Green Forest need to practice more

③ Mountain Pear can sing very well

④ Silent Hill have a promising future

問 4　One **opinion** from the judges' comments and shared evaluation is that ⬚ 9 ⬚.

① each evaluated band received the same total score

② Ms Wells' suggestion about originality was agreed on

③ Silent Hill really connected with the audience

④ the judges' comments determined the rankings

問 5　Which of the following is the final ranking based on the judges' shared evaluation? ⬚ 10 ⬚

	1st	2nd	3rd
①	Green Forest	Mountain Pear	Silent Hill
②	Green Forest	Silent Hill	Mountain Pear
③	Mountain Pear	Green Forest	Silent Hill
④	Mountain Pear	Silent Hill	Green Forest
⑤	Silent Hill	Green Forest	Mountain Pear
⑥	Silent Hill	Mountain Pear	Green Forest

2021 第 1 日程 英語（リーディング）

（下 書 き 用 紙）

英語（リーディング）の試験問題は次に続く。

B You've heard about a change in school policy at the school in the UK where you are now studying as an exchange student. You are reading the discussions about the policy in an online forum.

New School Policy ＜Posted on 21 September 2020＞
To: P. E. Berger
From: K. Roberts

Dear Dr Berger,

On behalf of all students, welcome to St Mark's School. We heard that you are the first Head Teacher with a business background, so we hope your experience will help our school.

I would like to express one concern about the change you are proposing to the after-school activity schedule. I realise that saving energy is important and from now it will be getting darker earlier. Is this why you have made the schedule an hour and a half shorter? Students at St Mark's School take both their studies and their after-school activities very seriously. A number of students have told me that they want to stay at school until 6.00 pm as they have always done. Therefore, I would like to ask you to think again about this sudden change in policy.

Regards,
Ken Roberts
Head Student

2021 第 1 日程 英語 (リーディング)

Re: New School Policy ＜Posted on 22 September 2020＞

To: K. Roberts

From: P. E. Berger

Dear Ken,

Many thanks for your kind post. You've expressed some important concerns, especially about the energy costs and student opinions on school activities.

The new policy has nothing to do with saving energy. The decision was made based on a 2019 police report. The report showed that our city has become less safe due to a 5% increase in serious crimes. I would like to protect our students, so I would like them to return home before it gets dark.

Yours,

Dr P. E. Berger

Head Teacher

問 1　Ken thinks the new policy 　11　 .

① can make students study more

② may improve school safety

③ should be introduced immediately

④ will reduce after-school activity time

問 2　One **fact** stated in Ken's forum post is that 　12　 .

① more discussion is needed about the policy

② the Head Teacher's experience is improving the school

③ the school should think about students' activities

④ there are students who do not welcome the new policy

問 3　Who thinks the aim of the policy is to save energy? 　13　

① Dr Berger

② Ken

③ The city

④ The police

2021 第 1 日程 英語 (リーディング)

問 4　Dr Berger is basing his new policy on the **fact** that ⬚14⬚ .

① going home early is important

② safety in the city has decreased

③ the school has to save electricity

④ the students need protection

問 5　What would you research to help Ken oppose the new policy? ⬚15⬚

① The crime rate and its relation to the local area

② The energy budget and electricity costs of the school

③ The length of school activity time versus the budget

④ The study hours for students who do after-school activities

— 13 —

第３問 （配点 15）

A You are planning to stay at a hotel in the UK. You found useful information in the Q&A section of a travel advice website.

I'm considering staying at the Hollytree Hotel in Castleton in March 2021. Would you recommend this hotel, and is it easy to get there from Buxton Airport?   (Liz)

- -

Answer

Yes, I strongly recommend the Hollytree. I've stayed there twice. It's inexpensive, and the service is brilliant! There's also a wonderful free breakfast. (Click *here* for access information.)

Let me tell you my own experience of getting there.

On my first visit, I used the underground, which is cheap and convenient. Trains run every five minutes. From the airport, I took the Red Line to Mossfield. Transferring to the Orange Line for Victoria should normally take about seven minutes, but the directions weren't clear and I needed an extra five minutes. From Victoria, it was a ten-minute bus ride to the hotel.

The second time, I took the express bus to Victoria, so I didn't have to worry about transferring. At Victoria, I found a notice saying there would be roadworks until summer 2021. Now it takes three times as long as usual to get to the hotel by city bus, although buses run every ten minutes. It's possible to walk, but I took the bus as the weather was bad.

Enjoy your stay!   (Alex)

― 14 ―

Access to the Hollytree Hotel

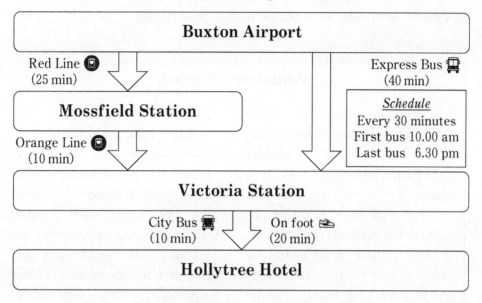

問1 From Alex's answer, you learn that Alex [16].

① appreciates the convenient location of the hotel
② got lost in Victoria Station on his first visit to Castleton
③ thinks that the hotel is good value for money
④ used the same route from the airport both times

問2 You are departing on public transport from the airport at 2.00 pm on 15 March 2021. What is the fastest way to get to the hotel? [17]

① By express bus and city bus
② By express bus and on foot
③ By underground and city bus
④ By underground and on foot

B Your classmate showed you the following message in your school's newsletter, written by an exchange student from the UK.

Volunteers Wanted!

Hello, everyone. I'm Sarah King, an exchange student from London. I'd like to share something important with you today.

You may have heard of the Sakura International Centre. It provides valuable opportunities for Japanese and foreign residents to get to know each other. Popular events such as cooking classes and karaoke contests are held every month. However, there is a serious problem. The building is getting old, and requires expensive repairs. To help raise funds to maintain the centre, many volunteers are needed.

I learnt about the problem a few months ago. While shopping in town, I saw some people taking part in a fund-raising campaign. I spoke to the leader of the campaign, Katy, who explained the situation. She thanked me when I donated some money. She told me that they had asked the town mayor for financial assistance, but their request had been rejected. They had no choice but to start fund-raising.

Last month, I attended a lecture on art at the centre. Again, I saw people trying to raise money, and I decided to help. They were happy when I joined them in asking passers-by for donations. We tried hard, but there were too few of us to collect much money. With a tearful face, Katy told me that they wouldn't be able to use the building much longer. I felt the need to do something more. Then, the idea came to me that other students might be willing to help. Katy was delighted to hear this.

Now, I'm asking you to join me in the fund-raising campaign to help the Sakura International Centre. Please email me today! As an exchange student, my time in Japan is limited, but I want to make the most of it. By working together, we can really make a difference.

Class 3 A
Sarah King (sarahk@sakura-h.ed.jp)

セーラ・キング

— 16 —

問 1 Put the following events (①～④) into the order in which they happened.

18 → 19 → 20 → 21

① Sarah attended a centre event.
② Sarah donated money to the centre.
③ Sarah made a suggestion to Katy.
④ The campaigners asked the mayor for help.

問 2 From Sarah's message, you learn that the Sakura International Centre 22 .

① gives financial aid to international residents
② offers opportunities to develop friendships
③ publishes newsletters for the community
④ sends exchange students to the UK

問 3 You have decided to help with the campaign after reading Sarah's message. What should you do first? 23

① Advertise the events at the centre.
② Contact Sarah for further information.
③ Organise volunteer activities at school.
④ Start a new fund-raising campaign.

第4問 (配点 16)

Your English teacher, Emma, has asked you and your classmate, Natsuki, to help her plan the day's schedule for hosting students from your sister school. You're reading the email exchanges between Natsuki and Emma so that you can draft the schedule.

Hi Emma,

We have some ideas and questions about the schedule for the day out with our 12 guests next month. As you told us, the students from both schools are supposed to give presentations in our assembly hall from 10:00 a.m. So, I've been looking at the attached timetable. Will they arrive at Azuma Station at 9:39 a.m. and then take a taxi to the school?

We have also been discussing the afternoon activities. How about seeing something related to science? We have two ideas, but if you need a third, please let me know.

Have you heard about the special exhibition that is on at Westside Aquarium next month? It's about a new food supplement made from sea plankton. We think it would be a good choice. Since it's popular, the best time to visit will be when it is least busy. I'm attaching the graph I found on the aquarium's homepage.

Eastside Botanical Garden, together with our local university, has been developing an interesting way of producing electricity from plants. Luckily, the professor in charge will give a short talk about it on that day in the early afternoon! Why don't we go?

Everyone will want to get some souvenirs, won't they? I think West Mall, next to Hibari Station, would be best, but we don't want to carry them around with us all day.

Finally, every visitor to Azuma should see the town's symbol, the statue in Azuma Memorial Park next to our school, but we can't work out a good schedule. Also, could you tell us what the plan is for lunch?

Yours,
Natsuki

— 18 —

Hi Natsuki,

Thank you for your email! You've been working hard. In answer to your question, they'll arrive at the station at 9:20 a.m. and then catch the school bus.

The two main afternoon locations, the aquarium and botanical garden, are good ideas because both schools place emphasis on science education, and the purpose of this program is to improve the scientific knowledge of the students. However, it would be wise to have a third suggestion just in case.

Let's get souvenirs at the end of the day. We can take the bus to the mall arriving there at 5:00 p.m. This will allow almost an hour for shopping and our guests can still be back at the hotel by 6:30 p.m. for dinner, as the hotel is only a few minutes' walk from Kaede Station.

About lunch, the school cafeteria will provide boxed lunches. We can eat under the statue you mentioned. If it rains, let's eat inside.

Thank you so much for your suggestions. Could you two make a draft for the schedule?

Best,
Emma

Attached timetable:

Train Timetable
Kaede — Hibari — Azuma

Stations	Train No.			
	108	109	110	111
Kaede	8:28	8:43	9:02	9:16
Hibari	8:50	9:05	9:24	9:38
Azuma	9:05	9:20	9:39	9:53

Stations	Train No.			
	238	239	240	241
Azuma	17:25	17:45	18:00	18:15
Hibari	17:40	18:00	18:15	18:30
Kaede	18:02	18:22	18:37	18:52

Attached graph:

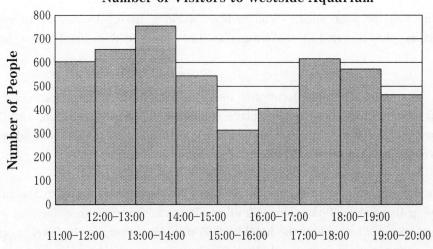

問 1 The guests from the sister school will arrive on the number [24] train and catch the number [25] train back to their hotel.

① 109   ② 110   ③ 111
④ 238   ⑤ 239   ⑥ 240

問 2 Which best completes the draft schedule? [26]

A : The aquarium   B : The botanical garden
C : The mall   D : The school

Draft schedule for visit from sister school

9:30 → 13:30 → 15:30 → 17:00

2021 第 1 日程 英語 (リーディング)

① D→A→B→C

② D→B→A→C

③ D→B→C→A

④ D→C→A→B

問 3　Unless it rains, the guests will eat lunch in the 　27　 .

① botanical garden

② park next to the school

③ park next to the station

④ school garden

問 4　The guests will **not** get around 　28　 on that day.

① by bus

② by taxi

③ by train

④ on foot

問 5　As a third option, which would be the most suitable for your program?
　　　28　 29　

① Hibari Amusement Park

② Hibari Art Museum

③ Hibari Castle

④ Hibari Space Center

— 21 —

第5問 (配点 15)

Using an international news report, you are going to take part in an English oral presentation contest. Read the following news story from France in preparation for your talk.

Five years ago, Mrs. Sabine Rouas lost her horse. She had spent 20 years with the horse before he died of old age. At that time, she felt that she could never own another horse. Out of loneliness, she spent hours watching cows on a nearby milk farm. Then, one day, she asked the farmer if she could help look after them.

The farmer agreed, and Sabine started work. She quickly developed a friendship with one of the cows. As the cow was pregnant, she spent more time with it than with the others. After the cow's baby was born, the baby started following Sabine around. Unfortunately, the farmer wasn't interested in keeping a bull—a male cow—on a milk farm. The farmer planned to sell the baby bull, which he called Three-oh-nine (309), to a meat market. Sabine decided she wasn't going to let that happen, so she asked the farmer if she could buy him and his mother. The farmer agreed, and she bought them. Sabine then started taking 309 for walks to town. About nine months later, when at last she had permission to move the animals, they moved to Sabine's farm.

Soon after, Sabine was offered a pony. At first, she wasn't sure if she wanted to have him, but the memory of her horse was no longer painful, so she accepted the pony and named him Leon. She then decided to return to her old hobby and started training him for show jumping. Three-oh-nine, who she had renamed Aston, spent most of his time with Leon, and the two became really close friends. However, Sabine had not expected Aston to pay close attention to her training routine with Leon, nor had she expected Aston to pick up some

— 22 —

2021 第 1 日程 英語 (リーディング)

tricks. The young bull quickly mastered walking, galloping, stopping, going backwards, and turning around on command. He responded to Sabine's voice just like a horse. And despite weighing 1,300 kg, it took him just 18 months to learn how to leap over one-meter-high horse jumps with Sabine on his back. Aston might never have learned those things without having watched Leon. Moreover, Aston understood distance and could adjust his steps before a jump. He also noticed his faults and corrected them without any help from Sabine. That's something only the very best Olympic-standard horses can do.

Now Sabine and Aston go to weekend fairs and horse shows around Europe to show off his skills. Sabine says, "We get a good reaction. Mostly, people are really surprised, and at first, they can be a bit scared because he's big—much bigger than a horse. Most people don't like to get too close to bulls with horns. But once they see his real nature, and see him performing, they often say, 'Oh he's really quite beautiful.'"

"Look!" And Sabine shows a photo of Aston on her smartphone. She then continues, "When Aston was very young, I used to take him out for walks on a lead, like a dog, so that he would get used to humans. Maybe that's why he doesn't mind people. Because he is so calm, children, in particular, really like watching him and getting a chance to be close to him."

Over the last few years, news of the massive show-jumping bull has spread rapidly; now, Aston is a major attraction with a growing number of online followers. Aston and Sabine sometimes need to travel 200 or 300 kilometers away from home, which means they have to stay overnight. Aston has to sleep in a horse box, which isn't really big enough for him.

"He doesn't like it. I have to sleep with him in the box," says Sabine. "But you know, when he wakes up and changes position, he is very careful not to crush me. He really is very gentle. He sometimes gets lonely, and he doesn't like being away from Leon for too long; but other than that, he's very happy."

Your Presentation Slides

30

Central High School
English Presentation Contest

Who's Who?

Main figures

☐ , ☐ , ☐

Minor figures

☐ , ☐

| 31 |

Pre-fame Storyline

Sabine's horse dies.
↓
| 32 |
↓
| 33 |
↓
| 34 |
↓
| 35 |
↓
Aston and Sabine start going to shows.

Aston's Abilities

Aston can:
- learn by simply watching Leon's training.
- walk, gallop, and stop when Sabine tells him to.
- understand distance and adjust his steps.
- | 36 | .
- | 37 | .

Aston Now

Aston today:
- is a show-jumping bull.
- travels to fairs and events with Sabine.
- | 38 | .

2021 第 1 日程 英語 (リーディング)

問 1 Which is the best title for your presentation? $\boxed{30}$

① Animal-lover Saves the Life of a Pony

② Aston's Summer Show-jumping Tour

③ Meet Aston, the Bull who Behaves Like a Horse

④ The Relationship Between a Farmer and a Cow

問 2 Which is the best combination for the **Who's Who?** slide? $\boxed{31}$

	Main figures	Minor figures
①	309, Aston, the farmer	Sabine, the pony
②	Aston, Aston's mother, Sabine	309, the farmer
③	Aston, Leon, the farmer	Aston's mother, Sabine
④	Aston, Sabine, the pony	Aston's mother, the farmer

問 3 Choose the four events in the order they happened to complete the **Pre-fame Storyline** slide. $\boxed{32}$ ~ $\boxed{35}$

① Aston learns to jump.

② Sabine and Aston travel hundreds of kilometers together.

③ Sabine buys 309 and his mother.

④ Sabine goes to work on her neighbor's farm.

⑤ Sabine takes 309 for walks.

— 25 —

問 4 Choose the two best items for the **Aston's Abilities** slide. (The order does not matter.) 36 · 37

① correct his mistakes by himself
② jump side-by-side with the pony
③ jump with a rider on his back
④ pick up tricks faster than a horse
⑤ pose for photographs

問 5 Complete the **Aston Now** slide with the most appropriate item. 38

① has an increasing number of fans
② has made Sabine very wealthy
③ is so famous that he no longer frightens people
④ spends most nights of the year in a horse trailer

2021 第 1 日程 英語（リーディング）

（下 書 き 用 紙）

英語（リーディング）の試験問題は次に続く。

第6問 (配点 24)

A You are working on a class project about safety in sports and found the following article. You are reading it and making a poster to present your findings to your classmates.

Making Ice Hockey Safer

Ice hockey is a team sport enjoyed by a wide variety of people around the world. The object of the sport is to move a hard rubber disk called a "puck" into the other team's net with a hockey stick. Two teams with six players on each team engage in this fast-paced sport on a hard and slippery ice rink. Players may reach a speed of 30 kilometers per hour sending the puck into the air. At this pace, both the players and the puck can be a cause of serious danger.

The speed of the sport and the slippery surface of the ice rink make it easy for players to fall down or bump into each other resulting in a variety of injuries. In an attempt to protect players, equipment such as helmets, gloves, and pads for the shoulders, elbows, and legs, has been introduced over the years. Despite these efforts, ice hockey has a high rate of concussions.

A concussion is an injury to the brain that affects the way it functions; it is caused by either direct or indirect impact to the head, face, neck, or elsewhere and can sometimes cause temporary loss of consciousness. In less serious cases, for a short time, players may be unable to walk straight or see clearly, or they may experience ringing in the ears. Some believe they just have a slight headache and do not realize they have injured their brains.

In addition to not realizing the seriousness of the injury, players tend to worry about what their coach will think. In the past, coaches preferred tough players who played in spite of the pain. In other words, while it would seem

---

— 28 —

logical for an injured player to stop playing after getting hurt, many did not. Recently, however, it has been found that concussions can have serious effects that last a lifetime. People with a history of concussion may have trouble concentrating or sleeping. Moreover, they may suffer from psychological problems such as depression and mood changes. In some cases, players may develop smell and taste disorders.

The National Hockey League (NHL), consisting of teams in Canada and the United States, has been making stricter rules and guidelines to deal with concussions. For example, in 2001, the NHL introduced the wearing of visors—pieces of clear plastic attached to the helmet that protect the face. At first, it was optional and many players chose not to wear them. Since 2013, however, it has been required. In addition, in 2004, the NHL began to give more severe penalties, such as suspensions and fines, to players who hit another player in the head deliberately.

The NHL also introduced a concussion spotters system in 2015. In this system, NHL officials with access to live streaming and video replay watch for visible indications of concussion during each game. At first, two concussion spotters, who had no medical training, monitored the game in the arena. The following year, one to four concussion spotters with medical training were added. They monitored each game from the League's head office in New York. If a spotter thinks that a player has suffered a concussion, the player is removed from the game and is taken to a "quiet room" for an examination by a medical doctor. The player is not allowed to return to the game until the doctor gives permission.

The NHL has made much progress in making ice hockey a safer sport. As more is learned about the causes and effects of concussions, the NHL will surely take further measures to ensure player safety. Better safety might lead to an increase in the number of ice hockey players and fans.

Making Ice Hockey Safer

What is ice hockey?
- Players score by putting a "puck" in the other team's net
- Six players on each team
- Sport played on ice at a high speed

Main Problem: A High Rate of Concussions

Definition of a concussion
An injury to the brain that affects the way it functions

Effects

Short-term	Long-term
· Loss of consciousness	· Problems with concentration
· Difficulty walking straight	· ☐ 40 ☐
· ☐ 39 ☐	· Psychological problems
· Ringing in the ears	· Smell and taste disorders

Solutions

National Hockey League (NHL)
- Requires helmets with visors
- Gives severe penalties to dangerous players
- Has introduced concussion spotters to ☐ 41 ☐

Summary
Ice hockey players have a high risk of suffering from concussions. Therefore, the NHL has ☐ 42 ☐ .

2021 第 1 日程 英語 (リーディング)

問 1　Choose the best option for ☐39☐ on your poster.

   ① Aggressive behavior

   ② Difficulty thinking

   ③ Personality changes

   ④ Unclear vision

問 2　Choose the best option for ☐40☐ on your poster.

   ① Loss of eyesight

   ② Memory problems

   ③ Sleep disorders

   ④ Unsteady walking

問 3　Choose the best option for ☐41☐ on your poster.

   ① allow players to return to the game

   ② examine players who have a concussion

   ③ fine players who cause concussions

   ④ identify players showing signs of a concussion

問 4　Choose the best option for ☐42☐ on your poster.

   ① been expecting the players to become tougher

   ② been implementing new rules and guidelines

   ③ given medical training to coaches

   ④ made wearing of visors optional

— 31 —

B You are studying nutrition in health class. You are going to read the following passage from a textbook to learn more about various sweeteners.

Cake, candy, soft drinks—most of us love sweet things. In fact, young people say "Sweet!" to mean something is "good" in English. When we think of sweetness, we imagine ordinary white sugar from sugar cane or sugar beet plants. Scientific discoveries, however, have changed the world of sweeteners. We can now extract sugars from many other plants. The most obvious example is corn. Corn is abundant, inexpensive, and easy to process. High fructose corn syrup (HFCS) is about 1.2 times sweeter than regular sugar, but quite high in calories. Taking science one step further, over the past 70 years scientists have developed a wide variety of artificial sweeteners.

A recent US National Health and Nutrition Examination Survey concluded that 14.6% of the average American's energy intake is from "added sugar," which refers to sugar that is not derived from whole foods. A banana, for example, is a whole food, while a cookie contains added sugar. More than half of added sugar calories are from sweetened drinks and desserts. Lots of added sugar can have negative effects on our bodies, including excessive weight gain and other health problems. For this reason, many choose low-calorie substitutes for drinks, snacks, and desserts.

Natural alternatives to white sugar include brown sugar, honey, and maple syrup, but they also tend to be high in calories. Consequently, alternative "low-calorie sweeteners" (LCSs), mostly artificial chemical combinations, have become popular. The most common LCSs today are aspartame, Ace-K, stevia, and sucralose. Not all LCSs are artificial—stevia comes from plant leaves.

Alternative sweeteners can be hard to use in cooking because some cannot be heated and most are far sweeter than white sugar. Aspartame and Ace-K are 200 times sweeter than sugar. Stevia is 300 times sweeter, and sucralose

— 32 —

2021 第 1 日程 英語 (リーディング)

has twice the sweetness of stevia. Some new sweeteners are even more intense. A Japanese company recently developed "Advantame," which is 20,000 times sweeter than sugar. Only a tiny amount of this substance is required to sweeten something.

When choosing sweeteners, it is important to consider health issues. Making desserts with lots of white sugar, for example, results in high-calorie dishes that could lead to weight gain. There are those who prefer LCSs for this very reason. Apart from calories, however, some research links consuming artificial LCSs with various other health concerns. Some LCSs contain strong chemicals suspected of causing cancer, while others have been shown to affect memory and brain development, so they can be dangerous, especially for young children, pregnant women, and the elderly. There are a few relatively natural alternative sweeteners, like xylitol and sorbitol, which are low in calories. Unfortunately, these move through the body extremely slowly, so consuming large amounts can cause stomach trouble.

When people want something sweet, even with all the information, it is difficult for them to decide whether to stick to common higher calorie sweeteners like sugar or to use LCSs. Many varieties of gum and candy today contain one or more artificial sweeteners; nonetheless, some people who would not put artificial sweeteners in hot drinks may still buy such items. Individuals need to weigh the options and then choose the sweeteners that best suit their needs and circumstances.

— 33 —

問 1 You learn that modern science has changed the world of sweeteners by
43 .

① discovering new, sweeter white sugar types

② measuring the energy intake of Americans

③ providing a variety of new options

④ using many newly-developed plants from the environment

問 2 You are summarizing the information you have just studied. How should
the table be finished? 44

Sweetness	Sweetener
high	Advantame
	(A)
	(B)
	(C)
low	(D)

① (A) Stevia   (B) Sucralose
  (C) Ace-K, Aspartame   (D) HFCS

② (A) Stevia   (B) Sucralose
  (C) HFCS   (D) Ace-K, Aspartame

③ (A) Sucralose   (B) Stevia
  (C) Ace-K, Aspartame   (D) HFCS

④ (A) Sucralose   (B) Stevia
  (C) HFCS   (D) Ace-K, Aspartame

— 34 —

2021 第 1 日程 英語 (リーディング)

問 3 According to the article you read, which of the following are true?
(Choose two options. The order does not matter.) 45 ・ 46

① Alternative sweeteners have been proven to cause weight gain.

② Americans get 14.6% of their energy from alternative sweeteners.

③ It is possible to get alternative sweeteners from plants.

④ Most artificial sweeteners are easy to cook with.

⑤ Sweeteners like xylitol and sorbitol are not digested quickly.

問 4 To describe the author's position, which of the following is most
appropriate? 47

① The author argues against the use of artificial sweeteners in drinks and
desserts.

② The author believes artificial sweeteners have successfully replaced
traditional ones.

③ The author states that it is important to invent much sweeter products
for future use.

④ The author suggests people focus on choosing sweeteners that make
sense for them.

— 35 —

2024-駿台　大学入試完全対策シリーズ
大学入学共通テスト実戦問題集

英語リーディング

2023年7月6日　2024年版発行

編　　者	駿　台　文　庫
発 行 者	山　﨑　良　子
印刷・製本	日経印刷株式会社

発 行 所　　駿台文庫株式会社
〒 101-0062　東京都千代田区神田駿河台 1-7-4
小畑ビル内
TEL. 編集 03 (5259) 3302
販売 03 (5259) 3301
《共通テスト実戦・英語リーディング 608pp.》

Ⓒ Sundaibunko 2023
許可なく本書の一部または全部を，複製，複写，
デジタル化する等の行為を禁じます。

落丁・乱丁がございましたら，送料小社負担にて
お取り替えいたします。

ISBN978-4-7961-6441-2　Printed in Japan

駿台文庫 Web サイト
https://www.sundaibunko.jp

外国語　解答用紙

マーク例

良い例	悪い例
●	⊗ ⊙ ◐ ◯

③
- 1科目だけマークしなさい。
- 解答科目欄が無くマーク又は複数マークの場合は、0点となることがあります。

解答科目欄

英語（リーディング）	ドイツ語	フランス語	中国語	韓国語
◯	◯	◯	◯	◯

注意事項

1　訂正は、消しゴムできれいに消し、消しくずを残してはいけません。
2　所定欄以外にはマークしたり、記入したりしてはいけません。
3　汚したり、折りまげたりしてはいけません。

① 受験番号を記入し、その下のマーク欄にマークしなさい。

受験番号欄

千位	百位	十位	一位	英字
－	⓪	⓪	⓪	Ⓐ
①	①	①	①	Ⓑ
②	②	②	②	Ⓒ
③	③	③	③	Ⓗ
④	④	④	④	Ⓚ
⑤	⑤	⑤	⑤	Ⓜ
⑥	⑥	⑥	⑥	Ⓡ
⑦	⑦	⑦	⑦	Ⓤ
⑧	⑧	⑧	⑧	Ⓧ
⑨	⑨	⑨	⑨	Ⓨ
－	－	－	－	Ⓩ

② 氏名・フリガナ、試験場コードを記入しなさい。

フリガナ	
氏　名	

試験場コード	十万位	万位	千位	百位	十位	一位

駿　台　文　庫

解答欄（解答番号 1〜25）

解答番号	1	2	3	4	5	6	7	8	9
1	①	②	③	④	⑤	⑥	⑦	⑧	⑨
2	①	②	③	④	⑤	⑥	⑦	⑧	⑨
3	①	②	③	④	⑤	⑥	⑦	⑧	⑨
4	①	②	③	④	⑤	⑥	⑦	⑧	⑨
5	①	②	③	④	⑤	⑥	⑦	⑧	⑨
6	①	②	③	④	⑤	⑥	⑦	⑧	⑨
7	①	②	③	④	⑤	⑥	⑦	⑧	⑨
8	①	②	③	④	⑤	⑥	⑦	⑧	⑨
9	①	②	③	④	⑤	⑥	⑦	⑧	⑨
10	①	②	③	④	⑤	⑥	⑦	⑧	⑨
11	①	②	③	④	⑤	⑥	⑦	⑧	⑨
12	①	②	③	④	⑤	⑥	⑦	⑧	⑨
13	①	②	③	④	⑤	⑥	⑦	⑧	⑨
14	①	②	③	④	⑤	⑥	⑦	⑧	⑨
15	①	②	③	④	⑤	⑥	⑦	⑧	⑨
16	①	②	③	④	⑤	⑥	⑦	⑧	⑨
17	①	②	③	④	⑤	⑥	⑦	⑧	⑨
18	①	②	③	④	⑤	⑥	⑦	⑧	⑨
19	①	②	③	④	⑤	⑥	⑦	⑧	⑨
20	①	②	③	④	⑤	⑥	⑦	⑧	⑨
21	①	②	③	④	⑤	⑥	⑦	⑧	⑨
22	①	②	③	④	⑤	⑥	⑦	⑧	⑨
23	①	②	③	④	⑤	⑥	⑦	⑧	⑨
24	①	②	③	④	⑤	⑥	⑦	⑧	⑨
25	①	②	③	④	⑤	⑥	⑦	⑧	⑨

解答欄（解答番号 26〜50）

解答番号	1	2	3	4	5	6	7	8	9
26	①	②	③	④	⑤	⑥	⑦	⑧	⑨
27	①	②	③	④	⑤	⑥	⑦	⑧	⑨
28	①	②	③	④	⑤	⑥	⑦	⑧	⑨
29	①	②	③	④	⑤	⑥	⑦	⑧	⑨
30	①	②	③	④	⑤	⑥	⑦	⑧	⑨
31	①	②	③	④	⑤	⑥	⑦	⑧	⑨
32	①	②	③	④	⑤	⑥	⑦	⑧	⑨
33	①	②	③	④	⑤	⑥	⑦	⑧	⑨
34	①	②	③	④	⑤	⑥	⑦	⑧	⑨
35	①	②	③	④	⑤	⑥	⑦	⑧	⑨
36	①	②	③	④	⑤	⑥	⑦	⑧	⑨
37	①	②	③	④	⑤	⑥	⑦	⑧	⑨
38	①	②	③	④	⑤	⑥	⑦	⑧	⑨
39	①	②	③	④	⑤	⑥	⑦	⑧	⑨
40	①	②	③	④	⑤	⑥	⑦	⑧	⑨
41	①	②	③	④	⑤	⑥	⑦	⑧	⑨
42	①	②	③	④	⑤	⑥	⑦	⑧	⑨
43	①	②	③	④	⑤	⑥	⑦	⑧	⑨
44	①	②	③	④	⑤	⑥	⑦	⑧	⑨
45	①	②	③	④	⑤	⑥	⑦	⑧	⑨
46	①	②	③	④	⑤	⑥	⑦	⑧	⑨
47	①	②	③	④	⑤	⑥	⑦	⑧	⑨
48	①	②	③	④	⑤	⑥	⑦	⑧	⑨
49	①	②	③	④	⑤	⑥	⑦	⑧	⑨
50	①	②	③	④	⑤	⑥	⑦	⑧	⑨

解答欄（解答番号 51〜75）

解答番号	1	2	3	4	5	6	7	8	9
51	①	②	③	④	⑤	⑥	⑦	⑧	⑨
52	①	②	③	④	⑤	⑥	⑦	⑧	⑨
53	①	②	③	④	⑤	⑥	⑦	⑧	⑨
54	①	②	③	④	⑤	⑥	⑦	⑧	⑨
55	①	②	③	④	⑤	⑥	⑦	⑧	⑨
56	①	②	③	④	⑤	⑥	⑦	⑧	⑨
57	①	②	③	④	⑤	⑥	⑦	⑧	⑨
58	①	②	③	④	⑤	⑥	⑦	⑧	⑨
59	①	②	③	④	⑤	⑥	⑦	⑧	⑨
60	①	②	③	④	⑤	⑥	⑦	⑧	⑨
61	①	②	③	④	⑤	⑥	⑦	⑧	⑨
62	①	②	③	④	⑤	⑥	⑦	⑧	⑨
63	①	②	③	④	⑤	⑥	⑦	⑧	⑨
64	①	②	③	④	⑤	⑥	⑦	⑧	⑨
65	①	②	③	④	⑤	⑥	⑦	⑧	⑨
66	①	②	③	④	⑤	⑥	⑦	⑧	⑨
67	①	②	③	④	⑤	⑥	⑦	⑧	⑨
68	①	②	③	④	⑤	⑥	⑦	⑧	⑨
69	①	②	③	④	⑤	⑥	⑦	⑧	⑨
70	①	②	③	④	⑤	⑥	⑦	⑧	⑨
71	①	②	③	④	⑤	⑥	⑦	⑧	⑨
72	①	②	③	④	⑤	⑥	⑦	⑧	⑨
73	①	②	③	④	⑤	⑥	⑦	⑧	⑨
74	①	②	③	④	⑤	⑥	⑦	⑧	⑨
75	①	②	③	④	⑤	⑥	⑦	⑧	⑨

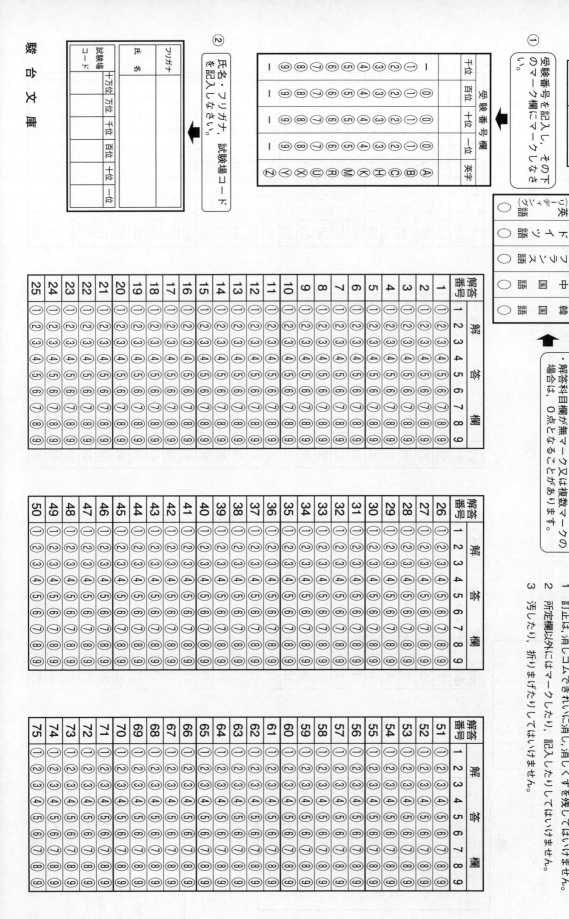

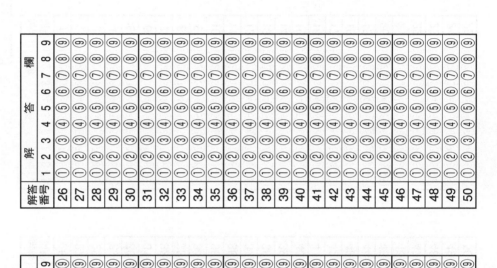

外国語　解答用紙

マーク例
良い例	悪い例
●	⊗ ◑ ◯

① 受験番号を記入し、その下のマーク欄にマークしなさい。

受験番号欄

千位	百位	十位	一位	英字
－	⓪	⓪	⓪	Ⓐ
①	①	①	①	Ⓑ
②	②	②	②	Ⓒ
③	③	③	③	Ⓗ
④	④	④	④	Ⓚ
⑤	⑤	⑤	⑤	Ⓜ
⑥	⑥	⑥	⑥	Ⓡ
⑦	⑦	⑦	⑦	Ⓤ
⑧	⑧	⑧	⑧	Ⓧ
⑨	⑨	⑨	⑨	Ⓨ
				Ⓩ

② 氏名・フリガナ、試験場コードを記入しなさい。

フリガナ	
氏　名	
試験場コード	十万位 万位 千位 百位 十位 一位

解答科目欄

英語	ドイツ語	フランス語	中国語	韓国語
○	○	○	○	○

③
・1科目だけマークしなさい。解答科目欄が無マーク又は複数マークの場合は、0点となることがあります。

注意事項

1 訂正は、消しゴムできれいに消し、消しくずを残してはいけません。
2 所定欄以外にはマークしたり、記入したりしてはいけません。
3 汚したり、折りまげたりしてはいけません。

解答番号	解答欄 1 2 3 4 5 6 7 8 9
1	① ② ③ ④ ⑤ ⑥ ⑦ ⑧ ⑨
2	① ② ③ ④ ⑤ ⑥ ⑦ ⑧ ⑨
3	① ② ③ ④ ⑤ ⑥ ⑦ ⑧ ⑨
4	① ② ③ ④ ⑤ ⑥ ⑦ ⑧ ⑨
5	① ② ③ ④ ⑤ ⑥ ⑦ ⑧ ⑨
6	① ② ③ ④ ⑤ ⑥ ⑦ ⑧ ⑨
7	① ② ③ ④ ⑤ ⑥ ⑦ ⑧ ⑨
8	① ② ③ ④ ⑤ ⑥ ⑦ ⑧ ⑨
9	① ② ③ ④ ⑤ ⑥ ⑦ ⑧ ⑨
10	① ② ③ ④ ⑤ ⑥ ⑦ ⑧ ⑨
11	① ② ③ ④ ⑤ ⑥ ⑦ ⑧ ⑨
12	① ② ③ ④ ⑤ ⑥ ⑦ ⑧ ⑨
13	① ② ③ ④ ⑤ ⑥ ⑦ ⑧ ⑨
14	① ② ③ ④ ⑤ ⑥ ⑦ ⑧ ⑨
15	① ② ③ ④ ⑤ ⑥ ⑦ ⑧ ⑨
16	① ② ③ ④ ⑤ ⑥ ⑦ ⑧ ⑨
17	① ② ③ ④ ⑤ ⑥ ⑦ ⑧ ⑨
18	① ② ③ ④ ⑤ ⑥ ⑦ ⑧ ⑨
19	① ② ③ ④ ⑤ ⑥ ⑦ ⑧ ⑨
20	① ② ③ ④ ⑤ ⑥ ⑦ ⑧ ⑨
21	① ② ③ ④ ⑤ ⑥ ⑦ ⑧ ⑨
22	① ② ③ ④ ⑤ ⑥ ⑦ ⑧ ⑨
23	① ② ③ ④ ⑤ ⑥ ⑦ ⑧ ⑨
24	① ② ③ ④ ⑤ ⑥ ⑦ ⑧ ⑨
25	① ② ③ ④ ⑤ ⑥ ⑦ ⑧ ⑨

解答番号	解答欄 1 2 3 4 5 6 7 8 9
26	① ② ③ ④ ⑤ ⑥ ⑦ ⑧ ⑨
27	① ② ③ ④ ⑤ ⑥ ⑦ ⑧ ⑨
28	① ② ③ ④ ⑤ ⑥ ⑦ ⑧ ⑨
29	① ② ③ ④ ⑤ ⑥ ⑦ ⑧ ⑨
30	① ② ③ ④ ⑤ ⑥ ⑦ ⑧ ⑨
31	① ② ③ ④ ⑤ ⑥ ⑦ ⑧ ⑨
32	① ② ③ ④ ⑤ ⑥ ⑦ ⑧ ⑨
33	① ② ③ ④ ⑤ ⑥ ⑦ ⑧ ⑨
34	① ② ③ ④ ⑤ ⑥ ⑦ ⑧ ⑨
35	① ② ③ ④ ⑤ ⑥ ⑦ ⑧ ⑨
36	① ② ③ ④ ⑤ ⑥ ⑦ ⑧ ⑨
37	① ② ③ ④ ⑤ ⑥ ⑦ ⑧ ⑨
38	① ② ③ ④ ⑤ ⑥ ⑦ ⑧ ⑨
39	① ② ③ ④ ⑤ ⑥ ⑦ ⑧ ⑨
40	① ② ③ ④ ⑤ ⑥ ⑦ ⑧ ⑨
41	① ② ③ ④ ⑤ ⑥ ⑦ ⑧ ⑨
42	① ② ③ ④ ⑤ ⑥ ⑦ ⑧ ⑨
43	① ② ③ ④ ⑤ ⑥ ⑦ ⑧ ⑨
44	① ② ③ ④ ⑤ ⑥ ⑦ ⑧ ⑨
45	① ② ③ ④ ⑤ ⑥ ⑦ ⑧ ⑨
46	① ② ③ ④ ⑤ ⑥ ⑦ ⑧ ⑨
47	① ② ③ ④ ⑤ ⑥ ⑦ ⑧ ⑨
48	① ② ③ ④ ⑤ ⑥ ⑦ ⑧ ⑨
49	① ② ③ ④ ⑤ ⑥ ⑦ ⑧ ⑨
50	① ② ③ ④ ⑤ ⑥ ⑦ ⑧ ⑨

解答番号	解答欄 1 2 3 4 5 6 7 8 9
51	① ② ③ ④ ⑤ ⑥ ⑦ ⑧ ⑨
52	① ② ③ ④ ⑤ ⑥ ⑦ ⑧ ⑨
53	① ② ③ ④ ⑤ ⑥ ⑦ ⑧ ⑨
54	① ② ③ ④ ⑤ ⑥ ⑦ ⑧ ⑨
55	① ② ③ ④ ⑤ ⑥ ⑦ ⑧ ⑨
56	① ② ③ ④ ⑤ ⑥ ⑦ ⑧ ⑨
57	① ② ③ ④ ⑤ ⑥ ⑦ ⑧ ⑨
58	① ② ③ ④ ⑤ ⑥ ⑦ ⑧ ⑨
59	① ② ③ ④ ⑤ ⑥ ⑦ ⑧ ⑨
60	① ② ③ ④ ⑤ ⑥ ⑦ ⑧ ⑨
61	① ② ③ ④ ⑤ ⑥ ⑦ ⑧ ⑨
62	① ② ③ ④ ⑤ ⑥ ⑦ ⑧ ⑨
63	① ② ③ ④ ⑤ ⑥ ⑦ ⑧ ⑨
64	① ② ③ ④ ⑤ ⑥ ⑦ ⑧ ⑨
65	① ② ③ ④ ⑤ ⑥ ⑦ ⑧ ⑨
66	① ② ③ ④ ⑤ ⑥ ⑦ ⑧ ⑨
67	① ② ③ ④ ⑤ ⑥ ⑦ ⑧ ⑨
68	① ② ③ ④ ⑤ ⑥ ⑦ ⑧ ⑨
69	① ② ③ ④ ⑤ ⑥ ⑦ ⑧ ⑨
70	① ② ③ ④ ⑤ ⑥ ⑦ ⑧ ⑨
71	① ② ③ ④ ⑤ ⑥ ⑦ ⑧ ⑨
72	① ② ③ ④ ⑤ ⑥ ⑦ ⑧ ⑨
73	① ② ③ ④ ⑤ ⑥ ⑦ ⑧ ⑨
74	① ② ③ ④ ⑤ ⑥ ⑦ ⑧ ⑨
75	① ② ③ ④ ⑤ ⑥ ⑦ ⑧ ⑨

駿台文庫

外国語 解答用紙

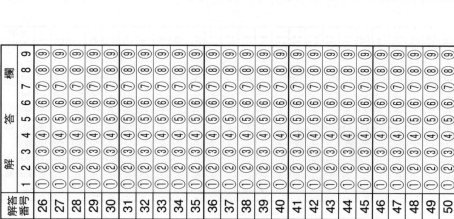

駿台文庫

マーク例

良い例	悪い例
●	⦸ ⊗ ◕ ○

① 受験番号を記入し、その下のマーク欄にマークしなさい。

受験番号欄

千位	百位	十位	一位	英字

② 氏名・フリガナ、試験場コードを記入しなさい。

フリガナ					
氏名					
試験場コード	十万位	万位	千位	百位	十位	一位

解答科目欄

○ 英語
○ ドイツ語
○ フランス語
○ 中国語
○ 韓国語

外国語　解答用紙

③
・1科目だけマークしなさい。
・解答科目欄が無マーク又は複数マークの場合は、0点となることがあります。

注意事項

1　訂正は、消しゴムできれいに消し、消しくずを残してはいけません。
2　所定欄以外にはマーク、記入したりしてはいけません。
3　汚したり、折りまげたりしてはいけません。

解答番号 1〜25（解答欄 1〜9）

解答番号 26〜50（解答欄 1〜9）

解答番号 51〜75（解答欄 1〜9）

外国語　解答用紙

マーク例

良い例	悪い例
●	⦸ ⊗ ◑ ◯

① 受験番号を記入し、その下のマーク欄にマークしなさい。

受験番号欄

千位	百位	十位	一位	英字
	⓪	⓪	⓪	Ⓐ
①	①	①	①	Ⓑ
②	②	②	②	Ⓒ
③	③	③	③	Ⓗ
④	④	④	④	Ⓚ
⑤	⑤	⑤	⑤	Ⓜ
⑥	⑥	⑥	⑥	Ⓡ
⑦	⑦	⑦	⑦	Ⓤ
⑧	⑧	⑧	⑧	Ⓧ
⑨	⑨	⑨	⑨	Ⓨ
—	—	—	—	Ⓩ

② 氏名・フリガナ、試験場コードを記入しなさい。

フリガナ						
氏　名						
試験場コード	十万位	万位	千位	百位	十位	一位

③

解答科目欄

	英語	ドイツ語	フランス語	中国語	韓国語
◯	◯	◯	◯	◯	◯

注意事項

1　訂正は、消しゴムできれいに消し、消しくずを残してはいけません。

2　所定欄以外にはマーク又は記入したりしてはいけません。

3　汚したり、折り曲げたりしてはいけません。

・1科目だけマークしなさい。
・解答科目欄が無マーク又は複数マークの場合は、0点となることがあります。

解答欄（1〜25／26〜50／51〜75）

各解答番号 1〜75 について、選択肢 1 2 3 4 5 6 7 8 9 のマーク欄。

駿台文庫

外国語　解答用紙

マーク例

良い例	悪い例
●	⊗ ● ◐ ○

① 受験番号を記入し、その下のマーク欄にマークしなさい。

受験番号欄

| 千位 | 百位 | 十位 | 一位 | 英字 |

③ ・1科目だけマークしなさい。
・解答科目欄がマーク又は複数マークの場合は、0点となることがあります。

解答科目欄

リーディング英語	ドイツ語	フランス語	中国語	韓国語
○	○	○	○	○

② 氏名・フリガナ、試験場コードを記入しなさい。

フリガナ	
氏名	
試験場コード	十万位 万位 千位 百位 十位 一位

注意事項

1　訂正は、消しゴムできれいに消し、消しくずを残してはいけません。
2　所定欄以外にはマークしたり、記入したりしてはいけません。
3　汚したり、折りまげたりしてはいけません。

駿　台　文　庫

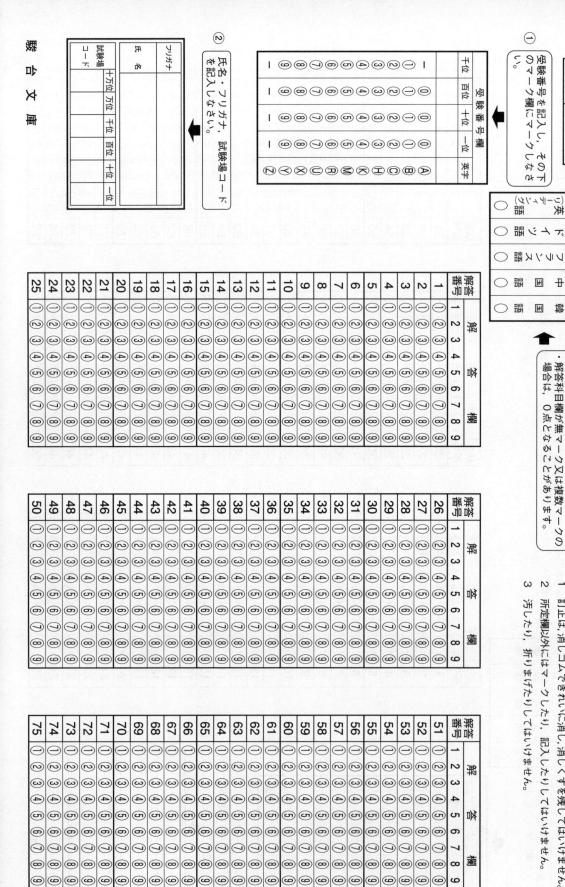

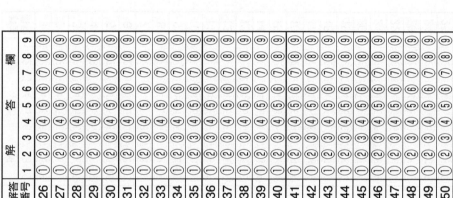

駿台文庫

マーク例
良い例	悪い例
●	◐ ⊗ ◖ ○

① 受験番号を記入し、その下のマーク欄にマークしなさい。

受験番号欄

千位	百位	十位	一位	英字

② 氏名・フリガナ、試験場コードを記入しなさい。

フリガナ	
氏名	
試験場コード	十万位 万位 千位 百位 十位 一位

解答科目欄

英ドイツ語	フランス語	中国語	韓国語
リーディング	○	○	○

③ ・1科目だけマークしなさい。
・解答科目欄が無マーク又は複数マークの場合は、0点となることがあります。

外国語 解答用紙

注意事項
1 訂正は、消しゴムできれいに消し、消しくずを残してはいけません。
2 所定欄以外にはマークしたり、記入したりしてはいけません。
3 汚したり、折りまげたりしてはいけません。

外国語 解答用紙

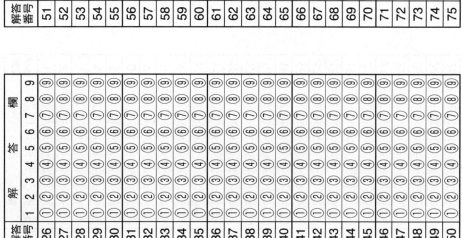

外国語　解答用紙

マーク例

良い例	悪い例
●	◑ ✕ ● ○

① 受験番号を記入し、その下のマーク欄にマークしなさい。

受験番号欄

千位	百位	十位	一位	英字

② 氏名・フリガナ、試験場コードを記入しなさい。

フリガナ							
氏　名							
試験場コード	十万位	万位	千位	百位	十位	一位	

解答科目欄

○ 英語	○ 中国語
○ フランス語	○ 韓国語
○ ドイツ語	

③
- 1科目だけマークしなさい。
- 解答科目欄が無マーク又は複数マークの場合は、0点となることがあります。

注意事項

1. 訂正は、消しゴムできれいに消し、消しくずを残してはいけません。
2. 所定欄以外にはマークしたり、記入したりしてはいけません。
3. 汚したり、折りまげたりしてはいけません。

駿　台　文　庫

外国語 解答用紙

外国語　解答用紙

注意事項

1　訂正は、消しゴムできれいに消し、消しくずを残してはいけません。
2　所定欄以外にはマーク又は記入したりしてはいけません。
3　汚したり、折りまげたりしてはいけません。

- ・1科目だけマークしなさい。
- ・解答科目欄が無マーク又は複数マークの場合は、0点となることがあります。

解答科目欄

	英語	ドイツ語	フランス語	中国語	韓国語
リーディング	○	○	○	○	○

マーク例

良い例	悪い例
●	⊘ ⊗ ◑

① 受験番号を記入し、その下のマーク欄にマークしなさい。

受験番号欄

千位	百位	十位	一位	英字
	⓪	⓪	⓪	Ⓐ Ⓑ Ⓒ
①	①	①	①	Ⓓ Ⓔ Ⓕ
②	②	②	②	Ⓖ Ⓗ Ⓘ
③	③	③	③	Ⓙ Ⓚ Ⓛ
④	④	④	④	Ⓜ Ⓝ Ⓞ
⑤	⑤	⑤	⑤	Ⓟ Ⓠ Ⓡ
⑥	⑥	⑥	⑥	Ⓢ Ⓣ Ⓤ
⑦	⑦	⑦	⑦	Ⓥ Ⓦ Ⓧ
⑧	⑧	⑧	⑧	Ⓨ Ⓩ
⑨	⑨	⑨	⑨	

② 氏名・フリガナ、試験場コードを記入しなさい。

フリガナ	
氏名	
試験場コード	十万位　万位　千位　百位　十位　一位

駿台文庫

駿台

2024
大学入学共通テスト
実戦問題集

英 語 リーディング
【解答・解説編】

駿台文庫編

直前チェック総整理

　共通テスト・リーディング問題の特徴は，英語の読解力そのものというよりむしろ，読解力をツールとして正解に必要な情報を引き出す「情報検索能力」にある。そのためには本文とイラストや図表といった視覚情報のさまざまな箇所に目を向けなければならず，その正確さと迅速さが高得点への鍵となろう。以下で2022年に出題された3つの問題を通して「情報処理」の過程を具体的に見ていくことで，注意するべきポイントを明示し，共通テスト対策における必要不可欠なステップとしていきたい。

　　　　　　　　　　　　　　　情報収集能力

まず，2022年度第4問を検討してみる。

2022年度（本試）第4問：2つのブログ記事とイラストおよび図表からなる
　　　　　　　問5：最安値の電子レンジが購入できる店と5年保証付きの最安値のテレビが購入できる店を問う問題

設問文　　You have decided to buy microwave from [28] because it is the cheapest. You have decided to buy a television from [29] because it is the cheapest with a five-year warranty. (Choose one for each box from options ①～④.)「あなたは最も値段が安いという理由で [28] で電子レンジを購入することにした。あなたは5年保証つきで最も値段が安いという理由で [29] でテレビを購入することにした。（それぞれの空欄に対し選択肢①～④から1つずつ選べ）」

　　① Cut Price　　　「カットプライス」
　　② Great Buy　　　「グレートバイ」
　　③ Second Hand　　「セカンドハンド」
　　④ Value Saver　　「バリューセーバー」

---

[28] （電子レンジを最安値で購入できる店）

＜第1段階：イラストと図表に掲載されている電子レンジの価格＞
　それぞれの店における電子レンジの価格は以下の通り。

① 「カットプライス」（シンディのブログに掲載された図表）：$88
② 「グレートバイ」（シンディのブログに掲載された図表）：$90
③ 「セカンドハンド」（レンのブログに掲載されたチラシのイラスト）：$85
　（イラストと図表に掲載されている価格だけを比較すると最安値）
④ 「バリューセーバー」（シンディのブログに掲載された図表）：$95

— 英R1 —

レンのブログに掲載された図表　　　　シンディのブログに掲載された図表

<第2段階：本文中の割引情報>
　シンディのブログの第4段落第5文で，グレートバイでは学生証を提示すれば図表に掲載されている価格から10%割引される，と述べられている。リード文から「あなた」はロビンソン大学の新入生であるとわかるので，この学生割引が適用され，グレートバイでは電子レンジを提示価格 $90 の 10% 引き＝$81 で購入できることになる。この価格は ③「セカンドハンド」の $85 を下回って最安値となるので，正解は ② 「グレートバイ」となる。

[29]　（テレビを 5 年保証付きの最安値で購入できる店）

<第1段階：イラストと図表に掲載されているテレビの価格>
　それぞれの店におけるテレビの価格は以下の通り。

① 「カットプライス」（シンディのブログに掲載された図表）：$300
② 「グレートバイ」（シンディのブログに掲載された図表）：$295
③ 「セカンドハンド」（レンのブログに掲載されたチラシのイラスト）：$250
　　（5年保証付きという条件を抜きにして，イラストと図表に掲載されている価格だけを比較すると最安値）
④ 「バリューセーバー」（シンディの記事に掲載された図表）：$305

レンのブログに掲載された図表　　　　シンディのブログに掲載された図表

<第2段階：5年保証付きという条件を加味する>

それぞれの店における保証に関する条件は以下の通り。

① 「カットプライス」：シンディのブログの第4段落最終文で，カットプライスでは5年保証をつけるには商品ごとに $10 払わなければならない，と述べられていることから，5年保証付きのテレビの価格は提示価格 $300 + $10 = $310 ということになる。

② 「グレートバイ」：シンディのブログの第4段落第5文で，グレートバイではすべての家庭用品に1年保証を付与している，と述べられているだけで5年保証に関する言及はないために条件から外れる。

③ 「セカンドハンド」：セカンドハンドはレンのブログで紹介されているが，保証に関する言及はないために条件から外れる。

④ 「バリューセーバー」：シンディのブログの第4段落第3～4文で，バリューセーバーはすべての家庭用品に無料で1年保証を付与し，さらに $300 以上の商品は保証期間をさらに4年延長している，と述べられている。バリューセーバーのテレビの提示価格は $305 であるので，この特典が利用できることになり，保証期間が1年から4年延長されて5年となり，価格は提示価格である $305 のままということになる。この価格は①「カットプライス」の $310 を下回って最安値となるので，正解は④「バリューセーバー」となる。

> Note that warranties are available for all items. So, if anything stops working, replacing it will be straightforward. Value Saver provides one-year warranties on all household goods for free. If the item is over $300, the warranty is extended by four years. Great Buy provides one-year warranties on all household goods, and students with proof of enrollment at a school get 10% off the prices listed on the table above. Warranties at Cut Price are not provided for free. You have to pay $10 per item for a five-year warranty.
>
> Things go fast! Don't wait or you'll miss out!

第2段階

（シンディのブログ第4段落）

2021年度（第1日程）第3問Aはさらに手の込んだ問題となっていたので，こちらもあわせて検討してみたい。

2021年度　第3問A：Q&A形式になっている英語の本文とイラストからなる
（第1日程）　　問2：バクストン空港からホリーツリーホテルまで最も速く行く方法を問う問題

設問文　　　You are departing on public transport from the airport at 2.00 pm on 15 March 2021. What is the fastest way to get to the hotel?「あなたは2021年3月15日の午後2時に空港から公共の交通機関に乗って出発するところだ。ホテルまで最も速く行く方法はどれか」

① By express bus and city bus　「高速バスと市バス」
② By express bus and on foot　「高速バスと徒歩」
③ By underground and city bus　「地下鉄と市バス」
④ By underground and on foot　「地下鉄と徒歩」

— 英R3 —

＜第1段階：アクセス図＞

　バクストン空港からホリーツリーホテルまでの交通アクセスを図示したイラストがあることから，まずはイラスト内で示されている情報を検討する。

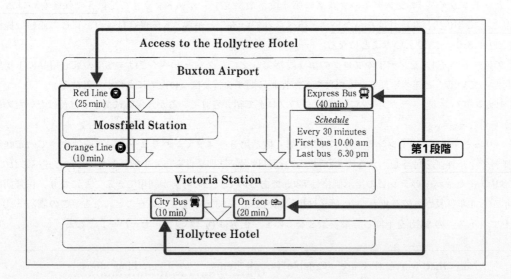

① 高速バスでヴィクトリア駅まで40分，ヴィクトリア駅からホテルまで市バスで10分，合計 50分。
② 高速バスでヴィクトリア駅まで40分，ヴィクトリア駅からホテルまで徒歩で20分，合計 60分。
③ 地下鉄でモスフィールド駅まで25分，さらに地下鉄を乗り換えてヴィクトリア駅まで10分，ヴィクトリア駅からホテルまで市バスで10分，合計 45分（この時点で最速）。
④ 地下鉄でモスフィールド駅まで25分，さらに地下鉄を乗り換えてヴィクトリア駅まで10分，ヴィクトリア駅からホテルまで徒歩で20分，合計 55分。

＜第2段階：本文中の道路工事情報＞

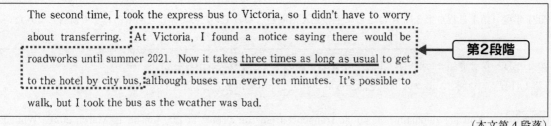

(本文第4段落)

　設問文に「2021年3月15日」と日付が記されているが，本文から，2021年夏までは道路工事が行われるために市バスを使うと通常よりも3倍の時間（30分）がかかる，ということがわかる。よって市バスを利用する選択肢①と③には20分加算されることになる。

① 50分 + 20分 = 70分
② 60分
③ 45分 + 20分 = 65分
④ 55分（この時点で最速）

　この第2段階までを考慮すると最速の行き方は④となり，本試で正解として④をマークした受験生は少なくなかったのではないかと思われる。センター試験でも複数箇所の情報統合は2箇所であることが多かったために，その印象が影響を及ぼしたということもあるかも知れない。だが，共通テストで大学入試センターが用意したハードルはこれだけにとどまらなかったのである。

＜第3段階：本文中の地下鉄乗り換え情報＞

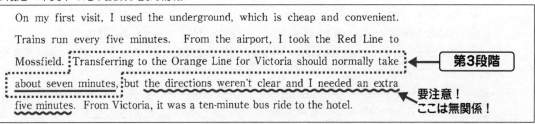

(本文第3段落)

　本文から，地下鉄の乗り換えには通常7分ほどかかる，ということがわかる。よって地下鉄の乗り換えを含む選択肢③と④には7分加算され，この時点での最速の選択肢は②となり，これが正解となる。

① 70分
② 60分（この時点で最速）
③ 65分 + 7分 = 72分
④ 55分 + 7分 = 62分

　大学入試センターが用意した「これでもか」というほどの仕掛けはさらにあり，乗り換え時間に関する記述の直後では，このQ&A解答者のアレックス（Alex）の場合，乗り換え案内がはっきりしなかったためにさらに5分多くかかった，と述べられていた。しかしこれはアレックスの個人的な経験に属するもので，正解を得るのに必要な情報ではなく，結果としてかなりやっかいな情報検索が求められたことになる。

> ## 情報判断能力

2021 年度　第 3 問 B：交換留学生のクラスメートが学校新聞に書いたボランティア募集の記事
（第 1 日程）　　問 1：交換留学生が参加することになった，ある施設を維持するための募金活動にまつわる出来事の順番を問う問題

設問文　Put the following events （① ～ ④） into the order in which they happened.

「以下の出来事（① ～ ④）を発生した順番に並べよ」

① Sarah attended a centre event.　　　　　「セーラはセンターのあるイベントに参加した」

② Sarah donated money to the centre.　　　「セーラはセンターにお金を寄付した」

③ Sarah made a suggestion to Katy.　　　　「セーラはケイティにある提案をした」

④ The campaigners asked the mayor for help.「募金運動をしている人たちは町長に援助を求めた」

I learnt about the problem a few months ago. While shopping in town, I saw some people taking part in a fund-raising campaign. I spoke to the leader of the campaign, Katy, who explained the situation. She thanked me when I **選択肢②** donated some money. She told me that they had asked the town **要注意！過去完了（大過去）！** mayor for financial assistance, but their request had been rejected. **選択肢④** They had no choice but to start

Last month, I attended a lecture on art at the centre. Again, I saw people trying to raise money, and I decided to help. **選択肢①** They were happy when I joined them in asking passers-by for donations. We tried hard, but there were too few of us to collect much money. With a tearful face, Katy told me that they wouldn't be able to use the building much longer. I felt the need to do **選択肢③** something more. Then, the idea came to me that other students might be willing to help. Katy was delighted to hear this.

（本文第 3・4 段落）

　本文で述べられている出来事を追っていくと，数カ月前のことを述べた第 3 段落で「私［交換留学生のセーラ］がいくらかのお金を寄付すると彼女［募金運動のリーダーであるケイティ］は私に感謝してくれた（She thanked me when I donated some money.）」と述べられており，これが選択肢②にあたると判断できる。その直後の文には「ケイティが私に語ったところによると，彼女たちは町長に経済的援助を求めたが…（She told me that they had asked the town mayor for financial assistance, but …）」とあり，この内容が選択肢④と対応するので，早合点して②→④と続くと判断してしまった受験生も少なくなかったかもしれないが，もちろん had asked は過去完了形で大過去を示しているので，実際は④→②という順番になる。さらに，第 4 段落の冒頭（Last month, I …）で述べられている「先月，私はセンターの美術に関する講演に参加した」という内容が選択肢①にあたり，最後の 2 つの文（Then, the idea …）（Katy was delighted …）で述べられている「そのとき，他の学生が進んで援助してくれるかもしれないという考え

— 英 R 6 —

が私の頭に浮かんだ。そのことを聞いてケイティは喜んだ」ということが選択肢③を示唆していると推測できるので，正解は④→②→①→③という順番になるとわかる。

センター試験から共通テストに変わって文法問題がなくなったが，今後もリーディング問題においてこのような形で文法的知識が問われていくのではないだろうか。

以上実際の問題に沿って具体的に見てきたように，共通テストのリーディング問題の特徴が読解力をツールとしての「情報検索能力」にあることはわかっていただけただろうか。こうした問題への対策としては，「複数箇所の情報を統合する問題が出題される可能性が高い」という，さらに「検索した情報を正しく判断することを求める問題が出題される可能性が高く，その中には文法要素も含まれうる」という意識を常に持ち，十分な練習を積んでいくことが重要だろう。相手の出方を知り，戦略を立て，十分な練習を積むことでこそ，本番でベストパフォーマンスを発揮することができるだろう。諸君の健闘を心から祈る。

以下では，読解力の養成に役立つポイントと重要な語彙知識を紹介しておく。ぜひ力をつけてほしい。

パラグラフ（段落）について

「パラグラフ」は，書き手が伝えようとする内容を，読者に効率よく伝えるために，いくつかの文を1つのまとまりとして示したものである。書き手はパラグラフを適切に並べることで，自分の伝えたいことが読者に分かりやすく伝わるように工夫する。

1つのパラグラフは，ある**主題**（topic）に関してまとまりのある内容となっており，その主題が何であり，そして，それについてどのような説明や主張をしているかを捉えることが大切である。あるパラグラフの主題を含む文は**トピック・センテンス**と呼ばれる。トピック・センテンスは，パラグラフの冒頭にあることが多いが，常に決まって冒頭にあるわけではないので，固定した考え方はしないで，書かれている英文に即して判断する必要がある。

パラグラフの主題は，1つ1つのパラグラフで異なるという場合もないわけではないが，いくつかのパラグラフがまとまってある主題について述べている場合の方が多い。その場合，そのまとまった複数のパラグラフ間の内容的な関係を捉えることが必要になる。その関係は，例えば，1つめのパラグラフで概略を説明し，後ろのパラグラフでその具体例を紹介したり，1つめのパラグラフに出した主題について，それに続くパラグラフで別の側面から説明を加えたり，さらに掘り下げた内容を提示したりするなど，具体的には様々である。

1つの主題について内容的なまとまりのある複数のパラグラフ間や，新たに別の主題を提示するパラグラフの出だしには，次項目の「談話の展開を明示する語句」にあるそれぞれの語句や，another, the same, similar, such などの語が新たなパラグラフの最初の文で用いられて，パラグラフ間の内容的な関係を捉える手がかりとなることが多いので，それらの語句に着目する読み方ができるようにしたい。

談話の展開を明示する語句

「談話（ディスコース）」とは，いくつかの文が連なったもので，全体としてまとまった内容を持っている。談話を構成する文から文への流れが円滑に進み，その内容が効果的に伝達されるために，「談話の展開を明示する語句」が用いられることが多い。これらの語句は**ディス**コース・マーカーと呼ばれる。それぞれのディスコース・マーカーの意味を理解することで，談話の展開が把握しやすくなる。

以下のリストに挙げたものは，主に書き言葉で用いられる代表的なディスコース・マーカーである。<…>に意味関係を，「…」に日本語訳を示している。なお，これらの語句は文頭や主語の後ろなど，文の前の方に置かれることが多い。

<追加> 「さらに，また」
besides, furthermore, moreover, in addition, also, what is more, on top of that
<逆接> 「しかし，それでも」
however, nevertheless, nonetheless, still, yet, in spite of this
<対比> 「いっぽう，これに対して」
on the other hand, in contrast
<譲歩> 「たしかに…だが」
to be sure, certainly, it is true, of course
<論理> 「したがって，だから」
therefore, thus, then, so, hence, as a result, consequently, accordingly
<例示> 「例えば」
for example, for instance, say, such as ...
<列挙> 「まず第一に（など）」
first(ly), second(ly), lastly, finally, in the first place, to begin with, for one thing
<要約> 「要するに」
in conclusion, in short, to sum up, in a word, briefly
<類似> 「同様に」
similarly, in the same way
<言い換え> 「言い換えると，すなわち」
that is, in other words
<焦点・強調> 「とりわけ，特に」
in particular, above all, especially, more importantly
<事実への言及> 「実を言うと」
in fact, actually, as a matter of fact, to tell the truth
<話題の転換> 「ところで」
by the way, incidentally
<その他>
after all「なにしろ…だから」, on the contrary「とんでもない，それどころか」

名詞について

A．可算名詞と不可算名詞

英語の名詞には可算名詞と不可算名詞があり，それぞれの意味合いと用法の違いに慣れておくことは大切である。また，常に可算名詞または不可算名詞である名詞がある一方で，意味に応じて可算名詞としても不可算名詞としても用いられる名詞が多いことも，しっかり理解する必要がある。

1．可算名詞

(a) ある一定の形を持ち，ひとつひとつ目に見える（手に取れる）ものを表す名詞

apple, boy, cat, doctor, hotel, letter, machine, poem, table, tree など

(b) 具体的な形はないが，ひとつひとつ個別に捉えられるものを表す名詞

day, dream, game, job, mile, promise, song, story, village など

(c) 人やものの集合体を表す名詞

audience, class, committee, crowd, family, team など

可算名詞の用法

・単数形と複数形がある。
・単数形は，意味に応じて，その前に冠詞 (a / the)，所有格，this / that / one などを伴い，単独では用いられない。複数形は，一般的に述べるときは単独で用いられるが，意味に応じて，the, 所有格，these / those / two / some / many などを伴っても用いられる。

2．不可算名詞

(a) 一定の形のない物質・材質などを表す名詞

air, bread, meat, milk, rice, salt, snow, tea, water など

(b) 抽象的な概念を表す名詞

beauty, fun, love, money, progress, truth など

(c) 集合的な概念として「…というもの」という意味を表す名詞

clothing (衣類), fiction (フィクション), machinery (機械類), poetry (詩歌), scenery (風景), traffic (交通) など

不可算名詞の用法

・複数形はない。
・その前に some / a lot of / (not) much など量を表

す語句を伴うことはあるが，a / one / two / few / several / many など数を表す語句は伴わない。また，数える必要があるときは，名詞に応じて，a slice of bread / two glasses of milk などのようにする。

3．間違えやすい不可算名詞

次に挙げる語は日本語に訳すと可算名詞のように感じられるかも知れないが，不可算名詞であり，入試でよく狙われるので，しっかり覚えよう。

advice (忠告), baggage (荷物), evidence (証拠), furniture (家具), homework (宿題), information (情報), knowledge (知識), news (ニュース), permission (許可), research (研究)

4．意味に応じて可算名詞としても不可算名詞としても用いられる名詞

可算・不可算の両方の用法を持つ名詞は多いが，以下に代表的なものを挙げる。それぞれ，上の方の用法が基本である。

・They keep *chickens* in the backyard. (ニワトリ)
　This *chicken* is tender. (鶏肉)
・I like *coffee* better than tea. (コーヒーという飲み物)
　Two *coffees*, please. (2杯のコーヒー)
・I boiled some *eggs*. (卵)
　You've got some *egg* on your face. (卵のしみ・かけら)
・*Experience* is the best teacher. (経験すること)
　I had a pleasant *experience* yesterday. (経験した事柄)
・All his efforts ended in *failure*. (失敗)
　He thinks himself to be a *failure*. (失敗した人)
・They are short of *food*. (食物，食糧)
　I'm trying to cut down on fatty *foods*. (特定の食物の種類)
・*Glass* breaks easily. (ガラス)
　Be careful not to break the *glasses*. (グラス，コップ)
・He has a good command of five *languages*. (ある特定の言語)
　Only humans have *language*. (言語というもの)
・*Light* travels faster than sound. (光)
　All the *lights* went out suddenly. (明かり)
・This envelope is made from recycled *paper*. (紙という材質)
　I take a local *paper*. (新聞)
・He picked up a *stone* and threw it. (小石)
　That bridge is made of *stone*. (石という材質)
・I have a lot of *work* to do today. (仕事)
　The museum possesses many *works* by Picasso. (作品)

— 英R9 —

B．意味・扱いに注意を要する名詞

1．複数形が単数形にはない意味を持つ名詞

　次のような名詞の複数形は，単数形の意味での複数形の他に，単数形にはない意味も表す。

arm（腕）— arms（武器）

custom（習慣）— customs（税関，関税）

manner（方法）— manners（マナー，行儀）

　　It's bad *manners* to put on makeup in public.
　　「人前で化粧をするのは無作法だ」

measure（基準，寸法）— measures（公的な対策）

　　We should take strong *measures* against drunk driving.
　　「飲酒運転には強硬な対策を取るべきだ」

quarter（4分の1）— quarters（方面，宿舎）

pain（苦痛，痛み）— pains（苦労，骨折り）

　　She took great *pains* in bringing up her children.
　　「彼女は子育てに非常に骨を折った」

term（期間，用語）— terms（人との関係，契約などの条件）

　　She is on good *terms* with her neighbors.
　　「彼女は近所の人と仲がいい」

2．常に複数形で用いられる名詞

　glasses（眼鏡），goods（商品），pajamas（パジャマ），pants（ズボン），scissors（はさみ）など

3．複数形の名詞を含む表現

　make *friends*（仲良くなる），shake *hands*（握手する），change *trains*（列車を乗り換える），take *turns*（交替で行う）など

4．単複同形の名詞

　Chinese（中国人），deer（鹿），fish（魚），Japanese（日本人），means（手段），series（連続），species（種）など

C．名詞＋前置詞…

　英語では2つの名詞が連続する時，通例，間に前置詞の of を入れるのが一般的であり，またその名詞に対応する動詞や形容詞の用法から類推できる場合が多い。

例：destroy the building → the destruction *of* the building

　　anxious about the result → anxiety *about* the result

以下に名詞と前置詞の結びつきの代表的な例を挙げる。なお，of と結びつく例は，特に注意すべきもの以外は省いている。

　また，記述が煩雑になるのを避けるために，見出しの名詞はすべて無冠詞で記載し，前置詞との結びつき方がいくつかある場合は，一般的なものを挙げた。繰り返し見直し，語感を養うとよい。

affection for [toward] ...	「…に対する愛情」
appeal for ...	「…を求める訴え」
approval for ...	「…に対する是認」
authority over ...	「…に対する権威」
・ — on [about] ...	「…の権威者」
charge for ...	「…に対する料金」
・ — against ...	「…に対する非難」
claim for ...	「…に対する要求」
committee for [on] ...	「…の委員会」
confidence in ...	「…に対する信頼；…への自信」
consent to ...	「…に対する同意」
contempt for ...	「…に対する軽蔑」
contrast to [with] ...	「…との対照」
cure for ...	「…に対する治療[解決策]」
decrease in ...	「…の減少」
・ — to ...	「…への減少」
defeat in ...	「…における敗北」
defect in ...	「…の欠点」
demand for ...	「…を求める要求」
description of ...	「…を記述すること」
desire for ...	「…への願望」
disadvantage in ...	「…の点での不利な立場」
doubt of [about; over; on] ...	「…についての疑い」
enthusiasm for ...	「…に対する熱狂[熱中]」
exception to ...	「…に対する例外」
excuse for ...	「…の言い訳」
experiment in ...	「…の分野における実験」
・ — on ...	「…を対象とする実験」
・ — with ...	「…を使った実験」
expert in [at; on] ...	「…に熟練した人」
faculty for ...	「…の才能」
failure in ...	「…での失敗」
faith in ...	「…に対する信頼」
fault in ...	「…の欠陥」
generosity in ...	「…に対して物惜しみしないこと」
gratitude for ...	「…に対する感謝の気持ち」
guarantee for [on] ...	「〈品質・物事〉の保証」
・ — against ...	「〈危険・損害など〉に対する保証」
hope for ...	「…に対する希望」
hunger for ...	「…に対する飢え[渇望]」
impatience with [at] ...	「人[事]に対してじれったいこと」

improvement in ...	「…の点での改良」
increase in ...	「…の増加」
independence of [from] ...	「…からの独立」
indifference to [toward] ...	「…への無関心」
inquiry (＝enquiry) about ...	「…についての質問」
investigation into ...	「…に対する調査」
invitation to ...	「…への招待」
key to ...	「…の解決のかぎ[秘訣]」
lament for ...	「…に対する悲しみ」
motive for ...	「…の動機」
obedience to ...	「…に対する従順」
obligation to ...	「…に対する義務」
obstacle to ...	「…に対する障害(物)」
offense against ...	「〈法律・習慣上〉の罪[違反]」
parallel to [with] ...	「…との平行線[面]・に対応[匹敵]するもの」
passion for ...	「…への熱中」
patience with ...	「…に対する忍耐(力)」
preference for ... over ～	「～よりも…が好きであること」
prejudice against [toward] ...	「…に対する偏見」
・－ for [in favor of] ...	「…に対する偏愛」
pride in ...	「…の誇り」
procedure for ...	「…の手順」
proposal for ...	「…の提案」
prospect for [of] ...	「…の見込み[見通し]」
protection from [against] ...	「…を防ぐための防護」
qualification for ...	「…の資格」
quest for [of] ...	「…の探求」
reaction to ...	「…に対する反応」
reason for ...	「…の理由」
reference to ...	「…への言及」
regard for ...	「…に対する尊敬」
regret for [at] ...	「…に対する遺憾[後悔]」
report on ...	「…に関する報告」
reputation for ...	「…という評判」
research into ...	「…についての研究」
respect for ...	「…に対する尊敬」
response to ...	「…への返答」
restriction on ...	「…に対する制限」
revenge on ... for ～	「～に対する…への復讐」
scorn for ...	「…への軽蔑」
sentiment on [about] ...	「…に対する心情[意見]」
specialist in [on] ...	「…の専門家」
standard for ...	「…の基準」
stimulus to ...	「…にとっての刺激」

substitute for ...	「…の代用品」
success in ...	「…における成功」
successor to ...	「…の後継者」
symbol of ...	「…の象徴」
・－ for ...	「…を表す記号」
sympathy for [with] ...	「人[事]への同情[共感]」
talent for ...	「…に対する才能」
test in [on] ...	「…の検査[試験]」
thirst for ...	「…を求める渇き[渇望]」
thought on [of; about] ...	「…に関する考え」
・－ for ...	「…に対する思いやり」
tolerance of [to] ...	「…に対する忍耐[我慢]」
triumph over ...	「…に対する勝利」
trust in ...	「…に対する信頼」
urge for [to] ...	「…への衝動」
victory over ...	「…に対する勝利」
・－ in ...	「…での勝利」
volunteer for ...	「…の志願者」
witness to ...	「…の目撃者」
zeal for ...	「…に対する熱意」

動詞＋名詞＋前置詞＋名詞

　「動詞＋名詞＋前置詞＋名詞」の結びつきで用いられる動詞のうち代表的なものを以下に挙げる。前置詞にも注意すること。なお、見出しの V は動詞を表し、A・B は名詞（相当語句）を表す。

◎ V A of B 「A に B を通知・説得する」
　convince「納得させる」
　　convince him of her sincerity
　　「彼に彼女の誠実さを納得させる」
　inform「知らせる」
　　inform him of her arrival
　　「彼女が到着したことを彼に知らせる」
　persuade「確信させる」
　　persuade her of his honesty
　　「彼が正直であることを彼女に信じさせる」
　remind「思い出させる」
　　This picture reminds me of our primary school days.
　　「この写真を見ると私は小学校時代を思い出す」
　warn「警告する；通知する」
　　warn her of the danger in front of her
　　「前途に横たわる危険を彼女に警告する」

◎ V A of B 「B に A を**要求・懇願**する」
ask 「頼む」
　ask too much of her
　「彼女に過大な要求をする」
　他に beg 「請う」, demand 「要求する」, expect 「期待する」, request 「頼む」, require 「要求する」。
　ask 以外は from も可。

◎ V A of B 「A から B を**分離・除去・軽減**する」
clear 「取り除く」
　clear the road of snow＝clear snow from/off the road
　「道の雪を取り除く」
cure 「和らげる；治療する」
　cure the patient of his disease
　「患者の病気を治療する」
deprive 「奪う」
　deprive people of their political rights
　「人民から政治上の権利を奪う」
ease 「楽にする；安心させる」
　ease her of her suffering
　「彼女の苦痛を楽にする」
free 「取り除く」
　free him of/from oppression
　「彼を抑圧から解放する」
rid 「取り除く」
　rid a house of mice ＝ rid mice from/out of a house 「家のねずみの駆除をする」
rob 「強奪する；盗む」
　rob the bank of its money
　「銀行から金を奪う」
strip 「剥ぎ取る」
　strip the tree of its bark ＝ strip the bark from/off the tree 「木の皮を剥ぐ」
relieve 「安心させる；和らげる」
　relieve him of/from sorrow
　「悲しみを除いて安心させる」

◎ V A for B 「B のことで A を**非難する・A に賞罰を
与える**」
blame 「非難する」
　blame her for having left there
　「そこを離れたことで彼女を責める」
condemn 「責める」
　condemn him for his mistake
　「彼の過失を責める」

excuse 「許す」
　excuse the child for his absence
　「その子の欠席をとがめない」
forgive 「許す」
　forgive him for his crimes
　「彼の罪を許す」
praise 「ほめる」
　praise him for saving her life
　「彼女の命を救ったことで彼をほめる」
punish 「罰する」
　punish him for being late
　「遅刻したことで彼を罰する」
thank 「感謝する」
　thank you for inviting me
　「招待していただいてあなたに感謝する」
scold 「叱る」
　scold the child for being lazy
　「怠けていたことで子供を叱る」
◎なお「非難」を表す以下の語にも注意：
　accuse A of B 「責める・訴える」
　charge A with B 「責める・非難する」
　reproach A for/with B 「非難する」

◎ V A from B 「A が B するのを**妨害・保護**する」
prevent 「妨げる」
　Illness prevented me from coming to school.
　「病気のために私は登校できなかった」
keep 「させない」
　keep the wagon from overturning
　「配膳台をひっくり返さないようにする」
stop 「止める」
　stop the child (from) playing with matches
　「子供がマッチをもてあそぶのを止めさせる」
hinder 「妨げる」
　Illness hindered me from attending the party.
　「病気で私はそのパーティーに出席できなかった」
discourage 「止めさせる；思い止まらせる」
　Urgent business discouraged me from attending the meeting.
　「私は急用で会合に出席するのをあきらめた」
prohibit 「禁止する」
　Our school prohibits us from going to the movies alone.
　「我々の学校では1人で映画を見に行くことは禁止されている」

－ 英 R 12 －

protect「保護する」

protect him from disease「彼を病気から守る」

save「不要にする」

Phoning saved me (from) writing a letter.

「電話をかけたので手紙を書く手間が省けた」

◎ V A from B「A と B を区別・識別する」

distinguish/tell「区別・識別する」

distinguish genuine pearls from imitation ones

「本物の真珠と模造真珠とを区別する」

know「見分けがつく」

never know black from white

「良否・善悪が分からない」

◎ V A with B「A に B を供給・付託する」

provide「供給する」

Cows provide us with milk. ＝ Cows provide milk for us.「雌牛はミルクを供給する」

supply「供給・支給する」

supply the villagers with food＝supply food for [to] the villagers「村人に食料を供給する」

feed「供給する」

feed the fire with logs ＝ feed logs to the fire

「火に丸太をくべる」

furnish「必要なものを備える」

furnish the kitchen with a cupboard

「台所に食器棚を取り付ける」

impress「認識させる」

impress him with the value of education

「彼に教育の価値を認識させる」

present「贈呈する」

The students presented their teacher with a gold watch.＝ The students presented a gold watch to their teacher.「生徒たちは先生に金時計を贈った」

＜動詞＋副詞＞の群動詞

動詞と up, down, on, in などが結びついて，全体が他動詞として用いられる群動詞の中には，目的語の位置に注意しなければならないものがある。

①目的語が「名詞」の場合には「動詞＋名詞＋副詞／動詞＋副詞＋名詞」のどちらでもよい。

②目的語が「代名詞」の場合には，必ず「動詞＋代名詞＋副詞」になる。

(例)　bring up「…を育てる」

They brought their child up well.　○

They brought up their child well.　○

「彼らは子供を立派に育てた」

They brought him up well.　　　　○

They brought up him well.　　　　×

＜動詞＋副詞＞の群動詞のうち，日常的にもよく用いられるものをリストアップしておく。

call up「…に電話をかける」

I'll call you up if I need help.

「助けが必要になったらあなたに電話します」

call back「…に電話をかけ直す；…を呼び戻す」

I'll call you back when I get more information.

「さらに情報が入ったら，こちらから電話をかけ直します」

carry out「…を実行する」

He carried out the plan without difficulty.

「彼はその計画を苦もなく実行した」

check out「…を確認する」

Will you ask him to check the information out?

「その情報を確認するよう彼に頼んでくれませんか」

figure out「…を理解する」＝ make out

She couldn't figure him out at all.

「彼女は全然彼を理解できなかった」

give up「…をやめる；あきらめる」

Jeff had a good job but he had to give it up.

「ジェフには良い仕事があったが，やめなければならなかった」

hand in「…を手渡す；提出する」

Please hand this message in at that office.

「このメッセージをあの事務所で渡してください」

look up「〈語彙・項目など〉を調べる」

If you come across a new word, look it up in a dictionary.

「新しい語に出合ったら，辞書で調べなさい」

lay off「…を一時解雇する」

They have laid him off from his job.

「彼は職を一時解雇になった」

pick up「…を拾う」

He picked the stone up.

「彼は石を拾い上げた」

point out「…を指摘する」

He pointed out the difficulties in carrying out the plan.

「彼はその計画を実行することの困難を指摘した」

put away「…を片づける」
　She put her clothes away in the closet.
　「彼女は衣服をタンスにしまった」
put on「衣服を身につける」
　Get your coat and put it on now.
　「すぐにコートを取ってきて着なさい」
see off「…を見送る」
　We'll come and see you off at the airport.
　「空港までお見送りにうかがいます」
　※ see off は，目的語が普通の名詞の場合でも必ず
　　 see＋O＋off の語順になる。
take off「衣服を脱ぐ」
　She took off her jacket.
　「彼女はジャケットを脱いだ」
turn down「…を却下する」
　He made a proposal, but the commitee turned it
　down.
　「彼は提案をしたが，委員会はそれを却下した」
turn in「…を提出する」
　You have to turn in your paper by the end of
　September.
　「9月末までに論文を提出しなければなりません」
turn on「〈電気〉をつける；〈ガス・水道〉を出す」
　The light is there. Turn it on.
　「電気はそこだ。つけろ」
turn off「〈電気〉を消す；〈ガス・水道〉を止める」
　They turned off the water supply.
　「彼らは給水を止めた」

第1回　実戦問題　解答・解説

☆下記の表は，「解答・解説」の中で用いた記号・略語の一覧表です。

S	主語または主部（Subject）	－	動詞の原形
S′	意味上の主語	to－	to 不定詞
V	動詞（Verb）	－ing	現在分詞または動名詞
O	目的語（Object）	p.p.	過去分詞
C	補語（Complement）	[ ]	置換可能な語句
M	修飾語句（Modifier）	（ ）	省略可能な語句
名動副,etc.	名詞, 動詞, 副詞, etc.	〈 〉	つながりのある語句

英語（リーディング）　第1回　（100点満点）

（解答・配点）

問題番号(配点)	設問		解答番号	正解	配点	自己採点欄	問題番号(配点)	設問	解答番号	正解	配点	自己採点欄
第1問 (10)	A	1	1	③	2		第4問 (16)	1	24	②	3	
		2	2	②	2			2	25	④	3	／
	B	1	3	④	2			3	26	④	3	
		2	4	③	2			4	27	②	2	
		3	5	②	2				28	①	2	
小　計								5	29	⑥	3	
第2問 (20)	A	1	6	①	2		小　計					
		2	7	④	2		第5問 (15)	1	30	④	3	
		3	8	②	2			2	31	①	3	
		4	9	④	2			3	32	①	3*	
		5	10	③	2				33	③		
	B	1	11	③	2				34	⑤		
		2	12	③	2				35	④		
		3	13	①	2			4	36 ― 37	① ― ⑤	3*	
		4	14	②	2			5	38	④	3	
		5	15	②	2		小　計					
小　計							第6問 (24)	A	1	39	④	3	／
第3問 (15)	A	1	16	②	3	／			2	40	③	3	
		2	17	④	3				3	41 ― 42	① ― ⑤	3*	／
	B	1	18	②	3*				4	43	①	3	
			19	④				B	1	44	④	2	／
			20	①					2	45	⑤	2	
			21	③					3	46	④	2	
		2	22	①	3				4	47 ― 48	① ― ②	3*	
		3	23	③	3				5	49	①	3	／
小　計							小　計					
							合　計					

（注）
1　＊は，全部正解の場合のみ点を与える。
2　－（ハイフン）でつながれた正解は，順序を問わない。

— 英 R 16 —

第1問

> **解答**
>
> A　問1－③　　　問2－②　　　　　　　　　　　　　　　　　　　　（各2点）
> B　問1－④　　　問2－③　　　問3－②　　　　　　　　　　　　　（各2点）

A

> **出典**　*Original Material*

> **全訳**
>
> 　あなたはカナダで勉強しているところで，午前中の活動に関する2つの提案のうちどちらの方がより興味深く思えるかを決める必要があります。あなたの先生が以下の投票指示書を配ります。

土曜日の活動の提案

バンクーバー・ハーバー 派手に濡れよう 鯨と一緒に帆走する	スタンレー・パーク 自転車で文化体験 バンクーバーを自転車で探検する
▶9時から13時まで毎時出発（50分のツアー） ▶スタッフによる，地元の海の生き物と地理についての詳細な紹介 ▶甲板や大きな窓からの眺め（飲み物の自動販売機が利用可能） ▶鯨を最初に目撃したお客様に無料の帽子を進呈！	▶2時間のツアーは10:30に出発し，ツアーに含まれる軽い飲食物をとるために20分間止まります（予約時に飲み物やベジタリアンオプションを選択してください） ▶熟練ガイドより名所にまつわる事実をお聞きください ▶自転車の乗り捨て場所で30ドルを超えるお土産の買い物をすれば10％割引になります

投票：青色の用紙（**派手に濡れよう**）または赤色の用紙（**自転車で文化体験**）に自分の名前を記入し，箱の中に入れてください。

> **設問解説**
>
> 問1　　1　　正解③
>
> 「指示書を読んだ後，あなたはどうするように言われているか」　　1
>
> 　① 用紙を入れる色のついた箱を選ぶ。
> 　② ツアー会社に直接連絡を取る。
> **　③ 箱の中に自分の名前を入れる。**
> 　④ 次の授業で投票する準備をする。
>
> 　正解は③。与えられた用紙の最後に「投票：青色の用紙（派手に濡れよう）または赤色の用紙（自転車で文化体験）に自分の名前を記入し，箱の中に入れてください」と記されていることから，この用紙を読んで2つの提案を検討した後，自分が選んだ提案に応じて青色か赤色の用紙に自分の名前を記入して，その用紙を箱の中に入れるように指示されていることがわかるので，正解は③となる。
>
> 　①，②，④に関しては，いずれの内容も与えられた用紙では言及されていないので誤り。

— 英 R 17 —

問2 　2　 正解 ②

「両方の活動に関して，どれが正しいか」　2

① 飲み物は別料金なしで飲用可能である。

② 社員はツアーを行う地域に関する知識が豊富である。

③ 毎朝数回出発する。

④ いくつかの特別商品に関しては割引を受けられる。

正解は ②。与えられた用紙において提案されている「バンクーバー・ハーバー」の説明の2つ目の項目（▶）には「スタッフによる，地元の海の生き物と地理についての詳細な紹介」とあり，「スタンレー・パーク」の説明の2つ目の項目（▶）では「熟練ガイドより名所にまつわる事実をお聞きください」と述べられていることから，これらの会社のスタッフはツアーが行われる地域に関する紹介や事実説明ができるほど知識が豊富であることがわかるので，正解は ② となる。

① は，「バンクーバー・ハーバー」の説明の3つ目の項目（▶）で「飲み物の自動販売機が利用可能」と言及されていることから，飲み物には別料金がかかることがわかるので誤り。③ は，「スタンレー・パーク」の説明の1つ目の項目（▶）で「2時間のツアーは10:30 に出発」と述べられていることから，自転車ツアーは1回のみの出発であると判断できるので誤り。④ の内容は，「スタンレー・パーク」の説明の4つ目の項目（▶）で「自転車の乗り捨て場所で30 ドルを超えるお土産の買い物をすれば10％割引になります」と割引に関することが言及されているが，「バンクーバー・ハーバー」の説明においては言及されていないので誤り。

〔主な語句・表現〕　・問題冊子を参照のこと。

[リード文]　◇ sound ＋〈形容詞〉「〈形容詞〉に思われる［響く］」

◇ suggestion 图「提案」　　　　　　　◇ voting instruction sheet「投票指示書」

[Vancouver Harbor]　◇ depart 動「出発する」　　　　　　　◇ marine life「海の生き物」

◇ geography 图「地理」　　　　　　　◇ vending machine「自動販売機」

◇ available 形「利用可能な」

[Stanley Park]　◇ refreshment 图「軽い飲食物」　　　　◇ book 動「予約する」

◇ landmark 图「（文化財などの）名所；歴史的建造物；陸標（目印になる建物・地形など）」

◇ drop-off 图「（レンタカー・レンタサイクルなどの）乗り捨て場所」

[設問・選択肢]　◇ extra cost「別料金；追加料金」　　　　◇ employee 图「社員；従業員」

B

〔出典〕　*Original Material*

〔全訳〕

　あなたは近所にオープンしたばかりのフィットネスクラブに入会することを考えています。あなたはそこのウェブサイトを訪問します。

— 英 R 18 —

レクサス・フィットネス

　レクサス・フィットネスは柔軟なプラン，手ごろな料金，そして最新の設備を提供します。我々の単純な目標は現代的で心地よい環境を提供することですが，その環境は，あなたの健康やフィットネスに関するあらゆる目標を達成するのを手助けするように特別に設計されています。あなたはトレーニングを新たな段階まで引き上げたいと思わずにはいられないでしょう。

　全ての新しい会員は**レクサス・フィットネス**のロゴが入った特別なタオルがもらえます。さらに，4月末までに登録すれば，抽選でオリジナルのジムバッグが当たるチャンスがあります。その上，特別企画として，4月末までにプラチナ会員になると，オリジナルTシャツがもらえます！　是非このすばらしい機会を逃さずに，我々のクラブに入会して目標を達成してください。

下記の会員オプションから選んでください。

施設を使える日時 そして含まれているもの (✔)	会員オプション		
	デイタイム (60ドル／月)	ゴールド (80ドル／月)	プラチナ (100ドル／月)
月曜日から金曜日， 午前9:00〜午後5:00	✔		✔
月曜日から金曜日， 午後5:00〜		✔	✔
土曜日と日曜日 (終日)	✔	✔	✔
無料駐車場	✔	✔	✔
グループエクササイズ・クラス		✔	✔
プールとスパ		✔	✔
水着の無料レンタル			✔
ジムシューズの無料レンタル			✔
個人トレーニング・プログラム			✔

☆入会金として50ドルいただきます。
☆4月20日より前にご入会いただいた場合，4月の会費を支払う必要はありません。
☆会費は毎月初めにお支払いいただきます。

デイタイム，ゴールド，プラチナのどの会員であっても，レクサス・フィットネスクラブの会員であることにご満足いただけるでしょう。さらに情報を得るために，または入会するためには，<u>ここ</u>をクリックしてください。

設問解説

問1　| 3 |　正解④

「全ての新しい会員は，| 3 |がもらえるだろう」

① フィットネス・バッグとタオル
② 必要なジム用品一式
③ タオルとTシャツ
④ **最低1つの実用的なプレゼント**

　正解は④。第2段落第1文（All new members ...）に，全ての新しい会員はタオルがもらえるとあり，第2文（In addition, if ...）には，4月末までに登録すれば抽選でバッグが

— 英 R 19 —

当たるとあり，さらに第3文（Plus, as a …）には，4月末までにプラチナ会員になった場合にTシャツがもらえると述べられている。つまり，新しい会員は最低1つは実用的なプレゼントがもらえるので，④が正解。

バッグやTシャツは全ての新会員がもらえるわけではないので，①と③は誤り。また，ジム用品を「一式」もらえるわけではないので，②も誤り。

問2　　4　　正解③

「ゴールド会員になったら，　4　　ことができるだろう」

① 火曜日の午前にグループエクササイズのクラスに参加する
② 無料でジムの履き物を借りる
③ 土曜日の午前にプールで泳ぐ
④ 日曜日にマンツーマン・レッスンを受ける

正解は③。表のゴールド会員の欄を見ると，土曜日に終日利用可能で，かつ，プールも利用可能であるとわかるので，③が正解。

ゴールド会員は火曜日は午後5時以降しか利用できないので，①は誤り。また，ジムシューズの無料レンタルや個人トレーニングのプログラムはゴールド会員の特典として含まれていないので，②と④も誤り。

問3　　5　　正解②

「もし4月15日にデイタイム会員になったら，12月の終わりまでに合計　5　支払うことになるだろう」

① 480ドル
② 530ドル
③ 540ドル
④ 590ドル

正解は②。表の後に続く注意書きに，入会金として50ドル必要であること，4月20日までに入会すれば4月の会費が無料になること，会費は毎月初めに支払うことが述べられている。以上のことから，4月15日に入会して12月末までデイタイム会員として在籍した場合，入会時の50ドルに加え，5月から12月までの月初めに60ドルずつ8ヵ月分を支払うことがわかる。したがって，合計530ドルとなり，②が正解。

主な語句・表現	
[本文]	・問題冊子を参照のこと。

[本文]
◇ flexible 形「柔軟な」　　　　　　　◇ affordable 形「手ごろな；無理なく買える」
◇ rate 名「料金」　　　　　　　　　◇ brand new「最新の」
◇ equipment 名「設備」　　　　　　◇ welcoming 形「心地よい；快適な」
◇ specifically 副「特に；具体的に」　◇ can't help but －「－せずにはいられない」
◇ motivate O to －「O に－する気を起こさせる」
◇ elevate 動「…を高める」　　　　　◇ workout 名「トレーニング；運動」
◇ enroll 動「登録する；入会する」　◇ lottery 名「抽選；くじ」
◇ plus 副「その上；さらに」　　　　◇ promotion 名「販売促進；キャンペーン」
◇ facility 名「施設」　　　　　　　◇ bathing suit「水着」
◇ charge 動「…を請求する」　　　　◇ enrollment 名「入会；登録」

[設問・選択肢]
◇ practical 形「実用的な」　　　　　◇ footwear 名「履き物」
◇ for free「無料で」　　　　　　　◇ one-on-one 形「1対1の；マンツーマンの」

— 英 R 20 —

第2問

解答

A	問1-①	問2-④	問3-②	問4-④	問5-③	（各2点）
B	問1-③	問2-③	問3-①	問4-②	問5-②	（各2点）

A

出典　*Original Material*

全訳

　あなたのマットレスが心地よくなく，騒々しい目覚まし時計が鳴って突然起きた後に苛立たしく感じることもしばしばです。イギリスのウェブサイトで睡眠に関する記事を読んでいて以下の広告を見つけます。

フォーティ・ウィンクスが新しいスィート・スリープ・シーツを提供します

今お使いのマットレスと一緒に，気分爽快になるスィート・スリープ・シーツが使用できます。このシーツはかしこく，睡眠を改善してくれます。

特性
「スィート・スリープ・シーツ」アプリをダウンロードして，あなたの睡眠の質を点検し，温度を管理してくれるセンサーにリンクさせてください。この製品はあなたが夜間に動いた量ばかりでなく，より深く休息する方法も教えてくれます。このアプリの有料会員登録をして定期的に睡眠のヒントをもらってください！

利点
気候に合わせた設定：季節を問わず，ベッドに入るときの最適温度を選び，夜の間中，あなたの体温に応じて温度を変化させます。
穏やかな起床：大きな目覚まし音の衝撃を避けて，マットレスが徐々に速くなる振動を始めるので，一日が穏やかに始まります。
健康の改善：ストレスがたまっていたり，気分がすぐれないときを感知するために，あなたがどれだけよく眠っているかについて追跡調査します。
個人に向けたフィードバック：あなたが好む睡眠習慣に関し，アプリ内のいくつかの質問に答えることで，特にあなたに合わせたアドバイスをもらいます。

お客様の声
● ちょっと音が大きめですが，扇風機やヒーター，他のスマートマットレスよりは静か。
● 無料でお試しできます！　2週間経って気に入らなければ，返送してください！
● 接続切れを避けるために，寝室には必ず電波の強い wi-fi を設置するようにしてください。
● 個人に適した呼吸トレーニングを行うことで睡眠が本当に改善しました！
● このマットレスカバーは柔らかすぎず，硬すぎません。
● 設定を行うのにかなり時間がかかりますが，私としてはそれ以外に不満はありません！
● 水を使った温度管理方式に必要なのは，毎月たった2～3さじの水を加えることだけです。

— 英 R 21 —

設問解説

問1 ☐6☐ 正解①

「会社が言っていることによると，どれがマットレスカバーのことを最もよく説明しているか」 ☐6☐

① 一年中適応できる
② 気分爽快になるが，季節が限定される
③ はっきりした目覚まし音が備わっていてかしこい
④ 洗濯ができて便利である

　正解は①。「利点」の中の「気候に合わせた設定」において，「季節を問わず，ベッドに入るときの最適温度を選び，夜の間中，あなたの体温に応じて温度を変化させます」と述べられていることから正解は①となる。

　②は「季節が限定される」という表現が，「利点」の中の「気候に合わせた設定」で述べられている「季節を問わず」ということに反するので誤り。③は「はっきりした目覚まし音が備わっていて」という表現が，「利点」の中の「穏やかな起床」で述べられている「大きな目覚まし音の衝撃を避けて」ということに反するので誤り。④は「洗濯ができて」という内容が言及されていないので誤り。

問2 ☐7☐ 正解④

「このカバーが提供するどの利点が，あなたに合っている可能性が最も高いか」 ☐7☐

① さまざまな睡眠方法を比較すること
② 不安な感情を軽減させること
③ 睡眠パターンを科学的に理解すること
④ よりゆったりと目覚めること

　正解は④。リード文の第1文から，あなたはしばしば「騒々しい目覚まし時計が鳴って突然起きた後に苛立たしく」感じていることがわかる。「利点」の中の「穏やかな起床」において，「大きな目覚まし音の衝撃を避けて，マットレスが徐々に速くなる振動を始めるので，一日が穏やかに始まります」と述べられていることから，起床時に騒々しい目覚まし時計の音で突然目覚める場合と比べて，よりゆったりと目覚めることになり，それがあなたに最も合っている可能性が高いと推測できるので，正解は④となる。

　①や②や③の内容は，リード文で述べられているあなたの悩みへの対策としてふさわしくないため誤り。

問3 ☐8☐ 正解②

「利用者によって述べられている1つの意見は ☐8☐ ということである」

① このカバーはすぐに故障する可能性が高い
② このカバーの硬さはちょうどよい
③ 温度システムはあまりに音が大きすぎる
④ 温度システムは定期的に水を必要とする

　正解は②。「お客様の声」の5つ目で「このマットレスカバーは柔らかすぎず，硬すぎません」と述べられていることから，正解は②となる。

　①と③の内容は「お客様の声」では言及されていないので誤り。④は「お客様の声」の最後で述べられている「水を使った温度管理方式に必要なのは，毎月たった2～3さじの水を加えることだけです」という内容に一致するが，これは意見ではなく事実であるので誤り。

— 英 R 22 —

問4 | 9 |　正解 ④

「ある利用者は個人に適した呼吸トレーニングに言及している。このコメントに関係が
あるのはどの利点か」| 9 |
　　① 気候に合わせた設定
　　② 穏やかな起床
　　③ 健康の改善
　　④ 個人に向けたフィードバック
　　正解は ④。「お客様の声」の４つ目には「個人に適した呼吸トレーニングを行うことで
睡眠が本当に改善しました！」とある。「利点」の中の「個人に向けたフィードバック（評
価的意見）」では「あなたが好む睡眠習慣に関し，アプリ内のいくつかの質問に答えること
で，<u>特にあなたに合わせたアドバイスをもらいます</u>」と述べられており，この利用者の言
う「個人に合わせた呼吸トレーニング」はこの「特にあなたに合わせたアドバイス」の一
例であると推測できるので，正解は ④ となる。
　　① や ② や ③ の利点の内容はこの利用者のコメントとは関係がないので誤り。

問5 | 10 |　正解 ③

「ある顧客の意見によれば，| 10 |ことが勧められている」
　　① アプリ内の質問に正直に答えること
　　② このカバーをさまざまなマットレスと比較すること
　　③ 寝室に十分な信号を備えた wi-fi を設置すること
　　④ 購入前に 30 日間このカバーを試すこと
　　正解は ③。「お客様の声」の３つ目に「接続切れを避けるために，<u>寝室には必ず電波の
強い wi-fi を設置するようにしてください</u>」とあることから，この顧客は「寝室に十分な信
号を備えた wi-fi を設置すること」を勧めていると判断できるので，正解は ③ となる。
　　① や ② の内容は「お客様の声」では言及されていないので誤り。④ は，「お客様の声」
の２つ目には「無料でお試しできます！　２週間経って気に入らなければ，返送してくだ
さい！」とあるように，お試し期間は 30 日ではなく２週間であることがわかるので誤り。

（主な語句・表現）　・問題冊子を参照のこと。

[リード文]　◇ mattress 图「（ベッドの）マットレス」　　◇ irritable 形「イライラして；苛立って」

[広告文]　◇ forty winks「うたたね；ひと眠り」　　◇ refreshing 形「気分爽快な；さわやかな」
　◇ existing 形「現在の；現行の」
　◇ app 图「アプリ；アプリケーション（application）」　アプリケーションソフトウェア（特
　　定の仕事をするために作られたソフトウェア）の略。
　◇ link A to B「A を B につなぐ」　　◇ rest 動「休息する」
　◇ subscribe to ...「…に有料会員登録する」　◇ tip 图「ヒント；秘訣；助言」
　◇ benefit 图「利益；特典；成果」　　◇ in relation to ...「…に関係して；…に対して」
　◇ in all seasons「四季を通じて；季節を問わず」
　◇ rising 图「起床」　　◇ calmly 副「穏やかに」
　◇ vibrate 動「振動する」　　◇ track 動「…について追跡調査する」
　◇ feedback 图「フィードバック；評価的意見」　軌道修正を促すための，相手の行動に対す
　　る評価的意見のこと。
　◇ for free「無料で」
　◇ make sure (that) S V「必ず［確実に］S V する」

— 英 R 23 —

◇wi-fi图「ワイファイ」Wireless Fidelity（ワイヤレス・フィデリティ）」の略で，デバイスとインターネット回線をつなぐ近距離対応の通信技術を指す。無線でインターネットに接続するのが特徴で，電波が届く範囲でのみ利用可能。

◇personalised形「特定の個人に適用された」

◇mattress cover「マットレスカバー」 ここではマットレスの上にかける「シーツ」のことを指している。

◇it takes〈時間〉to－「－するのに〈時間〉かかる」

◇other than that「それ以外は」

◇a couple of spoons of ...「2～3さじの…；スプーン2～3杯分の」

[設問文・選択肢]　◇adaptable形「適応可能な」　　　　　◇seasonal形「季節限定の；季節ごとの」

◇anxiety图「不安」　　　　　　　　　◇leisurely副「ゆったりと；のんびりと」

◇firmness图「硬さ」

◇advise －ing「－することを勧める［推奨する］」 問5の設問文では受動態として用いられている。

◇compare A with B「AをBと比較する」　◇install動「…を設置する」

◇signal图「（電波などの）信号」

B

出典 | *Original Material*

全訳 | 休暇で沖縄県の宮古島に行く前に，あなたはホテルを決める必要があるので，あるホテルについての案内と，そのホテルに関する宿泊客のコメントを読んでいます。

イムギャー

ロケーション：

イムギャーは宮古島にあり，宮古空港から車で20分，美しいホテル専用ビーチを備えております。近隣の名所としては平良橋や狩俣神社がございますし，下地アメリカンビレッジやシギラ植物園など人気の観光スポットもあります。スキューバダイビング，シュノーケリング，水上スキーもすぐ近くでできますので，海のアクティビティも数多くお楽しみいただけます。

ホテル詳細：

素敵なビーチで1日楽しんで過ごし戻られたら，イムギャー内にある5つのレストランのどこかでディナーをお楽しみください。全180室の客室は防音で，無料のWi-Fiやルームサービスも特色となっております。心ばかりのおもてなしとして，衛星チャンネルが備わった液晶テレビがございます。冷蔵庫やコーヒーメーカーなどの備品もご利用できます。

ホテル設備：

- 無料の空港送迎バス   - 18ホールのゴルフ場
- 土産物店／雑貨店   - インターネット
- ランドリー設備   - エレベーター
- 駐車場（1泊につき1,000円）   - スパサービス
- 季節営業の屋外プール   - テニスコート
- 24時間対応のフロント

客室内設備：

- ドライヤー   - バスタブ・シャワー別
- タオル   - 無料のペットボトルウォーター
- 携帯電話の充電器

料金（朝食込）：

- スタンダードダブル／ツイン・ガーデンビュー	1泊15,000円
- スタンダードダブル／ツイン・オーシャンビュー	1泊21,000円
- スーペリアダブル／ツイン・オーシャンビュー	1泊33,000円
- デラックスダブル／ツイン・オーシャンビュー	1泊42,000円

> 宿泊客レビュー（129件）　　　　　　　　　★★★★☆（平均 4.8）
>
> **イギリスからシンシアより**
> 　宮古島に来るのでしたら，ここに泊まるのが一番です。美しい白砂のビーチと感動的な青い海。ホテルの部屋もとてもきれいで快適です。プールとビーチはライフガードがいるので，子どもにはよいです。バイキング形式の朝食付きで，料理もたくさんありおいしかったです。唯一のマイナス面は宮古島の蒸し暑さだけでした。

設 問 解 説

問1 | 11 | 　**正解 ③**

「このホテルは | 11 | 位置している」

① ゴルフ場から遠く離れたところに
② 有名な遊園地の前に
③ **有名な橋の近くに**
④ 空港から徒歩圏内に

　正解は③。ロケーションに関する情報には「平良橋が近隣の名所」と書かれている。
　ホテル設備の項目に「18 ホールのゴルフ場」とあり，ゴルフ場はホテルの敷地内にあることから，①は誤り。②は本文に記載がない。また，空港から「車で 20 分」とあるので，④は誤り。

問2 | 12 | 　**正解 ③**

「このホテルに関する1つの事実は | 12 | ということである」

① 宮古島で最高の場所である
② 宿泊客は無料で駐車できる
③ **宿泊客は1年中プールが利用できるわけではない**
④ 唯一の問題は蒸し暑さである

　正解は③。ホテル設備に関する情報に「季節営業の屋外プール」という記述があることから，季節によってはプールが使用できないことになる。
　レビューに「ここに泊まるのが一番です」とあるが，これは宿泊者個人の意見であって，客観的な事実とは言えないので，①は誤り。②はホテル設備の項目に「1泊につき 1,000円（の駐車料金）」とあるので誤り。④に関しても，レビューに記載された宮古島に関する意見なので誤り。

問3 | 13 | 　**正解 ①**

「海が見える部屋に3泊滞在したいのなら，あなたは | 13 | 払うだろう」

① **最低でも 63,000 円**
② 最高で 99,000 円
③ 42,000 円より少なく
④ わずか 30,000 円

　正解は①。料金に関する記述に注目すると，「海が見える部屋」の最低金額は「1泊 21,000 円」のスタンダードダブル／ツイン・オーシャンビューであるから，3泊となると 21,000 円 × 3 泊 = 63,000 円である。したがって，それよりも低い金額である③と④は誤り。また，「海が見える部屋」の最高金額となる「1泊 42,000 円」のデラックスダブル／ツイン・オーシャンビューに泊まると，3泊で 42,000 円 × 3 泊 = 126,000 円なので，②のように「最高で 99,000 円」と考える根拠もない。

— 英 R 26 —

問4 　14　 正解 ②

「このホテルに関して述べられた意見の1つは　14　ということである」

① 食べ物やお土産が宿泊客にすぐに手に入る
② 子どもがビーチで遊ぶのは安全である
③ 宿泊客の大半が宿泊に満足している
④ 宿泊客が近くの海にスキューバダイビングをしに行くことができる

正解は ②。レビューの中に「プールとビーチはライフガードがいるので，子どもにはよい」という意見が載せられている。

① と ④ に関する記述もホテルの情報にあるが，どちらも事実なので誤り。また，レビューにある「5段階評価で平均4.8」という数値は，宿泊客の大部分がこのホテルに満足していることを示す客観的な事実と言えることから，③ は不正解となる。

問5 　15　 正解 ②

「このホテルの魅力の1つは何であるか」 　15

① 館内すべての無料 Wi-Fi
② 選択できる数々のレストラン
③ 屋内のテニスコート
④ 目の前の公共ビーチ

正解は ②。ホテル詳細に関する項目で「素敵なビーチで1日楽しんで過ごし戻られたら，イムギャー内にある5つのレストランのどこかでディナーをお楽しみください」と述べられているので，多様なレストランがこのホテルの魅力と言える。

「ホテル詳細」に「無料の Wi-Fi」とあるが，これは客室内の特色であり，館内すべてかは判断できないため ① は誤り。ホテル設備に「テニスコート」という記述があるが，屋内かどうかについてはこの情報だけでは判断できないので，③ は不正解となる。また，④ は「ロケーション」の「ホテル専用ビーチ」の記述と異なるので誤り。

主な語句・表現
・問題冊子を参照のこと。

[本文]
◇ notable 形「注目に値する」
◇ landmark 名「目印となる建物」
◇ attraction 名「呼び物」
◇ with ... nearby「…が近くにあるので」
◇ plenty of ...「多くの…」
◇ description 名「詳細；説明」
◇ return to −「戻って−する」
◇ dine 動「夕食をとる」
◇ soundproofed 形「防音の」
◇ feature 動「特徴として…がある」
◇ entertainment 名「娯楽；もてなし」
◇ LCD TV「液晶テレビ」
◇ satellite channel「衛星放送のチャンネル」
◇ convenience 名「便利な設備」
◇ fridge 名「冷蔵庫」
◇ amenity 名「快適な設備」
◇ laundry 名「洗濯」
◇ facility 名「設備；サービス」
◇ elevator 名「エレベーター」
◇ seasonal 形「ある季節に限った；季節ごとの」
◇ separate 形「別々の」
◇ charger 名「充電器」

[レビュー]
◇ gorgeous 形「見事な」
◇ lifeguard 名「ライフガード；水難救助員」
◇ buffet 名「バイキング形式の食事」
◇ option 名「選択する物」
◇ drawback 名「欠点；短所」
◇ humidity 名「湿気；蒸し暑さ」

— 英 R 27 —

第3問

解答		
A	問1 - ② 　問2 - ④	（各3点）
B	問1　18 - ②　19 - ④　20 - ①　21 - ③	（完答で3点）
	問2 - ①　問3 - ③	（各3点）

A

出典　*Original Material*

全訳

　　あなたはヨーロッパを旅行し，飛行機でロンドンからダブリンまで行く計画を立てています。旅行に関する助言をしてくれるウェブサイトのＱ＆Ａセクションで，有用な情報を見つけました。

2022年の4月にロンドンからダブリンへ飛行機に乗ろうと思っています。最もよい行き方は何か教えていただけないでしょうか。できる限りお金を節約したいです。ブルームズベリーに住んでいます。よろしくお願いします。　　　　　　　　　　　（グレイス）

回答

偶然にも私はロンドンの同じ地区に住んでいて，よく出張でダブリンに行きます。私はハムレット空港まで電車で行って（1時間くらいしかかかりませんし，費用も3ポンドです），ダーウィンエアラインズに乗るのが好きですね。ブルームズベリーからハムレット空港までは急行バスを使えば10分節約できますが，値段はずっと高いです（約8ポンド）。

いくつか代案を示しますね。

ハムレット空港ではなくてテンペスト空港を選ぶのであれば，ヨーロッパの航空会社の中で一番安いライオンエアラインズに乗ることができます。しかしテンペスト空港まで行くのに急行電車に乗る必要があり，20ポンドくらいかかります。

別の案です。ハムレット空港からアンツエアウェイズに乗れば，そこからダーウィンエアラインズに乗るのと比べてたいていはお金を節約できます。まぁ，アンツエアウェイズはオススメではないですけどね。サービスがよくないですし，スタッフはあまりよく訓練されていません。

フライトの価格は出発日によって違いますから，インターネットで調べてください。

旅を楽しんでくださいね！

（ロビン）

— 英R 28 —

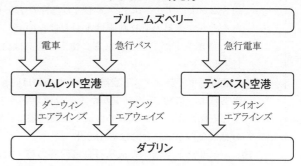

フライトの価格比較（2022年5月22日）

航空会社	価格	出発地	無料の手荷物制限	超過分の手荷物料金
ダーウィンエアラインズ	102ポンド	ハムレット	2	20ポンド／1個
アンツエアウェイズ	84ポンド	ハムレット	1	30ポンド／1個
ライオンエアラインズ	60ポンド	テンペスト	1	40ポンド／1個

設問解説

問1 　16　 正解 ②

「ロビンの回答から，あなたはロビンが　16　とわかる」

① ダーウィンエアラインズを薦めていない
② ブルームズベリーに住んでいてダブリンをよく訪れる
③ チケットをインターネットで買うよう強く勧めている
④ ハムレット空港へ行くのにたいてい急行バスを使っている

正解は②。ロビンの回答の冒頭で I happen to live in the same area of London「偶然にも私はロンドンの同じ地区に住んでいる」とあるが，この「同じ地区」とは質問者のグレイスと同じ地区ということなので，Bloomsbury「ブルームズベリー」のこと。またそれに続く部分で「よく出張でダブリンに行きます」と言っている。

回答の第2文（I prefer to ...）でロビンは「ハムレット空港まで電車で行って（…）ダーウィンエアラインズに乗るのが好き」と述べていることから，どちらかというとダーウィンエアラインズを薦めていると言えるので，①は誤り。「薦めていない」のは回答の第4段落第2文（If you take ...）にあるように，Ants Airways「アンツエアウェイズ」である。③は記述がない。インターネットで調べるように言っているのは当日のフライトの価格のこと。④は上述のように「ハムレット空港まで電車で行って（…）」と述べているため，一致しない。

問2 　17　 正解 ④

「あなたは2022年5月22日にブルームズベリーを出発しようとしている。2つの荷物を持っていく予定である。ダブリンへ行くのに最も経済的な方法は何か」　17

① 急行バスとアンツエアウェイズ
② 急行電車とライオンエアラインズ
③ 電車とアンツエアウェイズ
④ 電車とダーウィンエアラインズ

正解は④。ロビンの回答内の情報と Flight Price Comparison「フライトの価格比較」の表を照らし合わせて計算する必要がある。情報処理量が多いので見落としがないように注意。

— 英R 29 —

① 急行バスの料金は回答の第 1 段階最終文（From Bloomsbury to ...）にあるように約 8 ポンド。アンツエアウェイズの当日のフライト価格は 84 ポンドだが，荷物が 2 つあるうちで無料の荷物制限は 1 つだけなので，1 つ分の超過料金を払わなくてはならず，30 ポンドが上乗せされる。ゆえに合計は約 8 ポンド + 84 ポンド + 30 ポンドで約 122 ポンド。

② 急行電車でテンペスト空港に行くためには回答の第 3 段落最終文（However, to get ...）にあるように約 20 ポンドかかる。ライオンエアラインズの当日のフライトは 60 ポンドと安価だが，アンツエアウェイズと同様に荷物の超過料金がかかり，40 ポンド支払わねばならない。合計は約 120 ポンド。

③ ハムレット空港への電車料金は回答の第 1 段落第 2 文（I prefer to ...）にあるように 3 ポンド。アンツエアウェイズは① 同様に 84 ポンド + 30 ポンドかかる。よって合計で 117 ポンド。

④ ハムレット空港への電車料金は，③ 同様に 3 ポンド。当日のフライトの価格は表の中に 102 ポンドとある。ダーウィンエアラインズは 2 個まで荷物が無料なので，超過料金はない。よって合計で 105 ポンドとなる。

よってダブリンに行くのに最も安価な方法は ④ ということになる。

（主な語句・表現） ・問題冊子を参照のこと。
　　　[本文]
◇ aeroplane 名「飛行機」　　　　　　　◇ in advance「前もって」
◇ happen to -「偶然 - する」　　　　　　◇ on business「仕事で」
◇ prefer to -「- するのを好む」　　　　　◇ alternative 名「代案」
◇ instead of ...「…の代わりに」　　　　　◇ airline 名「航空会社」
◇ compared to ...「…と比べて」　　　　　◇ trained 形「教育を受けた」
◇ departure 名「出発」

[設問文・選択肢]　◇ economical 形「経済的な；お金のかからない」

B

（出典）　*Original Material*

（全訳）　あなたは海外留学をしたいと考えている人向けの雑誌で，以下の記事を見つけました。

コミュニケーションの隔たり
ティム・リーチ

　日本語と英語の会話のスタイルの隔たりのせいで，誤った伝達が行われてしまった私の経験について，お話しさせてください。

　私は高校生の時に文化交流プログラムの一環で日本に行きました。その時まで 2 年間日本語を学んでいましたから，日本人と実際に会話をする時だろうと思ったのです。私はクラスに紹介され，暖かい歓迎を受けました。最初は彼らが何を言っているのか理解するのに少し苦労しましたが，すぐに慣れることができました。

　ある日，グループでディスカッションをしている時に，奇妙なことに気がつきました。私が自分の意見を述べていると，そのグループのメンバーの 1 人がうなずいて「はい」と言いました。「はい」は日本語では "Yes" を意味するはずです。それで私は彼が私の意見に賛成したのだろうと思いました。しかし私がしゃべり終わると，彼は私が言っ

たばかりのことに反対し始めたのです。私は少し混乱してしまいました。ほんの少し前に彼は「はい」と言ってうなずいていたのに，今は私の意見に反対しているのです。

　授業の後で，先生にそのことを話しました。彼女は英語を教えていて，英語圏の文化をよく理解しているのです。彼女は私に，日本人は相手が言っていることを自分が理解していると示すために「はい」という言葉を使うことがあると教えてくれました。これは日本語で「あいづち」と呼ばれ，うなずきと一緒に使われることが多いとのことです。つまり，日本人が「はい」と言ってうなずいても，あなたが言っていることに同意しているということを意味しているとは限らない，ということです。私は理解しましたが，同時に，これは深刻な伝達の誤りを引き起こす可能性があると思いました。

　そこで，提案です。こうした経験，否定的な結果になってしまっていたかもしれないコミュニケーションスタイルの隔たりを感じた経験談を集めるのはどうでしょうか。あなたの経験を編集部までメールに書いて送ってください。連絡先はこの雑誌の最後のページに載っています。来月号のこのセクションで，皆さんが経験したことのリストを作成したいと思います。

設問解説

問1 　　18　　正解②, 　　19　　正解④, 　　20　　正解①, 　　21　　正解③

「次の出来事（①〜④）を起こった順番に並べなさい」

　① ティムはあるクラスメートの彼の意見に対する反応を，一貫性がないと思った。
　② ティムはクラスメートたちが言っていることをだいたい理解できると感じた。
　③ ティムは起こったことについて先生と話し合いをした。
　④ ティムは授業中に自身の意見を述べた。

　正解は②→④→①→③。

　②は，ティムが日本に来たばかりの頃に「最初は彼ら（クラスメート）が何を言っているのか理解するのに少し苦労しましたが，すぐに慣れることができました」という記述が第2段落最終文（At first I ...）にある。

　その後，授業中にディスカッションをしている時に，ティムが意見を述べると（④），1人のクラスメートがうなずいて「はい」と言い，それをティムは自分の意見を肯定する意思表示だととらえていたが（実際には，このクラスメートはあいづちをうっていただけ），その後にそのクラスメートがティムの意見に反対して，ティムが困惑した（①），という流れが第3段落に描かれている。続く第4段落第1文（After the class, ...）で，そのことをティムが先生に相談している（③）。

問2 　　22　　正解①

「この記事から，外国人の話を聞く際，日本人は　　22　　かもしれないとあなたはわかる」

　① 実際に考えていることについて誤った印象を与える
　② 理解していない時にうなずく
　③ 自分の意見を明確に述べない
　④ "Yes" と言う代わりに「はい」と言う

　正解は①。問1の解説で確認したように，この文章のティムの体験談では，日本人のあいづち（「はい」と言いながらうなずくことがある）が，外国人にとっては賛同を示すものと受け取られて誤解を招くことがある旨が述べられている。

　②は「理解していない時に」が誤り。第4段落第2文（She told me ...）にて，「日本人は相手が言っていることを自分が理解していると示すために『はい』という言葉を使うことがある」と述べられている。③は本文に記述がない。④もこの記事の記述からは誤りとなる。第3段落第2文（While I was ...）にあるように，ティムが「はい」と "Yes" が対応するものであると思い込んでいたがゆえに，本文で述べられている誤解が生じている。

— 英 R 31 —

このような状況では，第4段落第4文（This means that ...）にあるように，日本人は "Yes" の意味合いで「はい」と言っているのではないということになる。

問3　23　正解③

「あなたは編集部に自分の経験談を送ることに決めた。最初にすべきことは何か」

23
① ウェブサイトのアドレスを見つける。
② 編集部に提案をする。
③ 雑誌の最後のページを見る。
④ 自分の経験のリストを作る。

　正解は③。第5段落にて読者の体験談を募集する旨が述べられているが，第3文（Please write an ...）でメールを送るよう述べられた後に，続く第4文（Our contact address ...）でその連絡先が雑誌の最後のページに記載されていると述べられている。

　①は「ウェブサイトの」が誤り。見つけるべきは編集部のメールアドレスである。②は「提案」が誤り。「自分の経験」を送るのであり，「提案」をするのではない。④に関しては，読者の経験を集めて編集部がそのリストを作る旨が第5段落最終文（We are going ...）で述べられているが，読者自身がリストを作るとは書かれていないため誤りとなる。

（主な語句・表現）
[本文]
・問題冊子を参照のこと。
◇ miscommunication 图「伝達の失敗；誤解」
◇ cultural exchange「文化交流」　　　　◇ have trouble −ing「−するのに苦労する」
◇ get used to ...「…に慣れる」　　　　　◇ nod 動「うなずく」
◇ be supposed to −「−することになっている」
◇ slightly 副「少し」　　　　　　　　　◇ confused 形「困惑した」
◇ a while ago「少し前」　　　　　　　　◇ accompany 動「…を伴う」
◇ lead to「…につながる；…を引き起こす」
◇ serious 形「深刻な」　　　　　　　　　◇ misunderstanding 图「誤解」
◇ Why don't we ... ?「…しませんか？」　◇ account 图「説明；話」
◇ might have caused ...「…を引き起こしていたかもしれない」仮定法過去完了。
◇ editor 图「編集長；編集部」　　　　　◇ contact address「連絡先」
◇ issue 图「号」

[設問文・選択肢]
◇ inconsistent 形「一貫しない；矛盾した」　◇ follow 動「…についていく；…を理解する」
◇ state 動「〈意見など〉を言う」

第4問

解答

問1 — ②　　問2 — ④　　問3 — ④　　　　　　　　　　（各3点）
問4 — 27 — ②　　28 — ①　　　　　　　　　　　　　（各2点）
問5 — ⑥　　　　　　　　　　　　　　　　　　　　　　（3点）

出典　*Original Material*

全訳　あなたは外国の学生についての発表の準備をしています。あなたはクラスメートのジャックとメアリーにそれについてのデータをメールで送りました。彼らの返事をもとに，あなたは発表の概要を作成します。

データ：

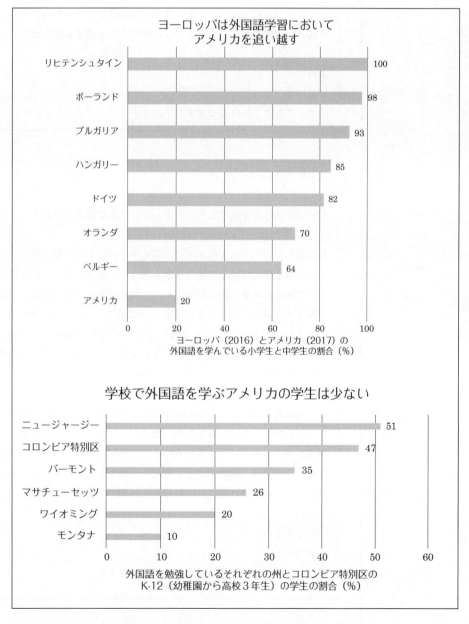

あなたのメールへの返事：

やあ，

メールありがとう。面白いデータだね。ヨーロッパ中のほとんどの小学生と中学生は彼らの教育の一部として少なくとも１つの外国語を勉強している。少なくとも１年，第二外国語を勉強することが20を超えるヨーロッパの国々で義務になっているということも聞いたことがある。外国語を学ぶということはヨーロッパ中の学生にとって共通の経験なんだね。僕はこのことについて発表したいと思うよ。

しかしながら，僕はこの問題についてより多くのことを知りたい。たとえば，この高い割合の理由を見つける必要がある。多くのヨーロッパ人はビジネスで成功するため，もしくは仕事を得るためにさえ，外国語を勉強する強い動機を持っているのだと僕は思うけれど，今後これについてさらなる調査をする必要があるね。

よろしく，
ジャック
追伸：このメッセージはメアリーにもいくよ。

こんにちは，

データを送ってくれてありがとう。とっても有益だったわ！

外国語を学ぶアメリカの学生がとても少ないことには驚いたし，外国語を学んでいないときに何を学んでいるのだろうとも思うわ。私はこのことについて話すわ。それに加えて，アメリカの学生が就活のために必要不可欠と考えているものについての情報を探してみようと思う。ジャックの考えには賛成で，ヨーロッパの学生が外国語を学ぶとき，仕事を見つけるということが彼らにとって重要な要因になっていると私も思う。それじゃあアメリカの学生はどうなのでしょう？　私は彼らが仕事を得るための準備をするときに重要視しているものについて知りたいわ。

私はあなたにアメリカの50州の間での違いについて話してほしいの。そうすると発表がもっと聴きごたえのあるものになるだろうから。あなたが送ってくれたグラフの中で示されているように，アメリカの中には外国語学習についての国家での基準というのはなく，この１つの国の中で多くの違いが存在している。きっと多くの人はなぜだか知りたいと思うわ。けれども，これはさらに調べる必要があるわ。

ではごきげんよう，
メアリー
追伸：このメッセージはジャックにもいきます。

発表の下書き：

> 発表のタイトル： ☐24☐
>
> 発表者　　　トピック
>
> 　ジャック： ☐25☐
>
> 　メアリー： ☐26☐
>
> 　私：　　　外国語学習に関するアメリカの州の間での違い
>
> 　　　　　　外国語学習のベルギーでの割合がリヒテンシュタインの約 ☐27☐
> 　　　　　　であるようにヨーロッパには一種の均一性が存在しているが，ア
> 　　　　　　メリカにおいては，モンタナの割合はニュージャージーのわずか
> 　　　　　　約 ☐28☐ である。
>
> 今後の研究テーマ： ☐29☐

設問解説

問1　☐24☐　正解 ②

「☐24☐に最適なものはどれか」

① 限られた数のやりがいのある仕事の機会をめぐるアメリカでの熾烈な競争
② **ヨーロッパとアメリカの学校での外国語教育**
③ 世界中での外国語学習への増加する支出
④ 外国語教育におけるヨーロッパの学校の均一性

　正解は②。ジャックはヨーロッパの学生の多くが外国語学習を行っていることについて発表するつもりである。またメアリーは，ヨーロッパに対してアメリカでは外国語学習をする学生の数が少ないことについて言及しており，自身はアメリカの学生は外国語の代わりに何を学んでいるのか発表するつもりである。「私」は外国語学習に関するアメリカの州の間での違いについて発表してほしいとメアリーに言われている。よって彼ら3人が扱おうとしているテーマは②「ヨーロッパとアメリカの学校での外国語教育」である。

　①，③については本文中に言及がない。④「外国語教育におけるヨーロッパの学校の均一性」はジャックの発表内容をまとめたものであるため，3人の発表全体をまとめたものとしては不適。

問2　☐25☐　正解 ④

「☐25☐に最適なものはどれか」

① ヨーロッパの学校とアメリカの学校の比較
② どのようにヨーロッパで外国語学習がますます多様化しているか
③ 第二外国語としての日本語の人気
④ **ヨーロッパにおける外国語学習の広範囲の実践**

　正解は④。ジャックは自身のメールの第1段落第3文（Most primary and ...）から最終文（I'd like to ...）において，ヨーロッパの学生の多くが外国語学習を行っていることを説明し，自分はそれについて発表したいと述べている。よって正解は④「ヨーロッパにおける外国語学習の広範囲の実践」。

問3　☐26☐　正解 ④

「☐26☐に最適なものはどれか」

① 高収入の仕事を求めるアメリカの学生の苦闘
② アメリカの州が持つ異なる学校政策
③ 多くのヨーロッパの学生がフランス語を勉強している理由
④ **外国語の代わりにアメリカの学生が勉強している科目**

— 英 R 35 —

正解は ④。メアリーは自身のメールの第 2 段落第 1 文（I was surprised ...）と第 2 文（I'll talk about ...）において，外国語学習をするアメリカの学生が少ないことに触れ，外国語学習をしていない時間で彼らは何を学んでいるのだろうと自身の疑問を提示した上で，それについて発表するつもりであると述べている。よって正解は ④「外国語の代わりにアメリカの学生が勉強している科目」。

問 4 　 27 　 正解 ②, 　 28 　 正解 ①

「あなたはメアリーの提案に同意しグラフを見る。 27 と 28 に最も適しているものを選びなさい」

① 　 5 分の 1
② 　 3 分の 2
③ 　 4 分の 3
④ 　 5 分の 4

1 つめのグラフを見れば，ベルギーの外国語学習の割合（64%）はリヒテンシュタイン（100%）の約 3 分の 2 であるとわかる。よって 27 には ② の「3 分の 2」が入る。また，2 つめのグラフにおいて，モンタナの割合（10%）はニュージャージーの割合（51%）の約 5 分の 1 である。よって 28 には ① の「5 分の 1」が入る。

問 5 　 29 　 正解 ⑥

「 29 に対する最適な組み合わせはどれか」

A：全世界的な言語としての英語への将来の傾向
B：外国語学習の母語への影響
C：アメリカにおいて外国語学習に違いがある理由
D：なぜヨーロッパでは多くの学生が外国語を学んでいるのか

正解は ⑥。ジャックは自身のメールの第 2 段落第 2 文（For example, I ...）と第 3 文（I suppose many ...）において，ヨーロッパにおいて外国語学習を行う学生の割合が高い理由について自分なりの考察を述べながら，これについてはさらなる調査が必要であると述べている。またメアリーは，自身のメールの第 3 段落において，アメリカは外国語学習に関して国内に違いがあることについて述べ，それについて発表してほしいと依頼しつつ，その理由については，さらに調べる必要があるとも書いている。

よって正解は C「アメリカにおいて外国語学習に違いがある理由」と D「なぜヨーロッパでは多くの学生が外国語を学んでいるのか」の組み合わせである ⑥ となる。

（主な語句・表現）・問題冊子を参照のこと。

[リード文]
◇ based on ...「…に基づいて」　　　　◇ response 图「返答」
◇ draft 動「…を起草する」图「下書き」　◇ outline 图「概略」

[添付データ]
◇ outpace 動「…にまさる」　　　　　　◇ primary 形「（学校などが）初等の」
◇ secondary 形「（学校・教育が）中等の」◇ district 图「地区」
◇ kindergarten 图「《米》（4-6 歳の子どものための）幼稚園」
◇ state 图「州」

[ジャックのメール]
◇ across 前「…の至る所に」　　　　　　◇ at least「少なくとも」
◇ education 图「教育」　　　　　　　　◇ compulsory 形「義務的な」
◇ common 形「共通の；ありふれた」　　◇ throughout 前「…の至る所に」
◇ suppose 動「…だと思う」　　　　　　◇ motive 图「動機」
◇ in order to-「-するために」　　　　　◇ successful 形「成功した」

— 英 R 36 —

◇ further 形「さらに付け加えた」
◇ best 名「（手紙などで）よろしくというあいさつ」

[メアリーのメール]

◇ informative 形「有益な」　　　　　　◇ wonder 動「…だろうかと思う」
◇ in addition「加えて」　　　　　　　◇ look for ...「…を探す」
◇ indispensable 形「不可欠な」　　　　◇ agree 動「意見が一致する」
◇ factor 名「要因」
◇ what about ...?「…についてはどう思いますか？」
◇ emphasis 名「重要視」　　　　　　　◇ difference 名「違い」
◇ among 前「…の間に」　　　　　　　◇ worth － ing「－する価値がある」
◇ As is shown ...　ここでの as は関係代名詞。先行詞は there is no ... in the one country。
　関係代名詞の as は，前の節全体や一部などを先行詞とする非制限用法で用いられることが
　ある。この文のように，as の導く節を先行詞となる主節の前に置くこともある。
◇ national 形「国全体の」　　　　　　◇ standard 名「基準」
◇ exist 動「存在する」　　　　　　　◇ sure 形「確信して」
◇ all the best「ではごきげんよう；ではご武運を願って」

[発表の下書き]

◇ presenter 名「発表者」　　　　　　◇ gap 名「相違」
◇ regarding 前「…に関して」　　　　◇ uniformity 名「均一性」
◇ theme 名「テーマ」

[設問文・選択肢]

◇ fierce 形「激烈な」　　　　　　　　◇ competition 名「競争」
◇ limited 形「限られた」　　　　　　◇ rewarding 形「やりがいのある」
◇ career 名「職業」　　　　　　　　◇ opportunity 名「機会」
◇ rise 動「上がる」　　　　　　　　◇ expenditure 名「支出」
◇ compare 動「…を比較する」　　　　◇ diverse 形「多様な」
◇ popularity 名「人気」　　　　　　◇ widespread 形「広範囲に及ぶ」
◇ practice 名「実践」　　　　　　　◇ struggle 名「苦闘」
◇ well-paid 形「給料のよい」　　　　◇ different 形「異なった」
◇ policy 名「政策」　　　　　　　　◇ instead of ...「…の代わりに」
◇ suggestion 名「提案」　　　　　　◇ combination 名「組み合わせ」
◇ tendency 名「傾向」　　　　　　　◇ toward 前「…の方へ」
◇ global 形「世界的な」　　　　　　◇ impact 名「影響」
◇ mother tongue「母語」

— 英 R 37 —

第5問

解答

問1 - ④　　問2 - ①　　　　　　　　　　　　　　　　　　（各3点）

問3 - ┃ 32 ┃ - ①　┃ 33 ┃ - ③　┃ 34 ┃ - ⑤　┃ 35 ┃ - ④　（完答で3点）

問4 - ① · ⑤　　　　　　　　　　　　（順不同・両方正解で3点）

問5 - ④　　　　　　　　　　　　　　　　　　　　　　　（3点）

出典　*Original Material*（参考資料：*The Economist*, Dec. 7th, 2006）

全訳　国際ニュースの記事を使って，あなたは英語の口頭発表コンテストに参加する予定です。発表用のメモを作成するために，アメリカで書かれた次のニュース記事を読みなさい。

　　アナイス・ボルディエとサマンサ・ファターマンは同じように笑い，同じように頬にそばかすがある。彼女たちは同じ髪型をしている。2人は一緒に育ったようにからかい，つつき合うが，一緒に育ったわけではないのだ。サマンサもアナイスも一卵性双生児の姉妹がいることを知らなかった。双子は2013年5月に初めてロンドンで会った。双子がエアビーアンドビー民泊アパートの居間で顔を合わせた時，2人は凝視することしかできなかった。最初彼女たちは，初デートをしているようで少しきまり悪く感じたが，その居心地の悪さはすぐに消え去った。その最初の日に一緒に昼寝までもしたのだった。

　　パリで育ったフランス人学生のアナイスはロンドンでファッションデザインを学んでいた。2012年12月のある土曜日，彼女がバスに乗っていた時，彼女の友だちがサマンサを特集したユーチューブ動画のスクリーン・ショットを送ってきた。アナイスはふと，「あら，誰が私の動画をユーチューブに載せたのかしら？」と思った。しかし後に，それは彼女ではなくてアメリカ人の女優であることがわかった。2005年の映画である『SAYURI』に出演したロサンゼルスに拠点を置く女優であるサマンサは，アナイスと同様に韓国で生まれたが，彼女と同じ日である1987年11月19日に生まれたのだった。2人とも生まれてすぐに養子に出され，アナイスはパリの夫婦に，サマンサは3人の男の子のいるニュージャージーの家族に引き取られた。彼女はフェイスブックを通じてサマンサに連絡することにし，友だちリクエストとメッセージを送った。

　　2013年2月21日，サマンサは新しい映画の公開日に向けて爪にマニキュアを塗ってもらうために友だちのアパートへ行った。彼女の友だちがマニキュアを塗っている間，彼女は携帯をいじり，アナイスという名前の若い女性からフェイスブックにリクエストが届いているのを見た。その女性の写真をじっと見て，自分の古い写真だと思った。彼女は画像をタップし，プロフィールを見た。すると，彼女たちは同じ誕生日で同じような活動をしてきたことがわかった。サマンサは最初，アナイスの友だちリクエストとメッセージをどう判断すればよいかわからなかった。返事をするのに数日かかったが，最終的に彼女は友だちリクエストを受け入れた。

　　フェイスブックでつながってから数日後，サマンサとアナイスはスカイプを使って初めて話をした。彼女たちにとって，それはブラインド・デートに行くようなもので，最初に何をたずねたらいいのかわからなかった。彼女たちは全てのことがどのように起こったのか，友だちは何と言っているのか話した。自分たちの鼻，歯，耳，手を比較した。現在の彼氏事情について話をした。彼女たちは話を続け，最後はただお互いを凝視していたのだった。90分間おしゃべりをするはずが，結局3時間話をすることになった。

　　後に彼女たちはDNAテストを受け，既にわかっていたことが証明された。つまり，

— 英 R 38 —

彼女たちは実際に双子だったのだ。彼女たちは，長い髪や鼻の周りに散りばめられたそばかす以外にも似ている点を発見した。2人ともピーマンと加熱した人参が嫌いで，ペプシよりもコカ・コーラが好きで，韓国バーベキューとハロウィンが好きである。2人は同じ色のマニキュアが好きで，ストレスを感じた時には昼寝が必要で，1日に10時間眠る。しかしながら，彼女たちの違いも明らかだ。サマンサはより社交的だが，それは彼女が思うに2人の兄と一緒に育った結果である。他方，一人っ子のアナイスは，はるかに気分屋で，自分が養子になったことや棄てられたという気持ちに苦しんでいる。

彼女たちは韓国人の生みの母親に連絡しようとしたが，母親は彼女たちとつながりを持ちたいと思っていない。「いつか彼女が私たちに連絡したくなったら，私たちはここにいるわ。私たちはその気があるし，準備もできているわ」とサマンサは言う。彼女たちは今でも地球の反対側に住んでいるが，今やパリでハンドバッグのデザイナーとなったアナイスとロサンゼルスにいるサマンサは毎日何度も携帯メッセージを送っている。サマンサは朝いつも携帯メッセージで起こしてくれるとアナイスは言う。彼女は「起きて，遅刻よ」といったメッセージを受け取るのだ。2人は赤ちゃんの時に引き離されたかもしれないが，今や永遠につながっていると彼女たちは言う。

あなたのメモ：

　　　　　　　　　　　　　　　　　　　　　 30 　　　　　　　セントラル高校
　　　　　　　　　　　　　　　　　　　　　　　　　　　　　英語口頭発表コンテスト

登場人物
- アナイス： ☐ ⎫
- サマンサ： ☐ ⎬ 31
　　　　　　　　⎭

双子の出会いの流れ
双子として生まれた。
→ 異なる家族に養子として受け入れられた。
→ 32 → 33 → 34 → 35

双子の共通の特徴
彼女たちは同じ：
- そばかすがある。
- 髪型をしている。
- 笑い方をする。
- 色の好みを持っている。
- 36 。
- 37 。

現在の双子
双子は今：
- 38 。
- お互いとつながっていると感じている。
- 多くのメッセージを送り合う。

設問解説　問1　30　正解④

「あなたの発表の最もよい題名はどれか」　30

①　いつも一緒にいる双子
②　母を探す双子
③　夢を追う双子
④　現代的な方法で再会した双子

正解は④。文章全体で双子が再会したいきさつが説明されているが，特に，ユーチューブで双子の姉妹の存在を知ったことや，フェイスブックやスカイプを使ってお互いと連絡を取ったという点で，再会方法が現代的であることがこのストーリーの特徴である。したがって，④が正解。

いつも一緒にいるわけではないので①は不適切であり，母親を探したり夢を追うことが主な記述内容ではないので②と③も誤り。

問2　31　正解①

「31 に最もふさわしい組み合わせはどれか」

	アナイス	サマンサ
①	韓国系のフランス人デザイナー	韓国系のアメリカ人女優
②	アメリカ系の韓国人女優	フランス系の韓国人デザイナー
③	フランス系の韓国人デザイナー	アメリカ系の韓国人女優
④	韓国系のアメリカ人女優	韓国系のフランス人デザイナー

第2段落第1文（Anais, a French ...）に，アナイスはフランス人学生であると述べられており，最終段落第3文（Though they still ...）より，今はハンドバッグのデザイナーになっていることがわかる。他方，サマンサについては，第2段落第4文（But later she ...）に，アメリカ人女優であると述べられている。また，第2段落第5文（Samantha, a Los ...）や最終段落第1文（They have tried ...）から，2人は韓国人の母親から韓国で生まれたことがわかる。

以上のことより，アナイスは韓国系のフランス人デザイナー，サマンサは韓国系のアメリカ人女優であると判断できるので，①が正解。

問3　32　正解①，　33　正解③，　34　正解⑤，　35　正解④

「5つの選択肢（①～⑤）から4つを選び，起こった順に並べ替えなさい」

①　アナイスはユーチューブでサマンサを見た。
②　サマンサはアナイスに友だちリクエストを送った。
③　フェイスブックで「友だち」になった。
④　初めて直接会った。
⑤　スカイプで話をした。

第2段落に，アナイスがサマンサのユーチューブ動画を見たことが述べられている。その後，アナイスがサマンサに対して友だちリクエストをしたことが同段落最終文（She decided to ...）に述べられており，さらに，第3段落の内容から，2013年2月21日にその友だちリクエストをサマンサが見て，その数日後にリクエストを受け入れてフェイスブック上の「友だち」になったことがわかる。また，その数日後にスカイプで会話をしたことが第4段落第1文（Several days after ...）から読み取れる。ここで第1段落第5文（The twins met ...）に戻ると，2人が初めて直接会ったのは2013年5月と述べられており，これはスカイプで連絡を取った後の出来事だとわかる。したがって，①→③→⑤→④の順番に決定する。なお，友だちリクエストはアナイスからサマンサに対して送ったので，②は誤り。

— 英 R 40 —

問4 36 ・ 37 正解①・⑤

「 36 と 37 に最もふさわしい２つの選択肢を選びなさい（順序は問わない。）」

① 食べ物の好み
② 家庭環境
③ 性格
④ 職業
⑤ 睡眠のパターン

正解は①・⑤。第５段落第３文（Both hate bell ...）に「２人ともピーマンと加熱した人参が嫌いで，ペプシよりもコカ・コーラが好きで，韓国バーベキューが好きだ」と述べられている。また，その次の文に「ストレスを感じた時には昼寝が必要で，１日に10時間眠る」とある。したがって，①と⑤が正解。

なお，同段落の最後から２番目の文（However, their differences ...）と最終文（On the other ...）から，２人の性格と家庭環境が異なることがわかるので，②と③は誤り。また，２人は同じ職業ではないことがわかるので④も誤り。

問5 38 正解④

「 38 に最も適切な選択肢を選びなさい」

① 生みの母親と連絡を取っている
② 毎朝お互いに電話をかける
③ 頻繁にお互いを訪問している
④ 離れた場所に住んでいる

正解は④。最終段落第３文（Though they still ...）より，２人は離れた場所に住んでいることがわかる。①，②については本文中の記述と異なり，③については本文中に記述がないので誤り。

主な語句・表現 ・問題冊子を参照のこと。

[リード文] ◇ oral 形「口頭の」 ◇ in preparation for ...「…に備えて」

[第１段落] ◇ freckled 形「そばかすのある」 ◇ tease 動「…をからかう」
(Anais Bordier ...) ◇ poke 動「…をつつく」 ◇ neither A nor B ...「A も B も…ない」
◇ identical 形「一卵性の」 ◇ come face to face「面と向かう」
◇ Airbnb「エアビーアンドビー」 アメリカの民泊企業。
◇ stare 動「凝視する」 ◇ awkward 形「きまりの悪い」
◇ discomfort 名「居心地の悪さ」 ◇ take a nap「昼寝する」

[第２段落] ◇ screen shot「スクリーン・ショット」 画面上に表示されたものを写した画像。
(Anais, a ...) ◇ feature 動「…を特集する」 ◇ automatically 副「自動的に；思わず」
◇ post 動「…を載せる；投稿する」 ◇ adopt 動「…を養子にする」
◇ via 前「…経由で」

[第３段落] ◇ have one's nails done「爪にマニキュアを塗ってもらう」 do one's nails で「爪にマニキュ
(On February ...) アを塗る；爪の手入れをする」。
◇ the opening day「（舞台などの）初日」 ◇ fiddle with ...「…をいじくる」
◇ tap 動「…をタップする；軽くたたく」
◇ what to make of ...「…をどう判断すべきか」
◇ eventually 副「最終的に」

— 英 R 41 —

[第4段落]	◇ status 图「状況」	◇ end up -ing「最終的に-することになる」
(Several days ...)		
[第5段落]	◇ similarity 图「類似点」	◇ spray 图「しぶき；飛散」
(Later they ...)	◇ bell pepper「ピーマン；パプリカ」	◇ prefer A to B「B よりも A の方を好む」
	◇ nail polish「マニキュア液」	◇ notable 形「顕著である；注目に値する」
	◇ outgoing 形「社交的な」	◇ moody 形「気分屋の；憂鬱な」
	◇ struggle with ...「…に苦しむ；…と戦う」	◇ abandonment 图「棄てられること」

[最終段落]	◇ halfway around the world「地球の反対側に」	
(They have ...)	◇ text message「携帯電話で送るメッセージ」	
	◇ multiple 形「多数の」	◇ tear ... apart「…を引き裂く」
	◇ bonded 形「(きずなで) 結ばれた」	

[設問・選択肢]	◇ pursue 動「…を追い求める」	◇ reunite 動「…を再会させる」
	◇ descent 图「系統；血統」	◇ preference 图「好み；嗜好」
	◇ profession 图「職業」	◇ be in touch with ...「…と連絡を取っている」
	◇ biological 形「生物学上の」	

— 英 R 42 —

第6問

解答

A 問1 - ④　　問2 - ③　　　　　　　　　　　　　　　　　　　　（各3点）
　問3 - ①・⑤　　　　　　　　　　　　　　　　（順不同・両方正解で3点）
　問4 - ①　　　　　　　　　　　　　　　　　　　　　　　　　　（3点）
B 問1 - ④　　問2 - ⑤　　問3 - ④　　　　　　　　　　　　　（各2点）
　問4 - ①・②　　　　　　　　　　　　　　　　（順不同・両方正解で3点）
　問5 - ①　　　　　　　　　　　　　　　　　　　　　　　　　　（3点）

A

出典　Linda Robinson Fellag: *From Reading to Writing 3* (adapted)

全訳

　現代社会の服装規定に関するクラスの研究課題に取り組んでいる最中，あなたは以下の記事を見つけました。あなたはそれを読み，発見したことについてクラスメートに話すためのメモを作成しています。

ネクタイの着用は本当に必要なのか

　ネクタイを身につけることは本当に必要なのだろうか。どうして聡明な男性たちは布きれを首に巻きつけ，締めつけるのか。アメリカのジャーナリストのリンダ・エラービーは「もし男性が世の中を動かすことができるのだとしたら，どうしてネクタイを身につけるのをやめられないのか」と問うた。多くの人々はこう答えるだろう。女性だけでなく，男性もファッションの名目で多くの愚行をしでかすものなのだ，と。

　世界中の多くの実業家が，現代のネクタイは無用だと今では主張している。ネクタイは帽子やシャツやズボンや靴のように暑さや寒さから体を守ってくれない。ネクタイは細長く薄い布きれなので，悪天候の中で体を覆うほど大きくない。また，ベルトのように他の衣料品を落ちないよう留めることもない。ネクタイはシャツの上からぶら下がっているので，何も留めることがないのだ。ネクタイは靴を快適に履けるようにする靴下と違い，着用者に快適性を提供することがない。実際，ほとんどの男性はネクタイが不快だと言っている。ネクタイに実用的な用途がないのは明らかだ。

　しかしネクタイはいつも無用だったわけではない。2世紀のローマでは，演説者や兵士がのどを暑さ，寒さ，埃から守るためにファカールというネックスカーフを身につけていた。後にクロアチア人が，天候から身を守るためにローマ人が首に巻いていた布を採用した。18世紀のイギリスでは，首に巻いた布が戦闘での負傷を防ぐほど分厚かったと伝えられている。アジアから南北アメリカでは，バンダナが働く男性の首を守る実用的な手段として役立ってきた。

　しかし時が過ぎるにつれ，ネクタイの実用性はなくなっていった。1600年代になると，上流階級のファッションを象徴するものだからという理由だけで，男性はネクタイを着用するようになった。フランスのルイ14世はきめの細かいシルク製のレースの布で首を覆っていた。その結果，多くの男性が王のスタイルに倣ったのである。17世紀から19世紀のヨーロッパの絵画には，軍隊や政府や上流階級に属する男性たちが，ほとんど首を回せないほど硬く幅の広い布を首に巻いた姿が描き出されている。しかし最終的に，首の布は身なりのよい男性にとって必須の衣料品になったのである。

　現代の多くの男性も，特定の職業においてより高い地位を求めようとする願望の結果としてネクタイを身につける。有望な重役や事務員や技師がネクタイを身につける

― 英 R 43 ―

のは，彼らの上司がそうしているからである。こうした男性はビジネス，政治，その他の職業に自分が帰属していることを示し，いかにも成功しているという見た目にしたり，上司を満足させたりするためにネクタイを着用している。このような要因のために，ネクタイの横行は世界中に広まったのである。アジア，アフリカ，南米では，ネクタイは男性のフォーマルな衣装において必要な一部となっている。それどころか現代の中国や日本では，ネクタイを身につけない男性は仕事に対して不真面目だと考えられ，伝統を軽んじているとみなされてしまう。もっとも，その親や祖父母の世代はネクタイを聞いたこともなかったのだが。

こうしたことを悪習であるとみなし，ネクタイを廃止しようとしてきた人もいる。金曜日に従業員がよりカジュアルな服装をすることを認める企業も増えてきており，その日は男性労働者がネクタイを身につけずに職場に行くことが許されている。また，男性が暑い夏にネクタイを身につけずにシャツを着用する場合もある。また，もはや男性のネクタイ着用がまったく要求されない職場も今日増えてきている。それにもかかわらず，職場にネクタイを着用していくことを要求されている男性はまだ多い。

今から数世紀後，あるいはほんの数十年先のことかもしれないが，人々は過去を振り返り，信じられないと言うかのように首を振るかもしれない。男性が実際にこのようなものを首に巻き，それを身につける必要があると考えていた理由が彼らには理解できないだろう。では，どうして現代世界の男性がネクタイを身につけずに職場の会議や結婚式に登場したからといって，不適切な身なりだとみなされてしまうのだろうか。将来，こうした状況にいるほとんどの人にとって，おそらく社会の非公式の服装規定よりも快適さの方が重要になるだろう。

あなたのメモ：

ネクタイの着用は本当に必要なのか

現代のネクタイに反対するいくつかの論拠

ネクタイには…という実用的な機能がない
- 天候から体を守る
- 39
- 身体の快適さを提供する

ネクタイの歴史的な背景

歴史におけるネクタイの実用的用途
- 古代ローマ：天候から男性ののどを守る
  →クロアチア人が 40
- 18世紀のイギリス：戦闘時の負傷から身を守る
- アジアと両アメリカ大陸：働く男性の首を守る

▽

ネクタイの意味の変化
- 17世紀以降のヨーロッパ：上流階級の象徴として機能
- 現代社会：41 と 42 を示す

最近の傾向

> ネクタイを悪習とみなす人が多い
> ・多くの会社が特定の状況でネクタイ非着用の服装規定を認めている
> ・ネクタイ着用をまったく要求しない企業もある
> 　→こうした試みにもかかわらず，ネクタイ着用の強要は完全にはな
> 　　くなっていない

筆者の予測
将来は大多数の人が　43　だろう。

設問解説

問1　　39　　正解 ④

「　39　に最もふさわしい選択肢を選びなさい」

① 着用者が成功するのに役立つ
② 着用者の見た目をよりよくする
③ 敵の攻撃から身を守る
④ **他の衣料品を留めておく**

　正解は ④。　39　を含むコラムの小見出しになっている「現代のネクタイに反対するいくつかの論拠」に関しては，第2段落に述べられている。とりわけ第3文（Also, it does ...）に「また，ベルトのように他の衣料品を落ちないよう留めることもない」とあるので，④ が当てはまる。hold up ≒ secure の対応がやや難しいが，この程度の言い換えは共通テストでも見られる。

　① は第5段落，③ は第3段落に該当する記述があるが，いずれもそのような実用的機能がないことが「現代のネクタイに反対するいくつかの論拠」となっているのではない。

問2　　40　　正解 ③

「　40　に最もふさわしい選択肢を選びなさい」

① ローマ人の服装規定を批判した
② 侵略から身を守った
③ **ローマ人の習慣に倣った**
④ 天気予報の方法を発明した

　正解は ③。　40　の前にある「クロアチア人」に関しては，第3段落第3文（Later, Croatians adopted ...）に「後にクロアチア人が，天候から身を守るためにローマ人が首に巻いていた布を採用した」とある。つまりローマ人が使用していた「ファカール」を模倣したということだから，③ が正解。

問3　　41　・　42　　正解 ①・⑤

「　41　と　42　に最もふさわしい2つの選択肢を選びなさい（順序は問わない。）」

① **仕事で成功したいという人々の野心**
② 努力せずに成功するという人々の期待
③ 他者に対する人々の友好的態度
④ 上司に対する人々の反抗的態度
⑤ **組織への人々の帰属意識**

　正解は ①・⑤。　41　と　42　を含むメモの小見出しになっている「ネクタイの意味の変化」については第4段落と第5段落で述べられている。第5段落第1文（Many men today ...）では「現代の多くの男性も，特定の職業においてより高い地位を求めようとす

— 英 R 45 —

る願望の結果としてネクタイを身につける」と述べられていることから，① が正解となる。また，第 5 段落第 3 文（These men wear ...）に「こうした男性はビジネス，政治，その他の職業に自分が帰属していることを示すためにネクタイを着用している」とあるので，⑤ も正解となる。

問 4　　43　　正解 ①

「ポスター中の　43　に最もふさわしい選択肢を選びなさい」

① 身体的な不快感を避けるためにネクタイ着用の習慣をやめる
② 公式の場でネクタイを着用していない人を不適切な服装だと見なす
③ いかなる規則にも従う必要がないと信じる
④ ネクタイの実用的価値を過小評価しない

正解は ①。　43　の前に記載されている「筆者の予測」に関しては，最終段落最終文（In the future, ...）に「将来，こうした状況にいるほとんどの人にとって，おそらく社会の非公式の服装規定よりも快適さの方が重要になるだろう」とある。「服装規定よりも快適さの方が重要になる」というのは，本文の文脈で言えば「不愉快なネクタイの着用をやめる」と解釈できるので，① が最もふさわしい。

主な語句・表現　・問題冊子を参照のこと。

[リード文]
◇ work on ...「…に取り組む」　　　　　◇ project 图「研究課題」
◇ dress code「服装規定」　　　　　　　◇ following 形「以下の」
◇ finding 图「発見［調査］結果」

[第 1 段落]
（Is wearing a ...）
◇ tie 图「ネクタイ」　　　　　　　　　◇ intelligent 形「聡明な」
◇ loop 動「…を巻きつける」　　　　　　◇ rag 图「布きれ」
◇ tighten 動「…をしっかり締めつける」　◇ run 動「…を動かす」

[第 2 段落]
（Many businesspeople ...）
◇ argue that ...「…と主張する」
◇ as　ここでは「…するように」という意味の接続詞として用いられている。
◇ strip 图「細長いもの」
◇ hold up ...［... up］「…を落ちないよう留める」
◇ clothing item「衣料品」　　　　　　　◇ comfort 图「快適さ」
◇ wearer 图「着用者」
◇ allow ... to −「…が−することを許可する［可能にする］」
◇ comfortably 副「快適に」　　　　　　◇ uncomfortable 形「不愉快な」
◇ practical 形「実用的な」　　　　　　　◇ purpose 图「目的」

[第 3 段落]
（The tie hasn't ...）
◇ not always ...「いつも…とは限らない」
◇ however 副「しかしながら」　この語は文頭の他，文中や文末にも置かれる。
◇ scarves　scarf 图「スカーフ」の複数形。　◇ throat 图「喉（のど）」
◇ Croatian 图「クロアチア人」　　　　　◇ adopt 動「…を採用する」
◇ guard against ...「…から身を守る」　against は前置詞で「…に反対して」の意味。
◇ so ... that ～「（とても）…なので～する；～するほど…だ」
◇ reportedly 副「報道によれば；うわさ［言い伝え］によると」
◇ bandana 图「バンダナ」　　　　　　　◇ serve as ...「…として役立つ」
◇ means 图「手段」

— 英 R 46 —

[第4段落]	◇ as ここでは「…するにつれて」という意味の接続詞として用いられている。
(As time ...)	◇ pass 動「過ぎる」
	◇ though 副「しかし」 though はこの副詞の用法では，文末もしくは文中に置かれる。
	◇ usefulness 名「実用性」　◇ symbolize 動「…を象徴する」
	◇ upper class「上流階級」
	◇ lace 名「レース」 ここでは形容詞的に用いられ，後ろの neck coverings を修飾している。
	◇ fine silk「きめの細かいシルク［絹］」　◇ covering 名「何かを覆うもの」
	◇ consequently 副「結果として」　◇ follow 動「…に倣う；…に従う」
	◇ stiff 形「硬い」
	◇ barely 副「ほとんど…ない；かろうじて…する」
	◇ in the end「最終的に」　◇ essential 形「必要不可欠な」
	◇ well-dressed 形「身なりの立派な」

[第5段落]	◇ as a result of ...「…の結果として」　◇ desire 名「願望」
(Many men ...)	◇ upward 形「上向きの；上位の」　◇ status 名「地位」
	◇ certain 形「(名詞の前に置いて) ある特定の；何らかの」
	◇ profession 名「職業」　◇ hopeful 形「有望な」
	◇ executive 名「重役」　◇ clerk 名「事務員」
	◇ technician 名「技師」　◇ successful 形「成功した」
	◇ please 動「…を満足させる」　◇ due to ...「…が原因で」
	◇ tyranny 名「横行；独裁 (政治)」　◇ spread 動「広まる」
	◇ across 前「…中に」　◇ globe 名「世界；地球」
	◇ male 形「男性の」　◇ disrespect 動「…を軽視する」
	◇ though ここでは「…だが」という意味の接続詞として用いられている。..., though ～という形は「…，もっとも～だが」という意味合いになることが多い。

[第6段落]	◇ see ... as ～「…を～とみなす」　◇ convention 名「慣習；慣例」
(Some people ...)	◇ get rid of ...「…をやめる；…を取り除く」　◇ casually 副「カジュアルに；気軽に」
	◇ professional 名「職業人」　◇ may 助「…してもかまわない」
	◇ no longer「もう…ない」
	◇ expect ... to －「…に－することを要求［期待］する」 ここでは受動態になっている。
	◇ 否定語 + at all「まったく…ない」　◇ nevertheless 副「それにもかかわらず」

[最終段落]	◇ decade 名「10 年」　◇ look back「〈過去を〉振り返る」
(In a few ...)	◇ disbelief 名「不信；疑念」　◇ actually 副「実際に」
	◇ inappropriately 副「不適切に」　◇ unofficial 形「非公式の」

[ポスター]	◇ argument 名「論拠」　◇ function 名「機能」
	◇ historical 形「歴史的な」　◇ context 名「背景」
	◇ ancient 形「古代の」　◇ from ... on「…以降」
	◇ regard ... as ～「…を～とみなす」　◇ occasion 名「場合；時」
	◇ require 動「…を要求する」　◇ despite 前「…にもかかわらず」
	◇ attempt 名「試み」　◇ pressure 名「強制；強要」
	◇ not completely「完全には…しない」　◇ expectation 名「予測；期待」

| [設問文・選択肢] | ◇ option 名「選択肢」　◇ help ... (to) －「…が－するのに役立つ」 |
| | ◇ make O －「O に－させる」　◇ enemy 名「敵」 |

— 英 R 47 —

◇ secure 動「…を固定する」　　　　　　◇ criticize 動「…を批判する」

◇ invasion 名「侵略」　　　　　　　　◇ imitate 動「…に倣う；…を模倣する」

◇ weather forecasting「天気予報」

◇ attitude toward ...「…に対する態度［考え方］」

◇ sense 名「感覚」　　　　　　　　　　◇ organization 名「組織」

◇ abandon 動「…を廃止する」　　　　　◇ custom 名「習慣」

◇ underestimate 動「…を過小評価する」

B

出典　*Original Material*（参考資料：https://www.darksky.org/light-pollution/）

全訳

　　あなたは，光が環境に与える影響について学んでいます。あなたは，それについて詳しく調べるために，インターネットサイトの次の文章を読もうとしているところです。

　　　大気汚染，水質汚染，土壌汚染は私たちのほとんどが知っているが，光もまた汚染物質となりうることをご存知だっただろうか？　人工光の不適切な使用や過剰な使用は，光害として知られており，人間や野生生物，気候に深刻な環境的結果をもたらす可能性がある。

　　　光害の１つに sky glow があり，それは主に都市部の上空で，自動車や街灯，オフィス，工場，屋外広告などの電灯のせいで夜空が明るくなり，日がとっぷり暮れても仕事や遊びをしている人たちのために，夜が昼になってしまうことである。2016 年の調査によると，世界の人口の 80% が sky glow の下で生活している。アメリカやヨーロッパでは，99% の大衆が自然の夜空を体験できないのだ！　他にも３種類の光害がある。それらは，clutter, light trespass, glare である。clutter とは，明るく混乱をさせるような過剰な光源の集まりのことだ。light trespass とは，望まれなかったり，必要とされていない場所に光が広がり入り込むことだ。glare とは，視覚的な不快感を引き起こす過剰な明るさのことだ。

　　　光害は，産業文明の副産物である。実際，夜間に使用される屋外照明の多くは，効率が悪く，明るすぎたり，おかしなところに当たっていたり，不適切に遮蔽されていたりして，多くの場合，まったく必要のないものである。これらの光とそれを作るために使用される電気は，人々が照らしてほしい現実の物や場所に当てられるのではなく，空に向かって無駄に放出されているのだ。

　　　地球上の多くの人々が光に汚染された空の下で生活しているため，過剰に光を当てることは国際的な懸念となっている。都市部や郊外に住んでいれば，夜，外に出て空を見上げるだけで，このような汚染を目にすることがでる。30 億年もの間，地球上の生命は，太陽，月，星の光だけで作られた明暗のリズムの中に存在していた。今では，人工的な光が闇を支配し，街が夜になると光り輝き，自然の昼と夜のパターンを崩し，環境の微妙なバランスを変えている。この天然資源の喪失による悪影響は，目に見えないもののように思えるかもしれない。しかし，夜空が明るくなることが，エネルギー消費量の増加，生態系や野生生物の混乱，人間の健康への害，犯罪や安全に関する悪影響を含むマイナスの影響に直接関連することを示す証拠が増えている。光害はすべての市民に影響を与える。幸いなことに，光害への関心は劇的に高まっている。自然な夜を取り戻すために行動を起こす科学者，環境保護団体，市民のリーダーが増えている。私たち一人一人が，地域，国内，国際的に光害に立ち向かうための現実的な解決策を選ぶことができる。

— 英 R 48 —

良いニュースは，光害は他の多くの形態の公害とは異なり，元に戻すことができ，私たち一人一人が変化をもたらすことができるということだ！　光害が問題であると認識するだけでは十分ではなく，行動を起こすことが必要だ。まずは，自分の家から出る夜の光を最小限にすることから始めることができる。そこで，家族や友人にその光害という言葉を広め，伝えてもらおう。多くの人は，光害や夜間の人工的な光がもたらす悪影響について知らないか，それほど理解していない。代表的人物になって他の人に問題を説明することで，この深刻化しつつある問題を認識してもらい，より多くの人に自然の夜空を守るために必要な行動をとってもらう一助となるだろう。

設問解説

問1　44　正解④

「あなたには光害が　44　によって引き起こされてきたことがわかる」

① 人間による自然光源の破壊
② 先進国での経済不況
③ 暗闇の危険性に対する高まる認識
④ 不必要な場所での不必要な光の使用

　正解は④。著者は，第3段落第2文（The fact is ...）で「実際，夜間に使用される屋外照明の多くは，効率が悪く，明るすぎたり，おかしなところに当たっていたり，不適切に遮蔽されていたりして，多くの場合，まったく必要のないものである」と述べ，続く最終文（This light, and ...）でも「これらの光とそれを作るために使用される電気は，人々が照らしてほしい現実の物や場所に当てられるのではなく，空に向かって無駄に放出されているのだ」と述べていることを根拠にする。
　①〜③のような記述は本文中にはない。

問2　45　正解⑤

「あなたは学んだばかりの情報をまとめている。表はどのように仕上げられるべきか」
45

光害の種類	簡単な説明
(A)	居住地域上空の明るさ
(B)	見ることを困難にする明るさ
(C)	さまざまな光源から集められた光
(D)	意図されていないところに入り込む光

① (A) clutter (B) glare (C) light trespass (D) sky glow
② (A) clutter (B) light trespass (C) sky glow (D) glare
③ (A) light trespass (B) glare (C) clutter (D) sky glow
④ (A) sky glow (B) clutter (C) light trespass (D) glare
⑤ **(A) sky glow (B) glare (C) clutter (D) light trespass**

　正解は⑤。表にまとめられている4種類の光害は第2段落に記述がある。sky glow に関しては第1文（One kind of ...）に「都市部の上空で，自動車や街灯，オフィス，工場，屋外広告などの電灯のせいで夜空が明るくなり」という記述があるので，(A)に該当するとわかる。第5文（Clutter is bright, ...）には clutter の説明があり，「明るく混乱をさせるような過剰な光源の集まりのことだ」とある。よって(C)が該当する。第6文（Light trespass is ...）には light trespass の説明があり，「望まれなかったり，必要とされていない場所に光が広がり入り込むことだ」と述べられているので(D)に該当する。最終文（Glare is excessive ...）には glare の説明があり，「視覚的な不快感を引き起こす過剰な明るさのこと」と述べられているので(B)がこれに該当する。

— 英 R 49 —

問3 ┃ 46 ┃ 正解 ④

「次のうち，光害の悪影響として含めるべきでないものはどれか」 ┃ 46 ┃

① 人体の生命と身体への危険
② 電気の無駄遣い
③ 自然環境への干渉
④ **文明の発展**
⑤ 社会における治安の悪化

　正解は ④。第4段落第6文（But a growing ...）で「しかし，夜空が明るくなることが，エネルギー消費量の増加，生態系や野生生物の混乱，人間の健康への害，犯罪や安全に関する悪影響を含むマイナスの影響に直接関連することを示す証拠が増えている」と述べられていることから，①「人体の生命と身体への危険（人間の健康への害に相当）」，②「電気の無駄遣い（エネルギー消費量の増加に相当）」，③「自然環境への干渉（生態系や野生生物の混乱に相当）」，⑤「社会における治安の悪化（犯罪や安全に関する悪影響に相当）」は光害の悪影響として言及されていると判断できる。一方，④「文明の発展」は本文中では光害の悪影響として取り上げられていないことから，正解は ④ となる。

問4 ┃ 47 ┃ · ┃ 48 ┃ 正解 ① · ②

「あなたが読んだ記事によると，次のうちどれが正しいか（選択肢を2つ選べ。順序は問わない。）」 ┃ 47 ┃ · ┃ 48 ┃

① 光害をなくすことは可能である。
② **地球上の生命は，非常に長い間，光と闇のリズムに沿って生きていた。**
③ 光害以外の種類の公害についても，人々はもっと知っておくべきだ。
④ 光害の悪影響は容易に理解できる。
⑤ 地球上の光の量を制御することはできない。

　正解は ① と ②。① に関しては最終段落第1文（The good news ...）に「光害は他の多くの形態の公害とは異なり，元に戻すことができ」とある。reversible「元に戻すことができる」というのは「光害をなくすことが可能である」と言い換えることができるので本文の内容に一致している。② に関しては第4段落第3文（For three billion ...）に「30億年もの間，地球上の生命は，太陽，月，星の光だけで作られた明暗のリズムの中に存在していた」とあり，これに一致している。

　③ に関しては本文最終文（By being an ...）に「この深刻化しつつある問題を認識してもらい，より多くの人に自然の夜空を守るために必要な行動をとってもらう一助となる」とあるが，光害以外の種類の公害についてもっと知るべきだという記述は本文中にはないため，本文の内容に一致しているとは言えない。④ に関しては最終段落第5文（Many people either ...）に「多くの人は，光害や夜間の人工的な光がもたらす悪影響について知らないか，それほど理解していない」とあるので，本文と一致しているとは言えない。⑤ に関しては最終段落第1文（The good news ...）の後半で「私たち一人一人が変化をもたらすことができる」と述べられていることと矛盾する。

問5 ┃ 49 ┃ 正解 ①

「著者の立場を表すには，次のうちどれが最も適切か」 ┃ 49 ┃

① **著者は，光害を減らすためには，人々の意識と行動が必要であると主張している。**
② 著者は，人間は自然光の美しさを思い出すべきだと考えている。
③ 著者は，光害をくい止めるためには，個人ではなく政府の努力が必要だと述べている。
④ 著者は，光をより放出しない製品を作る必要があることについて語っている。

　正解は ①。最終段落第2文（Just being aware ...）で「行動を起こすことが必要だ」と述べられていることと，本文最終文（By being an ...）で「この深刻化しつつある問題を

― 英 R 50 ―

認識してもらい，より多くの人に自然の夜空を守るために必要な行動をとってもらう一助
となるだろう」と述べられていることを根拠に ① を正解にする。

　② の「自然光の美しさ」や ④ の「光をより放出しない製品」といった内容の記述は本文
中にはない。③ に関しては，著者は最終段落で私たち一人一人の行動の重要性を説いてい
るので，著者の立場を説明したものとは言えない。

主な語句・表現　　・問題冊子を参照のこと。

[第1段落]
(Most of us ...)
◇ be familiar with ...「…をよく知っている」　◇ pollution 图「汚染」
◇ pollutant 图「汚染物質」　　　　　　　　◇ inappropriate 形「不適切な」
◇ excessive 形「過剰な」　　　　　　　　　◇ artificial 形「人工的な」
◇ serious 形「深刻な」　　　　　　　　　　◇ environmental 形「環境の」
◇ consequence 图「影響；結果」　　　　　　◇ wildlife 图「野生生物」

[第2段落]
(One kind of ...)
◇ glow 图「輝き；光」　　　　　　　　　　◇ brighten 動「…を明るくする」
◇ mostly 副「ほとんど；もっぱら」　　　　◇ urban 形「都市の」
◇ due to ...「…のせいで」　　　　　　　　◇ streetlamp 图「街灯」
◇ advertising 图「広告」　　　　　　　　　◇ turn ... into ～「…を～に変える」
◇ sunset 图「日没」　　　　　　　　　　　◇ the public「一般大衆」
◇ confusing 形「混乱させるような」　　　　◇ grouping 图「集団」
◇ source 图「源」　　　　　　　　　　　　◇ extend 動「広がる」
◇ brightness 图「明るさ」　　　　　　　　◇ visual 形「視覚の」
◇ discomfort 图「不快」

[第3段落]
(Light pollution ...)
◇ side effect「副作用」　　　　　　　　　◇ industrial 形「産業の」
◇ The fact is that ...「実は…」　　　　　　◇ inefficient 形「効率の悪い」
◇ overly 副「過剰に」　　　　　　　　　　◇ poorly 副「下手に」
◇ target 動「…を狙う」　　　　　　　　　◇ improperly 副「不適切に」
◇ shield 動「…を遮る」　　　　　　　　　◇ completely 副「完全に」
◇ waste 動「…を無駄にする」　　　　　　◇ spill 動「…を溢れさせる；流す」
◇ be focused on ...「…に集中している」　　◇ actual 形「実際の」
◇ object 图「物」
◇ areas that people want illuminated は，areas that people want to be illuminated と同じ
　で，to be が省略されたもの。that は関係代名詞で，want の目的語として働く。

[第4段落]
(With much ...)
◇ With much of the Earth's population living ...　with は付帯状況の with と呼ばれるもの。
　with A B で「A が B の状態で」という意味になる。この場合は A にあたるのが much of
　the Earth's population で B にあたるのが living ... である。
◇ over-...「過剰な…」　　　　　　　　　　◇ concern 图「懸念；関心」
◇ suburban 形「郊外の」
◇ all you have to do to see this type of pollution is go outside ...　all と you の間には関係
　代名詞が省略されていて，関係代名詞節は pollution まで。all が主語として機能していて is
　が動詞になっている。補語の位置の go outside ... は to go outside ... と不定詞の to を補っ
　て読む。補語の位置に置かれる名詞用法の不定詞は to が省略されて，原形が残ることがある。
◇ billion 图「10 億」　　　　　　　　　　　◇ rhythm 图「リズム」
◇ solely 副「…だけで；ただ」　　　　　　◇ illumination 图「照らすこと」
◇ power over ...「…を支配する力」　　　　◇ glow 動「輝く」
◇ disrupt 動「…を混乱させる」　　　　　　◇ shift 動「…を変える；移行する」

— 英 R 51 —

◇ delicate 形「繊細な」　　　　　　　　　◇ negative 形「否定的な」
◇ invisible 形「目に見えない」
◇ a growing body of ...「ますます増大していく大量の…」
◇ link ... to ～「…を～に結びつける；関連付ける」
◇ directly 副「直接に」　　　　　　　　　◇ impact 名「影響」
◇ including 前「…を含む」　　　　　　　　◇ energy consumption「エネルギー消費」
◇ disruption 名「混乱」　　　　　　　　　◇ ecosystem 名「生態系」
◇ adverse 形「有害な」　　　　　　　　　◇ regarding 前「…に関して」
◇ crime 名「犯罪」　　　　　　　　　　　◇ affect 動「…に影響する」
◇ fortunately 副「幸運にも」　　　　　　◇ dramatically 副「劇的に」
◇ a growing number of ...「ますます多くの…」　◇ take action「行動する」
◇ restore 動「…を復活させる」　　　　　◇ adopt 動「…を採用する」
◇ practical solution「実用的な解決策」　　◇ locally 副「地元で」

[最終段落]　　　◇ unlike 前「…とは違って」　　　　　　◇ reversible 形「元に戻せる」
(The good news ...)　◇ be aware that ...「…ということに気付いている」
　　　　　　　　　　◇ minimize 動「…を最小化する」　　　　◇ spread 動「…を広める」
　　　　　　　　　　◇ pass ... on「…を受け渡す」　　　　　◇ ambassador 名「代表的な人物；大使」
　　　　　　　　　　◇ issue 名「問題」　　　　　　　　　　◇ awareness 名「意識」
　　　　　　　　　　◇ inspire ... to -「…を-する気にさせる」　◇ take steps to -「-するための対策をする」
　　　　　　　　　　◇ protect 動「…を守る」

第 2 回　実戦問題　解答・解説

英語（リーディング） 第2回 （100点満点）

（解答・配点）

問題番号（配点）	設問		解答番号	正解	配点	自己採点欄	問題番号（配点）	設問		解答番号	正解	配点	自己採点欄
第1問（10）	A	1	1	①	2		第4問（16）		1	24	④	3	
		2	2	④	2				2	25	③	3	
	B	1	3	②	2				3	26	②	3	
		2	4	③	2				4	27	②	3	
		3	5	①	2				5	28	②	2	
小　計										29	③	2	
第2問（20）	A	1	6	②	2		小　計						
		2	7	②	2		第5問（15）		1	30	④	3	
		3	8	④	2				2	31 － 32	③ － ④	3*	
		4	9	③	2				3	33	⑤	3*	
		5	10	④	2					34	③		
	B	1	11	②	2					35	④		
		2	12	③	2					36	①		
		3	13	①	2				4	37	③	3	
		4	14	①	2				5	38	②	3	
		5	15	④	2		小　計						
小　計							第6問（24）	A	1	39	①	3	
第3問（15）	A	1	16	④	3				2	40	④	3	
		2	17	②	3				3	41	③	3	
	B	1	18	④	3*				4	42	③	3*	
			19	③						43	⑥		
			20	①				B	1	44	②	3	
			21	②					2	45	④	3	
		2	22	④	3					46	①	3	
		3	23	②	3				3	47 － 48	① － ⑤	3*	
小　計							小　計						
							合　計						

（注）
1　＊は，全部正解の場合のみ点を与える。
2　－（ハイフン）でつながれた正解は，順序を問わない。

— 英 R 54 —

第1問

解答

| A | 問1-① | 問2-④ | | (各2点) |
| B | 問1-② | 問2-③ | 問3-① | (各2点) |

A

出典 *Original Material*

全訳

　あなたはデンマークのコペンハーゲンへの旅行の準備をしています。あなたはこの都市の主要な地区のいくつかと，それらにおいて旅行者が楽しめることを紹介しているウェブサイトを見つけました。

コペンハーゲンの主要な地区	
ブリュッゲの島々	**クリスチャンスハウン**
▶有名ブランドのデザインも手掛けているような人を含む，若い芸術家たちがここにスタジオを構えています。 ▶太陽光発電のモーターボートで，ボートの旅を楽しむこともできます。	▶クリスチャンスハウンは主に住宅地です。 ▶美しい並木に彩られた運河沿いで，散歩やサイクリングを楽しむことができます。 ▶地元民が愛する，カフェや，流行の服を売る店などがたくさんあります。
ヴェスターブロ	**ノレブロ**
▶この地区は，かつてこの都市の食肉加工地区でした。今ではレストランや画廊が立ち並んでいます。 ▶ここで芸術家たちによって開かれるワークショップに参加するのもいいでしょう。	▶ノレブロはこの都市でおいしいコーヒーを見つけるには最高の場所の1つです。 ▶素敵な古着や中古家具，ヴィンテージのレコードなどを買うことができます。

設問解説

問1　　1　　正解①

「ブリュッゲの島々でもクリスチャンスハウンでも，　1　を楽しむことができる」
　　① 屋外活動
　　② 珍しい食べ物
　　③ 有名人に会うこと
　　④ ウインドウショッピング

　正解は①。ブリュッゲの島々では「太陽光発電のモーターボートで，ボートの旅が楽しめる」とあり，クリスチャンスハウンでは「運河沿いで，散歩やサイクリングが楽しめる」とあるので，どちらの地区でも屋外活動が楽しめるとわかる。

問2　　2　　正解④

「芸術作品を見て外食もしたければ，　2　を訪れるべきだ」
　　① クリスチャンスハウン
　　② ブリュッゲの島々
　　③ ノレブロ
　　④ ヴェスターブロ

　正解は④。「芸術作品を見る」ことができる可能性があるのは，ブリュッゲの島々のスタジオとヴェスターブロの画廊と考えられるが，「外食する」のに適しているのは，「レストランが立ち並んでいる」と記されているヴェスターブロであるので，④が正解となる。

— 英 R 55 —

主な語句・表現	・問題冊子を参照のこと。

[リード文]
◇ prepare for ...「…の準備をする」　　◇ introduce 動「…を紹介する」
◇ main 形「主要な」　　◇ district 名「地区」
◇ tourist 名「旅行客；観光客」

[Islands Brygge]
◇ studio 名「スタジオ；アトリエ」　　◇ including 前「…を含む」
◇ those who ...「…する人々」　those は前出の複数名詞を受けて，ここでは young artists
　のこと。
◇ design for ...「…のデザインを手掛けている」
◇ well-known 形「有名な；よく知られた」
◇ solar-powered 形「太陽光で動く；太陽発電による」

[Christianshavn]
◇ largely 副「主に；大部分が」　　◇ residential 形「住宅の；住宅向きの」
◇ stroll 動「ぶらつく；散歩する」　　◇ along 前「…に沿って」
◇ tree-lined 形「並木の；列になって樹が植わっている」
◇ canal 名「運河」　　◇ fashionable 形「流行の」
◇ the locals「地元の人々」

[Vesterbro]
◇ used to －「かつては－したものだ」　　◇ meatpacking area「食肉加工地区」
◇ be filled with ...「…で満たされている；…でいっぱいである」
◇ art gallery「画廊；アートギャラリー」　　◇ workshop 名「ワークショップ；作業場」

[Nørrebro]
◇ shop for ...「…を買い求める；…の買い物をする」
◇ secondhand 形「中古の」　　◇ vintage 形「ヴィンテージの；古い」
◇ record 名「(音楽の) レコード」

[設問文・選択肢]
◇ outdoor activity「屋外活動」
◇ artwork 名「芸術作品」「作品」を意味する work は可算名詞。
◇ eat out「外食する」

B

出典	*Original Material*

全訳	

あなたは「マンスリー・ブック・クラブ」という読書会のウェブサイトを見ています。
あなたは 6 月 17 日に開かれる，次の会に参加することを検討しています。

マンスリー・ブック・クラブ　タイラー・ブルーム氏を迎えて
本を読んで知性を養おう！

こんにちは，本好きの皆さん！　マンスリー・ブック・クラブの読書会を再び開催します！
今月は，ただのいつもと同じ読書会ではありません。というのも，若くて才能ある作家で，
つい最近，2022 年の『メイヤーズ・ブック・プライズ』を受賞した，タイラー・ブルー
ム氏をゲストに迎えるからです。

読書会の日程

ディスカッション	6 月 17 日 (土) 15:30 － 17:00
タイラー・ブルーム氏の講演	6 月 17 日 (土) 17:00 － 18:00

次回のマンスリー・ブック・クラブの読書会への参加方法

◆ウェブ申し込みフォームに記入してください。　　　　　　　　→ここをクリック！
　・読書会参加のお申し込みは，6月15日までに行ってください。
◆指定の本を読み，マンスリー・ブック・クラブの読書会に参加しましょう！
　・今月議論する本を，リストでチェックしましょう。　　　　　→リストはこちら！
　・開催場所　→地図はこちらをクリック。
　・読書会（ディスカッションおよび講演）には，オンラインでも参加できます。
　　→下記をご覧ください。
　・ディスカッションについては，ウェブ申し込みフォームを提出し，本を読んできて
　　さえいれば，出入りは自由です。

> **オンラインでの読書会参加方法：**
> お申し込み手続き完了後に，eメールをお送りください（monthlybookclub@
> example.com）。オンライン読書会のリンクをお送りします。

料金について：
◆ディスカッションは無料です。
◆講演を聴くためには，こちらのリンクに飛んでチケット（15ドル）をお求めください。
　クレジットカードか銀行振込でのお支払いが可能です。

設問解説

問1　 3 　正解②

「次回の読書会への申し込みは，少なくとも読書会の 3 前までにしなければならない」

① 　1日
②　2日
③ 　1週間
④ 　2週間

　正解は②。読書会が開かれるのは6月17日だが，「読書会への参加方法」の項目内に「申し込みは6月15日まで」と記されているので，2日前までに申し込めばよいとわかる。

問2　 4 　正解③

「ディスカッションに参加したい場合， 4 ならない」

① 　オンラインで参加しなければ
② 　15ドルでチケットを購入しなければ
③ 　リストに載っている本を読まなければ
④ 　17時に会が終わるまで席を離れては

　正解は③。「読書会への参加方法」の項目内に，「ディスカッションについては…本を読んできてさえいれば，出入りは自由」とあるため，指定の本を読んできていることがディスカッション参加の要件の1つだとわかる。また，指定の本については「リストでチェックしましょう」とあるため，③の「リストに載っている本を読まなければ（ならない）」が正解であるとわかる。
　オンラインでの参加については，「読書会への参加方法」の項目に「オンラインでも参加できます」とあるが，その直前で「開催場所」「地図はこちら」とあるように，オンラインでの参加が必須であるわけではないため，①は誤り。「料金について」の項目で「ディスカッションは無料」とあるため，②は誤り。「読書会への参加方法」の項目内に「出入りは自由」と記されているので，④も誤り。

— 英R 57 —

問3 　5　 正解 ①

「　5　 場合は，主催者に e メールを送るよう求められている」

① イベントにオンラインで参加する予定である
② 申し込みフォームの記入が完了できない
③ クレジットカードを持っていない
④ 6月15日よりも後に申し込みをしたい

　正解は ①。「e メール」への言及は，「オンラインでの読書会参加方法」の中にある。「申し込み手続き完了後に e メールを送ると，オンライン読書会のリンクが送られる」とのことなので，オンラインで参加する場合は e メールを送る必要があるとわかる。

　その他には，参加者が e メールを送るべき状況は記されていないので，他の選択肢は誤り。

主な語句・表現　　・問題冊子を参照のこと。

[リード文]
◇ monthly 形「月次の；月に1度の」　　　◇ book-reading circle「読書サークル」
◇ think about – ing「–することを考える［検討する］」
◇ take part in ...「…に参加する」
◇ the next meeting, to be held on ...「…に開催される，次回の読書会」

[本文]
◇ cultivate 動「…を耕す；（精神など）を養う」
◇ booklover 名「本好きの人」
◇ not just another ...「ただの，いつもと同じ…ではない」　another は「もう1つの；同じような」という意味。
◇ have O as a guest「O をゲストに迎える」　◇ talented 形「才能ある」
◇ win the prize「賞を獲る」　　　　　　　◇ fill in ...「…を埋める［記入する］」
◇ application form「申し込みフォーム［用紙］」
◇ apply 動「申し込む」　　　　　　　　　◇ selected 形「選ばれた；選りすぐりの」
◇ check the list for ...「リスト上で…を確認する」
◇ location 名「位置；場所」　　　　　　　◇ online 副「オンラインで」
◇ below 副「下で；下を」　　　　　　　　◇ at any time you like「いつでも好きな時に」
◇ as long as SV「S が V する限りは」　条件を表す接続表現。
◇ submit 動「…を提出する」　　　　　　　◇ email 動「…に e メールを送る」　他動詞。
◇ fee 名「入場料；参加費」　　　　　　　◇ free of charge「無料で」
◇ bank transfer「銀行振込」

[設問文・選択肢]
◇ apply for ...「…に申し込む」
◇ at least ... before the meeting「会議の少なくとも…前までに」
◇ organizer 名「主催者」

— 英 R 58 —

第2問

解答						
A	問1 - ②	問2 - ②	問3 - ④	問4 - ③	問5 - ④	（各2点）
B	問1 - ②	問2 - ③	問3 - ①	問4 - ①	問5 - ④	（各2点）

A

出典 ── *Original Material*

全訳 ──

　あなたはイギリスの大学で開かれるサマープログラムに参加する予定です。そのプログラムの期間中は大学の寮に滞在できます。あなたはその寮に関する情報を読んでいます。

コモンウェルスホール
寮生活ガイドブック 2022

自習室：2階21号室
　日曜日以外は，毎日午前10時から午後6時まで開室しています。日曜日は午後1時から午後6時までの開室です。無料のWi-Fiが利用可能です。ペットボトルに入った水のみ飲むことができます。部屋にある本はどれでも読むことができますが，部屋の外への持ち出しはできません。

食堂：1階5号室
　午前7時から9時（朝食）と午後6時から8時（夕食）に営業しています。土曜日と日曜日は朝食の代わりにブランチが午前9時から11時まで提供されます。食事を受け取るためには学生証を提示する必要があります。

ランドリー室：各階に設置
　ランドリー室を使用するためには，最初に3ポンドのランドリーカードを購入しなくてはいけません。その後，洗濯を行うためにカードにチャージする必要があります。洗濯と乾燥はそれぞれ1ポンドずつかかります。使用後は忘れずに服を回収し，その場所を掃除してください。

以前の学生たちからのコメント

- 自習室ではたいてい多くの人が熱心に勉強していますが，席はたくさんあるので，全ての席が埋まることは決してありません。

- 食堂では美味しい食事を食べることができます。食事の量はかなり多いので，食後はいつもお腹いっぱいです。

- ランドリー室はいつもきれいに保たれています。この寮の住民が素直にルールに従っているということですね。

- ランドリー室の機械は使いやすいと思いますので，それに関しては心配無用です。部屋の中には座る椅子がないということだけは気をつけてください。自分の衣服を洗濯している間は自分自身の部屋で待つべきでしょう。

- 4階には学生のための談話室があって，そこでは座ってリラックスし，友達と話すことができます。私はそこの雰囲気が大好きです！

設問解説

問1　6　正解②

「6　が，あなたが寮でできる２つのことだ」

A：自習室で Wi-Fi のネットワークに接続すること
B：毎日午前８時に朝食をとること
C：食堂で食事カードを購入すること
D：ランドリー室で座って待つこと
E：夕食ができるまで自習室を使うこと

① AとB
② AとE
③ BとC
④ CとD
⑤ DとE

　正解は②。A は，自習室の項の第３文（Free Wi-Fi is ...）に「無料の Wi-Fi が利用可能です」という記述がある。E は，自習室は午後６時まで利用可能であること，また夕食は午後６時から提供される，という２つの記述から判断して正しいとわかる。

　B は平日に関しては正しいものの，「土曜日と日曜日は朝食の代わりにブランチが午前９時から11時まで提供されます」と食堂の項の第２文（On Saturdays and ...）に書かれており，土日は午前８時に朝食をとれないため誤り。C は「食堂カード」なるものについては本文中に記述がないので誤り（食堂で必要なのは学生証であり，お金をチャージするカードが必要なのはランドリー室である）。D は「以前の学生たちからのコメント」の４つめで否定されている内容なので誤りとなる。

問2　7　正解②

「あなたは学生のための談話室にいて，自習室に行きたいと考えている。あなたは　7　必要がある」

① １階降りる
② ２階降りる
③ １階上がる
④ 同じ階にいる

　正解は②。談話室は「以前の学生たちからのコメント」の５つめから４階にあるとわかり，自習室は２階にあるので，２階降りればよいことになる。なお，イギリスでは１階を the ground floor，２階を the first floor，３階を the second floor，４階を the third floor … のように言うのが一般的。

問3　8　正解④

「この寮は　8　ための部屋がいくつかある」

① 朝食を食べる
② 勉強をする
③ 友達と話す
④ 衣服を洗う

　正解は④。ランドリー室の項に located on each floor「各階に設置」と書かれている。
　①は食堂，②は自習室，③は学生のための談話室のことだが，それぞれ１つずつしかないため誤り。

問4　9　正解③

「もしあなたがランドリーカードを持っておらず，ランドリー室で洗濯と乾燥をしたいと考えている場合，あなたは合計で　9　支払う必要がある」

— 英 R 60 —

① 3ポンド
② 4ポンド
③ **5ポンド**
④ 6ポンド

　正解は③。ランドリー室の項を見ると，第1文（In order to ...）にランドリーカードが3ポンドであることが書かれており，第3文（Washing and drying ...）では洗濯と乾燥にそれぞれ1ポンドずつかかると書かれている。よって，3ポンド（カード購入）＋1ポンド（洗濯）＋1ポンド（乾燥）で，合計5ポンドかかることになる。

問5　| 10 |　正解④

　「以前の学生によって述べられた**事実**の1つは| 10 |ということだ」
① 食堂は1階にある
② 洗濯機は新入生にとって使いやすい
③ たいてい自習室にはほとんど人がいない
④ **談話室では友達と話すことができる**

　正解は④。「以前の学生たちからのコメント」の5つめで，学生のための談話室では友達と話すことができる旨が述べられている。

　①は事実であり本文にも書かれているが，「以前の学生によって述べられた」ものではないので誤り。②は4つめのコメントに記載があるが，「使いやすいかどうか」は人によって意見が分かれるものであり，「事実」ではないので誤り。③は1つめのコメントで「たいてい多くの人が熱心に勉強しています」とあることから，本文の内容に反する。

主な語句・表現

・問題冊子を参照のこと。
◇ dormitory 图「寮」　　　　　　　　◇ available 形「利用可能な」
◇ brunch 图「遅めの朝食；朝食兼昼食（breakfast と lunch の混成語）」
◇ serve 動「…を提供する」　　　　　◇ instead of ...「…の代わりに」
◇ present 動「…を提示する」　　　　◇ laundry 图「洗濯」
◇ purchase 動「…を購入する」　　　◇ enthusiastically 副「熱心に」
◇ occupy 動「…を占有する」　　　　◇ fairly 副「かなり」
◇ resident 图「住民」　　　　　　　◇ be willing to –「–するのをいとわない」
◇ note 動「…に注意を払う」　　　　◇ atmosphere 图「雰囲気」

— 英 R 61 —

B

出典 | *Original Material*

全訳 | あなたは東京の高校で学校の英語新聞の編集者をしています。イギリスからの交換留学生のヒューが新聞に記事を書きました。

日本のどこを訪れるべきか？ これが先日あなたたちに私がした質問です。トモミとタクヤの力を借りて，回答を収集し終えました。京都が一番かなと思っていたのですが，実際には大阪が最もおすすめの場所として選ばれました。なんと，京都よりも北海道の方が人気があったのです。京都に続いたのは鹿児島でした。

どうして大阪はこんなにも人気なのでしょうか？ こちらがアンケートに書かれたコメントの一部です。

> ➤大阪は「天下の台所」として有名です。ここの食べ物は本当に素晴らしい！
> ➤人が友好的なんだよね。外国人のことも喜んで助けてくれるに違いないよ。
> ➤大阪の歴史と現代性の共存にはきっと満足できるよ！
> ➤場所が理想的です。奈良，京都，神戸，名古屋に大阪から簡単に訪れることができます。

一番私の興味をひいたのは最後のコメントです。私はできる限り多くの日本の都市を訪れたいので，まず大阪に行って，そこから行けるいくつかの都市に小旅行をするというのは良い考えです！ また，大阪は新幹線にも楽に乗ることができると聞きました。だから大阪に滞在すれば，私の友達が住んでいる広島まではるばる新幹線で行けるかもしれません。あるいは，そこに行くには夜行バスを使った方がいいと思いますか？ それについて教えてください！ いずれにせよ，大阪には絶対に行きます。答えてくれてありがとう！

設問解説 | 問1 　11　 正解 ②

「おすすめされた都道府県のランキングを<u>高い方から低い方へ</u>表しているのは次のうちどれか」 　11

① 大阪 — 北海道 — 鹿児島 — 京都
❷ **大阪 — 北海道 — 京都 — 鹿児島**
③ 大阪 — 鹿児島 — 北海道 — 京都
④ 大阪 — 鹿児島 — 京都 — 北海道
⑤ 大阪 — 京都 — 北海道 — 鹿児島
⑥ 大阪 — 京都 — 鹿児島 — 北海道

　正解は ②。第1段落第3文（I expected Kyoto ...）にて「京都が1位だと思っていたら大阪が1位だった」という旨が述べられた後，続く第4文（Actually, Hokkaido was ...）で「京都よりも北海道が上」だと述べられる。続いて最終文（Next to Kyoto ...）では「京都の次が鹿児島」と述べられているので，最終的な順位は大阪 — 北海道 — 京都 — 鹿児島となるとわかる。

— 英 R 62 —

問2　　12　　正解③

「アンケートのコメントによると，大阪を訪れる利点の1つは　12　ということだ」

① 大阪には多くの観光名所がある
② そこでは多くの人がツアーガイドとして働いている
③ **古いものも新しいものも両方楽しむことができる**
④ たいてい安い値段で食べ物を入手できる

　　正解は③。アンケートのコメントの3つめに「大阪の歴史と現代性の共存にはきっと満足できるよ！」とある。選択肢中の the old は〈the ＋形容詞〉の形で「古いもの」という抽象名詞になっている。the new も同様に「新しいもの」という意味。

　　他の選択肢に関する内容はいずれもコメントに書かれていない。

問3　　13　　正解①

「大阪への旅行に関して，ヒューの考えを最もよく要約しているものは次のうちどれか」
13

① **彼は大阪を拠点として，そこから旅行をするつもりだ。**
② 彼はできる限り多くの種類の食べ物を食べるつもりだ。
③ 彼はできる限り外国人を助けるつもりだ。
④ 彼は東京から大阪まで新幹線を使うつもりだ。

　　正解は①。大阪からは周辺のさまざまな都市に行きやすいというコメントを受けて，最終段落第2文（I want to ...）でヒューは「できる限り多くの日本の都市を訪れたいので，まず大阪に行って，そこから行けるいくつかの都市に小旅行をするというのは良い考えです」と述べている。

　　他の選択肢については全て記載がない。

問4　　14　　正解①

「なぜヒューは広島を訪れたいのか」　　14

① **そこに友達がいるから。**
② そこを一度も訪れたことがないから。
③ そこの食べ物が本当に好きだから。
④ 新幹線に乗りたいから。

　　正解は①。最終段落第4文（So if I ...）に「友達が住んでいる広島まで行けるかもしれません」とあり，他に広島を訪れる明確な理由の記載がないことから，友達がいることが広島を訪れる理由であると考えるのが適切。

問5　　15　　正解④

「ヒューの同級生は，この記事を読み終わった後にどんな情報を彼に与える可能性が最も高いか」　　15

① 大阪への夜行バスのチケットの取り方。
② 広島で彼が訪れるべき場所。
③ 関西地方でおすすめのレストラン。
④ **大阪から広島への最も良い行き方。**

　　正解は④。最終段落第4文（So if I ...）及び第5文（Or do you ...）で，大阪から広島に行くのに新幹線がよいか夜行バスを使うのがよいか，ヒューが迷っている旨が述べられた後に，第6文（Tell me about ...）で「それについて教えてください！」と読者に呼びかけている。よって，これを読んだ同級生たちは大阪から広島への最も良い行き方についてヒューに教える可能性が高いと言える。

　　他の選択肢についての情報をヒューが求めていると考えられる内容は書かれていない。

— 英 R 63 —

主な語句・表現　　・問題冊子を参照のこと。

◇ editor 图「編集者」　　　　　　　　　　◇ paper 图「新聞」　可算名詞で用いる。
◇ Next to Kyoto ranked Kagoshima.　Kagoshima ranked next to Kyoto. を倒置したもの。
◇ questionnaire 图「アンケート」　　　　　◇ lovely 形「素晴らしい」
◇ coexistence 图「共存」　　　　　　　　　◇ modernity 图「近代性；現代性」
◇ go as far as Hiroshima「はるばる広島まで行く」
◇ overnight bus「夜行バス」　　　　　　　◇ definitely 副「絶対に」
◇ prefecture 图「都道府県」

第3問

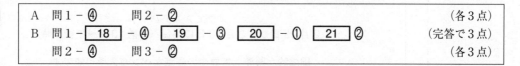

A

出典 *Original Material*

全訳

あなたはイギリスからの交換留学生と知り合いになりました。あなたは彼女ともっと仲良くなるために，彼女が書いたブログの投稿を読んでいます。

ヘレン・ポッター
2月28日月曜日，午後10時

先日，私がアパートに戻ると，郵便ポストに手紙が来ていることに気づいた。それは私の通っている日本の大学のクラスメートであるケンタから来たものだった。彼は私に，東京のデパートで催されている「世界の万年筆フェア」と呼ばれるイベントに行かないか，と誘ってきたのだ。

普段は私は勉強するために鉛筆かボールペンを使っており，万年筆は高価だからお金持ちの大人が使うのだと決めてかかっていた。しかしながら，私はケンタが添えてくれた，美しいペンの写真が載ったフェアのパンフレットを見た時，興味を持ったので，彼の誘いを受けるために彼に携帯電話でメールを送った。

今日，私はケンタとそのデパートのそばの地下鉄の駅で落ち合った。そのフェアには，世界中の多くの万年筆があった。日本文学を専攻する学生として，私は日本で作られている万年筆に興味を持った。店員さんが私に日本の万年筆を試し書きさせてくれたので自分自身の名前を書いたのだが，それを使うことに少々しっくりこない気がした。その店員さんの話によると，日本の万年筆は「漢字」を含めた日本語の文字を書くことに適しており，そのため，もし私が英語を書くために万年筆を使うのであれば，私はヨーロッパの国で作られた万年筆を使うべきだということだった。

はじめは，ケンタはドイツ製のモデルを買うつもりだと言っていたが，彼は私たちの会話を偶然耳にすると，パンフレットで宣伝されていた日本製のものを買おうと決心した。というのも，彼は主に日本語で文字を書くからだ。実際，私は普段は英語で文字を書くが，私もパンフレットに示されている日本製のものを買った。とはいっても，彼の万年筆よりも安物の万年筆ではあるが。というのも，ゆくゆくは日本語で文字を書くことを習得したいと思っているからだ。

世界の万年筆フェア				

スクエア・デパート
2月25日から3月10日に開催（午前10時ー午後5時）

国際的な販売：世界中の豪華なペンが入手可能です。

例	モデル A	モデル B	モデル C	モデル D
価格	3,000 円	12,000 円	30,000 円	75,000 円
国	日本	日本	ドイツ	イタリア

ペンクリニック：プロの職人たちが無料であなたのペンを修理します。
注記：1人につき1本

設問解説

問1 16 **正解 ④**

「ヘレンのブログから，あなたは彼女が 16 ということがわかる」

① 日本語で自分の名前を書ける
② 日本語の高い運用能力を持っている
③ ずっと自分自身の万年筆を持ちたいと思っていた
④ 漢字を書けるようになりたいと思っている

正解は④。最終段落最終文（Actually, I usually ...）の後半で「ゆくゆくは日本語で文字を書くことを習得したいと思っている」と述べられている。この日本語の文字については，第3段落最終文（The clerk said ...）の前半で「日本の万年筆は『漢字』を含めた日本語の文字を書くことに適しており」と述べられていることから，ヘレンは漢字を含めた日本語の文字を書けるようになりたいと思っていると推測できる。これが④に対応している。

①のようなことは本文中からは読み取れない。②については，第3段落第3文（As a student ...）で「日本文学を専攻する学生として，私は日本で作られている万年筆に興味を持った」という記述はあるが，日本語そのものをヘレンがどの程度運用できるのか本文では述べられていない（文字はあまり書けないことはうかがえるが，どの程度日本語を話したりできるのかなどの記述はない）。③については，第2段落第1文（Usually I use ...）で「普段は私は勉強するために鉛筆かボールペンを使っており，万年筆は高価だからお金持ちの大人が使うのだと決めてかかっていた」と述べられていることから，ヘレンは元々は万年筆に興味がなかったことがうかがえるので，不適である。

問2 17 **正解 ②**

「ケンタは 17 の万年筆を買った可能性が最も高い」

① モデル A
② モデル B
③ モデル C
④ モデル D

正解は②。最終段落第1文（At first Kenta ...）で「はじめは，ケンタはドイツ製のモデルを買うつもりだと言っていたが，彼は私たちの会話を偶然耳にすると，パンフレットで宣伝されていた日本製のものを買おうと決心した。というのも，彼は主に日本語で文字を書くからだ」と述べられていることから，パンフレットに掲載されているうち日本製のモデルAかモデルBが候補として絞れる。続く最終段落最終文（Actually, I usually ...）の前半で「実際，私は普段は英語で文字を書くが，私もパンフレットに示されている日本製

— 英 R 66 —

のものを買った。とはいっても，彼の万年筆よりも安物の万年筆ではあるが」と述べられており，ヘレンは，パンフレットに掲載されている万年筆のうち，日本製でより安い方の万年筆を購入したことがわかる。したがってヘレンがモデル A を購入し，ケンタはそれより高額のモデル B を購入したことが判断できる。

主な語句・表現

[リード文]
・問題冊子を参照のこと。
◇ become acquainted with ...「…と知り合いになる」
◇ exchange student「交換留学生」　　　◇ post 名「投稿」
◇ in order to –「–するために」　目的を表す表現。
◇ become friendly with ...「…と仲良くなる」

[第1段落]
(The other day, ...)
◇ the other day「先日」　　　　　　　◇ come back to ...「…へ戻る」
◇ flat 名「アパート」　イギリス英語。アメリカ英語の apartment に相当する。
◇ postbox 名「郵便ポスト」　イギリス英語。アメリカ英語の mailbox に相当する。
◇ ask O to –「O に–しないかと誘う」　　◇ event 名「催し物；イベント」
◇ fountain pen「万年筆」　　　　　　　◇ fair 名「フェア；博覧会；見本市」

[第2段落]
(Usually I use ...)
◇ usually 副「たいていは；ふつうは」　　◇ ballpoint pen「ボールペン」
◇ assume 動「…だと想定する；決めてかかる」
◇ expensive 形「高価な」　　　　　　　◇ brochure 名「パンフレット」
◇ attach 動「…を添える」　　　　　　　◇ text 動「…に携帯電話でメールを送る」
◇ offer 名「申し出」

[第3段落]
(Today, I met ...)
◇ meet 動「…と会う；…と落ち合う」
◇ underground 名「地下鉄」　イギリス英語。アメリカ英語の subway に相当。
◇ major in ...「…を専攻する」　　　　　◇ literature 名「文学」
◇ those　fountain pens の繰り返しを避けるために用いられている代名詞。
◇ clerk 名「店員」
◇ let O –「O に–させてあげる」　許可を表す。
◇ one　a fountain pen の繰り返しを避けるために用いられている代名詞。
◇ a bit「少々」
◇ strange 形「しっくりしない気がする；違和感がある」
◇ suitable 形「適した」　　　　　　　　◇ character 名「文字」

[最終段落]
(At first Kenta ...)
◇ at first「はじめのうちは」　　　　　　◇ model 名「モデル；型」
◇ overhear 動「…を偶然耳にする」　　　◇ advertise 動「…を宣伝する」
◇ eventually 副「最後には；ゆくゆくは」

[パンフレット]
◇ international 形「国際的な」　　　　　◇ sale 名「販売」
◇ splendid 形「豪華な」　　　　　　　　◇ available 形「入手可能な」
◇ professional 形「プロの」　　　　　　◇ craftspeople 名「職人たち」
◇ fix 動「…を修理する」　　　　　　　　◇ for nothing「無料で」
◇ note 名「注記」　　　　　　　　　　　◇ per 前「…につき」

B

出典 *Original Material*

全訳 　あなたは野外スポーツを楽しいと思っていて，自転車雑誌である面白い記事を見つけました。

5日未満で1,400キロメートル超

　数年前，私は連合王国を縦断する「ロンドン　エディンバラ　ロンドン」と呼ばれる長距離自転車行に参加しました。それは4年ごとに行われるもので，そこでは参加者たちはイングランドの首都であるロンドンからスコットランドの首都であるエディンバラまで行き，そしてその後ロンドンまで漕いで戻るんです，5日未満で。私の経験不足を補うために，私はアンとテッドとチームを組みましたが，2人とも私の地元の自転車クラブに属する，私よりもずっと経験豊富な自転車乗りです。

　7月30日，私たちは午前6時にロンドンから北に向けて出発しました。チェックポイントがおよそ80キロメートルごとにありました。やや平らな道のおかげで，私はチームの仲間たちと一緒に楽しんで自転車を漕ぎました。暗くなった後で私たちはポックリントンのチェックポイントに着いて，その夜はそこで過ごしました。でも，ベッドよりも多くの参加者がいたので，ベッドで眠るのを許されたのは皆3時間だけでした！このことで私たちは，それ以降はホテルの部屋を予約することに決めました。その翌日，寝不足だったにもかかわらず，私たちは前進しました。その日の終わりに，私たちは何とかモファットでホテルの部屋を見つけることができました。

　3日目，私たちは午前4時に起きて午前5時前に出発し，エディンバラに午前9時に着きました。今度は南向きの行程に就きました。でもすぐその後に，大雨が降り始めました。そしてその次に私の右足が痛み始めました。私は痛み止めを飲んで，私たちはどうにかバーナード・キャッスルに暗くなった後でたどり着くことができました。その翌日，テッドは首のことで文句を言い始めていましたが，私たちはともかく出発しました。しかし坂はより急になり，その次にやって来たのは向かい風でした。私の右足は，また痛み始めました。その日の終わりにラウスに着いた時には，テッドと私は激しい痛みがあり疲れ切っていました。アンは私たちにマッサージを申し出てくれました。彼女自身もまた明らかに疲れていたにもかかわらずです！

　最終日の朝，アンのマッサージのおかげで，私の痛みはかなり和らいでいました。でも，テッドはまだ痛がっていて，それでグレート・イーストンで彼は完全に漕ぐのをやめてしまいました。アンと私は1時間かけて彼を説き伏せて進み続けさせようとしましたが，効果はありませんでした。ついに私たちは彼を残していくことに決めました。今や私たちは時間切れになる前に難しい課題を終えるために，本当に急がなければなりませんでした。とうとう私たちは25分を残してゴール地点に着きました。私はそのことを嬉しく思いました。でもテッドが私たちと一緒にゴール地点に居たらよいのになあと，私は思いました。

設問解説　問1　18　正解④，　19　正解③，　20　正解①，　21　正解②
「次の出来事（①～④）を起こった順番に並べなさい」
① 漕いでいる最中に激しい雨が降り始めた。
② チームのメンバーの1人が完走しないことを選んだ。
③ チームはスコットランドの首都に着いた。
④ チームはチェックポイント会場の1つで睡眠をとった。
正解は④→③→①→②。

— 英 R 68 —

まず，第2段落第4文（After it got ...）に「暗くなった後で私たちはポックリントンの
チェックポイントに着いて，その夜はそこで過ごしました」という記述があるが，これは
④に該当する内容である。これは初日の行程の記述である。

次に，第3段落第1文（On the 3rd ...）に「私たちは午前4時に起きて午前5時前に出
発し，エディンバラに午前9時に着きました」という記述がある。これは，第1段落第1
文（Several years ago, ...）にエディンバラがスコットランドの首都であることが記され
ていたことを踏まえれば，③に該当する内容である。その後，第3段落第3文（But soon
after ...）に「でもすぐその後に，大雨が降り始めました」という記述があるが，これは①
に該当する内容である。これらは3日目の行程の記述である。

最後に，最終段落第2文（But Ted was ...）に「グレート・イーストシで彼［テッド］は
完全に漕ぐのをやめてしまいました」とあり，かつ第3文（Anne and I ...）に「アンと私
は1時間かけて彼を説き伏せて進み続けさせようとしましたが，効果はありませんでした」
という記述があるが，これは②に該当する内容である。これは最終日の行程の記述である。

問2　　22　　正解④

「筆者のチームがホテルで寝始めた理由は何だったか」　　22

①　ホテルはチェックポイントよりも高価でないことがわかった。
②　彼らが泊まっていたチェックポイントはあまりにも騒々しかった。
③　彼らはチェックポイントの1つで寝る場所をどこにも見つけられなかった。
④　彼らは最初の夜に十分な睡眠を得られなかった。

正解は④。第2段落第6文（This made us ...）に「このことで私たちは，それ以降はホ
テルの部屋を予約することに決めました」という記述があるが，これは設問文の「筆者の
チームがホテルで寝始めた」に該当する内容である。その中の「このことで」が指す内容は，
その直前の第2段落第5文（But as there ...）の「ベッドよりも多くの参加者がいたので，
ベッドで眠るのを許されたのは皆3時間だけでした」である。これは，④の内容に合致する。

①および②に関する記述は，本文中のどこにもない。③は，第2段落第5文の「ベッ
ドで眠るのを許されたのは皆3時間だけでした」という記述から，各人3時間ずつは寝た
と考えられるので，誤りである。

問3　　23　　正解②

「この記事からあなたが学んだのは，筆者が　　23　　ということである」

①　足の痛みで苦しんだのは1日だけだった
②　最終目的地に制限時間内に着いた
③　最終結果に完全に満足していた
④　チームの中で最も経験のある自転車乗りだった

正解は②。最終段落第6文（Finally we reached ...）に「とうとう私たちは25分を残
してゴール地点に着きました」という記述があるが，これは②に該当する内容である。

①にある，筆者が「自分の足の痛みで苦しんだ」ことに関する記述が本文中に現れるのは，
第3段落第3文（But soon after ...）の後半の「私の右足が痛み始めました」，および第3
段落第7文（My right leg ...）の「私の右足は，また痛み始めました」の2ヵ所である。
そのうちの前者は第3段落第1文（On the 3rd ...）から始まる3日目の内容で，後者は第
3段落第5文（The next morning, ...）から始まる4日目の内容にあたる。よって，筆者
が「自分の足の痛みで苦しんだ」のは「1日だけ」ではないことになるので，①は本文に
反する内容である。最終段落最終文（But I wished ...）に「でもテッドが私たちと一緒にゴー
ル地点に居たらよいのになあと，私は思いました」という記述があるが，これは③の「完
全に満足していた」に反する内容である。第1段落最終文（To make up ...）に「私の経
験不足を補うために，私はアンとテッドとチームを組みましたが，2人とも私の地元の自

— 英 R 69 —

転車クラブに属する，私よりもずっと経験豊富な自転車乗りです」とある。これは④に反する内容である。

主な語句・表現・問題冊子を参照のこと。

[第1段落]
(Several years ago, ...)

◇ participate in ...「…に参加する」　　◇ the United Kingdom「連合王国」
◇ take place「〈行事などが〉行われる；催される」
◇ every 形「《数字の前で》…ごとに」　　◇ participant 名「参加者」
◇ ride 動「（乗り物に）乗る；乗って行く」　◇ capital 名「首都」
◇ make up for ...「〈不足など〉を補う；埋め合わせる」
◇ lack of ...「…の不足」
◇ team up with ...「…と（チームを）組む；協力する」
◇ experienced 形「経験のある；経験豊富な」

[第2段落]
(On 30 July, ...)

◇ northwards 副「北方へ；北に向かって」　北米英語では northward。
◇ checkpoint 名「中間記録採点所；検問所」　◇ thanks to ...「…のおかげで」
◇ flat 形「平らな；平坦な」　　　　　　　◇ route 名「道；経路；ルート」
◇ book 動「〈部屋・座席など〉を予約する」
◇ despite 前「…にもかかわらず；…を顧みずに」
◇ press on「前進する；押し進む」
◇ manage to –「なんとか［どうにか］（して）–する」

[第3段落]
(On the 3rd ...)

◇ set off「出発する」　　　　　　　　　◇ set out on ...「…に向けて出発する」
◇ southbound 形「南へ向かう；南行きの」　◇ leg 名「（旅などの）一区間；一行程」
◇ ache 動「痛む；うずく」　　　　　　　◇ painkiller 名「鎮痛剤；痛み止め」
◇ complain about ...「…について不満［文句；ぐち］を言う」
◇ steep 形「傾斜の急な；険しい」　　　　◇ head wind「向かい風」
◇ exhausted 形「疲れ果てた；消耗した；へとへとになった」
◇ massage 名「マッサージ；もみ療治；あんま」

[最終段落]
(On the last ...)

◇ ease 動「〈痛みなどが〉軽くなる；楽になる」
◇ a lot「大いに；大変；とても」
◇ persuade 〈人〉to –「〈人〉を説得して［説き伏せて］–させる」
◇ keep – ing「–し続ける」　　　　　　　◇ to no effect「何の効果［効き目］もなく」
◇ at last「（努力や遅れの後で）やっと；ついに；ようやく」
◇ leave 〈人〉behind「〈人〉を後に残して行く［置き去りにする］」
◇ challenge 名「難問；難題；難しい仕事」
◇ run out「〈時間・資金などが〉なくなる；尽きる；切れる」
◇ with ... to spare「…を余らせ［残し］て；…の余裕をもって」
◇ wish (that) ...「…すれば［であれば］よいのにと思う［願う；祈る］」

[設問文・選択肢]

◇ come down「〈雨・雪などが〉（激しく）降る」
◇ choose not to –「–しない方を選ぶ［好む］；–しないことに決める」
◇ turn out to –「（結局は）–であることがわかる［判明する］」
◇ suffer from ...「…で苦しむ；…を患う」　◇ final destination「最終目的地；到達目標」
◇ time limit「時間（的）制限；タイムリミット」
◇ be satisfied with ...「…で満足している」　◇ result 名「（最終）結果［成績］」

第4問

解 答	問1 - ④　　問2 - ③　　問3 - ②　　問4 - ②　　　　　　（各3点）
	問5　28 - ②　　29 - ③　　　　　　　　　　　　　　　（各2点）

出典　*Original Material*

全訳

あなたはサウスシティに引っ越してきたばかりです。あなたは自転車の利用について2つの投稿を読んでいます。ひとつは自転車店が投稿したもので，もうひとつはエイミーが投稿したものです。

サウスシティに来てサイクリングを楽しんでください！
自転車店 BEN による 2022 年 4 月 2 日 午後 5 時の投稿

サイクリングは環境にやさしい交通手段であり，健康にも良いものです。サウスシティでサイクリングを楽しみませんか？　バスや車では行けないような裏通りに行くことができます。当店はセントラルパークの近くで自転車を貸し出しています。乗って行きたい場所によって，お好きな自転車をお選びください。さまざまなタイプの貸し自転車があり，料金は以下の通りです：

自転車店 BEN　貸し自転車

ロードバイク
50 ドル（1 日につき）

クルーザー
25 ドル（1 日につき）

マウンテンバイク
40 ドル（1 日につき）

折りたたみ式自転車
50 ドル（1 日につき）

電動自転車
60 ドル（1 日につき）

他のタイプの情報は→ https://rentalcycleben.example.web

料金は1日の金額です。自転車の貸出時間は午前10時〜午後1時で，利用した自転車は当日午後8時までに当店に返却してください。時間内に返却してもらえれば，どこに乗って行ってもらっても構いません。

シェアサイクルに乗ってみませんか？
エイミーによる 2020 年 5 月 5 日 午前 11 時 18 分の投稿

自転車シェアサービスをご存知でしょうか？　この度，サウスシティで始まったサービスです。アプリをダウンロードして登録すれば，このサービスを利用開始できます。自転車は，サイクルステーションのドックに施錠されています。会員番号を入力すると鍵が解除され，いつでも好きなときに自転車を利用することができます。空いてい

るドックがあれば，いつでもどこでも返却可能です。会社によって利用できることと，料金を比較した一覧表を作りました。会社のうちの1つはサウスシティに20ものステーションを持っています。近隣の都市で同じサービスを提供している会社もあります。私はよく自転車シェアサービスを利用しますが，とても便利です。サウスシティは坂が多いので，電動自転車はとても便利ですが，買うと高いです。貸し自転車は借りた場所に返さなければならないので，借りた場所から遠く離れていたり，天候が悪くなったりすると，ちょっと困ることがあります。この機会に，環境にやさしい自転車シェアサービスを体験してみてはいかがでしょうか。

会社名	Pedal More	BJ Cycles	Amazing Wheels
1時間あたりの料金	12 ドル	15 ドル（電動自転車） 10 ドル（クルーザー）	12 ドル（電動自転車） 10 ドル（クルーザー）
サウスシティ内の ステーションの数	12	20	15
自転車の種類	電動自転車	電動自転車 クルーザー	電動自転車 クルーザー
ステーションあたりの ドックの数	8	5	6
近隣の市でのサービス	利用できる	利用できる	利用できない

　なお，自転車の返却は，自転車ドックが空いている場合に可能です。アプリで自転車ステーションの位置やドックの空き状況を確認できますが，自転車を使い終わりたい場所の近くにドックが空いていない可能性があることを念頭に置いておく必要があります。

設問解説

問1　| 24 |　正解④

「自転車店 BEN はサウスシティでは | 24 | ことを勧めている」

　① 一番安い自転車を選んで借りる
　② 雨の日は自転車で出かけない
　③ 夜間は自転車に乗らない
　④ 車では行けない場所に行く

　正解は④。自転車店 BEN は投稿の中で，貸し自転車の良さについて語り，第1段落第3文（You can reach ...）で「バスや車では行けないような裏通りに行くことができます」と述べていることから④がふさわしいと判断できる。

　①や②のようなことは，BEN の投稿からは読み取れない。③の時間帯に関しては自転車の貸出時間や返却時間については言及しているが，それが夜は自転車に乗るべきではないという内容にはならないため正解ではない。

問2　| 25 |　正解③

「自転車のシェアサービスについて，エイミーは | 25 | と書いている」

　① ドックの数が他の会社の倍以上ある会社もある
　② サウスシティの市外でも，常に同じサービスが利用できる
　③ 自転車を受け取る時間や場所にほとんど制限がない
　④ 好みに合わせて多くの異なる種類の自転車を提供してくれる

— 英 R 72 —

正解は③。エイミーは投稿の第1段落第5文（Enter your membership ...）で「会員番号を入力すると鍵が解除され，いつでも好きなときに自転車を利用することができます」と述べていることから，時間に関する制限はないと判断できる。また，借りる場所の制限に関してはエイミーの投稿文中では言及されておらず，市内にいくつもあるステーションのドックに自転車が施錠されていれば利用可能であるということからも，場所に関する制限もほとんどないと判断する。

①に関しては，表中のステーションの数とステーションあたりのドックの数をかけ合わせてみれば判断できる。左から96，100，90となるので①は正解にはならない。②は表中の一番下の項目から，近隣の市では利用できない会社もあることがわかるので，always「常に」が誤りである。④に関しては表中の自転車の種類の項目で電動自転車とクルーザーの2種類しか貸し出されていないため「多くの異なる種類の自転車」とは言えない。

問3　26　正解②
「自転車店 BEN もエイミーも，26　と示唆している」
　　① 貸し自転車よりシェアサイクルの方が面倒が少ない
　　② **自転車は環境に害を与えない**
　　③ 自転車に乗ることは健康に良い
　　④ 自転車を使うとお金が節約できる

正解は②。自転車店 BEN は投稿の第1段落第1文（Cycling is an ...）でサイクリングは an environmentally sustainable means of transportation「環境にやさしい交通手段」であると述べ，エイミーは投稿の第1段落最終文（Why don't you ...）で an environmentally friendly bicycle sharing service「環境にやさしい自転車シェアサービス」と述べていることから②が正解となる。environmentally sustainable や environmentally friendly を don't harm the environment と言い換えているのがポイントとなる。

①は自転車店 BEN の言及がない。③はエイミーの言及がなく，④はどちらの投稿にもない内容である。

問4　27　正解②
「午後6時以降，いずれかの種類の自転車を最安値で利用し始めたい場合は，27　べきだ」
　　① お店の URL アドレスにアクセスする
　　② **エイミーが作成したリストを確認する**
　　③ 自転車店に連絡する
　　④ 他の市のサービスを利用する

正解は②。午後6時以降に自転車を利用し始めるという条件を考慮すると，自転車店 BEN は，第2段落第2文（Bicycles can be ...）で「貸出時間は午前10時～午後1時」と述べていることから，この店の貸し自転車は利用ができないとわかるので，①と③は正解にならない。エイミーは投稿の第1段落第5文（Enter your membership ...）で自転車シェアサービスは「いつでも好きな時に利用できる」と述べていることから，シェアサービスのうち一番安いところを調べるためにエイミーの作成したリストを確認するという②が正解になる。④は設問に与えられた条件とは無関係な内容である。

問5　28　正解②　　29　正解③
「あなたは，一番安い電動自転車であるという理由で，28　の電動自転車に午前10時から午後5時まで乗ろうと考えている。しかし，あなたは，隣の市で自転車を返したくなるかもしれないので，29　のクルーザーに乗ることも考えている（それぞれの空所に最適なものを，選択肢①～④の中から1つずつ選びなさい。）」

— 英 R 73 —

① Amazing Wheels
❷ 自転車店 BEN
❸ BJ Cycles
④ Pedal More

　まず，午前 10 時から午後 5 時は 7 時間で，電動自転車の料金は Amazing Wheels は 12 ドル×7 時間で 84 ドル，貸し自転車は 1 日 60 ドル，BJ Cycles は 15 ドル×7 時間で 105 ドル，Pedal More は 12 ドル×7 時間で 84 ドルとなる。よって条件に合う中で最も安い電動自転車を提供しているのは ❷ の自転車店 BEN ということになる。

　次に，隣の市で自転車を返すという条件になると ❸ の BJ Cycles と ④ の Pedal More が近隣の市でもサービスが利用できるので，このうちクルーザーを扱っている ❸ が正解となる。

主な語句・表現

・問題冊子を参照のこと。

[リード文]

◇ post 名「投稿」動「…を投稿する」

[自転車店 BEN の投稿]

◇ environmentally 副「環境的に」　　　◇ sustainable 形「持続可能な」
◇ means 名「手段」　　　　　　　　　　◇ transportation 名「交通機関」
◇ backstreet 名「裏通り」　　　　　　　◇ accessible 形「近づきやすい；入りやすい」
◇ rent 動「（お金を取って）…を貸す；（お金を払って）…を借りる」
◇ depending on ...「…に応じて」　　　　◇ for rent「借りることができる」
◇ available 形「利用可能な」　　　　　　◇ as follows「次のように」
◇ per 前「…につき」　　　　　　　　　◇ electric 形「電動の」
◇ fee 名「料金」　　　　　　　　　　　◇ check ... out / check out ...「…を借り出す」
◇ anywhere 副「どこにでも」　　　　　◇ as long as SV「S が V する限り」
◇ on time「時間通りに」

[エイミーの投稿]

◇ app 名「アプリ」　　　　　　　　　　◇ register 動「登録する」
◇ lock 動「…を施錠する」　　　　　　　◇ membership number「会員番号」
◇ unlock 動「…を開錠する」　　　　　　◇ anytime 副「いつでも」
◇ compare 動「…を比較する」　　　　　◇ as many as ...「…も」
◇ offer 動「…を提供する」　　　　　　　◇ neighboring 形「隣接している」
◇ convenient 形「便利な」　　　　　　　◇ hill 名「丘；山」
◇ troublesome 形「面倒な」　　　　　　◇ pick ... up / pick up ...「…を受け取る」
◇ environmentally friendly「環境にやさしい」
◇ unavailable 形「利用できない」　　　　◇ note 動「…に注意する」
◇ location 名「場所」　　　　　　　　　◇ availability 名「利用可能なこと」
◇ bear ... in mind / bear in mind ...「…を心に留めておく」

[設問文・選択肢]

◇ recommend 動「…を勧める」　　　　　◇ cheap 形「安い」
◇ regarding 前「…に関して」
◇ more than double the number of ...「2 倍を超える数の…」
◇ restriction 名「制限」　　　　　　　　◇ suit 動「…にぴったり合う」
◇ taste 名「好み」　　　　　　　　　　　◇ save 動「…を節約する」
◇ access 動「…にアクセスする」　　　　◇ contact 動「…に連絡する」
◇ consider −ing「−することを検討する」　◇ belong to ...「…に属する」

― 英 R 74 ―

第5問

解答

問1 - ④		（3点）
問2 - ③・④		（順不同・両方正解で3点）
問3 - 33 - ⑤　34 - ③　35 - ④　36 - ①		（完答で3点）
問4 - ③　　問5 - ②		（各3点）

出典　*Original Material*

全訳

あなたは高校生で，外国語として英語を学んでいます。来週ある研究者に関してプレゼンを行わなくてはいけません。あなたは以下の記事を見つけ，プレゼンに向けてメモの準備をしました。

　英文法は言語学と呼ばれる分野で研究されている。そして，何十年にもわたって，数えきれないほどの英文法の事実が明らかにされ，発見されてきた。誰もが英文法研究に最も貢献したと言う1人の研究者は，デンマーク人の言語学者，オットー・イェスペルセンである。

　彼は1860年にランダースの町で生まれた。若いころ，彼は言語を愛し，イタリア語やスペイン語などいくつかの外国語を独学した。1877年にコペンハーゲン大学に入学。最初は父や祖父と同じように法律を学んでいたが，時間さえあれば，外国語の文学を嗜（たしな）んでいた。当時，彼は生活費を稼ぐために，学校の先生とデンマーク議会の速記者としてアルバイトをしていた。

　1881年に彼の学問キャリアの大きな転機が訪れた。法律をすっかりやめ，本当に追求したいと思っていた言語の研究に完全に身を転じることに決めたのだった。そこでの先生の1人はヴィルヘルム・トムセンであった。彼は後にイェスペルセンに多大な影響を与えることとなる。イェスペルセンの主な研究テーマはフランス語であったが，英語やドイツ語も学んでいた。1887年，彼はフランス語で修士号を手にした。

　1887年に大学を卒業した後，イェスペルセンはイングランド，ドイツ，そしてフランスで1年近くを過ごし，その間，いくつかの言語学の授業を聴講した。イングランド訪問中，彼は当時非常に有名で影響力のある言語学者，ヘンリー・スウィートに出会った。イェスペルセンがこうして海外にいる間，トムセンは，英語の分野で大学のポストがまもなく空くだろうから，英語を専門にしてはどうか，と彼に助言した。イェスペルセンはこの助言に従い，1888年8月にコペンハーゲンに戻り，英語に関する博士論文に取り掛かった。1891年彼はついに博士号を取得した。イェスペルセンは1893年から1925年までコペンハーゲン大学の英語の教授であり，1920年から1921年にわたって大学の学長職をもこなした。

　彼は英語に関してたくさんの記事や本を発表した。そのほとんどはこれまで高く評価されてきた。彼の著作で最も重要なものの1つは『歴史原理に基づく近代英語文法』である。これは1909年から1949年までに出版された7巻からなる。これらは非英語母語話者によって書かれた英語に関する書物の中で最高傑作であるとみなされている。そこに見られる説明は非常に詳しく，中にはイェスペルセンは母語話者よりも英語のことをはるかに良くわかっていると示唆する者さえいるほどである。

— 英 R 75 —

イェスペルセンの研究や著作の何が特別なのだろうか？　まず挙げられるのは，それぞれの文法特性を説明するための例文が，たとえばシェークスピアの作品などの，本物の言語資料から採用されていることである。しばしば，英語の文法を分析する研究者は説明のためだけに例文を自分で作る。そうした言語学者は知らず知らずのうちに，英語のありのままを示すのではなく，彼らが見てほしいと思っている通りの英語を提示しがちだ。一方イェスペルセンは，常に実際の言語使用の例を参照しながら英語の真実を描き出そうとした。

　第二に，彼は英語の文法を説明するために，たくさんの新たな専門用語を作ったことが挙げられる。確かに多くの研究者が英文法を記述するための新しい概念や道具を編み出したが，そうしたものの大半は使われなくなったり，他の研究者に無視されたりしてきた。それに対して，死後およそ80年が経った今でさえ，イェスペルセンが作り出したものや明らかにしたことのほとんどは使われており，妥当だとみなされている。特に学習英文法においてはそうなのだ。学習文法とは，外国語学習者のために，コミュニケーションの中でどのように文法を活用するかを説明したものである。

　また，今日の言語学者の大半は自分の論文中でイェスペルセンの研究を引用したり触れたりしている。さらに，自分が発見したと感じていたことが，実はすでにイェスペルセンの著作の中で述べられていることにしばしば気づく研究者も多い。存命中のもっとも著名な言語学者の1人であるノーム・チョムスキーは，理論的な面でイェスペルセンの著作には多くの問題があるが，彼の英語の観察記録はおおむね正しいと書いた。

あなたのプレゼンのメモ：

オットー・イェスペルセン（1860 - 1943）

― 30 ―

最初の頃
　― 1860 年に生まれる
　― 31
　― 32

人生のいくつかの出来事の順序

　　　　　イェスペルセンは専門を言語に変えた。
　　　　　　33
　　　　　　34
　　　　　イェスペルセンは英語の教授になった。
　　　　　　35
　　　　　　36

研究と著作の1つの重要な特徴
　―イェスペルセンは英語の文法現象を 37 ことで説明した。

影響と評価
　―イェスペルセンは時に母語話者よりも英語のことをはるかによくわかっていると見なされることがある。
　― 38

設問解説

問1 ┃ 30 ┃ 正解 ④

「あなたのプレゼンの一番よいサブタイトルは何か」 ┃ 30 ┃

① 有名な言語学者兼法律家
② 母国語への強い愛情
③ 初心者向けの英文法
④ 英語の記述への貢献

正解は④。本文の第4段落までは研究面でのイェスペルセンの生涯が説明され，第5段落以降ではイェスペルセンの研究や著作の特徴について主に述べられている。第6段落で英語の実際の姿を描き出そうとしていたことが書かれており，最終段落最終文（Noam Chomsky, one ...）で「英語の観察記録はおおむね正しい」と評価されていることなどから，④が正解。また，第1段落第2文（One scholar who ...）で，イェスペルセンは英文法の研究に最も貢献した研究者の1人と見なされていると書かれており，これもヒントとなる。

①に関しては，イェスペルセンは法律を学んだものの，法律家になったわけではないので誤り。②に関しては，本文はあくまでイェスペルセンの英語とのかかわりがメインテーマであり，英語は彼にとっては外国語であることから，サブタイトルとしては適切ではない。③に関しては，該当する記述がない。

問2 ┃ 31 ┃・┃ 32 ┃ 正解 ③・④

「┃ 31 ┃ と ┃ 32 ┃ に入る最も適切な選択肢を2つ選び, <u>最初の頃</u>を完成させなさい(順序は問わない。)」

① ある英語の新聞の記者になった
② 気づかないうちにいくつかの法律を破っていた
③ 数年間父親と同じ道をたどった
④ 他者からの助けなしにヨーロッパ言語を学んだ
⑤ 大学に入る前に言語学を独学し始めた

正解は③と④。イェスペルセンは，1877年にコペンハーゲン大学に入学した後，1881年まで数年間，父や祖父と同じように法律を学んでいたことが，第2段落第3文（He entered Copenhagen ...）から第3段落第1文（In 1881 came ...）の間で述べられていることから，③は正しい。なお，第2段落第4文（At first he ...）中の as his father and grandfather had における had は had studied law の意味である。また，第2段落第2文（When he was ...）に「若いころ…イタリア語やスペイン語などいくつかの外国語を独学した」とあるので，④も正しい。

①，②，⑤に関しては該当する記述がない。

問3 ┃ 33 ┃ 正解 ⑤, ┃ 34 ┃ 正解 ③, ┃ 35 ┃ 正解 ④, ┃ 36 ┃ 正解 ①

「5つの出来事（①～⑤）から<u>4つの出来事</u>を起きた順番に選び, <u>人生のいくつかの出来事</u>の順序を完成させなさい」

① イェスペルセンは大学の学長になった。
② イェスペルセンは学校の先生として働き始めた。
③ イェスペルセンは博士号を取得するためのプロジェクトに取り掛かった。
④ 『歴史原理に基づく近代英語文法』の第1巻が出版された。
⑤ ヴィルヘルム・トムセンがイェスペルセンに英語を専攻するように勧めた。

正解は⑤→③→④→①。

まず ┃ 33 ┃ の前の「専門を言語に変えた」は第3段落から1881年だとわかる。②に該当する記述は第2段落にあるが，そこでは大学に入って法律を学んでいる頃に生活費のために学校の先生をした，と書かれている。よって，この内容は「専門を言語に変えた」よりも前の出来事であるから，②は解答から外れると判断する。

— 英 R 77 —

第4段落から⑤の内容は1887〜1888年の頃であるとわかるので，これは　33　以降に入れるのに適切である。③に関しては，同じく第4段落から1888年である。流れとしては，「トムセンが助言する→コペンハーゲンに戻る→博士課程に向けて取り組む」の順番なので，⑤の次に③が来る。同じく第4段落より，①にある「イェスペルセンは学長になった」のは1920年とわかる。　34　の後の「英語の教授になった」のは1893年なので，①は　35　か　36　に入ることになる。④に関しては，第5段落より，1909年と判断する。よって，①よりも④が先であるから，　35　が④で　36　が①である。

問4　37　正解 ③

「　37　に入れるのに最も適切な選択肢を選び，研究と著作の1つの重要な特徴を完成させなさい」

① 伝統的な理論的枠組みを採用する
② 自分で適切な例文を作る
❸ 実際に使われた英語の文を引用する
④ 初心者のための英語の教科書を書く

正解は③。第6段落第2文（First, example sentences ...）から，（自分で作ったものではなく）本物の素材（＝実際の言語資料）を用いて説明したと書かれているので，③が正しい。

②は正解と真逆で，イェスペルセン以外の多くの言語学者に当てはまるとされる内容なので誤り。①に関しては該当する記述がない。なお，第7段落で，独自の用語を作ったとあることからも，伝統的な理論的枠組みを採用していないことが推測される。④に関しては，第7段落で学習文法に影響を与えているとは書かれているものの，イェスペルセン自身が初心者向けの教科書を書いたとは書かれていないので誤りである。

問5　38　正解 ②

「　38　に入れるのに最も適切な選択肢を選び，影響と評価を完成させなさい」

① 言語学者として，イェスペルセンはヘンリー・スウィートと同じくらい偉大だと見なされている。
❷ イェスペルセンの研究は言語学習と言語研究の両方に大きな意義を持つ。
③ ノーム・チョムスキーはイェスペルセンの英語の理論に完全に同意した。
④ イェスペルセンによって開発された教育法は世界中の言語教育を大幅に改善した。

正解は②。第7段落で，イェスペルセンの研究成果が学習文法で使われており，妥当と見なされているとあるので，「言語学習に大きな意義を持つ」は正しいと判断できる。また，最終段落に書かれている，今日の言語学者が彼の研究を引用するといった内容から「言語研究に大きな意義を持つ」も正しいと判断できる。よって，②は適切。

①に関しては，該当する記述がない。③に関しては，本文最終文に，チョムスキーの言葉として「理論的には多くの問題がある」とあるので誤り。④に関しては，イェスペルセン自身が教育法を開発したという記述は本文中にないので誤り。

主な語句・表現	・問題冊子を参照のこと。

[第1段落]
(English grammar is ...)

◇ grammar 图「文法」　　　　　　　　◇ linguistics 图「言語学」
◇ contribute to ...「…に貢献する」

[第2段落]
(He was born ...)

◇ including 前「…を含む；たとえば…」　◇ by oneself「自分自身で；自分の力で」
◇ at first「最初は」
◇ literature 图「文学」　なお，第5段落に出てくる literature は「文献；書物」の意味。
◇ part-time 副「アルバイトで」　　　　◇ shorthand reporter「速記記者」

[第3段落] (In 1881 came...)	◇ turning-point 图「転換点」 ◇ devote oneself to ...「…に専念する」 ◇ be later to -「のちに-することとなる」	◇ altogether 副「一切をもって；完全に」 ◇ entirely 副「すっかり；完全に」 ◇ master's degree「修士号」
[第4段落] (After graduating from...)	◇ influential 形「影響力のある」 ◇ doctoral thesis「博士論文」　なお，doctoral dissertation と言うことの方が多い。 ◇ president 图「学長」	
[第5段落] (He published a ...)	◇ publish 動「…を発表する」 ◇ consist of ...「…から成る」	◇ regard 動「…を評価する」
[第6段落] (What is special ...)	◇ feature 图「特徴；特性」 ◇ authentic 形「本物の；実際に用いられた言語使用から採られた」 ◇ refer to ...「…を参照する；言及する」	◇ adopt 動「…を採用する」
[第7段落] (Second, he coined ...)	◇ coin 動「〈用語など〉を作り出す」 ◇ go out of use「使われなくなる」 ◇ valid 形「妥当である；有効な」	◇ technical term「専門用語」 ◇ by contrast「それに対して」 ◇ pedagogical 形「教育用の」
[最終段落] (Also, most linguists ...)	◇ cite 動「引用する」 ◇ renowned 形「著名な；高名な」 ◇ from a ... point of view「…の観点から（言えば）」 ◇ observation 图「観察（記録）」	◇ furthermore 副「さらに」
[設問文・選択肢]	◇ employ 動「…を採用する」 ◇ have a ... significance for ～「～に…な意義を持つ」	◇ quote 動「…を引用する」

— 英 R 79 —

第6問

解答	
A	問1-① 問2-④ 問3-③ （各3点）
	問4- 42 -③ 43 -⑥ （完答で3点）
B	問1-② （3点）
	問2- 45 -④ 46 -① （各3点）
	問3-①・⑤ （順不同・両方正解で3点）

A

出典　Andrea Pink: *Fact or Myth: Does Music Affect Plant Growth?*

全訳

　あなたの研究グループは「音楽が植物の成長を助けるかどうか」について学んでいます。あなたは共有したい記事を見つけました。次のミーティングのために，要約メモを完成させなさい。

事実か神話か：音楽は植物の成長に影響を与えるか？

　植物に音楽を聞かせると成長を助けるという説は本当だろうか，と考えたことはあるだろうか。植物はどのように「聴く」のだろうか。ヴィヴァルディやハリー・スタイルズが好みなのだろうか。植物が音楽に十分反応することを示唆する研究は実際に行われているが，この問題の真実はまだ不明である。とはいえ，この考えを裏付ける証拠は非常に説得力がある。

　この考え方はニューエイジ思想の最盛期に根付いたものだと知ってもあなたは驚かないかもしれない。1973年に出版されたクリストファー・バードとピーター・トンプキンスの共著『植物の神秘生活』は，「植物と人間の肉体的，感情的，霊的な関係」を描いたもので，この考えを広める一助となった。バードとトンプキンスは，音楽が植物の成長を助けるだけでなく，植物にもある程度の意識があり，人間に対して知的な反応を示すことができると示唆する科学的研究を引用した。

　音楽が植物に与える影響に関する最も初期の研究の1つは，1962年にアンナマライ大学の植物学部長であるT・C・シン博士によって行われたものだ。彼はバルサムの樹をクラシック音楽にさらして，対照群に比べ成長率が20％増加することを発見した。さらに，ラウドスピーカーでラーガ（インド音楽に見られる旋律の一種）を作物に聞かせたところ，全国平均より25〜60％収穫量が増えたことがわかった。

　『植物の神秘生活』が出版されたのと同じ年，コロラド女子大学の研究員であったドロシー・レタラックは，クラシック，ジャズ，ロックなど，さまざまな種類の音楽で実験を行った。クラシックやジャズなどの癒し系の音楽を聴かせた植物はスピーカーに向かって成長し，スピーカーに巻きついたりもした。一方でロック音楽を聞かせた植物はスピーカーから離れ，水をやりすぎた状態に似た兆候を示した。

　シンやレタラックを含めこれらの実験を行った研究者の多くは，植物は聴いている音楽によってなだめられるような反応をすると結論づけた。また彼らが，植物には何か不思議な能力があると考えていたことは注目に値する。レタラックはさらに，植物には超能力があり，歌詞に使われている言葉を恐れてロック音楽には近づかないようにしていたのだと考えていた。

— 英 R 80 —

音楽が植物の成長に役立つことについての最も有力な科学的理論は，音波の振動が植物に影響を与えることによるものである。植物は細胞質流動と呼ばれるプロセスによって，液体（細胞質）中のタンパク質などの栄養分を輸送している。ある種の音楽や音の振動は，このプロセスを刺激するのに役立つ可能性があり，自然界では鳥の鳴き声や強い風が吹く場所の周りで植物の成長が活発になることがある。

　カリフォルニア大学サンタバーバラ校の投稿により，これらの実験では光や水，気圧，土壌の状態など，適切な管理や考慮がなされていなかったかもしれない点が非常に多くあることが指摘されている。また，音楽の恩恵を受けるのは植物ではなく単に植物の世話をする人たちなのかもしれないことも示唆されている。世話をする人たちが単により注意を払うようになることから，植物に話しかけることが植物の成長を助けると言われるのも，これが理由かもしれない。

　しかし，少なくともある人気テレビ番組によればこの考え方にはまだ信憑性がある。その番組は 2004 年にこのテーマに取り組み，6 つの温室を用意し，1 つは音楽なし，1 つはクラシック音楽，1 つはデスメタル，2 つはネガティブな会話の録音を流し，1 つはポジティブな会話を流すという異なる条件を設定した。この実験では，他の植物よりもよく成長したのはデスメタルの植物であった。2 位はクラシック音楽，3 位はネガティブな会話とポジティブな会話を再生した温室でどちらも同じような成長を見せた。そして何も聞かせなかった植物は最下位になってしまった。

　音楽は精神の糧であるが植物にとってもそうなのだろうか。明確な答えはまだ出ていない。しかし，音楽を流すことが実際に植物の成長を助けるかどうかにかかわらず，植物をスピーカーのすぐそばに置き音量を上げ過ぎない限り，少なくとも損をすることはないだろう。

あなたの要約メモ：

事実か神話か：音楽は植物の成長に影響を与えるか？

過去の研究（1960 ～ 1970 年代）
・音楽が植物の成長に影響を与えるという仮説が生まれた。
・植物には霊的な力があり，植物は人間 ┃ 39 ┃ と考える科学者がいた。

現在の見解
・音楽が植物の成長に良い影響を与えるという決定的な証拠はない。
・科学的には，┃ 40 ┃。

興味深い内容
・1970 年代に行われたある実験と 2000 年代に行われた別の実験は ┃ 41 ┃。
・音楽だけでなく，┃ 42 ┃ も植物の成長と何らかの関係があるかもしれないと示す研究もある。
・この記事の著者は，┃ 43 ┃ を除けば，音楽はおそらく植物に悪い影響を与えないだろうと結論付けている。

設問解説

問1 　39　　正解①

「　39　に最もふさわしい選択肢を選びなさい」

① をある程度意識している
② に近づかない
③ のように意思の疎通ができる
④ を真似することができる

正解は①。　39　を含むコラムの小見出しになっている「過去の研究（1960 〜 1970年代）」に関しては，第2段落から第5段落で述べられている。第2段落最終文（Bird and Tompkins ...）に「バードとトンプキンスは，音楽が植物の成長を助けるだけでなく，植物にもある程度の意識があり，人間に対して知的な反応を示すことができると示唆する科学的研究を引用した」とあるので，①の内容に一致する。本文中の can intelligently respond to people「（植物は）人間に対して知的な反応を示すことができる」という部分を，①では plants had some awareness of humans「植物は人間をある程度意識していた」と言い換えている。

その他の選択肢は，いずれも本文中で述べられていないため誤り。

問2 　40　　正解④

「　40　に最もふさわしい選択肢を選びなさい」

① 騒がしい環境はたいてい植物の順調な成長を妨げる
② 植物は音楽を騒音と区別する能力を持っている
③ ある種の音楽の音は植物の体内組織に損傷を与えるかもしれない
④ 音波の振動は植物の栄養分の循環を良くする可能性がある

正解は④。　40　を含むコラムの小見出しになっている「現在の見解」に関しては第6段落から第7段落で述べられている。とりわけ　40　を含む文にある「科学的には」という表現に着目し，音楽と植物の関係について現在の科学的な見解が述べられている箇所を探すと，第6段落第1文（The best scientific ...）〜第3文（The vibration of ...）に「音波の振動が植物に影響を与えることで植物はタンパク質などの栄養分が輸送しやすくなる」ことが述べられているので，④が正解となる。

その他の選択肢は，いずれも本文中で述べられていないため誤り。

問3 　41　　正解③

「　41　に最もふさわしい選択肢を選びなさい」

① 人間と植物の関係が徐々に変化していることを説明している
② あらゆる種類の音楽は植物を全く同じ速度で成長させることを示している
③ 植物が好むと思われる音楽のジャンルの点で異なる結果を示している
④ 植物が他のどの音楽よりもクラシック音楽を好むという考えを支持している

正解は③。　41　を含む文にある「1970年代の実験」に関しては第4段落にレタラック氏が行ったと述べられており，その結果は第2文（Plants exposed to ...）に，実験で植物が好んだ音楽はクラシックやジャズで，ロックには拒否反応を示したというものであったことが記されている。一方で，同じく　41　を含む文にある「2000年代の実験」は第8段落にある2004年のテレビ番組で行われた実験のことであり，そこでは植物が最も好んだ音楽がデスメタル（ロックの一種）でありクラシックは2位であったことが述べられている。したがって，上記2つの実験結果では植物が好むと思われる音楽が異なっていることがわかるので③が最もふさわしい。

①・②の内容は本文中で述べられておらず誤り。④の内容は「2000年代の実験」の結果に矛盾する。

— 英 R 82 —

問4　| 42 |　正解③,　| 43 |　正解⑥

「| 42 |と| 43 |に最もふさわしい選択肢を選びなさい」

① 複雑なリズム
② デスメタル
③ **何らかの自然界の音**
④ 完全な無音
⑤ 交通騒音
⑥ **異常に大きな音**

| 42 |の正解は③。| 42 |を含む文の「植物の成長と何らかの関係があるかもしれないと示す研究」に関しては，第6段落第最終文（The vibration of ...）に「自然界では鳥の鳴き声や強い風が吹く場所の周りで植物の成長が活発になることがある」と述べられていることから，③が最も適切である。

| 43 |の正解は⑥。| 43 |を含む文は「| 43 |を除けば，音楽はおそらく植物に悪い影響を与えないだろうと結論付けている」という内容であるが，最終段落最終文（But regardless of ...）に「音楽を流すことが植物の成長を助けるかどうかにかかわらず，植物をスピーカーのすぐそばに置き音量を上げ過ぎない限り，少なくとも損をすることはないだろう」とあるので，植物の成長に悪影響を与える可能性があるものとしては⑥が最もふさわしいことがわかる。

（主な語句・表現）　・問題冊子を参照のこと。

[リード文]
◇ help ...（to）-「…が-するのに役立つ」　◇ article 名「記事」
◇ share 動「…を共有する」　◇ complete 動「…を完成させる」
◇ summary 名「要約」　◇ note 名「メモ」

[第1段落]
(Have you ever ...)
◇ truth 名「真実」　◇ theory 名「理論；説」
◇ prefer 動「…を好む」　◇ conduct 動「〈実験など〉を行う」
◇ suggest 動「…を示唆する」　◇ indeed 副「本当に；実際に」
◇ respond to ...「…に反応する」　◇ be up in the air「不明である」
◇ that being said「とはいえ」　◇ evidence 名「証拠」
◇ support 動「…を支持する」　◇ convincing 形「説得力がある」

[第2段落]
(It may not ...)
◇ take root「根付く」　◇ height 名「高さ；最盛期」
◇ New Age thinking「ニューエイジ思想」　◇ publish 動「…を出版する」
◇ account 名「説明；理論」　◇ physical 形「肉体的な」
◇ emotional 形「感情的な」　◇ spiritual 形「霊的な；精神的な」
◇ relation 名「関係」　◇ popularize 動「…を広める」
◇ cite 動「…を引用する」　◇ consciousness 名「意識」
◇ intelligently 副「知的に」

[第3段落]
(One of the ...)
◇ effect of ... on ～「…が～に与える影響」　◇ expose ... to ～「…を～にさらす」
◇ growth 名「成長」　◇ rate 名「率」
◇ compared to ...「…と比べて」　◇ control group「対照群」
◇ crop 名「作物」　◇ yield 動「…を産出する」
◇ national 形「全国の」　◇ average 名「平均」

[第4段落]
(The same year ...)
◇ experiment with ...「…を用いて実験をする」
◇ soothing 形「心を静める；癒し効果のある」

— 英 R 83 —

◇ wrap oneself around ...「…に巻き付く」　◇ away from ...「…から離れて」
◇ sign 名「気配；兆候」　◇ similar to ...「…に似ている」
◇ overwater 動「水をやり過ぎる」

[第5段落]　◇ conclude 動「…と結論付ける」　◇ as if ...「まるで…ように」
(Many of the ...)　◇ calm 動「…を静める；…を穏やかにする」　◇ be worth -ing「−する価値がある」
◇ magical 形「不思議な」　◇ supernatural 形「超自然的な」
◇ stay away from ...「…に近づかずにいる」

[第6段落]　◇ scientific 形「科学的な」　◇ as to ...「…に関する」
(The best　◇ vibration 名「振動」　◇ wave 名「波」
scientific ...)　◇ affect 動「…に影響を与える」　◇ transport 動「…を輸送する」
◇ nutrient 名「栄養分」　◇ protein 名「タンパク質」
◇ fluid 名「液体」　◇ process 名「プロセス；過程」
◇ certain 形「〈はっきりと言うのを避けて〉ある」
◇ stimulate 動「…を刺激する」　◇ nature 名「自然；自然界」
◇ advantageously 副「有利に」
◇ breeze 名「そよ風」　ここでは strong という形容詞が修飾しているので，strong breezes
　　で「強風」という意味になっている。

[第7段落]　◇ post 名「投稿」　◇ point out ...「…を指摘する」
(A post from ...)　◇ properly 副「適切に」　◇ manage 動「…を管理する」
◇ account for ...「…を考慮する」　◇ such as ...「たとえば…のような」
◇ air pressure「気圧」　◇ soil 名「土壌」
◇ condition 名「状態」　◇ benefit from ...「…の恩恵を受ける」
◇ caretaker 名「世話をする人」　◇ attentive 形「注意を払っている」

[第8段落]　◇ plausible 形「信憑性がある」　◇ at least「少なくとも」
(But the idea ...)　◇ according to ...「…によれば」　◇ tackle 動「…に取り組む」
◇ set up ...「…を用意する」　◇ negative 形「ネガティブな；悲観的な」
◇ positive 形「ポジティブな；前向きな」　◇ rest 名「その他；残り」
◇ follow 動「…の後に続く」　◇ exhibit 動「…を示す」
◇ dead last「最下位」

[最終段落]　◇ soul 名「心；精神」　◇ definitive 形「決定的な」
(Music is food ...)　◇ regardless of ...「…に関係なく」　◇ actually 副「実際に；現実に」
◇ aid 動「役立つ」　◇ at the very least「少なくとも」
◇ hurt 動「困ったことになる」　◇ as long as ...「…する限り」
◇ turn the volume up「音量を上げる」

[要約メモ]　◇ hypothesis 名「仮説」　◇ influence 動「…に影響を与える」
◇ possess 動「…を持っている」　◇ current 形「現在の」
◇ view 名「見解」　◇ conclusive 形「決定的な」
◇ scientifically 副「科学的に」　◇ detail 名「詳細；内容」
◇ have something to do with ...「…と何らかの関係がある」
◇ author 名「著者」　◇ probably 副「おそらく」
◇ except for ...「…は除いて」

— 英 R 84 —

[設問文・選択肢]

◇ awareness 图「意識」　　　　　　　◇ keep away from ...「…に近づかずにいる」
◇ be capable of －ing「－する能力がある」　◇ imitate 動「…を真似る」
◇ noisy 形「騒がしい」
◇ hinder ... from －ing「…が－するのを妨げる」
◇ steadily 副「着実に」　　　　　　　◇ ability 图「能力」
◇ tissue 图「(細胞の) 組織」　　　　　◇ improve 動「…を改善する」
◇ circulation 图「循環」　　　　　　　◇ relationship 图「関係」
◇ gradually 副「徐々に」　　　　　　　◇ indicate 動「…を示す」
◇ make O －「O に－させる」　　　　　◇ the exact same ...「全く同じ…」
◇ result 图「結果」　　　　　　　　　◇ in terms of ...「…の点で」
◇ genre 图「ジャンル；種類」　　　　　◇ total 形「完全な」
◇ silence 图「沈黙；音のない状態」　　◇ unusually 副「異常に」

B

出典　Sarah Zielinski: *Photographing wildflowers and other ways you can help fight climate change.*

全訳　　あなたは,「環境を守るために私たちに出来ることは何か」というテーマで科学のプレゼンテーションコンテストのためのポスターを準備している学生グループの一員である。あなたはポスターを作成するために以下の文章を読んでいる。

あなたは気候変動に立ち向かう手助けをすることができる: 科学者ではない人も研究に参加できる

　気候変動はあまりにも大きすぎる問題なので,あえて1人で立ち向かえるようなものとは思えません。もちろん科学者は,身の回りの世界で起こっていることを市民に知らせる手助けをすべく研究を行っています。こうした科学者の多くはいくらかの支援を必要としています。そして彼らは科学の専門家を必要としない場合もあるのです。一般の市民でも,彼らが必要とするものを提供できます。専門家はこうした支援者をシチズン・サイエンティストと呼んでいます。

　本当にすばらしいボランティアのプログラムがいくつかありますが,それらは2つのタイプに大別されます。その多くは,野生の動植物や自然環境の観察を含みますが,気候変動や環境破壊の原因となる人間の活動を報告することに関わるものもあります。

　SciStarter と Zooniverse という2つのウェブサイトは,あなたが参加できるシチズン・サイエンスのプロジェクトを一覧にしています。また,「シチズン・サイエンス」というキーワードと,あなたの住んでいる都市,州または国をインターネットで検索すれば,ボランティアを探している可能性のある地元のプロジェクトが出てくることもあります。そうしたプロジェクトと,それらに含まれているかもしれないもののいくつかの事例をここで紹介しましょう。

　Bird Count:このプロジェクトでは,世界中のボランティアが近隣の鳥の数をカウントします。このカウントが科学者に,さまざまな鳥が発見された場所とその数に関するデータを提供し,科学者はこれらのパターンが時と共にどう変化している可能性があるかを知ることができるのです。そこには,気候変動がそれらの鳥の個体数にどう影響を及ぼしうるかも含まれます。またこのプロジェクトは,バードウォッチングから得られた写真をできるだけ多く共有することもボランティアに求めています。

— 英 R 85 —

Household Waste Audit：環境保護庁によると，平均的なアメリカ人は1日に4.51ポンドのゴミを出しており，このゴミを燃やすことにより，二酸化炭素のような温室効果ガスが発生します。このプロジェクトでは，学生が1週間のうちに自分の家庭で出されるゴミの量を実測し，ゴミを減らしたり，再利用とリサイクルの両方，もしくはそのどちらかを行える独創的な方法を考案し，身の回りの環境の保護に対して積極的な役割を担うことが求められます。

Lunch Food Waste Audit：アメリカでは，食料が他のどの素材よりも多く埋め立て地に捨てられています。食料が埋め立て地に捨てられると，腐敗してメタン（二酸化炭素よりも強力な温室効果ガス）が発生します。食料を無駄にするのをやめるだけで，私たちは人間が発生させるすべての温室効果ガスのうち，おおよそ6％から8％を減らすことができるかもしれません。Lunch Food Waste Audit は自宅でできるプロジェクトで，みなさんに昼食の残り物の廃棄を追跡して，いくらか習慣を変えることをお願いしています。できる限り測定して，写真を撮ってください。

MeadoWatch：ワシントン大学発のこのプロジェクトは，レーニア山の野草に対して気候変動がどう影響しているかを観察しています。ボランティアはハイキング道を通りながら，野草が発芽し，開花し，果実をつけ，種を作る時期についてデータを集めます。またこのプロジェクトは，レーニア山国立公園一帯の野草の写真を収集しています。

Redmap：グレッタ・ピクルはホバートのタスマニア大学に勤めるオーストラリアの海洋生態学者です。彼女は海洋動物が気候変動に反応してどこに移動していくかを調査しています。彼女は Redmap というプログラムを始めました。このプログラムはオーストラリアの海域で見かけた"見慣れない"海洋種を報告することを求めています。「私たちは，どの種が生息域を変えつつあるかに関する初期の徴候を知ろうとしたのです」と彼女は説明している。

Water Monitoring：ミネソタ州の住民は，ミネソタ汚染管理局の水質監視のボランティアに参加申し込みをすることができます。ボランティアは湖か河川を指定されます。ボランティアは夏期に月に二度，水の透明度を測定します。このデータによって，政府はこれらの水路の衛生状態を評価するだけでなく，水の透明度が時と共に変化してきたかどうかを確認します。

Weather Rescue：人間は非常に長い間，天気のデータを収集してきました。しかし科学者がそれを利用するためには，紙に手書きされた記録データをデジタル化する，つまり，コンピュータに入力する必要があります。Weather Rescue では，イギリスの研究者がネット上のボランティアに依頼し，自宅のコンピュータを使って1860年代にヨーロッパで記録された過去の天気の測定値を入力してもらっています。これは地球の温暖化によって気温が上昇し始める前の時期です。このデータは将来の調査にとって有益な基準を提供するでしょう。

あなたの発表用ポスターの草案：

> ### 気候変動を防ぐために一般市民に何ができるか

シチズン・サイエンティストと気候変動に焦点を当てたプロジェクトについて
- シチズン・サイエンティストは専門家が科学研究を行うのを援助する一般市民である。
- 気候変動に関するプロジェクトには，自然を観察するものと人間の活動を報告するものの2つのタイプがある。
- 44

シチズン・サイエンスのプロジェクトの例

プロジェクト名	活動の例	タイプ
Bird Count	このプロジェクトは 45 を調査している。	自然観察
Household Waste Audit	このプロジェクトは，家庭でのゴミの量を知り， 46 ことを求めている。	人間の活動の報告
Lunch Food Waste Audit	このプロジェクトは食料の無駄を減らすために習慣を変えるよう求めている。	人間の活動の報告
MeadoWatch		

このプロジェクトのいくつかには共通の特徴がある：

> 47
> 48

設問解説

問1 44 **正解②**

「あなたのグループは，この文章で説明されているシチズン・サイエンスのプロジェクトについて紹介したいと考えている。次のうちどれが最も適切か」 44

① 一般市民は気候変動について科学者よりも優れた調査をすることが多い。

② インターネットで検索することで，あなたは自分の居住地周辺のそのようなプロジェクトを見つけることができる。

③ オンラインで申し込めば，あなたが住む自治体があなたに適したプロジェクトを選んでくれる。

④ Zooniverse は一般市民が参加できるシチズン・サイエンスのプロジェクトの1つである。

正解は②。本文の第3段落第2文（An internet search ...）に「また，『シチズン・サイエンス』というキーワードと，あなたの住んでいる都市，州または国をインターネットで検索すれば，ボランティアを探している可能性のある地元のプロジェクトが出てくることもあります」とあるので，②が正解。

④に関しては，第3段落第1文（SciStarter and Zooniverse ...）にあるように，Zooniverse は参加可能なプロジェクトを一覧にしているサイトであって，プロジェクトそのものではないことに注意。

— 英 R 87 —

問2 | 45 | 正解 ④ | 46 | 正解 ①

「あなたは Bird Count と Household Waste Audit に関する説明を書くよう頼まれた。| 45 | と | 46 | に最も適切な選択肢を選べ」

Bird Count | 45 |

① 長距離を飛ぶ鳥の能力
② 鳥はどのようにして新しい環境に順応するか
③ 鳥の行動における季節ごとの変化
④ **鳥に対する気候変化の影響**

Bird Count について説明している段落を見ると，第3文（That includes how ...）に「気候変動がそれらの鳥の個体数にどう影響を及ぼしうるか」という記述があるので，④が正解。

Household Waste Audit | 46 |

① **環境のためにどうすればそれを減らせるかを考える**
② 自分が住んでいる自治体のゴミの分別ルールに従う
③ 温室効果ガスの影響について学ぶ
④ それを燃やす適切な方法について考える

Household Waste Audit について説明している段落を見ると，第2文（In this project, ...）に「このプロジェクトでは，学生が1週間のうちに自分の家庭で出されるゴミの量を実測し，ゴミを減らしたり，再利用とリサイクルの両方，もしくはそのどちらかを行える独創的な方法を考案し，身の回りの環境の保護に対して積極的な役割を担うことが求められます」とあるので，①が正解。なお，it は（the amount of）waste を指している。

問3 | 47 | ・ | 48 | 正解 ①・⑤

「あなたはこれらのプロジェクトのいくつかに共通の特徴があることに気づいた。この記事によると，次のうち適切なものはどれか。2つ選びなさい（順序は問わない。）」
| 47 | ・ | 48 |

① **Household Waste Audit, Lunch Food Waste Audit, Water Monitoring, Weather Rescue には動植物の調査が含まれていない。**
② Bird Count, Redmap, Water Monitoring では水の調査が必要である。
③ Redmap と Water Monitoring はボランティアに海洋動物の報告をするよう求めている。
④ Bird Count, MeadoWatch, Redmap の調査には，野生動物の生態系の観察が含まれる。
⑤ **Bird Count, Lunch Food Waste Audit, MeadoWatch のボランティアは写真を撮ることを求められる。**
⑥ Household Waste Audit と Lunch Food Waste Audit 以外は，屋外での調査をする必要がある。

正解は①と⑤。それぞれのプロジェクトの解説を読むと，まず Household Waste Audit は「家庭ゴミ」，Lunch Food Waste Audit は「食料廃棄」，Water Monitoring は「水質」，Weather Rescue は「天候」の調査を行っており，それ以外のプロジェクトには動植物の調査が含まれている。よって①が1つめの正解。次に，Bird Count と Lunch Food Waste Audit と MeadoWatch の説明を見ると，それぞれ最終文に写真に関する記述が見られ，他のプロジェクトの説明にはない。よって⑤が2つめの正解。

②は，Redmap には海での調査，Water Monitoring には湖か河川での調査が含まれるが，Bird Count の調査では，水の調査が必要だとは書かれていない。③は，Redmap には海洋動物の報告が含まれるが，Water Monitoring には含まれない。④は，Bird Count には鳥の調査，Redmap には海洋動物の調査が含まれるが，MeadoWatch は野草の調査を行うだ

— 英 R 88 —

けであり，「野生動物」の調査は含まれない。⑥は，Household Waste Audit が家庭ゴミを対象とし，Lunch Food Waste Audit が食料廃棄を対象としているので，この２つに関して屋内のみでの調査が可能なのは間違いではないが，これら以外にも，自宅のコンピュータを使う Weather Rescue も屋内のみでの作業が可能である。

(主な語句・表現)	・問題冊子を参照のこと。	
[タイトル]	◇ climate change「気候変動」	◇ take part in ...「…に参加する」
[第1段落] (Climate change can ...)	◇ bother −ing「（主に否定文で）わざわざ−する」 ◇ tackle 動「…に立ち向かう」 ◇ could use ...「…を必要とする」	 ◇ inform ... about 〜「…に〜を知らせる」 ◇ refer to ... as 〜「…を〜と呼ぶ」
[第2段落] (There are some ...)	◇ roughly 副「おおよそ」 ◇ divide ... into 〜「…を〜に分ける」　ここでは受動態になっている。 ◇ involve 動「…を含む」 ◇ be related to ...「…と関係［関連］がある」 ◇ destruction 名「破壊」	 ◇ while 接「一方で」
[第3段落] (SciStarter and Zooniverse ...)	◇ list 動「…を一覧にする」 ◇ state 名「州」 ◇ bring up ... / bring ... up「…を（コンピュータの画面に）表示する」 ◇ local 形「地元の」	◇ internet search「インターネットの検索」 ◇ seek 動「…を探し求める」
[Bird Count]	◇ allow ... to −「…が−することを可能にする」 ◇ find out ... / find ... out「…を知る［調べる］」 ◇ affect 動「…に影響を及ぼす」 ◇ as ... as possible「できるだけ…」	 ◇ share 動「…を共有する」
[Household Waste Audit]	◇ waste 名「ゴミ；廃棄物；無駄（遣い）」 ◇ according to ...「…によると」 ◇ per 前「…につき」 ◇ carbon dioxide「二酸化炭素」 ◇ devise 動「…を考え出す」 ◇ role 名「役割」	◇ audit 名「検査」 ◇ generate 動「…を生み出す」 ◇ greenhouse gas「温室効果ガス」 ◇ measure 動「…を測定する」 ◇ active 形「積極的な」
[Lunch Food Waste Audit]	◇ landfill 名「埋め立て地」 ◇ rot 動「腐敗する」 ◇ potent 形「強力な」 ◇ emission 名「放出」 ◇ at-home 形「家庭での；家庭でできる」 ◇ habit 名「（個人の）習慣」	◇ material 名「素材」 ◇ methane 名「メタンガス」 ◇ human-caused 形「人間が引き起こした」 ◇ waste 動「…を無駄にする」 ◇ track 動「…を追跡する」 ◇ as best ... can「…のできる限り」
[MeadoWatch]	◇ meadow 名「草地」　ここでは watch「観察」とつなげた造語になっている。 ◇ wildflower 名「野草」 ◇ bud 動「発芽する」	 ◇ trail 名「道」 ◇ flower 動「開花する」

— 英 R 89 —

[Redmap]	◇ marine 形「海の」	◇ ecologist 名「生態学者」
	◇ in response to ...「…に反応して」	◇ set up ... / set ... up「…を始める」
	◇ waters 名「海；川；湖」	◇ indication 名「徴候」

[Water Monitoring]
◇ resident 名「住民」　　　　　　　◇ sign up「参加を申し込む」
◇ monitor 名「監視者」
◇ assign ... 〜「…に〜を指定する」　ここでは受け身になっている。
◇ stream 名「小川」　　　　　　　　◇ clarity 名「透明度」
◇ over time「時が経つにつれ」　　　◇ ... as well as 〜「〜と同様に…も」
◇ waterway 名「水路」

[Weather Rescue]
◇ handwritten 形「手書きの」　　　　◇ digitize 動「…をデジタル化する」
◇ enter 動「…を入力する」　　　　　◇ online 形「インターネット上の」
◇ transcribe 動「…を書き換える」　ここでは手書きの記録をコンピュータに入力すること
　を意味する。
◇ baseline 名「基準」

[ポスター]
◇ ordinary 形「一般的な」　　　　　◇ focus on ...「…に焦点を当てる」
◇ conduct 動「（調査など）を行う」　◇ concerning 前「…に関する」
◇ encourage ... to −「−するよう…を奨励する」

[設問文・選択肢]
◇ passage 名「文章」　　　　　　　◇ residence 名「居住」
◇ community 名「自治体；地域社会」　◇ suitable 形「適した」
◇ apply 動「申し込む」　　　　　　◇ adapt 動「適応する」
◇ seasonal 形「季節ごとの」　　　　◇ for the sake of ...「…のために」
◇ garbage 名「ゴミ」　　　　　　　◇ separation 名「分別」
◇ matter 動「問題である；重要である」　◇ require ... to −「−するよう…に要求する」
◇ ecosystem 名「生態系」　　　　　◇ except 前「…を除いて」

| 第3回 | 実戦問題　解答・解説 |

英語（リーディング）　第3回　（100点満点）

（解答・配点）

問題番号（配点）	設問		解答番号	正解	配点	自己採点欄	問題番号（配点）	設問		解答番号	正解	配点	自己採点欄
第1問（10）	A	1	1	③	2		第4問（16）		1	24	①	3	
		2	2	②	2				2	25	②	3	
	B	1	3	②	2				3	26	④	3	
		2	4	③	2				4	27	①	3	
		3	5	④	2				5	28	④	2	
小　計										29	②	2	
第2問（20）	A	1	6	②	2		小　計						
		2	7	④	2		第5問（15）		1	30	①	3	
		3	8	①	2				2	31	⑤	3*	
		4	9	③	2					32	③		
		5	10	①	2				3	33	②	3*	
	B	1	11	⑤	2					34	①		
		2	12	③	2					35	⑤		
		3	13	②	2					36	③		
		4	14	①	2				4	37	④	3	
		5	15	②	2				5	38	①	3	
小　計							小　計						
第3問（15）	A	1	16	②	3		第6問（24）	A	1	39	②	3	
		2	17	③	3				2	40	②	3	
	B	1	18	③	3*				3	41	③	3	
			19	①					4	42	③	3*	
			20	④						43	①		
			21	②				B	1	44	③	3	
		2	22	③	3				2	45	④	3	
		3	23	①	3					46	④	3	
小　計									3	47 — 48	① — ②	3*	
							小　計						
							合　計						

（注）
1　＊は，全部正解の場合のみ点を与える。
2　－（ハイフン）でつながれた正解は，順序を問わない。

— 英R 92 —

第1問

解答

| A | 問1 – ③ | 問2 – ② | | （各2点） |
| B | 問1 – ② | 問2 – ③ | 問3 – ④ | （各2点） |

A

出典　*Original Material*

全訳

　　あなたは家庭科の授業で，食べたり調味料として使ったりできる種子について勉強しています。そして，あなたは試してみたい4種類の種を見つけます。

食べてみたい4種類の種	
チーア種子	**ザクロの種**
▶食物繊維を多く含む ▶ヨーグルトやサラダにぴったりの，サクサク感あふれるトッピング ▶ジュースやアーモンドミルクに浸して柔らかくすると，プリンのようになる	▶ザクロの実の中にある，甘い宝石のようなビーズ状の種 ▶ビタミンCが多く，カロリーが低い ▶サラダや全粒粉の料理にジューシーな味わいと色を加えることができる。
亜麻の種（亜麻仁）	**麻の実**
▶紀元前9,000年から食べられている ▶健康的な脂肪と豊富な食物繊維が含まれている。 ▶オートミール，パンケーキ，新鮮な野菜に加える	▶たんぱく質をたっぷり含んでいる：（そのたんぱく質含有量は）亜麻仁やチーア種子よりもさらに多い ▶種を丸ごとサラダや全粒粉料理にまぶしたり，ヘンプミルクを作って普段消費している乳製品の一部の代替とすることができる。

設問解説

問1　　**1**　　正解③

「乳製品を食べすぎていると感じる人には，**1**を勧めることができる」

① チーア種子
② 亜麻の種
❸ 麻の実
④ ザクロの種

　　正解は③。「麻の実（Hemp Seeds）」の説明文の2つめ（You can use ...）に，「種を丸ごとサラダや全粒粉料理にまぶしたり，<u>ヘンプミルクを作って普段消費している乳製品の一部の代替とすることができる</u>」とある。③の「麻の実」を空所に入れれば，下線部の内容と合うことになる。

問2　　**2**　　正解②

「すべての種子は**2**とうまく合う」

① ミルク
❷ サラダ
③ 全粒粉料理
④ ヨーグルト

　　正解は②。4つの種子それぞれの説明文の中に，サラダ（salad(s)）や新鮮な野菜（fresh

— 英R 93 —

vegetables）という表現が登場しており，すべてサラダに使えるものとして紹介されていることがわかる。よって，正解は **②**。

主な語句・表現
・問題冊子を参照のこと。

[リード文]
◇ home economics「家庭の経済学→（学校で学ぶ教科としての）家庭科」
◇ seed 名「（植物の）種；種子」　　　　　　◇ seasoning 名「調味料；薬味」

[Chia Seeds]
◇ chia 名「（植物の）チーア［チア］」　シソ科の一年草。
◇ contain 動「…を含む」　　　　　　　　　◇ fiber 名「（食物）繊維」
◇ crunchy 形「サクサクの；カリカリの」
◇ topping 名「〈ケーキやアイスクリームなどの〉トッピング；上飾り」
◇ yogurt 名「ヨーグルト」　　　　　　　　　◇ soak 動「…を浸す；つける」
◇ pudding 名「プリン；プディング；デザート」

[Pomegranate Seeds]
◇ pomegranate 名「ザクロの実［木］」　　　◇ jewel 名「宝石」
◇ bead 名「ビーズ；ガラス玉」　　　　　　　◇ add A to B「A を B につけ加える［足す］」
◇ pop 名「ポン［パン］と弾けるような［弾むような］感じ・感覚」
◇ flavor 名「（独特の）味わい；風味」
◇ whole-grain 形「（穀物が）全粒の；無精白の」
◇ dish 名「料理」

[Flax Seeds]
◇ flax 名「（植物の）亜麻」　　　　　　　　◇ fat 名「脂肪（分）」
◇ a good dose of ...「十分な分量の…」　good は「十分な；申し分のない」, dose は名詞で「（薬などの）一服；量」という意味。
◇ oatmeal 名「オートミール」　　　　　　　◇ pancake 名「パンケーキ」

[Hemp Seeds]
◇ hemp 名「（植物の）麻；大麻」　　　　　　◇ plenty of ...「たくさんの…」
◇ protein 名「たんぱく質」　　　　　　　　◇ sprinkle 動「（…に）振りかける；まぶす」
◇ cut out「（…を）省く［やめる］；（…に）取って代わる」
◇ dairy 名「乳製品」　　　　　　　　　　　◇ consume 動「（…を）消費する；費やす」

[設問文・選択肢]
◇ explanation 名「説明」　＜ explain 動「…を説明する」
◇ recommend 動「（…を）勧める；推薦する」
◇ go well with ...「…と調和する；マッチする；（うまく）合う」

B

出典　*Original Material*

全訳

　あなたは学校の英語クラブの部長であり，クラブは次のようにチラシで説明されている
コンテストに参加する予定です。

第1回青年英語演劇コンテスト

　青年英語演劇協会は，最初となるコンテストを開催します。最高のエンターテインメントとしての形のひとつである演劇を通して，日本人の若者に積極的に英語を学んでもらうことをねらいとしています。

　このコンテストには3つのステージ（段階）があります。各ステージで勝者が選出され，3つのステージすべてに合格すると，グランドファイナル（本選）に参加することができます。

グランドファイナル	会場：センチュリーホール 日時：2023年2月5日

大賞賞品

優勝チームは，2023年3月にオーストラリアのキャンベラで開催されるインターナショナル・イングリッシュ・キャンプに参加できます。

コンテストについての情報：

ステージ	アップロードするもの 及びイベント	詳細	2022年の締切 及び日程
ステージ1	アンケートへの回答及び英語のエッセイ	エッセイの語数：150 - 200語	8月13日昼12時までにアップロードすること
ステージ2	あなたのチームが演じている様子を撮影した動画	（演技）時間：25 - 30分	10月25日昼12時までにアップロードすること
ステージ3	地域予選	このサイト上に，グランドファイナルへ進出する勝者（チーム）を発表します。	12月23日開催

グランドファイナルでの評価基準に関する情報

発音及び イントネーションなど	ジェスチャー及び パフォーマンス	発声及び アイコンタクト	チームワーク	審査員からの 質問への返答
40%	10%	10%	30%	10%

◆アンケート，英語のエッセイのタイトル，演劇用の台本をオンラインでダウンロードする必要があります。

<u>ここをクリック</u>してください。

◆資料はオンラインでアップロードする必要があります。すべての日時は日本標準時（JST）です。

◆ステージ1とステージ2の結果は，各ステージの締め切りから7日後にウェブサイトで知ることができます。

詳細については，<u>ここをクリック</u>してください。

設 問 解 説

問1 3 正解 ②

「ステージ1に参加するには，3 ことが必要である」

① 質問に答えて，パフォーマンスの動画を作成する

② 質問に答え，英語でエッセイを書く

③ 英語のエッセイを書いて，パフォーマンスの動画を作成する

④ 英語のエッセイを書いて，演劇（の台本）を書く

正解は ②。Contest information（コンテストについての情報）を記した一覧表を読み取る。各ステージに参加するための要件は，表の中の "Things to Upload & Events" の欄で示されており，ステージ1に参加するための要件としては，Answers to a questionnaire, and an English essay「アンケートへの回答及び英語のエッセイ」という記載がある。よって，② が正解。

問2 4 正解 ③

「ステージ1の結果はいつから確認できるか」 4

① 8月6日

② 8月13日

③ 8月20日

④ 8月27日

正解は ③。チラシの最後の◆（You can get ...）に，「ステージ1とステージ2の結果は，各ステージの締め切りから7日後にウェブサイトで知ることができます」とある。ステージ1の締め切り日は8月13日であり，それから7日後なので8月20日からステージ1の結果を確認することができるということになる。よって，③ が正解。

問3 5 正解 ④

「グランドファイナルで高得点を得るためには，自然な英語を話すことと 5 に最大の努力を注ぐ必要がある」

① 声や表情をコントロールすること

② 審査員にストーリーを丁寧に説明すること

③ ドラマチックなジェスチャーをすること

④ グループとしてよりうまく機能すること

正解は ④。Grand Final Grading Information（グランドファイナルでの評価基準に関する情報）の図表を見ると，Pronunciation & Intonation, etc.（発音及びイントネーションなど）の評価項目に最も重い40%の比重が置かれていて，これが「自然な英語を話すこと」に該当するとわかる。次に重い比重が置かれているのはTeamwork（チームワーク）で，30%であるが，チームワークに関わる内容としては，選択肢の ④「グループとしてよりうまく機能すること」が当てはまると考えられる。よって，正解は ④。

主な語句・表現

・問題冊子を参照のこと。

［リード文］

◇ chief 形「〈階級・重要度などにおいて〉最高の」

◇ flyer 名「（折り込み）チラシ」　　　　◇ as follows「以下の通り」

［チラシ］

◇ aim to −「−することをねらいとする」

◇ encourage A to −「Aが−するように勧める［励ます］；Aを励まして−させる［してもらう］」

◇ form 名「形；形態」　　　　◇ competition 名「競争；試合；コンテスト」

◇ participate in ...「…に参加する」（= take part in ...）

◇ Grand Final「グランドファイナル；（最終）本選」

— 英R 96 —

◇ questionnaire 名「アンケート」　　　　◇ video 名「動画；ビデオ」
◇ regional 形「地域の；地方の」　　　　◇ detail 名「詳細；詳しい内容」
◇ deadline 名「締切（日）」　　　　　　◇ script 名「〈演劇などの〉台本」
◇ play 名「演劇；戯曲」　　　　　　　　◇ material 名「資料」

[設問文・選択肢]　◇ expression 名「表情；表現」　　　　◇ dramatic 形「ドラマチックな；劇的な」

第2問

解答					
A	問1-②	問2-④	問3-①	問4-③	問5-① （各2点）
B	問1-⑤	問2-③	問3-②	問4-①	問5-② （各2点）

A

出典 *Original Material*

全訳　　あなたは，イギリスのサマープログラムに参加する予定なので，参加するコースについての情報と，昨年同じコースに参加した学生のコメントを読んでいます。

中級レベルの実用英語クラス

メアリー・ホワイト博士
white.mary@example-u.ac.uk
電話：020-8765-XXXX
執務時間：
月曜日と木曜日　午後 1:00 〜午後 2:00

2022 年 8 月 4 日〜 30 日
月曜日と木曜日
午後 2:00 〜午後 3:30
授業 8 時間につき 1 単位

コースの説明：
さまざまな国の人々と英語でよりよく交流する方法を学びます。英語は参加者の第一言語であってはなりません。また，すでに基本的な英語の文法を習得していることが前提です。

このコースでは，学生は自国に特有な文化の1つを紹介するスピーチまたはプレゼンテーションを英語で行います。

目標：
このコースを修了すると，次のことができるようになるでしょう。
― 日常生活の一般的なトピックについて，英語で人々とコミュニケーションをとったり，人々の前でそれらについて話す。
― 特に困難を感じることなく英語でテキストメッセージを書く。
― いくつかの社会問題について，英語で人々と意見交換を行う。

教科書：
サミュエル，B.（2020）『ゴー・フォワード！』
［中級］ロンドン：SDBK 出版

参加者の評価（76 人のレビューアー）
★★★★★（平均：4.78）

●メアリーは経験豊富な教師です。厳しいですが，とても親切で思いやりがあります。

●最初はこのコースが難しいと感じるかもしれませんが，すぐに慣れます。あなたはきっとあなたの英語力をよりスキルアップすることができます。

●メールの授業は楽しかったです。その授業は，私が今人々とコミュニケーションをとるのに本当に助けとなってくれています。

●コンピューターによる翻訳技術を最大限に活用する方法について学びたかった。それは将来のコミュニケーションにおいてますます有用で役に立つものになるでしょうから。

●世界にはたくさんの種類の英語があることに気づきました。このコースは私に「自分の」英語について自信を持たせてくれました。英語は確かに世界共通の言語です。

— 英 R 98 —

評価：
合格するには全体の 70% のスコア取得が必要
― 到達度テスト：60%
― 英語のスピーチまたはプレゼンテーション：30%
― 出席点：10%

設問解説

問1 　6　 正解 ②
「このコースの目的は何か」 　6
① スポーツ活動を行うことを通して英語を学ぶこと
② 英語のコミュニケーションスキルを向上させること
③ 有名な英語のスピーチを研究すること
④ 多くの英語圏の国々の歴史を学ぶこと
　正解は ②。Course description（コースの説明）に，You will be learning how to interact better with people from different countries in English.「さまざまな国の人々と英語でよりよく交流する方法を学びます」という記述がある。また，Goals（目標）の1つに，communicate with people in English about general topics in daily life and speak about them in front of people「日常生活の一般的なトピックについて，英語で人々とコミュニケーションをとったり，人々の前でそれらについて話せるようになる（こと）」がある。これらは選択肢の ② の内容に関わることであるので，② が正解。
　選択肢 ① 及び ④ の内容に関わる記述はない。また，選択肢 ③ については，本文に「学生は自国に特有な文化の1つを紹介するスピーチまたはプレゼンテーションを英語で行います」という記述や，「日常生活の一般的なトピックについて，英語で人々の前で話せるようになる（こと）」という記述はあるが，「有名な英語のスピーチを研究する」（Studying famous English speeches）という内容は記載がない。

問2 　7　 正解 ④
「　7　は，このコースの終了後にできるようになることの2つである」
　A：上級英文法をマスターする
　B：英語の新聞を読む
　C：人前で英語を話す
　D：英国の文化を理解する
　E：英語でメールを書く
① A と B
② A と D
③ B と C
④ C と E
⑤ D と E
　正解は ④。Goals（目標）の欄の記述に注目する。すると，そこには次の2つの記載があることがわかる。
　(1) speak about them（= general topics in daily life）in front of people「日常生活の一般的なトピックについて，英語で人々の前で話す」
　(2) write text messages in English without any particular difficulties「特に困難を感じることなく英語でテキストメッセージを書く」
　(1)は選択肢 C に当てはまることであり，(2)は選択肢 E に当てはまることである。そして，他の選択肢の内容に関わる記述は本文にはない。よって，④ が正解。

問3 | 8 | 正解①

「ホワイト博士についての1つの**事実**は | 8 | ということである」

① **自身の授業の1時間前にはいつもオフィスにいる**
② 英語でのチームティーチングが得意である
③ 厳しい先生であり，課題をたくさん出す
④ 手ごろな翻訳機の使い方を生徒に教える

正解は①。本文の左上部に，Office Hours：Monday & Thursday　1.00 pm – 2.00 pm（執務時間：月曜日と木曜日　午後1:00～午後2:00）とあり，授業については，Monday & Thursday　2.00 pm – 3.30 pm（月曜日と木曜日　午後2:00～午後3:30）という記載がある。つまり，授業は毎週月曜日と木曜日の週2回それぞれ午後2時に始まり，それより1時間前の午後1時から授業が始まる2時までの1時間の間はホワイト博士はオフィスにいる，ということである。よって，正解は①。

選択肢②と④についての内容は本文に記載がなく，選択肢③については，確かに「厳しい先生」という記述はある（She is strict）が，これは事実というよりは個人の意見であり，また「課題をたくさん出す」という記述はない。

問4 | 9 | 正解③

「クラスについてのある参加者の意見を最もよく要約しているのはどれか」 | 9 |

① 到達度テストが最も高く評価される。
② メールのクラスはお勧めしない。
③ **授業はそれほど難しくないことがわかる。**
④ 学生は週3時間授業を受ける。

正解は③。Participants' evaluations（参加者の評価）の2つめに At first you may find this course difficult, but soon you'll get used to it.「最初はこのコースが難しいと感じるかもしれませんが，すぐに慣れます」というコメントがある。これは，授業は慣れればそれほど難しくないことがわかるだろうという意見だと考えられるので，正解は③。

選択肢の①と④はこのクラスに関わる事実であって，参加者の「意見」（opinion）ではない。選択肢②については，参加者の評価の中では「メールの授業は楽しかったです。その授業は，私が今人々とコミュニケーションをとるのに本当に助けとなってくれています」という肯定的な評価がされており，②のような否定的なコメントは見当たらない。

問5 | 10 | 正解①

「このコースの単位を取得するために最も必要とされるものは何か」 | 10 |

① **テストでよい点数を取ること**
② 積極的に議論に参加すること
③ 良いスピーチとプレゼンテーションをすること
④ 授業を欠席していないこと

正解は①。Evaluation（評価）に関する説明箇所に注目する。評価の配点として最も大きなウエイトを占めるのは achievement tests（到達度テスト）であり，全体の60%の比重を占める。よって，正解は①。

選択肢②に関しては，具体的にそれがどのように評価されるのかということについての記述はない。選択肢③については，その評価のウェイトは30%であり，①の60%より低い。また選択肢④については，「出席点」は10%であり，いずれも「最も必要」というわけではない。

— 英 R 100 —

主な語句・表現	・問題冊子を参照のこと。

[リード文]
◇ summer programme「サマープログラム」 夏季の期間，欧米の大学等の施設で，英語を母語としない人々向けに行われる，主に英語の運用能力を高めることをねらいとする集中英語学習プログラム。なお，programme はイギリス英語の綴りであり，アメリカ英語では program となる。

[本文]
◇ intermediate 形「中級の；中くらいのレベルの」
◇ practical 形「実用的な」
◇ office hour「オフィスアワー；執務［勤務］時間」 勤務先で自らの常駐する部屋（オフィス）の中にいて，執務［勤務］する時間のこと。
◇ credit 名「(科目の) 履修単位」　　　　◇ description 名「描写；説明」
◇ interact 動「交渉する；関わる；やり取りをする」
◇ the first language = mother tongue「母語」
◇ participant 名「参加者」　　　　◇ unique 形「独特の；特有な」
◇ text message「(主に) E メールの本文やショートメッセージ」
◇ particular 形「特別の；著しい」　　　　◇ exchange 動「…を交換する」
◇ social 形「社会的な」　　　　◇ issue 名「問題；論点」
◇ evaluation 名「評価」　　　　◇ reviewer 名「批評者」
◇ experienced 形「経験豊富な」　　　　◇ strict 形「厳しい；厳格な」
◇ thoughtful 形「思いやりのある」
◇ at first「最初は」　cf. for the first time「初めて」
◇ get used to ...「…に慣れる」
◇ make the most of ...「〈有利な条件〉を最大限に活用する」
◇ translation 名「翻訳」　　　　◇ confident in ...「…に自信を持つ」
◇ common 形「共通の；共同の；共有の」　◇ overall 形「全部の；総体的な」
◇ require 動「必要とする；求める」　　◇ achievement 名「到達；達成；成就」
◇ participation 名「参加；出席」

[設問文・選択肢]
◇ advanced 形「上級の；高度な；先進的な」◇ in public「人前で；公然と；公衆の面前で」
◇ handy 形「手ごろな；役に立つ」　　　◇ summarise 動「…を要約する」
◇ value 動「価値を置く；評価する」　　◇ recommend 動「…を推薦する；勧める」
◇ turn out to be ...「結局…であることがわかる」

B

出典　*Original Material*

全訳

　あなたと英国からの交換留学生であるジョンは，学校の英字新聞の編集者です。彼はその新聞に，ある記事を書きました。

授業でタブレットを使うのは好きですか？　英国は ICT（情報通信技術）教育を推進してきていますが，順調に進んでいるとは言えないと思います。日本ではどうでしょうか？　日本の高校に関するいくつかの調査結果は，私たちにいくつかの答えを与えてくれています。

> ➤ 2018 年時点では，各々の生徒にタブレットを提供しなかった学校の数は，提供した学校の約 5 倍でした。
>
> 2020 年の状況は次のとおりでした：
> ➤ タブレットの導入を考えていなかった学校の数は，考えていた学校の 3 倍以上でした。
> ➤ 私立高校の 43.8％は，生徒ごとにめいめいがタブレットを持っていましたが，一方，公立高校においてはわずか 5.4％の学校だけが各生徒につき 1 台を提供していました。
> ➤ すべての生徒にタブレットを提供することを計画している高校は，公立高校よりも私立高校にずっと多くありました。

ご存知のように，私たちの学校では幸運にも個別のタブレットが提供されています。ただ，各生徒がきちんとかつ十分に使いこなしているかどうか，私はいぶかしく思っています。先生方はタブレットを使うのに十分熟練しているでしょうか？　先生方は，各生徒に日ごろの授業で自分の持つタブレットを最大限に活用させようとしているでしょうか？　私は校長先生からある情報を得ました。数学の教師の 10 人に 4 人は，ICT 教育の推進に熱心に取り組んでいます。これは英語教師の数よりも多いです。彼らの 11 人に 3 人は，生徒にタブレットを使用させています。そして，最も低い割合は国語の教師です。

実際，今後，このような電子ツールに，私たちはより依存する必要がはたしてあるのかどうかと私は思います。私たちの学校の生徒や先生方にアンケートなどをやらなくてはいけないと思いますし，そうすれば，現状の改善につながるであろうタブレットの使い方についてヒントを得ることになるかもしれません。

設問解説

問 1　　11　　正解 ⑤

「ICT 教育に熱心に取り組んでいるあなたたちの学校の先生方の比率の点で，次のどれが教科の先生の順位を高いものから低いものへと表しているか」　　11

① 英語教師 ― 国語教師 ― 数学教師
② 英語教師 ― 数学教師 ― 国語教師
③ 国語教師 ― 英語教師 ― 数学教師
④ 国語教師 ― 数学教師 ― 英語教師
⑤ **数学教師 ― 英語教師 ― 国語教師**
⑥ 数学教師 ― 国語教師 ― 英語教師

正解は ⑤。記事内の囲みの下の段落の第5文（I've got some ...）以降に，「数学の教師の10人に4人は，ICT教育の推進に熱心に取り組んでいます。これは英語教師の数よりも多いです。彼らの11人に3人は，生徒にタブレットを使用させています。そして，最も低い割合は国語の教師です」という記述がある。したがって，⑤ が正解。

問2 　12　 正解 ③

「ジョンの学校での現在のICT教育に関する彼のコメントは，　12　ということを表している」
　　　① 彼は自国のICT教育は劣っていると感じている
　　　② 彼は学校でのタブレットの効果的な使い方に満足している
　　　③ 彼は学校でタブレットが有効に活用されているかどうか懐疑的である
　　　④ 彼はもっと多くの種類のオンライン学習を見たいと思っている

　　正解は ③。記事内の囲みの下の段落の前半（As you know, ...）に，「ご存知のように，私たちの学校では幸運にも個別のタブレットが提供されています。ただ，各生徒がきちんとかつ十分に使いこなしているかどうか，私はいぶかしく思っています。先生方はタブレットを使うのに十分熟練しているでしょうか？　先生方は，各生徒に日ごろの授業で自分の持つタブレットを最大限に活用させようとしているでしょうか？」とある。ICT教育の一環として，生徒にはめいめいに1台ずつタブレットが配布されているが，果たして有効に活用されているかどうか疑わしいというジョンの気持ちが表れる文章になっている。よって，正解は ③。

　　① について，ジョンは記事の冒頭で「英国はICT（情報通信技術）教育を推進してきていますが，順調に進んでいるとは言えないと思います」とは述べているが，自国の英国が「劣っている」（inferior）と言っているわけではない。② については，「満足している」（satisfied）ということが読み取れる個所は本文中にはない。同様に，④ についても，その内容を裏付ける記述は本文中にない。

問3 　13　 正解 ②

「調査結果からわかることを最もよく反映している陳述は　13　である」
　　　① 「自分のタブレットを手に入れることができるのだから，私は公立学校の生徒だったらいいのに」
　　　② 「私の学校は公立です。そして，現時点ではICT教育を推進する予定はありません」
　　　③ 「2018年には，3校に1校の学校が各生徒めいめいにタブレットを提供しました」
　　　④ 「大多数の学校は，自校のICT教育を実践する授業を改善するつもりです」

　　正解は ②。記事内の囲みの最後の➤（There were many ...）に「すべての生徒にタブレットを提供することを計画している高校は，公立高校よりも私立高校にずっと多くありました」とある。逆に言うと，公立高校は私立高校に比べて，将来のICT教育推進については消極的である，ということである。よって，正解は ②。

　　他の選択肢については，タブレットが生徒1人につき1台行き渡っている高校は，公立よりも私立の方が多いので，① は誤りとなる。③ については，囲みの最初で「2018年時点では，各々の生徒にタブレットを提供しなかった学校の数は，提供した学校の約5倍でした」とあることから，約5校に1校の割合でしか生徒めいめいにタブレットが提供されていなかったということがわかるので誤りとなる。④ を正解とする根拠となる記述は調査結果には見当たらない。

問4 　14　 正解 ①

「ジョンの学校でのICT教育についての彼の意見を最もよく要約しているのはどれか」
　14

① 状況を改善するためには，いくつかの調査が必要である。

② タブレットは思ったほど役に立たない。

③ タブレットの使い方を教える先生向けの講座を実施する必要がある。

④ 生徒がタブレットを使いやすくする必要がある。

正解は①。記事の最終文 (I think we've ...) に，「私たちの学校の生徒や先生方にアンケートなどをやらなくてはいけないと思いますし，そうすれば，現状の改善につながるであろうタブレットの使い方についてヒントを得ることになるかもしれません」とある。よって，正解は①。

他の選択肢を正解とする根拠となる内容は本文中には書かれていない。

問5 ┃ 15 ┃ 正解 ②

「この記事に最もふさわしいタイトルはどれか」 ┃ 15 ┃

① タブレットのコストと性能

② タブレットの導入とその未来

③ タブレットの公立学校への配布戦略

④ タブレットの有用性と問題点

正解は②。この記事は，まず，日本の高校におけるタブレット端末の生徒1人1台の配置の現状について，調査結果をまとめている。言い換えれば，タブレットの導入に関する現状を述べている。その後，ジョンは自校におけるタブレットの生徒への配布状況の現実を確認し，また，教師も含む学校全体の教育や授業におけるタブレットの活用状況について現状とコメントをまとめ，最後に，それらの現状に基づいて将来自校においてどのようなICT教育が図られるべきかを探るために，アンケート調査などが必要なのではないかと問題提起している。よって，正解は②。

他の選択肢については，それらに関わる直接的な内容は本文中には見当たらない。③については，本文にはタブレットの配布に関する事実が調査結果により示されているが，その配布に関する「戦略」が述べられているわけではない。

主な語句・表現　　・問題冊子を参照のこと。

[リード文]　◇ an exchange student「交換留学生」

◇ UK = United Kingdom (of Great Britain and Northern Ireland)「連邦王国；イギリス」

◇ editor 图「編集者」　　　　　　　　　◇ paper 图「新聞」(= newspaper)

◇ article 图「〈新聞・雑誌・ネットなどの〉記事」

[本文]　◇ tablet 图「タブレット端末」(= tablet PC)

◇ promote 動「…を推進する」　　　　　◇ smoothly 圖「順調に；円滑に」

◇ How about ...?「…はどうでしょうか；…はいかがでしょうか」

◇ survey 图「調査」

◇ provide A for B「A を B に供給する [与える]」(= provide B with A)

◇ five times as large as that of schools which did in 2018　that = the number, which did = which provided a tablet for each student

◇ three times as large as that of schools which did　that = the number, which did = which thought of introducing tablets

◇ while 接「(…である) 一方，〜」 対照を表す。

◇ with one　one = a tablet

◇ many more private than public high schools「公立高校よりもはるかに多くの私立高校」

◇ individual 形「個々の；個別の」　　　◇ properly 圖「適切に；しっかりと」

◇ fully 圖「十分に」

— 英 R 104 —

◇ skillful 形「技術 [技能] のある；熟練 [熟達] した」
◇ use one　one = a tablet
◇ make the most of ...「〈有利な条件など〉を最大限に活用する」
◇ head teacher「《英》校長」《米》では principal。
◇ eager 形「熱心な；熱意のある」
◇ Three in eleven of them　them = English teachers
◇ depend on ...「…に頼る [依存する]」　　◇ electronic 形「電子の；電子工学の」
◇ we've [= we have] got to give ...　have got to は have to -「-しなければならない」
　の口語的な表現。
◇ questionnaire 名「アンケート（調査）；質問表」
◇ ... or something「…か何か」表現を柔らかくしてぼかす言い方。
◇ usage 名「使用（方法）；使うこと；使い方」
◇ lead to ...「…につながる；…へと導かれる」
◇ improvement 名「改善；改良；向上」
◇ present 形「現在の；現状の；今の」（= current）
◇ situation 名「状況；状態」

[設問文・選択肢]　◇ in terms of ...「…の点において；…という観点から」
◇ ratio 名「割合」　　　　　　　　　　◇ eagerly 副「熱心に」
◇ inferior 形「劣っている」⇔ superior 形「優れている」
◇ effective 形「効果的な」副詞形は effectively「効果的に」。
◇ skeptical 形「懐疑的な；疑い深い」　　◇ statement 名「陳述；述べること [内容]」
◇ reflect 動「…を反映する；映し出す」　　◇ finding 名「発見；所見」
◇ majority 名「大多数；大半」⇔ minority 名「少数（派）」
◇ intend to -「-しようとする；-しようと意図する」
◇ summarise 動「…を要約する；まとめる」《米》の綴りでは summarize となる。
◇ hold 動「…を催す；開催する」　　　　◇ suitable 形「適する；適合する」
◇ strategy 名「戦略；（戦略的）計画」　　◇ distribute 動「配布する」

第3問

解 答

A 問1 - ②　　問2 - ③　　　　　　　　　　　　　　　　　　（各3点）

B 問1 - 18 - ③　 19 - ①　 20 - ④　 21 - ②　（完答で3点）

問2 - ③　　問3 - ①　　　　　　　　　　　　　　　　　　（各3点）

A

出典　*Original Material*

全訳　　あなたのカナダ人の友人であるスーは，新しい動物園・水族館公園を訪れ，彼女の体験についてブログを投稿しました。

スーによって投稿されました
2021年10月3日午後8時47分

　　　　　　サンライズ動物園・水族館公園：訪れるべき素晴らしい場所

3週間前にオープンしたサンライズ動物園・水族館公園で，私は友達と楽しい時間を過ごしました。そこは，動物園と水族館の2つの主要なエリアがある巨大な公園です。

私たちは，パンダに会い，イルカのショーを楽しむのを本当に心待ちにしていました。最初にパンダに会うために動物園エリアに向かいましたが，あまりに人が多すぎたので，代わりにイルカショーに行きました。水族館エリアに入るのにしばらく並んでいました。しかし（並びはしましたが），ショーはとても素晴らしくてわくわくするものでしたので，それは並ぶ価値がありました！　私たちはオープンカフェで昼食をとり，その後パンダを見るために動物園エリアへ行く予定でした。しかし，カフェもパンダを見る場所も大変混雑していましたので，私たちはパークショップに行ってサンドイッチや飲み物を買うことにしました。そして，すぐ近くの休憩所で昼食をとりました。午後になって，ようやくパンダに会うことができました。彼らは信じられないくらいかわいらしかったです！　最後に私たちはまたパークショップに立ち寄って，友達や家族へのお土産を買いました。

サンライズ動物園・水族館公園は最高です！　この思い出に残る経験は，間違いなく決して忘れられないものになるでしょう！

— 英 R 106 —

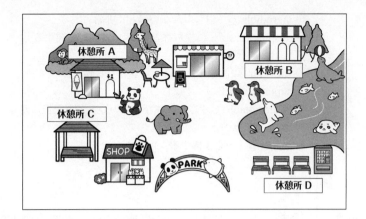

設問解説

問1 16 　正解 ②

「スーの投稿から，あなたは 16 ということがわかる」
① パンダを見るのにあまりにも時間がかかりすぎて，スーは疲れ切ってしまった
② スーと彼女の友達は自分たちの計画を変更したことを後悔していなかった
③ 混雑していたので，スーはイルカのショーを立って見ていた
④ オープンカフェよりレストランの方が混雑していた

正解は②。最初にパンダに会うという彼女たちの計画は，パンダ人気による大混雑のお陰で変更を余儀なくされたが，それを後悔しているような記述は一切読み取れない。代わりに向かった水族館エリアでのイルカショーでも，入場の際待たされたが，それについても「〈列に〉並ぶ価値があった」(We stood in a line for a while to enter the aquarium area. However, it was worth it ...) と述べている。よって，正解は②。

①については，「スーは疲れ切ってしまった」という記述は本文にはなく，③の「スーはイルカのショーを立って見ていた」ということも本文には書かれていない。また④については，レストランについての記述は本文中にない。

問2 17 　正解 ③

「スーと彼女の友達はどの休憩所で昼食をとったか」 17
① 休憩所A
② 休憩所B
③ 休憩所C
④ 休憩所D

正解は③。本文第2段落第6文 (But both the ...) には「私たちはパークショップに行ってサンドイッチや飲み物を買うことにしました。そして，すぐ近くの休憩所で昼食をとりました」とある。入園ゲートの横にあるパークショップから一番近い休憩所は，休憩所C (Rest Stop C) である。よって，正解は③。

主な語句・表現

・問題冊子を参照のこと。

[リード文]
◇ aquarium 图「水族館」
◇ post 動「〈ブログや動画など〉を（ネット上に）投稿する」，图「投稿」
◇ blog 图「ブログ」　ウェブログ (weblog) ともいう。

[本文]
◇ head for ...「…へ向かう」
◇ instead 副「その代わりに」
◇ for a while「しばらくの間」
◇ nearby 形「すぐ近くの；近所の」
◇ full with ...「…で一杯である」
◇ line 图「（人の並ぶ）列」
◇ worth 形「…の価値がある；…に値して」
◇ rest stop「休憩所」

◇ incredibly 形「信じられないほど；非常に」
◇ drop in at ...「…に立ち寄る；（短い時間）訪問する」
◇ lastly 副「最後に」
◇ souvenir 名「（旅の）土産；記念になる物」
◇ super 形「極上の；すばらしい」
◇ unforgettable 形「忘れられない；いつまでも記憶に残る」

[設問文・選択肢] ◇ regret 動「…を後悔する；悔やむ」

B

出典 (参考) https://www.myenglishpages.com/english/reading-bob-marley.php

全訳 　アメリカの友達が，彼のお気に入りのミュージシャンを紹介してくれました。あなたは
もっと知りたいと思い，ある音楽雑誌で次の記事を見つけました。

レゲエの魂，ボブ・マーリー

　ボブ・マーリーは 1945 年 2 月 6 日に生まれました。彼はジャマイカのレゲエ歌手
であり，また，ソングライター，ミュージシャン，ギタリストでもあり，国際的な名
声を獲得し，熱狂的なファンからは今なお高い評価を得ています。1963 年にグループ
The Wailers（ウェイラーズ）でスタートし，彼は独特の作詞作曲とボーカルスタイル
を作り出して，すぐにそれは世界中の聴衆に賞賛を持って受けとめられました。1974
年にウェイラーズが解散した後，マーリーはソロとして活躍し，1977 年 6 月のアルバ
ム『エクソダス』のリリースでそのピークを迎えました。そのアルバムが彼の世界的
な評価を確立し，また，7,500 万枚以上のレコード販売数を伴う，歴史に残る世界最
高の売り上げを誇るアーティストの 1 人としての彼の地位につながったということは
疑う余地もありません。
　ボブ・マーリーは，1930 年代にジャマイカで発展したアブラハムの宗教である（ラ
スタファリを信奉する），献身的なラスタファリアンでした。この宗教は彼にインス
ピレーションを与え，彼の音楽を精神的な感性で満たしました。ラスタファリ運動は
レゲエの発展における重要な要素でした。ラスタファリ（運動）の熱情的な支持者と
して，ボブ・マーリーはレゲエ音楽を，ジャマイカの社会的に恵まれない地域から国
際的な音楽シーンへと持ち上げました。
　1977 年 7 月，マーリーは足の 1 本の指の爪の下が，ある種の致命的な病気にかかっ
ていることが判明しました。彼の医者たちは彼に手術をするよう強く勧めました。し
かし，マーリーは彼の宗教的信念を持ち出して，彼らのアドバイスをはねのけました。
その病気にもかかわらず，彼は癌が彼の体全体に広がり，健康が悪化するまでツアー
を続けました。彼は，1981 年 5 月 11 日にマイアミのシダーズ・オブ・レバノン病院（現
在のマイアミ大学病院）で 36 歳で亡くなりました。彼の肺と脳への癌の広がりが彼
の死を引き起こしました。彼の息子ジギーへの彼の最後の言葉は，「お金は命を買え
ない」でした。

— 英 R 108 —

設問解説

問1 ⬚18⬚ 正解❸, ⬚19⬚ 正解❶, ⬚20⬚ 正解❹, ⬚21⬚ 正解❷

「以下の出来事（❶～❹）を起きた順に並べなさい」

  ❶ マーリーはソロで歌い始めた。

  ❷ マーリーは自分の病気を発見した後，ツアーを止めなかった。

  ❸ マーリーは *The Wailers* というグループの一員になった。

  ❹ アルバム『エクソダス』がリリースされた。

まず，第1段落第3文（Starting out in ...）に「1963年にグループ *The Wailers*（ウェイラーズ）でスタートし，彼は独特の作詞作曲とボーカルスタイルを作り出して，すぐにそれは世界中の聴衆に賞賛を持って受けとめられました」とある。

続けて第4文（After *The Wailers* ...）に「1974年にウェイラーズが解散した後，マーリーはソロとして活躍し，1977年6月のアルバム『エクソダス』のリリースでそのピークを迎えました」とある。

そして，最終段落第1文（In July, 1977, ...）以降に「1977年7月，マーリーは足の1本の指の爪の下が，ある種の致命的な病気にかかっていることが判明しました。... その病気にもかかわらず，彼は癌が彼の体全体に広がり，健康が悪化するまでツアーを続けました」とある。

以上のことを，具体的な年号や月なども手掛かりにして時系列でまとめると，❸→❶→❹→❷の順番になるとわかる。

問2 ⬚22⬚ 正解❸

「マーリーは ⬚22⬚ という理由で，医者からの治療を受けることを拒否した」

  ❶ 手術をするには遅すぎると思った

  ❷ コンサートツアーで忙しかった

  ❸ 自分の信仰に従っていた

  ❹ 彼の癌は初期段階だった

正解は❸。最終段落第2文から第3文（His doctors strongly .... However, Marley turned ...）に，「彼の医者たちは彼に手術をするよう強く勧めました。しかし，マーリーは彼の宗教的信念を持ち出して，彼らのアドバイスをはねのけました」とある。マーリーが自らが信じるところのラスタファリ運動の主義や信条に従う形で，手術を断ったことがわかる。よって，正解は❸。

問3 ⬚23⬚ 正解❶

「この話から，あなたは ⬚23⬚ ということがわかった」

  ❶ 宗教はマーリーの音楽に影響を与えた

  ❷ 宗教によってマーリーはジャマイカに移住した

  ❸ マーリーは彼のバンドメンバーとは反りが合わなかった

  ❹ マーリーの音楽は彼の国からお金を奪った

正解は❶。第2段落全体の内容を読むと，マーリーの信じるラスタファリが彼にいかに大きな影響を及ぼしていたかがわかる。とりわけ，第2文（This religion inspired ...）の「この宗教は彼にインスピレーションを与え，彼の音楽を精神的な感性で満たしました」という1文は，宗教がマーリーの音楽に影響を与えたということを明確に述べている。よって，正解は❶。

❷と❹については，それらが言及されている箇所は見当たらない。また，❸については，確かにマーリーが最初に所属した *The Wailers*（ウェイラーズ）というバンドは解散したが，「メンバーと反りが合わなかった」というような記述はどこにも見当たらない。

— 英 R 109 —

主な語句・表現

・問題冊子を参照のこと。

[第1段落]
(Bob Marley was born ...)

◇ Reggae 图「レゲエ」 狭義においては 1960 年代後半ジャマイカで発祥し，1980 年代前半まで流行したポピュラー音楽。広義においてはジャマイカで成立したポピュラー音楽全般のことをいう。2018 年にはユネスコの無形文化遺産に登録された。

◇ achieve 動「〈地位や名声など〉を得る；獲得する」

◇ fame 图「名声」　　　　　　　◇ praise 動「…を称賛する；褒め称える」

◇ enthusiastic 形「熱心な；熱情的な」

◇ distinctive 形「卓越した；傑出した；特筆に値する」

◇ admiration 图「称賛；褒めること」

◇ break up「〈グループなどが〉解散する；〈ペアなどが〉別れる」

◇ pursue 動「…を追い求める；追求する」　　◇ establish 動「…を確立する；打ち立てる」

◇ reputation 图「評判；評価」

[第2段落]
(Bob Marley was a ...)

◇ committed 形「献身的な；傾倒している」

◇ Rastafarian 图「ラスタファリアン（ラスタファリ運動の実践者）」 ラスタファリ運動（Rastafari movement）は，1930 年代にジャマイカの労働者階級と農民を中心にして発生した宗教的思想運動である。

◇ Abrahamic religion「アブラハムの宗教」 アブラハムの神の崇拝を支持する一神教のグループ。ユダヤ教，キリスト教，イスラム教などが含まれる。

◇ inspire 動「…を鼓舞する；刺激する；霊感を与える」

◇ fill A with B「A を B で満たす［一杯にする］」

◇ spirituality 图「霊性；霊的なこと；精神性」

◇ passionate 形「熱心な；情熱的な」　　◇ deprived 形「恵まれない；貧困の」

[第3段落]
(In July, 1977, ...)

◇ suffer from ...「〈病気など〉で苦しむ；…を患う」

◇ fatal 形「死に至る；致命的な；極めて重大な」

◇ operation 图「手術」

◇ turn down ...「…を断る［拒絶する］」（= decline）

◇ cite 動「…を引用する」　　　　　◇ in spite of ...「…にもかかわらず」

◇ spread 動「広がる；拡大する」 名詞形も spread「拡大；広がり」である。

◇ lung 图「肺」　　　　　　　　　◇ brain 图「脳」

[設問文・選択肢]

◇ refuse 動「拒否する；拒絶する」　　◇ influence 图「影響（力)」

◇ get along with ...「…とうまく［仲良く］やっていく［付き合う］」

◇ deprive A of B「A から B を奪う」

— 英 R 110 —

第4問

解答

問1 - ①	問2 - ②	問3 - ④	問4 - ①	（各3点）
問5　28 - ④		29 - ②		（各2点）

出典　（参考）https://www.slicktext.com/blog/2019/10/smartphone-addiction-statistics/
https://financesonline.com/smartphone-addiction-statistics/

全訳　あなたは現在，米国のロバート大学で勉強しています。社会科の授業で，スマートフォンが人々に与える影響についてレポートするよう求められています。あなたは，スマートフォンの使い方について考察している2人の学生ポールとリンダのブログを見つけました。

スマートフォン依存症では？
2022年9月5日午後4時52分にポールによって投稿されました。

　2007年に世界で最初のiPhoneが登場して以来，スマートフォンの使用は着実に私たちの日常生活の一部として受け入れられるようになりました — そして，スマートフォン依存症の統計はそれを証明しています。2022年の今，私たちは私たちのスマートフォンにべったりとへばり付けられています。私たちは通信と接続を私たちのスマートフォンに依存しているため，スマートフォンの過度の使用がいつ中毒になるかを判断するのは難しいかもしれません。しかしながら，次の統計は知っておく必要があります。

> 10代の若者の52％は，友人とぶらぶらしている間，スマートフォンを見ながら長時間黙って座って過ごしています。

> 調査対象の親の47％は，子供がスマートフォンに「病みつき」になっていると考えています。

> 調査対象の教師のうち，67％が，生徒たちはモバイルデバイスに集中力を削がれていることに気付いていました。

> 89％の親が，自分の子供のスマートフォンの使用に対する責任を感じています。

> 英国で調査された親のうち，46％が自分はモバイルデバイスに「病みつきになっている」と答えました。

　実際，私はかつて，おそらくスマートフォンが原因で，睡眠不足やストレスレベルの上昇，うつ症状や不安感に悩まされていました。それで，私はスマートフォンを使うのをやめました。デジタルデバイスへの依存症は，他の種類の依存症ほど深刻な健康への悪影響を及ぼしませんが，実際には確かに精神的健康面だけでなく身体的健康にも影響を及ぼします。ここで立ち止まって，「あなたの」スマートフォンの使い方についてよく考えてみませんか？

— 英 R 111 —

学校でのスマートフォンの（過剰）使用

2022年9月6日午前11時22分にリンダによって投稿されました。

　現代における人間の一番の親友であると主張するに最も値するものがあるとすれば，それは間違いなくスマートフォンでしょう。モバイルデバイスは，あらゆる種類の人間の活動に浸透しています。ほぼすべての人々が，自宅，学校，職場，および余暇の時間にスマートフォンを使用します。携帯電話にアクセスできないことが「ノモフォビア」，すなわち携帯電話との接触がなくなることへの恐れへの道を開いたほどです。そのため，現在のスマートフォン依存症に関する統計を理解することは，それが実際にどれほど深刻であるかを把握するために重要です。

　ここでは，学校におけるスマートフォンの使い方や使う習慣に光を当てたいと思います。スマートフォンは小さなコンピュータであることを考えれば，それは授業で役立つさまざまな機能を担うことができます。これにより，ユーザーはさまざまな方法でデバイスを楽しむことができます。残念なことに，楽しみが多すぎると非生産的になる可能性があります。スマートフォン依存症に関する統計が示唆しているように，携帯電話は学校においては学業の大きな妨げになることがわかっています。このことは，生産性の低下を引き起こしてしまうことになるのです。

パーセンテージ	（それぞれの）パーセンテージは何を示していますか？
20%	生徒がテキストメッセージのやり取りをしたり，ソーシャルメディアのチェックをしたりすることに費やした時間の授業に占める割合
45%	常にオンラインになっている生徒の割合。これには，彼らが授業に参加している時間が含まれる。
46%	教育者に，スマートフォンの使用と授業とをより融合する方法を見つけてもらいたいと思っている保護者の割合
49%	授業中にスマートフォンやその他のデジタルガジェットに気を取られている生徒の割合
80%	授業中の携帯電話の使用を制限する方針を持っている学校の割合

　もしあなたが今のあなたのスマートフォンとの深い関係性に不安感を持っているとしたら，あなたの生活におけるテクノロジーとのより健康的な関係を築く方法があります。毎日の使用状況を追跡し，ログオフを促すリマインダーを送信するアプリを使用して，スマートフォンに費やす時間を制限してみてください。携帯電話の設定によって，画面使用の平均時間にアクセスすることもできます。スマートフォンの使用を制限するのに役立つもう1つのやり方は，（画面の）カラー設定を白黒に変えることです。深夜の（暗い中での）画面スクロールでは，白黒の画面は（カラー画面ほど）視覚的には刺激がありません。そして，そうすることであなたはデバイスの使用をやめやすくなるのです。

設 問 解 説

問1 | 24 | **正解①**

「ポールは | 24 | という理由で，スマートフォンの使用をやめることを勧めている」

① スマートフォンは私たちの健康に有害である
② スマートフォンは人間関係を損なう可能性がある
③ スマートフォンは多額の費用がかかる
④ スマートフォンは対面でのコミュニケーションを妨げる

　正解は①。ポールのブログの最終段落第3文後半（it does indeed …）に「（デジタルデバイスに依存していることは，）実際には確かに精神的健康面だけでなく身体的健康にも影響を及ぼします」とある。実際，ポール自身，スマートフォンが原因でさまざまな健康被

— 英 R 112 —

害を被り，自分はスマートフォンの使用をやめたと言っている。したがって，正解は①。

　他の選択肢（②，③，④）については，それらの内容に関わる記述はポールのブログには見当たらない。

問2　[25]　正解②

　「リンダは[25]ということを示唆している」

　　①　スマートフォンの影響による身体面の健康に注意する必要がある

　　②　スマートフォンの画面の色を変更してみるべきである

　　③　スマートフォンの電源を自動的に切るアプリをインストールするべきである

　　④　他のデジタルガジェットを使って，スマートフォンを使う時間を制限すべきである

　正解は②。リンダのブログの最終段落第4文（Another trick that ...）に「スマートフォンの使用を制限するのに役立つもう1つのやり方は，（画面の）カラー設定を白黒に変えることです」とある。その理由として，続く最終文（Late night scrolling ...）で「深夜の（暗い中での）画面スクロールでは，白黒の画面は（カラー画面ほど）視覚的には刺激がありません。そして，そうすることであなたはデバイスの使用をやめやすくなるのです」と述べている。したがって，正解は②。

　他の選択肢（①，③，④）については，それらの内容に関わる記述はリンダのブログには見当たらない。

問3　[26]　正解④

　「ポールとリンダの両方が，あなたが[26]ことを勧めている」

　　①　通信技術の進歩に感謝する

　　②　スマートフォンが人々によってどれほど効果的に利用されているかを調べる

　　③　SNS（ソーシャル・ネットワーキング・サービス）の使用がいかに危険であるかを理解する

　　④　統計を通して，人々がスマートフォンによってどれほど影響を受けているかを把握する

　正解は④。ポールはブログの最初で，以下のように述べている。

Since the world saw the first iPhone in 2007, smartphone usage has steadily become an accepted part of our daily lives — and the smartphone addiction statistics prove it. ... However, it's necessary to know the following statistics:「2007年に世界で最初のiPhoneが登場して以来，スマートフォンの使用は着実に私たちの日常生活の一部として受け入れられるようになりました — そして，スマートフォン依存症の統計はそれを証明しています。…しかしながら，次の統計は知っておく必要があります」

　また，同じくリンダも，ブログの冒頭で次のように述べている。

If there's anything that most deserves the claim to being a man's best friend in the modern age, it has got to be the smartphone. ... As such, <u>understanding the current smartphone addiction statistics is important to get a grasp of how serious it really is.</u>「現代における人間の一番の親友であると主張するに最も値するものがあるとすれば，それは間違いなくスマートフォンでしょう。…そのため，<u>現在のスマートフォン依存症に関する統計を理解することは，それが実際にどれほど深刻であるかを把握するために重要です</u>」

　特に，それぞれの下線部は，統計を通して人々がスマートフォンによっていかに影響を被るかを把握することの重要性を指摘し，読者に統計を通して理解することを勧めていると読み取ることができる。よって，正解は④。

　他の選択肢（①，②，③）については，それらの内容に関わる記述は2人のブログには見当たらない。

問4 　27 　正解 ①
「授業中にデジタルガジェットに気を取られている生徒の割合は， 　27 　生徒の割合よりも高くなっている」
　① 常にインターネットに接続している
　② 自分のスマートフォンを適切に使用している
　③ 携帯電話の使用を制限するアプリを使用している
　④ 深夜にスマートフォンを使う

　正解は①。授業中にデジタルガジェットに気を取られている生徒の割合については，リンダのブログの中にある統計結果のひとつである Students who are distracted by smartphones and other digital gadgets in class「授業中にスマートフォンやその他のデジタルガジェットに気を取られている生徒の割合」を見れば，それが49％であることがわかる。一方，選択肢の①にある，常にインターネットに接続している生徒の割合については，同じくリンダのブログの Students who are constantly online. This includes the time that they are in class.「常にオンラインになっている生徒の割合。これには，彼らが授業に参加している時間が含まれる」を見れば，それが45％であることがわかる。両者を比較すると，前者の割合の方が後者よりも高いことがわかる。よって，正解は①となる。
　他の選択肢（②，③，④）それぞれの内容を表す割合の数値は，2人のブログのどちらにも示されていない。

問5 　28 　正解 ④ 　29 　正解 ②
「 　28 　ブログから， 　29 　保護者は半数未満であることがわかる（選択肢①～④から，それぞれ空所ごとに最も適切なものを1つ選択しなさい。）」
　① 学校でのスマートフォンの使用方法に満足している
　② 自分の子供がスマートフォンを使いすぎていると考えている
　③ リンダの
　④ ポールの

　選択肢の①の内容に関わる個所として，リンダのブログに Parents who want educators to find ways to integrate the use of smartphones into lessons more「教育者に，スマートフォンの使用と授業とをより融合する方法を見つけてもらいたいと思っている保護者の割合」とあり，それが46％であることが示されている。これは，言い換えれば，学校でのスマートフォンの使用方法に満足して<u>いない</u>保護者が半数未満ということであり，①の内容を示すものではない。一方，選択肢②の内容に関わる個所としては，ポールのブログに 47% of parents surveyed believe their children are "addicted" to their smartphones「調査対象の親の47％は，子供がスマートフォンに『病みつき』になっていると考えています」とある。これは，まさに②の内容である「自分の子供がスマートフォンを使いすぎていると考えている」保護者は半数未満，ということを示すものである。
　よって， 　28 　の正解は④， 　29 　の正解は②となる。

<table>
<tr><td>主な語句・表現</td><td>・問題冊子を参照のこと。</td></tr>
</table>

[リード文] 　◇ social studies「（教科としての）社会科」　◇ affect 動「…に影響を与える［及ぼす］」

[ポールのブログ] 　◇ addiction 名「常用癖；依存症；中毒」　　◇ steadily 副「着実に；どんどん；しっかりと」
　◇ statistics 名「統計；統計学」　　　　　　　◇ prove 動「…を証明する」
　◇ be glued to ...「…に（はりついたように）熱中している；夢中になっている」
　◇ rely on ...「…に頼る；依存する」　　　　　◇ determine 動「…を決定する；決心する」
　◇ excessive 形「過度の；行き過ぎた」　　　　◇ teen 名「10（歳）代の少年少女」
　◇ hang out「（…で）うろうろする；ぶらぶらする」

— 英 R 114 —

◇ survey 動「…を調査する」

◇ addict 動「〈人に〉（麻薬などを）常習させる；中毒にさせる」「〈人を〉（…に）ふけらせる（to ...）」 通例過去分詞で形容詞的に用いる（⇒ addicted）。

◇ distract 動「（…の）気持ちをそらす［散らす］；混乱させる」

◇ mobile device「モバイル機器」 携帯電話・スマートフォンや小型パソコンなど。

◇ device 名「器具；装置」

◇ take responsibility for ...「…に責任を負う；請負う」

◇ deprivation 名「はく奪；喪失；欠乏（状態）」

◇ depression 名「気分の落ち込み；うつ（状態）；憂うつ」

◇ anxiety 名「心配（事）；不安」   ◇ while 接「…である一方；…とは言え」

◇ impact 動「〈…に〉強い影響を与える」   ◇ indeed 副「実に；実際に；本当に」

◇ not only A but (also) B「A のみならず B も（また）；A だけでなく B も」

◇ physical 形「体の；肉体的な」   ◇ wellbeing 名「健康（な状態）」

[リンダのブログ]

◇ claim 名「権利（の主張）；資格」

◇ penetrate 動「…を貫く；染み込む；浸透する」

◇ nearly 副「ほとんど」

◇ Nearly everyone uses one at home, ...   one = a mobile device

◇ So much so that ...「そのような状況［程度］であるので，（結果として）…である」

◇ pave the way for ...「…への道を開く；…を容易にする」

◇ nomophobia 名 "no-mobile-phone phobia" の縮約形。phobia とは「恐怖症；病的恐怖」という意味の名詞で，nomophobia は「スマートフォンや携帯電話での連絡が取れなくなることへの病的な恐れ・不安感」という意味。

◇ as such「そのため；そのような状態であるので」

◇ current 形「今の；現在の」   ◇ get a grasp of ...「…を把握する；理解する」

◇ how serious it really is   it = nomophobia

◇ shine a light on ...「…に光を当てる」   ◇ habit 名「習慣」

◇ Given that ...「…ならば；…を考えれば」   ◇ take on ...「…を持つようになる；帯びる」

◇ counterproductive 形「逆効果の；非生産的な」

◇ prove to be ...「（結局）…となる；…であることがわかる」（= turn out to be ...）

◇ distraction 名「気を散らすもの［こと］」   ◇ dip 名「窪み；へこみ；低下」

◇ productivity 名「生産性」

◇ texting 名 主にスマートフォンや携帯電話などに備わる SMS（ショートメッセージサービス）などを利用してテキストメッセージのやりとりを行うこと，あるいは特にテキストメッセージの作成・送信をすること。

◇ constantly 副「常に；常時」   ◇ include 動「…を含む」

◇ educator 名「教育者」

◇ integrate 動「…を統合する；調和させる；まとめる」

◇ gadget 名「気のきいた小物；ちょっとした機械装置」

◇ policy 名「方針；方策」   ◇ restrict 動「…を制限する」

◇ attachment 名「付着；愛着；愛情」   ◇ cultivate 動「…を培う；求める；深める」

◇ app = application 名 スマートフォンなどの「アプリ」のこと。

◇ track 動「…を追跡する；探知する」

◇ reminder 名「〈思い出させるための〉注意；合図」

◇ trick 名「〈物事を上手にする〉やり方；こつ；要領；秘訣」

◇ stimulating 形「刺激する」

◇ visual 名「〈通例複数形で〉映像」 音声に対して写真・画面など。

— 英 R 115 —

◇ encourage 動「(…を) 促進する;助長する;奨励する」
◇ put down「(…を) 下に置く;(…を) 抑える;静める;やめる」

[設問文・選択肢]　◇ install 動「〈装置などを〉〈…に〉取り [据え] 付ける」
◇ automatically 副「自動的に」　　　　　◇ appreciate 動「…を感謝する」
◇ advance 名「進歩;前進;発展」　　　　◇ look into ...「…を調べる;研究する」
◇ utilize 動「…を利用する;活用する」　　◇ properly 副「適切に;正しく」

第5問

解答	問1 － ① （3点）

問1 － ①　　　　　　　　　　　　　　　　　　　　　　　　　　（3点）
問2 － 31 － ⑤　 32 － ③　　　　　　　　　　　　　（完答で3点）
問3 － 33 － ②　 34 － ①　 35 － ⑤　 36 － ③　（完答で3点）
問4 － ④　　問5 － ①　　　　　　　　　　　　　　　　　（各3点）

出典　（参考）https://www.myenglishpages.com/english/reading-edgar-allan-poe-biography.php

全訳

あなたは英語の授業で，世界の優れた作家についてのプレゼンテーションを行います。あなたは次の記事を見つけて，プレゼンテーション用のメモを用意しました。

エドガー・アラン・ポーは，1809年1月19日にマサチューセッツ州ボストンで生まれました。彼はアメリカ人の作家，詩人，編集者，そして文芸評論家でした。彼は，米国のロマン主義とアメリカ文学の中心的な人物として広く認められています。ポーはミステリーの物語で最もよく知られています。彼は最も初期のアメリカ人短編小説家の1人であり，一般的に探偵小説のジャンルの創始者と見なされています。

ポーの父と母はどちらもプロの俳優でした。彼らはその詩人（＝ポー）が3歳になる前に亡くなりました。ジョン・アランとフランシス・アランは正式に彼を養子にすることはありませんでしたが，バージニア州リッチモンドで里子として彼を育てました。ポーはバージニア大学に1学期間通いましたが，お金がなかったために大学を去りました。ポーは彼の教育資金とギャンブルの借金のことでジョンと喧嘩をしました。1827年に，彼は偽名でアメリカ陸軍に入隊しました。この時，彼の執筆活動は彼の最初の出版物で始まりましたが，それは，謙虚に，「ある1人のボストン市民」の作とのみ記された匿名の詩集である『タマレーン，その他の詩集』（1827年）という作品での始まりでした。1829年にフランシス・アランが亡くなると，ポーとジョン・アランは一時的に良好な関係を再構築しました。（しかし，）ポーは後にウェスト・ポイントで軍の士官の訓練生として失敗を犯してしまいました。彼は詩人兼作家になりたいという強い願いを固く表明し，そして，ジョン・アランと決別しました。

詩人として真剣にそのキャリアをスタートさせようとし始めたポーでしたが，そうするためには彼は困難な時期を選んでしまったことになります。アメリカの出版業界は，1837年恐慌，つまり，アメリカの金融危機によって特に大きな打撃を受けていました。利益，価格，賃金が下がったのです。失業率が上昇し，悲観論が広まりました。出版社はしばしば作家への支払いを拒否したり，約束の時よりもはるかに遅れて支払いをしたりしました。ポーは苦労したに違いありません。彼の初期における詩の試みの後，ポーは散文に注意を向けました。彼はその後の数年間，文学の雑誌や定期刊行物の業界で働いていました。彼は，彼独自の手法による文学評論家として活動し，有名になりました。彼は仕事によって，ボルチモア，フィラデルフィア，ニューヨーク市を含むいくつかの都市の間を行ったり来たりしなければなりませんでした。1835年，ボルチモアで，彼はいとこのヴァージニア・クレムと結婚しました。そしてこのことが，彼の著作の一部に影響を与えた可能性があります。

1845年1月，ポーは『大鴉』という詩を出版し，人気を博しました。ポーはその出版に対してたったの9ドルしか支払われませんでしたが，それはポーという名をほぼ一瞬の間に一般に馴染みのあるものにしました。彼の妻はその出版の2年後に結核で

— 英R 117 —

亡くなりました。何年もの間，彼は彼自身のジャーナル，『ペン』（後に『スタイラス』と改名）を作成することを計画していましたが，それが出版されないうちに彼は亡くなりました。1849年10月7日，40歳で，ポーはボルチモアで亡くなりました。彼の死因は不明であり，アルコール，脳疾患，コレラ，薬物，心臓病，自殺，結核，およびその他の原因など，さまざまな要因と結びつけられてきています。

エドガー・アラン・ポーと彼の作品は，米国および世界中の文学に影響を与えると同時に，執筆の専門分野の草分けとしてもその役割を果たしました。彼はホラー及び探偵小説の両方の創始者の1人として見なされています。彼はまた，現代の短編小説の「構築者」としても認められています。評論家として，彼は（文学の）スタイルと構造の効果というものを強調した最初の作家の1人でした。したがって，彼は「芸術のための芸術」運動の先駆者でした。ポーは，シャルル・ボードレールによる初期の翻訳のおかげもあって，とりわけフランスで尊敬されています。ボードレールの翻訳は，その芸術的な出来栄えにより，ヨーロッパ全体でポーの作品の決定版となりました。

ポーと彼の作品は，文学，音楽，映画，そしてテレビにおける大衆文化全体に登場します。彼の住んだ家の多くは今日，博物館として寄贈されています。米ミステリー作家協会は，ミステリージャンルの傑出した作品に対して，エドガー賞として知られる毎年恒例の賞を授与しています。

プレゼンテーションのためのメモ：

エドガー・アラン・ポー

彼は1809年1月19日に生まれ，探偵小説のジャンルの創始者と考えられている。

若齢期
- ジョンとフランシス・アランに世話を受けた。
- 彼はジョンと口論になったが，後に彼と仲直りした。
- ┃ 30 ┃

新しい人生と結婚
- 彼は自身の関心の中心を ┃ 31 ┃ に切り替えた。
- 彼は ┃ 32 ┃ における彼自身のスタイルで有名になった。
- 彼はいとこであるヴァージニア・クレムと結婚した。

成功と死

┃ 33 ┃

彼は偽名を使って陸軍に入隊した。

┃ 34 ┃

┃ 35 ┃

┃ 36 ┃

彼は原因不明のままボルチモアで亡くなった。

影響
- 彼と彼の作品は，文学，音楽，映画，テレビにおける大衆文化全般に登場する。
- ┃ 37 ┃

業績及び評価
―彼はホラーと探偵小説の分野を創始した。 ―彼は（文学の）スタイルと構造が物語にどのような影響を与えるかについて，最初に焦点を当てた。 ― 38

設問解説

問1 30 正解①

「 30 に最適な文を選びなさい」

① 彼は，詩人兼作家になると宣言して，ジョンとの接触を断ち切った。
② 彼の父親は家族を捨てて家を出た。
③ 彼の最初の詩集によって，彼の名前は人々によく知られるようになった。
④ ポーは軍に入隊した直後，再びジョンと険悪な関係となった。

　正解は①。第2段落第10文（He firmly stated ...）に「彼は詩人兼作家になりたいという強い願いを固く表明し，そして，ジョン・アランと決別しました」とあることから，①が正解とわかる。

　②については，父親はポーが3歳になる前に亡くなったという記述があるだけで，「家族を捨てて家を出た」ということがわかる記述はない。③については，彼の最初の詩集は『タマレーン，その他の詩集』であり，それは匿名の詩集であったので，ポーの名前が明らかになることはなかった。④については，ポーが陸軍に入隊した2年後に（フランシスが亡くなって）2人は良好な関係を再構築した，とあるので，誤りである。

問2 31 正解⑤　 32 正解③

「新しい人生と結婚を完成させるのに， 31 と 32 に入る最適なものを選びなさい」

① 探偵小説
② 雑誌の編集
③ 文芸批評
④ ミステリーの筋立て
⑤ 散文の著述

　 31 については，第3段落第6文（After his early ...）に「彼の初期における詩の試みの後，ポーは散文に注意を向けました」とあることから，⑤が入る。

　 32 については，同じ第3段落第8文（He became well-known, ...）に「彼は，彼独自の手法による文学評論家として活動し，有名になりました」とある。よって，③が正解。

問3 33 正解②， 34 正解①， 35 正解⑤， 36 正解③

「5つの出来事（①～⑤）の中から4つを起こった順序で選び，成功と死を完成しなさい」

① 匿名の詩集が出版された。
② 彼はバージニア大学に入学した。
③ 妻が病気で亡くなった。
④ 『ペン』が創刊された。
⑤ 『大鴉』が出版され，大ヒットした。

　まず，第4段落に「『ペン』が出版される前にポーは亡くなった」（... he died before it could be published）とあるので，彼の生前のことについてまとめている 33 ～ 36 の中には入らない。よって，④は正解から除外されることになる。

　 33 は，ポーが陸軍に入隊する以前の出来事である。残された選択肢で当てはまるのは，第2段落より②しかない。次に， 34 ～ 36 については，本文を時系列で整理

― 英 R 119 ―

して考える。まず，陸軍入隊中にポーは最初の匿名の詩集『タマレーン，その他の詩集』を1827年に出版した。その後，第4段落によると1845年1月に，ポーは『大鴉』という詩を出版して人気を博し，その出版の2年後にポーの妻は結核で亡くなった。以上のことを読み取れれば，正解は　34　-①，　35　-⑤，　36　-③となることがわかる。

問4　　37　　正解④

「影響を完成させるのに，　37　に入る最も適切な選択肢を選びなさい」

①　当時流行していた小説のスタイルや構造を改良した。
②　彼はボードレールにインスピレーションを与え，その作品はポーによって翻訳された。
③　短編小説に対する彼の文芸批評は，ミステリー小説に影響を与えた。
④　彼の作品はフランス語に翻訳され，ヨーロッパで高く評価されるようになった。

正解は④。第5段落第6文（Poe is particularly ...）に「ポーは，シャルル・ボードレールによる初期の翻訳のおかげもあって，とりわけフランスで尊敬されています。ボードレールの翻訳は，その芸術的な出来栄えにより，ヨーロッパ全体でポーの作品の決定版となりました」とある。ポーの作品が，シャルル・ボードレールによってフランス語に翻訳され，その翻訳がヨーロッパ中で読まれて，高い評価を得るようになったということが読み取れ，これは，選択肢④の内容を表している。

選択肢①については，同じ第5段落第4文（As a critic he ...）に「評論家として，彼は（文学の）スタイルと構造の効果というものを強調した最初の作家の1人でした」とあるが，①の中の「当時流行していた」や「改良した」の部分が本文からは読み取れない。選択肢②については，ボードレールがポーの作品を翻訳したわけであり，ポーがボードレールの作品を翻訳したわけではない。また，選択肢③の内容については，本文のどこにも触れられていない。

問5　　38　　正解①

「業績及び評価を完成させるのに，　38　に入る最も適切な選択肢を選びなさい」

①　毎年，著名なミステリー作家がポーの名のもとに表彰される。
②　彼は建築家として，自分の家を博物館に変えた。
③　彼は米ミステリー作家協会を設立した。
④　彼はミステリーを芸術的に批判する傾向に反対した。

正解は①。最終段落最終文（The Mystery Writers ...）に，「米ミステリー作家協会は，ミステリージャンルの傑出した作品に対して，エドガー賞として知られる毎年恒例の賞を授与しています」とある。これは，選択肢①の内容と一致する。

選択肢②については，同じ最終段落第2文（A number of ...）に「彼の住んだ家の多くは今日，博物館として寄贈されています」とあるが，「彼が建築家であった」という記述は本文のどこにもない。また，選択肢③についても，米ミステリー作家協会を「設立した」という記述は本文にはなく，選択肢④については，第5段落第5文に，He was thus a forerunner in the "art for art's sake" movement. 「したがって，彼は『芸術のための芸術』運動の先駆者でした」という記述はあるが，「ミステリーを芸術的に批判する傾向に反対した」という内容を表す記述は見当たらない。

主な語句・表現　・問題冊子を参照のこと。

［第1段落］
（Edgar Allan Poe was ...）

◇ critic 图「批評家」　　　　　　　◇ figure 图「人物」
◇ literature 图「文学」　　　　　　◇ tale 图「物語」
◇ practitioner 图「実践者」　　　　◇ detective fiction「探偵［推理］小説」
◇ genre 图「〈芸術作品の〉ジャンル；様式」

[第2段落]
(Both Poe's
father ...)

◇ adopt 動「…を養子として引き取る」　◇ raise 動「…を育てる」
◇ foster child「養子；里子」
◇ semester 名「(2学期制度での) 1学期；半学年」
◇ due to ...「…のせいで」(= because of ...)
◇ lack 名「欠乏；不足」　◇ quarrel 動「口げんかする；口論する」
◇ fund 名「資金」　◇ debt 名「借金；負債」
◇ enlist 動「(軍隊に) 入る」　◇ humbly 副「謙虚に；慎み深く；遠慮して」
◇ anonymous 形「匿名の；作者不明の」
◇ credit 動「(…に) 帰する」　(例) an invention *credited* to Edison（エジソンに権利のある発明）
◇ temporary 形「一時の；一時的な」　◇ trainee 名「訓練生」
◇ firmly 副「固く；しっかりと」　◇ state 動「…を述べる」
◇ part ways with ...「…とは離れて行く；…と決別する」

[第3段落]
(Although Poe
began ...)

◇ attempt 名「試み；企て」　◇ pessimism 名「悲観主義；悲観論」
◇ prevail 動「広がる；広まる」　◇ prose 名「散文」
◇ periodical 名「定期刊行物」

[第4段落]
(In January
1845 ...)

◇ raven 名「大鴉；ワタリガラス」　crow よりも大きいカラスで，不吉な鳥とされる。
◇ sensation 名「大評判；センセーション」
◇ household name「よく知られている人物や物の名前；おなじみの名前」
◇ tuberculosis 名「結核」　◇ attribute 動「(…に) 帰する」
◇ cholera 名「(病気の) コレラ」　◇ suicide 名「自殺；自死」

[第5段落]
(Edgar Allan
Poe and ...)

◇ originator 名「創始者；創設者；開祖」　◇ architect 名「建築家」
◇ forerunner 名「先駆者；先祖」
◇ sake 名〈for the *sake* of ... ／ for ...'s *sake* で〉「…のための [に]」
◇ definitive 形「決定的な；最も信頼のおける」

[最終段落]
(Poe and his ...)

◇ dedicate 動「(…に) ささげる；寄贈する」
◇ annual 形「年々の；例年の；毎年の」　◇ distinguished 形「抜群の；すぐれた」

[メモ]

◇ make up with ...「〈人と〉仲直りする」　◇ affect 動「…に影響を与える [及ぼす]」

[設問文・選択肢]

◇ statement 名「陳述」　◇ abandon 動「…を捨てる；見捨てる」
◇ become on bad terms with ...「…と仲が悪くなる；険悪な関係となる」
◇ plot 動「〈演劇や文学作品など〉の筋立てを行う；プロットを作る」
◇ pass away「〈人が〉亡くなる；死ぬ」　die の婉曲表現。
◇ prominent 形「傑出した；卓越した」　◇ honor 動「〈名誉賞など〉を与える [授与する]」
◇ in the name of ...「…の名において；…の権威のもとに」
◇ trend 名「傾向；趨勢；流行 (のスタイル)」

— 英 R 121 —

第6問

解 答

A　問1 - ②　　　問2 - ②　　　問3 - ③　　　　　　　　　　　　　　（各3点）

　　問4 - 42 - ③　　43 - ①　　　　　　　　　　　　　　　　（完答で3点）

B　問1 - ③　　　問2　45 - ④　　　　46 - ④　　　　　　　　　（各3点）

　　問3 - ① · ②　　　　　　　　　　　　　　　（順不同・両方正解で3点）

A

出典

（参考）https://unesdoc.unesco.org/ark:/48223/pf0000246740/PDF/246740eng.pdf.multi

全訳

　あなたは学校の生徒会のメンバーです。あなたはたまたまウェブサイトで，ある英語の記事を見つけました。その記事は，SDGs（持続可能な開発目標）の1つを達成することに対してどのように貢献できるかについての提案をあなたの学校に与えることができるかもしれません。生徒会の次の会議のための要約メモを完成させなさい。

学校は気候変動問題について何ができるでしょうか

　地球温暖化を含む気候変動は，人類に大きな脅威をもたらします。研究者やコミュニティは，気候変動がどこで人々が住み，食料を育て，インフラを維持し，健康を維持できるのかということに影響を及ぼすことを示してきました。気候変動は他の多くの地球規模の問題とも関係しています。たとえば，発展途上国は気候変動に対する責任が最も少ないですが，その影響によるリスクが最も高いため，気候変動は不平等と倫理に関連しています。

　問題を解決するために私たちは何ができるでしょうか。たとえば学校において，私たちは1人の人間または1つのグループとして，何かできることがあるはずです。そうです。あなたの学校の全員が，その学校の掲げる気候問題を解決するための目標に向けて取り組む役割を果たすことができるのです。実際，全員に参加してもらうことで，あなたは彼らに，より持続可能な社会を構築するために必要な共感を高める機会を与えることになるのです。

　生徒，教師，サポートスタッフ，家族，そして地域コミュニティのメンバー全員が果たすべき役割を担っています。女の子と男の子，女性と男性は等しく作業に従事し，活動的でなければなりません。たとえば，カフェテリアのスタッフは地元の食材を使ったヘルシーなスナックや食事を用意したり，生徒はエネルギー消費量について勉強したり，家族は家庭で気候にやさしい習慣を取り入れることで生徒が学校で学んでいることを補強したりすることができます。学校のメンバーがどのような役割を担うかを決める際には，全員を巻き込んで参加させることをお勧めします。各グループは，気候変動に関する学校の行動計画の策定，実施，査察などの調整を担当する気候対策行動チームに対して代表して話をし，行動する代表者を選出するのがよいでしょう。

　ブラジルのリオデジャネイロにある学校，Colégio Israelita Brasileiro A. Liessen は，環境責任の文化の創造に取り組んでいます。その学校は，学校の全員（800人の生徒と200人の従業員）がなぜ環境プロジェクトが行われているのかという理由を知っている必要があると考えています。また，誰もが自分たちはそのプロセスの一部なのだということを感じる必要があります。この目的のために，学校の環境チームは，教師，生徒，エンジニアなどの人々を，体験的で肩のこらない学習活動に参加するよう促してきました。彼らは屋上の緑化を行い，太陽光を使ったオーブンと竹製の自転車置き

— 英R 122 —

場を作り，スパイスや花を栽培し，瞑想の庭を作り，そして，使用済みの食用油を燃料に変えました。これらの活動は，学校コミュニティのさまざまなメンバー間の絆を生み出し，帰属意識と学校への誇りを呼び起こし，アイデアや情報が自由に共有される環境を構築しました。環境チームは，プロジェクトを成功させるために，学校のコミュニティメンバーにトレーニングも提供しています。たとえば，廃棄物の分別や食用油の収集に関するトレーニングが従業員に提供されました。また，ボランティアの生徒を対象にガーデニングワークショップを開催し，広がりつつある学校の庭をメンテナンススタッフが手入れをする手助けを，彼ら生徒が行うことができるようにしました。

あなたの要約メモ：

学校は気候変動問題について何ができるでしょうか

アクションの目的

　気候変動対策に参加することによって，　39　ことができる。

主なポイント

- 地球温暖化を含む気候変動は，人間にとって大きな問題である。
- 学校は　40　べきである。
- 学校ではいくつかのグループを編成して，より良い計画について体系的に話し合い，実行できるようにするべきである。

興味深い詳細

- ブラジルのある学校が，　41　ということを証明するために紹介されている。
- そのブラジルの学校は，人々に　42　に参加してもらおうと努力している。そしてそれは　43　を生み出した。

設問解説

問1　　39　　正解 ②

「　39　に入る最も適切な選択肢を選びなさい」

① 生徒に気候変動に関する情報提供を教師に求めさせる
② **持続可能な社会を維持する必要性を生徒に認識させる**
③ 自分たちの学校が環境にどれほどのダメージを与えているかを生徒に認識させる
④ 自分たちが CO_2 を産み出していることに対する生徒の罪悪感を減らす

　正解は ②。第2段落最終文（In fact, by ...）に，「実際，全員に参加してもらうことで，あなたは彼らに，より持続可能な社会を構築するために必要な共感を高める機会を与えることになるのです」とある。この文の最後の，the empathy needed for creating a more sustainable society「より持続可能な社会を構築するために必要な共感」がポイントである。気候変動対策に参加することで，このような「共感」を醸成することにつながると筆者は述べているわけであり，このことは選択肢 ② の内容と一致する。よって，正解は ②。

　他の選択肢（①，③，④）については，それぞれの内容に絡む記述は記事本文にはない。

問2　　40　　正解 ②

「　40　に入る最も適切な選択肢を選びなさい」

① ボランティアの生徒の全国的なネットワークを作るためにお互いと協力し合う
② **気候に関する目標を達成するのに役立つ活動に，すべての生徒と教職員を参加させる**

— 英R 123 —

③　学校の教育課程に，気候変動に焦点を当てた教科を導入する

④　天候パターンの変化による学校行事の中止を避けるためにより一層努力する

　正解は②。第2段落第4文（Everyone in your school ...）及び最終文（In fact, by ...）に，「あなたの学校の全員が，その学校の掲げる気候問題を解決するための目標に向けて取り組む役割を果たすことができるのです。実際，全員に参加してもらうことで，あなたは彼らに，より持続可能な社会を構築するために必要な共感を高める機会を与えることになるのです」とある。②は下線部の記述と合っていることから，これが正解となる。

　①のような「（学校同士が）ボランティアの生徒の全国的なネットワークを作るためにお互いと協力し合う」という趣旨の記述は本文中にはない。③や④のようなことも，本文では述べられていない。

問3　　41　　正解③

「　41　に入る最も適切な選択肢を選びなさい」

①　コミュニティ内での誤解を防ぐ方法を私たちに教えることができる

②　非常に長い間，気候変動対策に取り組んできた

③　誰でもが何らかの行動をとることができるということを示す良い例である

④　生徒の家族と協力して取り組んでいる

　正解は③。第4段落にある，ブラジルの学校での取り組み例を読むと，その学校は「学校の全員（800人の生徒と200人の従業員）がなぜ環境プロジェクトが行われているのかという理由を知っている必要があると考えています。また，誰もが自分たちはプロセスの一部なのだということを感じる必要があります」という目標と信念のもとに，学校に関わる誰でもが何らかの役割を持ち，行動しているということがわかる。このことと一致する内容を持つ選択肢は③である。

　②は，「非常に長い間」の部分が本文からは読み取れない。①や④のようなことも，本文からは読み取れない。

問4　　42　　正解③　　　43　　正解①

「　42　と　43　に最適な選択肢を選びなさい」

①　学校との一体感

②　高度な学術的議論

③　地球にやさしい活動

④　食品廃棄物の問題

⑤　お金の節約活動

⑥　リサイクルに関するいくつかのアイデア

ブラジルの学校で行われていることは，次のようなことである（第4段落より）。

・第5文（They have created ...）「彼らは屋上の緑化を行い，太陽光を使ったオーブンと竹製の自転車置き場を作り，スパイスや花を栽培し，瞑想の庭を作り，そして，使用済みの食用油を燃料に変えました」

・第8文〜最終文（For example, training ... 〜 Also, a gardening ...）「たとえば，廃棄物の分別や食用油の収集に関するトレーニングが従業員に提供されました。また，ボランティアの生徒を対象にガーデニングワークショップを開催し，広がりつつある学校の庭をメンテナンススタッフが手入れをする手助けを，彼ら生徒が行うことができるようにしました」

　これらの活動は，すべて選択肢③の「地球にやさしい活動」（earth-friendly activities）としてまとめることができる。よって，　42　には③が入る。

　また，これらの活動の結果，何が生まれたかということについては，同じく第4段落に次のように書かれている。

— 英 R 124 —

・第6文（These activities have ...）「これらの活動は，学校コミュニティのさまざまな
　メンバー間の絆を生み出し，帰属意識と学校への誇りを呼び起こし，アイデアや情報
　が自由に共有される環境を構築しました」
　①の「学校との一体感（a sense of identification with the school）」と，上の文の中の「帰
属意識（a sense of belonging）」とは同じものと考えられる。よって，　43　には①が
入る。

主な語句・表現	・問題冊子を参照のこと。

[リード文]
◇ student council「生徒会」　　　　　　◇ happen to -「たまたま［偶然］-する」
◇ contribute 動「寄与する；役に立つ」　　◇ sustainable 形「持続可能な」

[第1段落]
(Climate change,
including ...)
◇ pose 動「〈問題など〉を引き起こす；持ち出す」
◇ threat 名「脅威（となるもの）；恐れ」　　◇ humanity 名「人間；人類；人間性」
◇ infrastructure 名「（国家・社会などの経済的存続に必要な）基本的施設；インフラストラ
　クチャー」
◇ ethics 名「倫理（感）；道徳（観）」　　　◇ at risk「危険な状態で」

[第2段落]
(What can we ...)
◇ empathy 名「共感；感情移入」

[第3段落]
(Students, teachers,
support ...)
◇ engage 動「（…に）従事する；携わる」　◇ ingredient 名「（料理などの）原材料；素材」
◇ consumption 名「消費；使うこと」　　　◇ reinforce 動「…を強化する；補強する」
◇ practice 名「実践；実行；行い；行動」　◇ recommend 動「…を勧める；推薦する」
◇ involve 動「…を巻き込む；関わり合いを持たせる」
◇ take on「引き受ける；持つようになる；帯びる」
◇ elect 動「…を選ぶ；選出する」　　　　◇ representative 名「代表（者）；代理人」
◇ on one's behalf「…を代表して；…のために；…の代わりに」
◇ in charge of ...「…を担当［管理］している」
◇ coordinate 動「…を調整する；調和させる」
◇ implementation 名「実行；履行；実施」　◇ review 名「振り返り；反省」

[最終段落]
(Colégio Israelita
Brasileiro ...)
◇ take place「起こる；行われる；催される」
◇ end 名「目標；目的」
◇ experiential 形「体験［経験］的な；体験［経験］（上）の」
◇ convert 動「…を変える；変換［転換］する」
◇ bond 名「絆；結びつき」　　　　　　　◇ awaken 動「…を呼び起こす；呼びさます」
◇ sorting 名「分別；分けること」　　　　◇ collection 名「収集；集めること」
◇ offer 動「…を提供する；与える」　　　◇ expand 動「広がる；拡張［拡大］する」

[要約メモ]
◇ carry out ...「…を実行［実践］する；…に取り組む」
◇ systematically 副「体系的に；組織立って」
◇ prove 動「…を証明する」

[設問文・選択肢]
◇ sense of guilt「罪悪感」
◇ cancellation 名「中止；取り消し；キャンセル」
◇ miscommunication 名「誤解；（考えや気持ちの）行き違い」
◇ in cooperation with ...「…と協力［連携］して」
◇ identification 名「一体感；同一化；同一視」

B

出典 （参考）https://www.ccohs.ca/oshanswers/chemicals/whmis_ghs/pictograms.html
https://www.vumc.org/safety/sites/vumc.org.safety/files/public_files/osha/
what-pictograms-mean.pdf

全訳 　あなたは，「メッセージを送る方法」というタイトルでのポスタープレゼンテーションの準備をしているグループにいます。あなたのグループは，絵文字でメッセージを伝える方法であるピクトグラムに興味があり，次の文章を使用してポスターを作成することを計画しています。

ハザード・ピクトグラム
―メッセージをすばやく伝えることのできる記号―

　ここで紹介するピクトグラムとは，危険物を扱うユーザーに，どのような種類の危険性が存在するかを即座に示すグラフィック画像のことです。たとえば，（そのピクトグラムを用いれば）一目で，その製品が可燃性（すぐに燃焼する可能性がある）であるかどうか，あるいは別の点で健康に害を及ぼす可能性があるかどうかを確認できます。

　その中に，ひし型をしているピクトグラムがあります。そして，このひし形の中には，潜在的な危険（たとえば，火事を引き起こす，食べた場合に有害である，強酸性である，など）を表す記号が書かれています。その記号とひし型のデザインの両方を併せて，ピクトグラムと呼びます。ピクトグラムには，特定の危険等級あるいはカテゴリーが割り当てられています。

　ハザード・ピクトグラムは，国際的な「化学品の分類および表示に関する世界調和システム（GHS）」の一部を形成しています。GHSには2つのセットのピクトグラムが含まれています。1つは容器のラベル付けと職場での危険警告用に用いるもので，2つめのセットは危険物の輸送中に使用するためのものです。対象となる相手に応じてどちらか一方が選択されますが，2つを一緒には使用しません。ピクトグラムのこの2つのセットは，同じ危険性に対して同じ記号を使用しますが，輸送用のピクトグラムには用いる必要のない記号もあります。輸送用のピクトグラムにはよりさまざまな色があり，サブカテゴリー（下位の分類）を表す番号などの追加情報が含まれている場合もあります。

　ハザード・ピクトグラムは，GHSに基づく容器のラベル付けの重要な要素の1つであり，次のような他の情報を伴います。

・その製品の説明
・必要に応じて，「危険」または「警告」のいずれかの注意喚起のことば
・その製品によってもたらされるリスクの性質や程度を示す「危険性通告」
・ユーザー（及び他の人や一般的な環境）へのリスクを最小限に抑えるために，その製品をどのように取り扱うべきかを示す「予防措置的通告」
・（その製品の）供給元（それは製造業者あるいは輸入業者であるかもしれません）の身元

化学物質のGHSハザード・ピクトグラムは，（各国に対して）ハザード・ピクトグラムの国内システムについての基盤を提供したり，あるいは，それに取って代わることを目的としています。実際，GHS輸送ピクトグラムは，多くの国の国内規制で広く実施されている「危険物輸送に関する国連勧告」で推奨されているものと同じものです。

下の図は，ハザード・ピクトグラムの例をいくつか示したものです。

図1　ハザード・ピクトグラム

各ピクトグラムの意味を推測できますか？　それらは2つのグループに分けられます。1つのグループ（番号1及び2）は，上で述べたピクトグラムの最初のセットである，物理的危険性を示すピクトグラムを表しています。他方，もう1つのグループ（番号3，4，5，6及び7）には，2番目のセットである輸送用のピクトグラムが含まれています。それでは，最初のグループから始めて，それぞれを見ていきましょう。

最初のグループのピクトグラムには，それぞれ独自の名前があります。No. 1は「Flame（火炎）」，No. 2は「Flame over Circle（サークル上の炎）」と呼ばれています。前者は，水や空気にさらされたときに自ら発火しやすい，または可燃性ガスを放出して他の原料の燃焼を引き起こす可燃性の原料または物質を意味し，一方，後者は，何かが燃えるのを助ける，または火をより熱く，より長く持続させるような化学物質である酸化剤を意味します。

次に，2番目のグループに移りましょう。No. 3は，可燃性の固体，あるいは自己反応性物質を示しています。これらは，輸送中に遭遇する条件下で，発火したり，あるいは摩擦によって火災を引き起こしたりその一因となったり，注意深く取り扱わないと爆発する可能性があります。No. 4は，引火性液体，すなわち，引火点が60℃未満で，燃焼を維持し続けることができる液体を意味します。No. 5は，自然燃焼しやすい物質，すなわち，輸送中に遭遇する通常の状態で自然に熱くなったり，空気との接触により熱くなることから，発火しやすい物質を意味します。No. 6は，他への影響力のある物質を示しています。これらの物質は，それ自体は必ずしも可燃性ではありませんが，一般には酸素を放出することにより，他の物質の燃焼を引き起こしたり，その一因となる可能性があります。最後に，No. 7は有機毒を意味します。これは，ある特定の化学構造を持つ有害物質や危険物質を含む有機物質です。

それぞれのピクトグラムは特定の種類の危険を表し，危険物を扱う人なら誰でもすぐに認知できるように作られています。もっとも，これらのピクトグラムは一般の人々が理解するにはそれほど簡単なものではありませんが。

あなたのプレゼンテーション・ポスターの草案：

ハザード・ピクトグラムを知っていますか？

ハザード・ピクトグラムとは何か

・それは，製品にどのような種類の危険性が存在しているかを示すグラフィック画像です。

・ 44

何種類かのハザード・ピクトグラム

No.	ピクトグラム	危険性の内容	一般的な意味
1		・可燃性の原料または物質	それらは，燃焼または 45 可能性のある原料または物質です。
2		・酸化剤	46 化学物質です。
3		・可燃性固形物 ・自己反応性を有する物質	摩擦により発火しやすい原料または物質です。

共通のメッセージを持つピクトグラム

47

48

設問解説

問1 44 正解③

「ポスターの最初の見出しの下で，あなたのグループは，文章で説明されている通り，ハザード・ピクトグラムを紹介したいと考えている。次のうちのどれが最も適切か」

44

① 同じ危険が異なる記号で表されることがあります。
② 2つのセットがあり，同時に両方を使用できます。
③ **製品に関するその他の情報がそれに添えられます。**
④ 国連によって発明され，世界中で広く受け入れられています。

正解は③。第4段落第1文（Hazard pictograms are ...）に「ハザード・ピクトグラムは，GHS に基づく容器のラベル付けの重要な要素の1つであり，次のような他の情報を伴います」という記述があり，その後，何点か具体的な表記の例が箇条書きで示されている。つまり，製品にはピクトグラムだけでなく，普通その他の情報も添えられて，注意喚起されることになるということである。このことは，選択肢③の内容と一致する。

選択肢①と②については，本文の第3段落に次のような記述があることに注意する。

— 英 R 128 —

第3文〜第4文（Either one or ... 〜 The two sets ...）「対象となる相手に応じてどちらか一方が選択されますが，2つを一緒には使用しません。ピクトグラムのこの2つのセットは，同じ危険性に対して同じ記号を使用しますが，輸送用のピクトグラムには用いる必要のない記号もあります」

「同じ危険性に対して同じ記号を使用」する，とあるので，選択肢の① は誤りと見なされる。また，「2つを一緒には使用しません」とあるので，② についても誤りであることがわかる。

また，選択肢 ④ については，第5段落第2文（In fact, GHS ...）に「実際，GHS 輸送ピクトグラムは，多くの国の国内規制で広く実施されている『危険物輸送に関する国連勧告』で推奨されているものと同じものです」という記述があるが，「国連によって発明され」という内容は本文からは読み取れない。よって，④ も不正解である。

以上のことにより，正解は ③ となる。

問2 　45　 正解④ 　46　 正解④
「あなたは No. 1 と No. 2 のピクトグラムの一般的な意味を書くように頼まれた。 　45　 と 　46　 に入る最も適切な選択肢をそれぞれ選びなさい」
No. 1 　45　
　① 猛毒を含んでいる
　② 火の近くで爆発する
　③ 低温下でも溶ける
　④ **燃焼性のガスを放出する**

No. 2 　46　
　① 適切な制御をしないと活性化し，発火する可能性がある
　② 原料が爆発するのにかかる時間を短縮できる
　③ 酸素を吸収できる物質が含まれている
　④ **火の温度を上げたり，燃焼時間をより長くする**

No. 1 と No. 2 のピクトグラムについては，第8段落を見ると「No. 1 は『Flame（火炎）』，No. 2 は『Flame over Circle（サークル上の炎）』と呼ばれています。前者は，水や空気にさらされたときに自ら発火しやすい，または可燃性ガスを放出するような可燃性原料または物質を意味し，一方，後者は，何かを燃やすのを助ける，または火をより熱く，より長く持続させるような化学物質である酸化剤を意味します」とある。

よって，No. 1 　45　 については ④，No. 2 　46　 については ④ が選ばれることになる。

問3 　47　・　48　 正解①・②
「あなたは共通のメッセージを共有するいくつかのピクトグラムについて記述している。この記事によると，次の選択肢のうち，どの2つが適切か（順番は問わない。）」
　47　・　48　

　① No. 1 と No. 5 は，空気と接触させると危険になりうる。
　② No. 1 と No. 6 は，発火の原因となりうるガスを放出する。
　③ No. 1，6，7 は，有毒ガスが発生する可能性があることを意味している。
　④ No. 1 と No. 7 は，燃焼しやすく有害ガスを生み出すことを意味している。
　⑤ No. 2 と No. 6 は，可燃性であり，大火災の原因となりえることがあることを示している。
　⑥ No. 3，4，6 は，低温で燃焼し始めることを示している。

— 英 R 129 —

選択肢①：第8段落第2文（The former means ...）に，「前者（= No. 1）は，水や空気にさらされたときに自ら発火しやすい，または可燃性ガスを放出して他の原料の燃焼を引き起こす可燃性の原料または物質を意味し…」とあることから，No. 1 は①の内容と合っているとわかる。また，第9段落第5文（No. 5 means ...）に，「No. 5 は，自然燃焼しやすい物質，すなわち，輸送中に遭遇する通常の状態で自然に熱くなったり，空気との接触により熱くなることから，発火しやすい物質を意味します」とあることから，No. 5 も①の内容と合っている。したがって①は正しい。

選択肢②：上に引用した第8段落第2文に，「前者（= No. 1）は，水や空気にさらされたときに自ら発火しやすい，または可燃性ガスを放出して他の原料の燃焼を引き起こす可燃性の原料または物質を意味し…」とあることから，No. 1 は②の内容と合っている。また，第9段落第6文（No.6 shows ...）に，「No. 6 は，他への影響力のある物質を示しています。これらの物質は，それ自体は必ずしも可燃性ではありませんが，一般には酸素を放出することにより，他の物質の燃焼を引き起こしたり，その一因となる可能性があります」とあることから，No. 6 も②と合っている。したがって②は正しい。

選択肢③：No. 1 と No. 6 は「毒」とは関係ない。

選択肢④：No. 7 には「燃焼しやすい」という性質はない。

選択肢⑤：No. 2 も No. 6 もそれ自体は必ずしも「可燃性がある」わけではない。

選択肢⑥：No. 3 と No. 6 については，「低温で」燃焼し始めるということは書かれていない。

以上より，正解は①と②で，選択肢③〜⑥はすべて誤り。

主な語句・表現　・問題冊子を参照のこと。

[リード文]
◇ pictogram 名「ピクトグラム」 グラフィック・シンボルの典型。意味するものの形状などを使って，その意味概念を理解させる記号。
◇ pictorial 形「絵の；絵を用いた」

[第1段落]
(Pictograms introduced here ...)
◇ hazard 名「危険；ハザード」 形容詞は hazardous（危険な）。
◇ graphic 形「図表による；記号上の」
◇ glance 名「ちらっと見ること；一目；一瞥」
◇ flammable 形「可燃性の；燃えやすい」

[第2段落]
(Some pictograms have ...)
◇ represent 動「…を表す；表現する；表出する」
◇ potential 形「潜在的な；内に潜む」　◇ acid 名「酸；酸性のもの」
◇ be referred to as ...「…と呼ばれる；…と称される」
◇ assign 動「…を与える；あてがう」　◇ specific 形「（ある）特定の」
◇ class 名「等級」

[第3段落]
(Hazard pictograms form ...)
◇ form 動「…を形成する；形作る」　◇ classification 名「分類」
◇ chemical 名「化学物質［製品；薬品］」　◇ container 名「容器；コンテナ」
◇ require 動「…を要求する；求める」

[第4段落]
(Hazard pictograms are ...)
◇ nature 名「性質；本質」　◇ precautionary 形「予防の；用心の」
◇ supplier 名「供給者」
◇ manufacturer 名「（大規模な）製造業者；メーカー」
◇ importer 名「輸入者；輸入業者」

— 英 R 130 —

[第5～7段落]	◇ UN = United Nations「国際連合」　◇ regulation 图「規則；規制；ルール」
	◇ physical 形「物理的な」
[第8段落] (The pictograms of ...)	◇ the former「前者」　⇔ the latter「後者」　◇ material 图「原料；材料；素材」
	◇ substance 图「物質；物体」
	◇ (be) liable to ‐「‐しやすい；容易に‐してしまう」
	◇ emit 動「…を放出する；(外に) 出す」
	◇ identify 動「(…と) 同一であると見なす；同一視する」
	◇ oxidizer 图「酸化剤；酸化性物質」
[第9段落] (Next, let us ...)	◇ solid 图「固体」　　　　　◇ self-reactive 形「自己反応性の」
	◇ friction 图「摩擦」　　　　◇ liquid 图「液体」
	◇ flash point「引火点；引火温度」
	◇ be capable of ‐ing「‐することができる [可能である]」
	◇ sustain 動「…を維持する；保持する」　◇ spontaneously 副「自然に；自然発生的に」
	◇ in themselves　in oneself で「それ自体」という意味。
	◇ oxygen 图「酸素」　　　　◇ organic 形「有機の；有機体の」
[最終段落] (Each pictogram ...)	◇ recognizable 形「認知 [認識] することのできる」
	◇ handle 動「…を扱う；取り扱う」
[ポスター]	◇ common 形「共通の；共有の」
[設問文・選択肢]	◇ heading 图「見出し；表題」　　　◇ accompany 動「…に伴う；同時に起こる」
	◇ shorten 動「…を短くする；短縮する」　◇ absorb 動「…を吸収する」
	◇ length 图「長さ」　＜ long 形「長い」　◇ order 图「順序；順番」
	◇ matter 動「問題となる；重要である」　◇ poisonous 形「毒 (性) のある」

第4回　実戦問題　解答・解説

第4回　解答・解説

英語（リーディング） 第4回 （100点満点）

（解答・配点）

問題番号(配点)	設問		解答番号	正解	配点	自己採点欄	問題番号(配点)	設問	解答番号	正解	配点	自己採点欄
第1問(10)	A	1	1	②	2		第4問(16)	1	24	③	3	
		2	2	②	2			2	25	④	3	
	B	1	3	①	2			3	26	③	3	
		2	4	①	2			4	27	②	3	
		3	5	①	2			5	28	①	2	
小　計									29	④	2	
第2問(20)	A	1	6	②	2		小　計					
		2	7	③	2		第5問(15)	1	30	②	3	
		3	8	②	2			2	31	②	3	
		4	9	④	2			3	32	③	3*	
		5	10	⑤	2				33	④		
	B	1	11	①	2				34	⑤		
		2	12	①	2				35	②		
		3	13	①	2			4	36 — 37	① - ③	3*	
		4	14	③	2			5	38	③	3	
		5	15	③	2		小　計					
小　計							第6問(24)	A	1	39	④	3	
第3問(15)	A	1	16	②	3				2	40	①	3	
		2	17	②	3				3	41	②	3	
	B	1	18	②	3*				4	42	①	3	
			19	③				B	1	43	④	3	
			20	①					2	44	③	3	
			21	④					3	45	②	3	
		2	22	④	3				4	46 — 47	② - ④	3*	
		3	23	④	3		小　計					
小　計							合　計					

（注）
1　＊は，全部正解の場合のみ点を与える。
2　－（ハイフン）でつながれた正解は，順序を問わない。

— 英 R 134 —

第1問

解答
A	問1 – ②	問2 – ②		（各2点）
B	問1 – ①	問2 – ①	問3 – ①	（各2点）

A

出典　*Original Material*

全訳

　　あなたは自分の高校で何人かのインド人の生徒が催す料理コンテストの準備をしています。あなたの目標は，今まで知らなかった香味料を用いて，新しい料理を作ることです。あなたは日本ではあまり有名ではない香辛料についての記事を見つけます。

風味のよい香辛料	
ウルファ・ビーバー	**ポルチーニ・パウダー**
・甘いチョコレートのような味ですが，いぶしたような香りがするため，スープの味を損なうことがあります ・肉には合いますが，ケーキには合いません ・これを使えば野菜がとてもおいしくなります	・独特のキノコの香り ・木の実のような味ですが，ケーキよりもスープや野菜に合います ・パスタにぴったりです
ブレード・メイス	**カルダモン**
・このまろやかな味の種を丸ごと使って見事な味付けができます ・フルーツケーキに加えても，ミートボールに加えたのと全く同じくらいおいしくいただけます ・スープに入れると体が暖まります	・グリーンとブラックの2種類があります ・これはスープやパスタ料理をひときわスパイシーにしますが，ケーキには使わないでください ・豚肉のような，強い匂いがします

設問解説

問1　　1　　正解 ②

「ウルファ・ビーバーとブレード・メイスはどちらも　1　のために使うことができる」

① ケーキ
② ミートボール
③ キノコ
④ スープ

　　正解は②。ウルファ・ビーバー (Urfa Biber) の説明の2つめの項目（Great with meat ...）に「肉には合いますが，ケーキには合いません」とあり，ブレード・メイス（Blade Mace）の説明の2つめの項目（Just as delicious ...）に「フルーツケーキに加えても，ミートボールに加えたのと全く同じくらいおいしくいただけます」とあることから，②の「ミートボール」が正解となる。

　　①の「ケーキ」は，上に引用したウルファ・ビーバーの説明の中に「ケーキには合いません」とあることから誤り。③の「キノコ」は，この2つの香辛料の説明の中に記述がな

— 英 R 135 —

いので，正解にはなれない。④の「スープ」は，ウルファ・ビーバーの説明の中の1つめの項目（Sweet chocolatey taste ...）に，「甘いチョコレートのような味ですが，いぶしたような香りがするため，スープの味を損なうことがあります」とあることから，やはり正解になれない。

問2　　2　　正解②
　「もしあなたがパスタを辛くて肉の風味がする香辛料で味付けしたいと思ったら，2　を選ぶのがよい」
　　　① ブレード・メイス
　　　② カルダモン
　　　③ ポルチーニ・パウダー
　　　④ ウルファ・ビーバー

　正解は②。カルダモン（Cardamom）の説明の2つめの項目（Make your soup ...）に「これはスープやパスタ料理をひときわスパイシー（spicy）にしますが，ケーキには使わないでください」とある（spicy は hot とほぼ同じ意味である）。そして3つめの項目（Has a strong smell, ...）に「豚肉のような（like pork），強い匂いがします」とある（like pork は meaty とほぼ同内容である）。したがって②が正解となる。
　他の香辛料については，「辛い」とも「肉の風味がする」とも述べられていない。なお，ウルファ・ビーバーの説明の2つめの項目（Great with meat ...）に「肉には合いますが，ケーキには合いません」とあり，ブレード・メイスの説明の2つめの項目（Just as delicious ...）に「フルーツケーキに加えても，ミートボールに加えたのと全く同じくらいおいしくいただけます」とあるが，下線部の表現はこれらの香辛料が「肉の風味がする（meaty）」という意味ではないことに注意。

主な語句・表現　・問題冊子を参照のこと。
［リード文］◇ senior high school「高校」　　　　◇ flavor图「風味」

［本文］◇ chocolatey囮「チョコレートのような」　◇ smoky囮「いぶしたような」
　　　　◇ ruin動「…を台無しにする」　　　　　　◇ nutty囮「木の実のような」
　　　　◇ extra囮「普通以上に」

— 英R 136 —

B

出典 | *Original Material*

全訳 | ビルに入ったところで1人の学生が，あなたに興味を引く1枚のビラを渡しました。

「動物に意識を向ける週間」にご参加を

留学生の皆さんにお知らせします！「動物に意識を向ける週間」のために，皆さんの大陸の絶滅に瀕している動物について話を聞きたいと思っています。週間の終わりに学生が「世界の絶滅危惧種」に関する視覚資料を用いた30分の発表と選ばれた動物を救うために何ができるかの説明を行うまで，参加者はさまざまな活動を共にします。

我々は，アジア，ヨーロッパ，オセアニア，北米，南米の大陸から各10名の代表を集めたいと思っています。

日程表

8月16日	午前―生物学科長による歓迎スピーチ
	午後―自己紹介とグループ分け
8月17日	サファリパーク
	午前―パーク見学と絶滅危惧種に関するドキュメンタリー
	午後―現在の保護計画に関する講演
8月18日	午前―自然史博物館講習会―絶滅種のDNA摘出講習会
	午後―発表準備
8月19日	午前―討論―科学による歴史的動物の再生 – 是か否か
	午後―発表準備
8月20日	午前―発表
	午後―「最有益発表」賞表彰式

- 全ての活動／発表は英語で行われます。
- 可能な場合は大学からタブレット／必要な資材が提供されます。

プログラムに申し込む各大陸の最初の10人の学生の参加が認められます。
＊より詳細な情報の請求や申し込みには，理学部デスクにお立ち寄りください。

設問解説

問1 | **3** | 正解 ①

「このイベントの目的は，留学生が **3** ことである」

① **絶滅の危機にさらされた動物の将来について考える**
② 科学的により強健な動物を作り出す
③ 歴史的知識を用いて虚弱な動物を助ける

— 英 R 137 —

④　独特な動物を紹介する

　正解は①。ビラの最初のブロックの第3文（Participants will join ...）にあるように，イベントの最終日には「世界の絶滅危惧種」に関する発表と選ばれた動物を救うために何ができるかの説明が行われることや，日程表に記された各種の活動内容からも，①が正解と判断できる。

　②は，日程表の8月18日午前に絶滅種のDNA摘出講習会が組まれているが，これが「より強健な動物を作り出す」ことを目指したものであると判断するべき理由はないし，③，④に関係する内容の記述はないので，これらはいずれも正解とはならない。

問2　　4　　正解①

「このプログラムの間に学生は以下のうちどれをすることになるか」　　4

　①　DNA採取の授業に出席する
　②　どの動物が最も危険にさらされているかを決める
　③　近年の生物学の進歩について議論する
　④　動物園の珍しい動物と触れ合う

　正解は①。日程表の8月18日午前に「絶滅種のDNA摘出講習会」が組まれているので，①が正解となる。

　他の選択肢に合うような内容は記されていないため，いずれも正解とはならない。

問3　　5　　正解①

「イベントでは　　5　　ことになるため，理系の学生の役に立つだろう」

　①　絶滅した動物からクローンを作ることへの賛否両論について考察する
　②　考えをより科学的な方法でより良く説明する
　③　世界的に高名な科学者の理論を傾聴する
　④　現代の救命技術を活用する

　正解は①。日程表の8月19日午前に「討論―科学による歴史的動物の再生 – 是か否か」が組み込まれているので，①が正解となる。

　他の選択肢に合う活動は記されていないため，いずれも正解とはならない。

（主な語句・表現）・問題冊子を参照のこと。

[リード文]　◇ hallway 图「（ビルなどの）玄関 [廊下]」

[本文]　◇ Calling ...!「…に告ぐ [お知らせします]」 連絡事項を告げる際の定型表現。
◇ international student「（海外からの）留学生」
◇ endangered 厖「絶滅の危機にさらされた」◇ visual 图「視覚資料」
◇ workshop 图「講習会」　　　　　　　◇ extinct 厖「絶滅した」
◇ harvest 動「…を摘出する」　　　　　◇ award ceremony「授賞 [表彰] 式」
◇ where possible「可能な場合には」

[設問文・選択肢]　◇ threatened 厖「絶滅の危機にさらされた」
◇ clone 動「…からクローン [複製生物] を作る」
◇ world-renowned 厖「世界的に高名な [名声のある]」

― 英 R 138 ―

第2問

解答

A	問1－②	問2－③	問3－②	問4－④	問5－⑤ （各2点）
B	問1－①	問2－②	問3－①	問4－③	問5－③ （各2点）

A

出典 *Original Material*

全訳　あなたは来年，生徒会の選挙に立候補することを考えています。イギリスのウェブサイトに，高校の選挙の勝者たちによる，どうすれば支持を得てうまくいくかについての役立つ提案が見つかりました。

人気だけでは不十分！　生徒による選挙の勝ち方！

考察

1. 選ばれる秘訣は見つかっていない！　出来る限り多くの生徒に話しかけること―自分の仲間たちにだけでなく！
   ◇人々が何を望んでいるか探り出す。
   ◇積極的にクラスと共に行動する。
2. ソーシャルネットワーキングのアカウントを開設する。
   ◇自分の考えを投稿する。コメントを奨励する。
3. キャラクターとキャッチフレーズを作り出す！
   ◇わかりやすい目標を作る。
4. 人々に手伝わせる。
   ◇仲間たちに支持者のステッカーを身につけるよう頼む！
5. 自分の意見の弱みを見つける。
   ◇仲間にあなたの意見に反論するよう頼む。
   ◇選挙討論での賢い受け答えを用意する！
6. 強力なスピーチの計画を立てる。
   ◇クラスメートにとっての利益を明確にする。
   ◇スピーチにユーモアを取り入れる。気さくな人物に思われるだろう。
7. ユーチューブ向けにスピーチを撮影する！
   ◇学校の制服をきちんと着る（まじめに）。
8. ストレスに立ち向かう！
   ◇プレッシャーがかかるときには緊張を解くために呼吸しストレッチする。

— 英 R 139 —

アドバイスに対する高校の選挙の勝者による評価：

高校↓ ＼ 役立つ考察（評点）→	最高（＋2）	二番目（＋1）	最低（－1）
グレンジャー高校	2 & 5	1 & 6	3 & 8
ロングボトム・アカデミー	6	5 & 7	1 & 2
ポッター・アカデミー	3 & 6	1, 2 & 4	7 & 8
ウィーズリー中学校	4 & 7	5	3

設問解説

問1　　6　　正解②

「4つの高校からのフィードバックに基づくと，どの助言が最も役立たないか」　　6

① 誰にでも話しかけよ。
② ストレスを制御せよ。
③ キャラクターとキャッチフレーズを作れ。
④ 生徒たちから助力を得よ。

正解は②。①は「考察」の1，②は8，③は3，④は4のそれぞれの項目に相当する内容。それぞれの項目について，表の上の行から下の行に向かって，評価の出ている場合についてその評点を加算していくと，

①：＋1－1＋1＝＋1
②：－1－1＝－2
③：－1＋2－1＝±0
④：＋1＋2＝＋3

という計算になるので②が最も低評価ということになり，これが正解となる。

問2　　7　　正解③

「もし生徒会の選挙に立候補する際にこれらの助言を取り入れるなら，　　7　　を用いることになる」

① 豪華な服装
② レッスンの時間
③ ビデオ装置
④ よく知られたキャラクター

正解は③。7の項目の「ユーチューブ向けにスピーチを撮影する」に従うためには③を用いることになるので，これが正解。

①は7の項目の「学校の制服をきちんと着る」という指示に反し，②については特に記述がなく，④は3で新たにキャラクターを「作り出す」ようにとされているので，いずれも正解とはならない。

問3　　8　　正解②

「ウェブサイトによれば，生徒会の選挙への立候補に関する1つの事実は　　8　　ということである」

① 成功には援護が必要である
② 何が勝利を確実にするかは誰も知らない
③ あなたの意見を拒否する者もいるだろう
④ 今日，科学技術は重要である

正解は②。「考察」の1の「選ばれる秘訣は見つかっていない」は「事実」として紹介されているので、これに対応する②が正解となる。

①は4に通じる内容ではあるが「…が必要である」というのは資格や決まった金額など客観的な要素について言われている場合を除き、主観的「意見」であって「事実」ではないと考えられるため、正解とはならない。③、④は内容的にウェブサイトに書かれていることではないし、③は推測、④は価値判断であって「事実」ではないため、やはり正解とはならない。

問4　　9　　正解④

「ウェブサイトによれば、生徒会の選挙への立候補に関する1つの意見は　9　ということである」

① 名文句を借りてくることで票を得られる
② コメントに返答することでコミュニケーションが向上する
③ 深呼吸するとパニックが完全におさまる
④ **冗談を言うことで聞き手は引きつけられる**

正解は④。④は6の「スピーチにユーモアを取り入れる。気さくな人物に思われるだろう」に対応し、この「…だろう」という推測は「事実」ではなく「意見」なので、これが正解。

①、②はウェブサイトに書かれてない内容であるため、正解とはならない。③は8にストレス解消法として「緊張を解くために呼吸しストレッチする」ようにとあるが、「パニックが完全におさまる」といった極端な効果があるとは書かれていないため、やはり正解とはならない。

問5　　10　　正解⑤

「勝者による評価に基づけば、以下のうちどれが最も効果的な助言集か」　10

	第1	第2	第3
①	自分の意見の弱みを見つける。	人々に手伝わせる。	強力なスピーチの計画を立てる。
②	自分の意見の弱みを見つける。	強力なスピーチの計画を立てる。	人々に手伝わせる。
③	人々に手伝わせる。	自分の意見の弱みを見つける。	強力なスピーチの計画を立てる。
④	人々に手伝わせる。	強力なスピーチの計画を立てる。	自分の意見の弱みを見つける。
⑤	**強力なスピーチの計画を立てる。**	**自分の意見の弱みを見つける。**	**人々に手伝わせる。**
⑥	強力なスピーチの計画を立てる。	人々に手伝わせる。	自分の意見の弱みを見つける。

正解は⑤。選択肢は同じ3つの助言の組み合わせなので、より評点の高い助言を高い順位に位置付けたものの方が効果的、と考えられる。3つの助言の評点はそれぞれ、問1と同様の加算によって、

5「自分の意見の弱みを見つける」：＋2＋1＋1＝＋4
4「人々に手伝わせる」：＋1＋2＝＋3
6「強力なスピーチの計画を立てる」：＋1＋2＋2＝＋5

となるので、評点の高さが順位と一致している⑤が正解となる。

― 英 R 141 ―

主な語句・表現	・問題冊子を参照のこと。
[リード文]	◇ run for ...「…（の選挙）に立候補する」　◇ council 图「評議会」
	◇ UK 图「連合王国；イギリス」　United Kingdom の略。
[本文]	◇ consideration 图「考え；意見」　　　◇ formula for ...「…の秘訣［秘策］」
	◇ social networking「ソーシャルネットワーキング」　インターネットを利用した交流の場。
	◇ account 图「アカウント」　インターネット上のシステムへのアクセスの資格。
	◇ post 動「（インターネット上に）〈情報・メッセージなど〉を掲示［投稿］する」
	◇ recognisable 形「見分けがつく；それとわかる」　イギリス式の綴りで，アメリカ式では
	recognizable となる。
	◇ challenge 動「…に異議を唱える」　　　◇ good-natured 形「気さくな；好感のもてる」
	◇ tackle 動「…に取り組む［立ち向かう］」
	◇ secondary school「中等学校」　アメリカの high school，日本の中学校・高校にあたる
	もの。
[設問文・選択肢]	◇ feedback 图「（利用者などの）フィードバック；反応」
	B

出典　*Original Material*

全訳

　あなたは，この夏に自分が勉強しているイギリスの高校で，学習スタイルについてのネット上のフォーラムを見つけました。そのフォーラムの議論をいくつか読んでいます。

学習スタイル〈2021 年 7 月 21 日に投稿〉
S. パーキンスへ
J. ハーレーより

親愛なるパーキンス先生，
　問題解決型学習（pbl）すなわち，生徒を中心にした授業におけるグループで行う現実世界の問題解決に対する当惑から，pbl に不慣れな教師は立ち直れないでしょう。
　pbl では複数の科目を重なり合わせる必要がある場合も多いので，教師同士の協力が不可欠です。このことが原因で，科目ごとに分かれた国家試験で生徒は不安を覚えることを統計は証明しています。また費用も高額です。議論を観察し，生徒と定期的に会合を開くためにより多くの教師が必要になるのです。生徒はさまざまな情報源について評価を行いますが，これは収穫の得られない場合も多いので，時間の浪費になります。昔ながらの講義による学習の方が良くはないでしょうか。

よろしくお願いします。
ジョー・ハーレー
監督生

— 英 R 142 —

返信：学習スタイル〈2021 年 7 月 22 日に投稿〉

J. ハーレーへ
S. パーキンスより

親愛なるジョー
　貴重なご意見有難うございます。暗記は，やる価値がありはしますが，あなたの考えるほど効果的ではありません。ハーバード大学で行われたある研究は，講義の方が学習する内容が多いと生徒は感じているにもかかわらず，実はそんなことはないことを示しました。
　問題に取り組むには事前に知識を備えていることが不可欠であることが証明されています。ですから pbl では生徒が継続的に学習することを求められます。彼らはさまざまな可能性を考慮し，自分たちにとって最善と思われるものを選び，したがって「正しい」解答を受け入れるのではなく，賛否両論を真剣に分析します。

よろしく
シャウナ・パーキンス
カリキュラム責任者

設問解説

問1　11　正解①

「問題解決型学習は　11　」
　① 必ずしも 1 冊の特定の教科書に焦点を合わせない
　② 地球がより良い場所になることに助力する
　③ 世界中で議論の的となっている
　④ 教師の役割を重要ではなくする

　正解は①。ハーレーの投稿の第 2 段落第 1 文（Cooperation among teachers ...）に「pbl では複数の科目を重なり合わせる必要がある場合も多い」とあるので，① が正解。
　他の選択肢のうち② は，2 つの投稿と特に関わりのない内容であるため，正解とはならない。③ は pbl がこのフォーラムで議論の的になっていることだけをもって世界中でも事情は同様であると結論付けるわけにはいかないため，また ④ はハーレーの投稿の第 2 段落第 4 文（More teachers are ...）に「議論を観察し，生徒と定期的に会合を開くためにより多くの教師が必要になる」と述べられており，pbl での教師の役割が軽いものであるとは考え難いため，やはりいずれも正解とはならない。

問2　12　正解②

「ジョー・ハーレーの pbl に関するフォーラムへの投稿で述べられている 1 つの<u>事実</u>は　12　というものである」
　① それは費用が高額で，学校は既に予算案と格闘している
　② 科目で分かれている標準型の試験は生徒を混乱させることが多い
　③ 教師は数多くの科目に慣れなければならない
　④ 成功するために必要な時間が必ずしも賢明に使用されていない

　正解は②。ハーレーの投稿の第 2 段落第 2 文（Statistics prove that ...）に，pbl の影響で「科目ごとに分かれた国家試験で生徒は不安を覚えることを統計は証明して」いるとあるので，これと合った内容の② が正解となる。
　① は第 2 段落第 3 文（It's also expensive.）が「また（pbl は）費用も高額」であるという内容だが，「予算案との格闘」についての記述は見られないため，正解とはならない。③

— 英 R 143 —

は第2段落第1文（Cooperation among teachers ...）に「pblでは複数の科目を重なり合わせる必要がある場合も多いので，教師同士の協力が不可欠」とあるため，1人の教師が多科目に習熟することを求められるというより，多数の教師が共同してpblに当たるというのが現実の形態であると考えられるため，正解とはならない。④は第2段落第5文（And it consumes ...）の「生徒はさまざまな情報源について評価を行いますが，これは収穫の得られない場合も多いので，時間の浪費になります」に通じる内容と言えるが，「賢明に使用されていない」や「時間の浪費」というのは価値判断であり，「事実」というより「意見」であるため，やはり正解とはならない。

問3 　13　 正解①

「シャウナ・パーキンスがpblの支持となると考える1つの意見は　13　というものである」

  ① いくつかの解答となる可能性のあるものに向き合うことで，我々は問題を熱心に考えるようになると思われる

  ② それは他の学習スタイルとちょうど同等に費用が手頃である

  ③ 講義を通じての学習は，今日でも流行遅れではない

  ④ 我々はまず背景となる知識を把握しなければ問題を解決できない

　正解は①。パーキンスの投稿の第2段落第2文（They consider different ...）の，pblにおいて生徒は「さまざまな可能性を考慮し，自分たちにとって最善と思われるものを選び，したがって『正しい』解答を受け入れるのではなく，賛否両論を真剣に分析します」という記述は，複数の解答候補が存在することで問題への対処が真剣なものとなる，という考え方を示しており，①は同様の内容を「…と思われる」という「意見」として述べたものと言えるため，これが正解となる。

　②はパーキンスの投稿と特に関わりのない内容であるし，「意見」というよりは「事実」として述べられているため（「事実誤認」の可能性も高いが），正解とはならない。③は第1段落第3文（A study conducted ...）に講義による学習効率に疑問を投げかける研究結果が引用されているように，パーキンスはpblは支持，講義は不支持という立場なので，正解とはならない。④は第2段落第1文（It has been ...）の「問題に取り組むには事前に知識を備えていることが不可欠である」という内容を言い換えたものと言えるが，「意見」ではなく「事実」として述べられているため，やはり正解とはならない。

問4 　14　 正解③

「従来型の授業で生徒は自分で思うほどの量を学ばないと示したのは誰か」 　14　

  ① ジョー・ハーレー

  ② シャウナ・パーキンス

  ③ ハーバード大学である研究を行った人々

  ④ 若い教師たち

　正解は③。パーキンスの投稿の第1段落第3文（A study conducted ...）の「ハーバード大学で行われたある研究は，講義の方が学習する内容が多いと生徒は感じているにもかかわらず，実はそんなことはないことを示しました」という内容から，③が正解となる。

問5 　15　 正解③

「ジョー・ハーレーがpblに反対するのを助けるために，あなたは何を探し出そうとする可能性があるか」 　15　

  ① 過去20年の試験結果の点数

  ② 大学の研究がしばしば精密さを欠く証拠

  ③ 暗記の長所に関する科学的データ

— 英R 144 —

④　pbl に不慣れな教師の物語

　正解は③。パーキンスの投稿の第1段落第2文（Though worthwhile, memorising ...）の「暗記はあなたの考えるほど効果的ではありません」という記述からも読み取れるように，pbl と暗記学習は対立するものであり，ハーレーは暗記支持派と見なされているため，③が正解となる。

　①，②は pbl と特に関係が無いと言えるし，④も pbl に深く関わった者ならその欠点をよく理解し指摘できる場合もあろうが，不慣れな者の話はそれを肯定する材料としても否定する材料としても，十分なものとはなり得ないはずであるため，いずれも正解とはならない。

主な語句・表現	・問題冊子を参照のこと。

［リード文］
◇ come across ... 「…を（偶然）見つける」　◇ forum 图「フォーラム；公開討論」

［本文］
◇ problem-based learning「問題［課題］解決型学習」
◇ leave teachers who ... feeling overwhelmed「…である教師を当惑を感じたままにする」 leave (V) teachers (O) who ... (M) feeling overwhelmed (C) という構造で，overwhelmed は「…を圧倒［当惑］させる」という意味の他動詞の過去分詞。
◇ vital 形「きわめて重要な；不可欠な」
◇ pbl often makes it necessary to − 「pbl は−することをしばしば必要にする」 pbl (S) makes (V) it (形式 O) necessary (C) to − (真 O) という構造。
◇ have subjects overlap「科目を重なり合わせる」「have + O + 〈原形〉」で「O に−させる」という意味。overlap は，ここでは「（部分的に）重なり合う」という意味の動詞。
◇ consume 動「…を浪費［無駄遣い］する」
◇ evaluate 動「…を評価する」
◇ unproductively 副「収穫を得られずに；不毛に」
◇ regards 图「よろしく」 手紙や伝言での挨拶。
◇ prefect 图「風紀委員；監督生」 イギリスの学校で下級生の指導などを行う上級生。
◇ Though worthwhile「やる価値はあるが」 分詞構文の意味を明確化するために接続詞 though が添えられたとも（この場合 worthwhile の直前に being を補って考えることもできる），Though it [= memorising] is worthwhile という副詞節の it is が省略されたものとも考えられる。worthwhile は「（時間や労力を費やす）価値がある；やりがいがある」という意味の形容詞。
◇ previous 形「前もっての；事前の」　　　◇ pros and cons「賛否両論」

［設問文・選択肢］
◇ controversial 形「議論の的となる；物議をかもす」
◇ irrelevant 形「重要ではない；取るに足りない」
◇ struggle 動「格闘する」　　　◇ budget 图「予算（案）」
◇ familiarise oneself with ... 「…に習熟［精通］する」 familiarise はイギリス式の綴りで，アメリカ式では familiarize となる。
◇ One opinion that Shauna Perkins believes supports pbl「シャウナ・パーキンスが pbl を支持していると信じている1つの意見」 that 以下は One opinion を修飾する形容詞節で，Shauna Perkins believes (that) it [= the opinion] supports pbl.（シャウナ・パーキンスは，それが pbl を支持していると信じている）という文を元にして，it を関係代名詞 that に置き換えて先頭に出すことで出来上がったもの，と考えることができる。
◇ affordable 形「費用が手頃な；あまり金がかからない」
◇ inaccurate 形「精密さを欠く；ずさんな」

― 英 R 145 ―

第３問

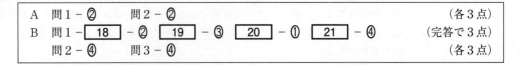

解 答
A　問１ー②　　問２ー②　　　　　　　　　　　　　　　　　　　（各３点）
B　問１ー　18　ー②　　19　ー③　　20　ー①　　21　ー④　　（完答で３点）
　　問２ー④　　問３ー④　　　　　　　　　　　　　　　　　　（各３点）

A

出典　*Original Material*

全訳
　あなたはイギリスの山頂からの眺めを見たいと思っています。バックパッカーのウェブサイトに役立つ情報が見つかりました。

> ジョージ山に登りたいのですが時間が限られています。パース駅からそこへ行く一番良い道筋を誰かご存知ですか。　　　　　　　　　　　　　　　　　　　　（ティム）

> 回答
> ケーブルカーが山頂まで行きます。鉄道の駅からケーブルカーの駅まで，無料のバスに乗ってください。人気があるのでたぶんその駅で，10分くらい待たなければならないでしょうか。いったん乗ってしまえば，ほんの３分で上に着きますけどね！
>
> タクシーにも乗れますが，10分か20分待たなければならないでしょう。ちょっと気を付けて欲しいんですが，無料バスもタクシーも大雨が降って道にいくらか水があふれると走りません。
>
> 11月から３月まで利用可能なスキーのリフトまで歩くこともできますが，でもケーブルカーの５倍遅いです。駅外の新聞の売店を過ぎると山道の入り口が見えます。ごく運が良ければ脇の川に鮭がいるのが見つかるかもしれませんよ。
>
> 　　　　　　　　　　　　　　　　　　　　　　　　　　　　　　　　　　（レジーナ）

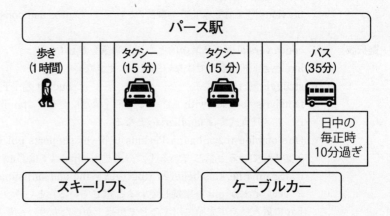

設問解説

問1 　16　 正解 ②

「レジーナの回答から　16　とわかる」

① 川には鮭があふれている
② 鉄道の駅の脇に店がある
③ その地域は嵐がよく来る
④ タクシーは前もってネットで予約できる

　正解は ②。レジーナの回答の最終段落第2文（Pass the newspaper ...）に「駅外の新聞の売店」という表現が出て来るので ② が正解となる。

　① は最終段落最終文（You might spot ...）に「ごく運が良ければ」鮭が見つかるかもしれないと書かれているので，鮭はそれほど多くはいないことになるため，③ は第2段落第2文（Just be warned, ...）に「大雨が降って道にいくらか水があふれると」という表現があるが，そのような事態になる頻度についての情報はないため，④ は同段落第1文（You can also ...）にタクシーは「10分か20分待たなければならないでしょう」とあるだけで，事前の予約が可能かどうかは不明なため，いずれも正解とはならない。

問2 　17　 正解 ②

「あなたは3月7日午前9時にパース駅に着く。天気は3日間晴れ続きである。山頂に着く最も速い道筋はどれか」　17

① バスとケーブルカー
② タクシーとケーブルカー
③ タクシーとスキーリフト
④ 徒歩とスキーリフト

　正解は ②。3月で天気が良いとなるといずれの交通手段も利用可能なはず。② は 9:00 に鉄道の駅で降りて10分から20分待ったタクシーでケーブルカーの駅に着くのは 9:25 から 9:35，そこでまた約10分待ってケーブルカーの所要時間は3分なので，9:38 から 9:48 に山頂に到着することになり，これが最も速い移動手段となるため，正解となる。

　① は 9:10 発の無料バスでケーブルカーの駅に到着するのが 9:45 なので，後の所要時間が同じ ② より速くはならないため，正解とはならない。③ はスキーリフト乗り場に着くのが ② でケーブルカーの駅に着くのと同じ 9:25 から 9:35 で，リフトは待ち時間が無いにせよケーブルカーの5倍の15分の時間をかけて，山頂に着くのは 9:40 から 9:50 になる。場合によっては ② より早く着くようにも見えるが，これはタクシーの待ち時間にその時々で幅があるためで，本問のような設定ではタクシーに乗る時刻が同じ場合の比較になるので，常に ③ は ② より遅くなるはずであるため正解とはならない。④ はスキーリフトの乗り場に着くのが 10:00 であるから，③ との比較で常に遅いことになるので，やはり正解とはならない。

主な語句・表現

・問題冊子を参照のこと。

［本文］

◇ backpacker 图「バックパッカー」　荷物を背負って低予算で旅行をする人。
◇ go up ...「…を登る」　この場合の up は「…を上方へ」という意味の前置詞。
◇ coach 图「バス」　　　　　　　　　◇ I'd say ...「まず…；…だろうか」
◇ just be warned, ...「一応警告しますが…；…なのでちょっと気を付けて」
◇ flood 動「…を水浸しにする」　　　　◇ pass 動「…のそばを通り過ぎる」
◇ mountain trail「山道」
◇ every ten minutes past the hour「毎正時10分過ぎ」　9時10分，10時10分などのこと。

［設問文・選択肢］

◇ book 動「…を予約する」　　　　　　◇ online 副「インターネット上で」
◇ in advance「前もって」

— 英 R 147 —

B

出典｜*Original Material*

全訳｜　あなたは，友人の１人が貸してくれた雑誌の中に，成功に関する以下の記事を見つけました。

ぼろから富へ
サリー・エリス

　ハワード・シュルツについてあなたは聞いたことがないかもしれないが，彼が変革した会社のことはおそらく知っているだろう。1953 年にニューヨークの貧しい家庭に生まれた彼の人生における第一の目標は成功してより明るい未来を築くことであり，彼は良い成績を収めようと学校で奮闘した。

　シュルツは後にスポーツの天才であると判明し，またその能力ゆえに大学では学費免除を受けた。卒業後シュルツは，他の会社と並んでコーヒーメーカーを扱う小さな会社でも販売業務を行い，そこで急速に昇進した。最終的に彼は，シアトルにいくつか店舗のあるコーヒー豆の会社の広告部長になった。この小さなチェーン店の名前はと言えば，スターバックスだった。

　イタリア旅行に行った際，シュルツは当地のカフェ文化に感銘を受け，人々が居心地良く集まっておしゃべりできる喫茶店を開くようスターバックスに提案した。着想が組織に合わないのではないかと最高経営者たちが疑うときでさえ，彼らはスタッフにその実行を許可する場合があった。そしてアメリカの大衆はシュルツの着想が大いに気に入ったのである。彼はそれからスターバックスから離れては戻ることを二度行い，最終的には企業の頭取となってそれをアメリカ合衆国中に広め，さらには 2012 年までに 39 ヵ国へと出店した。皮肉にも，隣接するスターバックスの店舗が互いに競合し閉店する場合もあった。ほどなくシュルツは，アメリカでトップの金持ちの１人としてフォーブズ誌に載った。

　シュルツは自分の会社のトップに上りつめて以来，持てる力のすべてを良い方向へと使ってきた。そしてよく知られているようにかつてある投資家を同性婚に反対していることについて批判し，その投資家に自分の金を別の会社を後援するために使うよう提案さえした。彼は職場で決して嘘をつかないことに対して賞を与えられ，公正な商慣習に関する講座を教えるようあるアメリカの大学に招かれた。彼は環境に優しい実業界という理念を支持しており，石油やガスへの課税がより厳しくなるよう望んでいる。

設問解説｜

問１　☐ 18 ☐　正解 ②，　☐ 19 ☐　正解 ③，　☐ 20 ☐　正解 ①，　☐ 21 ☐　正解 ④

「以下の出来事（①～④）を起きた順に並べよ」

① シュルツはスターバックスの頭取になった。
② シュルツはスターバックスへの新たなビジネス形態の導入を提案した。
③ シュルツはスターバックスで働くのをやめた。
④ シュルツは自分の影響力を建設的に使い始めた。

第３段落第１文（On an Italian …）にあるように「喫茶店を開くよう提案」した後，同段落第３文（He then left …）にあるように「スターバックスから離れては戻ることを二度行い」，さらに同文にあるように「最終的には企業の頭取」となってそれ以来，最終段落第１文（Schultz has used …）にあるように「持てる力のすべてを良い方向に使ってきた」

— 英 R 148 —

のであるから，それぞれに対応する②，③，①，④が，それぞれ 18 ， 19 ， 20 ， 21 に対する正解となる。

問2 　 22 　 正解④

「シュルツの人生についてわかっている1つの**事実**は，彼が 22 ということである」

① 学校で絶えず面倒を引き起こした
② 伝統的なアメリカの慣習を好んだ
③ 高価なエネルギー源を使用した
④ **アメリカで最も富裕な人々のうちの1人だった**

　正解は④。第3段落最終文（Soon after, Schultz ...）に「シュルツはアメリカでトップの金持ちの1人としてフォーブズ誌に載った」という記述が見られるので，④が正解。

　他の選択肢はいずれも，本文に書かれていない内容。

問3 　 23 　 正解④

「この話から，スターバックスは 23 ということがわかった」

① 貧しい暮らしの人にとって利用しやすい，安く利用できる店として始まった
② 早い時期に相当の難題に直面し，廃業しかなかった
③ 国際的なチェーン店を作り上げるために，自ら世界中のレストランからアイディアを集めた
④ **従業員の提案に耳を傾け，新しいことを試すことを厭わなかった**

　正解は④。第3段落第2文（Even when the ...）に「着想が組織に合わないのではないかと最高経営者が疑うときでさえ，彼ら［＝スターバックスの最高経営者たち］はスタッフにその実行を許可する場合があった」とあるため，④が正解。

　他の選択肢はいずれも，本文に書かれていない内容。

[主な語句・表現]
・問題冊子を参照のこと。

[本文]
◇ rag 名「ぼろ（きれ）」　　　　　　　　　◇ riches 名「富；財産」　通例複数扱いされる。
◇ most likely「たぶん；十中八九」
◇ Born into ...「…に生まれて」　分詞構文。意味上の主語である he［＝ Howard Schultz］が文の主語である his number one goal in life と一致していない点で厳密に言えば文法から外れているが，現実の英語ではそう珍しいことではない。
◇ natural 名「生来の達人；天才」　　　　　◇ free place「授業料免除の学籍」
◇ coffee-maker 名「コーヒーメーカー」　ここでは形容詞的に company を修飾している。
◇ socialize 動「うち解けて［社交的に］交際［おしゃべり］する」
◇ incorporate 動「…を組み入れる」　　　　◇ soon after「すぐ後に」
◇ list 動「…を名簿に載せる」
◇ Forbes Magazine「フォーブズ誌」　アメリカの経済雑誌。
◇ famously 副「よく知られているように」　◇ criticize O for ...「O を…のことで批判する」
◇ gay marriage「同性愛［間］結婚」
◇ even suggesting ...「…と提案しさえして」　分詞構文。
◇ boost 動「…を後援［宣伝］する」　　　　◇ business practice「商慣習」
◇ concept 名「概念；（基本）理念」　　　　◇ harshly 副「厳しく」

[設問文・選択肢]
◇ constructively 副「建設的に」
◇ accessible to ...「…にとって利用［入手］しやすい」
◇ in poverty「貧困のうちに」　　　　　　　◇ early on「早い時期［段階］に」
◇ go out of business「廃業する」

— 英 R 149 —

第4問

解答

問1 - ③	問2 - ④	問3 - ③	問4 - ②	（各3点）
問5 [28] - ①	[29] - ④			（各2点）

出典 *Original Material*

全訳

あなたには大学の交換留学生であるアメリカ人の友人がいます。彼女は部屋を探しており，2つの異なる不動産会社が出している，留学生に部屋を紹介する2つの記事を見つけました。あなたは彼女と一緒にその記事を読んでいます。

アパートをお探しですか？
AP不動産

　X大学の近くに1人暮らしする所を探している留学生向けの賃貸アパートを2つ紹介します。

　アパートAは築40年，鉄筋コンクリート造りで，部屋の広さは18㎡です。家賃は50,000円，管理費は5,000円，月々の支払いを保証する保険（保証委託料）が1,000円で，合計で月額56,000円になります。

　Bは築45年の木造アパートで，部屋の広さは15㎡です。月々，家賃が40,000円，管理費が2,000円，保証委託料が1,000円になります。

　どちらの部屋も状態が良く，キッチン，トイレ，風呂が完備です。どちらのアパートも大家への初期費用として，玄関の鍵を新しいものに交換するのに20,000円がかかります。敷金や，お客様との契約に同意する際に大家に支払う手数料である礼金は不要です。

シェアハウスはいかがですか？
SH不動産

　住む所を探している交換留学生に，シェアハウスをお勧めします。

　シェアハウスCは築10年で，X大学のすぐ近くにあります。高さ3階建ての鉄筋コンクリート造りです。各階に，リビングルームと8㎡の広さのプライベートベッドルームが3つあります。リビングルームとキッチンは共用スペース，風呂とトイレも共同使用です。ベッドルームのドアはロックできるので，プライバシーは守られます。月々，家賃25,000円，管理費15,000円となります。保証委託料は年間9,600円なので，月額では800円になります。その他の費用はありません。このシェアハウスにはX大学に通う多くの留学生が住んでいるので，共用スペースは国際交流の場として最適です。

　シェアハウスDは築9年で，建物の構造はCとほぼ同じです。大学からは少し離れていますが，駅まで徒歩5分圏内です。この物件は，プライベートスペースである各部屋の床面積が10㎡とやや広いので，月額賃料は30,000円になります。それ以外はシェアハウスCと同じ料金になります。

— 英R 150 —

設問解説

問1 | 24 | 正解③

「アパートAとBの部屋は | 24 | が同じである」

① 建築構造
② 床面積
③ 月額保険金
④ 月額管理費

正解は③。③の monthly insurance money とは，AP不動産の記事の第2段落にある the insurance to guarantee the monthly payment「月々の支払いを保証する保険（保証委託料）」を言い換えたものであり，アパートA，Bともに月額1,000円とあるので，これが正解。

①の建築構造は，Aが鉄筋コンクリートでBが木造，②の床面積は，Aが18㎡でBが15㎡，④の月額管理費は，Aが5,000円でBが2,000円となり，それぞれ異なるので誤り。

問2 | 25 | 正解④

「あなたの友人がアパートBに住みたい場合，家賃を含めた初期費用として | 25 | を支払う必要がある」

① 42,000円
② 43,000円
③ 54,000円
④ 63,000円

正解は④。アパートBの月々の支払いは家賃40,000円，管理費2,000円，保証委託料1,000円であるが，初期費用には鍵を新しいものに交換するための20,000円が必要となる。したがって，合計金額は63,000円となる。

問3 | 26 | 正解③

「シェアハウスCに住む利点の1つは，| 26 | ことだ」

① 管理費がアパートAまたはBよりも少ない
② 友人がお金を余分に払えば，部屋のドアの新しい鍵が手に入る
③ 友人が他国出身の友人を作れる可能性が高くなる
④ 友人にはアパートAやBに住むよりも大きなキッチンがある

正解は③。SH不動産の記事の第2段落最終文（As there are ...）に，シェアハウスCには多くの留学生が住んでいることや，共用スペースで国際交流する機会があることが紹介されている。これは他の部屋にはない特長なので，シェアハウスCの利点と言える。

①の管理費については，AP不動産の記事によるとアパートAが5,000円，Bが2,000円とあるので，シェアハウスCの管理費15,000円の方が少ないというのは誤り。②の新しい鍵については，AP不動産の記事第4段落第2文（Both apartment owners ...）にアパートに関する情報として記されているが，シェアハウスについては記述がない。④については，アパートやシェアハウスのキッチンの大きさに関する情報が本文中にないので，これを正しいと考える根拠はない。したがっていずれもシェアハウスCの利点とは考えられず，誤りである。

問4 | 27 | 正解②

「あなたの友人の毎月の予算が，2ヵ月目以降は45,000円未満ならば，彼女は | 27 | に住むことができる」

① アパートAとアパートB
② アパートBとシェアハウスC
③ アパートB，シェアハウスC，シェアハウスD

④　アパートBのみ

　　正解は②。アパートA，Bのドア鍵交換費用20,000円は初期費用なので，2ヵ月目以降に支払う月額費用には含まれないことに注意する。アパートAは月額56,000円とあり，アパートBは（家賃40,000円＋管理費2,000円＋保証委託料1,000円＝）月額43,000円。シェアハウスCは（家賃25,000円＋管理費15,000円＋1ヵ月あたりの保証委託料800円＝）月額40,800円。シェアハウスDは（家賃30,000円＋管理費15,000円＋1ヵ月あたりの保証委託料800円＝）月額45,800円。BとCならば45,000円の予算内で支払えるので，正解は②。

問5　　28　　正解①　　　29　　正解④

　　「あなたの友人が，コンクリート造りの建物で，自分専用のキッチン，トイレ，風呂がある場所に住みたいならば，彼女の選択は　28　となる。もし電車をかなり頻繁に使うつもりなら　29　を選択するとよい。（それぞれの空所に，選択肢①〜④の中から最も適切なものを1つずつ選べ。）」

　　①　アパートA
　　②　アパートB
　　③　シェアハウスC
　　④　シェアハウスD

　　アパートBを除くA，C，Dはコンクリート建築であるが，このうちシェアハウスではキッチン，トイレ，風呂は共用とされているので，　28　にはアパートAが入ることとなり，正解は①。

　　SH不動産の記事第3段落第2文（It is located ...）に，シェアハウスDは駅に近い物件であることが紹介されている。他の部屋の紹介では電車や駅の利便性について言及されていないことから，電車を頻繁に使うならばシェアハウスDが便利だと考えられるので，　29　には④が入る。

主な語句・表現
・問題冊子を参照のこと。

[リード文]　◇real estate company「不動産会社」

[AP不動産]　◇reinforce 動「…を強化する」　　　　　◇reinforced concrete「鉄筋コンクリート」
　　　　　　◇insurance 名「保険」
　　　　　　◇the insurance to guarantee the monthly payment「月々の支払いを保証するための保険」
　　　　　　　家賃等の支払いを保証する保証人を立てる代わりに加入する，いわゆる「保証委託料」のこと。
　　　　　　◇initial 形「最初の」　　　　　　　　　◇deposit 名「敷金；預金」
　　　　　　◇key money「礼金」　　　　　　　　　◇contract 名「契約」

[SH不動産]　◇recommend 動「…を推薦する」　　　　◇three stories high「3階建て」
　　　　　　◇is located (...) within a 5-minute walk of 〜「〜まで徒歩5分圏内に位置する」
　　　　　　◇with each room being 10㎡「それぞれの部屋が10㎡という状態で」 付帯状況を表すwithの表現。

— 英R 152 —

第５問

解答

問１－②　　問２－②　　　　　　　　　　　　　　　　　　　　（各３点）

問３－ 32 －③　 33 －④　 34 －⑤　 35 －②　　（完答で３点）

問４－①・③　　　　　　　　　　　　　（順不同・両方正解で３点）

問５－③　　　　　　　　　　　　　　　　　　　　　　　　（３点）

出典　*Original Material*

全訳

　あなたは大きな困難にもかかわらず偉大な事柄を達成したことについてあなたが讃嘆している人物について発表を行おうとしています。あなたが選んだ人物に関する以下の文章を読んで，発表用のスライドを完成させなさい。

　ケニアは何人かの感嘆すべきランナーを輩出している。テグラ・ロルーペは 1973 年にケニアの農村に生まれ，歩き始めるのとほぼ同時に 24 人の兄弟姉妹と同様にウシの世話をしに働きに出された。7 歳で毎日靴も履かずに学校までの 10 キロの行程を走るようになった。彼女が自分の走る潜在能力に気づいたのは学校でしばしば年上の子供相手にレースに勝ったときのことで，このことで彼女には卓越した運動選手になる野望，母親だけが支えとなってくれる夢が芽生えた。21 歳の時に彼女はアフリカ人の女性として初めてニューヨーク・マラソンで優勝し，アフリカ大陸全体の役割モデルとなった。

　そのいらつくことのない性格を指して Chametia というニックネームがつけられたテグラは，数知れぬ障害に直面しては克服した。彼女の父親がランニングはまともな女性のすることではないと言い張り彼女にやめるよう要求したばかりでなく，最初にケニア陸上連盟の目に留まったときには，虚弱過ぎて特別な存在にはなれないと判断された。彼女は否定的な批判に耳を貸すことや諦めることを拒んだ。そして 1988 年に有名な長距離レースに勝ち，ケニアのスポーツ当局者はようやく注目するようになった。1 年後，彼女は初めてのランニング・シューズを受け取ったが，可能な場合はそれをはかずに競争することを好んだ。

　テグラはますます成功をおさめ，いくつもの距離でライバルに勝ったばかりか，いくつもの世界記録を破った。2000 年のオーストラリアのシドニー・オリンピックのマラソンでは，彼女は金メダル候補の大本命だったが，何か食べ物にあたって前夜に非常な吐き気を覚えた。しかし，その後でさえ彼女は棄権することを拒み，酷い体調にもかかわらずレースで 13 位に入った。彼女の動機づけは，と言えばアフリカの彼女の支持者全てに対する義務感であった。1998 年から 2001 年まで彼女はフルマラソンの女性の世界記録を保持し，1999 年にはドイツで自身の記録を破ったが，この 3 年の期間のうちの多くは健康状態が悪かったのだった。

　テグラはいまやプロスポーツから引退しているが，世界規模の慈善団体オックスファムの代表者は彼女の人道的働きを「目覚ましい」と評している。2011 年には，4 ヵ国にまたがる多くの交戦中の共同体出身の生徒のために開校した学校であるテグラ・ロルーペ・ピース・アンド・リーダーシップ・センターに出資しその創設に助力した。彼女の目的は根深い否定的な感情を消し去り，貧困に陥った子供，とりわけ，良い機会をしばしば逃す少女たちにきちんとした教育を提供することである。彼女自身は父親に公然と反抗して兄弟と共に学校へ通ったわけだが，彼女と生い立ちを共にする多くの者が学校教育は男性の享受する贅沢だと信じているのである。

　実は，彼女が頭角を現すことは決してできないだろうという意見をケニア陸上連盟

― 英 R 153 ―

が表明したとき，テグラは純粋に人生を神に捧げることを考えた。彼女は身の回りの男性の態度に嫌気がさしており，教会のために働くこと，他の女性たちと質素に暮らすことが魅力的に思えたのである。幸運にも，彼女に対してやる気を削ぐ態度を取る者たちのことを間違っていると証明したいという彼女の意欲が強かった。男女は皆平等に扱われるべき人類であることに社会はゆるやかに気づきつつあるが，彼女は女性が重要視されることは男性と比べて依然として難しい場合があると気づいており，それがまだなお苦しい戦いであるのはなぜなのか釈然とせずにいるのである。

　女性の権利はテグラが擁護する唯一の大義というわけではない。いくつかの敵対する人種が住む地域の部族の出身であるため，テグラは常に自分の名声を紛争終結のために用いることを夢見てきた。彼女は年に一度の10キロのピース・レースを2006年に創設し，第1回には6つの敵対する共同体に属する2,000人の選手が，友好的に競うために集まった。さらには，同年に国際連合は彼女をスポーツ大使に指名した。戦闘中の部族にただ「やめるように」と言う代わりに，彼女は戦闘のない未来への確信を提供している。彼女が2003年に始めたテグラ・ロルーペ平和財団は生活を変え続けている。永遠の仲裁者たる，ドイツを本拠地とするテグラは，「彼女のキャリアを破壊しかけた」と自ら称する自分の父親をわが友と呼んでいるが，よくぞ彼の言うことに決して耳を傾けなかったものだ，と冗談で言うのである。

発表スライド

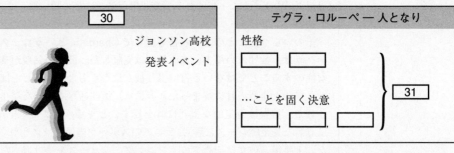

設問解説 問1 　30　 正解②

「あなたの発表に対する最良のタイトルはどれか」 　30

　① 男性中心社会？　いや平等な社会。

　② 自分を信じろ。変化を現実に！

　③ 行動で闘争に終結を！　言葉だけでは不十分。

　④ 女性？　貧困？　病気？　言い訳するのはやめなさい！

　正解は②。本文に描かれたテグラの行動は，性による不平等を解消したり闘争を終結させたりするために信念を貫き困難に立ち向かい続ける，という点で一貫している。これに合う②が正解となる。

　①，③は，テグラが「男性中心の社会」を否定し少しでも「男女平等」に近づこうと行動を取ったことも，彼女が闘争を終結させるために尽力したことも確かだが，その2つのうちのいずれか一方に当てはまる内容だけでは発表全体のタイトルとしては相応（ふさわ）しくないため，④は言い訳する態度を否定するような彼女の言動はまったく登場しないため，いずれも不正解となる。

問2 　31　 正解②

「どれが『テグラ・ロルーペ ― 人となり』というスライドのための最良の組み合わせか」
　31

	性格	…ことを固く決意
①	怒り，勤勉	有名になる，貧しい子供を助ける，部族の闘争を終えさせる
②	**冷静，勤勉**	**傑出した運動選手になる，貧しい子供を助ける，部族の闘争を終えさせる**
③	不注意，友好的	有名になる，部族の闘争を終えさせる，信仰生活を送る
④	内気，友好的	傑出した運動選手になる，貧しい子供を助ける，信仰生活を送る

　「性格」に関しては，第2段落第1文（Nicknamed 'Chametia,' a ...）に見られる「いらつくことのない性格」という表現があるように，世の不平等や闘争を止めるべく行動はするが，「怒り」を原動力にするというより「冷静」に理想の実現を図るタイプであることが窺（うかが）える。もちろん同文に「数知れぬ障害に直面しては克服した」とあるように粘り強く行動し続ける勤勉さも持ち合わせていた。これに対して，「不注意」，「内気」を思わせる描写はまったくなく，これほど積極的な行動力を持つ人物が「友好的」でないとは考え難いが，そうであったことを特に窺わせる記述もない。

　「固く決意」した内容については，第1段落第3文（Aged seven, she ...）に「彼女には卓越した運動選手になる野望が芽生えた」とあり，その後数多くの困難にもかかわらずその野望を実現していく様が描かれているので「傑出した運動選手になる」は適切であると言える。また第4段落第2文（In 2011 she ...）に書かれているテグラ・ロルーペ・ピース・アンド・リーダーシップ・センター創設への出資など「貧しい子供を助ける」ために尽力しているし，最終段落第3文（She established the ...）に書かれたピース・レースの創設は「部族の闘争を終えさせる」ことを目的としたものである。これに対して「有名になる」ことを固く決意していたことを思わせる記述は見られず，むしろ彼女の行動の結果として名声がもたらされたものと考えられるし，「信仰生活を送る」ことに一時魅力を感じたことは第5段落第1文（In fact, when ...），第2文（She was sick ...）に書かれているが，同段落第3文（Luckily, her drive ...）にあるように，俗世にあって敵対する者たちの誤りを証明する道を選んだのだからさほど固い決意があったわけではないと判断できる。

　以上より，すべてが正しい要素からなる②が正解となる。

問3 　32　 正解 ③, 　33　 正解 ④, 　34　 正解 ⑤, 　35　 正解 ②

「『テグラの人生』の年表を完成するために，出来事を起きた順に選べ」

① オリンピックで酷く負傷した
② 困窮する子供のために学校を建てた
③ スポーツをやめて宗教に専念することを考えた
④ 友情を促進するため組織を創設した
⑤ 敵対する部族の闘争をやめさせるためスポーツを利用した

①のような記述は本文中に見当たらない。

②については，第4段落第2文（In 2011 she ...）に 2011 年に困窮した子供のためにテグラ・ロルーペ・ピース・アンド・リーダーシップ・センター創設に助力したことが書かれている。

③については，第2段落第2文（Not only did ...）に，ケニア陸上連盟に「虚弱過ぎて特別な存在にはなれないと判断された」とあり，続く同段落第3文（She refused to ...）にその後 1988 年に「ケニアのスポーツ当局者はようやく注目するようになった」ことが書かれている。そして第5段落第1文（In fact, when ...）には「彼女が頭角を現すことは決してできないだろうという意見をケニア陸上連盟が表明したとき，テグラは純粋に人生を神に捧げることを考えた」とある。したがって，この③は 1988 年以前のことであるとわかる。

④については，最終段落第6文（The Tegla Loroupe ...）に紛争終結を目指す彼女の活動の一環として 2003 年にテグラ・ロルーペ平和財団を創設したことが書かれている。

⑤については最終段落第3文（She established the ...）に敵対する部族を平和的に競わせるピース・レースを 2006 年に創設したことが書かれている。

以上より空所にはそれぞれ，　32　に③，　33　に④，　34　に⑤，　35　に②を入れるのが正解となる。

問4 　36　・　37　 正解 ①・③

「『テグラの行動の影響』のスライドに対する2つの最良の項目を選べ（順番は問わない。）」 　36　・　37　

① 教育を受け始める少女が増えた。
② 体の弱いティーンエイジャーがより懸命に努力した。
③ 国連がテグラの努力を認めた。
④ 考え方が急速により現代的になった。
⑤ 幼い子供が大人の考えに異議を唱えるようになった。

正解は①・③。第4段落第3文（Her objective is ...）にあるように彼女が創設に尽力したテグラ・ロルーペ・ピース・アンド・リーダーシップ・センターは「貧困に陥った子供，とりわけ，良い機会をしばしば逃す少女たちにきちんとした教育を提供する」学校であるから，①は正解となる。また，最終段落第4文（Furthermore, the United ...）に国際連合が彼女をスポーツ大使に指名したことが書かれているため，③も正解となる。

他の選択肢②，④，⑤は，いずれもテグラの行動によって引き起こされてもおかしくはない事態と言えるが，本文中に言及がないので正解とはならない。

問5 　38　 正解 ③

「最も適切な項目で『なぜテグラは決して諦めなかったか？』のスライドを完成させよ」 　38　

① 彼女は世界記録を破ることを夢見ていた。
② 彼女は故郷での自身の安全を案じていた。
③ 彼女は自分に才能があるとわかっていた。

— 英 R 156 —

④　彼女は農場の生活から逃れたかった。

　正解は③。第1段落第3文（Aged seven, she ...）に，テグラが学校で年上の子供にレースで勝って自分の能力に気づき，運動選手として大成する野望を持つようになったことが書かれているので，③は彼女が努力を続ける原動力になっていたと考えられるため，これが正解となる。

　①，②，④は本文中に特に書かれていない内容であり，正解とならない。

主な語句・表現

・問題冊子を参照のこと。

[リード文]

◇ a person you admire for achieving ...「…を達成したことについてあなたが讃嘆する人物」you admire for achieving ... は形容詞節として a person を修飾しており，直前に関係代名詞の who などを補うことができる。admire O for ... で「…について O を讃嘆する」の意味で，補った場合の関係代名詞 who はこの O として働いている。

[第1段落]
(Kenya has ...)

◇ put O to work「O を働かせる」

◇ looking after cows「ウシの世話をして」 work を修飾する分詞構文。

◇ Aged seven「7歳の時に」 分詞構文。aged ... で「…歳で［の］」という意味。

◇ it was at school, often winning races against older kids, that she realized her running potential「彼女が自分のランニングの潜在能力に気づいたのは，学校でしばしば年上の子供にレースで勝つときであった」 副詞句の at school と分詞構文の often winning races against older kids が強調された強調構文。

◇ accomplished 形「秀でた；鍛え上げた」

◇ a dream her mother alone supported her in「彼女の母親だけが彼女を支持した夢」 her mother alone supported her in は a dream を修飾する形容詞節で，直前に関係代名詞の which または that を補うことができる。Her mother alone supported her in the dream. という文が元になったものと考えることができる。

◇ role model「役割モデル；模範人物」

◇ across 副「…の端から端まで（の）；…中に［の］」

[第2段落]
(Nicknamed 'Chametia,' ...)

◇ Nicknamed 'Chametia,' a reference to ...「…のことを指して言う Chametia というニックネームをつけられて」 分詞構文。'Chametia' と a reference to ... は同格の関係。reference to ... は「…への言及；…のことに触れること」という意味。

◇ relaxed 形「くつろいだ；あくせくしない」

◇ Not only did her father insist ...「彼女の父親が…と主張したばかりか」 not only A but (also) B（A ばかりでなく B も）の A が節の場合，その SV の要素は疑問文の語順に倒置される。 **(例)** *Not only are they* married *but also* they have children.「彼らは結婚しているばかりでなく，子供もいる」

◇ unladylike 形「淑女らしくない」

◇ did ... demand she quit「…彼女がやめるよう要求した」 demand (that) ... の ... では動詞は「(should +) 原形」の形を取る。

◇ when first spotted by the Kenyan Athletics Federation「最初にケニア陸上連盟の目に留まったときに」 spotted を中心とする分詞構文の意味を明確化するために接続詞 when が添えられたとも，when she was first spotted by ... という副詞節の she was が省略されたものとも考えられる。

◇ official 名「政府高官；当局者」　　　◇ take notice「注目する」

[第3段落]
(Tegla became ...)

◇ favorite 名「優勝候補；本命」

◇ drop out「（競技などへの）参加を取り止める」

— 英R 157 —

| [第4段落] | ◇ retired 形「引退した」 | ◇ spokesperson 图「代弁者；代表者」 |

[第4段落]
(Tegla is now ...)

◇ retired 形「引退した」　　　　　　　◇ spokesperson 图「代弁者；代表者」
◇ the worldwide charity Oxfam「世界規模の慈善団体であるオックスファム」 the worldwide charity と Oxfam は同格の関係。イギリスのオックスフォードで 1942 年に発足した貧困者救済機関。
◇ humanitarian 形「人道主義の」
◇ she invested in and helped found ...「彼女は…に投資しその創設を助けた」 invested in と helped found が and でつながれており, in と found の共通の目的語が ... となっている。
◇ a school set up for ...「…のために設立された学校」 直前のカンマで隔てられた Tegla Loroupe Peace and Leadership Centre と同格の関係。set ... up / set up ...（…を設立する）は他動詞相当で, その過去分詞である set up が a school を修飾している。
◇ warring 形「交戦中の」　　　　　　　◇ decent 形「きちんとした；恥ずかしくない」
◇ impoverished 形「貧困に陥った；貧窮化した」
◇ defy 動「…に（公然と）反抗［抵抗］する」
◇ miss out「良い機会を逃す」
◇ many from her background believing ...「彼女の生い立ちの多くの者は…と信じている」主節とセミコロンで隔てられた独立分詞構文。many はここでは many people の意味。

[第5段落]
(In fact, when ...)

◇ made clear their opinion that ...「…という意見を明らかにした」 made (V) clear (C) their opinion (O) の後に their opinion と同格関係の名詞節 that ... が置かれている。
◇ stand out「際立つ；卓越する」　　　　◇ genuinely 副「純粋に；心から」
◇ sick of ...「…にうんざりして；…が嫌になって」
◇ live simply「質素に暮らす」
◇ drive to −「−しようとする動因；−したいという意欲」
◇ prove those people ... wrong「…な人々は間違っていると証明する」 prove (V) those people ... (O) wrong (C) という構造。
◇ discouraging 形「やる気［張り合い］をなくさせるような」
◇ take O seriously「O を真剣に受け止める；O を重要と思う」
◇ struggle 图「苦闘」

[最終段落]
(Women's rights ...)

◇ cause 图「大義；大目的」　　　　　　◇ advocate 動「…を擁護［支持］する」
◇ Coming from ...「…の出身であり」 分詞構文。
◇ dispute 图「紛争」　　　　　　　　　◇ nominate 動「…を指名［推薦］する」
◇ peacemaker 图「仲裁人；調停者」
◇ ...-based 形「…に基礎を置いた；…を本拠地にした」（例）a Hamamatsu-based company「浜松に本社を置く会社」
◇ be grateful (that) ...「…ということを有難く［嬉しく］思う」

[スライド]

◇ determined to −「−しようと固く決意して」
◇ struggle on「苦闘し［頑張り］続ける」
◇ get along「仲良くやっていく；折り合っていく」

[設問文・選択肢]

◇ male-oriented 形「男性中心［本位］の」　◇ outstanding 形「傑出［卓越］した」
◇ injure oneself「怪我をする；負傷する」　◇ in need「困窮している」
◇ focus on ...「…に精神を集中させる」
◇ stop O (from) −ing「O が−するのをやめさせる［妨げる］」
◇ the UN「国際連合」 the United Nations の略。
◇ fear for ...「…について心配する；…を案じる」

— 英 R 158 —

第6問

解答				
A	問1 − ④	問2 − ①	問3 − ②	問4 − ①	(各3点)
B	問1 − ④	問2 − ③	問3 − ②		(各3点)
	問4 − ②・④				(順不同・両方正解で3点)

A

出典 *Original Material*

全訳

あなたは，自然災害とそれがある地域に与える影響に関する地理学の課題に取り組んでいて以下の記事を見つけました。あなたはそれを読み，発見したことをクラスメートに発表するためにポスターを作っています。

増加する自然災害 ― 総括的展望

地震，火山の噴火，台風，洪水，旱魃（かんばつ）といった自然災害の数は増加している。天候の顕著な変化は1960年代に始まり，1990年と比較してこうした災害は現在では35%増加している。赤十字は，10のうち8つを上回る災害は気候との関連が確認できるとしている。2020年に出版されたその「世界災害報告」では，とりわけ極度の高温と暴風雨が何千という人々に死をもたらしたと述べられている。

今世紀初頭以来，オーストラリアの各地が継続的な旱魃に苦しんできた。猛烈な高温と降雨不足により青果類の収穫が壊滅し，動物も命を落とした。2019年から2020年にかけての森林火災シーズンは記録上最悪のものに数えられ，多くの人々が全焼する前に自宅を見限ることを余儀なくさせられた。科学者たちは驚きを見せることなく，オゾン層破壊に関する予想に基づく仮説は間違っていなかったと述べている。

居住地もまた重大な意味を持つ。海岸近くに住む人々がかつてなく増えているのである。火山の斜面や河川系近くの肥沃な土地は，農業に恩恵をもたらす。同様に，大洋に近い地域には評価の定まった企業が多いため，求職者が惹きつけられる。海岸の都市は海外への交通の便の良さを利用してきたし，外国との貿易や取引から潤沢な利益を上げている。

比較的新しい用語として，『気候移住者』というものがある。人々はかつて，主に戦争や自らの信条への差別，その他の苦難から逃れるために祖国を離れた。疫病がジャガイモの収穫をほぼ全滅させた後で，1845年から1849年までに50万人がアイルランドを後にして合衆国に向かった。人々が故郷を捨てる当初からの理由は依然として存在しているが，今日においては，2世紀前のアイルランドにおけるのとちょうど同じく，残念ながら自分たちの生存にとって不適となってしまった故郷から，人々がひたすら逃れようとしている場合がはるかに多くなっている。

最初に姿を消す国は，数多くの島からなる太平洋の国家キリバスになるかもしれない。大洋に飲み込まれようとしており，陸地が急速に水面下へと消えようとしているのである。1999年には2つの無人島が完全に沈み込んだ。2100年までには全国土が水面下に沈む，という不可避の事態に備えて，キリバスの大統領は，住民を移住させる目的でフィジーから島を1つ買うに及んだ。海岸の浸食を減少させるべく厳しく法を施行するなどの手段を講じてはいるが，政府は既に国民の移住を奨励し始めているのである。

他の地域では，国際的移住は危険で違法な移動となる可能性が高い場合も多く，専門家でさえも目的地に到着して得るのは低賃金の職のみという場合がある。もちろん，地球温暖化現象を逆転させるには数十年もかかるだろうし，気象が原因の自然災害による難民は法による保護を与えられて然（しか）るべきである，と専門家は考えている。あるニューヨークの政治家は，国籍やアメリカ合衆国に住む理由の如何に関わらずあらゆる人に，健康上のまた経済的な援助を与える抱擁法を提案した。自然災害の数が近いうちに減少する見込みは少なく，政府は犠牲者救済の必要を理解すべきである。

自然災害と気候

事実
・天候の変化は 1960 年代に最初に目に留まった。
・1990 年と比べ現在は 35% 多くの自然災害がある。
・自然災害の 80% が気候と関連する可能性がある。

今世紀のオーストラリアの気候災害

何？		影響
・ 39 ・少な過ぎる降雨	➡	・ 40 ・命を落とす動物 ・大森林火災 ・自宅を後にする人々

今日なぜ海岸近くに住んでいる人が増えているのか ⇨

・土地が農業に適している
・ 41
・国際貿易に都合が良い

移住する理由

伝統的なもの		新たなもの
・戦争 ・信念 ・その他の苦難	⇨	・気候

島国キリバス	他の地域の移民が直面しがちな問題
国民は政府に移住を促されている	・ 42 ・技術に見合った職が得られない

設問解説

問1　 39 　正解④

「ポスターの 39 に最適な選択肢を選べ」

① 地震
② 大気質の悪さ
③ 暴風雨と台風
④ 高過ぎる気温

正解は④。問われているのは「少な過ぎる降雨」と並ぶ「今世紀のオーストラリアの気候災害」の内容である。第2段落（Since the beginning ...）に今世紀初頭以来のオーストラリアの旱魃の惨状が述べられており，その原因として第2文（Intense heat and ...）に挙げられているのは「猛烈な高温」と「降雨不足 [≒少な過ぎる降雨]」であることから，選択肢のうち「猛烈な高温」に対応する④の「高過ぎる気温」が正解となる。

問2　40　正解①

「ポスターの　40　に最適な選択肢を選べ」

① 壊滅しつつある農業
② 数が増えつつある砂漠
③ 地球の大気に対する急速な被害
④ 不十分な飲み水

正解は①。第2段落に挙げられている今世紀のオーストラリアの気候災害による影響のうち，第2文（Intense heat and ...）に挙げられている「青果類の収穫が壊滅」したことに対応する情報が現状ではポスターに含まれていないので，これにあたる①が正解となる。
その他の選択肢の内容は本文中に見られない。

問3　41　正解②

「ポスターの　41　に最適な選択肢を選べ」

① 周囲の島への交通の便が良い
② そこに多くの組織のオフィスがある
③ 移住する人々は船で移動する傾向がある
④ 水によって作られる電力がありふれている

正解は②。空所に入るのは「今日なぜ海岸近くに住んでいる人が増えているのか」という理由の1つであり，第3段落（Location is also ...）に挙げられているうちで，第4文（Similarly, communities near ...）の「評価の定まった企業が多い」に対応する情報が現状ではポスターに含まれていないので，これにあたる②が正解となる。
その他の選択肢の内容は本文中に見られない。

問4　42　正解①

「ポスターの　42　に最適な選択肢を選べ」

① 移動はしばしば法に違反する
② 彼らは目的地の気候に慣れていない
③ 彼らは新しい国に体調の悪い状態で到着する
④ 彼らは定住するのに十分な金を持っていない

正解は①。空所に入るのは「他の [＝キリバス以外の] 地域の移民が直面しがちな問題」の1つであり，最終段落（Elsewhere, international migrants ...）に挙げられているうちで，第1文の「国際的移住は危険で違法な移動となる可能性が高い場合も多い」に対応する情報が現状ではポスターに含まれていないので，これにあたる①が正解となる。
その他の選択肢の内容は本文中に見られない。

（主な語句・表現）
[リード文・タイトル]

・問題冊子を参照のこと。
◇ work on ...「…に取り組む」　　　　　◇ project 图「研究課題」
◇ disaster 图「災害；惨事」　　　　　　◇ on the increase「増加して（いる）」
◇ the big picture「大局観；総括的展望」　ここでは big が比較級 bigger として用いられているが，何かとの比較というより，漠然とした程度の高さを表す「絶対比較級」としての用法と考えられる。　**（例）** the *upper* class「上流階級」

— 英 R 161 —

[第1段落]
(The number ...)

◇ volcanoes erupting「火山の噴火」 自動詞 erupt（噴火する）の動名詞 erupting の直前にその意味上の主語を表す volcano（火山）の複数形が置かれた形。

◇ drought 图「旱魃(かんばつ)」　　　　　◇ noticeable 形「目立つ；顕著な」

◇ compared to ...「…と比較して」　　　◇ the Red Cross「赤十字」

◇ more than eight out of ten disasters「10 の災害のうち 8 つより多く」

◇ link O to ...「O を…と関連づける」 ここでは受動態で用いられている。

◇ in particular「とりわけ」

[第2段落]
(Since the ...)

◇ suffer from ...「…で苦しむ」

◇ A, as well as B「B と同様 A も；A ばかりか B も」 元は多くの人々が当然と受け取りそうな B よりも意外感を与えがちな A へと注意を促す表現であったが，近年は A と B の関係が逆転している場合も多く，ここでも，普通に考えて旱魃の影響を受けやすい青果類のみならず，動物までもが死に追いやられてきたことが強調されていると考えられる。

◇ forcing many people to desert their homes「多くの人々に家を見捨てることを強いて」 分詞構文。force O to - で「O に - することを強いる」，desert は他動詞で「…を見捨てる [放棄する]」の意味。

◇ burn down「全焼する；焼け落ちる」

◇ stating that ...「…であると述べて」 分詞構文。

◇ models based on predictions「予想に基づく仮説」 ここでの model は「(科学上の) 模式的な仮説」の意味で，過去分詞の導く based on ...（…に基づく）という形容詞句に修飾されている。

◇ regarding the destruction of the ozone layer「オゾン層の破壊に関する」 regarding は分詞構文に由来する「…に関する [関して]」という意味の前置詞で，regarding ... が形容詞句として predictions を修飾している。the ozone layer は太陽光線中の有害な紫外線を吸収して生物保護の役割を果たす「オゾン層」のこと。

◇ fit 動「合う；道理に適う」 models を主語とする述語動詞として働いている。

[第3段落]
(Location is ...)

◇ location 图「立地；居住地」　　　　　◇ reside 動「居住する」

◇ benefit from ...「…から利益 [恩恵] を得る」

◇ nutritious 形「栄養分のある」

◇ river system「水系」 川の本流とそれに合流する支流の全体。

◇ established 形「よく知られた；評価の高い」

◇ take advantage of ...「…を利用する」　◇ overseas access「海外への交通の便」

◇ profit from ...「…から利益を得る」　　◇ generously 副「気前よく；豊富に」

[第4段落]
(A relatively ...)

◇ migrant 图「移住者」　　　　　　　◇ flee 動「…から逃げる [避難する]」

◇ wipe ... out / wipe out ...「…を一掃する [絶滅させる]」

◇ inhospitable 形「住むのに適さない」

[第5段落]
(The first ...)

◇ Kiribati 图「キリバス共和国」　　　　◇ consist of ...「…から成る [構成される]」

◇ uninhabited island「無人島」 他動詞 inhabit（…に居住する）の過去分詞に un の付いた形容詞が island を修飾した形。

◇ the inevitable「避けられないこと」 inevitable は「避けられない；免れられない」という意味の形容詞。

◇ the whole country going underwater by 2100「2100 年までに国全体が水面下になること」 ダッシュを挟んで前に置かれている the inevitable の具体的な内容を表している。動名詞 going を中心とした表現で，the whole country はその意味上の主語を示している。

— 英 R 162 —

underwater は，ここでは「水面下に」という意味の副詞。

◇ go so far as to - 「- しさえする」 **(例)** She *went so far as to call* me a coward.「彼女は私を卑怯者とまで言った」

◇ relocate 動「…を移転［移住］させる」　◇ population 名「（ある地域の）全住民」

◇ enforce 動「〈法律など〉を施行する」　◇ erosion 名「浸食」

［最終段落］
(Elsewhere,
international ...)

◇ face 動「…の可能性［危険性］が高い」　◇ menial 形「熟練のいらない；低賃金の」

◇ it is essential that ...「…であることが不可欠［必須］である」 ... で用いられる動詞形は「(should ＋) 原形」となる。　**(例)** *It was essential that* everyone *do* it themselves.「誰もがそれを自分ですることが不可欠だった」

◇ refugee 名「難民；避難民」　　　　　◇ embrace 名「受け入れ；受容」

◇ benefit 名「便宜；援助」

［設問文・選択肢］

◇ air quality「大気質」　空気の非汚染度のこと。

◇ ruin 動「…を台無しにする［壊滅させる］」

B

(出典)　*Original Material*

(全訳)　　あなたは，運動の歴史に関する発表のためのポスターを準備する生徒のグループの一員です。健康状態がどのように変化したかを示すポスターを作るのに役立てるために，あなた方は以下の文章を読んできました。

健康の追求

我々は健康に取り憑かれた社会に生きており，スポーツクラブが至る所にある。ワールドワイド・ウェブにアクセスしてマウスボタンをクリックすれば，瞬時に最新のトレーニングやダイエットのトレンドを見て回ることができる。さらには，我々は素人の医者になりつつあって，自分が持っているかもしれない病気のどんな徴候についてでも調べ，自分で問題を特定し解決しようとする。これは精神衛生の問題が増加している一因かもしれない。今日，我々は肉体的のみならず精神的に我々がどのような状態であるかの重要性を認識しており，世界中の何百万という人々が幸福と，そしてもちろん「完璧な」体形を手にする秘訣を追求しているが，「完璧な」体形自体が各地，各文化で大きく異なるのだ。

もちろん，肉体的トレーニングは新たな概念ではないが，我々の最古の祖先たちは本能に従い健康を保っていた。自然の荒野に生きた人類は生き残るために絶えず，走り，這い，跳び，あらゆる大きさの重い物体を運び，物を投げ，戦闘に身を投じた。その後約 1 万年前に農業の時代が到来した。我々は狩猟採集をやめ，代わりに土地を耕し始め，単調な日々の作業を通じて同じ行動や動作を幾度となく繰り返した。生活はより単純なものとなった。たとえば，梯子を上るのに要する努力や動作は木のてっぺんに駆け上るよりはるかに少ないので，生活は肉体的に楽になった。

この平和な時期の後に，国家が形成され指導者が任命されるにつれて，土地と権力への渇望が戦争の時代へとつながり，戦闘用に男性を訓練するのが一大事業となった。教練と独特の訓練活動を通じて，こうした鍛錬された兵士たちは古代の人間と似た動き方をするようになったが，彼らが日々行う仕事の方が体系的だった。健康が成功へ

— 英 R 163 —

の鍵となり，彼らは信じ難いほど強健にならざるを得なかった。さらに後に，大文明においては強健な肉体と聡明な精神が結び付けられ，筋骨隆々で引き締まるならば知性もまた高まり得る，と人々は信じた。肉体的活動はそれほど激しくはなくなったが，人々は自らの体を大事に扱い，オリンピックのような運動能力を賛美するスポーツ・イベントが珍しくなくなった。

　西暦500年から1500年の間に，スポーツに対する見方には大転換が起きた。宗教が社会機能のあり方を支配し，肉体など重要ではないと我々は教わった。実際，我々の骨や皮膚や臓器は本質的には，来世を迎えるまで我々の魂を運ぶための精巧な容器に過ぎないと見なされた。さらには，この時代にはさまざまな疾病や自然災害という形で悲劇がもたらされ，人々は虚弱なままだった。しかしこの事態は長くは続かなかった。科学は医学の進歩と共に思考様式の変化をもたらし，大学が生物学的知識を広げる機会を提供した。近代教育の先駆者と見なされるヴィットリーノ・ダ・フェルトレは自分の働く機関の時間割に体育の授業を組み入れた。もう1人のイタリア人，メルクリアリスは運動と清潔さを確保するための定期的な洗浄の習慣を推奨する指導書を出版し，バランスの取れた食事をする必要を擁護した。彼は現在の健康に対する取り組み方に深い影響をもたらした。

　20世紀には系統だったスポーツやさまざまな当世風のダイエットの増加が見られ，健全，健康はメディアで大々的に主役扱いを受けている。見た目を魅力的にしたいという欲求によって，10億ドル規模の事業が生まれた。しかし，完璧な肉体を作り出すために我々が今日手にしているあらゆる道具にもかかわらず，1990年代に平均余命は世界的に下降し始めた。実のところ，今日ではいくらか体重超過であることは，ひどく恥ずかしいことであるとはみなされていない。そして我々は電子機器上のさまざまな健康アプリによって毒されてはいるが，ボタン1つでファストフードを注文し届けてもらうことが可能な機能によっても，同じだけ甘やかされている。ことによると，究極的には，健康を手にする秘訣は天然の食品と運動，新鮮な空気であって機械やアプリではないのである。自然があなたのスポーツクラブになり得るのだ。

あなた方の発表用ポスター：

運動の歴史

1.　現代の健康への姿勢
A.　自分自身の問題を診断しようとする傾向 **B.**　健康に関わる最新の流行についての情報を入手する機会 **C.**　肉体的なばかりでなく精神的健康の問題も意識すること **D.**　生い立ちによって異なる健康上の目標 **E.**　健康を保つための多くの施設

**2.　 44 **

- 自然からの食料源の採集に代えて土地の耕作
- スポーツ競技への愛好を生み出した，人間の肉体が達成することのできることへの正当な評価
- 宗教と科学の発展

> 3. どちらの時代の方が肉体は重要であったか
>
> | |
> |---|
> | 45 |
>
> 今日の社会の問題
>
> | 46 |
> |---|
> | 47 |

設問解説

問1　　43　　正解④

「あなたのグループは，ポスターの最初の見出しの下に本文で説明されている現代の健康への姿勢を記したい。誰もが１つの項目はふさわしくないと論じている。以下のうちどれを含めるべきではないか」　43

① A　　② B　　③ C　　④ D　　⑤ E

正解は④。A は第１段落第４文（We check any ...）の「我々は自分が持っているかもしれない病気のどんな徴候についてでも調べ，自分で問題を特定し解決しようとする」という記述に，B は同段落第２文（With access to ...）の「ワールドワイド・ウェブにアクセスしてマウスボタンをクリックすれば，瞬時に最新のトレーニングやダイエットのトレンドを見て回ることができる」という記述に，C は同段落第６文（Today we recognize ...）の「今日，我々は肉体的のみならず精神的に我々がどのような状態であるかの重要性を認識しており…」という記述に，E は第１文（We live in ...）の「スポーツクラブが至る所にある」という記述に，それぞれ相当する内容。これに対して D に相当する内容の記述は本文中に登場しないため，これが正解となる。

問2　　44　　正解③

「あなたはポスターの２つめの見出しを書くよう頼まれた。次のうちどれが最も適切か」
44

① 田舎と都会の環境における健康
② 男性の競争を好む本性と健康
③ 健康に強い影響を与える社会的変遷
④ 肉体と健康の進化

正解は③。ポスターの２つめの見出しの下に記されている「自然からの食料源の採集に代えて土地の耕作」は第２段落第４文（We stopped hunting ...）に書かれた「狩猟採集経済から農耕経済への変化」に，「スポーツ競技への愛好を生み出した，人間の肉体が達成することのできることへの正当な評価」は第３段落第４文（Later still, the ...），最終文（Though physical activity ...）に書かれた「戦闘能力重視から強健さや運動能力重視への変化」に，「宗教と科学の発展」は第４段落第２文（Religion started to ...）に書かれた「宗教の影響力増大による肉体の軽視」や同段落第６文（Science brought about ...）以降に書かれた「科学の発達のもたらした肉体の再評価」にそれぞれ対応する内容なので，これらすべてに通じる特徴と言える③が正解となる。

— 英 R 165 —

問3 ┃ 45 ┃ 正解 ②

「以下の4組の式のうち，どれがあなたのポスターに最も適切か」┃ 45 ┃

> [意味]
> 重要度が上位 ＞ 重要度が下位
> 重要度が下位 ＜ 重要度が上位

① 古代の人間 ＞ 農耕を行う人間
　農耕を行う人間 ＞ 戦闘を行う人間
　宗教的人間 ＞ 科学的人間
② **古代の人間 ＞ 農耕を行う人間**
　農耕を行う人間 ＜ 戦闘を行う人間
　宗教的人間 ＜ 科学的人間
③ 古代の人間 ＜ 農耕を行う人間
　農耕を行う人間 ＞ 戦闘を行う人間
　宗教的人間 ＜ 科学的人間
④ 古代の人間 ＜ 農耕を行う人間
　農耕を行う人間 ＜ 戦闘を行う人間
　宗教的人間 ＜ 科学的人間

正解は ②。「古代の人間」と「農耕を行う人間」の比較では，第2段落最終文（For example, going ...）にあるように，前者から後者への移行によって肉体的に楽な生活になり，その分肉体的能力の必要度は下がったため，前者の方が肉体の重要度は高かったと言える。

「農耕を行う人間」と「戦闘を行う人間」の比較では，第3段落第3文（Fitness was the ...）に端的に「健康が成功への鍵となり，彼ら［＝戦闘を行う人間］は信じ難いほど強健にならざるを得なかった」と書かれているように，究極的に健康かつ強健であることを求められた後者の方が肉体重視の傾向が強かった。

「宗教的人間」と「科学的人間」の比較では，第4段落第2文（Religion started to ...），第3文（In fact, our ...）に描かれているように前者は肉体軽視の傾向が強かったのに対し，同段落第6文（Science brought about ...）～第8文（Another Italian, Mercurialis, ...）に描かれているように，科学は肉体の再評価をもたらしたのであり，後者の方が肉体をより重要なものとして扱ったことになる。

したがって，以上の比較に合致する ② が正解となる。

問4 ┃ 46 ┃・┃ 47 ┃ 正解 ②・④

「あなたは本文に基づき，ポスターの最後の見出しの下に今日の社会のいくつかの問題点を指摘したい。以下の記述のうちどの2つを使うことができるか」┃ 46 ┃・┃ 47 ┃

① 健康を保つには非常に費用がかかる。
② **人々はかつてほど長生きしていない。**
③ メディアは，人々が自分を魅力的ではないと感じさせる原因となっている。
④ **身体が平均より大きいことについてほとんど恥じることがない。**
⑤ 我々は料理をすることより，食品を宅配してもらうことの方が多い。

最終段落第3文（Yet despite all ...）に「1990年代に平均寿命は世界的に下降し始めた」とあるので，かつてと比べ寿命は短くなっていると言えるため，② は正解となる。

同段落第4文（To tell the ...）に「今日ではいくらか体重超過であることは，ひどく恥ずかしいことであるとはみなされていない」とあり，肥満を恥じる風潮はないということになるため，④ は正解となる。

— 英 R 166 —

①，③は現在の社会に合致した内容と言えそうにも思えるが，本文にこれらに相当する記述は見られない。⑤は最終段落第4文（To tell the ...）にファストフードの宅配について記述はあるが，これと自炊の頻度の比較についての記述は本文に見られないので，正解とはならない。

主な語句・表現　　・問題冊子を参照のこと。
[リード文]　　◇ fitness 图「健康（状態）」

[第1段落]　　◇ health-obsessed 形「健康に取り憑かれた」 -obsessed は obsess（…に取り憑く）の過去
(We live in ...)　　　分詞からできた接尾辞。
　　◇ gym 图「ジム；スポーツクラブ」
　　◇ worldwide web「ワールドワイド・ウェブ」 インターネットの情報ネットワークのこと。
　　◇ surf through ...「（インターネット上で）…を見て回る」
　　◇ in an instant「瞬く間に；たちまち」
　　◇ what is more「その上（重要なことには）；さらには」
　　◇ identify 動「…を特定する」
　　◇ with millions of people around the world chasing ...「世界中の何百万もの人々が…を追
　　　及して」「付帯状況」を表す with を用いた with ... −ing で，「…が−している状態で」という意味。
　　◇ secret to ...「…の秘訣［こつ］」　　◇ in itself「それ自体；本来」
　　◇ location 图「位置；場所」

[第2段落]　　◇ stay fit「健康を維持する」 この fit は「体調が良い；健康な」という意味の形容詞。
(Naturally,　　◇ constantly 副「絶え間なく；連続的に」　　◇ hunting and gathering「狩猟と採集」
physical ...)　　◇ farm 動「…を耕作する」
　　◇ repeating the same actions and movements「同じ行動や動作を繰り返し」 分詞構文。
　　◇ unvaried 形「単調な」
　　◇ going up a ladder「梯子を上ること」 この場合の up は「…を上方へ」という意味の前
　　　置詞。
　　◇ existence 图「暮らし（ぶり）；生活（状況）」◇ demanding 形「骨の折れる；きつい」

[第3段落]　　◇ nations were formed and leaders appointed「国家が形成され，指導者が任命された」
(After this ...)　　　appoint は「…を指名［任命］する」という意味の他動詞。appointed の直前には繰り返し
　　　を避けるために were が省略されている。
　　◇ hunger for ...「…への渇望［切望］」
　　◇ result in ...「…という結果になる；…に終わる」
　　◇ operation 图「事業；計画」　　　　　◇ drill 图「教練；演習」
　　◇ specific 形「独特［特別］の」　　　　◇ discipline 動「…を訓練［鍛錬］する」
　　◇ routine 图「日常業務」　　　　　　　◇ structure 图「体系；規則性」
　　◇ drive O to −「O を−する［−である］よう追いやる；O に余儀なく−させる［−である
　　　ようにする］」
　　◇ athlete 图「筋骨たくましい［強健な］人」 ◇ sharp 形「利口［聡明］な」
　　◇ muscular 形「筋骨たくましい」
　　◇ celebrate 動「…をほめたたえる［賛美する］」

[第4段落]　　◇ reversal 图「反転；転換」
(Between 500 ...)　　◇ deem O (to be) C「O は C であると見なす」 ここでは受動態で用いられている。

— 英 R 167 —

◇ afterlife 图「来世」

◇ a variety of sicknesses and natural calamities that left people weak「人々を虚弱なまま
　にする，さまざまな病気や自然災害」 calamity は「災害；惨事」という意味の名詞。that
　は sicknesses and natural calamities を修飾する形容詞節を導く関係代名詞。leave O C
　は「O を C のままにしておく」という意味。

◇ state of affairs「事態；情勢」　　　　　　◇ mindset 图「心的態度；思考様式」

◇ P.E. 图「体育」　physical education の略。◇ cleanliness 图「清潔」

◇ champion 動「…を擁護［支持］する」

[最終段落]　　◇ fashionable 形「当世風の」
(The twentieth ...)　◇ feature 動「主要部分を占める；需要な役割を果たす」

◇ all the tools we have to build perfect bodies today「完璧な体を作るために今日われわれ
　が持つすべての道具」 we 以下は形容詞節として all the tools を修飾しており，直前に関
　係代名詞 that を補うことができる。that (O) we (S) have (V) to build ... (M) today (M)
　という構造で，to build ... は「目的」を表す副詞用法の to 不定詞で have を修飾している。

◇ life expectancy「平均余命」　　　　　　◇ overweight 形「体重超過の；太り過ぎの」

◇ embarrassing 形「まごつかせる；恥ずかしがらせる」

◇ spoil 動「…を台無しにする［損なう］」

◇ app 图「アプリケーション（ソフト）」 application program の略。

◇ indulge 動「…を甘やかす」　　　　　　◇ trick 图「こつ；秘訣」

[ポスター]　　◇ diagnose 動「…を診断する」

◇ access to ...「…に接近する［…を入手する］機会」

◇ background 图「素性；生い立ち」

[設問文・選択肢]　◇ heading 图「表題；見出し」　　　　　◇ competitive 形「競争を好む」

◇ shift 图「変化；変遷」

◇ feel unattractive「自分が魅力がないと感じる」 この feel ... は feel (V) oneself (O) ... (C)
　の oneself が省略されてできた形で「自分が C であると感じる」という意味を表す。　**(例)**
　He likes to *feel important.*「彼は自分が大物だと思いたがる」

| 第 5 回 | 実戦問題　解答・解説 |

英語（リーディング） 第5回 （100点満点）

（解答・配点）

問題番号（配点）	設問		解答番号	正解	配点	自己採点欄
第1問（10）	A	1	1	②	2	
	A	2	2	④	2	
	B	1	3	③	2	
	B	2	4	②	2	
	B	3	5	①	2	
小　計						
第2問（20）	A	1	6	②	2	
	A	2	7	①	2	
	A	3	8	②	2	
	A	4	9	①	2	
	A	5	10	④	2	
	B	1	11	③	2	
	B	2	12	②	2	
	B	3	13	③	2	
	B	4	14	④	2	
	B	5	15	②	2	
小　計						
第3問（15）	A	1	16	①	3	
	A	2	17	④	3	
	B	1	18	③	3*	
			19	④		
			20	①		
			21	②		
	B	2	22	③	3	
	B	3	23	②	3	
小　計						

問題番号（配点）	設問	解答番号	正解	配点	自己採点欄
第4問（16）	1	24	③	3	
	2	25	④	3	
	3	26	③	3	
	4	27	①	2	
		28	②	2	
	5	29	⑥	3	
小　計					
第5問（15）	1	30	③	3	
	2	31	④	3*	
		32	①		
		33	②		
		34	③		
	3	35	①	3	
	4	36 — 37	③－⑤	3*	
	5	38	④	3	
小　計					
第6問（24）	A	1	39	③	3	
	A	2	40	④	3	
	A	3	41	①	3	
	A	4	42	①	3	
	B	1	43	②	3	
	B	2	44	③	3	
	B	3	45 — 46	①－⑤	3*	
	B	4	47	②	3	
小　計						
合　計						

（注）
1 ＊は，全部正解の場合のみ点を与える。
2 －（ハイフン）でつながれた正解は，順序を問わない。

第1問

解答	A 問1-②	問2-④	（各2点）
	B 問1-③	問2-② 問3-①	（各2点）

A

出典 *Original Material*

全訳

あなたはフランスに留学している。同じ市内にある別の学校で勉強しているイギリス人の友人からテキストメッセージを受け取る。

> こんにちは！　世界中からやってきた人たちを紹介する手段として，市役所がコミュニティセンターで「歌う」日の準備をしているところで，いろいろな言語で歌ったり歌を聴いたりする機会になるよ！　音楽はカラオケスタイルで楽器やステージはなし。おいでよ！　そしてクラスメートも連れておいでよ！

> やあ、サイモン。その話，聞いてたよ！　そこに行く予定でいるよ！　歌の種類はまだ決めてないんだけどね。人によって好きな音楽の種類は違うことが多いだろ。僕は何を歌ったらいいかな？

> そうだな，ほとんどが若者だろうから，好きな曲に合わせて踊れるように，テンポのいい歌の方がいいとは思うけどね。僕は早めに行くけど，センターで会おう！

設問解説

問1 　　1　　正解②

「あなたの友人はあなたが　1　ことを望んでいる」

① ロックバンドを組むための人を何人か探す
② 他の人たちをこのイベントに参加するよう誘う
③ ステージで伝統的な踊りを踊る
④ 学生たちにあなたの国の歌を教える

サイモンは最初のテキストメッセージの第2文（The city hall ...）で，市役所がコミュニティセンターで「歌う」日の準備をしていて，それはいろいろな言語で歌ったり歌を聴いたりする機会になると伝えた後，第4文（Come!）以降で，あなたに対して「おいでよ！　そしてクラスメートも連れておいでよ！」と述べているのだから，あなたに他の人たちもこのイベントに参加するよう誘って欲しいと思っていることがわかる。よってその内容に一致する②が正解。

①に関しては，「ロックバンドを組む」という内容がテキストメッセージ上にはないので誤り。③に関しては，サイモンが最初のテキストメッセージの第3文(The music will ...)で，「ステージはなし」と述べているので誤り。④に関しては，「学生たちにあなたの国の歌を教える」という内容がテキストメッセージ上にはないので誤り。

— 英 R 171 —

問2 　2　 正解 ④

「サイモンの２つ目のメッセージに対してあなたはどのように返信するか」　2

① わかった。歌詞を訳し始めることにするよ！
② わかった。昔の歌を調べた方がいいね！
③ ゴメン，そんなに早くは行けないよ。
④ **確かに！　かっこいいＪポップをいくつか選ぶことにするよ！**

あなたは「歌う」日に歌う歌のジャンルをまだ決めかねていて，テキストメッセージの最終文（What should I ...）でサイモンに「僕は何を歌ったらいいかな？」と尋ねると，サイモンが２つ目のテキストメッセージの第１文（Well, most people ...）で「テンポのいい歌の方がいいとは思うけどね」と答えてくれる。それに対して「確かに！　かっこいいＪポップをいくらか選ぶことにするよ！」と返信すれば，自然なやりとりとなるので，正解は④となる。

①に関しては，「歌詞を訳す」という内容がテキストメッセージ上からはうかがえないので誤り。②に関しては，「昔の歌を調査する」という内容がテキストメッセージ上からはうかがえないので誤り。③に関しては，サイモンは２つ目のテキストメッセージの最終文（I'll go early ...）で「僕は早めに行くけど，センターで会おう！」と述べているが，具体的に何時に行くとは言っていないので，③の内容では自然なやり取りとは言えず，誤り。

（主な語句・表現）・問題冊子を参照のこと。

[リード文] ◇ study abroad「留学する」

[メッセージ] ◇ city hall「市役所」　　　　　　　　　◇ organise 動「…を準備する［催す］」
◇ community centre「コミュニティセンター」　教育・文化・厚生・社交などの設備がある社会事業センター。centre は center のイギリス英語表記。
◇ the opportunity to –「–するための機会」◇ introduce 動「…を紹介する」
◇ musical instrument「楽器」　　　　　　◇ category 名「種類；部類」
◇ right?「（文尾に〈, right?〉の形で付加的につけ，自分の発言を相手に確認して）わかったね；いいね；…だよね」　（例）Then you won't come, *right?*「それじゃ来ないんだね」
◇ I should think「私としては…と思いますが」　この should はよく say, think, like, prefer などの動詞の前に置かれて，控え目・ためらい・丁寧の気持ちを表す。（例）He's over fifty, *I should think.*「彼は 50 歳は過ぎていると思いますが」
◇ so that S can –「（目的を表して）S が–するために［–できるよう］」
◇ dance to ...「…に合わせて踊る」

[設問文・選択肢] ◇ invite ... to –「…に–するよう誘う［勧める；依頼する］」
◇ reply to ...「…に返信を書く［返事をする；答える］」
◇ Got it.「わかった」　Got の前には I または I have が省略されている。この get は「…を理解する」という意味。
◇ translate 動「…を翻訳する」　　　　　　◇ song word「歌詞」
◇ would better 原形「〈原形〉した方がよいだろう」
◇ research 動「…を調査［研究］する」　◇ sure 副「（返答として）確かに；その通り」
◇ cool 形「かっこいい」
◇ J-pop「J（ジェー）ポップ」　Japanese Pop (music) の略。日本のポップス音楽の総称。

— 英 R 172 —

B

出典 | *Original Material*

全訳 | あなたの先生が興味深い講義の案内を配布した。

英語に関する特別講義

　言語の研究分野で先導的な学者の1人である Swain 教授が，本校で英語に関する無料の連続講義を来月行ってくださいます。この特別講義は3つのセクションに分かれています：

	講義日	開催場所	内容
講義A	3月6日	南ホール	・英語の統語論
講義B	3月8日	中央ホール	・英語の語彙 ・英語の音韻論
講義C	3月10日	講堂	・英語の歴史

☆学生は1人につき最大で2つの講義まで登録可能です。
☆前提知識は不要です。
☆それぞれの講義の後，短いレポートを書いてもらいます。

講演者について
　Bolic 大学の教授。主に英語統語論（英語の文法を扱う分野）に関して多くの論文を発表されていますが，英語の音声の研究である英語音韻論に関する研究でも著名な先生です。

講演者からのメッセージ
　皆さんこんにちは！　私は日本の文化と日本食が大好きです。ですから，それぞれの講義の後にそれらについて皆さんとお話しすることを本当に楽しみにしています！　これが，皆さんが英語を話す練習をする良い機会になればと思っています。

＊高橋先生に今月末までに申し込み用紙を提出しなくてはいけません。
＊これらの講義にはご家族を招待することができます。

— 英 R 173 —

設問解説

問1 　3　 正解③

「特別講義に参加するためには，あなたは 　3　 いけない」

① 少なくとも２つの講義に出席しなくては
② いくらかの背景知識がなくては
③ **２月中に申し込み用紙を提出しなくては**
④ 家族を一緒に連れてこなくては

本文第１文（Professor Swain, one ...）の「連続講義が来月行われる」という記述と，１つ目の＊（You must hand ...）の「申し込み用紙の提出期限は今月末」という記述から，提出期限は開催月の前月中だとわかる。さらに表から，講義が行われるのは３月だとわかるので，以上を合わせると「申し込み期限は２月中」ということになり，③が正解となる。

①に関しては，１つ目の☆（Each student can ...）に「最大で２つの講義まで」とあるので誤りである。②に関しては，２つ目の☆（No prior knowledge ...）の「前提知識は不要」という記述に反する。２つ目の＊（You can invite ...）に「家族を招待することができる」と記されているが，これは「連れてこなくてはいけない」という意味ではないので，④も誤りである。

問2 　4　 正解②

「講義の後に，Swain 教授は 　4　 可能性が高い」

① 他の先生たちと日本食を食べる
② **日本について会話をする**
③ 日本の習慣についての本を出版する
④ 日本についての短いレポートを書く

講演者からのメッセージ欄（Message from the lecturer）の第３文（So I am ...）に「講義の後にそれら（＝日本の文化と日本食）について話すのを楽しみにしている」とあるので，②が正解となる。

①，③，④については，本文中に該当する記述がない。

問3 　5　 正解①

「英語の文法について学びたい場合，あなたが最もする可能性があるのは 　5　 である」

① **南ホールで開かれる講義に出席すること**
② ３月10日に講堂に行くこと
③ ３月８日に行われる講義に参加すること
④ Bolic 大学で講義を受けること

講演者についての欄（About the lecturer）の第２文（He has published ...）に「主に英語統語論（英語の文法を扱う分野）に関して多くの論文を発表されています」とあるので，syntax が文法を扱う分野だとわかる。表を見ると，その syntax が扱われるのは南ホールで開かれる講義Ａだとわかるので，①が正解となる。

②と③はそれぞれ講義Ｃと講義Ｂに関する記述で，これらは文法を扱う講義ではないので誤りである。講演者についての欄から，Swain 教授が Bolic 大学で教えているとわかるので，確かにそこで講義を受ければ英語の文法について学べる可能性はあるが，日本の高校で行われる講義の案内という文脈から考えて，④の内容が「最もする可能性がある」ことにはならないので，④も誤りとなる。

— 英 R 174 —

主な語句・表現	・問題冊子を参照のこと。	
[リード文]	◇ notice 名「案内；広告」	◇ lecture 名「講義；講演」

[案内]
◇ leading scholar「先導的な学者；一流の学者」
◇ field 名「分野」　　　　　　　　　　◇ a series of ...「連続した…；一連の…」
◇ consist of ...「…から構成される；…に分かれている」
◇ content 名「内容」　　　　　　　　　◇ syntax 名「統語論」
◇ vocabulary 名「語彙」　　　　　　　◇ phonology 名「音韻論」
◇ auditorium 名「講堂」　　　　　　　◇ register for ...「…に登録する」
◇ up to ...「最大で…」　　　　　　　◇ prior knowledge「前提知識」
◇ require 動「…を必要とする」　　　　◇ lecturer 名「講演者」
◇ publish 動「…を出版する；…を発表する」◇ article 名「論文；記事」
◇ mainly 副「主に」　　　　　　　　◇ deal with ...「…を扱う」
◇ famous for ...「…のことで有名な」　◇ research 名「研究」
◇ look forward to −ing「−することを楽しみにする」
◇ opportunity 名「機会」　　　　　　◇ practice −ing「−することを練習する」
◇ hand in ...「…を提出する」　　　　◇ application 名「申し込み用紙」
◇ invite 動「…を招待する」

[設問文・選択肢]
◇ in order to −「−するために」　　　◇ take part in ...「…に参加する」
◇ attend 動「…に出席する」　　　　　◇ at least「少なくとも」
◇ background knowledge「背景知識」　◇ submit 動「…を提出する」
◇ be likely to −「−するだろう；−する可能性が高い」
◇ conversation 名「会話」　　　　　　◇ custom 名「慣習；習慣」
◇ brief 形「短い」
◇ held 動「開催される」　hold「…を開催する」の過去分詞形。
◇ participate in ...「…に参加する」

第2問

解 答						
A	問1 - ②	問2 - ①	問3 - ②	問4 - ①	問5 - ④	(各2点)
B	問1 - ③	問2 - ②	問3 - ③	問4 - ④	問5 - ②	(各2点)

A

出典 *Original Material*

全訳

　あなたはバレンタインデーに向けてイギリスのロンドンにあるレストランを探しており，その地域のレストラン対決についての文章を読んでいる。デートのために1軒のレストランに予約を取りたいと思っている。

<table>
<tr><th colspan="5">レストラン評論家による星★ランキング</th></tr>
<tr><th>　　　　　項目
レストラン名</th><th>料理
★★★★★</th><th>サービス
★★★★★</th><th>内装
★★★★★</th><th>合計</th></tr>
<tr><td>ファンク・シャック</td><td>1.3</td><td>2.0</td><td>1.7</td><td>5</td></tr>
<tr><td>メドウ・イン</td><td>3.9</td><td>3.8</td><td>5.0</td><td>12.7</td></tr>
<tr><td>オサリバンズ</td><td>4.1</td><td>4.7</td><td>3.9</td><td>12.7</td></tr>
<tr><td>ザ・ローズ・パブ</td><td>4.3</td><td>3.9</td><td>4.5</td><td>12.7</td></tr>
</table>

<table>
<tr><th colspan="2">評論家の意見</th></tr>
<tr><td>フルーム氏</td><td>ザ・ローズ・パブで給仕スタッフのタイミングが，特にのろのろして面白みのないメドウ・インのサービス提供と比較して，すばらしいと感じた。オサリバンズの中華料理とイギリス料理の融合は巧みだったが，常にうまくいっていたわけではなかった。</td></tr>
<tr><td>キング氏</td><td>オサリバンズは意表をついた料理をいくつか提供した！　誰にとってもとは多分ならないだろうが，私にとっては勝者だ！　給仕スタッフはメニューを熟知。ザ・ローズ・パブではスタッフが当てにならないように思われた。メドウ・インの陽気な雰囲気は大いに気に入った！</td></tr>
<tr><td>タッカー氏</td><td>大好物の料理を出してくれたオサリバンズに感謝！　だがメドウ・インからヒントをもらった方がいい。壁をもっと明るく，もっと陽気な色に塗ることだ。</td></tr>
</table>

評論家の共同判定（キング氏による要約）

　1店の例外はあるが，すべてのレストランが同点となった！　料理に関しては，その3店はどれも悪いところは何1つとしてなかったので，我々評論家は，サービスがランキングのトップとなる要素であるべき，ということで全員の意見が一致した。

　2位と3位を決める際，タッカー氏はほとんどの人は料理がおいしければ内装はそれほど気にしないと指摘した。フルーム氏と私もそう考える。

設問解説

問1 　6　 **正解②**

「評論家の最終判定に基づけば、どのレストランの装飾が最もよかったか」 　6　

① ファンク・シャック
② メドウ・イン
③ オサリバンズ
④ ザ・ローズ・パブ

「レストラン評論家による星★ランキング」表にある３つの項目のうち、Décor の意味がわからなくとも、Food は「料理」、Service は「サービス」であることから、残る項目の Décor が「装飾；内装」といった意味を表す語だと推測できるはずである。この項目で最も高い 5.0 ポイントを獲得しているのがメドウ・インであるので、正解は②となる。

問2 　7　 **正解①**

「好意的なコメントと批判的な意見の両方を述べているのはどの審査員か」 　7　

① 審査員全員
② フルーム氏
③ キング氏
④ タッカー氏

フルーム氏は、好意的な意見として、ザ・ローズ・パブで給仕スタッフのタイミングがすばらしかったこととオサリバンズの中華料理とイギリス料理の融合が巧みだったことを評価し、批判的な意見として、メドウ・インのサービス提供がのろのろして面白みがなかったことと、オサリバンズの中華料理とイギリス料理の融合が常にうまくいっていたわけではなかったと指摘している。

キング氏は、好意的な意見として、オサリバンズが意表をついた料理をいくつか提供したことと給仕スタッフがメニューを熟知していたこと、さらにメドウ・インの陽気な雰囲気がよかったことを評価し、批判的な意見として、ザ・ローズ・パブではスタッフが当てにならないように思われたと指摘している。

タッカー氏は、好意的な意見として、オサリバンズが大好きな料理を出してくれたことを評価し、批判的な意見として、同店の壁の色は明るく陽気な色に塗り替える必要があると指摘している。

以上のことから、審査員全員が好意的なコメントと批判的な意見の両方を述べていることがわかるので、①が正解となる。

問3 　8　 **正解②**

「評論家独自の意見における１つの事実は　8　ということである」

① ザ・ローズ・パブでは長く料理を待つことは決してない
② オサリバンズは２カ国の食文化を融合させている
③ ファンク・シャックに関し、審査員は意見を一致させることができなかった
④ メドウ・インの壁の色は魅力的である

フルーム氏はその意見の第２文（O'Sullivan's fusion of ...）で「オサリバンズの中華料理とイギリス料理の融合は巧みだったが、常にうまくいっていたわけではなかった」と述べているが、中華料理とイギリス料理の融合が「巧みだった」こと、あるいはその融合が「常にうまくいっていたわけではなかった」ことはフルーム氏の主観に基づいた「意見」だとしても、オサリバンズが中華料理とイギリス料理を融合させていたことは「事実」であるとみなせるので、正解は②となる。

①に関しては、フルーム氏がその意見の第１文（I felt that ...）で「ザ・ローズ・パブで給仕スタッフのタイミングがすばらしいと感じた」と述べていることから、「ザ・ローズ・パブでは長く料理を待つことは決してない」というのは事実ではなく意見であるとみなせ

— 英 R 177 —

るので誤り。③に関しては,評論家3人が述べている独自の意見の中では,ファンク・シャックに関する言及がまったくなされていないので誤り。④に関しては,タッカー氏がその意見の第2文（But take a ...）〜第3文（Paint the walls ...）で,オサリバンズに関し,メドウ・インからヒントをもらって壁をもっと明るく陽気な色に塗った方がいい,と述べていることから,タッカー氏にとってメドウ・インの壁の色は魅力的だったと推測できるが,これは事実ではなく,タッカー氏の主観に基づく個人的意見であるとみなせるので,誤り。

問4　　9　　正解①

「評論家の共同判定から得られる1つの意見は　9　ということである」
　　①　トップのレストラン3店はみな満足できる料理を提供している
　　②　料理の質より内装を改善することの方が必要となる技術は少なくて済む
　　③　タッカー氏はあることを指摘し,他の者も同意した
　　④　評論家は話し合いによって勝者を選んだ

　評論家の共同判定における第2文（When it comes ...）で,「料理に関しては,その3店はどれも悪いところは何1つとしてなかった」とある。この店の料理はすばらしいとか別の店より劣っているといった評価は主観に基づく意見であるとみなせるので,①が正解となる。

　②に関しては,「料理の質より内装を改善することの方が必要となる技術は少なくて済む」という内容は言及されていないので誤り。③に関しては,評論家の共同判定における第2段落第1文（When deciding second ...）〜最終文（Mr Frome and ...）で,「2位と3位を決める際,タッカー氏はほとんどの人は料理がおいしければ内装はそれほど気にしないと指摘した。フルーム氏と私もそう考える」と述べられているが,これは意見ではなく事実であるとみなせるので誤り。④に関しては,評論家の共同判定から,3店が同じ12.7ポイントを獲得して同点首位となったが,サービスがランキングのトップとなる要素であるべきということで評論家全員の意見が一致し,それを基準とした話し合いによって勝者を選んだと推測できるが,それは意見ではなく事実であるとみなせるので誤り。

問5　　10　　正解④

「評論家の共同評価に基づけば,以下のうちのどれが最終ランキングとなるか」　　10

	第1位	第2位	第3位
①	メドウ・イン	オサリバンズ	ザ・ローズ・パブ
②	メドウ・イン	ザ・ローズ・パブ	オサリバンズ
③	オサリバンズ	メドウ・イン	ザ・ローズ・パブ
④	**オサリバンズ**	**ザ・ローズ・パブ**	**メドウ・イン**
⑤	ザ・ローズ・パブ	メドウ・イン	オサリバンズ
⑥	ザ・ローズ・パブ	オサリバンズ	メドウ・イン

　評論家の共同判定から,3店が同じ12.7ポイントを獲得して同点首位となったが,第1段落第2文（When it comes ...）後半で「我々評論家は,サービスがランキングのトップとなる要素であるべき,ということで全員の意見が一致した」と述べられていることから,同点首位3店の中でサービスのポイントが4.7と最も高かったオサリバンズが第1位を獲得したことがわかる。さらに,第2段落第1文（When deciding second ...）〜最終文（Mr Frome and ...）に「2位と3位を決める際,タッカー氏はほとんどの人は料理がおいしければ内装はそれほど気にしないと指摘した。フルーム氏と私もそう考える」とあり,このことは第2位と第3位を決定するにあたっては内装のポイントよりも料理のポイントの方が優先されることを意味する。メドウ・インとザ・ローズ・パブの料理のポイントはそれぞれ3.9と4.3であるので,ザ・ローズ・パブが第2位,メドウ・インが第3位と確定したことがわかる。以上のことから正解は④となる。

― 英R 178 ―

主な語句・表現	・問題冊子を参照のこと。

[ランキング表]
◇ critic 名「批評家；評論家」　　　　　　　◇ condition 名「条項；項目」
◇ decor 名「(室内) 装飾；内装」　フランス語由来の語で décor とも綴る。

[意見・共同判定]
◇ server 名「給仕する人；ウェイター，ウェイトレス」
◇ compared to ...「…と比較して」　　　　◇ delivery 名「配達；サービスの提供」
◇ fusion 名「融合」
◇ serve up ...「〈レストランなどがある種の料理〉を出す」
◇ wait staff「給仕スタッフ」　　　　　　　◇ summarise 動「…を要約する」
◇ exception 名「例外」　　　　　　　　　　◇ tie 動「同点になる」
◇ when it comes to ...「…ということになると；…に関しては」
◇ point out that ...「…と指摘する」　　　　◇ care about ...「…を気にする」

[設問文・選択肢]
◇ based on ...「…に基づけば」　　　　　　◇ decorate 動「…を装飾する」
◇ critical 形「批判的な」　　　　　　　　　◇ original 形「独自の」
◇ evaluation 名「評価」　　　　　　　　　　◇ decent 形「満足できる；立派な」
◇ take 動「…を必要とする」　　　　　　　　◇ indicate 動「…を指摘する」
◇ pick 動「…を選ぶ」

B

出典 *Original Material*

全訳　あなたの英語の先生が，あなたが次の授業でのディベートの準備をする手助けとなる記事をくれた。記事に対するコメントのうちの１つとともにこの記事の一部が以下に挙げてある。

生徒は制服を着用すべきか？

ロジャー・ホワイト　ニューヨーク

2019 年 10 月 20 日　17：15

アメリカは少しずつ学校での制服の使用を取り入れている。国立教育統計センターが2018 年に公表した数値によれば，生徒に学校用制服の着用を求める公立学校の割合は，1999 年の 12 パーセントから 2015 年には 21 パーセントに上昇した。別の調査からは，大都市の公立学校に通う生徒の 41 パーセントが制服を着用していることが明らかとなった。特にフィラデルフィアでは，公立学校の全生徒が制服を着るよう求められている。

では，学校用制服を着用することの利点は何だろうか。ある教員は次のように述べた。「まず，生徒間での平等を推進し，いじめを減らすことができるのです。生徒の中には高価な服を持っている者がいますが，そうでない者もいます。これが時としていじめにつながるのです。さらに，部外者が校内に侵入した場合でも，制服がある方が容易にその人物が部外者だとわかります。安全の観点からも，この方針は望ましいのです」

しかしながら，すべての親がこの方針に賛成しているわけではない。ある親たちは「学校用制服を着用するという方針は，生徒の持つ表現の自由を侵害しています。生徒は自分の気に入った服を着るべきなのです」と言った。また別の親たちはこう述べた。「今は移民の子どもたちがたくさんいて，彼らは私たちとは異なる価値観や習慣を持っています。こういった時代には，多様性を尊重しなくてはいけません。『画一性』ではなくてね」

---

17 コメント

最新

ケイト・トンプソン　2019 年 10 月 22 日　21：05

この方針わかります。毎朝何を着たらよいか考える必要がないんですから。その上，一体感が生まれる可能性もありますし。でも同時に，制服を買う余裕がない生徒がいるかもしれませんね。時には値段が 500 ドルを超えてしまうこともあるそうですから。

設問解説

問1 　11　正解③

「記事によると，フィラデルフィアの公立学校の生徒は　11　」

① 親に学校の制服を買うように頼むことを強制されている
② 自分たちが好きなものを何でも自由に着られる
③ 自分たちが望むような服を着ることが許されていない
④ 毎日服装を変える気がない

　フィラデルフィアの公立学校の生徒に関する記述は第1段落最終文（In Philadelphia, especially, ...）にあり，「全生徒が制服を着るよう求められている」と述べられているので，これと一致する③が正解である。

　①のような内容は本文中で述べられていない。②は第1段落最終文の内容に合わないので誤り。④のような内容も，本文中で全く述べられていない。

問2 　12　正解②

「あなたのチームは『すべての生徒は学校の制服を着用すべきである』というディベート・テーマを支持する。記事の中で，あなたのチームに役立つ1つの<u>意見</u>は　12　ということだ」

① 学校の制服を着る方が何を着るかを選ぶよりも費用が安い
② 学校の制服は生徒にとってより安全な環境を生み出す
③ 公立学校のイメージが本当に改善される
④ 犯罪を犯す生徒の数が減少する

　制服の着用を支持するチームにとって役立つ意見は，制服を着用することの長所が述べられている第2段落に記されている。この段落では一教員の意見として，「生徒間での平等を推進していじめが減る」という長所と「部外者の判別がつきやすく安全面で望ましい」という長所が述べられており，後者の長所に一致する②が正解となる。

　他の①・③・④の各選択肢の内容は，制服着用の長所として本文中で述べられてはいないので，正解とはならない。

問3 　13　正解③

「相手のチームはこのディベート・テーマに反対する。記事の中でそのチームに役立つ1つの<u>意見</u>は　13　ということだ」

① 公立学校の教員が自分たちの好きな服を着るのは公平ではない
② 制服を要求することは公立学校の社会的地位に影響を及ぼさない
③ 学校の制服は生徒の持つ自己表現の能力を制限する
④ 一部の親は自分たちの好きな服を子どもに買ってあげられない

　制服の着用に反対するチームにとって役立つ意見は，制服を着用することの短所が述べられている第3段落に記されている。この段落では親の発言として，「生徒の表現の自由を侵害するものだ」という短所と「多様性の尊重につながらない」という短所が述べられており，前者の短所に一致する③が正解となる。

　他の①・②・④の各選択肢の内容は，制服着用の短所として本文中で述べられてはいないので，正解とはならない。

問4 　14　正解④

「記事の第3段落において，『こういった時代には』は『　14　時代には』という意味である」

① すべての人々が何らかの種類の制服を着用しなくてはならない
② 個人の人権がある程度まで制限されている
③ 情報が人々の生活の中で大変重要な役割を果たしている
④ 様々な文化的背景を持った人々が一緒に暮らしている

— 英 R 181 —

この「こういった時代には (In this day and age)」という表現の this が指しているのは，直前の英文 (And others said, ...) の「今は移民の子どもたちがたくさんいて，彼らは私たちとは異なる価値観や習慣を持っています」という内容と考えられ，そのように判断すれば，「多様性を尊重しなくてはいけません」という後続の文脈とも合う。よって，この内容に最も近い ④ が正解となる。

他の ①・②・③ の選択肢の内容は，いずれも本文中で述べられていない。

問5 　15　 正解 ②

「コメントから判断すると，ケイト・トンプソンは記事で述べられている方針に 　15　 である」

① 無関心
② 部分的に賛成
③ 全面的に賛成
④ 全面的に反対

ケイト・トンプソンのコメントでは，第2文 (You don't need ...) と第3文 (Moreover, a sense ...) で制服着用の長所として，「毎朝何を着たらよいか考える必要がない」「一体感が生まれる」の2点を挙げている。しかし彼女は，第4文 (But at the ...) と最終文 (I hear the ...) では「経済的に制服を買えない生徒もいるかもしれない」という短所も挙げている。以上より，正解は ②「部分的に賛成」となる。

（主な語句・表現）　・問題冊子を参照のこと。

[リード文]
◇ article 图「記事；論文」
◇ prepare for ...「…の準備をする」
◇ help O − 「O が−するのを助ける」
◇ below 副「以下に」

[第1段落]
◇ adopt 動「…を取り入れる」
◇ figure 图「数値」
◇ statistics 图「統計」
◇ public school「（米国の）公立学校」
◇ increase 動「増加する」
◇ survey 图「調査」
◇ according to ...「…によると」
◇ publish 動「…を公表する」
◇ proportion 图「割合；比率」
◇ require A to − 「A に−するように求める」
◇ another 形「別の；もうひとつの」
◇ especially 副「特に」

[第2段落]
◇ advantage 图「利点」
◇ equality 图「平等」
◇ bullying 图「いじめ」
◇ besides 副「さらに；他にも」
◇ recognize 動「…だとわかる」
◇ security 图「安全」
◇ desirable 形「望ましい」
◇ promote 動「…を推進［促進］する」
◇ reduce 動「…を減らす」
◇ lead to ...「…につながる」
◇ outsider 图「部外者」
◇ in terms of ...「…の観点から」
◇ policy 图「方針；政策」

[第3段落]
◇ agree with ...「…に賛成［同意］する」
◇ freedom 图「自由」
◇ favorite 形「お気に入りの；大好きな」
◇ value 图「価値（観）」
◇ in this day and age「こういった時代には」
◇ respect 動「…を尊重［尊敬］する」
◇ uniformity 图「画一性；同一性」
◇ violate 動「…を侵害する」
◇ expression 图「表現」
◇ immigrant 形「移民（の）」
◇ custom 图「習慣；慣習」
◇ diversity 图「多様性」

— 英 R 182 —

[コメント]	◇ moreover 副「さらに；その上」	◇ a sense of togetherness「一体感」

[コメント]
◇ moreover 副「さらに；その上」　　◇ a sense of togetherness「一体感」
◇ at the same time「同時に」
◇ can't afford ...「…を買う（経済的な）余裕がない」
◇ reach over ...「…を超えるところまで達する」

[設問文・選択肢]
◇ force O to −「O に−するよう強制する」　◇ ask O to −「O に−するよう頼む」
◇ free to −「自由に−して［できて］」　　◇ permit O to −「O が−するのを許す」
◇ dress 動「服装をする；服を着る」　　◇ the way S V ...「S V…するように」
◇ willing to −「−する気がある」　　　◇ support 動「…を支持する」
◇ opinion 名「意見」　　　　　　　　　◇ helpful for ...「…に役立つ」
◇ it will cost less to −「−する方が費用が安い（だろう）」
◇ create 動「…を造る；…を生み出す」　◇ improve 動「…を改善する」
◇ commit crimes「犯罪を犯す」　　　　◇ decrease 動「減少する」
◇ oppose 動「…に反対する」　　　　　◇ fair 形「公平な」
◇ as they like「彼らが好きなように」　◇ effect 名「影響；効果」
◇ social status「社会的地位」　　　　　◇ limit 動「…を制限する」
◇ ability to −「−する能力」　　　　　◇ individual 形「個人（の）」
◇ human rights「人権」　　　　　　　◇ restrict 動「…を制限する」
◇ to some extent「ある程度」　　　　　◇ play a ... role「…な役割を果たす」
◇ various 形「様々な」　　　　　　　　◇ cultural 形「文化的な」
◇ background 名「背景」　　　　　　　◇ judging from ...「…から判断すると」
◇ mention 動「…に言及する；…のことを述べる」
◇ partly 副「部分的に；ある程度は」　◇ totally 副「完全に；全面的に」
◇ disagree with ...「…に反対する；…と意見が異なる」

第3問

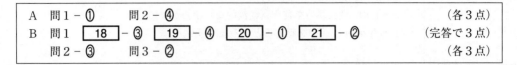

A
出典 *Original Material*

全訳
あなたの友人であるイギリス人のピッパが少し前にしゃれた博物館から戻って来て，自分のホームページにそれに関する投稿をしたところだ。

> **ようこそ，もう一つの世界ペブルトン科学博物館へ。**
> 〈ピッパの投稿—2021年3月16日20時21分〉
>
> ペブルトン科学博物館についてはすばらしい話を聞いていましたが，ついに今日そこへ行ってきました！ しゃれたものがたくさんあって，とってもインタラクティヴ(双方向型)なんです！
>
> 4Dシアターはすてきでした。ロケットショーで月まで飛んでいく体験を非常に楽しみにしていました。その前に，1階の恐竜エリアを巡るガイド付きツアーに参加する時間がありました…がそう思えただけの話。モダンモデルは超リアルでした！ とてもよかったので私たちは時間が経つのも忘れて，2階上のちょっとわかりにくい未来のモデル都市の街路を苦労して通り抜けてロケットショーへと続くエスカレーターにたどり着いた時には，ショーは半分終わっていました。でも気にしません。その代わりに帰路につく直前に別のショーを見ることができたのですから！
>
> 未来のモデル都市は見逃しちゃダメです。運転手のいない乗り物や環境にやさしいテクノロジーが印象的で，AIロボットたちは実際とてもキュート！ たくさんのボタンがあって，押すとワクワクドキドキの結果に―これ以上は言わないようにしましょう！ あっそうだ，長い興奮の1日の後に，もしお腹が空いていたらカフェに行くのを忘れないで。お薦めはムーンケーキ。このカフェの中に入らなければ博物館見学は完璧だとは言えません。私はそこですてきな休憩をとってから1階上の私たちにとっての終着点へと昇って行きました。

4階	4Dシアター
3階	カフェ，未来のモデル都市
2階	プラネタリウム
1階	恐竜エリア

設問解説

問1 ☐16☐ **正解①**

「ピッパの投稿から ☐16☐ ことがわかる」

① モデル都市の設計は少し複雑だった
② 恐竜のガイドが語った話は恐ろしかった
③ 本物のロケットの中に座る体験ができる
④ カフェの食べ物はモデル都市の中に持ち込める

ピッパの投稿の第2段落第5文（It was so ...）に「…2階上のちょっとわかりにくい未来のモデル都市の街路を苦労して通り抜けてロケットショーへと続くエスカレーターにたどり着いた時には…」とあることから，「モデル都市の設計は少し複雑だった」と推測できるので，正解は①となる。

②，③，④に関しては，ピッパの投稿には言及されていない内容なのでいずれも誤り。

問2 ☐17☐ **正解④**

「ピッパは博物館での1日を何階で終えたか」 ☐17☐

① 1階
② 2階
③ 3階
④ 4階

イラストで示されたペブルトン科学博物館のフロアガイドの各階は上から順に 3rd Floor, 2nd Floor, 1st Floor, The Ground Floor となっているが，これはイギリス英語の表記であり，アメリカ英語および日本語ではそれぞれ 4th Floor「4階」，3rd Floor「3階」，2nd Floor「2階」，1st Floor「1階」のことになる。

ピッパの投稿の第3段落最終文（I had a ...）に「私はそこですてきな休憩をとってから1階上の私たちにとっての終着点へと昇って行きました」とあるが，「そこで」というのは3文前の「カフェ」のことを指しており，カフェはフロアガイドのイラストから3階にあるとわかる。ピッパはその後「1階上の私たちにとっての終着点へと」昇って行ったのだから，その日の終着点は4階（4Dシアターがある）であると判断できる。よって正解は④。

主な語句・表現
・問題冊子を参照のこと。

[リード文]
◇ cool 形 「しゃれた；かっこいい；すてきな」
◇ post 動 「〈ウェブ上にメッセージなどを〉投稿する」
◇ webpage 名 「ウェブページ；ホームページ」

[投稿文]
◇ alternative 形 「別の；もう一つの」　　　◇ plenty of ... 「多くの…」
◇ stuff 名 「〈漠然と〉物」
◇ interactive 形 「〈コンピューターなどが〉インタラクティヴな；双方向の」
◇ 4D theatre 「4Dシアター」　4Dとは音声・映像といった視覚や聴覚以外の，嗅覚や触覚といったリアルな体感要素のこと。theatre はイギリス英語の表記。アメリカ英語では theater。
◇ or so S thought 「気のせいかも；わからないけど；そう思えただけ」　結果的にちょっと考えたら間違っていたかもしれないということを表す場合に使う。（例）He hates me, *or so I thought*.「彼はわたしが嫌いなんでしょ。気のせいかもしれないけど」
◇ terribly 副 「とても；すごく」　　　　　◇ realistic 形 「本物のような；リアルな」
◇ so good (that) we lost ...　《so +〈形容詞・副詞〉+ that ...》構文「とても〈形容詞・副詞〉なので…」の that はしばしば省略される。
◇ lose track of time 「時間の経過を忘れる」　◇ by the time S V 「S V する時までに（は）」
◇ find one's way 「苦労して進む」　　　　◇ slightly 副 「少し；わずかに」
◇ confusing 形 「わかりにくい」　　　　　◇ over 形 「終わる」

— 英 R 185 —

◇ (We) never mind「気にしない」　　　　　◇ vehicle 名「乗り物」
◇ environmentally-friendly「環境にやさしい」
◇ cute 形「キュートな；かわいい；魅力的な」
◇ not ... anymore「これ以上…ない」　　　◇ recommend 動「…を薦める」
◇ ... before －ing「…してから－する；－する前に…する」（例）You should think *before* speaking.「考えてから言いなさい」

[設問文・選択肢]　◇ layout 名「設計」　　　　　　　　◇ complicated 形「複雑な」
◇ frightening 形「恐ろしい」

B

出典　*Original Material*

全訳

　あなたは海外からの留学生向けの雑誌で次のような話を見つけた。

祖父にとって学問の意味

　ある日，僕が家に帰ると，同居している祖父が大学入試に関する本を読んでいるのに気づきました。なぜそんな本を読んでいるのかと尋ねると，祖父は，また大学に通う準備をしているのだと言いました。最初は，僕は祖父の言うことを信じず，冗談を言っているだけだと思っていました。ところが，祖父は本気だとわかりました。祖父は，英語や数学といった科目の教科書も買っていたのです。祖父は家族の誰にも何も言っていなかったので，僕たちはみんな驚きました。

　数日後，僕は思い切って，何を勉強するつもりなのかと祖父に聞いてみました。児童心理学のような，教師としての祖父の仕事に関連した科目だろうと僕は思っていました。祖父ははっきりと話してはくれなかったのですが，「私は，田舎に住んでいた幼い頃，夜空を見上げて，恒星や惑星の名前を言おうと試みるのが大好きだったんだ。恒星や惑星が本当に魅力的に感じられたんだよ。歴史の教師として働いている時ですら，星の神秘について私の興味をいっそう引いてくれるような本をたくさん読んだものさ。だから私は大学に行こうと決心したんだ。もっと学びたいんだよ」と語ってくれました。祖父の話を聞いて，僕は祖父の知的好奇心を深く尊敬するようになりました。

　それ以来，祖父と僕はリビングでよく一緒に勉強しています。祖父の隣に座っているのがこんなに心地よく感じられるなんて思いもしませんでした。それは，僕たちが目標に向かってともに一生懸命頑張っている友人であるかのような気分です。そして，祖父が知識を得るためだけに勉強している様子を目にして，なぜ自分が勉強するべきなのかに関する僕の考えは変わりました。何かを学ぶためには実用的な目的は必要ではないということが，僕にははっきりしたのです。今では僕は，入試に合格することが実用的な問題であるとは必ずしも思っていません。それは実際は，広大な知識の世界に入っていくための１つの道なのかもしれないのです。

　　　　　　　　　　　　　　　　　　　　　　　　　アキヤマ　サトル（高校生）

設問解説

問1　正解　　18　③　　19　④　　20　①　　21　②

「この物語によると，祖父に対するサトルの感情は以下の順序で変化した：　18　→　19　→　20　→　21　」

　　① 称賛　　　　　　② 親密さ　　　　　③ 疑い　　　　　④ 驚き

　第1段落第2文（When I asked ...）で祖父から「また大学に通う準備をしている」と聞いたサトルは，続く第3文（At first, I ...）で「僕は祖父の言うことを信じず，冗談を言っているだけだと思っていました」と述べているので，最初に来るべき感情は③「疑い」である。次に，同段落最終文（He had said ...）に，家族に黙って大学入試を受ける準備を進めていた祖父の行動を知って，「僕たちはみんな驚きました」とあるので，2番目に来る感情としては④「驚き」が適切である。第2段落で，大学で何を勉強したいのかと祖父に尋ねたサトルに対し，祖父は自分の考えを告白している。その考えを聞いたサトルは，第2段落最終文（Hearing his story, ...）で「祖父の話を聞いて，僕は祖父の知的好奇心を深く尊敬するようになりました」と述べている。選択肢に含まれる単語の中で，「尊敬」にもっとも近い意味を持つのは① admiration「称賛」なので，これが3番目に来る。

— 英 R 187 —

最後に，同じ目標に向かって祖父と一緒に勉強するようになったサトルの心情が説明されている最終段落第2文（I never thought ...）および第3文（It is almost ...）で「祖父の隣に座っているのがこんなに心地よく感じられるなんて思いもしませんでした。それは，僕たちが目標に向かってともに一生懸命頑張っている友人であるかのような気分です」と述べられており，選択肢に含まれる単語の中でこの感情を表すのにもっとも適切な単語は② closeness「親密さ」と判断できる。よって正解は③→④→①→②の順番になる。

問2　　22　　正解 ③

「サトルの祖父はおそらく大学で　22　について勉強するつもりである」

① 児童心理学
② 田舎での生活
③ **宇宙**
④ 世界史

　第2段落の祖父のセリフの引用の中で，祖父は，自分が子どもの頃から夜空の星に対して興味を持っており，教師として働いている間も，星の神秘に関する興味深い書物を数多く読んできたと述べている（... interested in their secrets の their は the stars and planets を指している）。このような内容を受けて，告白の最後の2文（That's why I've ...・I want to ...）で「だから私は大学に行こうと決心したんだ。もっと学びたいんだよ」と祖父が述べているので，③の the universe「宇宙」が正解となる。

　第2段落第2文（I thought it ...）に「児童心理学のような，教師としての祖父の仕事に関連した科目だろうと僕は思っていました」と述べられているが，これはサトルの誤った思い込みであると判明するので，①は正解ではない。②に関しては，祖父は第2段落のセリフの中で自分が田舎に住んでいたときの話をしているが，これは「田舎での生活」について祖父が勉強する予定であるということを意味するものではない。④に関しても，第2段落のセリフの中で祖父は「（自分が）歴史の教師として働いている間も…」と述べているが，これは祖父が新たに入学しようと思っている大学で「歴史」を勉強するつもりであることを示してはいないので，④「世界史」も誤りである。

問3　　23　　正解 ②

「この物語からわかったのは，サトルの祖父は　23　ということである」

① 学問の意味を理解していなかったので大学では非常に不幸に感じていた
② **新しい物事を学ぶためだけに勉強をすることもできるのだとサトルに気づかせた**
③ 自分の願いを実現するために若い頃はとても一生懸命勉強した
④ サトルが人生の意味を見つけ出すのを手助けするために自分の家族の話をした

　第2段落最終文（Hearing his story, ...）で「祖父の話を聞いて，僕は祖父の知的好奇心を深く尊敬するようになりました」と述べたサトルは，最終段落第4文（And seeing the ...）および第5文（It's clear to ...）で，「そして，祖父が知識を得るためだけに勉強している様子を目にして，なぜ自分が勉強するべきなのかに関する僕の考えは変わりました。何かを学ぶためには実用的な目的は必要ではないということが，僕にははっきりしたのです」と，自分の心情の変化を述べている。空所に②が入れば，「サトルの祖父は『新しい物事を学ぶためだけに勉強をすることもできるのだとサトルに気づかせた』」という文意になり，上記の文脈に合うので，②が正解となる。

　「サトルの祖父が大学で不幸に感じていた」という内容の記述は本文中にないので，①は誤りである。祖父は現在は「自分の願いを実現するために」一生懸命勉強しているが，若い頃もそうであったという内容の記述は本文中にないので，③も正解にはならない。④のような内容も本文中ではまったく述べられていない。

主な語句・表現	・問題冊子を参照のこと。	

[リード文]
◇ following 形「次に述べる；以下の」　　◇ overseas 副「海外（から）の；海外へ」

[タイトル]
◇ meaning 名「意味」

[第1段落]
(One day, when ...)
◇ one day「（過去の）ある日；（未来の）いつの日か」
◇ find O -ing「O が―しているのに気づく」
◇ entrance exam「入学試験」　　◇ prepare to -「―する準備をする」
◇ at first「最初（のうち）は」　　◇ make a joke「冗談を言う」
◇ it turned out S V ...「S V…ということがわかった」　S V ... の直前に接続詞の that が省略されている。
◇ serious 形「本気の；真面目な」　　◇ textbook 名「教科書」
◇ such as ...「（たとえば）…のような；…といった」
◇ amazed 形「驚いた；びっくりした」

[第2段落]
(A few days ...)
◇ ... later「…後に」　　◇ dare to -「思い切って―する；あえて―する」
◇ subject 名「科目」　　◇ related to ...「…に関連した」
◇ career 名「職業；仕事」　　◇ child psychology「児童心理学」
◇ directly 副「はっきりと；直接に」　　◇ the country「田舎」
◇ look up at ...「…を見上げる」　　◇ try to -「―しようと試みる」
◇ name 動「…の名前を言う」　　◇ star 名「星；恒星」
◇ planet 名「惑星」　　◇ completely 副「完全に；すっかり」
◇ fascinating 形「魅力的な」　　◇ all the more ...「いっそう［ますます］…」
◇ interested in ...「…に興味を持った」　　◇ That's why ...「だから…；それが…の理由だ」
◇ decide to -「―しようと決心する」　　◇ deeply 副「深く」
◇ respect 動「…を尊敬する」　　◇ intellectual 形「知的な；知性の」
◇ curiosity 名「好奇心」

[最終段落]
(Since then, we've ...)
◇ comfortable 形「心地よい；快適な」　　◇ next to ...「…の隣に」
◇ as if ...「まるで…かのように」　　◇ goal 名「目標；目的」
◇ the way S V ...「S V…する方法［様子］」　　◇ purely 副「ただ単に；純粋に」
◇ gain 動「…を得る」　　◇ knowledge 名「知識」
◇ practical 形「実用的な；現実的な」　　◇ purpose 名「目的」
◇ not necessarily ...「必ずしも…とは限らない」　部分否定を表す。
◇ regard O as ...「O を…と見なす［思う］」　　◇ pass 動「…に合格する」
◇ actually 副「実際は；本当は」　　◇ huge 形「広大な；巨大な」

[設問文・選択肢]
◇ according to ...「…によると」　　◇ order 名「順序」
◇ admiration 名「称賛；敬服」　　◇ closeness 名「親密さ；近いこと」
◇ doubt 名「疑い；疑念」　　◇ surprise 名「驚き」
◇ plan to -「―するつもりである」　　◇ universe 名「宇宙」
◇ unhappy 形「不幸な；悲しい」　　◇ realize 動「…だと気づく；…を認識する」
◇ simply 副「ただ単に」
◇ make his wishes come true「自分の願いを実現する」　make は使役動詞（make O 原形動詞「O を―させる」）。come true で「〈夢や願いが〉実現する」という意味。
◇ help O -「O が―するのを手助けする」

第4問

問1 － ③　　問2 － ④　　問3 － ③　　　　　　　　　　　　　　　　（各3点）
問4　27 － ①　　28 － ②　　　　　　　　　　　　　　　　　　　（各2点）
問5 － ⑥　　　　　　　　　　　　　　　　　　　　　　　　　　　　（3点）

出典　*Original Material*

全訳　あなたはペットに関する研究会を開催する計画を立てている。あなたが見つけた国際的なペット飼育の習慣についての資料を2人のイギリス人パートナーであるメラニーとダスティンにメールした後，あなたは自分たちが話すことのための原案を作成する。

資料：

図1．*ペットを所有することにかかる費用*（10億ドル単位）

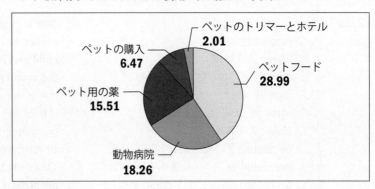

表1．*世界のペット数*

国	ペットの犬の数 （単位：100万匹）	国	ペットの猫の数 （単位：100万匹）
アメリカ	55.3	アメリカ	80.6
ブラジル	35.7	中国	58.1
中国	27.4	ロシア	18.0
ロシア	12.5	ブラジル	12.5
日本	12.0	フランス	11.4
フィリピン	11.6	イギリス	8.5
インド	10.2	ドイツ	8.2
アルゼンチン	9.2	イタリア	7.5
イギリス	8.5	日本	7.3
フランス	7.4	トルコ	3.1

（参考：Euromonitor, APPA, FEDIAF and sportrichlist.com, via GfK: *"Finding your opportunities in the Chinese pet food & treats market,"* Petfood Forum China 2015）

あなたのメールに対する返信：

こんにちは
メールをありがとう！　ペット用品がとても大きなビジネスになっているなんて知らなかった！　ブラジル人はホント大の犬好きね。ブラジルの約半分の家庭に犬がいるということが読んでわかったわ！　それももっともなことだと思う。この10年の間にブラジルは裕福になったことを知っているから。最近では，子どもを持つ代わりにペットを飼うブラジル人が多いということも耳にしたわ。

私たちの都市の至るところでペットショップを見かけるから，ペットの健康にとてもたくさんのお金が使われていることに驚きはないわね。ペットを購入する前に人々がそのことに気づいてくれたらいいのだけれど。ペットが道に捨てられる話を聞くのはもううんざり。私としてはこの点に焦点を当てたいと思う。

今後数年で人気になるのはどんなペットかしら。都会の暮らしで最新の傾向はヘビやトカゲだって！　でも今回は，あなたは猫や犬を飼う傾向について話した方がいいんじゃないかしら。

ではまた。
メラニー
追伸：このメッセージはダスティンにも送信しました。

こんにちは
すばらしい資料！　なんと役に立つことか！

ペットの飼い主が使うお金のグラフは，ペットホテルに使われるお金という点では誤解を招きやすいかも知れない。この業界は，利用可能なペットの世話関連のサービス数とともに，急速に成長しているから。僕はそのことについてみんなに説明したいと思う。

アメリカは猫と犬の数を示す表のトップに立っているけど，近い将来，この通りにはならないかも知れないというのは興味をそそる。北京では以前，犬をペットとして飼うことは違法だったことを知ってたかい。もはやそうではないが。どうやら特に北京の高齢者が連れ合いとして犬を飼っているようだ。

動物が捨てられることに関するメラニーの主張は適切だ。飼い主のいない動物は数百万匹に上るが，動物の権利がますます改善されるようになったために，この状況は変わりつつある。ロシアの首都は野良犬が有名で，よく地下鉄のエスカレーターに乗っており，親切な見知らぬ人が野良犬をかわいがって餌をあげている！　僕はもっと探してみるつもりでいる。このことはまた別の機会に発表できる面白いテーマとなり得るだろう。

ではご機嫌よう。
ダスティン
追伸：このメッセージはメラニーのところにも届くことになっている。

あなたの発表原案：

発表のテーマ：　　　　　　　| 24 |

発表者　　　　　　　　テーマ

メラニー：　　　　　　　| 25 |

ダスティン：　　　　　　| 26 |

私：　　　　　　　現在のペット飼育に関する統計

　　　　　　　観察例：
　　　　　　| 27 | の国民が飼っている犬の数は猫の約3分の2である
　　　　　　が，| 28 | の人々が飼っている猫の数とほぼ同じである。

さらなる研究テーマ：　　| 29 |

設問解説

問1　| 24 |　正解 ③

「| 24 | に最も適するのはどれか」

① 猫 vs. 犬：どっちが人々の票を勝ち取るか？
② 世界規模でペットをより温かく受け入れている社会
③ **人間の動物に対する関係および好み**
④ 人々がペットを飼う主な理由

　メラニーの返信の第1段落第2文 (I had no ...) に「ペット用品がとても大きなビジネスになっている」とあり，第2段落第1文 (I see pet ...) には「ペットの健康にとてもたくさんのお金が使われている」と，また同段落第3文 (I'm fed up ...) には「ペットが道に捨てられる話を聞くのはもううんざり」とある。さらにダスティンの返信の第2段落第2文 (This industry is ...) に「この業界［ペットホテル業界］は，利用可能なペットの世話関連のサービスの数とともに，急速に成長している」とあり，それらはいずれも人間とペットとしての動物との関係に言及した内容となっている。

　加えて，メラニーの返信の第3段落第3文 (But it'd be ...) で述べられている猫や犬を飼う傾向と，ダスティンが返信の第3段落第1文 (It's interesting that ...) で言及している猫と犬の数を示す表は，どちらも人間のペットとしての動物に対する好みに触れている。

　以上のことから正解は③となる。

　①に関しては，「猫 vs. 犬」は発表原案にある表の観察例にすぎず，リード文で述べられている「ペットに関する研究会」という内容には足りないので誤り。②と④に関しては，どちらも2人の返信メールや発表原案で今回の発表のテーマとしては言及されていないので誤り。

問2　| 25 |　正解 ④

「| 25 | に最も適するのはどれか」

① ペットをどこで手に入れたらいいかということに関して人々を教育すること
② ペットの安全を守ることを専門的に行う組織
③ ペットに関連したサービスの経済的成功
④ **ペットを買う前によく考える**

　| 25 | はメラニーの発表テーマである。メラニーは返信の第2段落 (I see pet ...) で，ペットの健康を保つにはとてもたくさんのお金がかかることを人々が認識しないままペットを購入するために，後になって持て余したペットを捨てる人がいることを批判し，最終文 (I'd like to ...) で「私としてはこの点に焦点を当てたいと思う」と述べていることから，正解

— 英 R 192 —

は④の「ペットを買う前によく考える」となる。

問3 26 正解③

「 26 に最も適するのはどれか」
① ペットを飼うという点で，中国がアメリカを追い抜くこと
② 飼い主のいない動物を見つける方法
❸ ペットの世話に関連したサービスが人気を増していること
④ ペットが公共の交通機関に乗るのを許されること

 26 はダスティンの発表テーマである。ダスティンは返信の第2段落（The chart on ...）で，ペットホテル業界は，利用可能なペットの世話関連のサービス数とともに，急速に成長しているために，ペットのトリマーとホテルにかかる費用をかなり少なく示している円グラフは誤解を招きやすいかも知れないと指摘し，最終文（I want to ...）で「僕はそのことについてみんなに説明したいと思う」と述べていることから，正解は③の「ペットの世話に関連したサービスが人気を増していること」となる。

問4 27 正解① 28 正解②

「あなたはメラニーの考えに同意し，資料に目を向ける。 27 と 28 に最も適するのはどれか」
① フランス
❷ 日本
③ ロシア
④ イギリス

発表原案の観察例にある文には「 27 の国民が飼っている犬の数は猫の約3分の2であるが， 28 の人々が飼っている猫の数とほぼ同じである」と述べられている。「世界のペット数」を示している表において，飼っている犬の数が猫の約3分の2となっている国は，選択肢の中では① フランス（犬740万匹，猫1,140万匹）と③ ロシア（犬1,250万匹，猫1,800万匹）であるとわかる。さらにその2カ国のどちらかが飼っている犬の数とほぼ同じ数の猫を飼っている国は，選択肢の中では② 日本（フランスで飼われている犬740万匹，日本で飼われている猫730万匹）であるとわかる。以上から， 27 に入る選択肢は①， 28 に入る選択肢は② ということになる。

問5 29 正解⑥

「 29 に最も適する組み合わせはどれか」
A：家族や友だちがいないことで残された空白を動物が埋めてくれること
B：ペットの飼育に関する法律がより緩和されること
C：人々が路上で生活する動物を助ける話
D：より流行となりつつあるペットの種類

発表原案の最終項目より 29 には「さらに研究するべきテーマ」が入るとわかる。

メラニーは返信の第3段落（I wonder what ...）で，「今後数年で人気になるのはどんなペットかしら。都会の暮らしで最新の傾向はヘビやトカゲだって！ でも今回は，あなたは猫や犬を飼う傾向について話した方がいいんじゃないかしら」と述べていることから，今後人気になるペットに関心があることがわかる。よって「さらに研究するべきテーマ」の組み合わせの一つは選択肢Dの「より流行となりつつあるペットの種類」であると判断できる。

ダスティンは返信の第4段落第3文（In Russia's capital ...）〜第5文（It could be ...）で「ロシアの首都は野良犬が有名で，よく地下鉄のエスカレーターに乗っており，親切な見知らぬ人が野良犬をかわいがって餌をあげている！ 僕はもっと探してみるつもりでい

— 英 R 193 —

る。このことはまた別の機会に発表できる面白いテーマとなり得るだろう」と述べている。彼が「もっと探してみるつもりでいる」のは，前文で述べられているような親切な人たちが餌をあげるなどして飼い主のいない動物を助けてあげているような事例であると推測でき，それを受けて第5文で「このことはまた別の機会に発表できる面白いテーマとなり得るだろう」と言っていることから，「さらに研究するべきテーマ」の組み合わせのもう一つは選択肢Cの「人々が路上で生活する動物を助ける話」であると判断できる。

　以上から，正解は⑥C，Dということになる。

　A，Bに関しては，2人の返信メールや発表原案で「さらに研究するべきテーマ」としては言及されていない。

主な語句・表現	・問題冊子を参照のこと。

[リード文]
◇ seminar 图「研究会；セミナー」
◇ come up with ...「〈必要な物〉を作成［生産］する」
◇ draft 图「草案；原案」

[グラフ・表]
◇ purchase 图「購入」
◇ groomer 图「トリマー；グルーマー」　ペットの美容師で，毛の手入れや入浴などの世話をする。

[メール]
◇ have no idea (that) S V「S Vすることを知らない」　that は同格の名詞節を導く接続詞。
◇ read (that) S V「S Vすることを読んで知る」
◇ make sense「道理にかなう；もっともである」
◇ I wish S would ...「…すればいいのだが」　これからの期待感の薄い願望を表す。（例）I wish he *would* do his best.「彼には最善を尽くしてもらいたい（ものだが）」
◇ be fed up of ...「…にうんざりしている」　　◇ abandon 動「…を捨てる」
◇ it'd be better for you to ...「あなたは…した方がいいでしょう」
◇ for now「今のところ（は）；さしあたり」
◇ chat soon「ではまた」　英文メールの末尾に用いるカジュアルな表現。
◇ chart 图「図表；グラフ」　　　　　　　　◇ misleading 形「誤解を招きやすい」
◇ in terms of ...「…の点から（見ると）」　◇ along with ...「…と共に；…と一緒に」
◇ pet-sitting 形「ペットの世話の」
◇ available 形「利用可能な」　直前の pet-sitting services にかかっている。
◇ top 動「〈リストなど〉のトップになる［首位に立つ］」
◇ used to −「以前−だった」　　　　　　　◇ illegal 形「違法の」
◇ Beijing 图「北京（中華人民共和国の首都）」◇ not anymore「もはやそうではない」
◇ apparently 副「どうやら［たぶん］…らしい」
◇ especially 副「特に」　　　　　　　　　◇ for company「連れ（合い）として」
◇ point 图「主張；論点」　　　　　　　　◇ throw away ...「…を捨てる」
◇ millions of ...「数百万の…」　　　　　　◇ due to ...「〈理由を表して〉…のために」
◇ animal rights「動物の権利」　　　　　　◇ capital city「首都」
◇ metro 图「地下鉄」　　　　　　　　　　◇ pet 動「…をかわいがる」
◇ feed 動「…に餌を与える」　　　　　　　◇ present 動「発表する」
◇ cheers「さようなら」　英文メールの末尾に用いるカジュアルな表現。

[発表原案]
◇ current 形「現在の」　　　　　　　　　◇ statistics 图「統計」
◇ example observation「観察例」　　　　　◇ roughly 副「おおよそ；大体」

[設問文・選択肢]

◇ A versus B「A 対 B；A vs. B」 　　　◇ win 動「…を勝ち取る」
◇ vote 名「票」 　　　　　　　　　　　◇ taste 名「好み」
◇ dedicated to ...「…に専念する；…にささげられた」
◇ overtake 動「…を追い越す［追い抜く］」 　◇ spot 動「…を見つける」
◇ homeless 形「ホームレスの；飼い主のいない」
◇ allow 動「…を許す」 　　　　　　　　◇ gap 名「空白」
◇ lack 名「欠落；いなくなること」 　　　◇ relax 動「〈規制など〉を緩和する」
◇ fashionable 形「流行の；はやりの」

第5問

解答

問1 − ③ （3点）

問2 ┃31┃ − ④ ┃32┃ − ① ┃33┃ − ② ┃34┃ − ③ （完答で3点）

問3 − ① （3点）

問4 − ③・⑤ （順不同・両方正解で3点）

問5 − ④ （3点）

出典

David Cotton, David Falvey, Simon Ken: *Language Leader Intermediate CourseBook*
問題作成のためのやむを得ない事情から，省略・改変した箇所があります。

全訳

　あなたは宿題をしている。その宿題であなたは，クラスメートに自分が調べたことを発表するために，以下の雑誌記事からの情報を使って，アメリカに多大な影響を及ぼした男性に関するプレゼンテーションメモを作らなければならない。

　レイモンド・ローウィは，「アメリカを形作った男」と呼ばれているが，あらゆる時代を通じて最も影響力のあるデザイナーの1人に違いない。彼はデザイン業界に革命を起こし，200社を超える企業のコンサルタントとして働き，包装紙から冷蔵庫，自動車から宇宙船の内装まで，あらゆるもののデザインを作り出した。彼は様々な産業にまたがりデザインの努力をすることの重要性で名声を獲得したのである。

　レイモンド・ローウィは1893年にパリで生まれた。彼はまだ十代のころにデザインの素晴らしい才能を見せ始めた。彼がデザインした模型飛行機はとてもうまくできていたので，1908年に模型飛行機の有名な賞を勝ち取った。第一次世界大戦で彼はフランス軍に従軍していたのだが，戦後1919年にニューヨークへ移住した。彼はそこに到着するとすぐに，ファッションイラストレーターの仕事を見つけた。彼は1929年に，イギリスのメーカーのためにコピー機のデザインを変更することで，工業デザインの仕事を始めた。彼のデザインのおかげで，そのコピー機の売上げは大幅に増加した。これをきっかけに，人々は工業製品のデザインの重要性により多くの注意を払うようになった。さらなる注文が相次ぎ，その中には冷蔵庫のデザインもあった。工業デザイナーとしての彼の名声を確立したのはこの製品だった。1937年以降，彼は，ペンシルバニア鉄道やアメリカの自動車メーカーのスチュードベーカーなどのような，様々な企業との関係を築き上げた。

　ローウィのデザインにはすべて，1つの共通点があった。それらは，デザインは非常に先進的であると同時に節度があるものでもなければならないという原則によって形作られていた。彼の考えは，人々は新奇なものに引きつけられるが未知のものは怖がる，ということだった。ローウィのデザインの外見上の特徴は流線型であった。流線型のものは，空中や水中を素早く，あるいは効率的に動くことを可能にする形をしている。1929年のコピー機は流線型を使った多くのデザインの始まりだった。彼は流線型を「機能と簡素化を通じての美」と評した。彼が流線型を発明して以降，それを使う傾向が何十年にもわたって工業デザインの様々な分野で強まっていった。流線型は，スピード，進歩，現代性の象徴とみなされた。彼はその後の50年間を，郵便切手や企業のロゴから店舗の内装まで，あらゆるものを流線型にすることに費やした。

　ローウィはことによると，アメリカのタバコの銘柄であるラッキーストライクの包装デザインを改めたことで最も有名であるかもしれない。1940年に，彼はその箱の背景色を緑から白に変えた。それから彼は，箱の両側に赤色の大当たりの的を置いた。こうすることでそれはより人目を引くものになり，売上げは大幅に増加した。ローウィのロゴ

— 英R 196 —

デザインは「視覚による記憶」を目指していた。彼は，短時間でもロゴを見た者は誰でも絶対にそれを忘れないようにしたかったのである。彼は有名企業のために非常に目立つロゴを数多くデザインした。

20世紀の半ばまでには，彼の工業デザイン会社はとても有名になっていたので，ローウィは，彼の会社がデザインした「ものやサービスや建造物のうちのいくつかに，普通の生活を送っている平均的な人はきっと日常的に接しているはずだ」と述べることができた。晩年に，ローウィはNASAの仕事をした。彼は，有人宇宙船内の人々の心理状態，安全性，快適性を向上させた。ローウィは1980年に87歳で引退して母国のフランスへ戻り，1986年にそこで亡くなった。

プレゼンテーションメモ：

タイトル： 30

レイモンド・ローウィの生涯
☆ローウィは子ども時代をフランスで過ごした。
☆ 31
☆ 32
☆ 33
☆ 34
☆ローウィは母国へ戻った。

ローウィのデザインに関して
☆彼のすべてのデザインに共通する概念は「 35 」だった。
☆彼のデザインにはいくつかの際立った特徴がある： 36 ・ 37

デザインの革命家であるローウィ
☆彼はデザイン業界に革命を起こした。
☆彼は多くの点でデザインにおいて偉業を成し遂げた： 38

設問解説

問1 30 正解③

「あなたの発表に最も適したタイトルはどれか」 30

① 広告におけるアメリカ人の巨匠
② 複雑で洒落たデザインが良質であることを示す
③ **産業の顔をデザインし直すこと**
④ ファッションから宇宙への旅

リード文から本文は「アメリカに多大な影響を及ぼした男性」を扱った記事であることがわかるが，その「多大な影響」のまとめとして，第1段落（Called "the man ...）に「レイモンド・ローウィは，『アメリカを形作った男』と呼ばれているが，あらゆる時代を通じて最も影響力のあるデザイナーの1人に違いない。彼はデザイン業界に革命を起こし，200社を超える企業のコンサルタントとして働き，包装紙から冷蔵庫，自動車から宇宙船の内装まで，あらゆるもののデザインを作り出した。彼は様々な産業にまたがりデザインの努力をすることの重要性で名声を獲得したのである」とある。

さらに，第3段落最終文（He spent the ...）では，ローウィのデザインの具体的特徴をまとめて，「彼はその後の50年間［流線型のデザインを発明した1929以降］の50年間を，

— 英R 197 —

郵便切手や企業のロゴから店舗の内装まで，あらゆるものを流線形にすることに費やした」
と述べられている。

「デザイン業界に革命を起こしあらゆるもののデザインを作り出した」というのは，「あ
らゆる産業の顔とも言えるデザインを作り変えた」ということを意味しているので，正解
は③となる。

①，②，④に関しては，本文には言及されていない内容なのでいずれも誤り。

問2 ┃ 31 ┃ 正解④ ┃ 32 ┃ 正解① ┃ 33 ┃ 正解② ┃ 34 ┃ 正解③
「あなたはローウィの生涯における重要なできごとを一覧表にした。そのできごとを
┃ 31 ┃ ～ ┃ 34 ┃ の空所に起きた順に入れよ」

 ① ローウィはファッションイラストレーターとして働き始めた。
 ② ローウィはコピー機のデザインを変更した。
 ③ ローウィは鉄道会社と自動車メーカーの仕事を引き受けた。
 ④ ローウィは自作の模型飛行機で賞を勝ち取った。

1900年代については，第2段落第3文（The model aircraft ...）の「彼がデザインした
模型飛行機はとてもうまくできていたので，1908年に模型飛行機の有名な賞を勝ち取った」
という記述から，④が入る。1910年代については，同段落第4文（After World War ...）と
第5文（On arriving there, ...）の「（彼は）第一次世界大戦後1919年にニューヨークへ移
住した。彼はそこに到着するとすぐに，ファッションイラストレーターの仕事を見つけた」
という記述から，①が入る。それ以降については，同段落第6文（He started his ...）の「彼
は1929年に，イギリスのメーカーのためにコピー機のデザインを変更することで，工業デ
ザインの仕事を始めた」，同段落最終文（After 1937, he ...）の「1937年以降，彼は，ペン
シルバニア鉄道やアメリカの自動車メーカーのスチュードベーカーなどのような，様々な
企業との関係を築き上げた」という記述から，② → ③という順番になることがわかる。以
上から，正解は順に④①②③となる。

問3 ┃ 35 ┃ 正解①
「以下のうちどれがローウィのデザインを最も適切に説明しているか」 ┃ 35 ┃

 ① 先進的でありそのうえ許容できる
 ② 美しいだけでなく伝統的
 ③ スピードと快適さの結合
 ④ 最新の流行の追従

ポスターを見ると，空所には「彼のすべてのデザインに共通する概念」を説明するも
のが入ることがわかる。第3段落第1文（Loewy's designs all ...），第2文（They were
shaped ...）および第3文（His idea was ...）に，「ローウィのデザインにはすべて，1つ
の共通点があった。それらは，デザインは非常に先進的であると同時に節度があるもので
もなければならないという原則によって形作られていた。彼の考えは，人々は新奇なもの
に引きつけられるが未知のものは怖がる，ということだった」とある。この内容に最も近
いのは①なので，これが正解である。

②，③，④に該当する記述は本文中にはない。

問4 ┃ 36 ┃・┃ 37 ┃ 正解③・⑤
「以下の記述のうち，どの2つがポスターでの使用に最も適切か。（順不同とする）」
┃ 36 ┃・┃ 37 ┃

 ① 特定の色と文字の組み合わせが彼のデザインで使われていた。
 ② 円と直線のモチーフが彼のデザインで使われていた。
 ③ 人々は彼のデザインを一目見ただけで覚えていることができた。

— 英R 198 —

④　彼のデザインがあまりにも芸術的だったので人々はそれを理解できなかった。

⑤　彼のデザインは簡素で機能的であるにもかかわらず美しかった。

　ポスターを見ると，空所には「彼のデザインに見られるいくつかの際立った特徴」が入ることがわかる。第4段落第4文（This made it ...），第5文（Loewy's logo designs ...）および第6文（He wanted to ...）の「こうすること（＝タバコの包装デザインを変更したこと）でそれはより人目を引くものになり，売上げは大幅に増加した。ローウィのロゴデザインは『視覚による記憶』を目指していた。彼は，短時間でもロゴを見た者は誰でも絶対にそれを忘れないようにしたかったのである」という記述から，タバコの売上げが大きく増えたのは，ローウィの意図した通り，人々が変更された包装デザインを短時間でも目にしただけで覚えていた結果であると考えることができるので，③は正しい。また，第3段落第6文（The copying machine ...）と第7文（He described streamlining ...）の「1929年のコピー機は流線型を使った多くのデザインの始まりだった。彼は流線型を『機能と簡素化を通じての美』と評した」という記述から，⑤も正しい。①，②，④に該当する記述は本文中にない。

問5　　38　　正解④

「以下のできごとのどの組み合わせがポスターでの使用に最も適切か」　　38

　A：ローウィは先進的で現代的な工業デザインを作り出した。

　B：ローウィは1930年代以降のデザインの潮流を確立した。

　C：ローウィは，たとえデザインが複雑でも売り上げは増えることを知った。

　D：ローウィはNASAの依頼で宇宙船のエンジン設計を改善した。

　E：ローウィは工業デザインの重要性を人々に認識させた。

　F：ローウィはデザインを定期的に変更することの有効性を証明した。

　ポスターを見ると，空所には「ローウィがデザインにおいて成し遂げた偉業」が入ることがわかる。第1段落第2文（He revolutionized the ...）の「彼はデザイン業界に革命を起こした」，第3段落第2文（They were shaped ...）の「デザインは非常に先進的である（…）という原則」，および同段落第9文（It was seen ...）の「（ローウィが発明した）流線型は，スピード，進歩，現代性の象徴とみなされた」という記述から，Aは正しい。また，第3段落第8文（After his invention ...）の「彼が流線型を発明（＝1929年）して以降，それを使う傾向が何十年にもわたって工業デザインの様々な分野で強まっていった」という記述から，Bも正しい。さらに，第2段落第7文（Thanks to his ...）および第8文（This led to ...）の「彼のデザインのおかげで，そのコピー機の売上げは大幅に増加した。これをきっかけに，人々は工業製品のデザインの重要性により多くの注意を払うようになった」という記述から，Eも正しい。CやFのような内容は本文では述べられていない。また，第1段落第2文（He revolutionized the ...）に「彼は（…）自動車から宇宙船の内装まで，あらゆるもののデザインを作り出した」という記述があり，最終段落第3文（He improved the ...）にも「彼は，有人宇宙船内の人々の心理状態，安全性，快適性を向上させた」という記述はあるが，「宇宙船のエンジン設計を改善した」とは述べられていないので，Dも誤りである。以上から，正解は④となる。

（主な語句・表現）

[リード文]

・問題冊子を参照のこと。

◇ require O to – 「Oに－するよう要求する」

◇ below副「以下の」　　　　　　　◇ present動「…を発表する」

[第1段落]

（Called "the man ...）

◇ influential形「影響力のある」　　◇ of all time「あらゆる時代を通じて」

◇ revolutionize動「…に革命を起こす」　◇ industry名「産業；…業界」

◇ consultant名「コンサルタント；顧問」　◇ packaging名「包装材料」

— 英 R 199 —

◇ refrigerator 图「冷蔵庫」　　　　　◇ interior 图「内装」
◇ spacecraft 图「宇宙船」　　　　　　◇ achieve 動「…を獲得する」
◇ fame 图「名声」　　　　　　　　　　◇ effort 图「努力」
◇ a variety of ...「様々な…」

[第2段落]　　◇ exhibit 動「〈才能など〉を示す [見せる]」　◇ aircraft 图「飛行機」
(Raymond Loewy ...)　◇ award 图「賞」　　　　　　　　　　◇ serve 動「軍務に就く；従軍する」
　　　　　　　◇ on −ing「−すると（すぐに）」　　　　◇ career 图「仕事；キャリア」
　　　　　　　◇ re-design 動「…をデザインし直す」　　◇ copying machine「コピー機」
　　　　　　　◇ manufacturer 图「製造業者；メーカー」　◇ thanks to ...「…のおかげで」
　　　　　　　◇ lead to ...「…という結果になる；…を引き起こす」
　　　　　　　◇ pay attention to ...「…に注意を払う」　◇ further 形「さらなる」
　　　　　　　◇ commission 图「注文；依頼」　　　　　◇ follow 動「続いて起こる」
　　　　　　　◇ including ...「…を含めて」
　　　　　　　◇ It was this product that established ...「…を確立したのはこの製品だった」 強調構文。
　　　　　　　◇ establish 動「…を確立する」　　　　　◇ reputation 图「名声」
　　　　　　　◇ ..., and so on「…など」

[第3段落]　　◇ in common「共通して」　　　　　　　◇ principle 图「原則」
(Loewy's designs ...)　◇ progressive 形「先進的な」　　　　　◇ moderate 形「節度がある;極端に走らない」
　　　　　　　◇ attract 動「…を引きつける」　　　　　◇ novel 形「新奇な；真新しい」
　　　　　　　◇ external 形「外部の」　　　　　　　　◇ feature 图「特徴」
　　　　　　　◇ streamlining 图「流線型」　streamline は「…を流線型にする」という動詞。
　　　　　　　◇ object 图「物体」
　　　　　　　◇ allow O to −「O が−するのを許す [可能にする]」
　　　　　　　◇ efficiently 副「効率的に」
　　　　　　　◇ describe ... (as 〜)「…を（〜だと）評する；…を説明する」
　　　　　　　◇ function 图「機能」　　　　　　　　　◇ simplification 图「簡素化」
　　　　　　　◇ trend 图「傾向；流行」　　　　　　　　◇ decade 图「10 年」
　　　　　　　◇ see ... as 〜「…を〜だとみなす」　　　◇ progress 图「進歩；発展」
　　　　　　　◇ modernity 图「現代性」
　　　　　　　◇ spend〈時間〉−ing「〈時間〉を−することに費やす」
　　　　　　　◇ postage stamp「郵便切手」
　　　　　　　◇ logo 图「〈商標・社名などの〉ロゴ；シンボルマーク」

[第4段落]　　◇ brand 图「銘柄；ブランド」　　　　　◇ background 图「背景」
(Locwy is　　◇ packet 图「(小) 箱」　　　　　　　　◇ lucky strike「大当たり」
perhaps ...)　◇ target 图「(標) 的」　　　　　　　　　◇ eye-catching「人目を引く」
　　　　　　　◇ aim at ...「…を目指す [狙う]」　　　　◇ visual 形「視覚による」
　　　　　　　◇ retention 图「記憶（力）」　　　　　　◇ make sure that ...「確実に…する」
　　　　　　　◇ highly 副「非常に」　　　　　　　　　◇ visible 形「目立つ」

[最終段落]　　◇ firm 图「会社」　　　　　　　　　　◇ lead a ... life「…な生活を送る」
(By the mid-20th ...)　◇ be bound to −「必ず−する；きっと−するはずだ」
　　　　　　　◇ be in daily contact with ...「…に日常的に接している」
　　　　　　　◇ structure 图「建造物；構造」　　　　　◇ late in life「晩年に」
　　　　　　　◇ improve 動「…を改善する」　　　　　◇ psychology 图「心理状態；心理学」

◇ comfort 图「快適性」
◇ manned 形「〈宇宙船などが〉人間を乗せた；有人の」
◇ retire 動「引退する」　　　　　　◇ native 形「母国の；出生地の」

[ポスター]
◇ concept 图「概念」　　　　　　　◇ distinctive 形「際立った」
◇ characteristic 图「特徴」　　　　　◇ revolutionist 图「革命家」
◇ achievement 图「業績」　　　　　◇ in a number of ways「多くの点で」

[設問文・選択肢]
◇ presentation 图「発表」　　　　　◇ master 图「巨匠」
◇ complex 图「複雑」　　　　　　　◇ cool 形「かっこよい；洒落た」
◇ quality 图「上質；良質」　　　　　◇ list 動「…を一覧表にする」
◇ order 图「順序」　　　　　　　　◇ take on ...「…を引き受ける」
◇ following 形「以下の」　　　　　　◇ advanced 形「先進的な」
◇ acceptable 形「許容できる」　　　◇ traditional 形「伝統的な」
◇ combine 動「…を結合する」　　　◇ latest 形「最新の」
◇ description 图「記述；説明」　　　◇ appropriate 形「適切な」
◇ specific 形「特定の」　　　　　　◇ letter 图「文字」
◇ motif 图「モチーフ；主題」　　　　◇ glance 图「一目見ること」
◇ despite 前「…にもかかわらず」　　◇ functional 形「機能的な」
◇ combination 图「組み合わせ」　　　◇ onward 副「…以降」
◇ find out「…を知る；…とわかる」　◇ complicated 形「複雑な」
◇ aware of ...「…を認識した；…に気づいた」
◇ prove 動「…を証明する」　　　　　◇ effectiveness 图「有効性」
◇ regularly 副「定期的に；規則正しく」

第6問

解答

A 問1 - ③ 問2 - ④ 問3 - ① 問4 - ① (各3点)
B 問1 - ② 問2 - ③ (各3点)
  問3 - ①・⑤ (順不同・両方正解で3点)
  問4 - ② (3点)

A

出典

What makes reading a social justice issue? (America THE JESUIT REVIEW)
問題作成のためのやむを得ない事情から，省略・改変した箇所があります。

全訳

　あなたは授業で行う，読書が及ぼす影響に関するクラスの研究課題に取り組んでいる。あなたは以下の記事を見つけた。あなたは，クラスメートに自分が調べたことを発表するために，その記事を読んでポスターを作っているところだ。

なぜ読書が社会正義の問題になるのか

　ニューヨーク・タイムズ紙で報告された最近の研究では，読書をする人が読書をしない人よりも平均して2年近く長生きをすることが突き止められた。実際，読書をする人の人生は，より長いだけでなく，より深いものである可能性が高い。読書は他者の気持ちを理解する能力を育み，より多くの喜びや愛情を得る能力を築くのを助けうるのだ。

　現在のアメリカ人の読書活動は，少々評価が難しい。10年以上前だが，『危機的状況にある読書』(2004) と呼ばれる報告書は，文学を読むアメリカの成人の割合が劇的に落ち込んだと結論づけた。しかし2005年のある調査では，全く反対の結果になった。全アメリカ人のほぼ半数がその調査の時期に本を読んでいたが，これは1990年の割合よりも増えていて，1957年の割合の2倍以上であった。より最近には，2015年の調査報告で，16歳から29歳までの年齢のアメリカ人の80パーセントが過去1年の間に本を読んでいることがわかり，その年齢層にいる人は30歳より上の年齢の人々よりも本を読む人になる可能性が高いとまで示されたのだった。

　しかし，そうしたデータのいくつかは励みになるかもしれないが，明らかに心配の種となるものもまた存在する。利用可能な最も近年のものである2012年と2014年に集められた読み書き能力調査のデータでは，16歳から65歳までの年齢のアメリカ人の17パーセントが，測定された読解力の4つのレベルのうち，最も低いレベルかそれ以下のレベルで読んでいると示されている。さらに，読解力が欠けている人の割合は，失業者の間での方が高かった。

　社会経済的地位と読解力の関係がどのようなものであったとしても，その関係性は複雑だ。学校制度において資源が不均等に分配されていることと，十分に財政的支援が投入されていないことは，確実にその一因であるだろう。裕福な家庭の方が，親が自身の望み通りに子どもと読書ができる時間を多くとることができ，そうした融通が利くという事実もまたそうだ。貧困と読み書き能力をつなぐものが厳密には何であるのかに関わらず，こうした統計上のデータは，読書がぜいたく品として扱われてはならず，社会的な対応を要する根本的に人間が必要とするものとして扱わなければならないということ

— 英 R 202 —

を思い出させてくれるのに役立っているのだ。

　学校での読書活動もまた強化されるべきであり，それは，生徒の読解力を高めるためだけでなく，本が読者に与える様々な世界や洞察へと彼らを導くためでもある。昔からある名著も，より広範な種類の著者によるより近年の作品も，どちらも生徒の視野を広げ，他者の人生に対する好奇心を促進するのを助けるためには重要だ。最近，3つの異なる公立高校の英語の授業を1年にわたって観察したある著者が気づいたのは，3つすべての高校の教師が，生徒に対して，ヘミングウェイのような古典だけでなくアリス・ウォーカーやエイミ・タンのような近年の著者も読む気にさせようと決意していることであった。

　その生徒たちは創造的な課題や教室内での真剣な討論に熱意を持って取り組むようになった。私たちが持つ最も古い科学技術の1つである本が，最も現代的なソーシャルメディアネットワークが提供しうるよりも深く，彼らを異なる経験や文化や考えへとつなげるのを助けてくれたのだ。

　読解力は現代の経済活動にいかなる形で参加するのにも必要なものだ。しかしさらに重要なことに，読書，特に小説を読むことは，読者を感化し，他者の感情に対してより興味を持たせて，読者が精神性や政治的責任を育むのを助けてくれる。読書が大好きだという気持ちを促進することは，経済面での生活の質を向上させる可能性が高いだけでなく，社会で共有される人生を深め，豊かなものにしてくれる可能性も高いのである。

なぜ誰もが読書をするべきなのか

読書は危機的状況にあるのか？　誰が文学を読んでいるのか？
・1957―成人の約4分の1
・2005―成人の約2分の1
・2015―成人の約80%
⇒ 今日ではさらに多くの人々が読書をしている

主な問題：16歳〜65歳のアメリカ人の17%が基本的な読解力を欠いている

なぜ一部の人々は読解力を欠いている可能性が高いのか？

誰が	考えられる理由
・失業者	・自分が通っていた学校に資源が不足していたこと
	・ 39
	・彼らに本を読んでやる時間が親になかった
	・彼らに本を読んでやる欲求／能力が親になかった

教室での解決策	読書の恩恵
・もっと読書に取り組むこと	・寿命が2年延びること
・昔からある本と最近の本を利用すること	・ 41
・創造的な課題を与えること	・愛情を得る能力を築くこと
・ 40	・生徒の視野を広げること

> **要約**
>
> 読書は我々の社会にとって重要である。
>
> それは [42] ばかりでなく，我々をより思いやりのある人間にもする。

設問解説

問1 [39] **正解③**

「ポスターの [39] に最も適する選択肢を選べ」

① 読書を重要であるとみなさない
② 長期にわたって学校を欠席すること
③ **教育に十分なお金が投入されていないこと**
④ 書物にかかる費用が高額であること

ポスターの [39] には，失業者が読解力を欠いていると考えられる理由の1つが入る。

第3段落最終文（Furthermore, the share ...）から第4段落第2文（Unequal distribution of ...）前半にかけて「さらに，読解力が欠けている人の割合は，失業者の間での方が高かった。社会経済的地位と読解力の関係がどのようなものであったとしても，その関係性は複雑だ。学校制度において資源が不均等に分配されていることと，十分に財政的支援が投入されていないことは，確実にその一因であるだろう」と述べられている。したがって，社会経済的地位の低い失業者が読解力を欠いている理由としてここでは「学校制度において資源が不均等に分配されていること」（これが [39] の上の理由に当たる）と「学校制度において十分に財政的支援が投入されていないこと」が挙げられていることがわかるので，正解は③となる。

①，②，④に関しては，本文には言及されていない内容なのでいずれも誤り。

問2 [40] **正解④**

「ポスターの [40] に最も適する選択肢を選べ」

① 他の文化との関係を説明すること
② ソーシャルネットワーキングサイトを組み込むこと
③ 教師の経験を共有すること
④ **授業での真剣な討論を始めること**

ポスターの [40] には，読解力を欠いていることに対する教室で行う解決策の1つが入る。

第5段落（Commitment to reading ...）では，生徒の読解力を高めるためだけでなく，本が読者に与える様々な世界や洞察へと生徒を導くためにも，学校での読書活動を強化するべきであり，実際3つの公立高校の英語の授業では，教師が古典だけでなく，近年の著者も読むよう生徒たちを促している，と説明されている。その内容を受けて，第6段落第1文（These students became ...）では「その生徒たちは創造的な課題や教室内での真剣な討論に熱意を持って取り組むようになった」と述べられ，「読書活動の強化」と「創造的な課題や教室内での真剣な討論への取り組み」の間には相補的関係があることが読み取れる。よって正解は④となる。「創造的な課題への取り組み」が [40] の上の解決策に当たる。

①，②，③に関しては，本文には言及されていない内容なのでいずれも誤り。

問3 [41] **正解①**

「ポスターの [41] に最も適する選択肢を選べ」

① **感情の理解**
② 経験を表現したいという欲求
③ 生徒のマナーの向上
④ もっと上手に文章を書きたいという意欲

ポスターの [41] には，読書がもたらす恩恵の1つが入る。

— 英R 204 —

第1段落最終文（Reading can help ...）で「読書は他者の気持ちを理解する能力を育み，より多くの喜びや愛情を得る能力を築くことを助けうるのだ」と述べられていることから，読書がもたらす恩恵の1つが「他者の気持ちを理解する能力」であるとわかる。よって正解は ① となる。「他者の気持ち」に関しては，最終段落第2文（But even more ...）においても「読書，特に小説を読むことは，読者を感化し，他者の感情に対してより興味を持たせて，読者が精神性や政治的責任を育むのを助けてくれる」という言及があるが，この箇所も「読書が他者の気持ちを理解する能力」を育むことを示唆していると言えるだろう。

　②，③，④ に関しては，本文には言及されていない内容なのでいずれも誤り。

問4　　42　　正解 ①
　「ポスターの　42　に最も適する選択肢を選べ」
　① 経済を促進する
　② テクノロジーを発展させる
　③ 税金を納めるよう我々を促す
　④ 犯罪発生率を下げる
　ポスターの　42　には，要約文の一部が入る。

　筆者は最終段落（Reading skills are ...）でタイトルの「なぜ読書が社会正義の問題になるのか」という問いかけの答えとなる自身の主張をまとめているが，その最終文（Encouraging a love ...）では「読書が大好きだという気持ちを促進することは，経済面での生活の質を向上させる可能性が高いだけでなく，社会で共有される人生を深め，豊かなものにしてくれる可能性も高いのである」と述べている。これは，読書が個人のものとしての「経済を促進する」ばかりでなく，第2文（But even more ...）で述べられているように他者の感情に対してより興味を持たせて，「思いやりのある人間にする」ことで，他者と共有する人生を深め，豊かなものにしてくれる可能性も高い，ということを意味している。よって正解は ① となる。

　②，③，④ に関しては，本文には言及されていない内容なのでいずれも誤り。

（主な語句・表現）　・問題冊子を参照のこと。

[リード文]
◇ work on ...「…に取り組む」　　　　◇ project 名「研究課題」
◇ article 名「記事；論文」　　　　　◇ below 形「以下の」

[タイトル]
◇ social 形「社会の」　　　　　　　◇ justice 名「正義；公正」
◇ issue 名「問題」

[第1段落]
（A recent study ...）
◇ determine 動「…を突き止める」　　◇ average 名「平均」
◇ indeed 副「実際（に）」　　　　　◇ help － 「－するのを助ける」
◇ capacity 名「能力」

[第2段落]
（Americans'
current ...）
◇ current 形「現在の」　　　　　　　◇ engagement 名「取り組み；活動」
◇ somewhat 副「やや；少し」　　　　◇ evaluate 動「…を評価する；…を測定する」
◇ decade 名「10年間」　　　　　　　◇ risk 名「危険；リスク」
◇ conclude that ...「…と結論づける」　◇ literature 名「文学」
◇ dramatically 副「劇的に」　　　　◇ survey 名「調査」
◇ the exact opposite「正反対」　　　◇ more than double ...「…の2倍以上で」
◇ range 名「範囲」　　　　　　　　　◇ those over 30「30歳より上の年齢の人々」

— 英R 205 —

[第3段落]
(As encouraging ...)

◇ As encouraging as some of that data may be「そうしたデータのいくつかは励みになる かもしれないが」（as ＋）〈形容詞・副詞〉＋ as ＋ S be「S は〈形容詞・副詞〉だけれど も」（譲歩）。encouraging は「励みになる」という意味の形容詞。

◇ concern 名「心配」　　　　　　　　　　◇ literacy 名「読み書き能力」
◇ available 形「入手［利用］可能な」　　　◇ furthermore 副「さらに」
◇ share 名「割合；割り当て」動「…を共有する」
◇ those lacking reading skills「読解力が欠けている人々」　lack は「…を欠いている」と いう意味の動詞。
◇ population 名「人々；人口」　　　　　　◇ unemployed 形「失業した；求職中の」

[第4段落]
(Whatever the ...)

◇ relationship 名「関係」　　　　　　　　◇ socioeconomic 形「社会経済的な」
◇ status 名「地位；身分」　　　　　　　　◇ complicated 形「複雑な」
◇ unequal 形「不平等な」　　　　　　　　◇ distribution 名「分配」
◇ resource 名「資源」　　　　　　　　　　◇ insufficient 形「不十分な」
◇ funding 名「財政的支援」　　　　　　　◇ contribute 動「一因となる」
◇ as does the fact that ...「…という事実と同じように」
◇ better-off 形「より裕福な」　well-off「裕福な」の比較級。
◇ flexibility 名「柔軟さ；融通がきくこと」　◇ act on ...「…に基づいて行動する」
◇ regardless of ...「…に関係なく；…に関わらず」
◇ link 動「…をつなぐ」　　　　　　　　　◇ poverty 名「貧困」
◇ statistics 名「統計；統計上の数字［データ］」
◇ serve as ...「…として役立つ」　　　　　◇ reminder 名「思い出させるもの」
◇ treat 動「…を扱う」　　　　　　　　　　◇ luxury 名「ぜいたく品」
◇ call for ...「…を要求する」　　　　　　　◇ response 名「反応；対応」

[第5段落]
(Commitment to ...)

◇ commitment to ...「…への関わり；…への参加」
◇ strengthen 動「…を強める」　　　　　　◇ introduce 動「…を導く；…を導入する」
◇ insight 名「洞察」　　　　　　　　　　　◇ traditional 形「伝統的な；古くからある」
◇ variety 名「種類」
◇ broaden one's horizons「〈人〉の視野を広げる」
◇ encourage 動「…を促進する」　　　　　◇ curiosity 名「好奇心」
◇ monitor 動「…を観察する」　　　　　　◇ motivate O to －「O を－する気にさせる」
◇ classic 名「古典」　ここでは古典的な文学作品のこと。

[第6段落]
(These students ...)

◇ passionately 副「熱心に」　　　　　　　◇ involved 形「参加した；取り組んだ」
◇ creative 形「創造的な」　　　　　　　　◇ assignment 名「課題」
◇ earnest 形「真剣な」　　　　　　　　　◇ connect 動「…をつなぐ」
◇ depth 名「深さ」

[最終段落]
(Reading skills ...)

◇ participation 名「参加」
◇ even more important「さらに重要なことには」　副詞句として働いている。even は「さ らに；いっそう」という意味で，比較級を強調している。
◇ especially 副「特に」　　　　　　　　　◇ fiction 名「小説；フィクション」
◇ inspire 動「…を鼓舞する；…を感化する」◇ spirituality 名「精神性」
◇ political 形「政治的な」　　　　　　　　◇ responsibility 名「責任」
◇ improve 動「…を向上させる；…を改善する」
◇ deepen 動「…を深める」　　　　　　　　◇ enrich 動「…を豊かにする」

[ポスター]	◇ solution 图「解決策」	◇ benefit 图「利益；恩恵」
	◇ caring 形「思いやりのある」	
	◇ A as well as B「B ばかりでなく A；A ばかりでなく B も」	

[設問文・選択肢]　◇ see A as B「A を B とみなす［考える］」　◇ link to ...「…との関係」
　　　　　　　　◇ incorporate 動「…を組み込む」　　　　◇ comprehension 图「理解」
　　　　　　　　◇ boost 動「…を高める；…を促進する」　◇ encourage O to −「−するよう O を促す」
　　　　　　　　◇ crime rate「犯罪（発生）率」

B

出典　Lillian Steenblik Hwang: *Analyze This: Sleep patterns vary widely across the world*
　　　問題作成のためのやむを得ない事情から，省略・改変した箇所があります。

全訳

　　あなたは十分な睡眠をとることの重要性に関心を持っていて，異なる人間集団の睡眠パターンに関する以下の記事を読もうとしている。

　　睡眠は重要である。実際，最近のデータが示しているのは，一貫した睡眠スケジュールを維持することが，適切な量の質の良い睡眠をとることとまさに同じくらい重要であるかもしれないということだ。他の霊長類の動物と比べると，人間の進化には，より短い時間でより深い睡眠をとることへ移行するという特徴が生じ，それにより，文化が発展していくにつれ，新たな技術や知識を身につけるための時間がより多く得られた。人間はまた，日々の仕事のスケジュールや環境的要因に基づいて，睡眠のスケジュールを修正する能力も進化させたのである。

　　興味深いことに，世界中のあらゆる人が同じタイプの睡眠スケジュールに従っているわけではない。最近の研究で，科学者たちは4つの人間集団の睡眠パターンに注目した。ハッツァ族は，東アフリカの国であるタンザニアに住む狩猟採集民族である。マラガシー族は，アフリカ南東部の沿岸沖に浮かぶ巨大な島国であるマダガスカルの村に暮らしている。どちらの集団も電気のない生活をしている。これらの人々が，西洋（アメリカ合衆国やヨーロッパのような場所）で暮らす人々と比較され，さらには，今からおよそ200 ～ 500年前，産業革命以前に暮らしていた西欧の人々とも比較された。

　　世間一般の通念に反して，電気のない社会に住む人々は，工業社会に住む人々より必ずしもたくさん睡眠をとっているわけではない。これは，1つには，この研究におけるマラガシー族やハッツァ族を含めた，非西洋諸国の狩猟採集民族や村人たちは，日中のうちで自然の太陽光を浴びて過ごしている時間がより長いからかもしれない。また，1日に1回か2回昼寝をすることも彼らに何らかの影響を及ぼしているのかもしれない。狩猟採集民族や村人たちはたいていの場合，家族や集団の様々なメンバーと一緒の空間で睡眠をとっており，西洋の人々について報告されている状況に比べ，夜の間に目を覚ます頻度が高いのである。

　　昼寝を別にすれば，マラガシー族の村人たちの睡眠パターンは，産業革命以前の西欧の人々と非常によく似ている。どちらの事例においても，大人たちは午後6時よりも少し後に眠りについていた。それから彼らは2回に分けて睡眠をとっていた。最初の睡眠は午前0時近くに終わり，その後，1時間かそこら目を覚ましたまま過ごしたあと，再び眠りに落ちていた。それに対して，アメリカ合衆国で9時から5時まで仕事をしている成人のような現代の西洋人は，概して，午前0時の少し前に眠りにつき，朝6時頃に起床している。そして，彼らのうちの大多数はまったく昼寝をしていないのである。

― 英 R 207 ―

これらの集団のそれぞれにおける異なった睡眠パターンは，人間の睡眠の柔軟性を強調し，また，現代の西洋人の睡眠のあり方における健康面での潜在的な危険性を示している。狩猟採集民族と村人たちは，屋内の照明やコンピュータ画面からのブルーライトにさらされる量がより少ないが，ブルーライトは，体内時計を混乱させる可能性がある。スマートフォンや他のデジタル機器から放出される青い波長の光は，人が眠りに落ちるのを促すホルモンであるメラトニンの生成を抑制し，睡眠を遅らせる可能性があるのだ。現代社会に生きる人々は，この研究から教訓を得ることができるだろう。すなわち，質の良い睡眠を取るためには，日中はもっとたくさん日光を浴びるようにし，暗くなった後は青い波長の光にさらされるのを減らすべきなのである。

設問解説

問1　43　正解②

「人間はより短い時間でより深い睡眠をとるように進化したが，それによって，　43　」
① 人間は独力で睡眠スケジュールを修正することができるようになった
② **人間はより知能が高く，より有能になることが可能になった**
③ 日中に昼寝をする機会がよりたくさん与えられた
④ 狩猟や採集をするための時間がはるかに多く与えられた

　人間がより短い時間でより深い睡眠をとるように進化したことは，第1段落第3文 (Compared with other ...) に述べられており，その文の後半に「…それにより，文化が発展していくにつれ，新たな技術や知識を身につけるための時間がより多く得られた」という記述がある。よって，新たな技術を身につけた状態を more competent，新たな知識を身につけた状態を more intelligent と言い換えている ② が正解となる。

　① の「睡眠スケジュールの修正をする能力」については，第1段落最終文 (Humans also evolved ...) に述べられているが，これは「より短い時間でより深い睡眠をとることへの進化」とは別の人間の進化として挙げられたものであり，両者に因果関係はない。③，④ についても，「より短い時間でより深い睡眠をとることへの進化」との直接の結びつきは本文中では述べられていない。

問2　44　正解③

「4つの図表のうち，どれが記事に一致しているか」　44

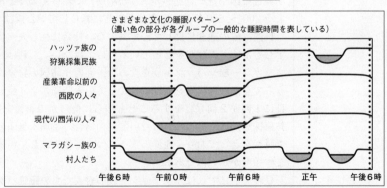

　図表は4つの人間集団の睡眠パターンを表したものだが，これに関する記述は第2～4段落にある。選択肢の4つの図表において，それぞれ左側に示されている4つの人間集団を整理しておくと，Hadza hunter-gatherers は「タンザニアに住む狩猟採集民族であるハッツァ族」，Preindustrial Western Europeans は「今からおよそ200～500年前，産業革命以前に暮らしていた西欧の人々」，Present-day Westerners は「現代の西洋諸国に暮らす人々」，Malagasy villagers は「マダガスカルの村に暮らすマラガシー族」である。そ

れぞれの集団の睡眠パターンに関して判断材料となる記述は以下の3点である。

(1) 第3段落第3文（Napping once or ...）に「1日に1回か2回昼寝をすること」がマラガシー族とハッツァ族の特徴として挙げられている。よって，図表の右側の日中（6 a.m. から 6 p.m. の範囲）に睡眠が見られる2つが，マラガシー族とハッツァ族になる。

(2) 第4段落第1文（Except for the ...）に「昼寝を別にすれば，マラガシー族の村人たちの睡眠パターンは，産業革命以前の西欧の人々と非常によく似ている」，第2文（In both cases, ...）と第3文（Then they slept ...）に「どちらの事例においても，大人たちは午後6時よりも少し後に眠りについていた。それから彼らは2回に分けて睡眠をとっていた」と述べられている。よって，図表の左側の夜間（6 p.m. から 6 a.m. の範囲）の睡眠が2回に分かれているもののうち，昼寝を示す時間帯が含まれているものがマラガシー族，昼寝が見られないものが産業革命以前の西欧の人々とわかる。

(3) 第4段落第6文（By comparison, present-day ...）と最終文（And no mid-day ...）に「現代の西洋人は，概して，午前0時の少し前に眠りにつき，朝6時頃に起床し，彼らのうちの大多数はまったく昼寝をしていない」と述べられている。すなわち，夜間の睡眠が1回で，昼寝が見られないものが現代の西洋人となる。

よって，以上の(1)，(2)，(3)をすべて満たしている ③ が正解となる。

問3 　45 ・ 46 　正解①・⑤

「記事によれば，以下の記述のうち，どの2つが正しいか。（順不同とする）」 　45 ・ 46

　　① 青い波長の光が，人間に対して健康面での危険をもたらす可能性がある。
　　② 狩猟採集民族は，自然の太陽光にもっとさらされるべきである。
　　③ ある種のブルーライトは，睡眠ホルモンの生成を促進する可能性がある。
　　④ 今日の西洋の人々は，定期的に昼寝をするべきである。
　　⑤ 今日の西洋の人々の体内時計は，非常に狂いやすい。

最終段落第1文（Different sleep patterns ...）に「異なった睡眠パターンが，現代の西洋人の睡眠のあり方における健康面での潜在的な危険性を示している」という記述があり，この危険性について述べているのが，最終段落第2文（Hunter-gatherers and villagers ...）の「ブルーライトは，体内時計を混乱させる可能性がある」という部分である。さらに，ブルーライトが及ぼす影響は，続く第3文（Blue-wave light emitted ...）で「スマートフォンや他のデジタル機器から放出される青い波長の光は，人が眠りに落ちるのを促すホルモンであるメラトニンの生成を抑制し，睡眠を遅らせる可能性がある」と説明されている。以上のことから，「ブルーライトによって，睡眠障害という健康被害がもたらされる可能性がある」（①に合致）と言え，「スマートフォンやデジタル機器に触れる時間が長い現代の西洋人の体内時計は，ブルーライトによって狂わされやすい」（⑤に合致）と言える。

最終段落最終文（People in modern ...）で述べられているように，もっと自然の太陽光を浴びるべきなのは狩猟採集民族ではなく現代社会に生きる人々なので，②は本文の内容に合わない。③は，「ブルーライトは，睡眠ホルモンの生成を促進する」という点が誤りである（最終段落第3文に「青い波長の光は，人が眠りに落ちるのを促すホルモンであるメラトニンの生成を抑制する」とある）。④のような記述は本文にはない。

問4 　47 　正解②

「この記事に最適なタイトルは， 　47 　である」
　　① 人間の睡眠量の進化
　　② 人間の柔軟な睡眠パターン
　　③ 現代における睡眠障害
　　④ 電気なしでの睡眠習慣

— 英 R 209 —

この記事は，4つの人間集団の異なる睡眠パターンを調べた研究結果を基盤にして，そのような睡眠スケジュールの違いが意味することや，その重要性について考察したものである。第1段落最終文（Humans also evolved ...）では，人間は「日々の仕事のスケジュールや環境的要因に基づいて，睡眠のスケジュールを修正する能力も進化させた」と述べられており，第2～4段落では，様々な人間集団の睡眠スケジュールが具体的に詳述されている。さらに最終段落第1文（Different sleep patterns ...）には，「これらの集団のそれぞれにおける異なった睡眠パターンは，人間の睡眠の柔軟性を強調し」とあり，同段落最終文（People in modern ...）に記された，健康的な睡眠習慣をもたらすための現代人への助言で文章全体が締めくくられている。以上のように，記事全体を通して「人間の睡眠の柔軟性」への言及がなされていることから，② が正解になる。

　① については第1段落で，③ については最終段落で，④ については第3段落と第4段落でそれぞれ言及がなされているが，いずれも記事全体から見ると部分的な記述にとどまっており，記事のタイトルとしては適切ではない。

主な語句・表現	・問題冊子を参照のこと。

[リード文]
◇ be interested in ...「…に関心［興味］を抱いている」
◇ adequate 形「十分な；適当な」　　◇ following 形「以下の；次の」
◇ article 名「記事；論文」

[第1段落]
(Sleep is important ...)
◇ in fact「実際に」　　◇ recent 形「最近の」
◇ suggest 動「…を示唆する」　　◇ consistent 形「首尾一貫した；変わらない」
◇ schedule 名「スケジュール」　　◇ quality sleep「質のよい睡眠」
◇ compared with ...「…と比べると」　　◇ primate 名「霊長類の動物」
◇ evolution 名「進化」＞ evolve 動「進化する」
◇ feature 動「…を呼び物［特徴］にする」　　◇ shift 名「変化；移行；交替」
◇ provide 動「…を提供する」　　◇ expand 動「発展する；拡大する」
◇ revise 動「…を見直す［修正する］」　　◇ based on ...「…に基づいて」
◇ environmental 形「環境の」　　◇ factor 名「要因；要素」

[第2段落]
(Interestingly, not everyone ...)
◇ interestingly 副「興味深いことに」　　◇ keep to ...「…に従う」
◇ hunter-gatherer「狩猟採集民」　　◇ electricity 名「電気」
◇ be compared to ...「…と比較される」　　◇ the Industrial Revolution「産業革命」

[第3段落]
(Contrary to ...)
◇ contrary to ...「…に反して；…とは違って」
◇ conventional 形「従来の；世間一般の」　　◇ wisdom 名「一般的な考え；通念；知恵」
◇ industrial society「工業社会」　　◇ in part「部分的に；1つには」
◇ including 前「…を含めた」　　◇ nap 名「昼寝をする；昼寝」
◇ effect 名「影響；効果」　　◇ various 形「様々な」
◇ frequently 副「頻繁に」　　◇ Westerner 名「西洋の人々」

[第4段落]
(Except for the ...)
◇ except for ...「…を除けば；…を別にすれば」
◇ be similar to ...「…に似ている」　　◇ preindustrial 形「産業化以前の」
◇ midnight 名「午前0時；夜の12時」
◇ remain up「目が覚めたままである；起きたままでいる」
◇ ... or so「…かそこら」
◇ fall back to ...「〈元の状態など〉に戻る［帰る］」
◇ by comparison「それに対して；対照的に」

— 英 R 210 —

◇ present-day 形「現代の；今日の」　　　◇ typically 副「典型的に；概して」
◇ mid-day 形「真昼の」　　　　　　　　　◇ majority 名「大多数；大部分」

[最終段落]
（Different sleep ...）
◇ highlight 動「…を強調する」　　　　　◇ flexibility 名「柔軟性；適応性」
◇ point to ...「…を示す［表す］」　　　◇ potential 形「潜在的な；可能性を秘めた」
◇ be exposed to ...「…にさらされる」　◇ indoor lighting「屋内（の）照明」
◇ confuse 動「…を混乱させる」　　　　　◇ internal 形「体内の；内部の」
◇ emit 動「…を発する［出す］」　　　　　◇ device 名「機器；装置」
◇ suppress 動「…を抑える」　　　　　　　◇ production 名「生成；生産」
◇ melatonin 名「メラトニン」　ホルモンの一種。
◇ hormone 名「ホルモン」　　　　　　　　◇ fall asleep「寝入る；眠りに落ちる」
◇ delay 動「…を遅らせる」　　　　　　　◇ research 名「研究；探究」
◇ that is「つまり；すなわち」　　　　　◇ exposure 名「さらされること」

[設問文・選択肢]
◇ allow O to -「O が-するのを許す」　　　◇ on one's own「独力で；1 人で」
◇ enable O to -「O が-するのを可能にする」
◇ intelligent 形「知能が高い；聡明な」　◇ competent 形「有能な」
◇ offer 動「…を与える；…を提供する」　◇ opportunity 名「機会」
◇ chart 名「図表；グラフ」　　　　　　　◇ typical 形「典型的な；普通の」
◇ according to ...「…によると」　　　　◇ statement 名「記述；意見；文」
◇ option 名「選択肢」　　　　　　　　　　◇ matter 動「重要である；関係がある」
◇ pose 動「…をもたらす」　　　　　　　　◇ hazard 名「危険；危険要素」
◇ stimulate 動「…を刺激する；…を促進する」
◇ daytime 形「日中の；昼間の」　　　　　◇ regularly 副「定期的に」
◇ body clock「体内時計」　　　　　　　　◇ quantity 名「量」
◇ flexible 形「柔軟な；適応性に富んだ」　◇ disorder 名「不調；障害」
◇ habit 名「習慣；癖」

2023 年度

大学入学共通テスト 本試験
英語（リーディング）

解答・解説

■ 2023 年度（令和 5 年度）本試験「英語（リーディング）」得点別偏差値表
下記の表は大学入試センター公表の平均点と標準偏差をもとに作成したものです。

平均点　53.81　　標準偏差　20.99　　　　　　　受験者数　463,985

得 点	偏差値	得 点	偏差値
100	72.0	50	48.2
99	71.5	49	47.7
98	71.1	48	47.2
97	70.6	47	46.8
96	70.1	46	46.3
95	69.6	45	45.8
94	69.1	44	45.3
93	68.7	43	44.8
92	68.2	42	44.4
91	67.7	41	43.9
90	67.2	40	43.4
89	66.8	39	42.9
88	66.3	38	42.5
87	65.8	37	42.0
86	65.3	36	41.5
85	64.9	35	41.0
84	64.4	34	40.6
83	63.9	33	40.1
82	63.4	32	39.6
81	63.0	31	39.1
80	62.5	30	38.7
79	62.0	29	38.2
78	61.5	28	37.7
77	61.0	27	37.2
76	60.6	26	36.8
75	60.1	25	36.3
74	59.6	24	35.8
73	59.1	23	35.3
72	58.7	22	34.8
71	58.2	21	34.4
70	57.7	20	33.9
69	57.2	19	33.4
68	56.8	18	32.9
67	56.3	17	32.5
66	55.8	16	32.0
65	55.3	15	31.5
64	54.9	14	31.0
63	54.4	13	30.6
62	53.9	12	30.1
61	53.4	11	29.6
60	52.9	10	29.1
59	52.5	9	28.7
58	52.0	8	28.2
57	51.5	7	27.7
56	51.0	6	27.2
55	50.6	5	26.7
54	50.1	4	26.3
53	49.6	3	25.8
52	49.1	2	25.3
51	48.7	1	24.8
		0	24.4

英語（リーディング） 2023年度　本試験　（100点満点）

（解答・配点）

問題番号（配点）	設問		解答番号	正解	配点	自己採点欄
第1問（10）	A	1	1	①	2	
	A	2	2	④	2	
	B	1	3	③	2	
	B	2	4	④	2	
	B	3	5	③	2	
小　計						
第2問（20）	A	1	6	②	2	
	A	2	7	②	2	
	A	3	8	②	2	
	A	4	9	④	2	
	A	5	10	①	2	
	B	1	11	④	2	
	B	2	12	①	2	
	B	3	13	①	2	
	B	4	14	①	2	
	B	5	15	②	2	
小　計						
第3問（15）	A	1	16	②	3	
	A	2	17	③	3	
	B	1	18	③	3*	
			19	④		
			20	②		
			21	①		
	B	2	22	③	3	
	B	3	23	②	3	
小　計						

問題番号（配点）	設問	解答番号	正解	配点	自己採点欄
第4問（16）	1	24	①	3	
	2	25	①	3	
	3	26	②	2	
		27	⑤	2	
	4	28	①	3	
	5	29	②	3	
小　計					
第5問（15）	1	30	④	3	
	2	31	③	3	
	3	32	②	3*	
		33	④		
		34	⑤		
		35	③		
	4	36	③	3	
	5	37 － 38	① － ⑤	3*	
小　計					
第6問（24）	A 1	39	③	3	
	A 2	40	④	3	
	A 3	41 － 42	④ － ⑥	3*	
	A 4	43	①	3	
	B 1	44	④	2	
	B 2	45 － 46	① － ⑤	3*	
	B 3	47	③	2	
	B 4	48	④	2	
	B 5	49	④	3	
小　計					
合　計					

（注）
1　＊は，全部正解の場合のみ点を与える。
2　－（ハイフン）でつながれた正解は，順序を問わない。

第1問

A

〈全訳〉

　あなたは米国で勉強中で，午後の活動として2つの公演のうち1つを選んで見に行く必要があります。担任の先生から次のようなプリントをもらいます。

金曜日の公演

パレス劇場 「どこでも一緒に」	グランド劇場 「ギター・クイーン」
笑いあり涙ありの恋愛劇	華やかな衣装が特徴のロックミュージカル
▶午後2時から（休憩はなく，上演時間は1時間45分）	▶午後1時開演（2度の15分休憩を含めて3時間の上演）
▶上演後にロビーで俳優たちと話ができます	▶開演前に衣装を着た出演者たちを迎える機会があります
▶飲食物は販売していません	▶軽い飲食物（スナックやドリンク）や，特製Tシャツなどのグッズをロビーで販売します
▶幸運な方5名にTシャツをプレゼントします	

申込方法：どちらの公演を見に行きたいですか。下の書式に記入して担任の先生に今日中に提出してください。

- -

1つ選んでください（✓）：
「どこでも一緒に」□　　「ギター・クイーン」□

氏名：＿＿＿＿＿＿＿＿＿＿＿

〈設問解説〉

問1　1　正解－①

「あなたはプリントを読んだ後で何をしなさいと言われているか」

① 一番下の部分に記入してそれを提出する。
② 2つの公演についてより多くのことを調べる。
③ 自分が決めたことを担任の先生に話す。
④ 自分の名前を書いて自分の選択を説明する。

　正解は①。本文下部の Instructions の第2文（Fill in the ...）に，「下の書式に記入して担任の先生に今日中に提出してください」とあり，①はこの内容と合っている。

他の選択肢のようなことは本文からは読み取れない（④は「自分の選択を説明する」が誤り）。

問2　2　正解－④

「2つの公演のどちらについても言えることはどれか」

① 上演前に飲み物を購入することはできない。
② 数枚のTシャツがおみやげにもらえる。
③ どちらも同じ時刻に終演する。
④ 劇場で俳優たちに会うことができる。

　正解は④。「パレス劇場（Palace Theater）」での公演についての説明の中に「上演後にロビーで俳優たちと話ができます（Actors available to ...）」とあり，「グランド劇場（Grand Theater）」での公演についての説明の中に「開演前に衣装を着た出演者たちを迎える機会があります（Opportunity to greet ...）」とあり，④はこれらの内容と合っている。

　①や②は，グランド劇場に当てはまらない。③については，パレス劇場の公演は，「午後2時から（休憩はなく，上演時間は1時間45分）（From 2:00 p.m. ...）」とあることから，終演時間は3時45分であり，グランド劇場の公演は，「午後1時開演（2度の15分休憩を含めて3時間の上演）（Starts at 1:00 p.m. ...）」とあることから，終演時間は午後4時であるとわかるので，③も誤りである。

〈主な語句・表現〉

performance 图「（音楽・演劇などの）催し物」／handout 图「刷り物；プリント」／break 图「小休止；休憩」／running time「上演時間」／free 形「無料の」／feature 動「…を特徴［呼び物］とする」／two 15-minute breaks「2度の15分休憩」／greet 動「…に挨拶する；…を歓迎する」／cast 图「出演者（全員）」／light refreshments「軽い飲食物」／instructions 图「指示；命令」／fill in ...「…を埋める；…に記入する」／the form below「下の書式」／hand ... in「…を提出する」

— 英 R 215 —

B

〈全訳〉

　あなたは夏休みに英語の力を伸ばしたいと思っている高校3年生です。あるインターナショナルスクールが提供する夏期集中英語キャンプのウェブサイトを見つけます。

夏期集中英語キャンプ
ギャリー・インターナショナルスクール（GIS）は，1989年から日本の高校3年生に夏期集中英語キャンプを提供してきました。2週間英語だけの環境で過ごしてみませんか！

日程：2023年8月1－14日
場所：山梨県・河口湖青年の家
費用：食事と宿泊代込みで12万円（カヤッキングやカヌーイングなどの自由選択活動は別料金）

コース設定

◆フォレスト：基本的な文法構造をマスターし，簡単なトピックについての短いスピーチを行い，発音のコツを身につけます。指導教官は数ヵ国で20年以上の英語の指導経験があります。キャンプの最終日にはスピーチコンテストに参加して，他のキャンプ参加者全員に聞いてもらいます。

◆マウンテン：グループで作業をして，英語の寸劇を書いて演じます。このコースの指導教官はニューヨーク市，ロンドン，シドニーの演劇学校で働いた経験があります。8月14日に寸劇を演じて，キャンプ参加者全員に楽しんでもらいます。

◆スカイ：このコースではディベート力と批判的思考法を身につけます。指導教官は多くの国でディベートチームを指導した経験を持ち，このテーマでベストセラーになったテキストを出版した人たちもいます。最終日には他のキャンプ参加者全員の前で短いディベートを行います。（注：受講を認められるのは上級レベルの英語力を持つ人に限られます）

▲申し込み

ステップ1：2023年5月20日までにここにあるオンライン申込書に記入してください。

ステップ2：あなたの英語力を評価したり希望のコースを尋ねるための面接を設定するため，私たちからあなたに連絡をします。

ステップ3：あなたにコースが割り当てられます。

〈設問解説〉

　　問1　　3　　正解－③

「GIS のすべての指導教官は　3　」

① 1989年以来ずっと日本にいる

② 国際大会で優勝したことがある

③ 他の国々で働いたことがある

④ 人気のある本を何冊か書いたことがある

　正解は③。GIS は3つのコースを提供しているが，FOREST コースの説明には「指導教官は数ヵ国で20年以上の英語の教授経験があります（Your instructors have taught ...）」とあり，MOUNTAIN コースの説明には「このコースの指導教官はニューヨーク市，ロンドン，シドニーの演劇学校で働いた経験があります（Instructors for this course ...）」とあり，SKY コースの説明には「指導教官は多くの国でディベートチームを指導した経験を持ち…（Your instructors have been to ...）」とある。これらの記述から③は正しいとわかる。

　他の選択肢はいずれも，GIS の指導教官全員に当てはまることとは考えられない。

　　問2　　4　　正解－④

「キャンプの最終日にキャンプ参加者たちは　4　」

① お互いの成果を評価し合う

② 最優秀賞をもらうために競い合う

③ 将来についてのプレゼンを行う

④ キャンプで身につけたことを披露する

　正解は④。キャンプで提供される3つのコースのうち，FOREST については「キャンプの最終日にはスピーチコンテストに参加して，他のキャンプ参加者全員に聞いてもらいます（On the final day ...）」とあり，MOUNTAIN については「8月14日（つまりキャンプの最終日）に寸劇を演じて，キャンプ参加者全員に楽しんでもらいます（You'll perform your skit ...）」とあり，SKY については「最終日には他のキャンプ参加者全員の前で短いディベートを行います（You'll do a short debate ...）」とある。これらの内容と合っている④が正解となる。

　①については，お互いの成果を「評価し合う」とは本文では述べられていないので，正解にはなれない。②や③のようなことも，本文からは読み取れない。

　　問3　　5　　正解－③

「あなたがキャンプの申込書を提出するとどうなるか」

— 英 R 216 —

① あなたは英語の指導教官たちに電話をする。
② あなたは英語の筆記試験を受ける。
③ **あなたの英語のレベルが調べられる。**
④ あなたの英語のスピーチのトピックが送られてくる。

正解は③。本文の「申し込み (Application)」のステップ2に，「あなたの英語力を評価したり希望のコースを尋ねるための面接を設定するため，私たちからあなたに連絡をします (We'll contact you ...)」とあることから，下線部の内容と合っている③が正解となる。

他の選択肢のようなことは，本文では述べられていない。

〈主な語句・表現〉

senior 形「最高学年の」／ intensive 形「集中的な」／ run 動「…を運営［提供］する」／ provide A for B「AをBに提供する」／ location 名「場所；所在地」／ prefecture 名「県」／ accommodation 名「宿泊(施設)」／ additional fees「追加料金」／ optional 形「選択の；任意の」／ Courses Offered「提供されるコース」／ grammar structure「文法構造」／ tip 名「ヒント；秘訣」／ take part in ...「…に参加する」／ skit 名「寸劇」／ debating skills「ディベート［討論］の技術」／ critical thinking「批判的思考(法)」／ have been to ...「…に行ったことがある」／ subject 名「主題；学科」／ those with ...「…を伴う［持っている］人々」／ advanced 形「上級の」／ accept 動「〈受講を〉認める」／ application 名「申し込み(書)」／ set up「…を設定する」／ assess 動「…を評価する」／ course preference「コースについての好み」／ assign 動「…を割り当てる」

第2問
A
〈全訳〉

あなたは長い距離を歩いて学校へ通っていて，しばしば足が痛くなることから，良い靴を1足買いたいと思っている。英国のあるウェブサイトで探していると，このような広告を見つける。

ナビ55が提供する新しいシューズ
スマートサポート

スマートサポート・シューズは丈夫で長持ち，しかもお手頃な価格です。3つのカラーとスタイルの中からお求めになれます。

ナノチップ

特徴

スマートサポート・シューズに組み込まれたナノチップは，iSupportアプリに接続するとあなたの足の形を調べます。このアプリをあなたのスマートフォン，パソコン，タブレット，スマートウォッチのいずれか，あるいはすべてにダウンロードしてください。それからシューズを履いている間に，あなたの足のデータをチップに収集させると，シューズの内側が自動的に調節されて，インソールが正確でパーソナライズされたものとなります。ナビ55の他の製品と同様に，このシューズにも定評あるルートメモリー機能が搭載されています。

優れた点

より良いバランス：パーソナライズされたインソールが，あなたの立ち方を調節することによって，足，脚部，背中が痛むのを防ぎます。

運動の促進：とても履き心地がいいので，定期的に歩こうという気持ちになります。

ルートメモリー：歩いている間，チップがあなたの毎日のルート，距離，ペースを記録します。

ルートオプション：デバイスで現在地を見たり，道案内の音声を自動的にイヤホンで流したり，スマートウォッチで道案内を読むことができます。

お客様の声

● 私は道案内の方法を選べるのが気に入っていますが，ビジュアルガイダンスよりオーディオガイダンスの方が好きです。

● 1ヵ月で2キロもやせました！

● 今は自分のシューズをとても気に入っていますが，履き慣れるのに数日かかりました。

● 雨でも滑らないので，一年中履いています。

● 軽くて履き心地がいいので，自転車に乗る時も履いています。

● あちこち簡単に出かけられます！ 道に迷う心配は無用です。

● とてもかっこいいです。アプリの基本機能は使いやすいですが，お金を払ってオプションの上級機能を利用することはないと思います。

〈設問解説〉

問1 6 正解－②

「メーカーの説明によれば，この新しいシューズを最も適切に言い表しているものはどれか」

① 安価な夏向きのシューズ

② ハイテクなふだん履きのシューズ

③ 軽くて快適なスポーツシューズ

④ スタイリッシュでカラフルなサイクリングシューズ

正解は②。広告中のAdvantagesの項には，「運動の促進：とても履き心地がいいので，定期的に歩こうという気持ちになります（Promotes Exercise: ...）」，「ルートメモリー：歩いている間，チップがあなたの毎日のルート，距離，ペースを記録します（Route Memory: ...）」といった記述がある。これらの中の下線部の表現から，これは「ふだん履きのシューズ（everyday shoes）」と考えることができる。また，ナノチップが組み込まれていて，使用者がアプリを使って様々な機能を利用できると述べられていることから，このシューズは「ハイテク（high-tech）」であると考えることもできる。したがって②が正解として最適である。

このシューズが「夏向き（①）」であるとか，「スポーツ（③）」や「サイクリング（④）」に向いているとは，メーカーの説明からは読み取れないので，他の選択肢はいずれも誤りとなる（この問いでは「メーカーの説明（the maker's statements）」として正しいものを選ぶことが求められているので，「お客様の声（Customers' Comments）」の項にある内容を正解の根拠にすることはできない）。

問2 7 正解－②

「このシューズが提供する利点の中で，あなたが気に入る可能性が最も高いものはどれか」

① 定期的な運動をよりたくさんすること［より規則正しい運動をすること］

② パーソナライズされたインソールを備えていること

③ あなたの歩く速さを知っていること

④ 履くとかっこよく見えること

正解は②。問題の冒頭文（You want to ...）に，「あなたは長い距離を歩いて学校へ通っていて，しばしば足が痛くなることから，良い靴を1足買いたいと思っている」とあることに注意する。下線部から，足が痛くならない機能が「あなた」が最も気に入る利点となると考えることができる。その利点とは，Advantagesの最初の項に「より良いバランス：パーソナライズされたインソールが，あなたの立ち方を調節することによって，足，脚部，背中が痛むのを防ぎます（Better Balance: ...）」とあることから，「パーソナライズされたインソール（the personalised support）」が「あなたが気に入る可能性が最も高い利点」であることになる。したがって正解は②に決まる。

他の選択肢を正解とする根拠はない。

問3 8 正解－②

「利用客が述べた意見の1つに，8というのがある」

① アプリは早歩きを促す

② アプリの無料機能は利用しやすい

③ このシューズはお買い得だ

④ このシューズはサイクリングの速度を上げる

正解は②。「お客様の声（Customers' Comments）」の内容と合っているものが正解となる。最後の意見（They look great. ...）に「とてもかっこいいです。アプリの基本機能は使いやすいですが，お金を払ってオプションの上級機能を利用することはないと思います」とあることから，この内容と合っている②が正解となる（アプリの基本機能が無料であることは，後半の「お金を払って…」という記述からわかる）。

①のように「アプリが早歩きを促す」や，④のように「シューズがサイクリングの速度を上げる」という意見を述べた利用客はいない。③のようなことも「お客様の声」の中では述べられていない。

問4 9 正解－④

「ある利用客は，オーディオ機器の利用についてコメ

— 英 R 218 —

ントしている。このコメントは次のどの利点に基づく
ものか」

① より良いバランス

② 運動の促進

③ ルートメモリー

④ ルートオプション

　正解は④。「オーディオ機器の利用」について触れて
いるのは，「お客様の声」の最初の意見（I like the ...）
のみである。そこには「私は道案内の方法を選べるの
が気に入っていますが，ビジュアルガイダンスよりオー
ディオガイダンスの方が好きです」とあることから，
このコメントは「道案内（directions）」に関する利点
に基づくものである。4つの選択肢の中で，「道案内」
と関連があるのはルートオプション（これについては，
「デバイスで現在地を見たり，道案内の音声を自動的に
イヤホンで流したり，スマートウォッチで道案内を読
むことができます」と述べられている）のみなので，
④が正解となる。

問5　10　正解－①

「ある利用客の意見では，10が勧められている」

① シューズを履き慣れるのにかかる時間を見込ん
でおくこと

② 体重を減らすのに役立つ時計を買うこと

③ シューズを履く前にアプリに接続すること

④ お金を払って iSupport の上級機能を利用するこ
と

　正解は①。「お客様の声（Customers' Comments）」
の3つ目のコメント（I love my ...）に，「今は自分の
シューズをとても気に入っていますが，履き慣れるの
に数日かかりました」とある。このコメントは，この
シューズを履き慣れるにはある程度時間がかかるので，
最初は自分に合わないと感じても，しばらく様子を見
るのが良いと勧めている，つまり靴を履き慣れるまで
「時間を見込んでおくこと（allowing time）」を勧めて
いると考えられることから，①は適切な内容である。

　②のように「時計」を買うことを勧めているコメン
トはない。③や④のようなことを勧めているコメント
もない。

〈主な語句・表現〉

sore 形「痛い」／ advertisement 名「広告」／ line
名「製品の種類；製品群」／ long-lasting 形「長持ち
する」／ reasonably priced「手頃な価格の」／
feature 名「特徴」／ nano- [接頭辞]「10億分の1」／

chip 名「チップ；半導体（の小片）」／ analyse 動「…
を分析する」／ application 名「アプリ」／ A, B, C,
and/or D「A, B, C, D のすべてまたはそのどれか」／
personalised 形「個人向けにした；パーソナライズさ
れた」／ foot support「靴底［足裏］サポート；インソー
ル」／ as with ...「…と同様に」／ function 名「機能」／
help (to) 原形「－するのに役立つ」／ keep ... free
from pain「…が痛くならないようにし続ける」／
back 名「背中」／ promote 動「…を促す」／ be
willing to－「－するのをいとわない」／ directions 名「行
き方；道順」／ prefer A to B「B よりも A を好む」／
get used to them「シューズに慣れる」　them は my
pair (of shoes) を指している。／ all year round「一年
中」／ They are so light and comfortable (that) ...
「それはとても軽くて快適なので…」／ get around「あ
ちこち動き回る」／ get lost「道に迷う」／ cool 形「かっ
こいい」／ be based on ...「…に基づいている」／
recommend 動「…を勧める」／ put ... on「…を身に
つける」

— 英 R 219 —

B

〈全訳〉

　あなたは生徒会の委員です。委員たちは生徒が時間を効率よく使うのに役立つ生徒プロジェクトについて議論してきました。あなたはアイディアを得ようとして，あるスクール・チャレンジについてのレポートを読んでいます。それは日本の他の学校で学んでいた交換学生が書いたものでした。

通学チャレンジ

　私の学校では，ほとんどの生徒はバスか列車で通学しています。多くの生徒が携帯電話でゲームをしたり，おしゃべりしているのをよく見かけます。けれども，この時間を読書や宿題に使うこともできるはずです。私たちは生徒たちが通学時間をより有効に使うのを助けるためにこの活動を始めました。生徒たちには1月17日から2月17日までの通学時の活動のチャートを完成させることが求められました。合計300人の生徒が参加しましたが，その3分の2以上は2年生で，およそ4分の1は3年生でした。1年生で参加したのはわずか15名でした。1年生の参加者がこんなに少なかったのはなぜでしょう。（以下に示す）参加者たちの感想によれば，どうやらこの問題には答えがあるようです。

参加者たちの感想

HS：このプロジェクトのおかげで，私は英語の単語テストで過去最高点を取ることができました。小さな目標をいくつも設定して，それをクリアしながら通学するのは楽でした。

KF：私の友人は参加できなかったので残念そうでした。彼女は家が近いので，歩いて通学しています。他の参加方法もあったらよかったのですが。

SS：私の乗る列車はいつも混んでいて立っていなければならないので，本やタブレットを開けるスペースはありません。耳で聞く教材しか利用できませんでしたが，量が全然足りませんでした。

JH：私は学習日誌を作りましたが，このおかげで自分が時間をどう使っているのかに気づきました。どういうわけか，私の1年生のクラスメートのほとんどは，このチャレンジについて知らなかったようでした。

MN：私はバスに乗っている時間はほとんど，ビデオを見て過ごしていて，それは授業をより理解するのに役立ちました。時間がとても速く流れるように感じました。

〈設問解説〉

問1　11　正解 — ④

「通学チャレンジの目的は，生徒たちが 11 のを助けることだった」

① より敏速に通学する

② 試験の点数を上げる

③ 英語の授業によりうまく対処する

④ 時間をよりうまく使う

　正解は④。本文中の「通学チャレンジ（Commuting Challenge）」に関する説明文の第4文（We started this ...）に，「私たちは生徒たちが通学時間をより有効に使うのを助けるためにこの活動を始めました」とあることから，下線部の内容に最も近い④が正解となる。

　他の選択肢は，このチャレンジの目的とは考えられない。

問2　12　正解 — ①

「通学チャレンジに関する1つの事実は，12 ということである」

① 1年生の参加者は10パーセント未満だった

② 冬季に2ヵ月間行われた

③ 生徒たちはバスの中で携帯機器を使わなければならなかった

④ 参加者の大多数は列車で通った

　正解は①。「通学チャレンジ（Commuting Challenge）」に関する説明文の第6文（A total of ...）以降に，「合計300人の生徒が参加しましたが，その3分の2以上は2年生で，およそ4分の1は3年生でした。1年生で参加したのはわずか15名でした」とある。下線部の内容から①は正しいとわかる。

　②は「2ヵ月」を「1ヵ月」に直さないと，第5文（Students had to ...）の内容と合わない。③のようなことは本文からは読み取れない。④は「列車」を「バスか列車」に直さないと，第1文（Most students come ...）の内容と合わない。

問3　13　正解 — ①

「参加者たちの感想によると，13 が参加者たちが報告した活動の中にあった」

A：学習記録をとること

B：言語を学ぶこと

C：タブレットでメモを取ること

D：授業ノートを携帯電話で読むこと

　正解は①。本文中の「参加者たちの感想（Feedback from participants）」の内容に合うものを選ぶ。Aは

— 英 R 220 —

JH の感想（私は学習日誌を作りましたが…）と合っている。B は HS の感想（このプロジェクトのおかげで，私は英語の単語テストで過去最高点を取ることができました…）と合っている。

C や D のようなことを述べた生徒はいない。

問4　　14　　正解－①

「通学チャレンジに関する参加者の意見の１つに，14 というのがある」

① それは徒歩で通学する生徒たちを含むこともできたであろうに

② 列車内は本を読むには良い場所だった

③ 勉強のためのオーディオ教材は豊富にあった

④ 娯楽のためにビデオを見ることは，時間の経過を早めるのに役立った

正解は①。本文中の「参加者たちの感想（Feedback from participants）」を参照する。KF の感想に「私の友人は参加できなかったので残念そうでした。彼女は家が近いので，歩いて通学しています。他の参加方法もあったらよかったのですが」とある。この感想は，徒歩で通学する生徒たちもチャレンジに参加できるようにするべきだったという意味に解せることから，① が正解となる（① の中の could have p.p. は「（その気になれば）…することもできたであろう（がしなかった）」という意味を表している）。

② や ③ のような感想を述べた生徒はいない。④ は「娯楽のために（for fun）」が MN の感想と合わない。

問5　　15　　正解－②

「筆者の疑問は 15 によって答えられている」

① HS

② JH

③ KF

④ MN

⑤ SS

正解は②。「筆者の疑問」とは，「通学チャレンジ（Commuting Challenge）」に関する説明文の下から３行目にある「１年生の参加者がこんなに少なかったのはなぜでしょう（How come ...?）」である。この疑問に答えていると考えられるのは，JH の感想の第２文（For some reason ...）の「どういうわけか，私の１年生のクラスメートのほとんどは，このチャレンジについて知らなかったようでした」である。この発言は，「１年生の参加が少なかったのは，彼らへの告知不足が原因」と解せる発言であるから，上の疑問の答えに相当

する発言と考えられる。したがって ② が正解に決まる。

他の生徒の感想の中に，上の疑問への答えと考えられるものは含まれていない。

〈主な語句・表現〉

student council「生徒会」／ efficiently 副「効率よく」／ challenge 名「難題；チャレンジ」／ commute 動「通学する」／ they could also use ...「彼らは（その気になれば）…を使うこともできるだろう」／ effectively 副「効果的に；有効に」／ complete 動「…を完成させる；記入する」／ chart 名「図表；グラフ；チャート」／ participate 動「参加する」／ two thirds「３分の２」／ first [second; third] -years「１［２；３］年生の生徒たち」／ a quarter「４分の１」／ How come ... ?「どうして…なのか」／ based on ...「…に基づくと」／ feedback 名「反応；意見；感想」／ the highest score ever「今までで最高の得点」／ goals to complete「達成すべき目標」／ on my way「途中で」／ There should have been ...「…がある方が良かった」／ take part「参加する」／ audio materials「オーディオ［耳で聞く］教材」／ not nearly ...「…に近いどころではない；全然…でない」／ enough = enough materials「十分な量の教材」／ keep a log「記録をとる；日誌をつける」／ for some reason「何らかの理由で；どういうわけか」／ spend O −ing「O を−ing して過ごす」

— 英 R 221 —

第3問
A
〈全訳〉

　あなたはシドニーのキャンバーフォード大学で勉強しています。クラスのキャンプ旅行に行くことになっていて，準備のためにキャンプクラブの会報を読んでいます。

キャンプに行くのなら，読んでください！

　こんにちは，私はケイトリンです。私が最近行ったクラブ旅行から得た2つの実用的なキャンプの教訓をお話ししたいと思います。1つ目は，バックパックを大きく3つの部分に分けて，一番重いものを中間部に入れ，バックパックのバランスを取ることです。次に，より頻繁に使う日常必需品は，上部に入れるのが良いです。つまり，寝袋は下部に入れて，食べ物や料理器具やテントは中間部に，服は上部に入れるのです。良いバックパックにはたいてい，すぐに取り出せる小物を入れておくための「ブレーン（補助ポーチ）」が付いています。

　去年，私たちは晩に屋外で楽しく料理を作って食べました。私はキャンプファイアーの近くに座っていましたが，テントに戻る頃には，寒さでこごえていました。寝る前に何枚も重ね着をしましたが，それでも寒く感じました。すると友達が私に，上に着ている重ね着を脱いで，それを寝袋に詰め込んですき間を少しふさいでみなさいと言いました。この詰め物方式は私には初めてでしたが，一晩中暖かく過ごせたので驚きました！

　私のアドバイスが，あなたが暖かく快適に過ごすのに役立てば幸いです。キャンプ旅行を楽しんでくださいね。

〈設問解説〉
問1　16　正解─②
「ケイトリンのアドバイスに従えば，バックパックをどのように詰めるべきか」

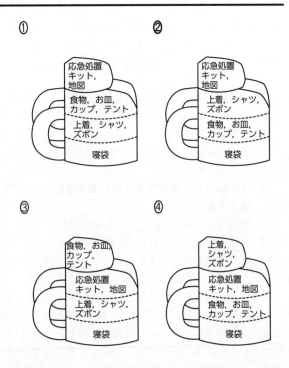

　正解は②。ケイトリンが書いた会報記事の中で，バックパックの詰め方に関するアドバイスは，第1段落第3文（The first thing ...）以降の「1つ目は，バックパックを大きく3つの部分に分けて，一番重いものを中間部に入れ，バックパックのバランスを取ることです。次に，より頻繁に使う日常必需品は，上部に入れるのが良いです。つまり，寝袋は下部に入れて，(A)食べ物や料理器具やテントは中間部に，(B)服は上部に入れるのです。良いバックパックにはたいてい，すぐに出せる小物を入れておくための『ブレーン（補助ポーチ）』が付いています」という部分である。下線部(A)から，図中の「中間部（middle section）」に「食べ物や料理器具やテント（food, plates, cups, tent）」が入っている②か④が正解だとわかる。次に下線部(B)から，「服（clothes）」，つまり「上着やシャツやズボン（jackets, shirts, trousers）」が，「上部（top section）」に入っている②が正解に決まる。②は上記のアドバイスの他の内容とも矛盾しない。

問2　17　正解─③
「ケイトリンの話によると，17が，夜通し暖かくして過ごすのに最適な方法である」
① テントから出るのを避けること
② キャンプファイアーのそばで温かいものを食べること

③ 寝袋の中のすき間をふさぐこと
④ 着替えをすべて身につけること

正解は③。ケイトリンが書いた記事の第2段落最終文（This stuffing method ...）に，「この詰め物方式（stuffing method）は私には初めてでしたが，一晩中暖かく過ごせたので驚きました！」とあることから，下線部に相当するものが正解となる。「この詰め物方式」とは，直前にある「すると友達が私に，上に着ている重ね着を脱いで，それを寝袋に詰め込んですき間を少しふさいでみなさいと言いました（Then, my friend ...）」という文の中の下線部分に相当するので，この内容と合っている③が正解となる。

〈主な語句・表現〉

newsletter 名「会報」／ practical 形「実用的な」／ divide A into B「AをBに分ける」／ frequently used「頻繁に使われる」／ daily necessities「日常必需品」／ place 動「置く」／ sleeping bag「寝袋」／ cookware 名「料理器具」／ come with ...「…が付いてくる」／ additional 形「追加の；補助的な」／ easy-to-reach「簡単に手が届く」／ have fun −ing「−して楽しむ」／ close to ...「…の近くに」／ by the time I got back to ...「私が…に戻るまでには」／ freeze 動「凍るほど寒く感じる」／ put on ...「…を身につける」／ extra 形「余分の；追加の」／ layers of ...「何重もの…」／ take off ...「…を脱ぐ」／ outer 形「外側の」／ stuff A into B「AをBに詰め込む」／ fill up ...「…を埋める［ふさぐ］」

B

〈全訳〉

あなたの英語クラブは学校祭のために「アドベンチャールーム」を作ります。あなたはアイディアを得るために，ある英国人男性が作ったルームについてのブログを読んでいます。

自分だけの「ホームアドベンチャー」を作ってみよう。

去年，私は「アドベンチャールーム」の体験会に参加しました。本当に楽しかったので，私は子どもたちのためにルームを作ってみました。あなたが自分独自のルームを作る際のヒントを紹介しましょう。

アドベンチャーを作るための重要な手順
テーマ→筋書き→パズル→衣装

まず最初に，テーマを選びます。私の息子たちはシャーロック・ホームズの大ファンなので，私は探偵推理ものに決めました。私は居間の家具の配置を変えたり，持っていた古い絵やランプを加えてシーン設定をしました（→問1③）。

次に，物語の筋書き作りをします。私たちは，「消えたチョコレート事件」という筋書きにしました。子どもたちが探偵になって，行方不明になったお菓子を見つける手がかりを探すというものです。

3つめのステップは，パズルや難問を考案することです。ここで役に立つ発想は，解答からさかのぼりながら作業することです。たとえば課題が，3けたの数字でロックされた南京錠の付いた箱を開けることだとしたら，3けたの番号を隠す方法を考えてください。古い本は，メッセージの隠し場所としてぴったりです。いろいろなページの語にアンダーラインをして謎めいた文章を作り上げる作業はとても楽しいものでした。忘れてはいけないのは，最終ゴールが近づくにつれて，パズルをますます難しくするべきだということです。雰囲気を出すために，私はそれから子どもたちに衣装を着せました（→問1④）。私が虫メガネを渡すと長男はとても興奮して，ただちにシャーロック・ホームズのように振る舞い出しました。その後子どもたちは，第1の手がかりを探し始めました（→問1②）。

— 英 R 223 —

この「アドベンチャールーム」は，私の家族向けに特別にデザインされたので，難問の中には我が家独自のものを含めました。最後の課題として，私は2つの小さなカップを持ってきてそれぞれにプラスチックのステッカーを貼り，それからヨーグルトをたっぷりと入れました。「探偵たち」が手がかりを明らかにするには，ヨーグルトをカップの底まで食べ進めなければなりませんでした（→問1①）。子どもたちはどちらもヨーグルトを食べたがらないので，これは本当に彼らには辛いものでした。アドベンチャーをしている間，子どもたちは完全に集中してとても楽しめたので，私たちは来月また別のものをやることにします。

〈設問解説〉
　問1　正解　[18]－③，[19]－④
　　　　　　[20]－②，[21]－①
「次の出来事（①～④）を，それらが起こった順に並べなさい」
　① 子どもたちは好きではないものを食べた。
　② 子どもたちはお菓子を探し始めた。
　③ 父親は家の居間の飾り付けをした。
　④ 父親は息子たちに着る物を与えた。
　正解は③→④→②→①である。各選択肢に相当する本文中の記述は，「全訳」中の下線部を参照のこと。本文は基本的に出来事が起こった順序通りに述べられているので，本文の記述の順序通りに並べればよい。

　問2　[22]　正解－③
「この父親のアドバイスに従って，あなた独自の『アドベンチャールーム』を作ろうとするならば，あなたは[22]べきである」
　① 3文字の単語に集中する
　② ランプの下に秘密のメッセージを残しておく
　③ チャレンジを少しずつ難しくする
　④ シャーロック・ホームズのように振る舞う練習をする
　正解は③。ブログ本文の第4段落第6文（Remember that the ...）に，「忘れてはいけないのは，最終ゴールが近づくにつれて，パズルをますます難しくするべきだということです」とあり，③はこの内容と合っているので正解となる。
　他の選択肢の内容は，「あなた独自の『アドベンチャールーム』を作ろうとする」場合に，従うべきアドバイスとは考えられない。

　問3　[23]　正解－②
「この話から，この父親は[23]ことがわかる」
　① お菓子を探すことに集中するようになった
　② 特に自分の子どもに体験してほしいものを作った
　③ アドベンチャーゲームを準備するのにある程度苦労した
　④ 部屋の装飾にたくさんのお金を費やした
　正解は②。ブログ本文の最終段落第1文（This "adventure room" ...）に，「この『アドベンチャールーム』は，私の家族向けに特別にデザインされたので，難問の中には我が家独自のものを含めました」とある。下線部中の「家族（family）」とは，「子どもたち」のことと考えられることから，下線部の内容と合っている②が正解となる。他の選択肢の内容は，本文からは読み取れない。

〈主な語句・表現〉
　take part in ...「…に参加する」／ tip 图「ヒント；秘訣」／ storyline 图「筋立て」／ rearrange 動「…を配列し直す」／ some old paintings and lamps (that) I had「私が持っていたいくつかの古い絵やランプ」／ to set the scene「状況を設定するために〈…を加えた〉」／ missing 形「あるべきところにない」／ clue 图「手がかり；かぎ」／ locate 動「…を捜し出す」／ challenge 图「難題；チャレンジ」／ backwards 副「後ろ向きに；逆さに」／ three-digit「3けたの」／ padlock 图「南京錠」／ code 图「暗号；番号」／ Old books are fantastic for hiding messages in「古い本は（その中に）メッセージを隠すにはすばらしい」／ have fun －ing「－して楽しむ」／ progressively 副「次第に；ますます」／ get into the spirit「熱中する」／ magnifying glass「拡大鏡；虫メガネ」／ specifically 副「明確に；とりわけ」／ made some of ... personal「…の一部をパーソナル［私的］なものにした」／ fill A with B「AをBで満たす」／ eat one's way to ...「どんどん食べて…まで進む」／ reveal 動「…を明らかにする」／ be focused「集中している」／ concentrate on ...「…に集中する」／ have trouble －ing「－するのに苦労する」／ spend O －ing「－するのにOを費やす」

－ 英 R 224 －

第4問
〈全訳〉
あなたは先生から，効果的な勉強法についての2つの投稿記事を読むように求められました。あなたは次の授業で，学んだことを議論します。

効果的な学習法とは：文脈学習です！
ティム・オックスフォード
ストーンシティ中学校　理科教諭

理科の教師である私は，学習に苦労している生徒をどうやって助けたらよいかいつも気にかけています。最近私が知ったのは，生徒たちの主な学習法は，新しい情報を全部思い出せるようになるまで繰り返し学習するというものでした。たとえば試験勉強をする時には，下の例のようなワークブックを利用して，空欄に入る用語を繰り返し唱えようとするのです。「黒曜石は火成岩で，黒っぽくて，ガラス質で…　黒曜石は火成岩で，黒っぽくて，ガラス質で…」こういった生徒たちは，その情報を覚えたと感じるでしょうが，すぐに忘れて，試験で低い点数を取るでしょう。また，このような反復式の学習は退屈で，やる気がそがれます。

生徒たちの学習の役に立つようにと，私は「文脈学習」を応用してみました。この種の学習では，新しい知識は生徒自身の経験を通じて積み上げられていきます。私の理科の授業のために，生徒たちはさまざまな種類の石の特徴を学びました。私は生徒たちにワークブックにある用語を暗記させるのではなく，いろいろな石の入った大きな箱をクラスに持っていきました。生徒たちは石を調べて，観察した特徴に基づいて名前を特定しました。

この経験のおかげで，これらの生徒たちは学習した石の特徴をいつでも説明できるようになると思います。しかし1つ問題なのは，私たちにはいつも文脈学習をする時間があるとは限らないので，生徒はやはりドリル方式で勉強するだろうということです。私はこれが最良の方法だとは思いません。今でも生徒の学習を改善する方法を模索しています。

石の名前	黒曜石
石の種類	火成岩
色	黒っぽい
質感	ガラス質
画像	

反復学習を効果的に行う方法
チェン・リー
ストーンシティー大学教授

オックスフォード先生の文脈学習に関するお考えはとても鋭いものでした。それが有益になりうることには私も賛成です。けれども反復も役に立つことがあります。しかしながら，先生が話題にされた反復的学習法は「集中学習」と呼ばれるもので，これは効果的ではありません。別の種類の反復学習に，「分散学習」と呼ばれるものがあります。これは学習者が新しい情報を記憶したら，より長い間隔をあけて復習するというものです。

学習の間隔が重要な差となります。オックスフォード先生の例では，生徒たちはおそらくワークブックを使って短期間で勉強しようとしたのでしょう。この場合，生徒は復習を続けるにつれ，内容に注意が向かなくなっていったのかもしれません。こうなる理由は，内容がもはや新しくないので，おそらく無視されるだろうからです。これに対して，間隔がより長いと，内容についての生徒の記憶は弱くなります。それゆえ，生徒は前に覚えたことを思い出すのにより大きな努力を払わなければならないので，より大きな注意を払うのです。たとえば，生徒がワークブックを使って勉強して，3日間置いてからまた勉強すれば，おそらく教材をよりよく覚えられるでしょう。

これまでの研究で，分散学習の利点を支持する証拠が得られています。ある実験では，AとBのグループに分けられた生徒たちが，50の動物の名前を覚えようとしました。どちらのグループも4回学習しましたが，グループAは1日間隔で学習し，グループBは1週間間隔で学習しました。右の図が示すように，最後の学習セッションから28日たつと，テストにおいて想起される名前の平均的割合は，分散学習のグループの方が高かったのです。

生徒はしばしば短期間でたくさんの情報を覚える必要があり，学習の間に長い休止期間を設けるのは現実的ではないかもしれません。しかし理解していただきたいのは，集中学習が長期の想起力にとっては良くないかもしれないということです。

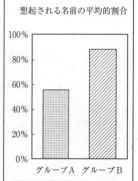

想起される名前の平均的割合

〈設問解説〉

本文を読み，効果的な学習法に関する2人の投稿者の評価について，基本的に以下のように理解できればよい。

	オックスフォード氏	リー氏
反復学習 (repetitive learning)	(A)否定的	(B)集中型 (massed) には否定的 (C)分散型 (spaced) には肯定的
文脈学習 (contextual learning)	(D)肯定的	(E)肯定的

これらの点を踏まえた上で，問いに取り組むことが大事である。

問1　正解　[24]－①

「オックスフォード氏は[24]と考えている」

① **連続する反復学習は退屈だ**
② 用語の説明を読むのは役に立つ
③ 生徒たちは科学に興味がない
④ ワークブックで勉強すればうまくいく

正解は①。表中の(A)に関する問題。オックスフォード氏の投稿記事の第1段落最終文 (Also, this sort ...) に「また，このような反復式の学習は退屈で，やる気がそがれます」とあり，この内容と合っている①が正解となる。本文中の「このような反復式の学習 (this sort of repetitive learning)」と①の中の「連続する反復学習 (continuous drilling)」がほぼ同じ意味であることがわかればよい。

他の選択肢を正解とする根拠はない。

問2　[25]　正解－①

「リー氏によって論じられた研究においては，生徒たちは最後のセッションの[25]後にテストを受けた」

① **4週間**
② すぐ
③ 1日
④ 1週間

正解は①。リー氏の投稿記事の第3段落最終文 (As the figure ...) に，「右の図が示すように，最後の学習セッションから28日たつと，テストにおいて想起される名前の平均的割合は，分散学習のグループの方が高かったのです」とあることから，下線部と同じ意味である①が正解となる。

問3　[26]　正解－②，[27]－⑤

「オックスフォード氏が論じた[27]学習の不利な点を克服するために，リー氏は[26]間隔での学習を伴う分散学習を紹介している（①～⑥の中からそれぞれの空所に最適なものを選びなさい）」

① 文脈の
② **長期の**
③ 固定された
④ 不規則な
⑤ **集中した**
⑥ 実用的な

[26]には，表中の(C)にあるように，リー氏が推奨する分散学習の特徴を表す語が入る。リー氏の投稿記事の第1段落最終文 (There is another ...) に，「別の種類の反復学習に，『分散学習』と呼ばれるものがあります。これは学習者が新しい情報を記憶したら，より長い間隔をあけて復習するというものです」とあることから，[26]には「より長い (longer)」に等しい意味の語が入ることがわかる。選択肢の中でこの意味に最も近いのは，②の extended（延長された；長期の）である。

リー氏が分散学習を紹介した目的は，表中の(B)にあるように，集中型の反復学習に対しては否定的，つまり集中型には不利な点があると考えるためである。このことはリー氏の投稿の第1段落第4文以降 (However, the repetitive ...) の「しかしながら，（オックスフォード）先生が話題にされた反復的学習法は『集中学習』と呼ばれるもので，これは効果的ではありません。別の種類の反復学習に，『分散学習』と呼ばれるものがあります。（以下略）」などの記述から明らかである（この集中型の持つ「不利な点 (disadvantages)」とは，具体的には「内容に注意が向かなくなるかもしれないこと（リー氏投稿文の第2段落第3文：In this case, ...）」，「長期の想起力にとって良くないかもしれないこと（同最終段落最終文：You should understand, ...）」などが挙げられている）。したがって[27]には⑤の「集中した (massed)」が入る。

問4　正解　[28]－①

「2人の投稿者は，[28]は新しい情報を覚えるのに役に立つことで意見が合っている」

① **経験に基づく学習**
② 適切な休息をとること
③ 長期間の注意
④ ワークブックを使った学習

正解は①。表中の(D)と(E)に示されているように，2

— 英 R 226 —

人の投稿者の両方が肯定的に評価している学習法は文脈学習（contextual learning）である。このことは、オックスフォード氏の投稿記事の第2段落第1・2文（To help them ...・In this kind ...）に、「生徒たちの学習の役に立つようにと、私は『文脈学習』を応用してみました。この種の学習では、新しい知識は生徒自身の経験を通じて積み上げられていきます」とあり、リー氏の投稿記事の第1段落第1・2文（Mr. Oxford's thoughts ...・I agree that ...）に、「オックスフォード先生の文脈学習に関するお考えはとても鋭いものでした。それが有益になりうることには私も賛成です」とあることからわかる。また、上に引用した文から、文脈学習とは、新しい知識が生徒自身の「経験（experience）」を通じて積み上げられるということもわかる。したがって2人の投稿者はいずれも、「経験に基づく（experiential）」学習の有用性を支持していることになるので、①が正解に決まる。

②の「適切な休息」については、リー氏が紹介した「分散型の反復学習」のことを指すと考えることはできるが、オックスフォード氏はこれについては何も述べていないので、②は正解になれない。③については、両者とも触れていない。④については、オックスフォード氏の投稿文の第1段落（As a science ...）から、彼が否定的な立場をとっていることがわかるので、やはり正解になれない。

問5　正解　[29]－②

「分散学習に賛成するリー氏の主張をさらに支持するには、次のどの情報を追加するのが最適だろうか」
　① 理科の授業を魅力的にする主な要因
　② 分散学習にとって最も効果的な間隔の長さ
　③ 生徒のワークブックに視覚資料が含まれているかどうか
　④ オックスフォード氏の生徒たちはなぜ情報をよく覚えられなかったのか

正解は②。リー氏の投稿の第3段落（Previous research has ...）においては、長時間の間隔を置いて学習を行う分散学習に効果があることを示唆する実験結果が紹介されているが、具体的に「どのくらい長さの間隔を置くのが最も効果的か」ということについては明らかにされていない。したがって②の情報は、この学習法をさらに支持する有力な追加情報となりうることから、②が正解となる。

①や③は、分散学習とは無関係なことなので、正解にはなれない。④については、すでにリー氏の投稿記事の第2段落（The interval between ...）の中で考察がなされていることから、これがリー氏の主張をさらに支持する最適な追加情報になるとは考えられない。

〈主な語句・表現〉
リード文
　effective 形「効果的な」
オックスフォード氏の投稿文
　contextual 形「文脈上の；状況の」／ be concerned about ...「…を気にかけている」／ struggle to － 「－しようと奮闘する」／ term 名「用語」／ obsidian 名「黒曜石」／ igneous 形「火成の」／ glassy 形「ガラス状の」／ repetitive 形「繰り返しの」／ dull 形「退屈な」／ demotivating 形「やる気をそぐ」／ apply 動「…を適用［応用］する」／ construct 動「…を構築する」／ property 名「特徴；特性」／ rather than having them memorize ...「彼らに…を暗記させるのではなく」／ examine 動「…を調べる」／ identify 動「…を特定する」／ based on ...「…に基づいて」／ characteristic 名「特徴」／ thanks to ...「…のおかげで」／ describe 動「…を記述［説明］する」／ issue 名「問題」／ drill 名「練習；ドリル」／ improve 動「…を改善する」／ texture 名「感触；質感」

リー氏の投稿文
　insightful 形「洞察に富む」／ beneficial 形「有益な」／ repetition 名「反復；繰り返し」／ work well「うまく機能する」／ strategy 名「戦略；方策」／ massed 形「ひとかたまりになった；集中した」／ spaced 形「一定の間隔を置いた」／ review 動「…を見直す；復習する」／ interval 名「（時間的）間隔」／ key 形「重要な」／ pay attention to ...「…に注意を払う」／ content 名「内容」／ no longer「もはや…でない」／ could easily「おそらく…だろう」／ in contrast「対照的に」／ effort 名「努力」／ recall 動「…を思い出す」, 名「想起（力）」／ be likely to －「－しそうである」／ previous 形「以前の」／ evidence 名「証拠」／ advantage 名「利点」／ experiment 名「実験」／ memorize 動「…を暗記する」／ at one-day intervals「1日の間隔を置いて」／ the figure to the right「右側の図」／ 28 days after ...「…の28日後に」／ session 名「集団活動；セッション」／ ratio 名「比率」／ practical 形「実用的な；現実的な」

— 英 R 227 —

第5問
〈全訳〉
(全訳中の下線部については,設問解説の問3を参照のこと)

あなたの英語の先生はクラスの全員に,気持ちを高めてくれるストーリーを見つけて,メモを使ってそれを討論グループに発表するよう指示しました。あなたは英国の高校生が書いたストーリーを見つけました。

卓球が教えてくれたこと
ベン・カーター

　球は電光のような速さで僕のバックハンド側に飛んできた。それは全く予想外で,僕には反応する時間がなかった。僕はポイント,そして試合を落とした。敗北…また か！　僕が卓球をやり始めて最初の数ヵ月間はこんな感じでした。イライラがつのりましたが,このスポーツは僕に,単により優れた運動選手になる方法以上のものを教えてくれたことが,今の自分にはわかっています。

　僕は中学時代はサッカーが大好きでした。僕は得点王の1人でしたが,チームメートとはうまくいきませんでした。コーチからはよく,もっとチームプレーヤーになりなさいと言われました。この問題に取り組まなければならないことはわかっていましたが,僕はコミュニケーションをとるのが決して得意ではありませんでした。

　我が家が新しい町に引っ越す時に,僕はサッカー部を去らなければなりませんでした。いずれにせよサッカーはやめることにしていたので,動揺はしませんでした。新しい学校には,体育のトレント先生がコーチをしている卓球部があったので,僕は入部しました。正直に言うと,僕が卓球を選んだ理由は,自分には個人競技の方が楽だと思ったからです。

　最初の頃は,負け試合の数が勝ち試合を上回っていました。僕は欲求不満で,練習が終わると誰とも口を聞かずにまっすぐ帰宅することもよくありました。ところがある日のこと,トレント先生は僕に,「ベン,君はいい選手になれるかもしれないが,もっと試合のことを考える必要があるね。自分では何をする必要があると思うかい？」と言いました。「わかりません」と僕は答えました。「もっと球に集中することですか？」「そうだよ」とトレント先生は続けました。「だが相手の動きをよく見て,それに応じて自分のプレーを変えてい

くことも必要だね。いいかい,相手は人間なんだ。球じゃないんだよ」。(→問3②)この言葉は僕に強い印象を残しました。

　僕は相手の動きにより細かく注意して,自分のプレースタイルを意図的に修正しました。(→問3④)これは易しくはなく,多大な集中力を必要としました。けれども努力の甲斐あって,僕のプレーは上達しました。自信が深まり,僕は練習の後で居残りをするようになりました。僕はスタープレーヤーに変わりつつあり,クラスメートたちは以前よりも僕に話しかけようとしました。僕は人気者になりつつあると思いましたが,本当の会話が始まらないうちに僕たちは話すのをやめていました。僕のプレーは上達したかもしれませんが,会話術が上達していないのは明らかでした。

　兄のパトリックは,僕がうまく会話ができる数少ない人々の中の1人でした。ある日,僕はコミュニケーションの問題を彼に説明しようとしましたが,理解させることができませんでした。僕たちは話題を卓球に変えました。「実際には卓球のどこが面白いんだい？」と彼は興味ありげに僕に聞きました。僕は相手の動きを分析して次の動きを瞬時に判断するのが楽しいと言いました。(→問3⑤)パトリックは考え込んだ様子でした。「人がコミュニケーションをする時も,それと同じような技術を使うんじゃないかな」と彼は言いました。

　その時はわかりませんでしたが,兄と話した後すぐに,僕はある卓球のトーナメントで銀メダルを獲得しました。クラスメートたちは本当に喜んでいるようでした。その中の1人だったジョージが駆け寄ってきました。「やあ,ベン！」と彼は言いました。「お祝いのパーティーをやろうよ！」　僕は何も考えずに,「ダメだよ。練習があるんだ」と答えました。(→問3③)彼は少し傷ついたようで,他には何も言わずに立ち去りました。

　なぜ彼は気を悪くしたのだろう。僕はこの出来事についてしばらく考えました。なぜ彼はパーティーをしないかと言ったのだろう。僕は何か違うことを言うべきだったのか。たくさんの問いが頭に浮かびましたが,その後で僕は,彼はただ親切にしてくれただけなんだということに気づきました。もし僕が「それはいいね。ありがとう！　トレント先生と話して,練習を少し休めるかどうか調べてみるよ」と言っていたら,結果はもっと良くなっていたかもしれません。その時,パトリックの言葉の意味がわかりました。相手の意図を把握しようと試みることがなければ,自分がどう反応すればいいかがわかることはないでしょう。

--- 英 R 228 ---

僕はまだ，コミュニケーションが世界一上手だというわけではありませんが，今は以前よりも自分のコミュニケーション術に自信を持っていることには間違いありません。来年には，僕は友人たちと一緒に，他校との卓球リーグの編成の仕事をすることになっています。

あなたのメモ：

卓球が教えてくれたこと

著者（ベン・カーター）について
・中学ではサッカーをしていた。
・新しい学校で卓球を始めたのは，彼は 30 からだった。

他の重要人物
・トレント先生：ベンの卓球コーチで，彼のプレーが上達するのを助けた。
・パトリック：ベンの兄で，31 。
・ジョージ：ベンのクラスメートで，彼の勝利を祝いたいと思った。

ベンのコミュニケーションが上達する道のりにおいて影響を及ぼした出来事
卓球を始めた→ 32 → 33 → 34 → 35

ジョージとの会話の後でベンが気づいたこと
彼は 36 べきだった。

このストーリーから私たちが学べること
・ 37
・ 38

〈設問解説〉
問1　正解　30 － ④
「30 に最適な選択肢を選びなさい」
① それが彼がコミュニケーションをとるのに役立つだろうと考えた
② 学校で人気者になることを望んだ
③ 試合に簡単に勝てると思った
④ **チームスポーツをするの避けたいと思った**
　正解は④。空所には，ベンが新しい学校で卓球を始めた理由として正しいものが入る。ベンのストーリーの第3段落最終文（To be honest, ...）に，「正直に言うと，僕が卓球を選んだ理由は，自分には個人競技の方が楽だと思ったからです」とあることから，下線部とほぼ同じ内容である④が正解となる。

他の選択肢を正解とする根拠はない。

問2　正解　31 － ③
「31 に最適な選択肢を選びなさい」
① コミュニケーションの何が楽しいのかを彼に聞いた
② もっと自信を持つようにと彼を励ました
③ **彼が必要としている，人と付き合う技術を彼が身につけるのを助けた**
④ 彼が学校の友人たちに何を言うべきだったかを教えた
　正解は③。ベンの兄パトリックの役割として適切なものを選ぶ。第6段落第4文（"What do you ...）以降にある「『実際には卓球のどこが面白いんだい？』と彼は興味ありげに僕に聞きました。僕は相手の動きを分析して次の動きを瞬時に判断するのが楽しいと言いました。パトリックは考え込んだ様子でした。『人がコミュニケーションをする時も，それと同じような技術を使うんじゃないかな』と彼は言いました」というベンとパトリックのやり取りから，パトリックは下線部の発言において，人とうまくコミュニケーションをとるコツをベンに示唆したと考えられることから，③が正解となる。③の中の「人と付き合う技術（social skills）」とは，本文における「コミュニケーション術（communication skills）」を言い換えたものだと考えられればよい。
　①は上に引用した記述の中の「実際には卓球のどこが面白いんだい？」を誤解したものなので誤り。②や④のようなことは，ベンとパトリックのやり取りからは読み取れない。

問3　正解　32 － ②，33 － ④
34 － ⑤，35 － ③
「5つの選択肢（①〜⑤）の中から4つを選び，それらを起こった順序通りに並べ替えなさい」
① 卓球のチャンピオンになった
② 先生とうまくプレーする方法について話し合った
③ 自分のことを祝うパーティーを拒んだ
④ 相手の動きを観察するようになった
⑤ 兄と卓球について話した
　正解は②→④→⑤→③。各選択肢の本文における対応箇所は，全訳中の下線部を参照のこと。①については，（ベンは銀メダルを獲得したことはあるものの）本文中に該当する記述がない。

— 英 R 229 —

問4 　36　　正解－③

「　36　に最適な選択肢を選びなさい」

① 友人に彼の動機についてもっと多くのことを知るために質問をする

② トレント先生と他のクラスメートをパーティーに招待して感謝の気持ちを表す

③ **適切に振る舞うために友人の視点を理解しようと試みる**

④ うまくコミュニケーションをとるためによりよいチームプレーヤーになるよう懸命に努力する

正解は③。ジョージとの会話の後で，ベンが気づいたこととして適切なものを選ぶ。ジョージとの会話の後でベンが考えたことは，第8段落（Why was he ...）に書かれている。この段落の最終文（Without attempting to ...）に「相手の意図を把握しようと試みることがなければ，自分がどう反応すればいいかがわかることはないでしょう」とある。選択肢③の中の「友人の視点を理解しようとする（tried to understand his friend's point of view）」が，上の文の中の「相手の意図を把握しようと試みる（attempting to grasp someone's intention）」とほぼ同内容で，③の中の「適切に振る舞う（act appropriately）」が，上の文の中の「自分がどう反応すればいいかがわかる（know how to respond）」に対応していると考えられれば，③が正しいとわかる。

他の選択肢のようなことに，ベンがジョージとの会話の後で気づいたとは，本文では述べられていない。

問5 　37　・　38　　正解－①・⑤

「　37　と　38　に最適な2つの選択肢を選びなさい（順序は問わない）」

① **周囲の人々のアドバイスが私たちを変えるのに役立つことがある。**

② コミュニケーションが上手くなるには自信が大切だ。

③ 友人に自分の意図をはっきりと伝えることが大切だ。

④ チームメートが互いに与え合う支えは助けになる。

⑤ **あることから学んだことを別のことに応用することができる。**

正解は①と⑤。このストーリーから得られる教訓として適切なものを2つ選ぶ。①については，「周囲の人々」とはストーリー中のトレント先生や兄のパトリックのことで，「私たちを変える」とは，ベンが人々とのコミュニケーションが上手にとれるようになることを指していると考えれば，本文から得られる教訓の1つと考えることができる。⑤については，「あることから学んだこと」を「卓球から学んだこと」，つまり「相手の動きを瞬時に読んで自分の反応を決めること」と考えて，「別のこと」を「人とのコミュニケーション」と考えれば，本文の内容に合ったものとなるので，これがもう1つの正解となる。

②については，ベンは「コミュニケーションが上手くなって自信がついた」とは言える（最終段落第1文：I'm still not the best ...）が，本文の内容から「コミュニケーションが上手くなるには自信が大切だ」と考えることはできない。③については，本文の内容から「友人の意図をはっきりと理解することが大切だ」ということは言える（第8段落最終文：Without attempting to grasp ...）が，「友人に自分の意図をはっきりと伝えることが大切だ」と考えることはできない。④のように，チームメートと支え合うことの重要性も，本文では述べられていない。

〈主な語句・表現〉

リード文

inspirational 形「インスピレーションを与える；気持ちを高めてくれる」

第1段落（The ball flew ...）

at lightning speed「電光石火の速さで」／unexpected 形「予期しない」／This is how it was in the first few months「最初の数ヵ月間はこのような有様だった」 it は漠然と「状況」を表す。／frustrating 形「挫折感を起こすような」／athlete 名「運動選手」

第2段落（In middle school, ...）

middle school「中学校」／get along with ...「…とうまくやっていく」／work on ...「…に取り組む」／strong point「長所；得意」

第3段落（I had to ...）

be upset「動揺する；気分を害する」／PE「体育（physical education）」／to be honest「正直に言うと」／individually 副「個人で」

第4段落（At first, I ...）

at first「最初の頃は」／focus on ...「…に集中する」／opponent 名「対戦相手」／adjust 動「…を調整する」／accordingly 副「それに応じて」／impression 名「印象」

第5段落（I deliberately modified ...）

deliberately 副「意図的に」／modify 動「…を修正する」／concentration 名「集中（力）」／pay off「利

— 英 R 230 —

益を産む；引き合う」／confidence 名「自信」／stay behind「居残る」／turn into ...「…に変わる」／get started「始まる」／obviously 副「明らかに」

第6段落（My older brother ...）

communicate with ...「…と気持ちを伝え合う」／problem with ...「…に関する問題」／switch to ...「…へ切り換える」／analyse 動「…を分析する」／instant 形「瞬時の」／thoughtful 形「考え込んだ」／That sounds like ...「それは…のように聞こえる」

第7段落（At that time, ...）

seem pleased「喜んでいるようだ」／come running over「駆け寄ってくる」／celebrate 動「お祝いする」／look a bit hurt「少し傷ついたように見える」／walk off「歩き去る」

第8段落（Why was he ...）

incident 名「出来事」／should have p.p.「…すべきだった」／was just being kind「ただ親切にしているだけだった」／get some time off practice「練習をしばらく休む」／outcome 名「結果」／make sense「意味をなす」／grasp 動「…を把握［理解］する」／intention 名「意図」／respond 動「応答する」

最終段落（I'm still not ...）

definitely 副「確かに；絶対に」／feel confident in ...「…に自信がある」／co-ordinate 動「…を組織する；まとめ上げる」

第6問

A

〈全訳〉

　あなたは学校で討論のグループに入っています。あなたは次の記事を要約するよう頼まれました。あなたはメモだけを使ってそれについて話します。

コレクション活動

　コレクション活動は昔から，社会のあらゆる層で，文化や年齢集団の壁を越えて行われてきました。博物館は，物が集められ，保管され，将来の世代に伝えられてきたことの証です。コレクションを始める理由は様々です。例えば女性のＡさんは，毎週土曜日の朝に子どもたちと一緒にヤードセールへ行くのが楽しみです。ヤードセールでは，不用品が人の家の前で売られます。ある日のこと，彼女は骨董品のお皿を見ていると，珍しい絵に目が釘付けになり，それをわずか数ドルで買いました。彼女は時間をかけて心に残る同じような物をいくつも見つけて，今ではささやかな美術品のコレクションを所有しています。その中のいくつかには，支払った金額以上の価値があるかもしれません。ある人にとってのガラクタは，別の人にとっては宝物になることがあるのです。人がどのようにしてコレクションを始めるのであろうと，物を集めるのは人間の性なのです。

　1988年に，ブレンダ・ダネットとタマール・カトリエルという研究者が，10歳未満の子どもたちについての80年にわたる数々の研究を分析して，約90パーセントの子どもが何かを集めていたことを知りました。このことは，人は幼時から物を集めるのが好きであることを私たちに示しています。大人になった後でも，人は物を集め続けます。この分野の研究者たちは一般に，大人のおよそ3分の1がこういった行動を続けるということで意見が一致しています。これはどうしてなのでしょう。最も代表的な説明は情緒と関連しています。友人や家族からもらったグリーティングカードや，特別な行事で使ったドライフラワー，海岸で過ごした日に拾った貝殻，古い写真などをとっておく人がいます。人によっては，コレクションが若かった日々への架け橋となるのです。子どもの頃から集めた野球カードや，漫画本，人形，ミニカーを持っているかもしれません。また歴史への愛着を持っている人もいて，歴史的な文書や，有名な人の署名の入った手紙やサインなどを探し求めてずっととっておくのです。

— 英 R 231 —

人によっては，社交的な理由もあります。分けてあげたり，見せたり，さらには交換するためのピンなどを集め，これによって新しい友達を作るのです。他にも，一部のギネス世界記録保持者のように，独特のコレクションをすることで勝ち取る名声を享受する人たちもいます。カード，ステッカー，切手，コイン，玩具が「普通の」コレクションのリストの上位を占めてきましたが，一部のコレクターは，もっと意外な物に傾いていきます。2014年の9月に，ギネス世界記録はドイツのハリー・スパールさんを，3,724点にものぼるハンバーガー関連の世界最大級のコレクション保持者として表彰しました。Tシャツから枕，犬の玩具に至るまで，スパールさんの部屋は「ハンバーガー」関連のありとあらゆる物でいっぱいでした。同様に，中国のリウ・フーチャンさんはトランプのコレクターです。彼は異なる種類の11,087組ものトランプを持っています。

最も理解しやすい動機は，喜びかもしれません。純粋に楽しむためにコレクションを始める人たちがいます。しばしば眺めるためだけの絵画を買って掛けておくこともあれば，お気に入りの音楽を聴くために録音素材や古風なアナログレコードを集めることもあります。こういった種類のコレクターは，宝のように大切な音楽の金銭的価値にはあまり関心を持ちそうにありませんが，明確に投資対象として物を集める人もいます。ある特定の名作ゲームは無料でダウンロードできますが，同じゲームを未開封のまま最初の包装状態，つまり「ミントコンディション」で持っていると，ゲームに大きな値打ちが出ることがあります。さまざまな価値ある「コレクターアイテム」を所有すれば，経済的な安全性が保証されるかもしれないのです。

このようなコレクション活動は，遠い未来まで続くことは間違いありません。人が物を持ち続ける理由はおそらく変わらないでしょうが，テクノロジーの進歩はコレクションに影響を及ぼすでしょう。テクノロジーは物理的な制約を取り除くことができるため，今や個人が30年前は考えられなかったような膨大な音楽や芸術のデジタルコレクションを持つことが可能となっています。けれども，テクノロジーがコレクションにそれ以外のどんな影響を及ぼすかははっきりしません。次の世代のコレクションがどんな形や規模のものになるか想像することさえ大変です。

あなたのメモ：

コレクション活動

導入部
- ◆コレクション活動は昔から人間の経験の一部となっている。
- ◆ヤードセールの話は私たちに $\boxed{39}$ ということを教えてくれる。

諸事実
- ◆$\boxed{40}$
- ◆ギネス世界記録
  - ◇スパール：ハンバーガーに関するものが3,724点
  - ◇リウ：11,087組のトランプ

コレクションをする理由
- ◆コレクションをする動機は情緒的なものも，社交的なものもある。
- ◆次のような様々な理由が挙げられている。$\boxed{41}$，$\boxed{42}$，歴史への興味，子ども時代の熱中，有名になること，分け合うことなど。

将来のコレクション
- ◆$\boxed{43}$

〈設問解説〉

問1 $\boxed{39}$ 正解—③

「$\boxed{39}$に最適な選択肢を選びなさい」

① 人々がコレクターに物を高い値段で売るのにぴったりの場所はヤードセールだ

② 人々は物を不正確に評価し，その結果ジャンク品に法外なお金を払ってしまうことがある

③ ある人にとって大事でない物が，別の人には価値ある物になるかもしれない

④ かつて収集されて別の人の庭に捨てられた物は，他の人々には価値があるかもしれない

正解は③。ヤードセールの話が教えてくれることとして適切なものを選ぶ。ヤードセールについては，本文第1段落で述べられているが，その第8文（One person's trash ...）に「ある人にとってのガラクタは，別の人にとっては宝物になることがあるのです」とあることから，この内容と合っている③が正解となる。

他の選択肢のようなことは，本文からは読み取れない。

— 英 R 232 —

問2　　40　　正解－④

「　40　に最適な選択肢を選びなさい」

① 子どもの約3分の2は，普通の物を集めない。
② 大人のほぼ3分の1が，娯楽で物を集め始める。
③ 子どものおよそ10パーセントが，友達と同じようなコレクションを持っている。
④ 人々のだいたい30パーセントが，大人になるまでコレクション活動を続ける。

正解は④。本文中で述べられている事実として正しいものを選ぶ。第2段落第1文（In 1988, researchers ...）から第4文（Researchers in the ...）に，「1988年に，ブレンダ・ダネットとタマール・カトリエルという研究者が，10歳未満の子どもたちについての80年にわたる数々の研究を分析して，約90パーセントの子どもが何かを集めていたことを知りました。このことは，人は幼時から物を集めるのが好きであることを私たちに示しています。大人になった後でも，人は物を集め続けます。この分野の研究者たちは一般に，大人のおよそ3分の1がこういった行動を続けるということで意見が一致しています」とあり，下線部の内容と合っている④が正解となる。

他の選択肢はいずれも上の引用部分の一部を誤解したものであり，正解にはなれない。

問3　　41・42　　正解－④・⑥

「　41　と　42　に最適な選択肢を選びなさい（順序は問わない）」

① テクノロジーを進歩させたいという願望
② 予期せぬ機会を逃すことへの恐れ
③ 空虚感を埋め合わせること
④ 大切な出来事の記念
⑤ 将来のために物を再利用すること
⑥ 何らかの種類の利潤を求めること

正解は④と⑥。コレクション活動を行う理由として本文中に挙げられているものを2つ選ぶ。④については，コレクション活動を続ける大人が多い理由を説明している第2段落第6・7文（The primary explanation ...）に「最も代表的な説明は情緒と関連しています。友人や家族からもらったグリーティングカードや，特別な行事で使ったドライフラワー，海岸で過ごした日に拾った貝殻，古い写真などをとっておく人がいます」とあり，④の「大切な出来事の記念」は，この部分を一般的に表したものと考えられるため，正解の1つとなる。

⑥については，第4段落第4文（This type of ...）に，「こういった種類のコレクターは，宝のように大切な音

楽の金銭的価値にはあまり関心を持ちそうにありませんが，明確に投資対象として物を集める人もいます」とあることなどと合っている。

他の選択肢のようなことは，コレクション活動を行う理由として挙げられていない。

問4　　正解　　43　－①

「　43　に最適な選択肢を選びなさい」

① コレクションはおそらく規模や形態を変え続けるだろう。
② 新品状態のゲームのコレクターは，より多くのデジタルコピーを持つようになるだろう。
③ コレクション活動への情熱を失った人々が，再びコレクションを始めるだろう。
④ テクノロジーの進歩のせいで，コレクション活動をする理由は変わるだろう。

正解は①。コレクション活動の未来について当てはまるものを選ぶ。これについて述べられているのは最終段落だが，その最終文に，Can you even imagine the form and scale that the next generation's collections will take? とある。これはいわゆる修辞疑問文で，文字通りには「あなたは次の世代のコレクションがとる形や規模を想像することさえできるだろうか」という意味だが，実質的には「あなたは次の世代のコレクションがとる形や規模を想像することとさえできないだろう」，つまり「次の世代のコレクションは形や規模が大きく変化する」ことを示唆している。したがってこの内容と合っている①が正解となる。

②や③のようなことは本文では述べられていない。④は，最終段落第2文（Although the reasons ...）に「人が物を持ち続ける理由はおそらく変わらないでしょうが，テクノロジーの進歩はコレクションに影響を及ぼすでしょう」とあるのと合わない。

〈主な語句・表現〉

第1段落（Collecting has existed ...）

age group「年齢集団」／ proof that ...「…という証拠」／ pass down「…を（次の世代へ）渡す」／ unwanted 形「不必要な」／ antique 形「骨董品の」／ ... catch one's eye「…に目が釘付けになる」／ buy A for B「A（＝品物）を B（＝金額）で買う」／ over time「長い期間にわたって」／ impression on ...「…への印象」／ modest 形「適度の；ささやかな」／ be worth more than ...「…以上の価値がある」／ trash 名「ゴミ」／ treasure 名「宝物」／ regardless of ...「…に関係なく」／

— 英 R 233 —

it is human nature to ～「～するのは人間の性質［本質］だ」

第2段落（In 1988, researchers ...）

　analyze 動「…を分析する」／ stuff 名「もの」／ approximately 副「およそ」／ one third「3分の1」／ primary 形「主要な」／ be related to ...「…と関係がある」／ emotion 名「感情；情緒」／ seashell 名「貝殻」／ ... and so on [forth]「…など」／ connection to ...「…とのつながり」／ youth 名「青春時代；若さ」／ miniature car「ミニカー」／ attachment to ...「…への愛着」／ hold onto ...「…を手放さない［取っておく］」／ autograph 名「サイン」

第3段落（For some individuals ...）

　appreciate 動「…をありがたく思う」／ fame 名「名声」／ top 動「…のトップに載っている」／ lean toward ...「…の方に（心が）傾く」／ the more unexpected「より意外なもの」／ recognize A for B「AをBのことでたたえる」／ hamburger-related 形「ハンバーガー関連の」／ be filled with ...「…で満たされている」／ all things "hamburger"「ハンバーガーに関するあらゆるもの」／ playing card「トランプ」／ set 名「（トランプの）組」

第4段落（Perhaps the easiest ...）

　the easiest motivation to understand「最も理解しやすい動機づけ」／ pleasure 名「喜び」／ pure enjoyment「純粋な楽しみ」／ put up「（絵画を）掛ける」／ paintings just to gaze at frequently「しばしば眺めるためだけの絵画」／ vinyl record「アナログレコード」／ be unlikely to ～「～しそうにない」／ monetary value「金銭的価値」／ treasured 形「宝のように大切な」／ specifically 副「とりわけ；はっきりと」／ investment 名「投資（の対象）」／ certain 形「ある特定の」／ for free「無料で」／ packaging 名「包装（材料）」／ mint condition「新品状態；ミントコンディション」／ ensure 動「…を保証する」／ financial security「経済的な安全性」

最終段落（This behavior of ...）

　definitely 副「確かに」／ likely 副「おそらく」／ have an influence on ...「…に影響を及ぼす」／ remove 動「…を取り除く」／ physical constraint「物理的制約」／ unimaginable 形「想像できない」／ what other impacts「他のどんな影響」　what は疑問形容詞。／ have an impact on ...「…に影響を与える」／ take 動「（ある形を）とる」

B

〈全訳〉

　あなたは生徒たちのあるグループに入っていて，国際科学プレゼンテーションコンテストの準備をしています。あなたは次の文章を利用して，珍しい生き物についてのプレゼンテーションの自分の担当箇所を作成しています。

　世界で最も強靭な動物の名前を挙げてくださいと誰かに言えば，その人は摂氏50度の高温でも生きられるからフタコブラクダだとか，マイナス58度以下の低温でも生きられるからホッキョクギツネだと言うかもしれません。ところが，緩歩動物が地球で最も強靭な生き物と広く考えられていることから，上の答えはどちらも間違いとなるでしょう。

　緩歩動物は，クマムシという名でも知られている微生物で，体長は0.1ミリから1.5ミリです。6,000メートルの高山から，4,600メートルの海底まで，ほぼあらゆる場所に生息しています。厚い氷の下や，熱い温泉の中でも見つけることができます。緩歩動物のほとんどは水中に生息していますが，地球で最も乾燥した土地の一部に見られることもあります。ある研究者は，緩歩動物が25年間降水記録のない砂漠の中の岩の下に生息しているのを見つけたことを報告しました。それが必要とするのは，生活の場となる数滴の水あるいは薄く張った水だけです。水が干上がると，それらも干上がります。それらは水分の大半を失って3パーセントのみを残し，新陳代謝のスピードは通常の0.01パーセントに落ちます。干上がった緩歩動物は今や「タン（樽）」と呼ばれる一種の熟睡状態に入ります。この状態は再び水に浸されるまで続きます。するとそれはスポンジのように水を吸収して，まるで何事も起こらなかったかのように復元するのです。緩歩動物のタンの期間が1週間なのか10年間なのかは，あまり大事な問題ではありません。水に囲まれた瞬間に，それは再び元気になるのです。緩歩動物はタンの状態ではとても強靭で，摂氏マイナス272度の低温，そして151度の高温の中でも生きることができます。一体どうやってこれを成し遂げるのかは，完全にはわかっていません。

　緩歩動物の地球上での生存能力（約5億4千万年前から地球にいるのです）よりもさらに驚くべきは，その宇宙における生存能力かもしれません。2007年に，ヨーロッパの研究者のチームが，何匹もの生きている緩歩動物を宇宙空間に送り出し，ロケットの外側に10

— 英 R 234 —

日間放置しました。地球に戻る際, 68 パーセントがまだ生きているのを研究者たちは知って驚きました。つまり大部分は 10 日の間, この地球上よりも 1,000 倍強烈な X 線や紫外線に耐え抜くことができたのです。その後 2019 年に, イスラエルの宇宙船が月面に衝突し, タン状態にあった非常に多くの緩歩動物が月面に放り出されました。誰もこれらを回収しに行った人がいないので, これらがまだ生きているかどうかはわかりません。残念なことです。

緩歩動物は短いキュウリのような形をしています。胴体のそれぞれの側に 4 本の短い足があります。それぞれの足先に付着盤が付いている種もあれば, 爪が付いている種もあります。爪には 16 の変種があることがわかっていて, それは爪を持っている種を区別するのに役立ちます。すべての緩歩動物には眼窩(がんか)がありますが, すべての種が眼を持っているわけではありません。眼は単純な作りで, 全部で 5 つの細胞しかなく, 光を感知するのはその中の 1 つだけです。

緩歩動物は基本的に, 植物を食べるものと, 他の生き物を食べるものとに分けることができます。植物を食べる種には, 腹口（サメのように, 頭の下部に付いている口）があります。他の生き物を食べる種には終端口があります。つまりマグロのように, 口は頭の最先端に付いているのです。緩歩動物の口には歯はありません。しかし吻針(ふんしん)と呼ばれる 2 本の鋭い針を持っていて, それで植物の細胞やより小さな生き物の体を突き刺し, 中身を吸い出せるのです。

どちらのタイプの緩歩動物も, 消化器系はかなり単純です。口は咽頭（のど）につながり, そこで消化液と食物が混ぜ合わされます。咽頭の上方には唾液腺があります。これは口の中へ流れ込んで消化を助ける液体を分泌します。咽頭を過ぎると, 食物を消化器官に運ぶ管があります。この管は食道と呼ばれます。中腸は, 簡単な胃や腸に当たる器官ですが, これは食物を消化して栄養分を吸収します。それから残存物はそこを通り抜けて最終的に肛門まで移動します。

あなたのプレゼンテーションのスライド：

緩歩動物：

極限まで生き残る地球の生物

1．基本情報

- 体長 0.1 ミリから 1.5 ミリ
- 短いキュウリのような形
- ・
- ・ 44
- ・
- ・

2．生息地

- ほぼあらゆる場所に生息する
- 以下のような過酷な環境
  - ✓ 海抜 6 キロメートル
  - ✓ 海底 4.6 キロメートル
  - ✓ 砂漠の中
  - ✓ −272 度から 151 度まで
  - ✓ （おそらく）宇宙空間

3．生き延びる秘訣

 ⇔

「タン」　　　　　活動状態

- 45
- 46

4．消化器系 47

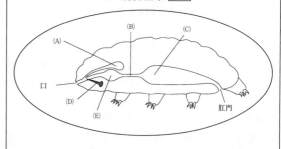

5．最後に

48

〈設問解説〉

問1　44　正解－④

「次の中で，44に含めるべきでないものはどれか」

① 8本の短い足

② 目が見えないものと見えるもの

③ 植物を食べるものと生き物を食べるもの

④ **16の異なる足の種類**

⑤ 歯の代わりに2本の吻針

　正解は④。緩歩動物の基本情報として正しくないものを選ぶ。この生物の基本的特徴については，本文の第4・5段落に，次のように述べられている。

・第4段落 (Tardigrades are shaped ...)：緩歩動物は短いキュウリのような形をしています。胴体のそれぞれの側に4本の短い足があります（→①）。それぞれの足先に付着盤が付いている種もあれば，爪が付いている種もあります。爪には16の変種があることがわかっていて（→×④），それは爪を持っている種を区別するのに役立ちます。すべての緩歩動物には<ruby>眼窩<rt>がんか</rt></ruby>がありますが，すべての種が眼を持っているわけではありません（→②）。眼は単純な作りで，全部で5つの細胞しかなく，光を感知するのはその中の1つだけです。

・第5段落 (Basically, tardigrades can ...)：緩歩動物は基本的に，植物を食べるものと，他の生き物を食べるものとに分けることができます（→③）。植物を食べる種には，腹口（サメのように，頭の下部に付いている口）があります。他の生き物を食べる種には終端口があります。つまりマグロのように，口は頭の最先端に付いているのです。緩歩動物の口には歯はありません。しかし吻針と呼ばれる2本の鋭い針を持っていて（→⑤），それで植物の細胞やより小さな生き物の体を突き刺し，中身を吸い出せるのです。

　それぞれの下線部の後に，対応する選択肢の番号を示してある。これらの内容から，④の「16の異なる足の種類」が誤りだとわかるので，これが正解となる。

問2　正解　45・46－①・⑤

「『生き延びる秘訣』のスライドに入れるために，緩歩動物が生き延びるのに最も役立つ2つの特徴を選びなさい（順序は問わない。)」

① **乾燥した状況では，その新陳代謝は通常の1パーセント未満まで低下する。**

② タンの状態にある緩歩動物は摂氏151度を超える温度の中で生き延びることができる。

③ 緩歩動物の体内の水分が0.01パーセントを超えるとタンの状態は止まる。

④ そのサメのような口によって，より簡単に他の生き物を食べることができる。

⑤ **極度の放射線レベルに耐える能力を持っている。**

　正解は①と⑤。①については，第2段落第7・8文 (When the water ...・They lose all ...) に「水が干上がると，それらも干上がります。それらは水分の大半を失って3パーセントのみを残し，新陳代謝のスピードは通常の0.01パーセントに落ちます」とあるのと合っている。⑤については，第3段落第4文 (This means that ...) に「つまり大部分は10日間，この地球上よりも1,000倍強烈なX線や紫外線に耐え抜くことができたのです」とあるのと合っている。

　②は第2段落第14文 (When tardigrades are ...) に「緩歩動物はタンの状態ではとても強靭で，摂氏マイナス272度の低温，そして151度の高温の中でも生きることができます」を誤解したもので，下線部の内容から②のように「摂氏151度を超える温度の中で生き延びることができる」と考えることはできない。③は上に引用した第2段落第7・8文の内容を誤解したもので，③のようなことは本文からは読み取れない。④は第5段落第2文 (Those that eat ...) に「植物を食べる種には，腹口（サメのように，頭の下部に付いている口）があります」とあるのと合わない。

問3　正解　47－③

「『消化器系』のスライドにある緩歩動物のイラスト上の空欄を埋めなさい」

① (A) 食道　　(B) 咽頭　　(C) 中腸
　 (D) 吻針　　(E) 唾液腺

② (A) 咽頭　　(B) 吻針　　(C) 唾液腺
　 (D) 食道　　(E) 中腸

③ **(A) 唾液腺　(B) 食道　　(C) 中腸**
　 (D) 吻針　　(E) 咽頭

④ (A) 唾液腺　(B) 中腸　　(C) 吻針
　 (D) 食道　　(E) 咽頭

⑤ (A) 吻針　　(B) 唾液腺　(C) 咽頭
　 (D) 中腸　　(E) 食道

　正解は③。緩歩動物の消化器系については，最終段落 (Both types of ...) で次のように述べられている。「どちらのタイプの緩歩動物も，消化器系はかなり単純です。(ア) 口 (mouth) は咽頭（のど）につながり，そこで消化液と食物が混ぜ合わされます。咽頭の上方には唾液腺があります。これは口の中へ流れ込んで消化を

— 英 R 236 —

助ける液体を分泌します。(イ)咽頭を過ぎると，食物を消化器官に運ぶ管があります。この管は食道と呼ばれます。(ウ)中腸は，簡単な胃や腸に当たる器官ですが，これは食物を消化して栄養分を吸収します。それから残存物はそこを通り抜けて最終的に肛門（Anus）まで移動します」。下線部(ア)の記述から，スライドの中の(E)が咽頭（Pharynx）で，その上方にある(A)が唾液腺（Salivary gland）であることがわかる。さらに下線部(イ)の記述から，(B)が食道（Esophagus）であるとわかる（この時点で正解は③に決まる）。そして下線部(ウ)の記述から，(C)が中腸（Middle gut）であることがわかる。また，第5段落第4文と5文(The mouths of ... ／They do, however, ...)に「緩歩動物の口には歯はありません。しかし吻針と呼ばれる2本の鋭い針を持っていて，それで植物の細胞やより小さな生き物の体を突き刺し，中身を吸い出せるのです」とあることから，通常の動物の歯の位置と考えられる(D)が吻針（Stylets）であるとわかる。

問4　48　正解－④
「最後のスライドに最もふさわしい言葉はどれか」
① 何千何万年もの間，緩歩動物は地球や宇宙の最も過酷な環境のいくつかを生き抜いてきた。この生き物は人類よりも長生きするだろう。
② 緩歩動物は宇宙から来て，ホッキョクギツネやフタコブラクダの限界を超える温度下で生きることができるので，この生き物はきっと人間よりも強い。
③ 緩歩動物は間違いなく地球で最も強靭な生き物である。それは山の頂上でも，海の底でも，温泉の中でも生き延びることができる。そして月面にも生息することができるのだ。
❹ 緩歩動物は地球上の最も過酷な状況のいくつか，そして少なくとも一度の宇宙旅行を生き抜いてきた。この驚くべき生き物は，人間よりも長く生きながらえるかもしれない。

正解は④。プレゼンテーションを締めくくる結びの言葉として適切なものを選ぶ。④の第1文の「緩歩動物は地球上の最も過酷な状況のいくつか，そして少なくとも一度の宇宙旅行を生き抜いてきた」は，本文第2段落（Tardigrades, also known ...）や第3段落（Perhaps even more ...）の内容と合っている。そして④の第2文の「この驚くべき生き物は，人間よりも長く生きながらえるかもしれない」は，この文章に基づく推量として適切な内容である。したがって④が正解

となる。
①については，本文第3段落第1文（Perhaps even more ...）に，「緩歩動物の地球上での生存能力（約5億4千万年から地球にいるのです）よりもさらに驚くべきは…」とあるので，①の第1文中の「何千何万年もの間（For thousands of years）」という表現は正確とは言えない。また，本文では緩歩動物の未来についての考察は基本的になされていないため，本文の内容から第2文のように「この生き物は人類よりも長生きするだろう（will live）」と結論づけるのも無理がある（正解の④は，第2文の中で「この驚くべき生き物は，人間よりも長く生きながらえるかもしれない（might outlive）」という，①よりも非断定的な推量の表現を用いていることに注意）。②については，「緩歩動物は宇宙から来て」の部分が本文からは読み取れないので誤りである。③については，宇宙船から月面に放出された緩歩動物に関して本文第3段落最終文（Whether these are ...）に「誰もこれらを回収しに行った人がいないので，これらがまだ生きているかどうかはわかりません。残念なことです」とあることから，③の第2文のように「そして月面でも生息することができるのだ」と考えることはできない。

問5　49　正解－④
「緩歩動物を宇宙に送り出すことに関して推測できることは何か」
① 緩歩動物が宇宙で生き延びることができるかどうかは，重要と考えられことが一度もなかった。
② 緩歩動物は，何百万年もの間地球上にいる他の生物と同様に，X線や紫外線放射に耐えることができる。
③ イスラエルの研究者たちは，あんなにも多くの緩歩動物が宇宙の過酷な環境で生き延びるとは予想しなかった。
❹ 緩歩動物が月面で生き延びることができるかどうかを誰も見に行ってきていない理由が，筆者の注意を引きつけた。

正解は④。問4の解説でも引用した第3段落最終文（Whether these are ...）の「誰もこれらを回収しに行った人がいないので，これらがまだ生きているかどうかはわかりません。残念なことです」という記述は，月面に残された緩歩動物を誰も調べに行っていないのはなぜかと筆者は疑問に思ったことだろう（つまりその理由が筆者の注意を引きつけただろう），と推測するのに十分な根拠となりうることから，④が正解となる。

— 英 R 237 —

①のように推測する根拠は本文中にはない。②についても、「何百万年もの間地球上にいる緩歩動物以外の生物も、X線や紫外線放射に耐えることができるだろう」と推測する根拠は本文中にはないので、やはり誤りとなる。③については、「イスラエル」を「ヨーロッパ」に変えれば正しいが、「イスラエル」のままでは適切な内容にならない（第3段落参照）。

〈主な語句・表現〉
第1段落（Ask someone to ...）
tough 形「丈夫な」／ Bactrian camel「フタコブラクダ」／ Arctic fox「ホッキョクギツネ」
第2段落（Tardigrades, also known ...）
tardigrade 名「緩歩動物」／ water bear「クマムシ」／ microscopic creature「微生物」／ length 名「長さ；全長」／ hot spring「温泉」／ desert 名「砂漠」／ All they need are ...「彼らが必要とするものは…だけだ」／ layer 名「層」／ so do they ＝ they dry up, too「それらも干上がる」／ all but ...「…を除く全て」／ metabolism 名「新陳代謝」／ dried-out 形「乾燥した」／ state 名「状態」／ soak 動「…を漬ける；浸す」／ absorb 動「…を吸収する」／ spring back to life「復活する；息を吹き返す」／ as if ...「まるで…ように」／ the moment ...「…するとすぐに」／ come alive「生き生きとする」
第3段落（Perhaps even more ...）
more amazing（＝ C）than ... is（＝ V）their ability（＝ S）to －「…よりも驚くべきは、それらが－する能力だ」／ a number of ...「数多くの…」／ ultraviolet radiation「紫外線（放射）」／ intense 形「強烈な」／ spacecraft 名「宇宙船」／ crash 動「衝突する」／ spill 動「こぼす；吐き出す」／ pity 名「残念なこと」
第4段落（Tardigrades are shaped ...）
be shaped like ...「…のような形をしている」／ cucumber 名「キュウリ」／ species 名「（生物学上の）種」／ sticky pad「付着盤」／ claw 名「爪」／ variation 名「変異体」／ identify 動「…を特定する」／ primitive 形「原始的な；単純な」／ cell 名「細胞」／ light sensitive「光を感知する」
第5段落（Basically, tardigrades can ...）
basically 副「基本的には」／ divide A into B「A を B に分ける」／ plant matter「植物」／ creature 名「生き物；動物」／ vegetation 名「植物」／ ventral 形「腹の」／ located in ...「…の中に位置する［ある］」／ shark 名「サメ」／ terminal 形「終端の」／ tuna 名「マ

グロ」／ do ... have ～「（確かに；実際に）～を持つ」 do は強調の助動詞。／ needle 名「針」／ stylet 名「吻針」／ pierce 動「…を突き刺す；突き通す」／ so the contents can be sucked out「中身を吸い出すことができるように」
最終段落（Both types of ...）
digestive system「消化器系」／ lead to ...「…につながる」／ pharynx 名「咽頭」／ digestive juice「消化液」／ Located（＝ C）above ... is（＝ V）a salivary gland（＝ S）「…の上方に位置しているのは唾液腺である」／ digestion 名「消化」／ tube 名「管」／ transport 動「運ぶ」／ gut 名「消化器官；腸」／ esophagus 名「食道」／ stomach 名「胃」／ intestine 名「腸」／ organ 名「臓器；器官」／ digest 動「…を消化する」／ nutrient 名「栄養素」／ leftovers 名「残り物」／ eventually 副「結局は；最後には」／ anus 名「肛門」

2022 年度

大学入学共通テスト 本試験

英語（リーディング）

解答・解説

'22
本試験解答

■ 2022 年度（令和 4 年度）本試験「英語（リーディング）」得点別偏差値表
下記の表は大学入試センター公表の平均点と標準偏差をもとに作成したものです。

平均点　61.80　　標準偏差　20.30　　　　　　　受験者数　480,763

得 点	偏差値	得 点	偏差値
100	68.8	50	44.2
99	68.3	49	43.7
98	67.8	48	43.2
97	67.3	47	42.7
96	66.8	46	42.2
95	66.4	45	41.7
94	65.9	44	41.2
93	65.4	43	40.7
92	64.9	42	40.2
91	64.4	41	39.8
90	63.9	40	39.3
89	63.4	39	38.8
88	62.9	38	38.3
87	62.4	37	37.8
86	61.9	36	37.3
85	61.4	35	36.8
84	60.9	34	36.3
83	60.4	33	35.8
82	60.0	32	35.3
81	59.5	31	34.8
80	59.0	30	34.3
79	58.5	29	33.8
78	58.0	28	33.3
77	57.5	27	32.9
76	57.0	26	32.4
75	56.5	25	31.9
74	56.0	24	31.4
73	55.5	23	30.9
72	55.0	22	30.4
71	54.5	21	29.9
70	54.0	20	29.4
69	53.5	19	28.9
68	53.1	18	28.4
67	52.6	17	27.9
66	52.1	16	27.4
65	51.6	15	26.9
64	51.1	14	26.5
63	50.6	13	26.0
62	50.1	12	25.5
61	49.6	11	25.0
60	49.1	10	24.5
59	48.6	9	24.0
58	48.1	8	23.5
57	47.6	7	23.0
56	47.1	6	22.5
55	46.7	5	22.0
54	46.2	4	21.5
53	45.7	3	21.0
52	45.2	2	20.5
51	44.7	1	20.0
		0	19.6

英語（リーディング） 2022年度　本試験　（100点満点）

（解答・配点）

問題番号 （配点）	設問		解答番号	正解	配点	自己採点欄	問題番号 （配点）	設問		解答番号	正解	配点	自己採点欄
第1問 （10）	A	1	1	①	2		第4問 （16）		1	24	③	3	
		2	2	③	2				2	25	③	3	
	B	1	3	②	2				3	26	②	3	
		2	4	②	2				4	27	①	3	
		3	5	①	2				5	28	②	2	
小　計										29	④	2	
第2問 （20）	A	1	6	⑤	2		小　計						
		2	7	③	2		第5問 （15）		1	30	①	3	
		3	8	①	2				2	31 － 32	④ － ⑤	3*	
		4	9	③	2				3	33	②	3*	
		5	10	①	2					34	⑤		
	B	1	11	②	2					35	④		
		2	12	④	2					36	①		
		3	13	②	2				4	37	③	3	
		4	14	④	2				5	38	③	3	
		5	15	②	2		小　計						
小　計							第6問 （24）	A	1	39	③	3	
第3問 （15）	A	1	16	①	3				2	40	③	3	
		2	17	①	3				3	41	①	3	
	B	1	18	①	3*				4	42	⑥	3*	
			19	④						43	③		
			20	③				B	1	44	②	3	
			21	②					2	45	②	3	
		2	22	②	3					46	①	3	
		3	23	②	3				3	47 － 48	③ － ④	3*	
小　計							小　計						
							合　計						

（注）

1　＊は，全部正解の場合のみ点を与える。

2　－（ハイフン）でつながれた正解は，順序を問わない。

— 英 R 240 —

第1問

A

〈全訳〉

　あなたは高校の国際クラブで，ブラジルについて学んでいます。先生からブラジルの食物について調べるよう頼まれました。あなたはブラジル料理の本を見つけて，デザートを作るのに使われる果物について読みます。

人気のあるブラジルの果物	
クプアス	**ジャボチカバ**
・チョコレートのような香りと味 ・ケーキなどのデザートにしても，ヨーグルトに添えてもおいしい ・ブラジル人はこの果物で作るチョコレート風味のジュースを好む。	・ブドウに似ている ・収穫後3日以内に食べると甘い。 ・酸っぱくなったら，ジャムやゼリーやケーキ作りに使うのがよい。
ピタンガ	**ブリチ**
・赤と緑の2種類がある ・ケーキ作りには甘い赤の果実を使う。 ・酸っぱい緑の果実はジャムとゼリーにしか使わない。	・中身はオレンジ色で，桃やマンゴーに似ている ・とても甘くて，口の中で溶ける ・アイスクリームやケーキやジャムに最適

写真提供／Shutterstock

〈設問解説〉

問1　1　正解―①

「クプアスとブリチはどちらも，1 を作るために使うことができる」

① ケーキ
② チョコレート
③ アイスクリーム
④ ヨーグルト

　正解は①。クプアス（Cupuaçu）についての説明の第2の項目（Great for desserts, ...）に「ケーキなどのデザートにしても，ヨーグルトに添えてもおいしい」とあり，ブリチ（Buriti）の説明の最後の項目（Best for ice cream, ...）に「アイスクリームやケーキやジャムに最適」とあることから，①が正解となる。

　②の「チョコレート」については，クプアスの説明の中に，「チョコレートのような香りと味（Smells and tastes ...）」や「ブラジル人はこの果物で作るチョコレート風味のジュースを好む（Brazilians love ...）」とある

ものの，「クプアスを使ってチョコレートを作ることができる」とは書かれていないので，②は正解になれない。③や④を正解とする根拠もない。

問2　2　正解―③

「酸味のあるケーキを作りたければ，使うのに最適な果物は 2 である」

① ブリチ
② クプアス
③ ジャボチカバ
④ ピタンガ

　正解は③。ジャボチカバ（Jabuticaba）の説明文の最後の項目（After they get ...）に，「酸っぱくなったら，ジャムやゼリーやケーキ作りに使うのがよい」とあることから，正解は③に決まる。「酸味がある」と「ケーキ作りに利用できる」という2つの条件を両方とも満たしているのはジャボチカバだけなので，他の選択肢は正解になれない。

〈主な語句・表現〉

　senior high school「高等学校」／ smell［taste］like ...「…のような匂い［味］がする」／ chocolate-flavored 形「チョコレート味の」／ within A of B「BからA以内に」

B

〈全訳〉

　あなたはカナダのトロントにある公立動物園のウェブサイトを見ていて，興味深いコンテストの告知を見つけます。あなたはコンテストへの参加を考えています。

コンテストをやります！
キリンの赤ちゃんに名前を付けましょう
私たちの一番新しい動物を
公立動物園に暖かく迎えましょう！

健康なキリンの赤ちゃんが5月26日に
公立動物園で生まれました。
もう歩いたり走り回ったりしています！
体重は66キロで，体長は180センチです。
あなたにやっていただきたいのは，両親のビリーとノエルが
赤ちゃんの名前を選ぶのを助けることです。

参加方法

◆　ここのリンクをクリックして，赤ちゃんの名前の案を投稿して，指示に従ってください。　**→ ここから参加**

— 英 R 241 —

◆ 名前の受け付けは，6月1日の午前0時から，6月7日の午後11時59分までです。
◆ 名前を考える際の参考に，ライブウェブカメラでキリンの赤ちゃんをご覧ください。 →ライブウェブカメラ
◆ 投稿は1件につき5ドルです。お金はすべて，育ち盛りのキリンの赤ちゃんの餌代にあてられます。

コンテストのスケジュール	
6月8日	動物園のスタッフが，全エントリーの中から5つの最終候補に絞り込みます。 その名前は，動物園のウェブサイトで午後5時までに発表されます。
6月9日	キリンの両親は，第1位となる名前をどうやって決めるのでしょう。 午前11時から正午の間にライブストリームリンクをクリックすればわかりますよ！ →ライブストリーム 第1位となった名前については，正午以降に当ウェブサイトをチェックしてください。

賞品
5人の最終候補者全員に，7月末まで利用できる動物園の1日無料パスを贈呈します。
第1位となった名前の投稿者には，独り占めのナイト・サファリ・ツアー，さらにはキリンの赤ちゃんが家族と一緒に写っている特別な写真も進呈します！

〈設問解説〉
問1 ③ 正解ー②
「このコンテストには ③ の間に参加できる」
① 5月26日から5月31日
② 6月1日から6月7日
③ 6月8日から6月9日
④ 6月10日から7月31日
　正解は②。「参加方法（How to Enter）」の第2の項目（Names are accepted ...）に「名前の受け付けは，6月1日の午前0時から，6月7日の午後11時59分までです」とあることから，このコンテストに参加できるのは，6月1日から6月7日の間であることがわかるので，②が正解となる。

問2 ④ 正解ー②
「キリンの赤ちゃんの名前の案を投稿する際には，④ 必要がある」
① 1日パスを購入する
② 投稿料金を支払う
③ 公立動物園で5ドル使う
④ ウェブサイトでキリンを見る
　正解は②。「参加方法（How to Enter）」の最後の項

目（Each submission is ...）に「投稿は1件につき5ドルです」とあることから，投稿料金を支払う必要があることがわかるので，②が正解となる。
　①の「1日パスの購入」については本文中に記述がない。③は，5ドルの用途が正解の②とは異なるので誤り。④はキリンの赤ちゃんの名前の案を投稿するのに「必要な条件」ではないので，これも正解になれない。

問3 ⑤ 正解ー①
「あなたが投稿した名前が5つの最終候補に含まれていたら，あなたは ⑤ だろう」
① 無料で1日動物園に入園できる
② ライブウェブサイトに無料でアクセスできる
③ キリンの赤ちゃんに会って餌を与える
④ キリンの家族と写真を撮る
　正解は①。賞品（Prizes）の項の第1文（All five contest finalists ...）に「5人の最終候補者全員に，7月末まで利用できる動物園の1日無料パスを贈呈します」とあることから，下線部の内容と合っている①が正解となる。
　最終文（The one who ...）に「第1位となった名前の投稿者には，独り占めのナイト・サファリ・ツアー，さらにはキリンの赤ちゃんが家族と一緒に写っている特別な写真も進呈します！」とあり，④は下線部の内容と合わない。②は最終候補に選ばれなくてもできることなので誤り。③のようなことも，5人の最終候補者ができることとして述べられていない。

〈主な語句・表現〉
enter a contest「コンテストに参加する」／ giraffe 图「キリン」／ Your mission is to -「あなたの使命［任務］は-することだ」／ help (= V) his parents (= O) ... pick (= 原形) 〜「両親が〜を選ぶのを助ける」／ submit 動「…を提出［投稿］する」／ follow the directions「指示に従う」／ submission 图「提出（物）」／ go towards ...「…に使われる」／ finalist 图「決勝戦出場者」／ entry 图「参加者；出品物」／ post 動「…を投稿［発表］する」／ valid 形「有効な」／ as well as ...「…と同様に」

— 英 R 242 —

第2問

A

〈全訳〉

あなたはフューチャー・リーダーという夏期プログラムに参加していて，これは英国の大学のキャンパスで行われています。あなたはコースワークに取り組むため図書館についての情報を読んでいます。

アバマウス大学図書館
午前8時から午後9時まで開館
2022年度案内

図書館カード：あなたの学生IDカードは，図書館カードにもコピーカードにもなります。これはあなたのウェルカム・パックに同梱されています。

〜〜〜〜〜〜

図書を借りる

図書は1度に8冊まで7日間借りることができます。貸し出しの手続きをするには，2階にあるインフォメーション・デスクに来てください。期限までに図書が返却されない場合は，図書が返却された日から3日間は再び図書を借りることができなくなります。

コンピューターを利用する

インターネットに接続できるコンピューターは，2階の正面入口のそばにあるコンピューター・ワークステーションにあります。学生は自分のノートパソコンやタブレットを図書館に持ち込むこともできますが，使用できる場所は3階のスタディ・エリアに限られます。学生には静かに作業し，また友人のための席を取らないことが求められます。

図書館オリエンテーション

毎週火曜日の午前10時に，20分間の図書館オリエンテーションが4階のリーディング・ルームで行われます。詳しくはインフォメーション・デスクの職員にお尋ねください。

過去の学生からのコメント

- 図書館オリエンテーションは本当に良かったと思います。資料も大変充実していましたよ！
- スタディ・エリアはとても混雑することがあります。席を取るにはできるだけ早く行きましょう！
- 図書館内のWi-Fiはかなり遅いのですが，隣のコーヒーショップは良好です。ちなみに，図書館への飲み物の持ち込みはできません。
- インフォメーション・デスクの職員の方は私の質問に全て答えてくれました。困ったことがあったらここに行きましょう！
- 1階には図書館のビデオを見るためのテレビが何台かあります。ビデオを見ている時は，自分のイヤフォンやヘッドフォンを着ける必要があります。テレビの隣にはコピー機があります。

〈設問解説〉

問1　6　正解－⑤

「6 の2つは，図書館でできることに含まれる」

A：コーヒーショップで買ったコーヒーを持ち込む
B：スタディ・エリアで他の人のために席を取っておく
C：3階でコピー機を使う
D：自分のIDを使ってコピーを取る
E：スタディ・エリアで自分のノートパソコンを使う

正解は⑤の「DとE」。Dについては，「図書館カード（Library Card）」の説明の第1文（Your student ID card ...）に「あなたの学生IDカードは，図書館カードにもコピーカードにもなります」とあることと合っている。Eについては，「コンピューターを利用する（Using Computers）」の項の第2文（Students may bring ...）に「学生は自分のノートパソコンやタブレットを図書館に持ち込むこともできますが，使用できる場所は3階のスタディ・エリアに限られます」とあることと合っている。したがって⑤が正解となる。

Aについては，「過去の学生からのコメント（Comments from Past Students）」の3つめのコメントの最終文（By the way, ...）に「ちなみに，図書館への飲み物の持ち込みはできません」とあるのと合わない。Bについては，「コンピューターを利用する」の項の最終文（Students are asked ...）に「（スタディ・エリアでは）学生には静かに作業し，また友人のための席を取らないことが求められます」とあるのと合わない。Cについては，コピー機は1階（the ground floor）にあることは「過去の学生からのコメント」の最後のコメントの最終文（Next to the TVs ...）の中で述べられているが，3階（the second floor）にあるかどうかは本文の内容からはわからないので，正解にはなれない。

問2　7　正解－③

「あなたは図書館の正面入口にいて，オリエンテーションに行きたいと思っている。あなたは 7 必要がある」

① 1階下に降りる
② 1階上に昇る
③ 2階上に昇る
④ 同じ階にいる

正解は③。「図書館の正面入口」は，「コンピューターを利用する（Using Computers）」の項の第1文（Computers with Internet connections ...）に「インターネットに接続できるコンピューターは，2階の正

面入口（the main entrance on the first floor）のそばにあるコンピューター・ワークステーションにあります」とあることから，2階にあることがわかる。また，「図書館オリエンテーション（Library Orientations）」の第1文（On Tuesdays at ...）に「毎週火曜日の午前10時に，20分間の図書館オリエンテーションが4階のリーディング・ルーム（the Reading Room on the third floor）で行われます」とあることから，オリエンテーションは4階で行われることがわかる。したがって図書館の正面入口からオリエンテーションへ行くには，2階から4階に行く必要があるので，③の「2階上に昇る」が正解となる。

問3　8　正解—①

「8は図書館の正面入口の近くにある」
① コンピューター・ワークステーション
② リーディング・ルーム
③ スタディ・エリア
④ テレビ

正解は①。「コンピューターを利用する（Using Computers）」の項の第1文（Computers with Internet connections ...）に「インターネットに接続できるコンピューターは，2階の正面入口のそばにあるコンピューター・ワークステーション（the Computer Workstations by the main entrance）にあります」とあることから，①が正解となる。

正面入口は2階にあるが，②のリーディング・ルームは4階にあり（「図書館オリエンテーション」の第1文：On Tuesdays at ...），③のスタディ・エリアは3階にあり（「コンピューターを利用する」の第2文：Students may bring ...），④のテレビは1階（「過去の学生からのコメント」の最後のコメント：On the ground floor ...）にあるので，①以外は正解になれない。

問4　9　正解—③

「あなたが8月2日に本を3冊借りて，8月10日に返したとすれば，9だろう」
① 8月10日にさらに8冊の本を借りることができる
② 8月10日にさらに7冊の本を借りることができる
③ 8月13日になるまではそれ以上本を借りることができない
④ 8月17日になるまではそれ以上本を借りることができない

正解は③。「図書を借りる（Borrowing Books）」の項に，「図書は1度に8冊まで7日間借りることができます。（中略）期限までに図書が返却されない場合は，図書が返却された日から3日間は再び図書を借りることができなくなります」とある。本問の場合，返却期限は8月8日となるが，この日までに本を返却していないことから，図書が返却された日（8月10日）から3日間，すなわち8月12日まで本を借りることができなくなる。したがって③が正解となる。

問5　10　正解—①

「以前の学生が述べた1つの**事実**は10ということだ」
① ビデオを見ている時はヘッドフォンかイヤフォンが必要である
② 図書館は午後9時まで開いている
③ 図書館オリエンテーションの案内はすばらしい
④ スタディ・エリアには誰もいないことが多い

正解は①。「過去の学生からのコメント」の最後のコメントの第2文（When watching videos, ...）に「ビデオを見ている時は，自分のイヤフォンやヘッドフォンを着ける必要があります」とあるので，これと合っている①が正解となる。

②は事実であるが，学生の述べたコメントではないので誤り。③は1つめのコメントで述べられているが，これは主観的な意見であり，事実とは考えられない。④のようなことは本文中では述べられていないし，「過去の学生からのコメント」の2つめのコメント（The Study Area ...）とも合わない。

〈主な語句・表現〉

take place「行われる」／ handout图「配布資料」／ photocopy图「写真複写；コピー」／ a maximum of ...「最大で…」／ check ... out「〈本などを〉借り出す」／ the first floor「《英》2階；《米》1階」　本問では英国の大学という設定なので「2階」。／ due date「返却期限」／ the day (when) the books are returned「本が返却される日」／ reserve a seat for ...「…のために席を取っておく」／ for details「詳細については」／ by the way「ところで；ちなみに」／ the ground floor「《英》1階」／ photocopier图「コピー機」

— 英 R 244 —

B

〈全訳〉

　あなたは学校の英語新聞の編集者です。英国からの交換留学生であるデイビッドが，新聞に寄稿しました。

　あなたは動物が好きですか。英国は動物愛好家の国として知られていて，英国家庭の５件に２件はペットを飼っています。これは米国よりも少なく，米国では半分以上の家庭がペットを飼っています。しかしペットのいる家庭の比率が最も高いのはオーストラリアなんです！

　なぜそうなのでしょう。オーストラリアで行われた調査の結果が，私たちにいくつかの答えを示してくれます。

ペットの飼い主は，ペットと一緒に暮らす利点として以下のことを挙げています：
➤ペットが与えてくれる愛，幸福，友情（90％）；
➤家族に新しい一員が加わったという感じ（犬や猫の飼い主の60％超）；
➤ペットがもたらす幸福な時。ほとんどの飼い主は，毎日「毛皮のある子ども」と一緒に３，４時間過ごし，犬や猫の飼い主は全体の約半数が，ペットに添い寝をさせています！

１つ不都合なのは，飼い主が家をあける時には，誰かがペットの世話をしなければならないことです。ペットの世話の手配をするのは大変かもしれません。飼い主の25％は，ペットを連れて休暇や長距離ドライブに出かけるのですから。

　これらの結果は，ペットを飼うのはよいことだと示唆しています。一方，私は日本に来て以来，スペース，時間，費用といった他の問題も見てきました。それでも，ペットと一緒に小さなアパートで満ち足りた生活を送っている日本の人たちを私は知っています。日本では最近，小さなブタのペットとしての人気が高まっているそうです。飼っているブタ（たち）を連れて散歩する人もいて，それは楽しいに違いありませんが，ブタを家の中で飼うのはどれほど易しいのだろうかと私は疑問に思ってしまいます。

〈設問解説〉

　問１ 　11　　**正解 − ②**

　「ペットのいる家庭の比率に関して，３ヵ国の序列を最も高い国から最も低い国の順序で示しているのはどれか」

　正解は②。寄稿文の冒頭の段落の第２文（The UK is known ...）から第４文（However, Australia has ...）に「英国は動物愛好家の国として知られていて，英国家庭の５件に２件はペットを飼っています。⑴これは米国よりも少なく，米国では半分以上の家庭がペットを飼っています。しかしペットのいる家庭の比率が⑵最も高いのはオーストラリアなんです！」とある。下線部⑴から，ペットを飼う家庭の比率は「米国＞英国」であることがわかり，下線部⑵から「オーストラリア＞米国＞英国」であることがわかる。したがって正解は②に決まる。

　問２ 　12　　**正解 − ④**

　「デイビッドの報告によると，ペットを飼うことの１つの利点は　12　ということだ」
　① お金を節約できる
　② より長く眠れる
　③ 人気者になる
　④ 人生をより楽しくできる

　正解は④。寄稿文中の点線の枠内にある「ペットの飼い主は，ペットと一緒に暮らす利点として以下のことを挙げています：(Pet owners mention ...)」の項目には，以下の３つが挙げられている。「ペットが与えてくれる愛，幸福，友情 (The love, happiness, and ...)」，「家族に新しい一員が加わったという感じ (The feeling of ...)」，「ペットがもたらす幸福な時。ほとんどの飼い主は(中略)ペットに添い寝をさせています！(The happy times ...)」。選択肢の④は，これらの内容を端的に表したものと考えられることから，④が正解となる。

　他の選択肢は，いずれも上記の３つの利点とは無関係なので，正解にはなれない。

　問３ 　13　　**正解 − ②**

　「この調査からわかったことの１つを最も適切に反映している言葉は　13　である」
　① 「私は飼い猫と一緒にテレビを見ている時は居心地が悪い」
　② 「私は毎日ペットと一緒に約３時間過ごす」
　③ 「ほとんどのペットは自動車旅行に行くのが好きだ」

― 英 R 245 ―

④「ペットは自分だけの部屋を必要とする」

　正解は②。点線の枠内にある「ペットの飼い主は，ペットと一緒に暮らす利点として以下のことを挙げています：(Pet owners mention ...)」の３つめの項目の第２文 (Most owners spend ...) に「ほとんどの飼い主は，毎日『毛皮のある子ども』と一緒に３，４時間過ごし，犬や猫の飼い主は全体の約半数が，ペットに添い寝をさせています！」とあり，②は下線部の内容を反映した発言と考えられることから，これが正解となる。

　①や④のようなことは本文中では述べられていない。③のような「ペットが好むこと」についても，本文中では述べられていない。

問4　14　正解－④
「日本でペットを飼うことについてのデイビッドの意見を最も適切にまとめているのはどれか」

　①　ペットを飼うことは厄介ではない。
　②　人々はペットを飼うのをやめるかもしれない。
　③　ペットの飼い主の家族が増える。
　④　家の中でペットを飼って満足している人々もいる。

　正解は④。「日本でペットを飼うことについてのデイビッドの意見」については，寄稿文の最終段落で述べられている。この中の第３文 (Still, I know ...) に「それでも，ペットと一緒に小さなアパートで満ち足りた生活を送っている日本の人たちを私は知っています」とあり，④はこれと合っていることから正解となる。

　①については，同段落第２文 (On the other hand, ...) に「一方，私は日本に来て以来，スペース，時間，費用といった（ペットを飼うことに関する）他の問題も見てきました」とあることなどと合わない。なお，最終文の中に「ブタを家の中で飼うのはどれほど易しいのだろうかと私は疑問に思ってしまいます (I wonder how easy it is to keep pigs inside homes)」とあるが，これは「ブタを家の中で飼うのは難しいのではないか」ということを示唆する言葉である点にも注意したい。②のようなこともデイビッドは述べていない。③のようなこともデイビッドは述べていない（なお，点線の枠内に「家族に新しい一員が加わったという感じ (The feeling of ...)」という表現があるが，これは「オーストラリアで行われた調査の結果」を示しているのであり，「日本でペットを飼うことについてのデイビッドの意見」ではない）。

問5　15　正解－②
「この寄稿文に最適なタイトルはどれか」

　①　あなたのペットはあなたのベッドで眠りますか。
　②　ペットを飼うことは私たちに何を与えてくれるのでしょう。
　③　あなたはどんなペットを飼っていますか。
　④　ブタをペットにしてみませんか。

　正解は②。寄稿文は，第１段落 (Do you like animals? ...) においてペットを飼う家庭の比率を英・米・オーストラリアの３ヵ国で比較した後，その比率がオーストラリアにおいて最も高いことについて，「なぜそうなのでしょう (Why is this so?)」と問題提起をしている。そして続く点線の枠内では，オーストラリアにおいて行われた調査の結果を紹介している。この中では，飼い主が考える「ペットを飼う利点」の紹介，及び「ペットを飼うのに不都合な点」について触れている。この内容を踏まえて，デイビッドは最終段落で「これらの結果は，ペットを飼うのはよいことだと示唆しています」と述べた上で，日本のペット事情（スペースなどの問題もあるが，それでもペットと暮らすのに満足している人々がいる／小さなブタの人気が高まっている）について考察している。したがって端的に言えば本文全体はオーストラリアと日本における「ペットを飼うことの利点や難点」の紹介と考察ということになるが，「利点」の方に比重が置かれていると考えられることから，「ペットを飼うことの利点」を表していると考えられる②の「ペットを飼うことは私たちに何を与えてくれるのでしょう」が，選択肢の中ではタイトルとして最適である。

　①に関連することは，点線の枠内の「➤」の３つめ (The happy times ...) の中で触れられているのみであり，本文全体のタイトルとしては不適切である。③や④のような「飼うペットの種類」については，本文最終段落中で「日本では小さなブタの人気が高まっている」と指摘されているのみで，やはり本文全体のタイトルとしては不適切である。

〈主な語句・表現〉

　two in five UK homes「英国の家庭の５件につき２件」／ following 形「以下のような」／ fur baby「毛皮のある子ども」 ペットのこと。／ be cared for「世話をされる」／ go away「（休暇などで）出かける」／ organize 動「…を準備［計画］する」／ on the other hand「それに対して；他方」／ be content － ing「－することに満足している」／ flat 名「アパート」

第3問

A

〈全訳〉

　あなたは日本文化が他の国々でどのように表現されているかについて興味を持っています。あなたはある若い英国のブロガーの投稿を読んでいます。

エミリー・サンプソン
7月5日　月曜日　午後8時

毎年7月第1・2日曜日に，「日本の一面」と呼ばれる文化交流イベントがウィンズフィールドで開かれます。私は昨日そこへ行くことができました。これは絶対に訪れる価値がありますよ！　屋台と呼ばれる本場の食べ物売り場がたくさんあって，実地体験や見事な演芸なども行われていました。屋台では抹茶アイスクリームやたこ焼きや焼き鳥が売られていました。私は抹茶アイスクリームとたこ焼きを食べてみました。たこ焼きは特に美味でした。あなたも食べてみてくださいね！

演芸は3つ見ました。その1つは，英語で行われる落語でした。笑っている人もいましたが，どういうわけか私はおかしいと思いませんでした。それは私が日本文化についてあまり知らないからかもしれません。他の2つは太鼓と琴でしたが，私にはこれらが最も興味あるものでした。太鼓は力感あふれるもので，琴は気分がゆったりしました。

私はワークショップや文化体験にも参加しましたが，これらも楽しいものでした。ワークショップでは，おにぎりの作り方を学びました。私が作ったおにぎりは形が少し変でしたが，良い味がしました。流しそうめんは本当に面白い体験でした。これをするには，調理した麺が竹で作った水の滑り台から流れてくるのを，箸で掴もうとしなければなりませんでした。麺を掴むのはとても難しく感じました。

日本の一面を経験したければ，このフェスティバルがあなたにピッタリですよ！　チラシの写真を撮っておきました。チェックしてみてください。

日本の一面
カルチャーパーク，ウィンズフィールド
7月の第1・2日曜日に開催（午前9時から午後4時）

食べ物売り場	実地体験	伝統演芸
抹茶アイスクリーム	流しそうめん（ヌードル）体験	琴（ハープ）
たこ焼き（タコのスナック）	おにぎり（お米のボール）ワークショップ	太鼓（ドラム）
焼き鳥（鶏肉の串焼き）		落語(滑稽な語り)

〈設問解説〉

問1　16　正解－①

「あなたはエミリーのブログを読んで，彼女は 16 ということを知った」

① **日本の伝統的な音楽を楽しんだ**
② 和太鼓の演奏の仕方を学んだ
③ 竹から水の滑り台を作った
④ 屋台の食べ物をすべて試食できた

　正解は①。エミリーのブログ本文の第2段落第5文（For me, the other two, ...）と最終文（The *taiko* were ...）に「他の2つは太鼓と琴でしたが，私にはこれらが最も興味あるもの（the highlights）でした。太鼓は力感あふれる（powerful）もので，琴は気分がゆったり（relaxing）しました」とあり，下線部の表現からエミリーは太鼓と琴の演奏を楽しんだことがわかるので，①が正解となる。

　他の選択肢のようなことは，本文からは読み取れない。

問2　17　正解－①

「エミリーは落語を聞いていた時，おそらく 17 だろう」

① **困惑した**
② 納得した
③ 興奮した
④ 気分がゆったりした

　正解は①。落語を聞いていた時のエミリーの気持ちについては，ブログ本文の第2段落第3文（Some people were ...）で「笑っている人もいましたが，どういうわけか私はおかしいと思いませんでした」とあることから，下線部の内容に最も近い①が正解となる。

　他の選択肢はいずれも下線部とは明らかに異なる意味なので，正解にはなれない。

〈主な語句・表現〉

represent 動「…を表す；象徴する」／intercultural 形「異文化間で起こる」／worth visiting

「訪れる価値がある」／ authentic 形「本物の」／ hands-on 形「実地の；直接参加の」／ highlight 名「呼び物；最も興味あるもの［事件］」／ workshop 名「講習会」／ involve 動「…を（必然的に）伴う」／ chopsticks 名「箸」／ slide down ...「…を滑り降りる」／ bamboo 名「竹」／ slide 名「滑り台」／ flyer 名「チラシ」

B
〈全訳〉

あなたは屋外スポーツが好きで，登山の雑誌に面白い記事を見つけました。

スリー・ピークス・チャレンジに挑む
文：ジョン・ハイランド

ベン・ネビス
（▲1344 m）
スカーフェル・パイク
（▲977 m）
スノードン
（▲1085 m）

去る9月に，10人の登山者と2人のマイクロバスの運転手からなる私たち12人のチームは，英国の登山家の間で難度に定評のあるスリー・ピークス・チャレンジに参加しました。目標は，スコットランド最高峰（ベン・ネビス）とイングランド最高峰（スカーフェル・パイク）とウェールズ最高峰（スノードン）に24時間以内に登ることで，この時間の中には，これらの山々の間を車で移動するのにかかる約10時間も含まれます。このための準備として，私たちは数ヵ月間断続的にトレーニングを行い，ルートを入念に練りました。この難題は，ベン・ネビスの麓（ふもと）から始まり，スノードンの麓で終わることとなりました。

私たちは秋のある好天の朝，6時に最初の登山を始めました。トレーニングのおかげで，私たちは3時間足らずで山頂に到達しました。しかし下山の途中で，私は電話を落としたことに気づきました。幸いチームのみんなが助けてくれたので見つかりましたが，私たちは15分ロスしました。

私たちは次の目的地であるスカーフェル・パイクに，その日の夕方早くに着きました。マイクロバスの中で6時間休んだ後，私たちは元気いっぱいになって第2の登山を開始しました。しかし暗くなると私たちはペースを落とさなければなりませんでした。スカーフェル・パイクは踏破するのに4時間半かかりました。ここで

も計画時間をオーバーして，時間がなくなってきました。ところが道が空いていたので，最後の登山を始める時には計画通りに戻りました。制限時間内にこの難題を成し遂げられるという私たちの確信は，今やより強くなりました。

最後の登山を始めてまもなく，あいにく大雨が降り出し，私たちは再びペースを落とさなければなりませんでした。道は滑りやすく，前方の視界はとても悪くなりました。午前4時半に，私たちは24時間でゴールするのはもはや不可能であることに気づきました。にもかかわらず，私たちは最後の山に登る決意をまだ持ち続けていました。雨はますますひどくなり，チームのメンバーのうち2人がマイクロバスに戻ることにしました。残った私たちも疲れと悲しさのせいで，下山する覚悟ができていましたが，その時天気が回復し，私たちは山の頂上にもう少しのところまで来ていることがわかりました。突然私たちは疲れを感じなくなっていました。私たちは時間の難題については成功を収められませんでしたが，登山という難題については成功を収めることができたのです。私たちはやり遂げました。それは最高の気分でした！

〈設問解説〉
問1　正解　18 － ①，19 － ④
　　　　　　20 － ③，21 － ②

「以下の出来事（①～④）を，起こった順序に並べかえよ」
① メンバー全員がスコットランドの最高峰の頂上に到達した。
② 一部のメンバーがスノードンの登山を断念した。
③ 一行はウェールズまでマイクロバスで移動した。
④ チームのメンバーたちが筆者の電話を見つけるのを手伝った。

正解は 18 － ① → 19 － ④ → 20 － ③ → 21 － ② である。

3つの山の登頂の順序は，第1段落最終文（Our challenge would ...）に「この難題はベン・ネビスの麓から始まり，スノードンの麓で終わることとなりました」とあることから，「ベン・ネビス→スカーフェル・パイク→スノードン」であるとわかる。①の中の「スコットランドの最高峰」とはベン・ネビスのことである（第1段落第2文：The goal is ...）から，①は第1の山（ベン・ネビス）への登山中の出来事であるとわかる。また，②については最終段落第5文（The rain got ...）の中で触れられているが，これは第3の山（スノードン

への登山中の出来事である。③の中の「ウェールズ」はスノードンがある場所なので（第1段落第2文：The goal is ...）、③は第2の山（スカーフェル・パイク）から第3の山（スノードン）への移動を指しているとわかる。④については、第2段落第3文 (On the way ...) と第4文（Fortunately, I found ...）に「しかし下山の途中で、私は電話を落としたことに気づきました。幸いチームのみんなが助けてくれたので見つかりましたが、私たちは15分ロスしました」に対応する内容だが、この段落の第1文に We began our first climb ... とあることからもわかるように、④は第1の山（ベン・ネビス）への登山中の出来事である。この点では①と同じだが、④は「下山の途中」の出来事なので、①→④の順序になる。以上により、正しい順序は①→④→③→②に決まる。

問2　[22]　正解ー②
「彼らがスカーフェル・パイクを制覇した時に予定よりも遅れた理由は何だったか」
① ベン・ネビスの頂上に到達するのに、予定よりも時間がかかった。
② 暗闇の中で順調に進むのが難しかった。
③ 登山者たちはエネルギーを温存するために一休みした。
④ 状況が改善するまでチームは待たなければならなかった。

正解は②。「彼らがスカーフェル・パイクを制覇した時」については、第3段落（We reached our ...）で述べられている。この中の第3文（As it got ...）から第5文（Again, it took ...）に「しかし暗くなると私たちはペースを落とさなければなりませんでした。スカーフェル・パイクは踏破するのに4時間半かかりました。ここでも計画時間をオーバーして、時間がなくなってきました」とあることから、下線部分が「予定よりも遅れた理由」であると考えられる。したがってこれと同内容の②が正解となる。
他の選択肢はいずれも、「スカーフェル・パイクを制覇した時に予定よりも遅れた理由」とは考えられない。

問3　[23]　正解ー②
「この話から、あなたは筆者が[23]ことを知った」
① 満足感を得なかった
② 3つのすべての山に登頂した
③ 時間の難題を見事に達成した
④ マイクロバスの第2の運転手だった

正解は②。最終段落第8文（Even though we ...）以降に「私たちは時間の難題については成功を収められませんでしたが、登山という難題については成功を収めることができたのです。私たちはやり遂げました。それは最高の気分でした！」とある。下線部の表現から、筆者は3つの山の登頂に成功したと考えることができるので、正解は②に決まる。
①は上に引用した文の中の「それは最高の気分でした」と、③は「私たちは時間の難題については成功を収められませんでした」という部分と合わない。筆者は山に登っていることから、④のように「マイクロバスの第2の運転手だった」と考える根拠もない。

〈主な語句・表現〉
第1段落（Last September, a ...）
participate in ...「…に参加する」／ The goal is to -「目標は-することだ」／ approximately 副「約；およそ」／ on and off「断続的に」／ challenge 名「難題；挑戦」／ foot 名「麓（ふもと）」
第2段落（We began our ...）
thanks to ...「…のおかげで」／ in under three hours「3時間未満で」／ on the way down「下山の途中で」／ with the help of ...「…の助けを借りて」
第3段落（We reached our ...）
destination 名「目的地」／ full of energy「エネルギーがみなぎって；元気いっぱいで」／ it took longer than planned「計画されていたよりも長く時間がかかった」／ run out「（時間が）なくなる」／ the traffic was light「交通量が少なかった」／ right on schedule「予定通りに進んで」／ feel confident (that) SV「SV ということを確信する」
最終段落（Unfortunately, soon after ...）
soon after SV「S が V した後まもなく」／ slippery 形「滑りやすい」／ no longer「もはや…しない」／ be determined to -「-することを決意している」／ Exhausted and miserable, ...「非常に疲れていて惨めだったので…」／ the rest of us「私たちの残りの者」／ be successful with ...「…に関して成功した」／ What a feeling that was!「それは何という気持ち［感動］だったことか」→「それは最高の気分だった」

— 英 R 249 —

第4問
〈全訳〉
あなたは米国のロビンソン大学の新入生です。あなたはアパートで生活するための物を買える場所を見つけようとして，レンとシンディという2人の学生のブログを読んでいます。

ロビンソン大学の新入生ですか？
2021年8月4日午後4時51分にレンが投稿

　入学の準備の最中ですか？　家電や電子機器が必要だけど，あまりたくさんお金を使いたくないと思っていませんか。セカンド・ハンドという名前のとてもよいお店が大学の近くにありますよ。そこではテレビ，掃除機，電子レンジなどの中古品を売っています。多くの学生が好んでこのお店で自分の物を買ったり売ったりしています。今販売されているのは次のような物です。ほとんどの物はとてもお手頃な値段ですが，在庫には限りがあるので急ぎましょう！

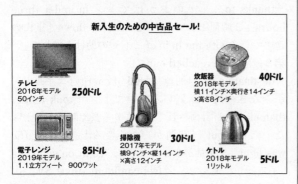

https://secondhand.web

　中古品を買うのは環境に優しいことです。さらに，セカンド・ハンドから購入することで，地元のお店を支えることになります。店主は実はロビンソン大学の卒業生なんです！

ロビンソン大学へようこそ！
2021年8月5日午前11時21分にシンディが投稿

　あなたはもうすぐロビンソン大学に入学するのですか？　新生活のために家電や電子機器を買う準備をしているかもしれませんね。

あなたはここに4年間いるわけですから，新品を買いましょう！　私は1年生の時，家電はすべて大学近くの中古品を売るお店で購入しました。新品よりも安かったからです。ところが，わずか1ヵ月で動かなくなってしまったものがあり，それらには保証は付いていませんでした。私はそれらをすぐに交換する必要があり，あちこちのお店を見て回ることができなかったので，すべてを1件の大きなチェーン店で買いました。買う前に複数のお店で値段を比較できればよかったのにと思います。

save4unistu.comというウェブサイトは，買い物に出かける前にいろいろなお店の品物の値段を比較するのにとても役に立ちます。下の表は，最も人気のある新しい商品の3つの大きなお店での現在の価格を比較しています。

品目	カット・プライス	グレート・バイ	バリュー・セーバー
炊飯器 (横11インチ×奥行き14インチ×高さ8インチ)	115ドル	120ドル	125ドル
テレビ　(50インチ)	300ドル	295ドル	305ドル
ケトル　(1リットル)	15ドル	18ドル	20ドル
電子レンジ (1.1立方フィート　900ワット)	88ドル	90ドル	95ドル
掃除機 (横9インチ×縦14インチ×高さ12インチ)	33ドル	35ドル	38ドル

https://save4unistu.com

　注目すべきは，すべての商品に保証を付けられることです。ですからいずれかの商品が動かなくなってしまったら，簡単に交換できます。バリュー・セーバーはすべての家電製品に無料で1年間の保証を付けています。300ドルを超える商品には，保証が4年間延長されます。グレート・バイもすべての家電製品に1年保証を提供していますが，学生は在学証明を持っていれば，上の表に挙げた価格の10％引きで購入できます。カット・プライスの保証は無料ではありません。5年保証を受けるには，商品1点ごとに10ドル払わなければなりません。

すぐに売り切れます！　待っていたらチャンスを逃しますよ！

〈設問解説〉

問1　正解　24 －③

「中古品を買うのをレンが勧める理由は 24 からである」

① それが大学の役に立つ
② それらの商品のほとんどが環境によい
③ **それらが学生には購入しやすい**
④ 必要なものを急いで見つけることができる

　正解は③。レンの投稿文の本文第1段落第2文（Do you need ...）に「家電や電子機器が必要だけど，あまりたくさんお金を使いたくないと思っていませんか」とあり，同段落最終文（Most of them ...）には「ほとんどの物はとてもお手頃な値段ですが，在庫には限りがあるので急ぎましょう！」とあることから，下線部の内容と合っている③が正解となる。

　①や④のようなことをレンは述べてはいない。②については，レンはブログ本文の最終段落第1文（Purchasing used goods ...）で「中古品を買うのは環境に優しいことです」と述べており，これは「（新品を買わずに）中古品を買う」という行為が環境に優しいという意味であるが，②は中古品自体に環境によい特性・性能が備わっているという意味になるので，これは正解になれない。

問2　25 　正解－③

「シンディは 25 買うことを提案している」

① 時間の節約になるので1件の大きなチェーン店で
② 最も良い価格で売っているのでウェブサイトから
③ **交換保証の付いている新品を**
④ 新品よりもはるかに安いので中古品を

　正解は③。シンディの投稿文の本文第2段落第1文（You're going to ...）に「あなたはここに4年間いるわけですから，新品を買いましょう！」とある。また，同段落第3文（However, some of ...）に「ところが，わずか1ヵ月で動かなくなってしまったものがあり，それらには保証は付いていませんでした」とあり，保証の付かない中古品を買ったことを後悔していることがわかる。そして第3段落（The website called ...）では新品を販売する店の価格を比較するウェブサイトを紹介し，第4段落（Note that warranties ...）では各店の保証制度を紹介していることから，シンディは保証付きの新品を購入することを勧めていることがわかるので，正解は③に決まる。

　第2段落第4文（I had to ...）と第5文（I wish I ...）に「私はそれらをすぐに交換する必要があり，あちこ

ちのお店を見て回ることができなかったので，すべてを1件の大きなチェーン店で買いました。買う前に複数のお店で値段を比較できればよかったのにと思います」とあることから，シンディは時間をかけていろいろな店で価格を比較したいと思っていたことが読み取れるので，彼女が①のようなことを提案するとは考えられない。シンディは，価格比較のウェブサイト（save4unistu.com）を参考にして実店舗から購入することを提案しているのであって，②のようにウェブサイトから直接購入することを提案しているのではない。④は上に引用した第2段落第1文（You're going to ...）の内容と合わない。

問3　26 　正解－②

「レンとシンディはどちらもあなたが 26 ことを勧めている」

① 大学の近くの店で買う
② **できるだけ早く家電製品を買う**
③ 学割を提供している店を選ぶ
④ 保証付きの品物を選ぶ

　正解は②。レンは投稿文本文の第1段落最終文（Most of them ...）で「ほとんどの物はとてもお手頃な値段ですが，在庫には限りがあるので急ぎましょう！」と述べており，シンディも投稿文本文の最後の2つの文（Things go fast!　Don't wait ...）で「すぐに売り切れます！　待っていたらチャンスを逃しますよ！」と述べている。したがって2人ともできるだけ早く家電製品を買うことを勧めていることから，②が正解に決まる。

　①はレンには当てはまるが，シンディには当てはまらない。③の「学割による購入」については，レンは触れていないし，シンディはこれができる店を紹介しているのみで，特にこれを勧めているわけではない。④はシンディが勧めていることだが，レンは勧めていない。

問4　正解　27 －①

「もしあなたが新しい家電製品をできるだけ安く買いたいのなら， 27 べきである」

① **シンディの投稿にある URL にアクセスする**
② レンの投稿にある URL にアクセスする
③ ある1件の大きなチェーン店に問い合わせる
④ キャンパスの近くにある複数の店に問い合わせる

　正解は①。シンディの投稿文の第3段落第1文（The website called ...）及び第2文（The following table ...）

— 英 R 251 —

に,「save4unistu.com というウェブサイトは，買い物に出かける前にいろいろなお店の品物の値段を比較するのにとても役に立ちます。下の表は，最も人気のある新しい商品の 3 つの大きなお店での現在の価格を比較しています」とあることから，本問のように「新しい家電製品をできるだけ安く買いたい」場合には，このウェブサイトを参照するために表の下の URL（https://save4unistu.com）にアクセスすればよいとわかる。したがって正解は ① に決まる。

レンは中古の家電製品を買うことを勧めているので，② は正解になれない。③ や ④ のようなことも本文からは読み取れない。

問 5　正解　28 ― ②，29 ― ④

「あなたは 28 から電子レンジを買うことに決めた。それが最も安いからだ。さらにテレビを 29 から買うことも決めた。それは最も安くて 5 年保証が付いているからだ（それぞれの空所に，選択肢 ① ～ ④ の中から 1 つずつ選べ。）」

① カット・プライス
② グレート・バイ
③ セカンド・ハンド
④ バリュー・セーバー

正解は 28 が ② で，29 が ④。「電子レンジ」の価格は，セカンド・ハンドが 85 ドル，カット・プライスが 88 ドル，バリュー・セーバーは 95 ドルである。そしてグレート・バイは 90 ドルだが，シンディの投稿文の表の下の段落の第 5 文（Great Buy provides ...）に「グレート・バイもすべての家電製品に 1 年保証を提供していますが，学生は在学証明を持っていれば，上の表に挙げた価格の 10% 引きで購入できます」とあることから，（90 × 0.9 ＝）81 ドルとなる（本問における you が学生であることは，本文の冒頭に You are a new student ... とあることからわかる）。したがってグレート・バイの価格が最も安くなるので，28 の正解は ② に決まる。

「5 年保証の付いたテレビ」はバリュー・セーバーとカット・プライスで購入できる。バリュー・セーバーについては，シンディの投稿文の表の下の段落の第 3 文（Value Saver provides ...）と第 4 文（If the item ...）に「バリュー・セーバーはすべての家電製品に無料で 1 年間の保証を付けています。300 ドルを超える商品には，保証が 4 年間延長されます（the warranty is extended by four years）」とあるので，ここで 305 ドルのテレビを買えば，5 年保証が付くことになる。他方，

カット・プライスについては，同段落第 6 文（Warranties at Cut Price ...）と第 7 文（You have to pay ...）に「カット・プライスの保証は無料ではありません。5 年保証を受けるには，商品 1 点ごとに 10 ドル払わなければなりません」とあることから，ここで 5 年保証の付くテレビを買うには，（300 ＋ 10 ＝）310 ドルかかることになる。したがってバリュー・セーバーの方が安く買えるので，29 の正解は ④ になる。

〈主な語句・表現〉

レンの投稿文

appliance 名「器具」／ electronics 名「電子機器」／ used goods「中古品」／ vacuum cleaner「電気掃除機」／ microwave 名「電子レンジ」／ on sale「売りに出した」／ stock 名「在庫」／ 50 in.「50 インチ（inches）」／ 1.1 cu. ft.「1.1 立方フィート（cubic feet）」／ W 9 in.「幅（width）9 インチ」／ L 14 in.「長さ（length）14 インチ」／ H 12 in.「高さ（height）12 インチ」／ D 14 in.「深さ〔奥行き〕（depth）14 インチ」／ eco-friendly 形「環境にやさしい」／ business 名「店」／ graduate 名「卒業生」

シンディの投稿文

buy（＝ V）your goods（＝ O）new（＝ C）「自分の物を新品で買う」／ brand-new 形「真新しい」／ warranty 名「保証（書）」／ replace 動「…を交換する」／ shop around「あちこちの店を見て回る」／ table 名「表」／ current 形「現在の」／ straightforward 形「簡単な；わかりやすい」／ for free「無料で」／ is extended by four years「4 年間延長される」 by four years は延長前と延長後の「差」が 4 年であることを表す。「4 年間に延長される」という意味ではないことに注意。／ proof of enrollment at a school「在学証明」／ per item「1 品目ごとに」／ Things go fast!「品物はすぐに売れてしまう」／ Don't wait or you'll miss out!「待ってはいけません。さもないとチャンスを逃しますよ」

— 英 R 252 —

第5問

〈全訳〉

（全訳中の下線部については，設問解説の問3を参照のこと）

あなたは英語の授業で，偉大な発明家についての発表を行います。あなたは以下の記事を見つけて，発表のためのノートを準備しました。

テレビを発明したのは誰でしょう。これは答えるのが簡単な問いではありません。20世紀の初頭に，機械テレビシステムと呼ばれるものがありましたが，これは成功しませんでした。発明家たちは競い合って，電子テレビシステムの開発にも取り組み，やがてこれが現在私たちが見るテレビの基礎となったのです。米国では，電子テレビシステムの特許権をめぐって争いが起こりましたが，これは1人の若者と大企業との間の争いだったので，人々の注意を引きつけました。この特許権を得れば，発明者はこのシステムの開発，使用，販売ができる唯一の人物となる正式な権利を得るのでした。

フィロ・テイラー・ファーンズワースは，1906年にユタ州にある丸太小屋の中で生まれました。彼の家には，彼が12歳になるまで電気がなく，一家が新しい家に引っ越した時，彼は発電機（電気を作る機械）を見つけて興奮しました。彼は機械や電気の技術にとても興味を持ち，このテーマに関して見つけた情報は何でも読みました。彼はしばしば，古い発電機を修理したり，母親の手動の洗濯機を電動の洗濯機に改造したりさえしました。

ある日，彼が父親のジャガイモ畑で働いていた時，振り返ってみると，そこには自分が作ってきた平行にまっすぐ並んだ土の列がありました。ふと彼は，この畑の列と全く同じように，平行な線を利用して画面上に電子映像を作り出せるのではないかと思いました。1922年，高校1年生の春学期に，彼はこのアイディアを化学の先生ジャスティン・トールマンに示して（→②），電子テレビシステムの構想についてアドバイスを求めました。黒板に下絵や図を描いて，彼は先生にそれがどのようにして可能となるかを示すと，トールマン先生はそのアイディアをさらに練るよう励ましました。

1927年の9月7日に，ファーンズワースは最初の電子映像の送信に成功しました（→A）。その後の数年間，彼はシステムの更なる改良を行い，生の映像を見事に放送できるようにしました。米国政府は1930年にこのシステムに対する特許権を彼に与えました（→④）。

しかしこのようなシステムに取り組んできたのは，ファーンズワースだけではありませんでした。RCA（ラジオ・コーポレーション・オブ・アメリカ）という巨大企業が，やはりテレビに明るい未来を見出し，その機会を逃したくないと思っていたのです。同社は，すでに電子テレビシステムに取り組んでいて，1923年に早くも特許権を得ていたウラジミール・ツウォリキン（→⑤）を雇いました。ところが，ファーンズワースのシステムはツウォリキンのものよりも優れていたので，1931年に同社は彼に大金を提示して，彼の特許権を売ってくれないかと持ちかけました。彼がこの申し出を断った（→①）ことにより，ファーンズワースとRCA社との特許戦争が始まったのです。

同社はファーンズワースに対して訴訟を起こし（→B），ツウォリキンの1923年の特許には，彼がこのシステムを実用化することは一度もなかったものの，優先権があると主張しました。ファーンズワースはこの訴訟の最初の2回の裁判に負けました（→③）。しかし最終審において，ファーンズワースが黒板に描いた図を写していた先生が，ツウォリキンの特許権が付与される少なくとも1年前にファーンズワースが電子テレビシステムのアイディアを確かに持っていたという証拠を示したのです。1934年にある裁判官が，かつての高校の先生トールマンが書いた手書きのメモを根拠にして，ファーンズワースの特許請求を認めました。

ファーンズワースは1971年に64歳で亡くなりました。彼は約300の米国及び外国の特許を持っていましたが，そのほとんどがラジオやテレビに関するものでした。そして1999年にタイム誌はファーンズワースを「タイム100：今世紀の最も重要な人々」に含めたのです。ファーンズワースの妻ペムは，彼の死後のインタビューの中で，ニール・アームストロングの月面着陸が放送されたことを回想しました。彼女と一緒にテレビを見ながらファーンズワースは，「ペム，これで今までのすべての苦労が報われたよ」と言いました。彼の話はいつまでも，動画を無線で送信するという10代の頃の夢と，高校で黒板に描いた例の図に結び付けられることでしょう。

— 英 R 253 —

あなたの発表ノート：

フィロ・テイラー・ファーンズワース
(1906 － 1971)
－ 30 －

子ども時代
－ 電気のない丸太小屋で生まれる
－ 31
－ 32

重要な事件の時系列

　↓ 33
　　34
　ファーンズワースは最初の映像の送信に成功した。
　　35
　　36
　↓ RCA がファーンズワースを告訴した。

結果
－ ファーンズワースは 37 のおかげで RCA との特許争いに勝った。

功績と評価
－ ファーンズワースは約 300 の特許を持っていた。
－ タイム誌は彼を 20 世紀の最も重要な人物の 1 人に挙げた。
－ 38

〈設問解説〉

問1　正解　30 － ①

「あなたの発表の副題として最適なものはどれか」
① **巨大企業と戦う若い発明家**
② 高校教師から成功を収める発明家へ
③ 尽きることのない発電への情熱
④ 電子テレビの未来

正解は①。記事本文の第 1 段落第 5 文（In the US, …）に「米国では，電子テレビシステムの特許権をめぐって争いが起こりましたが，これは 1 人の若者と大企業との間の争いだったので，人々の注意を引きつけました」とあるように，この話の中心は巨大企業（RCA）と若い発明家（ファーンズワース）の電子テレビシステムの特許権をめぐる争いにあると考えられるので，①が正解となる。

ファーンズワースは高校の教師をしていたわけではないので，②は誤り。また彼は発電への情熱を生涯持ち続けたわけではないので，③も正解になれない。本

文では電子テレビの「未来」については語られていないので，④も副題としては不適切である。

問2　正解　31 ・ 32 － ④・⑤

「 31 と 32 に入る最適な選択肢 2 つを選び，『子ども時代』を完成しなさい（順序は問わない。）」
① 家族に電気を供給するために発電機を買った
② 父親に手伝ってもらって電気がある丸太小屋を建てた
③ 学校のすべての科目に関する本を楽しく読んだ
④ **家族のために家庭用設備の修理や改良をした**
⑤ **畑で働いている間に電子テレビシステムのアイディアを得た**

正解は④と⑤。本文第 2 段落最終文（He would often …）に「彼はしばしば，古い発電機を修理したり，母親の手動の洗濯機を電動の洗濯機に改造したりさえしました」とあることから，この文の内容と合っている④が正解となる。また，第 3 段落第 1 文（One day, while …）と第 2 文（Suddenly, it occurred …）に「ある日，彼が父親のジャガイモ畑で働いていた時，振り返ってみると，そこには自分が作ってきた平行にまっすぐ並んだ土の列がありました。ふと彼は，この畑の列と全く同じように，平行な線を利用して画面上に電子映像を作り出せるのではないかと思いました」とあることから，下線部の内容と合っている⑤も正解となる。

①や②や③のようなことは本文では述べられていない。

問3　正解　33 － ②，　34 － ⑤
　　　　　 35 － ④，　36 － ①

「5 つの出来事（①～⑤）の中から 4 つを，起こった順序通りに選び，『重要な事件の時系列』を完成しなさい」
① ファーンズワースは RCA の申し出を断った。
② ファーンズワースは自分のアイディアを高校の先生に話した。
③ RCA は戦いの第 1 段階に勝利した。
④ 米国政府はファーンズワースに特許権を与えた。
⑤ ツウォリキンは彼のテレビシステムの特許権を与えられた。

発表ノートの中の「重要な事件の時系列（Sequence of Key Events）」の項にあらかじめ与えられている出来事は，(A)と(B)の 2 つである。

(A) ファーンズワースは最初の映像の送信に成功し

— 英 R 254 —

た（Farnsworth successfully sent ...）
(B) RCA がファーンズワースを告訴した（RCA took Farnsworth ...）

これらの出来事に対応する記述を「全訳」の中に下線部で示してある。これらの記述から，以下の順序が正しいとわかる。

重要な事件の連続
33 ② ファーンズワースは自分のアイディアを高校の先生に話した（1922 年）。
34 ⑤ ツウォリキンは彼のテレビシステムの特許権を与えられた（1923 年）。
(A) ファーンズワースは最初の映像の送信に成功した（1927 年 9 月 7 日）。
35 ④ 米国政府はファーンズワースに特許権を与えた（1930 年）。
36 ① ファーンズワースは RCA の申し出を断った（1931 年頃）。
(B) RCA がファーンズワースを告訴した。
(③ RCA は戦いの第 1 段階に勝利した。)

問4　37　正解－③
「37 に入れるのに最適な選択肢を選んで，『結果』を完成しなさい」
① 自分の競争相手が技術面で劣っていることを受け入れたこと
② トールマンが提供してくれた資金援助
❸ 自分の先生が長年の間持ち続けていた下絵
④ RCA が争いから撤退したこと

正解は③。ファーンズワースが RCA の特許争いに勝った原因と考えられるものを選ぶ。第 6 段落最終文（In 1934, a ...）に「1934 年にある裁判官が，かつての高校の先生トールマンが書いた手書きのメモを根拠にして，ファーンズワースの特許請求を認めました」とあることから，下線部の内容と合っている③が正解となる。

問5　38　正解－③
「38 に入れるのに最適な選択肢を選んで，『功績と評価』を完成しなさい」
① 彼と彼の妻は，RCA と協働したことに対して賞を与えられた。
② アームストロングの月面初着陸が放送された時に，彼はテレビ出演した。
❸ 彼の発明のおかげで，私たちは歴史的事件を生で視聴できるようになった。

④ 多くの 10 代の若者が，彼をテレビで見た後，自分たちの夢を追いかけた。

正解は③。最終段落第 3 文（In an interview ...）と第 4 文（Watching the television ...）に「ファーンズワースの妻ペムは，彼の死後のインタビューの中で，ニール・アームストロングの月面着陸が放送されたことを回想しました。彼女と一緒にテレビを見ながらファーンズワースは，『ペム，これで今までのすべての苦労が報われたよ』と言いました」とある。この記述からファーンズワースは，テレビを発明し普及させたことにより，（月面初着陸のような）歴史的事件を（自分を含めて）人々が生で視聴できるようにしたことに達成感を抱いていたことがわかる。したがってこの内容と合っている③が正解となる。

①や②のようなことは本文では述べられていない。④も，本文最終文（His story will ...）の「彼の話はいつまでも，動画を無線で送信するという 10 代の頃の夢と，高校で黒板に描いた例の図に結び付けられることでしょう」を誤解したもので，正解にはなれない。

〈主な語句・表現〉
第 1 段落（Who invented television? ...）
　mechanical 形「機械式の」／ electronic 形「電子の」／ inventor 名「発明家」／ compete 動「競争する」／ patent 名「特許権」／ corporation 名「大企業」
第 2 段落（Philo Taylor Farnsworth ...）
　log cabin「丸太小屋」／ electrical 形「電気の」／ change A into B「A を B に変える」／ hand-powered 形「手動の」
第 3 段落（One day, while ...）
　parallel 形「平行の」／ row 名「列」／ soil 名「土」／ it occurs to〈人〉that ...「…ということを〈人〉が思いつく」／ spring semester「春学期」／ diagram 名「図表」／ encourage〈人〉to -「〈人〉に-するよう励ます」
第 4 段落（On September 7, ...）
　succeed in ...「…に成功する」／ following 形「その後の」／ so that S can V「S が V できるように」／ live 形「生の」
第 5 段落（However, Farnsworth was ...）
　work on ...「…に取り組む」／ miss 動「〈機会を〉逃す」／ recruit 動「…を採用する」／ as early as 1923「早くも 1923 年に」／ offer〈人〉〈お金〉「〈人〉に〈お金〉を出すと申し出る」／ be superior to ...「…よりも優れている」／ that of Zworykin's「ツウォリキンのシステム」／ which started ...「それは…を始めた」

— 英 R 255 —

whichは He refused this offer を先行詞としている。／
patent war「特許戦争」

第6段落（The company took ...）

　legal action「法的手段；訴訟」／ priority 图「優先権」／
working 图「実用となる；実際に動く」／ the first
two rounds「最初の2回戦」／ court case「裁判事件；
訴訟」／ evidence that ...「…という証拠」／ at least
a year before SV「S が V する少なくとも1年前に」／
issue 颐「…を発表［交付］する」／ on the strength
of ...「…を根拠に」

最終段落（Farnsworth died in ...）

　recalled Neil Armstrong's moon landing being
broadcast「ニール・アームストロングの月面着陸が放
送されていたことを思い出した」 being は動名詞で，
Neil Armstrong's moon landing はその意味上の主
語。／ make it all worthwhile「その全てを価値あるも
のにする［全てが報われる］」／ be tied to ...「…に結
び付けられる」／ moving picture「動画」

第6問
A
〈全訳〉

　あなたの学習グループは，「時間帯は人にどのような
影響を及ぼすか」について学んでいます。あなたはみ
んなに読んでもらいたい記事を見つけました。次の会
合のための要約ノートを完成しなさい。

あなたの1日はいつから始まりますか？

　「あなたは朝型ですか？」と聞かれると，「いいえ，
私は夜ふかし人間（夜鳴きふくろう）です」と答える
人がいます。そういった人たちは夜に集中や創造がで
きるのです。時間の上でその対極にあるのは，「早起き
は三文の徳」と主張する有名なことわざで，これは朝
早くに起きることは，食べ物を手に入れたり，賞を取っ
たり，目標を達成する手段となることを意味していま
す。ひばりは朝に歌う鳥なので，ふくろう型の人とは
反対に，早起きする人はひばり型です。昼間に活動す
る生き物は「昼行性」，夜に現れる生き物は「夜行性」
です。

　また別のことわざに，「早寝早起きは人を健康で裕福
で賢明にする」というのがあります。ひばり型の人は
サッと起きて朝ご飯をたくさん食べ，朝を喜んで迎え
るかもしれませんが，ふくろう型は目覚ましのスヌー
ズボタンを押し，ギリギリになってから支度をして，
たいてい朝食を抜きます。食事をとることはより少な
いかもしれませんが，遅い時間に食べるのです。食事
の後で運動をしないと太ることがあります。ひばり型
の方が健康なのかもしれません。ふくろう型はひばり
型のスケジュールで働いたり学んだりしなければなり
ません。学校はたいてい午後4時までなので，若いひ
ばり型の人はある種の課題をより上手にこなせるかも
しれません。ビジネスの取引が早い時間に行われれば，
ひばり型の一部の人々がより裕福になるかもしれませ
ん。

　なぜある人はひばり型で，別の人はふくろう型にな
るのでしょう。ある理論は，昼と夜の好みが分かれる
のは，生まれた時間に関係があることを示唆していま
す。2010年にクリーブランド州立大学の研究者は，人
の体内時計は誕生した瞬間に作動し始めるだけでなく，
夜間に生まれた人は昼間の時間帯に物事をするのに生
涯苦労することを示す証拠を見つけました。たいてい
は，彼らの世界についての経験は，暗闇から始まるの

― 英 R 256 ―

です。伝統的に勉学の時間と職場での仕事は昼間なので，私たちは１日は朝から始まると思い込んでいるのです。寝ている人は遅れをとるため，チャンスを逃すかもしれないのです。

　すべての人が１日を朝から始めるシステムに従うのでしょうか。およそ6000年の歴史を持つ宗教集団であるユダヤ人が信じる１日の測り方は，日没から次の日没まで，つまり夕方から夕方までなのです。キリスト教徒はこの伝統をクリスマスイブで続けています。中国人は12の動物によるシステムを用いて，年を示すだけでなく，１日を２時間ずつに分けています。最初の時間帯である子の時間は，午後11時から午前１時です。中国文化においても，１日は夜から始まるのです。つまり，古代の慣習はふくろう型の時間の見方を支持しているのです。

　研究により，ふくろう型の人の方が利口で創造的であることがわかっています。ですから，ひばり型の人の方がより賢いとは限らないのです。言い換えれば，ひばり型は「健康」そして時には「裕福」を得るのですが，「賢明」は失うかもしれないのです。以前の報告書の中で，リチャード・D・ロバーツとパトリック・C・キロネンは，ふくろう型は知性がより高い傾向があると述べています。フランジス・プレケルによって行われたその後の包括的な研究は，ロバーツも共著者の一人でしたが，同じ結論に至りました。けれどもふくろう型の人にとっては，良いことばかりではありません。学業に取り組むのが難しくなるだけでなく，昼間働く仕事に就く機会を逃すかもしれず，「夜遊び」の悪習が身について，ひばり型の人が眠っている間に夜遊びをする可能性が高くなります。夜遊びは概して高くつきます。バルセロナ大学の研究は，ひばり型はきちょうめんで，完璧さを求め，ストレスをあまり感じないことを示唆しています。ふくろう型は，新しい冒険やわくわくする余暇活動を求めますが，しばしばリラックスするのに苦労します。

　人は変わることができるのでしょうか。結果がすべてわかっているわけではありませんが，若い成人の研究は，いや，私たちは簡単には変われないと言っているようです。そのため若者は成長してより多くの自由を得ると，結局は元のひばり型やふくろう型の性質に戻ってしまうのです。しかしながら，このような分類はすべての人には当てはまらないかもしれないという懸念が生じます。生まれた時間が１つの指標となりうるのに加えて，ネイチャー・コミュニケーションズが発表した報告書によると，DNAも私たちの時間に関す

る習慣に影響を与えるかもしれないのです。高齢化や病気のせいで一部の人々に起こっている変化に焦点を当てている論文もあります。この分野では新しい研究が常に行われています。ロシアの大学生の研究によると，６つのタイプがいるらしいので，世の中にはふくろうとひばり以外の鳥もいるのかもしれませんね。

あなたの要約ノート：

あなたの１日はいつから始まりますか？

用語

　diurnal（昼型）の定義： 39
　　⇔反意語：nocturnal（夜型）

主要な点

・私たちのすべてが普通の昼型のスケジュールに簡単になじめるわけではないが，私たちはそれに従うことを強制される。特に子どもの時はそうだ。
・私たち一人一人の最も活動的な時間は，私たちが生まれながらに持つ性質の一部であることを示す研究がある。
・基本的には， 40 。
・新しい研究によって見方は変わり続ける。

興味深い事項

・記事の中ではユダヤ教やキリスト教，及び中国の時間区分が， 41 ために触れられている。
・ 42 は人の体内時計を作動させるのかもしれないし，知性と 43 における違いの理由となるのかもしれないことを示す研究がある。

〈設問解説〉

　問１ 39 **正解ー③**

　「 39 に入れるのに最適な選択肢を選びなさい」

　① 目標を素早く達成する
　② ペットの鳥を飼うのを好む
　③ 日中に活発な
　④ 食物を見つけるのが巧みな

　正解は③。diurnal という語の定義として適切なものを選ぶ。記事の第１段落最終文（Creatures active during ...）に「昼間に活動する生き物は『diurnal』，夜に現れる生き物は『nocturnal』です」とあることから，下線部が diurnal の意味にほぼ等しいことがわかれば，正解は③に決まる。

　問２ 40 **正解ー③**

　「 40 に入れるのに最適な選択肢を選びなさい」

— 英 R 257 —

① より柔軟性のある時間や行動のスケジュールが将来開発されるだろう
② 午前中に社交的な活動を楽しむことは，私たちが歳をとるにつれて大切になる
❸ 私たちが1日のどの時間に仕事の出来栄えが最高になるかを変えることは難しいかもしれない
④ ふくろう型のスケジュールで生活することは，最終的には社会的及び経済的利益をもたらす

正解は❸。第5段落(Research indicates owls ...)で，ふくろう型（夜型）とひばり型（昼型）の人間の特徴の比較がなされ，その後の第6段落第1文(Can people change?)と第2文(While the results ...)では「人は変わることができるのでしょうか。結果がすべてわかっているわけではありませんが，若い成人の研究は，いや，私たちは簡単には変われないと言っているようです」と述べられている。つまり本文では，「夜型か昼型かを変えることは容易にはできないかもしれない」と述べられていて，「夜型か昼型か」ということは，❸の中の「1日のどの時間に仕事の出来栄えが最高になるか」と同内容と考えられることから，❸が正解に決まる。

他の選択肢のようなことは，本文からは読み取れない。

問3 41 正解ー①
「41に入れるのに最適な選択肢を選びなさい」
❶ ある種の社会は長い間1日は夜に始まると信じてきたことを説明する
② 夜型の人は，昔はより宗教的であったことを示す
③ 人々は長い間，朝に怠けているせいで機会を逃すと信じてきたと言う
④ ふくろう型の人はひばり型のスケジュールで職場や学校に行かなければならないという考えを支持する

正解は❶。41には，記事の中でユダヤ教やキリスト教，及び中国の時間区分が紹介された目的としてふさわしい表現が入る。「ユダヤ教やキリスト教，及び中国の時間区分」は記事の第4段落(Does everyone follow ...)で触れられている。この段落は，「すべての人が1日を朝から始めるシステムに従うのでしょうか(Does everyone follow ...)」という問いかけで始まり，上記の3種類の時間区分が紹介された後で，最終文(In other words, ...)で「つまり，古代の慣習はふくろう型の時間の見方を支持しているのです」と結んでいる。したがって，記事の中でこれらの時間区分が紹介され

た目的は，下線部分を示すためと考えられる。「ふくろう型の時間の見方」とは「1日は夜に始まる」ことと同内容と考えられるので，正解は❶に決まる。

他の選択肢を正解と考える根拠はない

問4 正解 42 ー❻, 43 ー❸
「42と43に入れるのに最適な選択肢を選びなさい」
① 睡眠の量
② 外見
❸ 行動
④ 文化的背景
⑤ 宗教的信念
❻ 生まれた時間

2つの空所を含む文(Some studies show ...)の意味は，「42は人の体内時計を作動させる（＝A）のかもしれないし，知性と43における違い（＝B）の理由となるのかもしれないことを示す研究がある」である。

第3段落第3文(In 2010, Cleveland ...)に「2010年にクリーブランド州立大学の研究者は，人の体内時計は誕生した瞬間に作動し始めるだけでなく，夜間に生まれた人は昼間の時間帯に物事をするのに生涯苦労することを示す証拠を見つけました」とある。下線部分は，上記の下線部(A)と同内容と考えられることから，42には，「誕生した瞬間(the moment of birth)」とほぼ同意である❻の「生まれた時間(time of birth)」を入れるのが正しい。

また，第5段落第7文(Not only can ...)に「学業に取り組むのが難しくなるだけでなく，昼間働く仕事に就く機会を逃すかもしれず，(ふくろう型の人は)『夜遊び』の悪習が身について，ひばり型の人が眠っている間に夜遊びをする可能性が高くなります」とある。この文の中の下線部に対応するのが，上の文の中の下線部(B)の「43における違い」と考えられることから，43には「夜遊び」，「眠る」，「遊ぶ」を一般的に表したものとして❸の「行動(behavior)」を入れるのが最適である。

〈主な語句・表現〉
第1段落(When asked ...)
　When asked " ...?" ＝When some are asked " ...?" ／ owl 名「ふくろう」／ The early bird catches the worm.「早起き鳥は虫を捕える；早起きは三文の徳」／ lark 名「ひばり」／ early bird「早起きの人」／ the

— 英 R 258 —

opposite of ...「…と正反対のもの」／ during the day「昼間に」／ emerge 動「現れる」
第2段落（Yet another proverb ...）
　snooze button「（目覚まし時計の）アラーム一時停止ボタン」／ at the last minute「ぎりぎりになってから」／ weight gain「体重増加；肥満」／ schooling 名「学校教育」／ certain 形「ある特定の」／ business deal「商売上の取引」／ wealthy 形「裕福な」
第3段落（What makes one person ...）
　What makes O + C?「何が O を C にするのか；なぜ O は C になるのか」／ preference for ...「…に対する好み」／ have to do with ...「…と関係がある」／ evidence that not only do S_1V_1, but that S_2V_2「S_1 は V_1 するだけでなく，S_2 は V_2 するという証拠」／ internal clock「体内時計」／ those born at night「夜に生まれた人々」／ have lifelong challenges -ing「－するのに一生苦労する」／ assume 動「思い込む」／ first in line「列の先頭に；第一候補に」
第4段落（Does everyone follow ...）
　approximately 副「約；およそ」／ sundown 名「日没」／ following 形「次に来る」／ eve 名「夕方；たそがれ」／ in other words「言い換えれば；すなわち」
第5段落（Research indicates *owls* ...）
　indicate 動「示す」／ that is to say「すなわち；つまり」／ comprehensive 形「包括的な」／ career opportunity「就業のチャンス」／ nightlife 名「夜遊び」／ have trouble -ing「－するのに苦労する」
最終段落（Can people change? ...）
　in 副「〈結果などが〉判明して；手に入って」／ hard-wired 形「固有で変化しにくい」／ end up -ing「結局－することになる」／ concerns arise that ...「…という懸念が生じる」 that は concerns と同格の名詞節をまとめる接続詞。／ categorization 名「カテゴリー化；分類」／ In addition to time of birth ... being an indication「生まれた時間が1つの指標であることに加えて」 being は動名詞で，time of birth はその意味上の主語。／ concerning 前「…についての」／ focus on ...「…に集中する」／ due to ...「…のせいで」／ aging 名「高齢化」

B

〈全訳〉

　あなたは，ある学生のグループに入っていて，「環境を守るために私たちが知っておくべきこと」というテーマの科学の発表会のためのポスターを準備しています。あなたはポスターを作成するために以下の文章を利用しています。

プラスチックのリサイクル
― 知っておくべきこと ―

　世界にはさまざまな種類のプラスチックが満ちています。見回せば，いくつものプラスチック製品が目に入るでしょう。もっと近づいて見れば，それらにはリサイクルのマークが付いているのに気づくでしょう。日本では，下の図1の中の最初のマークを見かけたことがあるかもしれませんが，米国やヨーロッパでは，より細かな分類がなされています。これらのリサイクルマークは，三角形で矢印が追い回しているデザインだったり，時には単純な三角形で中に1から7までの番号が書かれたりしています。このシステムは1988年に米国のプラスチック工業協会が始めましたが，2008年からは国際規格団体の ASTEM（米国試験材料協会）インターナショナルによって管理されています。リサイクルマークは，使用されているプラスチックの化学成分と，そのリサイクル可能性に関する重要な情報を与えてくれます。しかしながら，プラスチックのリサイクルマークが付いている物は，常にリサイクルできるというわけではありません。マークは単に，それがどんな種類のプラスチックでできているか，そしてそれはリサイクルできるかもしれない，ということを示すだけなのです。

図1　プラスチックのリサイクルマーク

　ではこれらの数字は何を意味するのでしょう。2, 4, 5番のグループは，人体に安全と考えられているのに対し，残りのグループ（1, 3, 6, 7番）は特定の状況で問題を起こす可能性があります。まずより安全な方のグループを見てみましょう。

高密度ポリエチレンは，リサイクルタイプ2のプラスチックで，普通はHDPEと呼ばれています。これは毒性がなく，人体に組み込んで心臓弁や人工関節として利用できます。それは強靭で，摂氏マイナス40度の低温や，100度の高温下でも利用できます。HDPEは再利用しても無害で，ビール瓶のケース，牛乳入れ，椅子，玩具にも適しています。タイプ2の製品は数回リサイクルが可能です。タイプ4の製品は低密度ポリエチレン（LDPE）から作られています。これは安全に使用できて，しなやかです。LDPEはスクイーズボトルやパンの包装紙に使われています。現在では，タイプ4のプラスチックはほとんどリサイクルされていません。タイプ5の原料であるポリプロピレン（PP）は，世界で2番目に広く生産されているプラスチックです。これは軽くて，伸縮性はなく，衝撃や熱や凍結への耐性が優れています。これは家具，食品容器，オーストラリアドルなどのポリマー紙幣に適しています。タイプ5のリサイクル率はわずか3パーセントです。

今度は第2のグループであるタイプ1，3，6，7を見てみましょう。これらは含有する化学物質やリサイクルの難しさのせいで，扱いはより難しくなります。リサイクルタイプ1のプラスチックは，一般にはPETE（ポリエチレンテレフタレート）という名で知られていて，主に食品や飲み物の容器に用いられています。PETEの容器（あるいは日本でよく見られる表記ではPET）は完全に洗浄するのが難しいので，使用回数は1回にとどめるべきです。また70度より高く熱することも勧められません。これによって一部の容器は柔らかくなったり変形することがあるためです。純粋なPETEはリサイクルが容易で，新しい容器や衣服やカーペットに変えることができますが，PETEにポリ塩化ビニル（PVC）が混じるとリサイクルできなくなることがあります。タイプ3であるPVCは，既知のプラスチックの中では最もリサイクルしにくいものの1つと考えられています。処理は専門家に任せるのがよく，家庭や庭先で燃やしては絶対にいけません。タイプ3のプラスチックは，シャワーカーテンやパイプや床材に見られます。タイプ6のポリスチレン（PS）は，しばしばスタイロフォームとも呼ばれますが，これはリサイクルが難しく，燃えやすいのです。けれども製造費が安くて軽量です。これは使い捨ての飲料コップやインスタント麺の容器やその他の食品包装材に使われています。タイプ7のプラスチック（アクリル樹脂，ナイロン樹脂，ポリカーボネート樹脂）はリサイクルが困難です。タイプ7のプラスチックはしばしば座席，

ダッシュボード，バンパーなど乗物のパーツの製造に用いられます。

現在では，リサイクルされるプラスチックはわずか20パーセントほどで，およそ55パーセントが埋立地行きとなります。したがって，さまざまな種類のプラスチックについての知識は，廃棄物を減らすのに役立ち，環境への意識を高めるのに貢献できるかもしれないのです。

あなたの発表ポスターの草案：

| あなたはプラスチックの |
| リサイクルマークを知っていますか？ |

（ プラスチックのリサイクルマークって何？ ）

| 44 |

（ プラスチックの種類とリサイクル情報 ）

種類	マーク	説明	製品
1	♺ PETE (PET)	この種のプラスチックはよく見られ，概してリサイクルが容易。	ドリンクボトル，食品容器など
2	♺ HDPE	この種のプラスチックはリサイクルが容易。 45 。	心臓弁，人工関節，椅子，玩具など
3	♺ PVC	この種のプラスチックは 46 。	シャワーカーテン，パイプ，床材など
4			

（ 共通の特質を持つプラスチック ）

| 47 |
| 48 |

〈設問解説〉

問1 　43 　正解ー②

「ポスターの最初の見出しの下に，文章中で説明されているプラスチックのリサイクルマークを紹介する文を入れたいとあなたのグループは思っている。次の中で最適なのはどれか」

① それはプラスチックのリサイクル可能性やその他の関連する問題を順位づけするマークです。

— 英 R 260 —

② それはプラスチックの化学成分とリサイクルの選択肢についての情報を与えてくれます。

③ それは使用者に，どの規格団体がそれらに一般的使用の認証を与えたかを教えてくれます。

④ それは ASTM が導入し，プラスチック工業協会が改善しました。

正解は②。説明文の第1段落第7文（Recycling symbols provide ...）に「リサイクルマークは，使用されているプラスチックの化学成分と，そのリサイクル可能性に関する重要な情報を与えてくれます」とあることから，この内容と合っている②が正解となる。

リサイクルマークを見ても，リサイクル可能性などの順位（rank）はわからないので，①は誤りである。このマークからは「規格団体」に関する情報も読み取れないので，③も誤りである。④は，第1段落第6文（This system was ...）の内容と矛盾している。

問2　正解　[45]—②，[46]—①

「あなたはタイプ2とタイプ3のプラスチックについての説明を書くように頼まれた。[45] と [46] に最適な選択肢を選びなさい」

タイプ2　[45]

① そして使い捨てのプラスチックとして広く知られている

② そして広範囲な温度の下で使われる

③ しかし人間には有害である

④ しかし飲み物の容器には不適である

正解は②。タイプ2のプラスチックの特徴については，第3段落第1文（High-density Polyethylene ...）から第5文（Type 2 products ...）で述べられている。この部分には「高密度ポリエチレンは，リサイクルタイプ2のプラスチックで，普通は HDPE と呼ばれています。これは毒性がなく，人体に組み込んで心臓弁や人工関節として利用できます（＝A）。それは強靭で，摂氏マイナス40度の低温や，100度の高温下でも利用できます（＝B）。HDPE は再利用しても無害で，ビール瓶のケース，牛乳入れ，椅子，玩具にも適しています（＝C）。タイプ2の製品は数回リサイクルが可能です（＝D）」とあり，②は下線部(B)の内容と合っているので正解となる。

①は下線部(D)の内容と合わない。③は下線部(A)の内容と合わない。④は下線部(C)の内容と合わない。

タイプ3　[46]

① リサイクルが難しく，庭先で燃やすべきではない

② 可燃性である。しかしながら，柔らかくて安く生産できる

③ 毒性のない製品として知られている

④ 容易にリサイクルできることで有名である

正解は①。タイプ3のプラスチックの主な特徴については，第4段落第7文（PVC, Type 3, ...）から第9文（Type 3 plastic ...）で述べられている。この部分には「タイプ3である PVC は，既知のプラスチックの中では最もリサイクルしにくいものの1つと考えられています。処理は専門家に任せるのがよく，家庭や庭先で燃やしては絶対にいけません。タイプ3のプラスチックは，シャワーカーテンやパイプや床材に見られます」とあることから，2つの下線部の内容と合っている①が正解となる。

②は「柔らかくて安く生産できる」の部分が本文からは読み取れない。③や④のようなことも本文からは読み取れない。

問3　正解　[47]・[48]—③・④

「あなたは共通の特徴を持ついくつかのプラスチックについて述べようとしている。この記事によると，次の中のどの2つが適切か（順序は問わない。）」

① 熱湯（摂氏100度）は，タイプ1とタイプ6のプラスチック容器には注ぐことができます。

② タイプ1，2，3のロゴが付いた製品はリサイクルが容易です。

③ 1，2，4，5，6のマークが付いた製品は，食品あるいは飲み物の容器に適しています。

④ タイプ5とタイプ6のマークが付いた製品は軽量です。

⑤ タイプ4と5のプラスチックは耐熱性があり，広くリサイクルされています。

⑥ タイプ6と7のプラスチックはリサイクルが容易で，環境に優しいものです。

正解は③と④。

①については，タイプ1について述べた第4段落第5文（Also, they should ...）に「また70度より高く熱することも勧められません。これによって一部の容器は柔らかくなったり変形することがあるためです」とあることから，正解にはなれない。

②については，タイプ1のプラスチックである PETE について述べている第4段落第4文（PETE containers ...）に「PETE の容器（あるいは日本でよ

— 英 R 261 —

く見られる表記では PET）は完全に洗浄するのが難しいので，使用回数は１回にとどめるべきです」とあり，同段落第７文（PVC, Type 3, ...）に「タイプ３であるPVC は，既知のプラスチックの中では最もリサイクルしにくいものの１つと考えられています」とあるのと合わない。

③については，第４段落第３文（Recycle-type 1 plastic ...）に「リサイクルタイプ１のプラスチックは，一般には PETE（ポリエチレンテレフタレート）という名で知られていて，主に食品や飲み物の容器に用いられています」とあり，第３段落第４文（HDPE can be reused ...）に「（タイプ２のプラスチックである）HDPE は再利用しても無害で，ビール瓶のケース，牛乳入れ，椅子，玩具にも適しています」とあり，同段落第８文（LDPE is used ...）に「（タイプ４のプラスチックである）LDPE はスクイーズボトルやパンの包装紙に使われています」とあり，同段落第12文（It is suitable ...）に「これ（＝タイプ５の原料であるポリプロピレン）は家具，食品容器，オーストラリアドルなどのポリマー紙幣に適しています」とあり，第４段落第12文（It is used for ...）に「これ（＝タイプ６のポリスチレン）は使い捨ての飲料コップやインスタント麺の容器やその他の食品包装材に使われています」とある。これらの記述から，③は正解となる。

④については，第３段落第11文（It is light, ...）に「これ（＝タイプ５の原料であるポリプロピレン）は軽くて，伸縮性はなく，衝撃や熱や凍結への耐性が優れています」とあり，第４段落第11文（However, it is ...）に「けれども（タイプ６のポリスチレンは）製造費が安くて軽量です」とある。これらの記述から，④も正しいとわかる。

⑤については，第３段落第９文（Currently, very little ...）に「現在では，タイプ４のプラスチックはほとんどリサイクルされていません」とあり，同段落最終文（Only 3% of Type 5 ...）に「タイプ５のリサイクル率はわずか３パーセントです」とあるので，⑤は正解になれない。

⑥については，第４段落第10文（Type 6, Polystyrene ...）に「タイプ６のポリスチレン（PS）は，しばしばスタイロフォームとも呼ばれますが，これはリサイクルが難しく，燃えやすいのです」とあり，同段落第13文（Type 7 plastics ...）に「タイプ７のプラスチック（アクリル樹脂，ナイロン樹脂，ポリカーボネート樹脂）はリサイクルが困難です」とあることから，⑥も誤りとなる。

〈主な語句・表現〉

第１段落（The world is ...）

figure 图「図」／ classification 图「分類」／ chase 動「…を追いかける」／ pointer 图「とがった物；指し棒」／ administer 動「…を管理する；執行する」／ chemical composition「化学成分［組成］」／ recyclability 图「リサイクルできること；リサイクル可能性」

第２段落（So, what do ...）

problematic 形「問題のある」／ certain 形「ある特定の」

第３段落（High-density Polyethylene is ...）

non-toxic 形「毒性のない」／ heart valve「心臓弁」／ artificial joint「人工関節」／ jug 图「水差し；ジョッキ」／ flexible 形「曲げやすい；しなやかな」／ squeezable 形「絞れる」／ non-stretching 形「伸びない」／ resistance 图「抵抗」／ polymer banknote「ポリマー紙幣」

第４段落（Now let us ...）

challenging 形「大変な；やりがいのある」／ chemicals 图「化学物質」／ beverage 图「飲み物」／ thoroughly 副「徹底的に；完全に」／ soften 動「柔らかくなる」／ contaminate 動「…を汚染する」／ dispose of ...「…を処理する」／ set fire to ...「…に火をつける」／ catch fire「火がつく」／ lightweight 形「軽量な」／ disposable 形「使い捨ての」

最終段落（Currently, only about ...）

currently 副「現在では」／ approximately 副「およそ」／ end up in ...「しまいには［結局］…行きとなる」／ landfill 图「埋立地；ゴミ処理場」／ waste 图「廃棄物；ごみ」／ contribute to ...「…に貢献する」

— 英 R 262 —

2021 年度

大学入学共通テスト 第 1 日程
英語（リーディング）

解答・解説

■ 2021 年度（令和 3 年度）第 1 日程「英語（リーディング）」得点別偏差値表
下記の表は大学入試センター公表の平均点と標準偏差をもとに作成したものです。

平均点　58.80　　　標準偏差　21.44　　　　　　　受験者数　476,174

得 点	偏差値	得 点	偏差値
100	69.2	50	45.9
99	68.8	49	45.4
98	68.3	48	45.0
97	67.8	47	44.5
96	67.4	46	44.0
95	66.9	45	43.6
94	66.4	44	43.1
93	66.0	43	42.6
92	65.5	42	42.2
91	65.0	41	41.7
90	64.6	40	41.2
89	64.1	39	40.8
88	63.6	38	40.3
87	63.2	37	39.8
86	62.7	36	39.4
85	62.2	35	38.9
84	61.8	34	38.4
83	61.3	33	38.0
82	60.8	32	37.5
81	60.4	31	37.0
80	59.9	30	36.6
79	59.4	29	36.1
78	59.0	28	35.6
77	58.5	27	35.2
76	58.0	26	34.7
75	57.6	25	34.2
74	57.1	24	33.8
73	56.6	23	33.3
72	56.2	22	32.8
71	55.7	21	32.4
70	55.2	20	31.9
69	54.8	19	31.4
68	54.3	18	31.0
67	53.8	17	30.5
66	53.4	16	30.0
65	52.9	15	29.6
64	52.4	14	29.1
63	52.0	13	28.6
62	51.5	12	28.2
61	51.0	11	27.7
60	50.6	10	27.2
59	50.1	9	26.8
58	49.6	8	26.3
57	49.2	7	25.8
56	48.7	6	25.4
55	48.2	5	24.9
54	47.8	4	24.4
53	47.3	3	24.0
52	46.8	2	23.5
51	46.4	1	23.0
		0	22.6

英語（リーディング） 2021年度　第1日程　（100点満点）

（解答・配点）

問題番号（配点）	設問		解答番号	正解	配点	自己採点欄
第1問（10）	A	1	1	①	2	
		2	2	②	2	
	B	1	3	④	2	
		2	4	④	2	
		3	5	③	2	
小　計						
第2問（20）	A	1	6	②	2	
		2	7	②	2	
		3	8	①	2	
		4	9	③	2	
		5	10	⑤	2	
	B	1	11	④	2	
		2	12	④	2	
		3	13	②	2	
		4	14	②	2	
		5	15	①	2	
小　計						
第3問（15）	A	1	16	③	3	
		2	17	②	3	
	B	1	18	④	3*	
			19	②		
			20	①		
			21	③		
		2	22	②	3	
		3	23	②	3	
小　計						

問題番号（配点）	設問		解答番号	正解	配点	自己採点欄
第4問（16）	1		24	①	2	
			25	⑤	2	
	2		26	②	3	
	3		27	②	3	
	4		28	②	3	
	5		29	④	3	
小　計						
第5問（15）	1		30	③	3	
	2		31	④	3	
	3		32	④	3*	
			33	③		
			34	⑤		
			35	①		
	4		36 － 37	① － ③	3*	
	5		38	①	3	
小　計						
第6問（24）	A	1	39	④	3	
		2	40	③	3	
		3	41	④	3	
		4	42	②	3	
	B	1	43	③	3	
		2	44	③	3	
		3	45 － 46	③ － ⑤	3*	
		4	47	④	3	
小　計						
合　計						

（注）
1　＊は，全部正解の場合のみ点を与える。
2　－（ハイフン）でつながれた正解は，順序を問わない。

第1問

A

〈全訳〉

　寮のルームメイトの Julie があなたの携帯電話に依頼のメッセージを送ってきました。

助けて！
昨日の夜，歴史の宿題を USB メモリースティックに保存したの。今日の午後に大学の図書館でプリントアウトするつもりだったけれど，USB メモリーを忘れてきちゃった。今日の午後4時までにコピーを1部先生に提出しなければならないの。USB メモリーを図書館に持ってきてくれる？　私の机の上にある歴史の本の上にあると思うわ。本はいらない。USB メモリーだけでいいわ ♡

ごめん Julie，見つからなかったわ。歴史の本は机の上にあったけど，USB メモリースティックはなかったの。ありとあらゆるところ，あなたの机の下まで探したわ。あなたが持っていないのは確かなの？　念のためあなたのノートパソコンを持っていくわ。

そのとおり！　確かに私が持っていたわ。バッグの底にあったの。ホッとしたわ。
いずれにせよありがとう ☺

〈設問解説〉

問1　1　正解－①

「Julie の依頼は何だったか」

① 彼女の USB メモリースティックを持ってくること
② 彼女の歴史の宿題を提出すること
③ 彼女に USB メモリースティックを貸すこと
④ 彼女の歴史の宿題をプリントアウトすること

　正解は①。Julie の最初のメッセージの第5文（Can you bring ...）に「USB メモリーを図書館に持ってきてくれる？」とあるので，これと合っている①が正解となる。他の選択肢のようなことを Julie は依頼していない。

問2　2　正解－②

「Julie の2つ目のメッセージにあなたはどのように応えるか」

① 心配しないで。見つかるわ。
② **それを聞いて本当に嬉しいわ。**
③ もう一度バッグの中を調べてみて。
④ がっかりしているでしょうね。

　正解は②。Julie は持ってくるのを忘れたと思っていた USB メモリーをバッグの中に見つけてホッとしている（What a relief!）。したがって，問題が解決して安堵している相手への言葉として，②が最適である。

〈主な語句・表現〉

　forget to －「－する（べき）ことを忘れる」／ bring the USB with me「USB（メモリースティック）を持参する」／ on top of ...「…の上に」／ just the USB「USB（メモリースティック）だけ（必要だ）」／ The history book was there「歴史の本はそこ（＝ Julie の机の上）にあった」／ Are you sure (that) ...?「確かに…ですか？」／ laptop computer「ノートパソコン」／ just in case「念のため」／ I did have it.「私は確かにそれを持っていた」 did は強調の助動詞。／ What a relief!「ホッと［安心］しました」／ Thanks anyway.「ともかくありがとう」

B

〈全訳〉

　あなたのお気に入りのミュージシャンが日本でコンサートツアーを開くことになっていて，あなたはファンクラブに入会しようかと考えています。あなたは公式のファンクラブのウェブサイトを訪れます。

TYLER QUICK　ファンクラブ

　TYLER QUICK（**TQ**）ファンクラブの会員になるのはとても楽しいですよ。常に最新のニュースを手に入れることができ，数多くのワクワクするファンクラブ会員のイベントに参加できます。新規会員になるともれなく，ニューメンバーズ・パックがもらえます。この中には会員証，無料のサイン入りポスター，**TQ** の3枚目のアルバム「**スピーディング・アップ**」が入っています。ニューメンバーズ・パックはご自宅に配送され，ファンクラブに入会後約1週間で届きます。

　TQ は世界中で愛されています。どの国からでも入会できて，会員証は1年間有効です。**TQ** ファンクラブの会員資格には，ペーサー，スピーダー，ズーマーの3種類があります。

— 英 R 265 —

下の会員資格オプションの中からお選びください。

会員特典（♪）	会員資格オプション		
	ペーサー （20 ドル）	スピーダー （40 ドル）	ズーマー （60 ドル）
定期メールとオンライン マガジン用のパスワード	♪	♪	♪
コンサートツアーの日程の 先取り情報	♪	♪	♪
TQ による毎週配信の ビデオメッセージ	♪	♪	♪
毎月発行の絵葉書		♪	♪
TQ ファンクラブ・ カレンダー		♪	♪
特別サイン会への招待状			♪
コンサートチケットの 20 パーセント割引			♪

要チェック！

◇ 5 月 10 日より前に入会すれば，会費が 10 ドル割引き！

◇ ニューメンバーズ・パックは 1 個につき 4 ドルの配送料がかかります。

◇ 初年度の終わりに，50 パーセント引きで更新またはアップグレードができます。

ペーサー，スピーダー，ズーマーのどの会員になっても，**TQ** ファンクラブをお気に入りいただけるでしょう。さらに詳しいことや入会については，こちらをクリックしてください。

〈設問解説〉

問 1 3 正解ー④

「ニューメンバーズ・パックは 3 」

① TQ の初のアルバムを含む

② 5 月 10 日に配送される

③ 10 ドルの配送料がかかる

❹ 到着まで約 7 日かかる

　正解は④。見出しの直後の説明文の第 1 段落最終文（The New Member's Pack ...）に「ニューメンバーズ・パックはご自宅に配送され，ファンクラブに入会後約 1 週間で届きます」とあることから，④が正解となる。他の選択肢のようなことは本文からは読み取れない。

問 2 4 正解ー④

「新しくペーサーの会員になると手に入るものは何か」

① コンサートの格安チケットとカレンダー

② 定期刊行のメールとサイン会への招待状

③ 月ごとのツアー情報と葉書

❹ ビデオメッセージとオンラインマガジンの購読権

　正解は④。What you get（会員特典）という見出しの表の Pacer の列を見ると，TQ's weekly video messages（TQ による毎週配信のビデオメッセージ）と Regular emails and online magazine password（定期メールとオンラインマガジン用のパスワード）には「♪」の印が付いていることから，ペーサーの会員になると，これらが特典として与えられることがわかるので，④が正解となる。これに対して，同じ列の 20% off concert tickets（コンサートチケットの 20 パーセント割引）や，TQ fan club calendar（TQ ファンクラブ・カレンダー）や，Invitations to special signing events（特別サイン会への招待状）や，Monthly picture postcards（毎月発行の絵葉書）の項には，「♪」の印が付いていないことから，これらは特典として与えられないことがわかるので，①や②や③は正解になれない。

問 3 5 正解ー③

「ファンクラブの会員になって 1 年経つと 5 ことができる」

① 50 ドルの料金でズーマーになる

② ニューメンバーズ・パックを 4 ドルで手に入れる

❸ 会員資格を半額で更新する

④ 会員資格を無料でアップグレードする

　正解は③。本文下部の Check it out! の 3 つ目の項目（At the end of ...）に「初年度の終わりに，50 パーセント引きで更新またはアップグレードができます」とあることから考えて，③は正しい。他の選択肢のようなことは本文からは読み取れない。

〈主な語句・表現〉

　keep up with ...「…に遅れずについていく」／ latest 形「最新の」／ take part in ...「…に参加する」／ a copy「（本や CD などの）1 部；1 冊」／ a week or so after SV ≒ about a week after SV「S が V しておよそ 1 週間後に」／ Pacer < pace 動「ゆっくりと歩く」／ Speeder < speed 動「速く進む」／ Zoomer < zoom 動「突っ走る」／ fee 名「料金」

— 英 R 266 —

第2問
A
〈全訳〉

　英国学校祭バンドコンテストを統括する学生として，あなたはランキングの理解と説明のために，3人の審査員の評点とコメントを調べています。

審査員の最終平均スコア

バンド名 ＼ 特性	演奏力 (5.0)	歌唱力 (5.0)	歌の独創性 (5.0)	合計 (15.0)
グリーン・ フォレスト	3.9	4.6	5.0	13.5
サイレント・ ヒル	4.9	4.4	4.2	13.5
マウンテン・ ペア	3.9	4.9	4.7	13.5
サウザンド・ アンツ	(演奏せず)			

各審査員のコメント

Hobbs 氏	サイレント・ヒルは演奏が素晴らしく，本当に聴衆と心が通いあっているようでした。マウンテン・ペアの歌も素晴らしかった。私はグリーン・フォレストのオリジナルの歌が気に入りました。見事な歌でした。
Leigh 氏	サイレント・ヒルは素晴らしい演奏をしてくれました。聴衆が彼らの音楽にあんなに反応するなんて信じられませんでした。サイレント・ヒルは有名になると本当に思います。マウンテン・ペアは素晴らしい歌声ですが，ステージではパッとしませんでした。グリーン・フォレストは素敵な新曲を披露しましたが，もっと練習が必要だと思います。
Wells 氏	グリーン・フォレストは新曲を出しました。私はそれが気に入りました。大ヒットするのではないかと思います。

審査員の共通評価（Hobbs 氏による要約）

　各バンドの合計スコアは同じですが，それぞれのバンドは非常に異なっています。Leigh 氏と私は，演奏力がバンドの一番大事な特性だという点で意見が一致しました。Wells 氏も同意しました。したがって第1位を決めるのは簡単です。

　2位と3位を決めるにあたり，歌唱力よりも歌の独創性を重視してはどうかとの提案が Wells 氏からありました。Leigh 氏と私もこの意見に同意しました。

〈設問解説〉

問1　6　正解－②

「審査員の最終平均スコアによると，歌が一番うまかったのはどのバンドか」

① グリーン・フォレスト

② マウンテン・ペア

③ サイレント・ヒル

④ サウザンド・アンツ

　正解は②。「審査員の最終平均スコア（Judges' final average scores）」の表中の「歌唱力（Singing）」のスコアが最高のバンドが正解となる。したがって 4.9 点を獲得している②のマウンテン・ペア（Mountain Pear）が正解。

問2　7　正解－②

「肯定的コメントと批判的コメントの両方を出した審査員は誰か」

① Hobbs 氏

② Leigh 氏

③ Wells 氏

④ 彼らの中の誰でもない

　正解は②。「各審査員のコメント（Judges' individual comments）」の欄を参照すればよい。すべての審査員が肯定的なコメントを出しているが，Leigh 氏のコメントの第4文（Mountain Pear have ...）及び最終文（Green Forest performed ...）には，「マウンテン・ペアは素晴らしい歌声ですが，ステージではパッとしませんでした。グリーン・フォレストは素敵な新曲を披露しましたが，もっと練習が必要だと思います」とあり，批判的な言葉も含まれている。したがって正解は②に決まる。

問3　8　正解－①

「各審査員のコメントからわかる1つの**事実**は　8　ということである」

① すべての審査員がグリーン・フォレストの歌を賞賛した

② グリーン・フォレストはもっと練習する必要がある

③ マウンテン・ペアはとても上手に歌うことができる

④ サイレント・ヒルは前途有望である

　正解は①。「各審査員のコメント（Judges' individual comments）」において，Hobbs 氏は最後の2文（I loved ... . It was ...）で「私はグリーン・フォレストのオリジナルの歌が気に入りました。見事な歌でした」と述べ，Leigh 氏は最終文（Green Forest performed ...）で「グリーン・フォレストは素敵な新曲を披露しましたが，もっと練習が必要だと思います」と述べ，Wells

— 英 R 267 —

氏は「グリーン・フォレストは新曲を出しました。私はそれが気に入りました。大ヒットするのではないかと思います」と述べている。下線部はいずれも，グリーン・フォレストの歌を賞賛する言葉と考えられることから，①は事実とみなすことができる。

②については，Leigh 氏のコメントの最終文（Green Forest performed ...）に，③については Hobbs 氏のコメントの第 2 文（Mountain Pear's singing ...）と Leigh 氏のコメントの第 4 文（Mountain Pear have ...）に，④については Leigh 氏のコメントの第 3 文（I really think ...）に，それぞれ同趣旨の指摘が見られるが，これらはいずれも一部の審査員の「意見」であり，客観的な「事実」とは言えないので，正解にはなれない。

問4　9　正解－③

「審査員のコメントと共通評価からわかる 1 つの意見は 9 ということである」
① 評価を受けた各バンドは，合計スコアが同じであった
② 独創性に関する Wells 氏の提案は同意された
③ **サイレント・ヒルは本当に聴衆と気持ちが通じ合った**
④ 審査員のコメントがランキングを決定した

正解は③。「各審査員のコメント（Judges' individual comments）」の Hobbs 氏の欄の第 1 文（Silent Hill are ...）に「サイレント・ヒルは演奏が素晴らしく，本当に聴衆と心が通いあっているようでした」とある。これは Hobbs 氏の見解（意見）であり，③の内容とも合っているので，③が正解となる。他の選択肢はいずれも（誰が見ても否定し得ない客観的な）事実であり，（人によって評価が変わる主観的な）意見と考えることはできないことから，正解にはなれない。

問5　10　正解－⑤

「次の中で，審査員の共通評価に基づく最終的なランキングはどれか」

	1位	2位	3位
①	グリーン・フォレスト	マウンテン・ペア	サイレント・ヒル
②	グリーン・フォレスト	サイレント・ヒル	マウンテン・ペア
③	マウンテン・ペア	グリーン・フォレスト	サイレント・ヒル
④	マウンテン・ペア	サイレント・ヒル	グリーン・フォレスト
⑤	**サイレント・ヒル**	**グリーン・フォレスト**	**マウンテン・ペア**
⑥	サイレント・ヒル	マウンテン・ペア	グリーン・フォレスト

正解は⑤。問 4 の①にあるように，各バンドの最終的な合計スコアは同じであったが，「審査員の共通評価（Judges' shared evalutation）」の第 1 段落第 2 文（Ms Leigh and I ...）及び最終文に「Leigh 氏と私は，演奏力がバンドの一番大事な特性だという点で意見が一致しました。Wells 氏も同意しました。したがって第 1 位を決めるのは簡単です」とあることから，第 1 位は「演奏力（Performance）」のスコアが 4.9 と最も高いサイレント・ヒルであることがわかる。

また，「共通評価」の第 2 段落（To decide between ...）に「2 位と 3 位を決めるにあたり，歌唱力よりも歌の独創性を重視してはどうかとの提案が Wells 氏からありました。Leigh 氏と私もこの意見に同意しました」とある。「歌の独創性（Song originality）」のスコアはグリーン・フォレストが 5.0 で，マウンテン・ペアが 4.7 であることから，グリーン・フォレストが 2 位，マウンテン・ペアが 3 位になるので，正解は⑤に決まる。

〈主な語句・表現〉

originality 图「独創性」／(be) connected with ...「…とつながっている」／It was incredible how ...「いかに…かということは信じられなかった」 It は形式主語で，how ... が真主語。／summarise 動「…を要約する」／suggest that S should V「S が V するべきではないかと提案する」

B

〈全訳〉

　あなたは現在自分が交換留学生として学んでいる英国の学校で，学校の方針が変わることを聞きました。あなたはインターネットの掲示板で，その方針に関する議論を読んでいます。

新しい学校方針〈2020年9月21日に投稿〉
宛先：P. E. Berger
差出人：K. Roberts

Berger 先生へ

　全生徒を代表して申し上げます。St Mark's School へようこそ。私たちは，先生はビジネス界出身の初の校長先生であるとお聞きしましたので，先生のご経験が私たちの学校に役立つことを望んでおります。

　先生が提案されている放課後の活動スケジュールへの変更について，1つ気がかりなことをお話ししたいと思います。エネルギーの節約は大切なことで，これから日が短くなっていくことはよくわかっております。先生がスケジュールを1時間半短縮されたのは，このためなのでしょうか。St Mark's School の生徒たちは，学業にも課外活動にも非常に真剣に取り組んでいます。何人もの生徒が私に，今までと同じように午後6時まで学校にいたいと言ってきました。そこで私は，この突然の方針転換についてご再考いただくよう先生にお願いしたいと思います。

よろしくお願いいたします。
Ken Roberts
生徒代表

Re: 新しい学校方針〈2020年9月22日に投稿〉
宛先：K. Roberts
差出人：P. E. Berger

Ken さんへ

　ご親切な投稿ありがとうございます。あなたは気がかりとなっているいくつかの重要なこと，特にエネルギー費と学校活動に関する生徒の意見について述べられました。

　新しい方針は，エネルギーの節約とは関係がありません。この決定は，2019年の警察の報告書をもとに行

われました。報告書によると，私たちの市では重大犯罪が5パーセント増加して，治安が悪くなったそうです。私は生徒たちを守りたいので，暗くなる前に帰宅してほしいと思うのです。

どうぞよろしく
Dr P. E. Berger
校長

〈設問解説〉

　問1　11　正解－④
　「Ken は新しい方針は11と思っている」
　① 生徒たちをより勤勉にできる
　② 学校の治安を改善するかもしれない
　③ 直ちに導入するべき
　④ 課外活動の時間を減らすだろう
　正解は④。Ken の投稿文本文の第2段落には，「先生が提案されている放課後の活動スケジュールへの変更について，1つ気がかりなことをお話ししたいと思います（第1文：I would like to ...）」，「先生がスケジュールを1時間半短縮されたのは，このためなのでしょうか（第3文：Is this why ...）」，「何人もの生徒が私に，今までと同じように午後6時まで学校にいたいと言ってきました（第5文：A number of students ...）」とある。これらの記述から，学校の新しい方針によって，課外活動の時間が短縮されると Ken が考えていることがわかる。したがって正解は④に決まる。他の選択肢のようなことを Ken が考えているとは，本文からは読み取れない。

　問2　12　正解－④
　「Ken の掲示板への投稿の中で述べられている1つの事実は12ということである」
　① この方針についてはより多くの議論を行う必要がある
　② 校長先生の経験は学校を改善しつつある
　③ 学校は生徒の活動について考えるべきだ
　④ 新しい方針を歓迎しない生徒が複数いる
　正解は④。Ken の投稿文本文の第2段落第5文（A number of students ...）に「何人もの生徒が私に，今までと同じように午後6時まで学校にいたいと言ってきました」とあり，ここから「（課外活動の時間を短縮する）新しい方針を歓迎しない生徒が複数いる」ことは事実であると考えられるので，④が正解となる。
　Ken の投稿文本文の第1段落第2文(We heard that ...)

― 英 R 269 ―

に「私たちは，先生はビジネス界出身の初の校長先生であるとお聞きしましたので，先生のご経験が私たちの学校に役立つことを望んでおります」とあるが，このことから②のように，「校長先生の経験は学校を改善しつつある」と考えることはできない。また，①や③のようなことを Ken は投稿文の中ではっきりと述べてはいないし，これらは（客観的な）事実と考えることもできないので，やはり正解にはなれない。

問3 13 **正解－②**

「この方針の目的は，エネルギーを節約することだと考えているのは誰か」

① Berger 先生
② **Ken**
③ 市
④ 警察

正解は②。Ken の投稿文本文の第2段落第2文（I realise that ...）と第3文（Is this why ...）に「エネルギーの節約は大切なことで，これから日が短くなっていくことはよくわかっております。先生がスケジュールを1時間半短縮されたのは，このためなのでしょうか」とある。この記述から，Ken は「新しい方針の目的はエネルギーを節約することだ」と考えている可能性が高いと言えることから，正解は②となる。Berger 先生の投稿文本文の第2段落第1文（The new policy has ...）に「新しい方針は，エネルギーの節約とは関係がありません」とあることから，①は誤りである。③や④を正解とする根拠もない。

問4 14 **正解－②**

「Berger 先生は，彼の新しい方針の根拠を 14 という事実に置いている」

① 早く帰宅することは重要だ
② **市の治安が悪化した**
③ 学校は電気を節約しなければならない
④ 生徒は保護が必要だ

正解は②。Berger 先生の投稿文本文の第2段落第2文（The decision was made ...）と第3文（The report showed ...）に「この決定は，2019年の警察の報告書をもとに行われました。報告書によると，私たちの市では重大犯罪が5パーセント増加して，治安が悪くなったそうです」とある。②の内容は，報告書に基づく「事実」と考えることができるので，これが正解となる。第2段落第1文（The new policy has ...）に「新しい方針は，エネルギーの節約とは関係がありません」と

あることから，③は正解になれない。①や④は「事実」と見なすことができないので，やはり誤りである。

問5 15 **正解－①**

「Ken が新しい方針に反対するのを助けるために，あなただったら何を調べるだろうか」

① **犯罪率とその地元地域との関係**
② 学校のエネルギー予算と電気コスト
③ 学校での活動時間の長さ対予算
④ 課外活動をする生徒にとっての勉強時間

正解は①。問4の解説からわかるように，Berger 先生が「課外活動の時間を短縮する」という新しい方針の根拠にしているのは，「市では重大犯罪が5パーセント増加して，治安が悪くなった」という事実である。したがって，新しい方針に反対するには，「生徒の課外活動時間を短縮し，帰宅時間を早めることによって，生徒が犯罪に巻き込まれる可能性が低くなるのかどうか」を検証するのが有効である。選択肢の中で，これと最も関連性が高いのは，①の「犯罪率とその地元地域との関係」である。これを調べれば，学校周辺の地域の治安が本当に悪くなっているかを検証するのに役立つと考えられ，新しい方針への転換に反対する根拠になりうる。したがって①が正解に決まる。

②や③や④は，いずれも「犯罪率」や「治安（の悪さ）」について全く触れていないので，これらを調べても，新しい方針への反対論の有効な根拠になるとは考えにくいため，これらは正解にはなれない。

〈主な語句・表現〉

online forum「インターネット掲示板」／ post 動「を投稿する」 名「投稿記事」／ on behalf of ...「…を代表して」／ head teacher「校長先生」／ concern 名「関心事；心配事」／ Is this why SV?「これが S が V する理由なのですか；このために S は V するのですか」／ made (= V) the schedule (= O) an hour and a half shorter (= C)「スケジュールを1時間半短くする」／ take O seriously「O を真剣に受け止める」／ a number of ...「いくつ〔何人〕もの…」／ as they have always done「これまでいつもそうしてきたように」 done は stayed at school until 6.00 pm の代わりをしている。／ regards「拝啓；敬具；草々」 手紙の結びの言葉。／ have nothing to do with ...「…とは全く関係がない」／ based on ...「…に基づいて」／ due to ...「…のせいで」／ yours「拝啓；敬具；草々」 手紙の結びの言葉。

第3問
A
〈全訳〉
　あなたは英国のホテルに宿泊する計画を立てています。旅行アドバイスのウェブサイトのQ&Aセクションで，あなたは役に立つ情報を見つけました。

　私は2021年の3月にキャッスルトンのホリーツリーホテルに宿泊することを考えています。このホテルはおすすめですか？　そしてバクストン空港からそこへ行くのは簡単でしょうか？
(Liz)

回答

はい，ホリーツリーを強くお勧めします。私はそこに2度泊まりました。安価で，サービスも最高です。豪華な無料朝食も付いています。(アクセス情報についてはこちらをクリックしてください。)

私がそこへ行った時の経験をお話しします。

初回訪問時には，安くて便利な地下鉄を利用しました。列車は5分間隔で運行しています。私は空港からレッドラインに乗ってモスフィールドまで行きました。ビクトリアへ行くオレンジラインへの乗り換え所要時間は，普通なら約7分ですが，私は行き方がよくわからず，5分余計にかかりました。ビクトリアからは，バスでホテルまで10分でした。

2回目は，ビクトリアまで高速バスを利用したので，乗り換えの心配は無用でした。ビクトリアで2021年の夏まで道路工事を行うという看板を見つけました。市バスは10分間隔で運行していますが，現在ではホテルまで行くには通常の3倍時間がかかります。歩くこともできますが，天気が悪かったので私はバスを利用しました。

楽しいご滞在を。
(Alex)

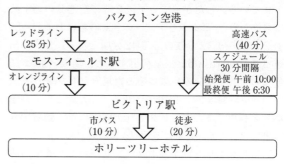

〈設問解説〉

問1　16　正解─③

「Alexの回答から，Alexは 16 ことがわかる」

① ホテルの立地が便利であることをありがたいと思っている
② 初めてキャッスルトンを訪れた時，ビクトリア駅で道に迷った
③ ホテルは金額に見合う価値が十分にあると思っている
④ 2回とも空港から同じルートを利用した

正解は③。Alexの回答文の第1段落第3文(It's inexpensive, ...)から第4文(There's also a ...)に，「(ホテルは)安価で，サービスも最高です。豪華な無料朝食も付いています」とあり，③はこの内容と合っている。①や④のようなことは，本文からは読み取れない。②は「ビクトリア駅」を「モスフィールド駅」に直さないと，本文の内容と合わない。

問2　17　正解─②

「あなたは2021年の3月15日の午後2時に，空港から公共交通機関で出発しようとしている。最も速くホテルへ行ける方法は何か」

① 高速バスと市バス
② 高速バスと徒歩
③ 地下鉄と市バス
④ 地下鉄と徒歩

正解は②。「ホリーツリーホテルへのアクセス(Access to the Hollytree Hotel)」の図を見ると，空港(Buxton Airport)からからビクトリア駅(Victoria Station)までは，地下鉄(underground)を利用した場合，レッドライン(Red Line)の乗車時間が25分，オレンジライン(Orange Line)の乗車時間が10分だが，途中のモスフィールド駅(Mossfield Station)で，乗り換えに約7分要することが，回答文(Answer)の第3段落

第4文（Transferring to the Orange Line ...）で述べられている。したがって，午後2時に空港発の地下鉄に乗った場合，ビクトリア駅への到着時刻はおよそ（25＋7＋10＝）42分後の2時42分頃となる。他方，高速バス（express bus）を利用すると，所要時間は40分なので，2時発のバスに乗った場合，ビクトリア駅への到着時刻は2時40分頃となる。したがって，高速バスを利用する方が，ビクトリア駅へは早く到着できる事になるので，正解は①か②に絞られる。

次にビクトリア駅からホリーツリーホテルまでの所要時間は，図では市バス（city bus）が10分となっているが，回答文の第4段落第3文（Now it takes ...）に「市バスは10分間隔で運行していますが，現在ではホテルまで行くには通常の3倍時間がかかります」とあることから，市バスを利用した場合の所要時間は（10×3＝）30分となるので，①の方法を選んだ場合，ホテルへの到着時刻は早くとも3時10分頃となる。これに対して徒歩（on foot）の所要時間は20分なので，②の方法を選ぶと，3時頃にホテルに到着できる。したがって正解は②に決まる。

〈主な語句・表現〉

free 形「無料の」／ access information「（ホテルへの）アクセス情報」／ underground 名「地下鉄」／ transfer 動「乗り換える」／ directions 名「行き方；道順」／ an extra five minutes「余分の5分間」／ a ten-minute bus ride「バスに乗って10分（の距離）」／ notice 名「看板；掲示」／ roadworks 名「道路工事」／ it takes three times as long as usual to －「－するのに普段より3倍の時間がかかる」

B

〈全訳〉

クラスメイトがあなたに，英国からの留学生が学校のニューズレターに寄せた次のようなメッセージを見せました。

ボランティア求む！

みなさん，こんにちは。私はロンドンからの交換留学生 Sarah King です。今日は大切なことをお話ししたいと思います。

サクラ国際センターのことをお聞きになったことがあるかもしれません。ここは日本人と外国人の住民同士が知り合う貴重な機会を提供してくれます。料理教室やカラオケ・コンテストなどの人気あるイベントが毎月開かれます。ところが深刻な問題があります。建物が老朽化していて，高価な修繕を必要としています。センターを維持するための資金調達を助けるために，多くのボランティアが必要とされます。

私はこの問題について数ヵ月前に知りました。街で買い物をしていると，何人かの人たちが資金調達キャンペーンに参加しているのを見かけました。私がキャンペーンのリーダーの Katy に話しかけると，彼女は状況を説明してくれました。私が寄付をすると，彼女はお礼を言ってくれました。彼女の話では，町長に財政支援をお願いしたのですが，要請は却下されてしまったそうです。資金集めの活動を始めるしかありませんでした。

先月私はセンターで芸術の講座に参加しました。ここでも人々がお金を募ろうとしているのを見かけて，私はお手伝いをすることにしました。私が彼らと一緒に通行する人々に寄付をお願いすると，彼らは喜びました。一生懸命やりましたが，たくさんのお金を集めるには人手が足りませんでした。Katy は泣きそうな顔で私に，建物の寿命もあまり長くはないでしょうと言いました。私はもっと何かしなければならないと感じました。すると，他の生徒たちも手伝う気になってくれるかもしれないという考えが私の頭をよぎりました。Katy はこれを聞くととても喜びました。

そこで，サクラ国際センターを助ける資金調達キャンペーンに私と一緒に参加していただけませんか。今日メールをください！　交換留学生として，私の日本での時間は限られていますが，できるだけのことをしたいのです。私たちが力を合わせれば，本当に変化を起こすことができるのです。

— 英 R 272 —

3 年 A 組
Sarah King（sarahk@sakura-h.ed.jp）

〈設問解説〉

問1　正解　 18 － ④,　 19 － ②
**　　　　　　 20 － ①,　 21 － ③**

「次の出来事（①～④）を，起こった順序通りに並べ替えなさい」

① Sarah はセンターのイベントに出席した。
② Sarah はセンターにお金を寄付した。
③ Sarah は Katy に提案をした。
④ キャンペーンの参加者たちは町長に援助を求めた。

正解は 18 － ④ → 19 － ② → 20 － ① → 21 － ③である。

①に対応するのは，本文第4段落第1文（Last month, I attended ...）の「先月私はセンターで芸術の講義に参加しました」という記述であり，これは「先月（Last month）」のことである。

②に対応するのは，第3段落第4文（She thanked me ...）の「私が寄付をすると，彼女はお礼を言ってくれました」という記述であり，これは第3段落第1文（I learnt about ...）からわかるように，「数ヵ月前（a few months ago）」のことであるから，これは①の出来事よりも前に起こったことである（②→①）。

③に対応するのは，第4段落第7文（Then, the idea ...）と最終文（Katy was delighted ...）の「すると，他の生徒たちも手伝う気になってくれるかもしれないという考えが私の頭をよぎりました。Katy はこれを聞くととても喜びました」という記述である。これは同段落の第1文で述べられている①の出来事の後に起こったことなので，②→①→③の順になる。

④に対応するのは，第3段落第5文（She told me ...）の「彼女の話では，町長に財政支援をお願いしたのですが，要請は却下されてしまったそうです」という記述であるが，この記述から，「町長に財政支援をお願いした」のは，彼女（Katy）と筆者（Sarah）が出会うよりも前の出来事であることがわかるので，④は②よりも前に起こったことになる。したがって，正しい順序は④→②→①→③となる。

問2　 22 　正解－②

「Sarah のメッセージから，サクラ国際センターは 22 ことがわかる」

① 外国人居住者に財政支援を行っている
② 親交を作り出す機会を提供している

③ 地域向けのニューズレターを発行している
④ 交換留学生を英国に派遣している

正解は②。第2段落第2文（It provides ...）に「ここ（＝サクラ国際センター）は日本人と外国人の住民同士が知り合う貴重な機会を提供してくれます」とあり，②はこの内容と合っている。他の選択肢のようなことをこのセンターが行っているとは本文に書かれていない。

問3　 23 　正解－②

「あなたは Sarah のメッセージを読んだ後，キャンペーンを手伝うことにした。あなたが最初にするべきことは何か」

① センターでのイベントの宣伝をする。
② Sarah と連絡をとってさらに情報を得る。
③ 学校でボランティア活動を組織する。
④ 新しい資金調達キャンペーンを始める。

正解は②。最終段落第1文（Now, I'm asking ...）と第2文（Please email me ...）に「そこで，サクラ国際センターを助ける資金調達キャンペーンに私と一緒に参加していただけませんか。今日メールをください！」とあることから，下線部の内容と合っている②が正解となる。他の選択肢のようなことを「最初にするべきこと」と考える根拠はない。

〈主な語句・表現〉

　share A with B「A を B と共有する；A を B に話す」／opportunities for ... to －「…が－する機会」／resident 图「住民」／get to know「知るようになる」／raise funds「資金を募る」／take part in ...「…に参加する」／donate 動「…を寄付する」／ask A for B「A に B を求める」／town mayor「町長」／have no choice but to －「－する以外にない」／join O in －ing「O と－することを共にする」／passer-by 图「通行人」／tearful 形「泣いている；泣き出しそうな」／the idea came to me that SV「S が V するという考えを私は思いついた」　that SV は，idea と同格の名詞節。／be willing to －「－することを厭わない；－する気がある」／be delighted to －「－してとても喜んでいる」／make the most of ...「…を最大限に活用する」／make a difference「違いを生じる；変化をもたらす」

— 英 R 273 —

第4問

〈全訳〉

　あなたの英語教師の Emma 先生が，あなたとクラスメートの Natsuki に，姉妹校から来る生徒をもてなす1日のスケジュールを立てるのを手伝ってほしいと頼んできました。あなたはスケジュールの下図を作れるように，Natsuki と Emma 先生がやりとりした電子メールを今読んでいます。

こんにちは，Emma 先生

来月12名のゲストの皆さんと出かけて一緒に過ごす日のスケジュールについて，私たちにはいくつかのアイディアと質問があります。先生がおっしゃったように，両校の生徒たちは午前10時から講堂でプレゼンテーションを行うことになっています。そこで私は添付した時刻表をずっと見てきました。ゲストは午前9時39分にアズマ駅に到着して，それからタクシーで来校するのでしょうか。

私たちは午後の活動についても話し合ってきました。科学に関連するものを見に行くのはどうでしょうか。私たちには2つのアイディアがありますが，別のアイディアが必要ならばお知らせください。

ウエストサイド水族館で来月開かれる予定の特別展をご存知ですか。これは海のプランクトンから作られる新しい栄養補助食品に関するものです。これは1つの良い選択肢ではないかと思います。人気があるので，一番混んでいない時に訪れるのが最も良いでしょう。水族館のホームページで見つけたグラフを添付します。

イーストサイド植物園は，私たちの地元の大学と共同で，植物から電気を起こす興味深い方法を開発してきました。運のいいことに，当日の午後早い時間に，開発責任者の教授が短いお話をしてくださいます。行ってみませんか？

みんなお土産を買いたいと思いますよね。私はヒバリ駅に隣接するウエストモールが一番良いと思いますが，1日中お土産を持って歩きたくはありません。

最後に，アズマを訪れるすべての人は，学校の隣のアズマ記念公園にある，町のシンボルとなっている像を見るべきですが，良いスケジュールを組むことができません。加えて，昼食の計画がどうなっているかも教えていただけますか。

よろしくお願いします。
Natsuki

こんにちは，Natsuki さん

メールをくれてありがとう。とても頑張っていますね。あなたの質問に関してですが，彼らは駅に午前9時20分に到着して，それからスクールバスに乗ります。

午後に訪れる主な2つの場所，水族館と植物園は良いアイディアですね。両校とも科学教育を重視しているし，このプログラムの目的は，生徒の科学に関する知識を高めるということですから。けれども，念のため3つ目の案も準備しておくのが賢明でしょうね。

お土産はその日の最後に買うことにしましょう。モールに行くバスに乗って，午後5時に向こうに着くことができます。これなら1時間近く買い物ができるし，ホテルはカエデ駅から歩いてほんの数分のところにあるので，ゲストの生徒たちはそれでも午後6時半までにホテルに戻って夕食を取ることができます。

お昼については，学校の食堂がお弁当を用意してくれます。あなたが挙げていた像の下で食べることができます。雨が降ったら屋内で食べましょう。

いろいろと提案してくれてありがとう。あなたたち2人でスケジュールの下図を作ってもらえませんか。

よろしく
Emma

添付された時刻表：

列車時刻表

カエデ － ヒバリ － アズマ

駅	列車番号			
	108	109	110	111
カエデ	8:28	8:43	9:02	9:16
ヒバリ	8:50	9:05	9:24	9:38
アズマ	9:05	9:20	9:39	9:53

駅	列車番号			
	238	239	240	241
アズマ	17:25	17:45	18:00	18:15
ヒバリ	17:40	18:00	18:15	18:30
カエデ	18:02	18:22	18:37	18:52

添付されたグラフ：

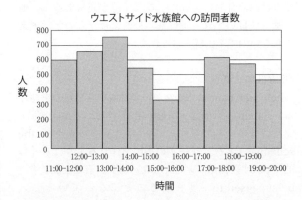

〈設問解説〉

問1　正解　24 －①，25 －⑤

「姉妹校からのゲストの生徒たちは，24 号の列車で到着し，25 号の列車でホテルへ帰るだろう」

① 109　　② 110　　③ 111
④ 238　　⑤ 239　　⑥ 240

Natsuki のメール本文の第1段落最終文（Will they arrive ...）に「ゲストは午前9時39分にアズマ駅に到着して，それからタクシーで来校するのでしょうか」とあり，Emma 先生のメールの第1段落最終文（In answer to ...）に「あなたの質問に関してですが，彼らは駅に午前9時20分に到着して，それからスクールバスに乗ります」とあることから，ゲストの生徒たちは，「午前9時20分にアズマ駅に到着する」ことがわかる。「添付された時刻表（Attached timetable）を参照すると，この列車は109号であることがわかるので，24 の正解は①となる。

Emma 先生のメールの第3段落最終文（This will allow ...）に「これなら1時間近く買い物ができるし，ホテルはカエデ駅から歩いてほんの数分のところにあるので，ゲストの生徒たちはそれでも午後6時半までにホテルに戻って夕食を取ることができます」とあることから，ゲストの生徒たちは，「午後6時半よりも数分前にカエデ駅に到着する列車」を利用してホテルに帰ることがわかる。この列車は時刻表で18:22にカエデ駅に到着する239号と考えられるので，25 の正解は⑤となる。

問2　26 　正解－②

「スケジュールの下図を完成させるのに最適なものはどれか」

A：水族館　　　　　B：植物園
C：モール　　　　　D：学校

① D→A→B→C
② D→B→A→C
③ D→B→C→A
④ D→C→A→B

正解は②。空欄の先頭（9:30）にDの学校が入ることは，すべての選択肢に共通している。

Emma 先生の第3段落第1文（Let's get souvenirs ...）と第2文（We can take ...）に「お土産はその日の最後に買うことにしましょう。モールに行くバスに乗って，午後5時に向こうに着くことができます」とあることから，図の17:00の欄にはCのモールが入ることがわかる。

残るAとBについては，Natsuki のメールの第3段落第4文（Since it's popular, ...）と第5文（I'm attaching ...）に「人気があるので，一番混んでいない時に訪れるのが最も良いでしょう。水族館のホームページで見つけたグラフを添付します」とある。「一番混んでいない時」というのは，「添付されたグラフ（Attached graph）」を参照すると，15:00から16:00の時間帯であることがわかるので，下図の15:30の欄にAの水族館が入ることがわかる。これによって13:30の欄はBの植物園ということになる。以上により正解は②に決まる。

問3　27 　正解－②

「雨が降らない限り，ゲストの生徒たちは昼食を 27 で食べるだろう」

① 植物園
② 学校に隣接する公園
③ 駅に隣接する公園
④ 校庭

正解は②。Emma 先生のメール本文の最後から2つ目の段落（About lunch, ...）に「お昼については，学校の食堂がお弁当を用意してくれます。あなたが挙げ

ていた像の下で食べることができます。雨が降ったら屋内で食べましょう」とある。この中の「あなたが挙げていた像」とは、Natsuki のメールの最終段落第1文（Finally, every visitor ...）の「最後に、アズマを訪れるすべての人は、学校の隣のアズマ記念公園にある、町のシンボルとなっている像を見るべきですが、良いスケジュールを組むことができません」という記述の中の下線部の像を指すので、昼食を食べるのは「学校の隣のアズマ記念公園」ということになる。したがって正解は②に決まる。

問4　正解　[28]─②

「ゲストの生徒たちは、当日 [28] 移動することは**ない**だろう」

① バスで
❷ タクシーで
③ 列車で
④ 徒歩で

　正解は❷。Natsuki がメールの第1段落最終文（Will they arrive ...）で「ゲストは午前9時39分にアズマ駅に到着して、それからタクシーで来校するのでしょうか」と質問したのに対して、Emma 先生はメールの第1段落最終文（In answer to ...）で「あなたの質問に関してですが、彼らは駅に午前9時20分に到着して、それからスクールバスに乗ります」と答えている。したがってゲストの生徒たちはタクシーは利用しないことになるので、②が正解となる。上に引用した文や、第3段落第2文（We can take ...）に「モールに行くバスに乗って、午後5時に向こうに着くことができます」とあることから、①は正解になれない。また、続く第3文（This will allow ...）に「これなら1時間近く買い物ができるし、ホテルはカエデ駅から歩いてほんの数分のところにあるので、ゲストの生徒たちはそれでも午後6時半までにホテルに戻って夕食を取ることができます」とあることから、④も正解ではない。そして問1からもわかるように、列車も利用するので、③も正解になれない。

問5　[29]　正解─④

「3番目の案として、どれがあなたのプログラムに最も適しているか」

① ヒバリ遊園地
② ヒバリ美術館
③ ヒバリ城
❹ ヒバリ宇宙センター

　正解は④。Emma 先生のメールの第2段落第1文（The two main afternoon locations, ...）に「午後に訪れる主な2つの場所、水族館と植物園は良いアイディアですね。両校とも科学教育を重視しているし、このプログラムの目的は、生徒の科学に関する知識を高めるということですから」とあることから、選択肢の中で下線部の目的に最も合っている④が正解となる。他の選択肢はいずれも下線部の目的に合うものとは考えられないので、正解にはなれない。

〈主な語句・表現〉

　help her plan ... 「彼女が…の計画を立てるのを助ける」「help ＋目的語＋原形不定詞」の形。／ host 動「…を接待する；もてなす」／ so that you can draft the schedule「スケジュールの下図を作れるように」「目的」を表す副詞節。／ day out「外出日；日帰り旅行」／ be supposed to −「−することになっている」／ assembly hall「講堂」／ attached 形「添付の」／ timetable 名「時刻表」／ something related to ... 「…と関係があるもの」／ exhibition 名「展示会」／ be on「〈事が〉予定［計画］されている」／ aquarium 名「水族館」／ food supplement「栄養補助食品」／ the best time to visit will be when SV「訪れるのに最適な時は、SがVする時でしょう」／ botanical garden「植物園」／ in charge「責任のある；統括している」／ souvenir 名「お土産」／ carry them around with us「それらを持ち歩く」／ statue 名「像」／ work out「〈計画などを〉作成する；練り上げる」

　in answer to ... 「…の返事として」／ place emphasis on ... 「…を強調［重視］する」／ the purpose of ... is to −「…の目的は−することだ」／ just in case「念のため」／ be a few minutes' walk from ... 「…から歩いて数分のところにある」／ boxed 形「箱入りの」／ draft 名「草稿；下図」動「下図を描く」

第5問

〈全訳〉

　国際的なニュース報道を利用して，あなたは英語による口頭プレゼンテーション・コンテストに参加しようとしています。話の準備として，次のフランスからのニュース記事を読みなさい。

───────────────────────

　5年前，Sabine Rouas さんは自分の馬を亡くした。馬が老齢で死ぬまで，彼女は馬と20年間過ごした。その時，彼女はもう二度と馬を飼うことはできないと感じた。彼女は寂しさから，近くの酪農場で牛を見て何時間も過ごした。その後ある日のこと，彼女は農場主に，牛の世話を手伝ってもいいですかと尋ねた。

　農場主は承諾して，Sabine は働き始めた。彼女はすぐに一頭の牛と友達になった。牛は子を宿していたので，彼女は他の牛よりも多くの時間をその牛と一緒に過ごした。牛に子が生まれ，その子牛は Sabine について回るようになった。あいにく農場主は酪農場で雄牛を飼うことには興味を示さなかった。農場主は309と呼ぶこの雄の子牛を精肉市場に売る計画を立てた。Sabine はそんなことはさせまいと決心したので，農場主に子牛とその母を売ってくれないかと尋ねた。農場主は承諾して，彼女は牛たちを買った。それから Sabine は，309を町へ散歩に連れて行くようになった。およそ9ヵ月後，牛たちを別の場所に移す許可を彼女はついに得て，牛たちは Sabine の農場に移った。

　その後まもなく，Sabine はポニーを飼わないかという話を持ちかけられた。最初彼女はポニーをあまり飼いたいとは思わなかったが，昔の馬の辛い思い出からはもう癒えていたので，ポニーを引き取り，Leon と名付けた。それから彼女は昔の趣味に戻ろうと決めて，ポニーに障害ジャンプの訓練をするようになった。309は，彼女によって Aston という名に改められていたが，ほとんどの時間を Leon と共に過ごし，2匹は本当に仲良しになった。けれども Sabine は，彼女が毎日 Leon に行う訓練に Aston が強い関心を持つようになることを期待していなかったし，Aston がいくつかの芸を身につけることも期待していなかった。この若い雄牛はすぐに，命令に応じて歩いたり，走ったり，止まったり，後ずさりしたり，ぐるりと回れるようになった。彼は馬とまったく同じように Sabine の声に反応した。そして体重が1,300キロあったにもかかわらず，彼はほんの18ヵ月で，Sabine を背中に乗せたまま高さ1メートルある馬術用の障害物を飛び越える方法を身につけた。Aston は，Leon を見ていなかったら，こういったものを決して身につけていなかったかもしれない。さらに Aston は距離を理解して，ジャンプするまでの足の運び方を調節することができた。彼はまた自分の欠点にも気づき，Sabine の助けなしでそれを矯正した。それは選りすぐりのオリンピックレベルの馬にしかできないことである。

　今では Sabine と Aston は，ヨーロッパ各地で週末に開かれるフェアやホースショーに出かけて，Aston の技を披露している。Sabine は言う。「人々の反応は良いです。ほとんどの場合，人々は本当に驚き，最初は少し怖がることもあります。Aston が大きい…馬よりもずっと大きいからです。ほとんどの人々は，ツノのある雄牛にあまり近づきたがりません。でもいったん Aston の本当の性質がわかって，彼の立ち振る舞いを見ると，『うわあ，本当はすごく美しいんですね』とよく言ってくれます」

　「ほら！」と言って Sabine はスマートフォンで Aston の写真を見せてくれる。そして続けて言う。「Aston がまだ幼かった頃，私は彼にひもを付けて犬のように散歩に連れて行きました。彼を人間に慣れさせるためです。だから彼は人を嫌がらないのかもしれません。彼はとてもおとなしいので，特に子供たちは彼を見て近寄るチャンスを得るのが本当に好きなんです」

　ここ数年間で，障害ジャンプをするこの大きな雄牛のニュースは急速に広まり，今や Aston は大きな呼び物となり，ネット上のファンも増えている。Aston と Sabine は，時に家から200あるいは300キロも離れたところへ移動する必要があるため，外泊しなければならないことがある。Aston は馬運搬車の中で眠らなければならないが，これは彼にはややきゅうくつだ。

　「彼はあれが好きじゃないんです。私は運搬車の中で彼と一緒に眠らなければなりません」と Sabine は言う。「でもね，彼は目を覚まして寝返りを打つ時，私を押しつぶさないようとても注意してくれるんです。本当に彼はとても優しいんです。彼は時々寂しくなり，Leon からあまり長い間離れることを好みません。でもそれ以外では，彼はとても満足しています」

あなたのプレゼンテーション・スライド

30
セントラル高校 英語プレゼンテーション・コンテスト

登場者の紹介
主要な登場者
□, □, □
それ以外の登場者　　⎫　31
□, □　　　　　　⎭

有名になるまでの経緯
Sabine の馬が死ぬ。
32
33
34
35
Aston と Sabine は見せ物に出かけるようになる。

Aston の能力
Aston にできるのは：
・Leon の訓練を見るだけで覚えること。
・Sabine の命令に応じて歩いたり，走ったり，止まったりすること。
・距離を理解して足の運び方を調節すること。
・ 36 。
・ 37 。

Aston は今
現在の Aston は：
・障害ジャンプをする雄牛である。
・Sabine とフェアやイベントに出かけている。
・ 38 。

〈設問解説〉

問1　正解　30 － ③

「あなたのプレゼンテーションのタイトルとして最適なものはどれか」

① 動物を愛する人がポニーの命を救う

② Aston の夏の障害ジャンプツアー

③ 馬のように振る舞う雄牛の Aston に会おう

④ ある農場主と牛の関係

正解は ③。消去法で考えるとわかりやすい。この話の最大の主役となっている動物は雄牛（bull）の Aston であり，ポニー（pony）の Leon ではないので，① はタイトルとして不適切である。また，② のような「夏の障害ジャンプツアー」についての話は本文中に出てこないし，「農場主と牛の関係」が話の中心になっているわけでもないので，④ も正解になれない。したがって正解は ③

に絞られる。③ の中の「馬のように振る舞う」という表現は，Sabine の呼びかけに「馬とまったく同じように応じ（第3段落第7文：He responded to ...）」，「障害ジャンプ（horse jump）」のやり方を覚えて，「ホースショー（horse show）」で人気者になった Aston にふさわしい表現であるし，「Aston に会おう」という表現も，第5段落第3文中の "When Aston was ..." という Sabine の言葉からわかるように，人と接することを嫌がらず，子供たちに人気があり，ネット上のファンも増えている（第6段落第1文：Over the last few years, ...）雄牛の Aston に適した表現である。

問2　31　正解 － ④

「『登場者の紹介』のスライドに最適な組み合わせはどれか」

　　　主要な登場者／それ以外の登場者

① 309, Aston, 農場主／ Sabine, ポニー

② Aston, Aston の母, Sabine ／ 309, 農場主

③ Aston, Leon, 農場主／ Aston の母, Sabine

④ Aston, Sabine, ポニー／ Aston の母, 農場主

正解は ④。消去法で考えると，この話の最も重要な登場者は，雄牛の Aston と，飼い主の Sabine であるから，この2人の両方が「主要な登場者（Main figures）」に含まれていない ① や ③ は誤りである。また，Aston と 309 は同じ（第3段落第4文：Three-oh-nine, ...）なので，この2つを別々の登場者として扱っている ② も正解になれない。したがって正解は ④ に絞られる。④ の中のポニー（the pony）とは Leon のことだが，Leon と Aston は仲睦まじく暮らす兄弟のような関係で，第3段落第9文（Aston might never ...）では「Aston は，Leon を見ていなかったら，こういったものを決して身につけていなかったかもしれない」と述べられており，最終段落最終文（He sometimes gets ...）の中で Sabine が，「彼（＝ Aston）は，Leon からあまり長い間離れることを好みません」と述べていることからも，Leon はこの話の中の重要な登場者と考えることができる。また，④ の中の「Aston の母」と「農場主（the farmer）」が登場するのは第2段落（The farmer agreed, ...）までで，それ以降は登場せず，いずれも話の展開の上で重要な役割を担っているわけではないので，彼らを「それ以外の登場者（Minor figures）」に分類するのも適切である。

問3　正解　32 － ④，　33 － ③
**　　　　　　34 － ⑤，　35 － ①**

— 英 R 278 —

「『**有名になるまでの経緯**』のスライドを完成させる
ため、4つの出来事を起こった順序で選びなさい」

① Aston がジャンプを覚える。
② Sabine と Aston は一緒に何百キロも移動する。
③ Sabine は 309 とその母を買う。
④ Sabine は近所の人の農場へ働きに出る。
⑤ Sabine は 309 を散歩に連れていく。

この話は、原則として出来事を起こった順序通りに
述べていく形で展開するので、本文の記述の順序と出
来事の起こった順序とは同じと考えてよい。本文の記
述順に並べると以下のようになる。

〈有名になるまでの経緯〉
Sabine の馬が死ぬ（第1段落第1文：Five years ago, ...）
　　　　　　　　↓
32 ④ Sabine は近所の人の農場へ働きに出る（第2段
　　　落第1文：The farmer agreed, and Sabine ...）
　　　　　　　　↓
33 ③ Sabine は 309 とその母を買う（第2段落第8文：
　　　The farmer agreed, and she ...）
　　　　　　　　↓
34 ⑤ Sabine は 309 を散歩に連れていく（第2段落
　　　第9文：Sabine then started ...）
　　　　　　　　↓
35 ① Aston がジャンプを覚える（第3段落第8文：
　　　And despite weighing ...）
　　　　　　　　↓
Aston と Sabine は見せ物に出かけるようになる（第4
段落第1文：Now Sabine and Aston ...）

　なお、② の「Sabine と Aston は一緒に何百キロも移
動する」については、第6段落第2文（Aston and
Sabine sometimes ...）で触れられているが、これは
Aston と Sabine が有名になった後の出来事なので、い
ずれの空所にも入らない。

問4　36・37　正解－①・③
「『**Aston の能力**』のスライドに最適な2つの項目を
選びなさい（順序は問わない）」

① **自分で誤りを矯正すること**
② ポニーと並んでジャンプすること
③ **人を背中に乗せてジャンプすること**
④ 馬よりも速く芸を身につけること
⑤ 写真用のポーズをとること

　正解は ① と ③。① については、第3段落第11文（He
also noticed ...）に「彼（＝ Aston）はまた自分の欠点

にも気づき、Sabine の助けなしでそれを矯正した」と
あるのと合っている。③ については、第3段落第8文
（And despite weighing ...）に「そして体重が 1,300 キ
ロあったにもかかわらず、彼（＝ Aston）はほんの
18 ヵ月で、Sabine を背中に乗せたまま高さ1メート
ルある馬術用の障害物を飛び越える方法を身につけた」
とあるのと合っている。他の選択肢のようなことは本
文では述べられていない。

問5　38　正解－①
「最適な項目を選んで『**Aston は今**』のスライドを完
成しなさい」

① ファンの数がますます増えている
② Sabine をとても裕福にした
③ とても有名になったのでもう人々を怖がらせない
④ 1年を通じてほとんどの夜を馬運搬車の中で過
　　ごしている

　正解は ①。「Aston は今」については、第4段落（Now
Sabine and Aston ...）以降で述べられている。第6段
落第1文（Over the last few years, ...）に「ここ数年
間で、障害ジャンプをするこの大きな雄牛のニュース
は急速に広まり、今や Aston は大きな呼び物となり、
ネット上のファンも増えている」とあり、① は下線部
の内容と合っている。② のようなことは本文では述べ
られていない。③ については、第4段落第2文（Sabine
says, ...）から始まる Sabine の言葉の中に「ほとんど
の場合、人々は本当に驚き、最初は少し怖がることも
あります（Mostly, people are ...）」や「ほとんどの人々
は、ツノのある雄牛にあまり近づきたがりません（Most
people don't like ...）」とあることから考えて誤りであ
る。④ については、第6段落第2文（Aston and
Sabine ...）及び最終文（Aston has to sleep ...）から
わかるように、Aston が馬運搬車の中で過ごすのは
「時々（sometimes）」であって、「ほとんどの夜（most
nights）」ではないので誤りである。

〈主な語句・表現〉
第1段落（Five years ago, ...）
　die of ...「〈病気など〉で死ぬ」／ out of loneliness「孤
独感から」／ spend O – ing「O を－して過ごす」／
cow图「牛」／ look after ...「…の世話をする」
第2段落（The farmer agreed, ...）
　pregnant图「妊娠した」／ follow O around「O の
後をついて回る」／ bull图「雄牛」／ have
permission to －「－してもよいという許可を得る」

— 英 R 279 —

第3段落 （Soon after, ...）

soon after「その後まもなくして」／ no longer ...「もはや…ではない」／ show jumping「（馬術などで行う）障害飛越競技；障害ジャンプ」／ pay close attention to ...「…に強い関心を持つ」／ nor had she expected ...「そして彼女は…も期待してはいなかった」／ pick up「〈芸事などを〉身につける」／ trick 图「芸（当）」／ gallop 動「ギャロップで駆ける」／ on command「命令で」／ it took him just 18 months to −「彼が−するのにほんの18ヵ月しかかからなかった」／ leap over ...「…を飛び越える」／ jump 图「跳躍障害物」／ with Sabine on his back「Sabine を背中に乗せたまま」付帯状況の表現。／ That's something の後には，do の目的語として働く関係代名詞が省略されている。／ very best「最高の」

第4段落 （Now Sabine and Aston ...）

horse show「ホースショー；馬術競技会」／ show off ...「…を見せびらかす［誇示する］」／ at first「最初の頃は」／ a bit「〈副詞的に〉少々」／ be scared「怖がる」／ once 腰「いったん…すると」

第5段落 （"Look!" ...）

used to −「昔は−したものだ」／ on a lead「ひもにつないで」／ get used to ...「…に慣れる」／ that's why ...「だから…だ」／ mind 動「…を気にする；嫌がる」／ in particular「特に；とりわけ」／ a chance to −「−する機会［チャンス］」

第6段落 （Over the last few years, ...）

the last few years「最近の数年間」／ massive 形「巨大な」／ a major attraction「主要な見せ物」／ a growing number of ...「ますます多くの…」／ follower 图「ファン；追っかけ」／ horse box = horse trailer「馬運搬車」

第7段落 （"He doesn't like it. ...）

change position「姿勢を変える」／ be careful not to −「−しないよう注意する」／ crush 動「…を押し潰す」／ for too long「あまりに長い間」／ other than that「それ以外では」

[スライド]

Who's Who?「誰が誰か」（氏名／職業／関係などについての情報）／ pre-fame storyline「有名になる以前の筋書き」

第6問

A

〈全訳〉

あなたはスポーツにおける安全についての授業課題に取り組んでいて，次の記事を見つけました。あなたは今それを読んでいて，わかったことをクラスメートに発表するためにポスターを作成しています。

アイスホッケーをより安全にする

アイスホッケーは，世界中でさまざまな人々が楽しんでいる団体競技です。この競技が目指すのは，「パック」と呼ばれる硬いゴム製の円盤をホッケー用のスティックで動かして，相手チームのネットの中に入れることです。各チームに6人のプレーヤーがいる2つのチームが，硬く滑りやすいアイススケート場で，このきびきびした競技を行うのです。プレーヤーは，時速30キロものスピードを出してパックを打ち飛ばすことがあります。この速さだと，プレーヤーもパックも重大な危険要因になりうるのです。

この競技のスピードと，スケート場の表面の滑りやすさのせいで，転倒やプレーヤー同士の衝突が起こりやすく，彼らはさまざまな怪我をすることになります。プレーヤーを保護するために，ヘルメット，グローブ，肩や肘や脚部用のパッドといった装備が，長い年月の間に導入されてきました。こういった努力にもかかわらず，アイスホッケーで脳しんとうが起こる率は高いのです。

脳しんとうは，脳の機能の仕方に影響を及ぼす脳の損傷で，頭や顔や首などの部位への直接的あるいは間接的な衝撃によってもたらされ，時に一時的に意識を失うこともあります。より軽い症状としては，短時間ですがプレーヤーが真っ直ぐに歩けなくなったり，物がはっきり見えなくなったり，耳鳴りがしたりすることがあります。プレーヤーの中には，軽い頭痛がするだけだと考えて，脳を傷つけたことに気づかない人もいます。

損傷の重大さに気づかないことに加えて，プレーヤーはコーチがどう思うかを心配する傾向があります。昔は，コーチは痛みに負けない屈強なプレーヤーを好みました。言い換えれば，負傷したプレーヤーは怪我をした後でプレーを中止するのが理にかなっているように思えるでしょうが，多くのプレーヤーはそうしなかったのです。しかし最近になって，脳しんとうは生涯続く深刻な影響を及ぼしうることがわかりました。脳し

んとうの既往歴がある人は，集中や睡眠に問題を抱えるかもしれません。さらには，うつや情緒変調などの精神的な問題で苦しむかもしれません。プレーヤーが嗅覚や味覚の異常を感じるようになる場合もあります。

カナダと米国のチームからなるナショナル・ホッケー・リーグ（NHL）は，脳しんとうに対処するためのより厳格な規則や指針を作成してきました。たとえば2001年にNHLはバイザー（ヘルメットに取り付けられた顔を保護する透明のプラスチック板）を導入しました。当初それは義務づけられていなかったので，多くのプレーヤーはそれを身につけない選択をしました。けれども2013年以降，それは義務化されました。さらに2004年にNHLは，他のプレーヤーの頭を故意に殴ったプレーヤーには，出場停止や罰金などのより厳しいペナルティーを課すようになりました。

NHLは2015年に脳しんとうスポッターシステムも導入しました。このシステムでは，NHLの職員が，ライブ映像とビデオリプレーを利用して，各試合中に視認可能な脳しんとうの症状を探します。当初は医学的訓練を受けていない2人の脳しんとうスポッターが，競技場で試合を監視しました。翌年には医学的訓練を受けた1人から4人の脳しんとうスポッターが加えられました。彼らはニューヨークにあるリーグの本部から各試合を監視しました。もしスポッターが，あるプレーヤーが脳しんとうを起こしたと考えれば，そのプレーヤーは試合から外されて，「クワイエット・ルーム」に連れて行かれて医師の診断を受けます。プレーヤーは医師の許可が降りるまで試合への復帰が許されません。

NHLはアイスホッケーをより安全な競技にすることにおいて大きく前進してきました。脳しんとうの原因や影響についてさらに多くのことがわかってくれば，NHLは必ずやさらなる対策を講じて，プレーヤーの安全を確保しようとするでしょう。安全性が高まれば，アイスホッケーのプレーヤーやファンが増えることになるかもしれません。

アイスホッケーをより安全なものに

アイスホッケーとは何か。
・プレーヤーは「パック」を相手チームのネットに入れることで得点を得る
・各チーム6人のプレーヤー
・氷上で高速でプレーする競技

主な問題：高い割合の脳しんとう

脳しんとうの定義
脳の機能の仕方に影響を及ぼす脳の損傷

影響	
短期	**長期**
・意識の喪失	・集中困難
・直進歩行の困難	・ 40
・ 39	・精神的問題
・耳鳴り	・嗅覚や味覚の異常

解決策

ナショナル・ホッケー・リーグ（NHL）
・バイザー付きヘルメットを義務化する
・危険なプレーヤーに厳格なペナルティーを課す
・ 41 ために，脳しんとうスポッターを導入した

要約
アイスホッケーのプレーヤーは脳しんとうを起こす危険性が高い。
したがってNHLは 42 。

〈設問解説〉

問1 39 正解—④
「ポスターの 39 に最適な選択肢を選びなさい」
① 攻撃的な動き
② 思考障害
③ 人格変化
④ 視界のぼけ

正解は④。「脳しんとうの短期的な影響」として適切なものを選ぶ。第3段落第2文（In less serious cases, ...）に「より軽い症状としては，短い時間ですがプレーヤーが真っ直ぐに歩けなくなったり，<u>物がはっきり見えなくなったり</u>，耳鳴りがしたりすることがあります」とあり，④は下線部の内容と合っているので正解となる。他の選択肢のようなことは，脳しんとうの短期的影響として述べられていない。

問2 40 正解—③
「ポスターの 40 に最適な選択肢を選びなさい」
① 視力の喪失
② 記憶障害
③ 睡眠障害
④ 歩行不安定

正解は③。「脳しんとうの長期的な影響」として適切なものを選ぶ。これについては第4段落第4文

— 英 R 281 —

（Recently, however, ...）以降で述べられている。続く第5文（People with a history ...）に「脳しんとうの既往歴がある人は，集中や睡眠に問題を抱えるかもしれません」とあり，③は下線部の内容と合っている。他の選択肢のようなことは，脳しんとうの長期的影響として述べられていない。

問3　41　正解—④
「ポスターの41に最適な選択肢を選びなさい」
① プレーヤーが試合に戻ることを許す
② 脳しんとうを起こしているプレーヤーを診断する
③ 脳しんとうをもたらすプレーヤーに罰金を課す
④ 脳しんとうの兆候を示すプレーヤーを特定する

正解は④。「NHLが脳しんとうスポッターを導入した目的」として適切なものを選ぶ。第6段落第2文（In this system, ...）に「このシステムでは，NHLの職員が，ライブ映像とビデオリプレーを利用して，各試合中に視認可能な脳しんとうの症状を探します」とある。また同段落第6文（If a spotter thinks ...）には「もしスポッターが，あるプレーヤーが脳しんとうを起こしたと考えれば，そのプレーヤーは試合から外されて，『クワイエット・ルーム』に連れて行かれて医師の診断を受けます」とある。これら下線部の内容から考えて，スポッター導入の目的は④の「脳しんとうの兆候を示すプレーヤーを特定する」ことと考えられるので，④が正解となる。①や②は，スポッターがすることではなく，医師（medical doctor）がすることなので，正解にはなれない。③もスポッターシステムの導入とは無関係である。

問4　42　正解—②
「ポスターの42に最適な選択肢を選びなさい」
① プレーヤーがより屈強になることを期待してきた
② 新しい規則や指針を履行してきた
③ コーチに医学的訓練を行ってきた
④ バイザーの着用を任意制にした

正解は②。「アイスホッケーのプレーヤーが脳しんとうを患う危険性が高いことから，NHLがこれまでやってきたこと」にあたる表現を空所に入れて，本文全体の要約（summary）として適切な表現を完成する。最終段落第1文（The NHL has made ...）に「NHLはアイスホッケーをより安全な競技にすることにおいて大きく前進してきました」とある。この下線部をより具体的に表現しているのが，第5段落第1文（The National Hockey League ...）の「カナダと米国のチー

ムからなるナショナル・ホッケー・リーグ（NHL）は，脳しんとうに対処するためのより厳格な規則や指針を作成してきました」である。したがって，下線部の内容と合っている②が正解となる。①のようなことは，「NHLが行ってきたこと」として本文では述べられていない。③は「コーチ」を「脳しんとうスポッター」に直さないと，本文と合わない（第6段落第4文：The following year, ...）し，本文全体の要約としても不十分な内容である。NHLはバイザーの着用を最終的には義務化した（第5段落第4文：Since 2013, ...）ので，④も正解になれない。

〈主な語句・表現〉
第1段落（Ice hockey is ...）
　a wide variety of ...「多種多様な…」／ The object ... is to -「目的は-することだ」／ engage in ...「…に従事する」／ slippery 形「滑りやすい」／ ice rink「アイススケート場」

第2段落（The speed of ...）
　make it easy for players to -「プレーヤーが-するのを容易にする」／ bump into ...「…にぶつかる」／ result in ...「…という結果になる」／ in an attempt to -「-しようと（努力）して」／ equipment 名「装備」／ over the years「長年にわたって」／ concussion 名「脳しんとう」

第3段落（A concussion is ...）
　the way (that) it functions「それが機能する方法」／ impact 名「衝撃」／ temporary 形「一時的な」／ loss of consciousness「意識の喪失」／ ringing 名「鳴り響く音」

第4段落（In addition to ...）
　in addition (to ...)「（…に）加えて」／ tough 形「頑丈［屈強］な」／ in spite of ...「…があるにもかかわらず」／ in other words「言い換えると」／ it would seem logical for ... to -「…が-するのは理にかなっているように思えるだろう」／ many did not = many injured players did not stop playing after getting hurt「多くの負傷したプレーヤーは怪我をした後でもプレーをやめなかった」／ last a lifetime「生涯続く」／ history 名「病歴」／ have trouble - ing「-するのに苦労する」／ depression 名「うつ病」／ mood change「情緒の変化」／ disorder 名「異常；障害」

第5段落（The National Hockey League ...）
　consist of ...「…からなる」／ strict 形「厳しい」／ deal with ...「…に対処する」／ attached to ...「…に

— 英 R 282 —

取り付けられた」／at first「最初（の頃）は」／optional形「選択制の；随意的な」／be required「要求される；必須である」／penalty名「罰」／suspension名「出場停止」／fine名「罰金」／hit O in the head「Oの頭を殴る」／deliberately副「故意に」

第6段落（The NHL also ...）

spotter名「監視員」／monitor動「監視する」／arena名「競技場」／the following year「その翌年（に）」／one to four concussion spotters「1人から4人の脳しんとうスポッター」／head office「本社；本部」／examination名「診察」／permission名「許可」

最終段落（The NHL has made ...）

make progress「進歩［前進］する」／As more is learned about ...「…についてより多くのことが知られるにつれて」／effect名「影響；結果」／take measures「対策を講じる」／ensure動「…を保証［確実に］する」／safety名「安全」／lead to ...「…につながる；…をもたらす」／increase in ...「…の増加」

B

〈全訳〉

　あなたは保健の授業で栄養の学習をしています。あなたは教科書に載っている次の文章を読んで，さまざまな甘味料についての知識を深めようとしています。

　ケーキ，キャンディー，ソフトドリンク。たいていの人は甘いものが大好きです。実際，若い人たちは英語で何かが「good」であるという意味で，「Sweet!」と言うくらいです。甘みについて考える時，私たちが想像するのは，サトウキビやサトウダイコンといった植物から作る普通の白砂糖です。しかし科学上の発見は，甘味料の世界を変えてしまいました。現在では砂糖を他の多くの植物から抽出できます。最も明らかな例がトウモロコシです。トウモロコシは豊富で，安価で，加工しやすいのです。高果糖コーンシロップ（HFCS）は，普通の砂糖よりも約1.2倍の甘さがありますが，かなり高カロリーです。科学者たちは科学をさらに一歩前進させて，過去70年間にわたって多種多様な人工甘味料を開発してきました。

　最近の米国の国民健康栄養調査が出した結論は，平均的なアメリカ人のエネルギーの14.6パーセントは，自然食品に由来しない糖分を指す「食品添加糖分」から摂取されているというものでした。たとえばバナナは自然食品ですが，クッキーには食品添加糖分が含まれています。食品添加糖分のカロリーの半分以上は，加糖飲料や加糖デザートによるものです。多量の食品添加糖分は，私たちの体に悪影響を及ぼす可能性があり，それには過剰な体重増加などの健康問題が含まれます。このため，多くの人は代わりに低カロリーのドリンクやスナックやデザートを選びます。

　白砂糖に代わる自然の甘味料としては，赤砂糖，ハチミツ，メープルシロップなどがありますが，これらもカロリーが高い傾向があります。その結果，大部分が人工化合物である代替「低カロリー甘味料（LCS）」の人気が高まりました。現在最も普及しているLCSは，アスパルテーム，アセスルファムK，ステビア，スクラロースです。LCSのすべてが人工物なのではありません。ステビアは植物の葉に由来します。

　代替甘味料は，一部が熱することができず，ほとんどが白砂糖よりもはるかに甘いため，調理に用いるのが難しい場合があります。アスパルテームとアセスルファムKは，砂糖より200倍甘く，ステビアは300倍甘く，スクラロースはステビアの2倍の甘みを持って

— 英 R 283 —

います。新しい甘味料の中には，さらに甘みが強いものもあります。ある日本企業が最近開発した「アドバンテーム」は，砂糖の2万倍の甘みがあります。この物質はごくわずかな量で，食物を甘くすることができるのです。

甘味料を選ぶ際に大切なのは，健康問題を考慮することです。たとえば多量の白砂糖を使って作られたデザートは，体重増加につながりかねない高カロリーの食べ物となります。まさにこの理由のために，LCSをより好む人々がいるのです。しかしながら，カロリーとは別に，人工のLCSの摂取を他のさまざまな健康問題と関連づけている研究もあります。LCSの中には，発癌性を疑われる強い化学物質を含むものもあれば，記憶や脳の発達に影響を与えることがわかっているものもあるので，特に幼い子供や妊娠中の女性やお年寄りには危険なものとなりうるのです。キシリトールやソルビトールといった，低カロリーの比較的自然に近い代替甘味料もいくつかあります。あいにくこれらは体内での移動速度が極めて遅いので，多量に摂取すると胃の病気を引き起こすことがあります。

人は何か甘いものが欲しくなると，こういったことをすべて知っていても，砂糖などの普通の高カロリー甘味料を変わらず使い続けるか，あるいはLCSを使うかを決められずに苦労します。今日の多くの種類のガムやキャンディーには，1種類以上の人工甘味料が含まれています。にもかかわらず，熱い飲み物には人工甘味料を入れようとしないのに，そういったお菓子は買うことがある人々がいます。私たち一人一人は，これらの選択肢を検討し，そして自分の必要と状況に最も合う甘味料を選ぶ必要があるのです。
（編集注：本書ではすべての問題を，実際の試験問題のまま収録・解説しています。）

〈設問解説〉
問1 　43　 正解－③
「現代科学は　43　によって甘味料の世界を変えたことをあなたは知る」
① 新しくてより甘みのある種類の白砂糖を発見すること
② アメリカ人のエネルギー摂取量を測定すること
③ さまざまな新しい選択肢を提供すること
④ 自然環境から新たに開発された多くの植物を用いること

正解は③。「現代科学が甘味料の世界を変えた」という趣旨の記述は，第1段落第4文（Scientific

discoveries, however, ...）にある。そしてその具体的内容については，続く第5文（We can now ...）以降で2つ述べられている。1つは第5文の「現在では砂糖を他の多くの植物から抽出できます」で，もう1つは同段落最終文（Taking science one step further, ...）の「科学者たちは科学をさらに一歩前進させて，過去70年間にわたって多種多様な人工甘味料を開発してきました」である。選択肢③の「さまざまな新しい選択肢を提供する」は，上の2つの下線部の内容を端的に言い換えたものと考えられることから，③が正解となる。

① は「白砂糖（white sugar）」を「甘味料（sweetener）」に直さないと，本文の内容と合わない。② は「甘味料の世界を変えた」こととは直接関係がないので，正解にはなれない。④ の中の「新たに開発された植物（newly-developed plants）」についての記述は本文中にない。

問2 　44　 正解－③
「あなたは調べたばかりの情報を要約している。次の表をどうやって仕上げるべきか」

甘み	甘味料
高	アドバンテーム
	(A)
	(B)
	(C)
低	(D)

① (A) ステビア
　 (B) スクラロース
　 (C) アセスルファムKとアスパルテーム
　 (D) HFCS
② (A) ステビア
　 (B) スクラロース
　 (C) HFCS
　 (D) アセスルファムKとアスパルテーム
③ (A) スクラロース
　 (B) ステビア
　 (C) アセスルファムKとアスパルテーム
　 (D) HFCS
④ (A) スクラロース
　 (B) ステビア
　 (C) HFCS
　 (D) アセスルファムKとアスパルテーム

正解は③。第1段落第8文（High fructose corn syrup ...）に「高果糖コーンシロップ（HFCS）は，普

— 英 R 284 —

通の砂糖よりも約1.2倍の甘さがありますが，かなり高カロリーです」とある。また，第4段落第2文（Aspartame and Ace-K ...）から第5文（A Japanese company ...）に「アスパルテームとアセスルファムKは，砂糖より200倍甘く，ステビアは300倍甘く，スクラロースはステビアの2倍の甘みを持っています。新しい甘味料の中には，さらに甘みが強いものもあります。ある日本企業が最近開発した『アドバンテーム』は，砂糖の2万倍の甘さがあります」とある。したがって，砂糖と比べた場合の甘さは，低い（low）ものから高い（high）ものへの順序で並べると，「HFCS（1.2倍）」，「アスパルテームとアセスルファムK（200倍）」，「ステビア（300倍）」，「スクラロース（600倍）」，「アドバンテーム（2万倍）」となるので，正解は③に決まる。

問3　正解　45 ・ 46 ─ ③・⑤
「あなたが読んだ記事によると，次の中でどれが正しいか（2つの選択肢を選びなさい。順序は問わない）」
① 代替甘味料は，体重増加を引き起こすことが証明されている。
② アメリカ人はエネルギーの14.6％を代替甘味料から得ている。
③ 植物から代替甘味料を得ることは可能である。
④ ほとんどの人工甘味料は調理に用いるのが簡単である。
⑤ キシリトールやソルビトールなどの甘味料は素早く消化されない。
正解は③と⑤。③については，第3段落最終文（Not all LCSs ...）に「LCS（低カロリー甘味料）のすべてが人工物なのではありません。ステビアは植物の葉に由来します」とあるのと合っている。⑤については，第5段落最終文（Unfortunately, these move ...）に「あいにくこれら（＝キシリトールやソルビトール）は体内での移動速度が極めて遅いので，多量に摂取すると胃の病気を引き起こすことがあります」とある。下線部の中の「体内での移動速度が極めて遅い」とは，「胃に到達して消化されるまでに時間がかかる」ことと考えられることから，⑤は正解となる。
①については，本文中の「体重増加」に関する記述は，第2段落第4文（Lots of added sugar ...）の「多量の食品添加糖分は，私たちの体に悪影響を及ぼす可能性があり，それには過剰な体重増加などの健康問題が含まれます」と，第5段落第2文（Making desserts with ...）の「たとえば多量の白砂糖を使って作られたデザートは，体重増加につながりかねない高カロリー

の食べ物となります」の2箇所であり，①のように「代替甘味料は，体重増加を引き起こすことが証明されている」とは述べられていない。②については，第2段落第1文（A recent US ...）に「最近の米国の国民健康栄養調査が出した結論は，平均的なアメリカ人のエネルギーの14.6パーセントは，自然食品に由来しない糖分を指す『食品添加糖分（added sugar）』から摂取されているというものでした」とあるので，②の中の「代替甘味料（alternative sweeteners）」が明らかな誤りである。④については，第4段落第1文（Alternative sweeteners can ...）に「代替甘味料は，一部が熱することができず，ほとんどが白砂糖よりもはるかに甘いため，調理に用いるのが難しい場合があります」とあるのと合わない。

問4　 47 　正解─④
「著者の立場を説明するには，次のどれが最も適切か」
① 著者は飲み物やデザートにおける人工甘味料の使用に反対している。
② 著者は人工甘味料は従来の甘味料に首尾よく取って代わったと考えている。
③ 著者は将来の利用のためにはるかに甘い製品を作り出すことが大事だと述べている。
④ 著者は人々が自分の理にかなう甘味料を選ぶことに重点を置くよう提案している。
正解は④。著者は最終段落最終文（Individuals need to ...）において「私たち一人一人は，これらの選択肢を検討し，そして自分の必要と状況に最も合う甘味料を選ぶ必要があるのです」と述べている。④の中の「自分の理にかなう（make sense）甘味料を選ぶ」は，上記引用文中の下線部を言い換えたものと考えられるため，④は著者の立場を説明したものとして適切である。
著者は人工甘味料の持ついくつかの問題点を指摘してはいるものの，①のようにその使用にはっきりと「反対している」わけではない。②や③のようなことも本文からは読み取れない。

〈主な語句・表現〉
第1段落（Cake, candy, soft drinks ...）
　white sugar「白砂糖」／ sugar cane「サトウキビ」／ sugar beet「サトウダイコン；テンサイ」／ extract 動「…を抽出する」／ easy to process「加工が容易な」／ Taking science one step further「科学をさらに一歩推し進めて」　分詞構文。／ a wide variety of ...「多種多様な…」／ artificial 形「人工の」／ sweetener 名「甘

― 英 R 285 ―

味料」< sweeten 動「…を甘くする」

第2段落（A recent US ...）

intake 名「摂取量」／ added sugar「食品添加糖分」／ refer to ...「…のことを言う」／ be derived from ...「…に由来している」／ whole food「自然食品」／ have negative effects on ...「…に悪影響を及ぼす」／ excessive 形「過度の」／ weight gain「体重増加」／ substitute 名「代替物」

第3段落（Natural alternatives to ...）

alternative 名「代わりとなるもの」形「代わりの」／ consequently 副「その結果」／ mostly 副「主に；ほとんど」／ chemical combination「化合物」／ Not all LCSs are artificial「すべての LCS が人工物だというわけではない」 部分否定。

第4段落（Alternative sweeteners can ...）

be hard to use in cooking「調理において使いにくい」／ far sweeter「はるかに甘い」／ has twice the sweetness of ...「…の2倍の甘みを持っている」／ even more intense「（甘みが）さらに強烈な」／ substance 名「物質」

第5段落（When choosing sweeteners, ...）

result in ...「…という結果になる」／ lead to ...「…につながる；…をもたらす」／ those who ...「…する人々」／ for this very reason「まさにこの理由で」／ apart from ...「…は別にして」／ link A with B「A を B に関連づける」／ consume 動「…を消費［摂取］する」／ health concern「健康問題」／ chemicals suspected of ...「…の疑いがある化学物質」／ pregnant 形「妊娠した」／ the elderly「年配の人々」／ stomach trouble「胃の問題［病気］」

第6段落（When people want ...）

whether to －「－するべきかどうか」／ stick to ...「…に固執する」／ nonetheless 副「それにもかかわらず」／ would not「…しようとしない」／ weigh 動「…を慎重に検討する」／ best suit ...「…に最も合う」

駿台文庫の共通テスト対策

過去問演習から本番直前総仕上げまで駿台文庫が共通テスト対策を強力サポート

2024共通テスト対策 実戦問題集

共通テストを徹底分析
「予想問題」+「過去問」をこの1冊で!

◆駿台オリジナル予想問題5回
◆2023年度共通テスト本試験問題
◆2022年度共通テスト本試験問題
◆2021年度共通テスト本試験問題(第1日程)
　　　　　　　　　　　　　計8回収録

科目	<全19点>
・英語リーディング	・生物
・英語リスニング	・地学基礎
・数学Ⅰ・A	・世界史B
・数学Ⅱ・B	・日本史B
・国語	・地理B
・物理基礎	・現代社会
・物理	・倫理
・化学基礎	・政治・経済
・化学	・倫理,政治・経済
・生物基礎	

B5判／税込 各1,485円
※物理基礎・化学基礎・生物基礎・地学基礎は税込各1,100円

● 駿台講師陣が総力をあげて作成。
● 詳細な解答・解説は使いやすい別冊挿み込み。
● 仕上げは、「直前チェック総整理」で弱点補強。
　（英語リスニングにはついておりません）
●『英語リスニング』の音声はダウンロード式(MP3ファイル)。
●『現代社会』は『政治・経済』『倫理,政治・経済』の
　一部と重複しています。

2024共通テスト 実戦パッケージ問題『青パック』

6教科全19点各1回分を、1パックに収録。

収録科目	
・英語リーディング	・生物
・英語リスニング	・地学基礎
・数学Ⅰ・A	・世界史B
・数学Ⅱ・B	・日本史B
・国語	・地理B
・物理基礎	・現代社会
・物理	・倫理
・化学基礎	・政治・経済
・化学	・倫理,政治・経済
・生物基礎	

B5判／箱入り　税込1,540円

● 共通テストのオリジナル予想問題。
●『英語リスニング』の音声はダウンロード式(MP3ファイル)。
● マークシート解答用紙・自己採点集計用紙付。
● わかりやすい詳細な解答・解説。

【短期攻略共通テスト対策シリーズ】

共通テスト対策の短期完成型問題集。
1ヵ月で完全攻略。　※年度版ではありません。

●英語リーディング<改訂版>	2023年秋刊行予定	価格未定
●英語リスニング<改訂版>	刀祢雅彦編著	1,320円
●数学Ⅰ・A基礎編	吉川浩之・榎明夫共著	1,100円
●数学Ⅱ・B基礎編	吉川浩之・榎明夫共著	1,100円
●数学Ⅰ・A実戦編	榎明夫・吉川浩之共著	880円
●数学Ⅱ・B実戦編	榎明夫・吉川浩之共著	880円
●現代文	奥村・松本・小坂共著	1,100円
●古文	菅野三恵・柳田縁共著	935円
●漢文	久我昌則・水野正明共著	935円
●物理基礎	溝口真己著	935円
●物理	溝口真己著	1,100円
●化学基礎	三門恒雄著	770円
●化学	三門恒雄著	1,100円
●生物基礎	佐野(恵)・布施・佐野(芳)・指田・橋本共著	880円
●生物	佐野(恵)・布施・佐野(芳)・指田・橋本共著	1,100円
●地学基礎	小野雄一著	1,045円
●地学	小野雄一著	1,320円
●日本史B	福井紳一著	1,100円
●世界史B	川西・今西・小林共著	1,100円
●地理B	阿部恵伯・大久保史子共著	1,100円
●現代社会	清水雅博著	1,155円
●政治・経済	清水雅博著	1,155円
●倫理	村中和之著	1,155円
●倫理,政治・経済	村中和之・清水雅博共著	1,320円

A5判／税込価格は、上記の通りです。

駿台文庫株式会社
〒101-0062 東京都千代田区神田駿河台1-7-4　小畑ビル6階
TEL 03-5259-3301　FAX 03-5259-3006
https://www.sundaibunko.jp

駿台文庫のお薦め書籍

多くの受験生を合格へと導き、先輩から後輩へと受け継がれている駿台文庫の名著の数々。

システム英単語〈5訂版〉
システム英単語Basic〈5訂版〉
霜 康司・刀祢雅彦 共著
システム英単語　　　B6判　税込1,100円
システム英単語Basic　B6判　税込1,100円

入試数学「実力強化」問題集
杉山義明 著　B5判　税込2,200円

英語 ドリルシリーズ

英作文基礎10題ドリル	竹岡広信 著　B5判　税込990円	英文法基礎10題ドリル	田中健一 著　B5判　税込990円
英文法入門10題ドリル	田中健一 著　B5判　税込913円	英文読解入門10題ドリル	田中健一 著　B5判　税込935円

国語 ドリルシリーズ

現代文読解基礎ドリル〈改訂版〉	池尻俊也 著　B5判　税込935円	古典文法10題ドリル〈漢文編〉	斉京宣行・三宅崇広 共著　B5判　税込 880円
現代文読解標準ドリル	池尻俊也 著　B5判　税込990円	漢字・語彙力ドリル	霜 栄 著　B5判　税込1,023円
古典文法10題ドリル〈古文基礎編〉	菅野三恵 著　B5判　税込935円		
古典文法10題ドリル〈古文実戦編〉〈三訂版〉	菅野三恵・福沢健・下屋敷雅暁 共著　B5判　税込990円		

生きる シリーズ
霜 栄 著
生きる漢字・語彙力〈三訂版〉　　　　　　B6判　税込1,023円
生きる現代文キーワード〈増補改訂版〉　　B6判　税込1,023円
共通テスト対応　生きる現代文 随筆・小説語句　B6判　税込 770円

開発講座シリーズ
霜 栄 著
現代文 解答力の開発講座 NEW　　　　　　　　A5判　税込1,320円
現代文 読解力の開発講座〈新装版〉　　　　　　A5判　税込1,100円
現代文 読解力の開発講座〈新装版〉オーディオブック　税込2,200円

国公立標準問題集 CanPass（キャンパス）シリーズ

英語	山口玲児・高橋康弘 共著	A5判 税込 990円	物理基礎＋物理	溝口真己・椎名泰司 共著　A5判 税込1,210円
数学Ⅰ・A・Ⅱ・B〈改訂版〉	桑畑信泰・古梶裕之 共著	A5判 税込1,210円	化学基礎＋化学	犬塚壮志 著　A5判 税込1,210円
数学Ⅲ〈改訂版〉	桑畑信泰・古梶裕之 共著	A5判 税込1,100円	生物基礎＋生物	波多野善崇 著　A5判 税込1,210円
現代文	清水正史・多田圭太朗 共著	A5判 税込 990円		
古典	白鳥永興・福田忍 共著	A5判 税込 924円		

東大入試詳解シリーズ〈第2版〉

25年 英語　　25年 現代文　25年 化学　　25年 世界史
20年 英語リスニング　25年 古典　25年 生物　25年 地理
25年 数学〈文科〉　20年 物理・上　25年 日本史
25年 数学〈理科〉　20年 物理・下

A5判〈物理のみB5判〉 全て税込2,530円
※2023年秋〈第3版〉刊行予定（物理・下は除く）

京大入試詳解シリーズ〈第2版〉

25年 英語　　25年 現代文　25年 化学　　20年 日本史
25年 数学〈文系〉　25年 古典　15年 生物　20年 世界史
25年 数学〈理系〉　25年 物理

A5判　各税込2,750円　生物は税込2,530円
※生物は第2版ではありません

2024-駿台 大学入試完全対策シリーズ
大学・学部別

A5判／税込2,750〜6,050円

2024-駿台 大学入試完全対策シリーズ
実戦模試演習

B5判／税込1,980〜2,530円

【国立】
- ■北海道大学〈文系〉　前期
- ■北海道大学〈理系〉　前期
- ■東北大学〈文系〉　前期
- ■東北大学〈理系〉　前期
- ■東京大学〈文科〉　前期※
- ■東京大学〈理科〉　前期※
- ■一橋大学　前期※
- ■東京工業大学　前期
- ■名古屋大学〈文系〉　前期
- ■名古屋大学〈理系〉　前期
- ■京都大学〈文系〉　前期
- ■京都大学〈理系〉　前期
- ■大阪大学〈文系〉　前期
- ■大阪大学〈理系〉　前期
- ■神戸大学〈文系〉　前期
- ■神戸大学〈理系〉　前期
- ■九州大学〈文系〉　前期
- ■九州大学〈理系〉　前期

【私立】
- ■早稲田大学　法学部
- ■早稲田大学　文化構想学部
- ■早稲田大学　文学部
- ■早稲田大学　教育学部-文系
- ■早稲田大学　商学部
- ■早稲田大学　社会科学部
- ■早稲田大学　基幹・創造・先進理工学部
- ■慶應義塾大学　法学部
- ■慶應義塾大学　経済学部
- ■慶應義塾大学　理工学部
- ■慶應義塾大学　医学部

※リスニングの音声はダウンロード式（MP3ファイル）

- ■東京大学への英語※
- ■東京大学への数学
- ■東京大学への国語
- ■東京大学への理科（物理・化学・生物）
- ■東京大学への地理歴史（世界史B・日本史B・地理B）

※リスニングの音声はダウンロード式（MP3ファイル）

- ■京都大学への英語
- ■京都大学への数学
- ■京都大学への国語
- ■京都大学への理科（物理・化学・生物）
- ■京都大学への地理歴史（世界史B・日本史B・地理B）
- ■大阪大学への英語※
- ■大阪大学への数学
- ■大阪大学への国語
- ■大阪大学への理科（物理・化学・生物）

駿台文庫株式会社
〒101-0062 東京都千代田区神田駿河台1-7-4　小畑ビル6階
TEL 03-5259-3301　FAX 03-5259-3006
https://www.sundaibunko.jp

① 20230706